Place-Names of Glamorgan

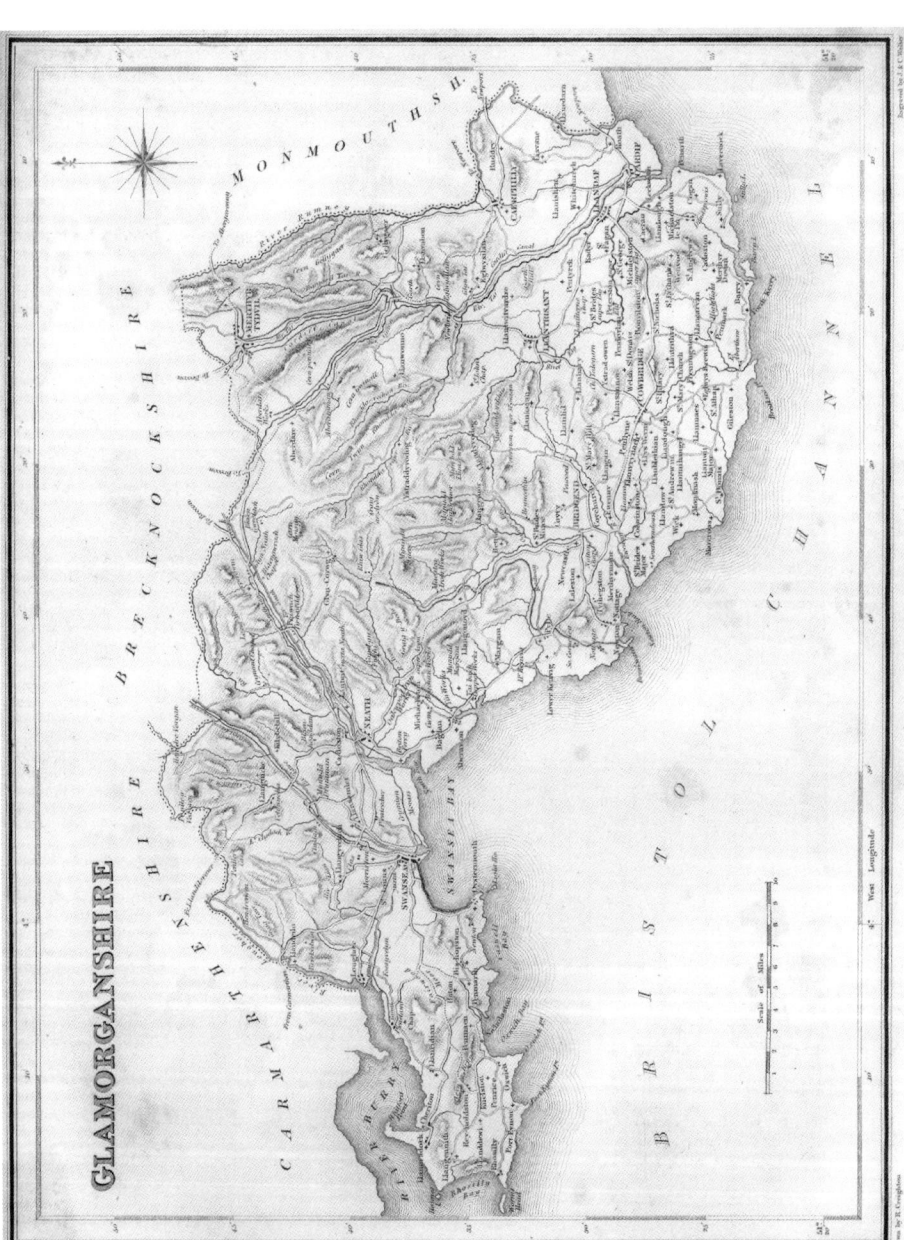

Glamorgan, from *A Topographical Dictionary of Wales* by Samuel Lewis, 1833.

Place-Names of
Glamorgan

Richard Morgan

welsh academic press
Cardiff

Published in Wales by Welsh Academic Press, an imprint of

Ashley Drake Publishing Ltd
PO Box 733
Cardiff
CF14 7ZY

www.welsh-academic-press.wales

First Edition - 2018

ISBN: - 978 1 86057 132 9

© Ashley Drake Publishing Ltd 2018
Text © Richard Morgan 2018

The right of Richard Morgan to be identified as author of this work has been asserted in accordance with the Copyright Design and Patents Act of 1988.

Every effort has been made to contact copyright holders. However, the publishers will be glad to rectify in future editions any inadvertent omissions brought to their attention.

Ashley Drake Publishing Ltd hereby exclude all liability to the extent permitted by law for any errors or omissions in this book and for any loss, damage or expense (whether direct or indirect) suffered by a third party relying on any information contained in this book.

All rights reserved. No part of this publication may be reproduced, stored in a retrieval system, or transmitted, in any form or by any means without the prior permission of the publishers.

British Library Cataloguing-in-Publication Data.
A CIP catalogue for this book is available from the British Library.

Typeset by Prepress Plus, India (www.prepressplus.in).

Printed in the Czech Republic by Akcent Media.

This volume has been published with the financial support of the Marc Fitch Fund and Cymdeithas Enwau Lleoedd Cymru/Welsh Place-Name Society

CONTENTS

Acknowledgements vii
List of Illustrations viii
Preface x
Introduction xii
    The importance of place-names xii
    Place-Names in Glamorgan xiii
    Selection of names xviii
    Editorial method xix
Guide to the International Phonetic Alphabet xxi
Abbreviations and Bibliography xxiv
Online Databases and Reference Resources xxxii
Glossary of Common Place-Name Elements xxxiv

A	Aberafan to Avan Vale	1
B	Bae Caerdydd to Byeastwood	9
C	Cadle to Cyntwell	28
D	Danescourt to Dynfant	65
E	Eaglebush to Ewenni	71
F	Faenor to Furzehill	76
G	Gabalfa to Gyfeillion	84
H	Hafod to Horton	100
I	Ilston to Is Caeach	107
J	Jersey Marine	108
K	Kendon to The Kymin	109
L	Laleston to Lunnon	112
M	Machen to Mynydd y Gwair	135
N	Nantgarw to Nurston	149
O	Oakdale to Oystermouth	155
P	Palmerstown to Pyle	159
Q	Quakers Yard to Quarella	187
R	Radur to Ruthin	188
S	St Andrews Major to Swffryd	198
T	Taf to Tythegston	211
U	Uchelola to Upper Killay	231
V	Vale of Glamorgan to Virginia Park	233
W	Wallston to Wyndham Park	235
Y	Ynysawdre to Ystumllwynarth	243

List of Subscribers 248

For Verona

ACKNOWLEDGEMENTS

The preparation of this publication has depended heavily upon many historians and specialists in place-name studies. In particular, I wish to acknowledge my deepest thanks to Professor Emeritus Gwynedd O. Pierce and Professor Hywel Wyn Owen whose contributions to the study of Welsh place-names are very well known in Wales and beyond. During the final stages of preparation I have also consulted Professor Prys Morgan, Gareth A. Bevan, J. Barry Davies, Dylan Foster Evans, Deric John, and Dai Thomas who have been especially helpful in providing critical advice and assistance with historical and linguistic evidence, and assisted me in avoiding errors. Brian Davies, former curator of Pontypridd Museum, was particularly helpful with regard to the bridges of Pontypridd. Any remaining errors and omissions, and all opinions in this publication, are entirely my own. I also wish to express my thanks to Keith H. Edwards and Frank Hartles for supplying two of the illustrations. The remaining illustrations are in the public domain.

LIST OF ILLUSTRATIONS

Glamorgan
Map of Glamorgan, from *A Topographical Dictionary of Wales* by Samuel Lewis, 1833.

Aberdare
Aberdare church. Engraved by William Woolnorth from a drawing by John Preston Neale for the *Beauties of England and Wales* (courtesy of Keith H. Edwards and Frank Hartles)

Barry
Entrance to Barry Docks c.1900. (courtesy of Glamorgan Archives ref. DCOMC/30/3/43)

Cardiff
Looking south from the castle, from an engraving by J.H. Lekeux, 1841.

Dinas
The landlord of the Gwaunadda Arms, Dinas, Rhondda, and a few of his regulars c.1920.

Ewenni Priory
From *Wales Illustrated* by Henry Gastineau (1830).

Fleur-de-lis
The High Street, looking northwards c.1935.

Gelli
The Eastern Colliery, Gelli, Rhondda, opened in 1877 and closed in 1937.

Hirwaun
The Lamb & Flag on Brecon Road c.1900. (courtesy of Rhondda Cynon Taf Libraries)

Ilston
The ruined chapel, Ilston valley, Parkmill c.1904.

Jersey Marine
Jersey Marine c.1900. (Courtesy of West Glamorgan Archive Service)

Kenfig Hill
Kenfig Hill c.1910.

List of Illustrations

Llangennith
St Cennydd's church c.1910.

Merthyr Tudful
Looking north along the river Taf towards Cyfarthfa castle c.1830. (courtesy of Keith H. Edwards and Frank Hartles)

Nash Point
From *Wales Illustrated* by Henry Gastineau (1830)

Oystermouth
Looking towards the Mumbles c.1930.

Porthcawl
The sea front c.1957.

Quakers Yard
Caerphilly Road.

Resolven
Commercial Road c.1910.

St Donats
The castle and church, from a nineteenth century print.

Tylorstown
East Road, looking north towards Pendyrys Colliery, c.1925.

Upper Boat
The bridge over the Glamorgan Canal at Upper Boat.

Vale of Glamorgan
Cowbridge, from *Wales Illustrated* by Henry Gastineau (1830).

Whitchurch
Merthyr Road, looking north c.1900.

Ynys-y-bŵl.
The old village c.1900. (courtesy of Rhondda Cynon Taf Libraries)

PREFACE

My interest in place-name studies was first sparked by consulting Gwynedd O. Pierce's *The Place-Names of Dinas Powys Hundred* (1968), R.J. Thomas's study of the names of rivers and streams of Wales *Enwau Lleoedd Afonydd a Nentydd Cymru* (1938) and B.G. Charles's *Non-Celtic Place-names in Wales* (1938) during the 1970s. They were and remain authoritative sources of reference on the subject of place-names in Wales but all three volumes raised questions. The most obvious was why there were so few publications on the subject in Wales. There was no lack of interest in the subject yet post-War research seemed to have produced little apart from the gazetteers compiled by Elwyn Davies in 1957 and Melville Richards in 1969 (see Bibliography). Possessing little knowledge of place-names, I concentrated during the following decade on publishing articles on medieval and local history which depended on accurate place-name identification and that often meant having to draw on poor and outdated local sources of reference. Fortunately, I made the acquaintance in 1980 of the late George Foxall who was gathering evidence from tithe maps for the English Place-Name Society survey of Shropshire under the editorship of Dr Margaret Gelling. The work of the society in Shropshire was drawing attention to the important contribution that Welsh-speakers had made to the toponymy of that county but those conducting the survey at that time were restricted by the paucity of comparative work on place-names in Wales. Much of what was available in print on the subject was uneven in quality and scattered through historical journals. Other relevant material – notably university dissertations and the place-name archive of the late Professor Melville Richards at Bangor University – was difficult to access at that time. In summary, Welsh place-name research was unco-ordinated, and depended heavily on a small number of historians and specialists sharing information through newsletters, journals and personal communication.

After 1984 I shifted from research in medieval history to place-names leading eventually to the publication of *Enwau Lleoedd Buallt a Maesyfed* (1993) in co-operation with the late G.G. Evans of Newtown and lengthier publications on four of our historic counties (mentioned in Abbreviations and Bibliography). All of these were written for local and non-specialist historians but were based on information taken from original historical sources and they proved to be of value to academics if only for comparative evidence. During the 1990s I began gathering evidence on Glamorgan. Fortuitously, a number of important publications on the subject appeared about that period, all of which proved valuable as sources of reference and comparison. These included the detailed surveys of Pembrokeshire by B.G. Charles (1992) and East Flintshire by Hywel Wyn Owen (1994), and more local, specialist studies by Gwynedd O. Pierce, Deric John and Michael Eyers. The first short draft of *Place-names of Glamorgan* was completed in 2001 but I put this on hold in order to complete *Place-names of Gwent* (2005) and to assist in the publication of the *Dictionary of the Place-names of Wales* (2007, 2008).

The delay proved to be advantageous. In 2002 Professor Pierce published *Place-names in Glamorgan*, a compilation of essays on 150 place-names in Glamorgan. This served as a source of reference when dealing with some of the more difficult place-names in Glamorgan. As part of the preparatory work on the *Dictionary* I extended my own database of place-name evidence gathered during research at Glamorgan Archives, West Glamorgan Archives, Gwent Archives, Cardiff University's Arts and Social Studies Library, Cardiff Central Library and The National Library of Wales, Aberystwyth. This task was greatly eased by the digitisation of the place-name archive of the late Professor Melville Richards in Bangor University (www.e-gymraeg.co.uk/enwaulleoedd), by the rapid growth of online websites offering access to primary and secondary historical sources, and the appearance of online indexes to the holdings of libraries and archives repositories (see Introduction: The Importance of Place-Names). This was set against a backdrop of growing recognition in Wales of the importance of place-name studies and the need for co-operation between historians, linguists, natural historians, archaeologists and others with particular skills and local knowledge. This led in part to the establishment of Cymdeithas Enwau Lleoedd Cymru/Welsh Place-name Society (www. cymdeithasenwaulleoeddcymru.org) in 2010. The work of the society in encouraging both research and respect for our historic place-names is already having a positive effect on place-name studies.

INTRODUCTION

The importance of place-names

Place-names have been a popular subject throughout our recorded history figuring prominently in chronicles, poetry, folk-lore, genealogies, geographies, topographical dictionaries and antiquarian tourism. Place-names were not mere geographical markers but possessed literary colour and meaning. They were the locations of real or imaginary battles, legends, natural marvels, man-made curiosities, and tragic or comical events. In Wales, the subject appears in the Historia Brittonum (9th century), saints' 'lives', the writings of Gerald of Wales (c.1146-1223), John Leland (1506-52), Humphrey Llwyd (c.1527-68), and Edward Lhuyd (c.1660-1709) who contributed to Gibson's edition of William Camden's *Britannia* in 1695. Many, unsurprisingly, offered interpretations for these place-names which were unwarranted and fanciful even by the standards prevalent in their day. The most prominent in this respect in Glamorgan were undoubtedly Rice Lewis (in Breviat, dated 1596-1600) and particularly Rice Merrick (c.1520-86/7) and Edward Williams (1747-1826) – better known as Iolo Morganwg. Iolo's writings, in particular, were frequently cited by his contemporaries and many later historians as sound historical evidence but it is now known that much of his work was fabricated, exaggerated and embroidered with mythology. That does not mean that his work is worthless, however; Iolo was a Welsh-speaker and a local man from the Vale of Glamorgan. He was particularly interested in the local spoken Welsh and occasionally provides valuable evidence on the Welsh language and the relationship between Welsh and English-speakers here during the late eighteenth and early nineteenth centuries.

Early sources have often been used as the starting-point of local historical research but the study of place-names – or *toponymy* – is best served by beginning with modern maps, local histories and the gazetteers of Elwyn Davies, Melville Richards and D. Geraint Lewis (2007). These provide the foundations of a name database which can then be expanded by gathering evidence from older sources. Over the past twenty-five years digitisation has simplified and speeded this task and now enables the organising, indexing and editing of large amounts of historical evidence. The appearance too of online websites and indexes created by archives repositories, libraries, museums, archaeological trusts, historical societies, universities and other bodies means that many of the practical difficulties which faced historians in gathering this evidence have been eradicated. Many websites now offer access to sources and materials which could once only be identified and consulted by means of frequent visits to libraries and archives. Major projects such as the digitising of the place-name collection of Melville Richards by Bangor University, and the probate and tithe records, newspapers and historical journals in The National Library of Wales, Aberystwyth, have proved especially valuable in this respect.

Introduction

Interpreting place-name evidence remains hard work. It has to be emphasised that it is not a simple matter of checking modern map forms against current dictionaries. Over a long period of time, words and names change their meaning, become obscured by re-interpretation and by shifts in pronunciation, and some lose currency. Gaps open up between local pronunciation and written forms – particularly when Welsh gives way to English as a local medium of conversation – and occasionally when standard Welsh displaces local usage. Understanding these developments takes time and demands specialist knowledge beyond the capabilities of any one person (including this author). Anyone offering an opinion on the meaning of a particular place-name has to be candid enough to admit doubts when evidence is inadequate. It is easy also to miss significant sources and spellings which may later prove to be critical in understanding the true meaning of a particular place-name. Ideally, every place-name dictionary should specify the sources of all historical forms which they cite in order to enable readers to check them and perhaps take the research further. Citing sources, however, can make publications lengthy and expensive and often have to be omitted. That is the case here but all historical forms in this publication may be identified online (see Selection of names below).

Place-Names in Glamorgan

Until recent years, more interest in Wales has been shown in the development of the Welsh language, its demographics and its literary history. Examples include the essays contained in *The Welsh Language before the Industrial Revolution* (1997) and, specifically in Glamorgan, the contribution by Ceri Lewis to *The Cardiff Region* (published by the British Association in 1960) and *Oes y Byd* (1992) by Siân Rhiannon Williams relating to the demographic history of the Welsh language in the Rhymni valley. *The Cardiff Region* also contains an essay by G.J. Williams on 'The Welsh literary tradition' which is especially valuable since it introduced the subject to English-only speakers. Williams was the leading authority on the literary history of the county – best shown in his *Traddodiad Llenyddol Morgannwg* (Cardiff 1948) – and he was well aware of the importance of place-name studies.

Interest in the history of the Welsh language and its literature ought to have lead on to investigation of both general and place-name vocabulary – as recognised in *The Welsh Dialect Survey*, edited by Alan R. Thomas (Cardiff 2000) – but little has so far appeared in print. A few characteristics of the local Welsh 'Gwentian' dialect are recorded by Iolo Morganwg (Richard Crowe, 'Iolo Morganwg and the Dialects of Welsh' in *A Rattleskull Genius. The Many Faces of Iolo Morganwg*, ed. Geraint H. Jenkins, Cardiff 2005, pp. 315-321), in the brief notes compiled by Frederic Evans published in *Tir Iarll* (Cardiff 1912), and the research of Ceinwen Thomas (see Nantgarw in Abbreviations and Bibliography). Some of these characteristics are readily identifiable in place-name evidence. In central and eastern Glamorgan, for example, colloquial *–a* is typically substituted for the common plural ending *–au* and *t* and *c* take the place of the 'softer' voiced consonants *d* and *g* found in the spoken language of other parts of Wales and in the modern written language. The first characteristic is identifiable in historic forms and current pronunciation of place-names such as Beddau ['beɪða]. The second characteristic (*c* for *g* and *t* for *d*) is found respectively in colloquial 'Rhicos, Ricos' for Rhigos and Tregatwg (the Welsh name of Cadoxton near Barry). Place-name evidence also enables us to identify and confirm some of the characteristics of the local English dialect and vocabulary. The best known example is the voicing of *f* as *v* witnessed in, for example, historic forms of Fernhill[2], in Gower. Similar evidence in Somerset – a few miles across the Bristol Channel – suggests that the English dialect of Glamorgan was heavily influenced by the language of that area and was reinforced by family and trading connections.

Place-name research has much else to offer and a thorough analysis of place-names in Glamorgan would undoubtedly shed more light, for example, on the historical inter-relationship of the Welsh and English languages. The meeting of the two languages in south Wales began more than a thousand years ago but it was the Anglo-Norman invasion during the twelfth century which brought them into truly close contact. The invasion was accompanied by immigration from England and further afield from Brittany, Normandy, other parts of France, and Flanders. This is proven not simply by incidental information in, for example, chronicles, conveyances of property and tax rolls but also in the names of individual fields, houses, villages and towns. The conquest brought with it distinctive English customary practices, personal names and vocabulary – many detectable in place-name evidence. What is surprising is how little investigation has been made into some of these matters such as the passage of English words into Welsh. Place-name evidence has much else to offer. Further research will certainly add words to our knowledge of both English and Welsh vocabulary (note Powndffald), provide earlier instances of particular elements and words, and add extensions of meanings (see Winsh-wen and Pen-iard) unrecognised in current dictionaries.

The importance of place-name evidence is more obvious when displayed in maps. This can be demonstrated by plotting, for example, the geographical distribution of English place-names. Seventy-four place-names are recorded before 1300 – less than 3% of the total place-names recorded in this publication. If we add names and anglicised place-names such as Aberthaw, Oystermouth and Roath recorded between 1301 and 1500, we can raise the figure to 115 or about 9% of the total. Any arguments based upon this evidence, however, must be heavily qualified. The problem is that place-names may not be recorded until many years after the date that they were first coined and we have no certain means of assessing how reliable these calculations may be. Our historical evidence plainly has large gaps and chance survival of evidence provides a poor foundation for definitive analysis. A more revealing method is to take this evidence as found, represent it as best we can geographically (see Map 2), and relate it to whatever other evidence (such as personal names) is available in order to test its reliability. Many of the publications relating to the medieval and early modern history of Glamorgan (specified in Abbreviations and Bibliography) will serve as a rough-and-ready comparison. Such geographical plotting shows that English place-names recorded before 1500 are concentrated in precisely those areas where non-Welsh personal names are more common in written records and where English law and custom had taken root. English and anglicised place-names dominate the western and southern parts of the Gower peninsula and the whole of the Vale of Glamorgan extending from the area around Pyle to St Mellons. Minor names (not covered in this publication) such as those of individual houses, fields and streets generally confirm this pattern and show also that English settlement in and immediately around Bridgend, Neath, Swansea, Cowbridge and Cardiff was extensive. In most of these areas, the English language has a continuous presence from the twelfth century down to the present day.

Introduction

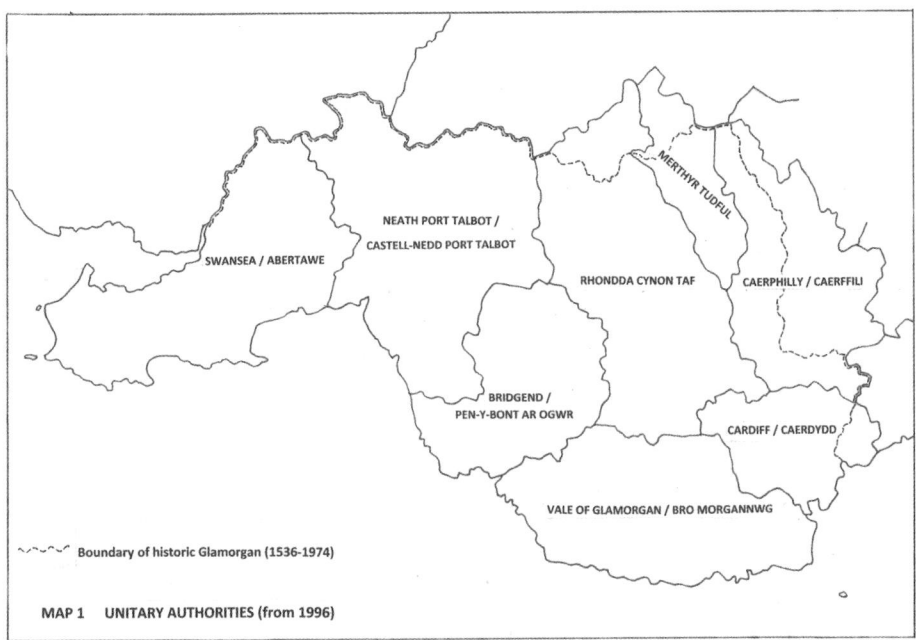

MAP 1   UNITARY AUTHORITIES (from 1996)

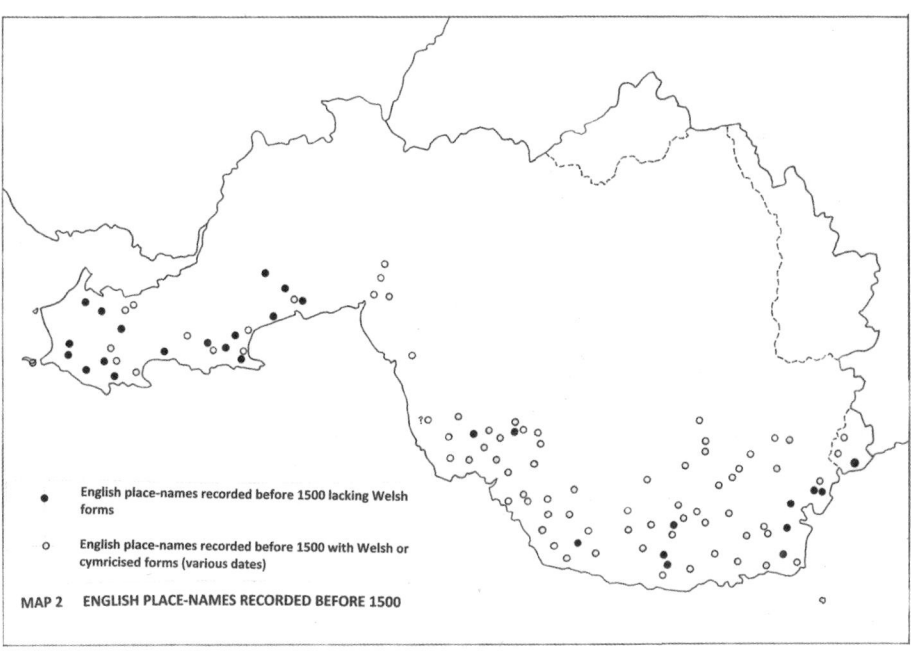

MAP 2   ENGLISH PLACE-NAMES RECORDED BEFORE 1500

The place-name landscape was, however, never static for long periods and place-names may only be reliable indications of the local spoken language at the time they were adopted. Some names, particularly those of larger rivers, lordships, townships and parishes, also have a much longer currency than the names of individual houses, streams and fields; these latter were more prone to change and as such are more reliable indicators of changes in local spoken language. One additional factor that has to be taken into account is that our sources are overwhelmingly English from the twelfth down to the eighteenth century and are typically taken from conveyances and surveys of property and from judicial and financial records kept by manorial, royal and ecclesiastical courts. That means that they are biased in favour of the languages – Latin, Norman French and English – used by their administrators and clerks and may not accurately reflect local usage. English influence sometimes imposed written forms which sidelined Welsh place-names and became regarded as the official form. It is interesting to note, for example, that a number of English parish names, such as Peterston-super-Montem (Llanbedr-ar-fynydd) and Michaelston-super-Avan (Llanfihangel Ynys Afan), were in areas which were – to judge from minor names and personal names – predominantly Welsh-speaking down to the mid nineteenth century. Some place-names may, in other words, have possessed little popular currency beyond the practices of a parish priest recording baptisms, marriages and burials, or a secular clerk compiling financial accounts. Evidence from purely Welsh sources by contrast is especially scarce before c.1500 and we sometimes have to rely upon literary sources such as poetry and late evidence in order to reach historical balance.

The English language introduced by Anglo-Norman lords and English settlers was, of course, laid over a Welsh foundation. This is evident in both anglicised place-names such as Oystermouth, Llancarfan, Penrice and St Lythans and in place-names such as St Brides Major which is probably an English translation of an unrecorded Llansanffraid – a place-name common in other parts of Wales. In this particular case, Welsh-speakers adopted the form Saint-y-brid (recorded from c.1566) as a cymricisation of the English name. Sometimes, as in the case of Marcross, it is exceptionally difficult to determine whether the place-name is Welsh or English and we can only present the evidence as it stands and offer a qualified opinion. It is also worth emphasising that the Welsh language was not in continuous retreat from the very moment that Anglo-Normans secured their conquest of Glamorgan. There is evidence to show that Welsh retained its hold on every part of Glamorgan with the exception of the westernmost and southerly parts of the Gower peninsula, parts of the eastern end of the Vale, and in and immediately around boroughs such as Swansea and Cardiff. In some areas, especially in the western part of the Vale, the English language seems to have weakened. This is manifest in the loss of English place-names such as Griffithsmoor and Poitevin Land, the dropping of the short form Afan/Avan used by English-speakers in favour of Aberafan (anglicised as Aberavon), and by a number of cymricisations of English place-names such as Tre-os. Welsh influence probably also accounts for the unusual development of English place-names such as Brackla and the Gnoll.

The English were not the only outsiders who settled in Glamorgan. Evidence for Irish settlement in the period before c.600 is attested in monumental inscriptions (one of the best known was at Kenfig) (Thomas Charles-Edwards, *Wales and the Britons 350-1064* (2013) 112-4, 631-2) but Irish influence has also been recognised in personal names (note Caerphilly/Caerffili) and river-names, especially those containing the suffix *–ach* (Bradach, Caeach, Clydach). The names of large rivers were far less likely to change than place-names so that river-names containing *–ach* are likely to be much older than their first recorded written forms. The extent of Irish settlement and how long it lasted is very difficult to gauge on the basis of such evidence. There are similar problems too with regard to Scandinavian settlement in Glamorgan. The subject received the attention of D.R. Paterson in a number of articles published in the historical and archaeological journal Archaeologia Cambrensis in the 1920s but he made many errors and most of his research is now widely discredited. Gwynedd O. Pierce has made some perceptive comments on the matter but it is one that needs re-examination based on detailed local studies. Names such as Womanby Street (in Cardiff) and Lamby (in Rumney) certainly look Scandinavian and Dunraven seems to be Irish-Scandinavian in Celtic word-order but we have no absolute means of testing the reliability of their historic forms or knowing how and exactly when they arose. The poor survival of such place-names and their concentration in coastal areas suggests that any Scandinavian settlement was relatively shortlived – ninth to the eleventh century at most – and very limited geographically.

For the greater part of its recorded history Glamorgan was a predominantly agricultural county of small market towns with a thinly scattered rural population, particularly in the uplands (Blaenau). Few new major place-names emerged between the late thirteenth and late eighteenth century when the rapid expansion of the coal and metal industries led to mass immigration, mainly from England and Ireland. Hundreds of new settlements appeared, linked by canal, rail and road to docks at Swansea, Barry, and Cardiff. Some adopted the names of nearby farms or streams but others took new, English names. Thirty-three of the place-names in this publication (Butetown, Elliots Town, Hopkinstown, Morriston, Tylorstown, Wattsville, for example) incorporate the elements -town, -ton and –ville, often coupled with the name of an industrial entrepreneur. Others took the names of local works (Merthyr Vale, Spelter, Trehafod), landowners (Jersey Marine, Llandarcy, Port Talbot, Wyndham Park), imperial battles (Balaclava, Waterloo) and public houses (Cross Keys, Fleur-de-lis, Mountain Hare, Nelson). Developments such as these have parallels in other parts of industrialised Britain, of course, but the effect in south Wales was especially marked and had a sharp cultural edge. A few adopted Welsh names on the same pattern: Cap-coch recalls a public house, Trealaw commemorates a bard, and Treherbert is named from ancestors of the marquesses of Bute, but the great majority took English names.

These developments drew the wrath of Welsh scholars at a time when Welsh cultural identity seemed to be threatened both by the incomers and by the gradual introduction of universal elementary education from 1870 which promoted English as the language of empire, the gentry and 'progress'. Some comfort was presumably found when a small number of English place-names were dropped: Newbridge made way for Pontypridd and Lewistown for Trelewis, or when towns and villages adopted Welsh alternatives: Aberpennar was added to Mountain Ash, Glynrhedynog to Ferndale, Tregŵyr to Gowerton. No doubt everyone was pleased that Sodom and Gomorrah (see Pontlotyn) never achieved official status. The great majority of the new English place-names, however, have survived down to the present day. The new place-names also set a pattern which was copied in the names chosen for new housing estates (Danescourt, Fernlea, Mornington Meadows) constructed in the twentieth century and in the names of streets. Unfortunately, attempts to redress the imbalance led some developers and local authorities to adopt names which possess no historical base (Glanyrafon for Riverside), misinterpretations (Glenboi. Trecenydd), historical errors (Ystum Taf for Llandaff North) and mistranslations (Trelluest for Grangetown). Some of these are likely to stay with us. New names, of course, are sometimes essential and it is a positive sign that the Welsh language is acquiring legal and social status which was long denied. Some of these linguistic developments also have a long pedigree. Re-interpretation, for example, is a phenomenon which can be identified in some of our oldest place-names (note Highlight for Uchelola, Oystermouth for Ystumllwynarth) and was a natural development before mass literacy. What is most remarkable, however, is how easily some modern names have been adopted with such little consideration as to their meaning. Bishwell Park (see Mynydd-bach y Cocs), as I have been reminded, ultimately draws its name from a place-name which signifies 'cattle dung, urine' (*biswail*). In Cardiff, Tiger Bay is still in semi-official use ('Porth Teigr' appears on tourist buses) though it is a euphemism for 'a place of ill repute'.

Selection of names

The choice of place-names as lead entries in dictionaries is always difficult. Toponymists often receive complaints from readers that particular names have been omitted but too wide a choice usually makes a publication lengthy and expensive. Publications of this nature – local and county surveys which take the analysis down to the level of individual field-names and house-names – are essential for academic reference but are beyond the pocket of most local historians. *Place-Names of Glamorgan* covers 1129 entries – hopefully enough to satisfy most demands – and, as the name indicates, concentrates overwhelmingly on places and excludes most topographical names. Exceptions are made for larger rivers and a few major topographical features. Some compensation for excluded names will be found within individual entries which frequently cite topographical and comparative place-name evidence in Glamorgan as well as other parts of Wales.

Selected place-names are drawn from:
(1) The OS map *Wales & West Midlands* (1:250 000) 1997.
(2) Larger-case place-names on the OS 1:25,000 Explorer (2012) maps of Brecon Beacons National Park/Parc Cenedlaethol Bannau Brycheiniog, Cardiff & Bridgend, Gower/Gŵyr, Llanelli & Ammanford/Rhydaman, Rhondda & Merthyr Tydfil/Merthyr Tudful, and Swansea/Abertawe.
(3) Historic parishes, lordships and manors from WATU (with exceptions such as Drefechan at Coety for which there seems to be no reliable evidence)
(4) Larger-case place-names on OS maps (1:50,000) *Brecon Beacons* (1997), *Cardiff, Newport & surrounding area* (1991), *Swansea, Gower & surrounding area* (1987) and *Vale of Glamorgan & Rhondda area* (1992) and
(5) *Philip's Street Atlas. Cardiff, Swansea & the Valleys* (2007)

The area chosen is that of the present eight unitary authorities (Map 1) which cover the historic county of Glamorgan (1889-1974), part of Breconshire (Faenor and Penderyn) transferred to Mid Glamorgan in 1974, and that part of historic Monmouthshire now in Caerphilly County Borough and the area around St Mellons and Rumney transferred to Cardiff County Borough Council in 1937 and 1951. The disappearance of our historic counties and county boroughs in 1974 (merged to form the counties of West

Glamorgan, Mid Glamorgan and South Glamorgan) and subsequent local government changes in 1996 means that an increasing number of people are now more familiar with the boundaries of their present unitary authority than extinct administrative divisions. A strict adherence to the county boundary of Glamorgan as it existed before reorganisation in 1974 might have been particularly confusing to those who live in the Rhymni valley and in the area of Faenor and Penderyn. I have added the names Breconshire and Monmouthshire where appropriate in order to provide a geographical link to historic counties and added the names of parishes (where the name differs from the lead entry) as they existed before 1896 to help in distinguishing identical place-names.

Editorial method

Dictionary entries comprise the following elements:

1. The lead-form in **bold** arranged according to the English alphabet. Spelling generally follows that on current Ordnance Survey maps giving precedence to English and anglicised place-names over the Welsh forms as appropriate in an English-language publication. Lead-forms are shown followed by any other official form, eg. **Swansea**, **Abertawe**. Exceptions have been made where the difference between current Ordnance Survey map spelling and the regular Welsh form is only a matter of a letter or two, eg. **Llanwynno** (Llanwonno) and **Bedwellte** (Bedwellty). The Ordnance Survey forms are shown in brackets. Such variations are not cross-referred unless the alphabetical sequence is significantly different, eg. **Aberavon** and **Risca** are referred to **Aberafan** and **Rhisga**. General guidance on Welsh spellings conventions are to be found in Guidelines for Standardizing Place-names in Wales issued by the Welsh Language Commissioner (2016) (www.comisynyddygymraeg/cymru). The Ordnance Survey has issued an explanatory guide 'The Welsh origin of place names in Britain' and an explanation of its Welsh Language Scheme (www.ordnancesurvey.co.uk/resources).
2. Six-figure National Grid references for precise locations taken from Ordnance Survey maps (not the OS Gazetteer which sometimes fails to correspond with historical nuclei) and four-figure references for wider areas. No grid references are given for very large areas such as local authorities.
3. Current unitary authority (in English/anglicised form) followed by the name of the historic parish, eg. Bridgend (Llangeinwyr). The historic county is not specified except in the case of those places which lay in the counties of Brecon and Monmouth before local government re-organisation in 1974.
4. A concise interpretation of the place-name with an identification of place-name element(s) in bold *italic* listed in the concise glossary at the end of this volume. This is based partly on the fuller glossary of *The Dictionary of the Place-names of Wales* (DPNW) supplemented by *Geiriadur Prifysgol Cymru* (GPC), the glossary in *The Place-Names of Pembrokeshire* (PNPemb), and *English Place-Name Elements* (EPNE). Any elements not contained in the glossary are in *italic* print, eg. Aber-carn appears as *aber*, rn. *Carn*. Any elements found as lead entries elsewhere in the volume appear in **bold** print, eg. Cefn Rhigos appears as *cefn*, pn. **Rhigos**. Personal names are excluded from the glossary.

5. A sample of historic spellings in ordinary *italics* and date. No indication of the source of spellings is provided in order to reduce both the length and cost of this publication. A full record of the sources is accessible online on the website of Cymdeithas Enwau Lleoedd/Welsh Place-Name Society: www.cymdeithasenwaulleoedd.cymru and www.welshplace-namesociety.wales. It has to be stressed that the reliability of some spellings is difficult to gauge when they occur in later manuscripts since copyists sometimes amended names or miswrote them. Rather than waste space, I have ignored the date of the copy unless it is considerably later than the original form; the date in these cases is given in brackets. Some historic forms also lack precise dates in their original sources and the usual practice, especially in edited printed sources, is to use the form 1160 x 1180 indicating the earliest and latest possible dates for a particular form. In this publication an arbitrary medial date has been adopted, i.e. c.1170.
6. Analysis of individual place-names. The length of this section varies according to the complexity of the name. Whenever possible, cross-references are made to similar or identical place-names found elsewhere. This section also contains relevant background information on the general history or topography of the place-name with limited referrals to secondary sources.
7. Whenever there is significant doubt over pronunciation I have added a simplified form of the International Phonetic Alphabet in brackets. A guide to this is set out below.

The use of some technical language in a work of this nature is inevitable but the opportunity is taken to explain further where appropriate. Some specialist terms, however, occur so frequently in Welsh that repetition would waste space. The main example is lenition, more widely known as soft mutation, which belongs to a group of sound changes found in all modern Celtic languages. Lenition in Welsh is the process in which the initial letters B, C, D, Ll [ɫ], M, P, and Rh [r̥] are displaced by F [v], G, Dd [ð], L, F [v], B and R, and G drops out altogether. These are most often caused by prepositions such as *i* 'to' and *o* 'from', and by the def.art. *Y, Yr* (before a vowel and H) and its affixed form `*r* (found after a vowel as in Cae'r-eithin). Elements in place-name entries are simply shown in the radical form, i.e. **pebyll** (for Cilybebyll) and **magwyr** (for Clwydyfagwyr) and lenition may be assumed to account for the change to *bebyll* and *fagwyr*. The other mutations – aspirate and nasal – are much less common and are explained within individual entries. The rules are, however, consistent and can be checked in a standard Welsh grammar (such as CWG and GC). All nouns and adjectives are also either masculine or feminine (noted as nm., adj.m., nf. and adj.m.), though a few vary in gender (nmf., adj.mf.); these are best identified in Geiriadur Prifysgol Cymru (geiriadur.ac.uk/gpc.html).

GUIDE TO THE INTERNATIONAL PHONETIC ALPHABET

The following represents a simplified form of the IPA and should be used only as an approximate guide to pronunciation. It has to emphasised that local pronunciation in both Welsh and English often varies from standard or expected form. Differences between Welsh and English pronunciation – even where a particular place-name has a common spelling – often varies.

IPA	Welsh	English	Examples of Glamorgan place-names
Consonants			
b	**b**ach, cw**b**l, ma**b**	**b**e	**B**aglan, **B**ryncethin, Cefncri**b**wr
d	**d**ydd, ca**d**w, ta**d**	**d**o	**D**yffryn, Pen**d**re
ʤ	gare**j**, **di**engyd (coll.)	**j**ust	**G**iants Grave, **G**range**t**own, **J**ersey Marine
ð	**dd**oe, be**dd**	**th**e	Be**dd**au, Caer**dy**dd, Llanble**th**ian
f	**ff**enest, cor**ff**	**f**ind	**F**erndale, **F**onmon, Pantyf**f**ynnon
g	**g**lan, ce**g**in	**g**et	Blaene**g**el, Fa**g**wr, Tyn-y-**g**arn
h	**h**aul	**h**ave	**H**endy, **H**ollybush, Fern**h**ill
j	**i**aith, ge**i**riadur	**y**ou	Pen-**i**ard, Tir **I**arll
k	**c**ig, a**cw**	**c**an	Bra**ck**la, **C**efn, **K**endon, Treor**c**i
l	**l**eicio, bo**l**	**l**ike	Gi**l**fach, **L**ogin
ɬ	**ll**yfr, cy**ll**ell		Cwm**ll**ynfell, **L**landaf, **Ll**wyn-onn, Tra**ll**wn
m	**m**ab, di**m**	**m**e	**M**an-**m**oel, **M**orriston
m̥	**mh**en	wor**mh**ole	Cw**m**-**h**wnt
n	**n**erth	**n**o	**N**elson
n̥	fy **nh**ad	u**nh**appy	Pen-**h**ydd, Town**h**ill
ŋ	fy **ng**wely	thi**ng**	Hardi**ng**s Down, Penyre**ng**lyn, Rhw**ng** Nedd a Tawe
ŋ̊h	fy **ngh**ŵn	Sha**ngh**ai	Se**ngh**ennydd
p	**p**en, co**p**a	**p**lease	Ca**p**-coch, **P**antyffynnon, **P**enderyn

xxi

r	radio, garw	right (trilled)		Darran, Riverside
r̥	rhestr, anrheg			Blaenrhymni, Rhiw, Rhondda
s	Saesnes, sws	see		City, Cyntwell, Seven Sisters
ʃ	siarad, brwsh	she		Llanisien, Shwt, Winsh-wen
t	tatws	time		Nottage, Taff Vale
tʃ	tseina, wats	chance		Birchgrove, Cheriton
θ	athro, peth	think		Brithdir, Cwmcothi, Thistleboon
v	faint, afal	very		Cefn, Fan, Fochriw, Pant-y-fid
w	wedyn, gwlân	was		Derwen, Walterston
χ	chwaer, bwlch			Blaenllechau, Glyn-fach, Machen
ʒ		decision		Cosmeston, Williamstown

Monopthongs

a	sant	sand	Aberaman, Ystrad
ɑː	mab, sâl	father, tar	Balaclava, Cwar, Parkmill, Pentretân
e	peth		Pelenna, Trefforest
eː	trên		Bryn-teg
ə	cymydog	about	Abercynon, Dyffryn, Llanwynno
ɛ	perth, mes	well	Berry, Gelli, Pelenna
ɛː		air, dare	Aberdare, Fairoak
iː	hir, tîm	be	Blackweir, Ely, Tir-nest
ɪ	tipyn	it, sit	Bryn, Cyncoed, Pen-prysg, Tresimwn
i̵ː	llun, bûm	tea	Clun-du, Galon Uchaf, Ysguborneywdd
oː	bro, ôl	toe (Scots)	Bryn-coch, Drope, Lônlas, Tre-os
ɔ	bron	gone	Ffontygari, Onllwyn
ɔː		stall	Stalling Down, Wallston
uː	cwch, dŵr	pool	Llwyn-y-bwch, Ynys-y-bŵl
ʌ		run	Burry, Dunraven, Loughor, Mumbles, Tutt
ʊ	cwm, mŵg	put	Betws, Cibwr, Swffryd
y	llu (north Wales)		
yː	bûm (north Wales)		

Dipthongs

ai	tai	eye	Abercannaid, Craigybwldan, Glais
ai̵	cau, nesáu	pie	Bryngolau

ʌɪə		fire	
au	llaw	around	Cae-mawr, Pen-clawdd, Ty-draw
aʊ		how	Beggars Pound, Cowbridge, Gower
aʊə		sour	
ɑːɨ	hael, cae		Baedan, Faenor, Llys-faen
ɛu	llew	wayward	Ewenni, Llanddewi
əi	Seisnig		Creigiau, Tonbreigam
ɔɨ	gwneud		Creunant, Llanfeuthin
eɪ		say	Lisvane, Oakdale
eɔ	heol		Heolgerrig
əu	bywyd		Glywysing
ɪu	lliw	stew	Butetown, Llan-giwg, Mewslade, Skewen
iu	Duw, menyw		
ɔi	osgoi	boy	Coychurch, Oystermouth
ɔi	coeden		Argoed, Treboeth
ɔː		caw, paw	Mawdlam (E pronunciation)
ʊə		poor	Landore, Moore Town, Po
ʊɨ	mwy, gŵyl		Abergwynfi, Gŵyr

ABBREVIATIONS AND BIBLIOGRAPHY

The following includes all sources cited in this publication, all abbreviations within individual entries and other relevant publications.

Abertawe	*Abertawe a'r cylch*, gol. Ieuan M. Williams (Bro'r Eisteddfod. Llandybïe 1982)
AC	*Archaeologia Cambrensis*. The Journal of the Cambrian Archaeological Association (1846-) [Followed by year of publication]
ADG[1]	Gwynedd O. Pierce, Tomos Roberts a Hywel Wyn Owen, *Ar Draws Gwlad* (Llanrwst 1997)
ADG[2]	Gwynedd O. Pierce a Tomos Roberts, *Ar Draws Gwlad 2* (Llanrwst 1999.)
adj.	adjective
adv.	adverb
AELIM	R.J. Thomas, 'Astudiaeth o enwau lleoedd cwmwd Meisgyn gyda sylw arbennig i blwyf Llantrisant', unpubl. MA thesis, Cardiff (NLW Aberystwyth 1933) [copy in Arts and Humanities Library, Cardiff University]
AF	Anglo-French
AN	Anglo-Norman
APNW	Scott Lloyd, *Arthurian Place Names of Wales* (Cardiff 2017)
ASEG	W. Ll. Morgan, *An Antiquarian Survey of East Gower* (London 1899)
ASFL	Charles F. Shepherd, *Annals of St. Fagans With Llanillterne* (Cardiff 1938)
ASG	Marianne Robertson Spencer, *Annals of South Glamorgan* (Carmarthen 1930)
asp.mut.	aspirate mutation
BCKenfig	Thomas Gray, *The Buried City of Kenfig* (London and New York 1909)
BG	Rice Merrick. *Morganiæ Archaiographia. A booke of Glamorganshire Antiquities* (1578), ed. J.A. Corbett (London 1887) [c.1580 collated with Queens College, Oxford, MS c.1660-80]
BirchM	Walter de Gray Birch, *A History of Margam Abbey* (London 1897)
BirchN	Walter de Gray Birch, *A History of Neath Abbey* (London 1902)
Blaencwm	Chris Evans, *Blaencwmdulais: a short history of the social and industrial development of Onllwyn and Banwen Pyrddin* (Cardiff 1977)
BPN	Adrian Room, *The Penguin Dictionary of British Place Names* (London 2003)
BRC	Biological Records Centre, CEH Wallingford, online: <www.brc.ac.uk>
Breviat	*A Breviat of Glamorgan, c.1598, by Rice Lewis* [c.1598], ed. William Rees in South Wales and Monmouthshire Record Society, no. 3 (1954)

Abbreviations and Bibliography

Brit	British
BroM	Aneirin Talfan Davies, *Bro Morgannwg* (Swansea 1976)
BWGwent	*The Buildings of Wales. Gwent*, by John Newman (Penguin/University of Wales (2000)
BZN	*Beiträge zur Namenforschung* (1949-)
Camden	*Britannia*, with an English translation by Philemon Holland (The Philological Museum), ed. Dana F. Sutton (University of California)
CardV	Brian Dicks, *Portrait of Cardiff and its valleys* (London 1984)
Cartae	*Cartae et Alia Munimenta*, ed. G.T. Clark (2nd ed. London 1910)
CAS	*Carmarthenshire Antiquarian Society Transactions*
CDEPN	*The Cambridge Dictionary of English Place-Names*, ed. Victor Watts (Cambridge 2004)
ch(s).	church, -es
chp(s).	chapel, -s
cmt(s).	commote, -s
CofiantCE	T.J. Jones, *Cofiant Canon Evans, Rhymni. "Un o Gymry Duw," sef Cofeb Fechan am William Evans, Canon Llandaf a Ficer Rhymni* (Lampeter 1904)
CofiantJD	*Cofiant y Parch. J. Davies* (Caerdydd 1883)
coll.n.	collective noun
conj.	conjunction
Coxe	William Coxe, *An Historical Tour in Monmouthshire* (2 vols. London 1801)
CPNE	O.J. Padel, *Cornish Place-name Elements* (English Place-Name Society vol. lvi/lvii, 1985)
CR	*Cardiff Records*, ed. John Hobson Mathews (Cardiff 1898-1911) [online: www.british-history.ac.uk/cardiff-records]
CVPN	Deric John, *Cynon Valley Place-Names* (Llanrwst 1998)
CWG	David Thorne, *A Comprehensive Welsh Grammar* (Oxford 1993)
dat.	dative
def.art.	definite article
DEPN	Eilert Ekwall, *The Concise Oxford Dictionary of English Place-Names* (Oxford, 4th edition, 1960)
dim.	diminutive
DPNW	Hywel Wyn Owen and Richard Morgan, *Dictionary of the Place-Names of Wales* (Gomer. Llandysul 2007, 2008)
DWB	*The Dictionary of Welsh Biography down to 1940*. Honourable Society of Cymmrodorion (London 1959) [online: http://yba.llgc.org.uk/en/index]
DWT	*The Diary of William Thomas, 1762-1795*, abstracted and edited by R.T.W. Denning (South Wales Record Society 1995)
E	English
EANC	R.J. Thomas, *Enwau Afonydd a Nentydd Cymru* (Cardiff 1938)
ECB	Dafydd Davies ac Arthur Jones, *Enwau Cymreig ar Blanhigion. Welsh Names of Plants* (Cardiff 1995)
ed.	edited, edition
EDD	Joseph Wright, *The English Dialect Dictionary* (London 1898-1905)
EHOSW	John Lloyd, *The Early History of the Old South Wales Ironworks (1760 to 1840)* (London 1906)

el(s).	element(s)
Elfen	Bedwyr Lewis Jones, *Yn ei Elfen* (Capel Garmon 1992)
ELl	Ifor Williams, *Enwau Lleoedd* (Liverpool 1969 impression)
ELlMeisgyn	R.J. Thomas, 'Astudiaeth o enwau lleoedd cwmwd Meisgyn gyda sylw arbenning i blwyf Llantrisant', unpubl. MA thesis, Cardiff (NLW Aberystwyth 1933)
EMaldwyn	Richard Morgan, *Enwau Lleoedd ym Maldwyn*, addasiad Dai Hawkins (Llanrwst 2001)
EnWales	*The Welsh Academy Encyclopaedia of Wales*, ed. John Davies, Nigel Jenkins, Menna Baines and Peredur I. Lynch (Cardiff 2008)
EPNE	A.H. Smith, *English Place-Name Elements* (English Place-Name Society, Cambridge 1956)
ETG	Melville Richards, *Enwau Tir a Gwlad*, gol. Bedwyr Lewis Jones (Caernarfon 1998)
Fr	French
fem.	feminine
fm(s).	farm(s)
fm.n(s).	farm-name(s)
fn(s).	field-name(s)
GazWPN	*A Gazetteer of Welsh Place-names. Rhestr o Enwau Lleoedd*, ed. Elwyn Davies (Cardiff 1957; 3rd edn.1967)
GC	David Thorne, *Gramadeg Cymraeg* (Llandysul 2000)
GCH II, III	*Glamorgan County History: II. Early Glamorgan. Pre-History and Early History*, ed. H.N. Savory (Cardiff 1984), and *III. The Middle Ages*, ed. T.B. Pugh (Cardiff 1971)
gen.	genitive
gen.sg.	genitive singular
GGower	*A Guide to Gower* (Gower Society. 2nd edn. 1966)
GlamLM	J.S. Corbett, *Glamorgan: Papers & Notes on the Lordship and its Members*, ed. D.R. Paterson (Cardiff 1925)
GLH	Gwent Local History (1976-)
Gower	*Gower. Journal of the Gower Society* (1948-)
GowerH	Paul Ferris, *Gower in History. Myth, people, landscape* (Armaleg Books 2009)
GPC	*Geiriadur Prifysgol Cymru* (Caerdydd 1950-2002) [online: https://geiriadur.ac.uk/gpc]
GPNG	C.J. Evans, *A Short Glossary of the Place-Names of Glamorgan* (Cardiff 1908)
GuideHTV	Mary Gilham, John Perkins and Clive Thomas, *A Guide to the Historic Taff Valley from Quakers' Yard to Aberfan* (Merthyr Tydfil and District Naturalists' Society 1979)
GwCH I, II	*The Gwent County History*, ed. Ralph A. Griffiths: Vol. 1. Gwent in Prehistory and Early History (Cardiff 2004); Vol. 2. The Age of the Marcher Lords, c.1070-1536 (Cardiff 2008)
HBryn	Enoch Rees, *Hanes Brynamman a'r cylchoedd* (Ystalyfera 1896; facsimile 1992)
HBT	*A Handbook for Travellers in South Wales* (John Murray. London 1860)
hd(s).	hundred(s)

HE	Glenda Carr, *Hen enwau o Arfon, Llŷn ac Eifionydd* (Caernarfon 2011)
HGower	Derek Draisey, *A History of Gower* (Logaston Press 2002)
HLlangynwyd	Thomas Christopher Evans (Cadrawd), *History of Llangynwyd* (Llanelli 1887)
HLlanwyno[1, 2]	William Thomas (Glanffrwd), *Plwyf Llanwyno*, ed. David J. Hopkin (Pontypridd 1888; 2nd ed. Aberdare 1913)
HLlanwyno[3]	*Llanwynno Glanffrwd*, ed. Henry Lewis (Cardiff 1949) [3rd ed. of HLlanwyno[1] with modernised spellings and a fuller index]
HM	Glenda Carr, *Hen enwau o Ynys Môn* (Caernarfon 2015)
HMA	*History of Mountain Ash by William Bevan 1896*, a translation by A.V. Jones (1990) of *Hanes Mountainash: traethawd buddugol yn Eisteddfod y Pasc* (Caernarfon 1897)
HMerth	Charles Wilkins, *The History of Merthyr Tydfil* (Merthyr Tydfil 1867; 1908)
HMON I-IV	J.A. Bradney, *A History of Monmouthshire I-IV* (London 1904-33). 4 vols.
HMON V	J.A. Bradney, *A History of Monmouthshire... V*, ed. Madeleine Gray (South Wales Record Society, Cardiff and The National Library of Wales, Aberystwyth, 1993)
HMorg	David Watkin Jones (Dafydd Morganwg), *Hanes Morganwg* (Aberdare 1874)
ho(s).	house(s)
ho.n(s)	house-name(s)
HSeven	Christopher Evans, *A History of Seven Sisters* (1964)
HSoar	Erastus Jones, *Hanes Eglwys Gyffredin: Eglwys Annibynnol Soar, Blaendulais, 1872-1951* (Glyn-nedd 1951)
ht(s).	hamlet(s)
HTonyrefail	Thomas Morgan [d.1890], *Hanes Tonyrefail. Yr hen amser gynt. Tonyrefail a'i amgylchoedd. Adgofion am y tadau*, rhagymadrodd gan Owen Morgan (Morien) (1899) [online: www.hanestonyrefail.org]
IHCS	Dennis Morgan, *The Illustrated History of Cardiff's Suburbs* (Derby 2003)
IoloMor	G.J. Williams, *Iolo Morganwg* (Cardiff 1956)
Ir	Irish
John SPN	Deric John, 'Some place-names in south Wales and their etymologies' <someplacenames.mysite.wanadoo-members.co.uk/index.jhtml>
KeyEPN	Key to English Place-Names, Nottingham University <http.://kepn.nottingham.ac.uk>
Lat	Latin
Leland	*The Itinerary in Wales of John Leland, in or about the years c.1536-9*, ed. Lucy Toulin-Smith (London 1906)
len.	lenition (soft mutation)
LewisTD	Samuel Lewis, *A Topographical Dictionary of Wales* (London 1843; 3rd edn. 1845; 4th edn. 1849)
LimbPat	G.T. Clark, *Limbus Patrum Morganiæ et Glamorganiæ, being the Genealogies of the Lordships of Morgan and Glamorgan* (London 1886)
LL	*Liber Landavensis. The Text of the Book of Llan Dav*, ed. John Gwenogvryn Evans and John Rhŷs (Oxford 1893; facsimile Aberystwyth 1979)

LlEnwau	D. Geraint Lewis, *Y Llyfr Enwau. Enwau'r Wlad. A check-list of Welsh Place-names* (Llandysul 2007)
Lloffyn	Thomas Morgan, *Lloffyn llenorol: sef, gweithiau buddugol Eisteddfod Salem, Spelter, Maesteg* (J.T. Thomas. Aberdare 1857)
LLR	*Llandaff Records*, ed. J.A. Bradney and R. Rickards (Cardiff and London 1905-14)
LLRees	*Liber Landavensis*, ed. William Jenkin Rees (Welsh Manuscripts Society. Llandovery 1840)
LlUF	*Llawlyfr Undeb Ferndale a'r Cylch* (Undeb yr Annibynwyr Cymraeg. Mehefin 1957. Swansea 1957)
lp(s).	lordship, -s
LWS	G.H. Doble, *Lives of the Welsh Saints*, ed. D. Simon Evans (Cardiff 1971)
MachenR	*Machen Revisited*, compiled Delphine Coleman and Dennis Spargo (Images of Wales. Stroud 2001)
Malkin	Benjamin Heath Malkin, *The Scenery, Antiquities, and Biography of South Wales* (London 1807)
masc.	masculine
MCPP	Michael Eyers, *Masters of the Coalfield. People and Place-Names in Glamorgan and Gwent* (Risca 1992)
ME	Middle English (c.1150-c.1500)
MedSwans	www.medievalswansea.ac.uk
Merrick	*Rice Merrick. Morganiae Archaiographia. A Book of the Antiquities of Glamorganshire*, ed. B.Ll. James (South Wales Record Society 1983)
mess.	messuage
MethC	Rev. John Hughes, *Methodistiaeth Cymru: sef hanes blaenorol a gwedd bresenol y Methodistaid Calfinaidd yn Nghymru* (Wrexham 1851, 1854, 1856)
MMF	D. Morgan Rees, *Mines, Mills and Furnaces. An introduction to industrial archaeology in Wales* (National Museum of Wales. London 1969)
ModE	Modern English (c.1500 to present)
ModW	Modern Welsh
MSM	Royal Commission on Ancient and Historical Monuments, *An Inventory of the Ancient Monuments in Glamorgan*, Volume III, Part 1b, Medieval Secular Monuments, The later Castles from 1217 to the Present (2000)
MW	Middle Welsh
n(s).	name(s), noun(s)
Nantgarw	Ceinwen Thomas, *Tafodiaith Nantgarw: Astudiaeth o Gymraeg Llafar Nantgarw yng Nghwm Taf, Morgannwg* (Cardiff 1993)
NCDL	Rev. C.A.H. Green, *Notes on churches in the diocese of Llandaff* (Aberdare 1906, 1907)
NCPN	B.G. Charles, *Non-Celtic Place-Names in Wales* (Cardiff 1938)
NCR	Gareth Pierce, *Nabod Cwm Rhymni* (Whitchurch 1990)
nf.	feminine noun
NGG	Lewis D. Nichol, *The Normans in Glamorgan, Gower and Kidweli* (Cardiff 1936)
NLW	The National Library of Wales, Aberystwyth
NLWJ	*The National Library of Wales Journal*
nm.	masculine noun
nmf.	masculine or feminine noun

n.pl.	plural noun
n.sg.	singular noun
NTC	*The Names of Towns and Cities in Britain*, ed. Margaret Gelling, W.F.H. Nicolaisen and Melville Richards (London 1970)
OBret	Old Breton
ODan	Old Danish
ODEPN	A.D. Mills, *Oxford Dictionary of English Place-Names* (2nd edn., Oxford 1998)
OE	Old English
OED	*The Oxford English Dictionary*, ed. J. A. Simpson and E. S. C. Weiner (2nd edn. Oxford 1989)
Oes y Byd	Sian Rhiannon Williams, *Oes y Byd i'r Iaith Gymraeg. Y Gymraeg yn ardal ddiwydiannol Sir Fynwy yn y bedwaredd ganrif ar bymtheg* (Cardiff 1992)
OIr	Old Irish
ON	Old Norse
OPemb	*The Description of Penbrokshire, by George Owen of Henllys, Lord of Kemes*, ed. Henry Owen, notes by Egerton Phillimore (London 1872-1906) [1603]
OPN	Rev. Thomas Morgan, *Handbook of the Origin of Place-Names in Wales and Monmouthshire* (Merthyr Tudful 1871)
OS	Ordnance Survey
OScand	Old Scandinavian
OW	Old Welsh
Par	*Parochialia*, ed. R.H. Morris (Archaeologia Cambrensis supplements 1909-11)
p(s).	parish(es)
p.ch(s).	parish church(es)
pers.n(s).	personal name(s)
pn(s).	place-name(s)
PNANG	Gwilym T. Jones and Tomos Roberts, *The Place-Names of Anglesey* (Bangor 1996)
PNBangor	<www.e-gymraeg.co.uk/enwaulleoedd>
PNBont	Deric John, *Notes on Some Place-Names in and around the Bont* (Aberdare 1999)
PNBre	Richard Morgan and R.F. Peter Powell, *A Study of Breconshire Place-Names* (Llanrwst 1999)
PNCrd	Iwan Wmffre, *The Place-Names of Cardiganshire* (BAR British Series 379 (I) 2004) (3 vols.)
PND	Bedwyr Lewis Jones, *Place-name Detective*, trans. Anthony Lias (Llanrwst 2008)
PNDPH	Gwynedd O. Pierce, *The Place-Names of Dinas Powys Hundred* (Cardiff 1968)
PNF	Hywel Wyn Owen and Ken Lloyd Gruffydd, *Place-Names of Flintshire* (Cardiff 2017)
PNEF	Hywel Wyn Owen, *The Place-Names of East Flintshire* (Cardiff 1994)
PNG	E.T. Davies, *The Place-Names of Gwent* (Risca 1982)
PNGlam	Gwynedd O Pierce, *Place-Names in Glamorgan* (Cardiff 2002)
PNGwent	Richard Morgan, *Place-names of Gwent* (Llanrwst 2005)
PNIG	Howard C. Jones, *Place Names in Glamorgan* (Barry 1978)

PNMont	Richard Morgan, *A Study of Montgomeryshire Place-Names* (Llanrwst 2001)
PNPemb	B.G. Charles, *The Place-Names of Pembrokeshire* (Aberystwyth 1992)
PNRad	Richard Morgan, *A Study of Radnorshire Place-Names* (Llanrwst 1998)
PNRB	A.L.F. Rivet and Colin Smith, *The Place-Names of Roman Britain* (Cambridge 1979)
PNSHR I	Margaret Gelling, *The Place-Names of Shropshire*, Part I (English Place-Name Society 1990)
PNWales	Hywel Wyn Owen, *The Place-Names of Wales* (Cardiff 2015)
PNWB	Anthony Lias, *Place Names of the Welsh Borderlands* (Ludlow 1991)
PNWG	Graham Osborne and G.J. Hobbs, *The Place-Names of Western Gwent* (Abertillery 1992)
Porthcawl	Alun Morgan, *Porthcawl Newton and Nottage* (Cowbridge 1987)
prep.	preposition
pron.	pronunciation
q.v.	*quod vide* as a cross-referral
r(s).	river(s)
RB	Romano-British
ref(s).	reference(s)
RFWM	*Roman Frontiers in Wales and the Marches*, ed. Barry C. Burnham and Jeffrey L. Davies (Royal Commission on the Ancient and Historical Monuments of Wales. Aberystwyth 2010)
rn(s).	river-name(s)
SalemN	Peter Brooks, *Hanes Eglwys y Bedyddwyr Salem Newydd Welsh Baptist Church 1877-1994* (Ferndale 2008)
Scand	Scandinavian
sing.	singular
SIR	*Swansea and Its Region*, ed. W.G.V. Balchin (University College of Swansea. Swansea 1971)
SLBM	S. Phillips and William Rees, 'The story of the Lower Borowes of Merthyrmawr', South Wales and Monmouthshire Record Society 1 (1949)
SNW	John and Sheila Rowlands, *The Surnames of Wales. Updated & Expanded* (Llandysul 2013)
sp(s).	spelling(s)
Spurrell	*Spurrell's Welsh-English Dictionary*, ed. J. Bodvan Anwyl (Carmarthen 1913)
StAbercynon	Thomas Evans, *The Story of Abercynon* (2nd ed. Tonypandy 1955)
StBenson	Dorothy M. Bayliffe and Joan N. Harding, *Starling Benson of Swansea* (Cowbridge and Bridgend 1996)
StC	*Studia Celtica* (1996-)
StTaibach	A. Leslie Evans, *The Story of Taibach and District* (Port Talbot 1963)
t(s).	township(s)
TAMDHS	*The Transactions of the Aberafan & Margam Historical Society* (followed by year)
terr.n.	territorial name
THPM	William Edmunds, *Traethawd ar Hanes Plwyf Merthyr o'r cyfnod boreuaf hyd yn bresenol* (Aberdare 1864)
Trib	*Tribannau Morgannwg*, ed. Tegwyn Jones (Llandysul 1976)

TVD	Thomas V. Davies, *The Farms and Farmers of Senghenydd Supra Prior to the Industrial Revolution* (1990)
vb.	verb
VGS	*Stewart Williams' Vale of Glamorgan Series* 1: History on my Doorstep (Cowbridge 1959); 2: Vale of History (Cowbridge 1960); 3: The Garden of Wales (Cowbridge 1961); 4: Saints and Sailing Ships (Cowbridge 1963)
VNeath	D. Rhys Phillips, *History of the Vale of Neath* (Swansea 1921; facsimile with foreword 2014)
VSB	*Vitae Sanctorum Britanniae et Genealogiae*, ed. A.W. Wade-Evans (Board of Celtic Studies. Cardiff 1944)
W	Welsh
WATU	Melville Richards, *Welsh Administrative and Territorial Units* (Cardiff 1969; 1973)
WB	Thomas M. Charles-Edwards, *Wales and the Britons 350-1064* (The History of Wales) (Oxford University Press 2013)
WLlR	*The Welsh Language before the Industrial Revolution*, ed. Geraint H. Jenkins (Cardiff 1997)
WP	Griffith Jones, *Welch Piety or a Collection of the several Accounts of the Circulating Welsh Charity Schools, 1737-76* (annual reports. London)
*	Hypothetical form
>	Developing into
<	Developing from

ONLINE DATABASES AND REFERENCE RESOURCES

Archives Network Wales:
www.archivesnetworkwales.info

Archives of Welsh colleges and universities:
www.archiveshub.ac.uk

British History Online (miscellaneous sources):
www.british-history.ac.uk

Geiriadur Prifysgol Cymru:
www.geiriadur.ac.uk/gpc

Glamorgan Archives, Archifau Morgannwg:
www.glamorganarchives.gov.uk, www.archifaumorgannwg.gov.uk

National Archives, London:
www.nationalarchives.gov.uk

National Library of Wales, Aberystwyth:
www.llgc.org.uk

Ordnance Survey 1:50 000 scale gazetteer:
data.ordnancesurvey.co.uk/datasets/50k-gazetteer

Ordnance Survey first edition 1:63 360 maps:
www.visionofbritain.org.uk/maps

Ordnance Survey historic maps (various scales):
www.old-maps.co.uk

Ordnance Survey website:
www.ordnancesurvey.co.uk/website

Online Databases and Reference Resources

Place-Name Research Centre, Canolfan Bedwyr, Bangor University: Archif Meville Richards:
www.e-gymraeg.co.uk/enwaulleoedd

Places of Wales (Discover the tithe maps of Wales):
https.//places.history.wales

Royal Commission on Ancient and Historical Monuments for Wales: online catalogue of archaeology, buildings, industrial and maritime heritage in Wales:
www.coflein.gov.uk

Tithe Maps of Wales, Mapiau Degwm Cymru (Coflein):
cynefin.archiveswales.org.uk

Welsh Place-Name Society/Cymdeithas Enwau Lleoedd Cymru:
www.cymdeithasenwaulleoedd.cymru and www.welshplace-namesociety.wales

Welsh Coal Mines:
www.welshcoalmines.co.uk

West Glamorgan Archive Service, Gwasanaeth Archifau Gorllewin Morgannwg:
www.swansea.gov.uk/westglamorganarchives,
www.abertawe.gov.uk/archifaugorllewinmorgannwg

Glossary of Common Place-name Elements

This covers all elements marked in bold in the main text with the exception of:

1. The Welsh def.art. (*y*, *yr*, `*r*) and English def.art. (*the*).
2. Place-names which serve as qualifiers, eg. **Blaenau Morgannwg** in the text, is referred to the elements *blaen* (in italic and bold) pl. *blaenau* in the Glossary and the qualifier **Morgannwg** (ordinary case and bold) is cross-referred in the text to **Glamorgan, Morgannwg**.

Discussions of individual elements are necessarily brief and readers should check these against the glossaries in DPNW and PNPemb. Infrequent elements and individual Welsh words within the body of each entry are excluded. These should be checked in GPC. English elements are covered by EPNE and authoritative English dictionaries. All place-name elements are assumed to be Welsh unless stated otherwise.

abbey E

aber, nf., earlier nm., pl. *ebyr*, 'confluence (of two rivers); mouth of a river' and 'stream, rivulet; creek'

-ach Ir suffix

acre E see *æcer* OE

aderyn variant *ederyn* nm., *adar* pl., 'bird'

æcer OE 'plot of arable land; measure of land which a yoke of oxen could plough in a day; statute acre'

æsc OE 'ash-tree'

afall, *afallen* nf. 'apple-tree'

afon nf., pl. *-ydd*, *-oedd*, 'river'

āld, *eald* OE 'old, former'

allt, *gallt* nf., *alltau*, *elltydd*, *eillt* pl., 'hill(side); wooded slope'

-an dim. suffix

anchor E

ar prep. 'near, at, by, on'

aradur 'oratory'

ardd[1] nf., adj., 'hill, highland'; cf. I *ard*, 'height, hill'

argoed (*ar* + *coed*) coll.n., pl. *–ydd*, 'trees, forest, edge or border of forest'

arlwydd variant *arglwydd* nm. 'lord, feudal lord, the Lord'

ash see *æsc* OE

atten OE 'at the'

awel nf. '(light) wind, breeze'

bach[1] adj. 'small, little; lesser'

bach[2] nmf. 'hook, nook, angle, bend'

bad[2] nm. 'boat, ferry'

bae nm. 'bay'

ban[1] nf., *bannau*, **benni* pl., 'top, summit, peak'

banhadlog, *banhalog* adj. 'abounding with broom'

bank E, *banke* ME, 'bank, hill-slope'

banw nm. 'pig or young pig'

bar[2] nm. 'head, top, summit'

bāt 'boat, ferry'

bay E 'broad inlet of the sea where the land curves in'

bechan see *bychan*

bedd nm., *-au* pl., 'grave'

bedlwyn, *bedwlwyn* nmf., 'birch-grove'

bedw n.pl. and nf. 'birch, birch-grove', *bedwen* nf. 'birch-tree'

bedyddiwr nm. *bedyddwyr* pl. 'baptist'

Glossary of Common Place-name Elements

beggar E 'person who begs, a poor person'
ben¹ nf., *benni* pl., 'cart, wagon'
beorg OE 'hill, tumulus', E *burrow*
ber see *byr*
*berran (*ber* + *rhan* 'part, share') nf. 'short share-land'
betws¹ (< OE *bed-hūs*) nm., *betysau* pl., 'house of prayer, chapel of ease'
beu, *beau* Fr 'fair, beautiful'
bī OE 'by, near'
bid¹ nmf., *bid(i)au* pl., 'hedge, quickset hedge, fence'
birce OE, *birch* E 'birch-tree'
birch see *birce* OE
biscop OE 'bishop, senior member of the clergy'
black E see *blæc* OE
blæc OE 'black, dark-coloured, overgrown'
blaen nm., *-au* pl., and adj., 'end, point, tip, apex, summit; source or upper reaches of river or stream; extremity, uplands', etc'
blāw OE 'blue pigment'
blue E see *blāw* OE
boat E see *bāt* OE
boch nf. 'cheek, jaw'
bod¹ nmf., *-ydd*, *-au* pl., 'permanent home, dwelling place, abode'
bôn¹ nm. 'bottom, base; tree-trunk, stump'
brād OE, *brode* ME, 'broad'
brǣc 'a brushwood, a thicket'
bracty variant *bragdy* nm. 'brewery, malthouse'
brain see *brân*
braith see *brith*
brân nf., *brain* pl., 'crow, rook, raven'
brēc, *brǣc* OE 'land broken up'
brech see *brych*
brende, *brente* ME 'burnt'
brenin nm. 'king, sovereign'
bridge see *brycg* OE

brith¹ adj., *braith* fem., 'marked with different colours, mottled, speckled'
bro nf., *broydd* pl., 'vale, lowland' and 'region, country, land'
broad see *brād* OE
brōc OE 'brook, stream'
broch¹ nm. 'badger'
brode ME see *brād* OE
brōm OE 'broom'
brook see *brōc* OE
brwydr¹ nf., *brwydrau* pl. 'pitched battle, attack; dispute'
brycg OE, 'a bridge'; *brigge*, *brugge* ME
brych adj., *brech* fem., 'brindled, spotted, speckled'
bryn nm., *-iau*, *-nau* pl., 'hill, mount, rise, bank; heap' etc
bugeilydd nm. 'shepherd'
burh dat. *byrig*, 'fortified place, fort'
busc OE 'bush, shrub'
bush E see *busc* OE
bwch nm. 'buck, he-goat; roebuck'
bŵl (< ME *boule*) 'ball; bowl'
bwlch nm., *bylchau* pl., 'breach, gap; pass'
bwlwarc (< E *bulwark*) nm., *bwlwarcau* pl., 'bulwark'
by see *bī* OE
bychan adj., *bechan* fem., *bychain*, *bychan* pl., 'little, small, lesser'
byr¹ adj., *ber* fem., 'short, small'
býr ON 'yard, courtyard, farmhouse; village'
cadle nm. 'battlefield, battle'
cadlys nf. 'castle bailey; court-yard, enclosure'
cae nm., *caeau* pl., 'hedge, hedge-row, fence' but more widely 'field, enclosure' in field-ns.
caer nf., *caerau* pl., 'a fortified place, a fortification, a fort' and 'city'.
cærse OE 'cress'
cafn nm. 'vat; trough; gutter

cald OE 'cold; inhospitable, bleak, exposed'

caled adj. 'hard; rough'

cam² adj. 'crooked, bent'

canol, cenol nm, *-au, -ydd* pl., and adj. 'middle, centre'

cap nm. 'cap; hood'

capel nm., pl. *-au, -i, -ydd, -oedd*, 'chapel', esp. 'chapel of ease, Nonconformist meeting-house or chapel'

car¹ nm., *ceir* pl., 'cart, car'

câr nm. 'kinsman, relative; friend, dear one'

carn nmf., *–au* pl., and adj., 'cairn, barrow, tumulus, mound, rock; heap, pile'; nm. 'hoof, foot'

carreg nf., *cerrig* pl., 'stone, rock'

carw nm., *ceirw* pl., 'deer, hart, stag'

caseg nm., *cesig* pl., 'mare'

castel(l) ME 'castle'

castell nm., *castellau, cestyll, cystyllau, -e* pl., 'castle, fort, stronghold'

castle see *castel(l)* ME

cat OE, ME 'cat, wild cat'

cath nf. 'cat'

cawg nm. 'dish, bowl, basin'

cawl nm. 'soup, pottage; cabbage, colewort'; *cawl y môr* 'sea-cabbage, sea-kale'

cefn, dial. *cefen* nm., *–i, -au* pl., 'back, fig. support; ridge, butt of ploughed land'

ceibr nm. 'rafter, beam, joist'

ceiliog, ceilog nm. 'cock'

ceirw see *carw*

celli nf. 'grove, copse, woodland'

celyn¹ n.pl. or coll.n. 'holly', *celynnen* nf. 'holly-tree'

cenol see *canol*

cerddin, cerddinen, cerdin nf. 'rowan-tree, mountain-ash'

ceri, cerïen n.pl. or coll.n. 'service-tree(s); berries of dog-rose or wild briar, hips, kernels; medlar-tree(s)'

cethin adj. 'dark, swarthy; wild'

ceubalfa (*ceubal* 'a boat', *-fa*) nf. 'ferry'

channel ME, E 'sea-channel'

church see *cirice* OE

chwith adj. 'left, left-handed; strange, unusual, sinister'

chwyth nm. 'breath; a blowing, gust, breeze'

cil¹ nm., sometimes nf., *ciliau, cilion* pl., 'retreat, corner, nook' and, with a rn., 'source'

cilfach nf., *-au, -oedd, -fechydd* pl., 'nook, recess, corner, sheltered or secluded spot; retreat' etc

cimle, cimla (<*cymfei, cymfai*) nm., variants *cimdda, cymdda, cymfa* 'common, common land'

cirice, cyrice OE 'church'

city E 'large town'

clas nm. 'monastic community'

clawdd nm., *cloddiau*, 'trench, earthwork; ditch'

clif OE 'cliff, bank'

cliff see *clif* OE

clog¹ nf. 'rock, cliff, precipice'

clun² nm., 'meadow, moor; brake'

clwyd nf., *clwydau* 'movable hurdle; gate, door'

cnæp(p) OE 'hill-top, short sharp ascent'

cnap¹ nm. 'knap, lump; boss, knob'

cnocc OE

cnol OE 'hill top, knoll, hillock'

cnol (< OE *cnol*, E *knoll*) nm., ?nf. 'knoll, hillock'

coal see *col* OE

coch adj. 'red, ruddy; brown' etc.

cocket ME, E 'hillock'

cocos, cocs pl. 'cockles'

coed nm. and coll.n. 'forest, wood, trees', pl. of *coeden* nf., 'tree'

coedcae, coetgae nm., 'quickset, a hedge of trees; land enclosed with a hedge, field, close' etc.

coes nmf. 'leg, shank'

coetgae see *coedcae*

coetref nm. 'woodland homestead or dwelling'

col OE 'coal, charcoal'

cōl OE 'cool'

*coll*² coll.n., *collen* nf., *cyll* pl., 'hazel; sapling'

collen see *coll*²

cor nm. 'dwarf, pigmy'

cored nmf. 'weir, dam'

corlan, *corddlan* nf., *corlannau* pl., 'fold, pen'

corn OE 'crane, heron'

corn nm., *cyrn* pl., 'horn; point'

cors nf. and coll.n. 'swamp, bog, marsh'

corun OE, *corune* ME 'crown, top'

cot OE 'cottage, hut, shelter'

court OFr, ME, 'a space enclosed by walls or houses, a yard' and 'a large house, a manor' (from late 13cent); sometimes confused with *cort(e)* OE, ?'a short plot of ground, a piece of land cut off'. Locally 'monastic grange'; cf. *cwrt*¹ nm. 'enclosure, yard, farm-yard; grange, court'

cow see *cū* OE

cragen nf., *cregyn* pl., 'shell; shell-fish'

craig nf., *creigiau*, *creigydd* pl., 'a rock, cliff',

*crau*¹ nmf. 'blood, gore'

crāwe OE 'a crow'

creigiau see *craig*

cribwr nm. 'comber, one who cards wool'

croes nf., *crwys*, later *croesau*, pl.; 'a cross, crossroads'

crofft nf., -*au* pl., 'small enclosed field'

croft OE 'small enclosed field'

cron see *crwn*

cros OE 'a cross, the Cross; crossroads'

crow E see *crāwe* OE

crug nm., -(*i*)*au* pl., 'hillock, knoll; cairn, tumulus; heap, mass'

crwm adj., *crom* fem., 'crooked, bent, curved'

crwn adj., *cron* fem. 'round, circular'

crwys see *croes*

crynwr nm., *crynwyr* pl., 'Quaker, member of Society of Friends'

cū OE 'a cow'

culfre OE, ME 'pigeon'

curn, *cyrn* nf. 'heap, mound'

*cwar*¹ nm., *cwarrau* pl., 'quarry'

*cwarel*¹ nm., *chwarel*¹ nmf, *cwarelau* pl., 'quarry; mine'

cwm nm., *cymoedd*, -*au*, -*ydd* pl., 'a deep, narrow valley, coomb, glen, dale; hollow, bowl-shaped depression'

cwmwr nm. 'footbridge'

*cwmin*³ variants *comin*, *cymin* (< ME *cumin*, *comin*) nm. 'common'

*cwrt*¹ nm., 'court, mansion; courtyard, enclosure, farmyard' and 'monastic grange'

cwter nf. 'gutter, channel; rain-trough'

*cyfarth*¹ nm. 'barking, baying', vb. 'to bark, bay', earlier 'barking made by a bear'

*cyfeilltion (*cyf*-, *eilltion* as dual pl. of *allt*)

cyff nm., *cyffiau*, *cyffion*, 'trunk (of a tree), stump, log'

cyfraith nf. 'law; statute; custom'

cylen, *cyln* OE, E *kiln* dialect *kill* 'a kiln'

cymdda, *cymfa* see *cimle*, *cimla*

*cymer*¹ nm., *cymerau* pl., 'confluence of two or more rivers or streams, meeting of waters'

cynhaeaf-dre, *cynhawdre* nm. (*cynhaeaf* 'harvest; harvest-time', *tref*)

cynnud nm. 'fuel, firewood'

cȳta OE 'kite (bird-of-prey)'

cyw nm., *cywion* pl., 'young bird, chick; young animal'

dafad nf., *defaid* pl., 'sheep, ewe'

dale E 'valley'

dan see *tan*

dâr nf., *deri* pl., 'oak-tree'

dau variant *deu*, number and adj., *dwy* fem., 'two; pair'

defaid see *dafad*
deme see *dime*
deri see *dâr*
derwen nf., *derw* pl., 'oak-tree'
deu see *dau*
deunaw number and nm. 'eighteen; eighteen pence'
dīc OE, 'a ditch', esp. 'an excavated trench', also 'defensive work, bank'
dime, *deme* ME 'tenth, tithe'
din nm., *–au* pl., 'city, fort, fortress, fastness, stronghold (eg. defensive hill)'
dinas nm., later nf., *-oedd* pl., 'city, large town, town (fortified or unfortified); fortress; refuge'
disgwylfa nf. 'watching-place, look-out'
ditch see *dīc* OE
dôl[1] nf., *dolau* pl., 'meadow, water-meadow'
down see OE *dūn*
draen[1], *drain* nmf., *drain* pl., 'thorn, thorn-bush'
draenen nf. 'thorn, thorn-bush'
draw, *traw* adv. 'yonder, there, beyond'
dreiniog adj. 'thorny, prickly'
drum, *drumau* see *trum*, *drum*
du, *duf* adj., *duon* pl., 'black, sable, dark; overgrown; bitter'
duke E 'duke (as a title)'
dūn OE 'a hill', *doun* ME, 'a hill, an expanse of open hill-country'
duon see *du*, *duf*
dwfn, *dyfn* adj. 'deep; dense'
dŵr, *dwfr* nm., *dyfroedd* pl., 'water'
dwy see *dau*
dwys adj. 'serious; intense; dense'
Dwyw, *Duw* nm. 'God'
dyffryn nm. 'valley, vale, bottom' etc
dyrys adj. 'wild, rough, uncultivated'
eagle E 'eagle (the bird of prey)'
ēast, *ēasterne* OE adj., adv., 'eastern, east'. The adj. is applicable where the place named lies eastwards of some older place or faces east; as an adv. elliptically '(place) east of (something)'
eglwys nf. 'church'
eithin n.pl. or coll.n. 'furze, gorse'
-ell dim. suffix
-en suffix
end see *ende* OE
ende OE 'end, the end of something'
*englyn (*an-*, *glyn*) ?'deep valley'
eos nf. 'nightingale'
erw nf., *-au* pl., 'Welsh measure of land varying in size throughout Wales; area of land equivalent to the English statute acre; a plot of land, field' etc.
erydd[2], *eryr*[1] nmf. 'eagle'
esgair nf. 'ridge, mountain spur; leg, shank'
estate ME, E 'estate, later housing estate'
ey ON 'island'
-fa, see *ma(n)*, *-fa*
fæger OE
fair E see *fæger* OE
feld OE 'open land, land for pasture or cultivation', later 'enclosed land, field'
fern, *fearn* OE, 'fern(s)'
ferry E 'ferry, boat conveying people and goods across water'
ffald nf., *ffaldau* pl. 'fold, pen, pound'
fforch nf. 'fork'
ffordd nf., *ffyrdd* pl., 'road, way, street'
fforest nf. 'forest, park for hunting'
ffranc[1] nm. 'foreign mercenary, enemy; Frenchman'
ffranc[2] adj. and nm. 'free, frank'
ffriw nf. 'face; nose, snout', fig. 'promontory'
ffrwd nmf. 'swift stream, torrent'
ffynnon nf., *ffynhonnau* pl., 'spring, fountain, well; source, origin'
ffyrlling, *ffyrlin*, *-g* nf. 'farthing'
field see OE *feld*

flat OE 'flat' 'flat piece of ground, level ground' and adj. for '(something) flat, low'

flatr ON 'flat'

fleur-de-lis Fr, *flour de lys* ME, 'fleur-de-lis, flower of the lily'

font OE, ME 'fountain'

ford OE 'shallow place in a river by which a crossing can be made; way, road'

forge ME 'forge, smithy'

foundry E 'building used for the founding of metal, ironworks'

fountain ME 'fountain, spring'

foxhole E 'a hole dug by a fox; concealed place'

fyrs OE 'furze'

gallt see *allt*

garden E 'garden', loosely 'an area notable for its greenery, i.e. hedges and pl. trees; forest, wood'

garth[1] nmf. 'mountain ridge, promontory'

garth[2] nm. 'field, enclosure'

garw adj. 'rough, rugged; coarse'

gate see *gatu* OE

gatu OE 'opening, gap; gate'

geard OE E 'yard, enclosure'

gefail nf. 'smithy, forge'

genau nm. 'mouth; entrance to a valley'

giant E 'imaginary or mythical creature superhuman in size; abnormally tall or large person'

glais variant of *glas*[2] nm. 'stream'

glan nf., –*nau*, *glennydd* pl., 'river-bank, edge; slope'

glanfa[1] nf. 'landing-place, quay'

glas[1] adj., *gleision* pl., 'blue, greenish blue; green, verdant'

glas[2] see *glais*

glaw nm. 'rain, shower'

glebe ME 'glebe, portion of land belonging to a clergyman's benefice'

glo nm., coll.n., 'coal; charcoal'

glyn nm. 'narrow valley, glen, dingle'

gnoll see *cnol* OE

godre nm. 'foot, bottom'

golau, *goleu* adj. 'light, source of light, bright'

golchfa nf. 'washing-place, bath'

gores[2], *gorest* adj. 'open, fenceless, uninclosed, waste', nm. 'a waste'

gōs OE 'goose'

grāf(a), *græfe* OE 'grove, copse, thicket'

grange ME 'granary, barn, grange, farm belonging to a religious house or feudal lord'

grēat OE, *great* ME 'large, bulky'

green E see *grēne* OE

grēne OE 'green in colour; village green, grass-grown'

grove E see *grāf(a)* OE

grug coll.n. 'heather, ling'

gwaelod nm. 'bottom; base'

gwair[1] nm. 'grass (grown for harvesting); hay'

gwaith[1] nm. 'work; a working place, works, factory'

gwaun nf., *gweunydd* pl., 'high and wet level ground, moorland, heath'

gwden nf., *gwdyn* pl., 'withy; rope of plaited withes'

gwen see *gwyn*

gwern nmf. 'alder-tree(s); alder-grove, alder-marsh, swamp'

gweryn[2] 'a worm or bot, that breeds in the backs of cattle; ?serpent, snake'

gweunydd see *gwaun*

gwig[1] nf. 'wood, forest'

gwin nm. 'wine'

gwlad nf. 'country, land'

gwlyb adj., pl. and coll.n.?*gwlybion*, 'wet, damp'

gwryd[1], *gwrhyd* nm. 'length of the outstretched arms; fathom', 'small gap in a ridge, pass'

gwŷdd coll.n. and pl.trees; forest, woods'

gwyddfa nf. 'height, eminence; promontory; burial-mound'

gwyll³, gwyllt adj. 'wild; angry; rushing, rapid'

gwyn adj., adj.f. ***gwen***, pl. *gwynion*

gŵyr¹ adj. 'askew, slanting, crooked, bent'

gwyrai, *gw(y)rhai* nf. 'saw-set, saw-rest'

(ge)hæg OE, *hay* ME 'enclosure, area within a fence'

hæth OE 'heath'

haf nm. 'summer'

hafod nf. 'summer residence, upland farmstead occupied in summer months'

halog adj. 'dirty, soiled'

*****halog*** containing *hâl³* nf. 'moor, moorland' and *–og*

hawthorn E 'hawthorn, thorny shrub'

hay ME see ***(ge)hæg*** OE

head E see OE ***hēafod***

hēafod 'head, top of something'

hēah OE adj., 'high, important; lying high up, prominent'

heath see ***hæth*** OE

helyg¹ coll.n. and adj., sing. *helygen* 'willow-tree, sallow-tree'

hen adj. 'old, aged, former'

hendref nf., 'winter dwelling located in the valley to which the family and its stock returned after transhumance, permanent residence, old or ancestral home'

heol nf., *heolydd* pl., 'way, road, street'; locally *hewl* and 'path, track'

heulog¹ adj. 'sunny, exposed to the sun'

high see ***hēah*** OE

hill see ***hyll*** OE

hin² nm. 'side, edge, limit'

hir adj., pl. *hirion*, 'long, tall, extensive'

hnot OE 'close-cropped, pollard'

holegn OE 'holly'

holly see ***holegn***

holmr ON 'island'

horu OE 'mud'

house E see ***hūs*** OE

hræfn OE 'raven'

hrycg OE, *rugge* ME, 'ridge'

hudd adj. 'dark, dusky, gloomy'

hūs OE, 'house, dwelling house; building used for a particular purpose'

hwch nmf. 'sow'

hwit OE adj., 'white; infertile, dry'; in fns. sometimes 'dry, open pasture'

hwnt adv. and adj. 'yonder, beyond; away'

hydd¹ nm. 'stag, hart'

hyfryd adj. 'pleasant, agreeable'

hyll*, **hull*** OE 'hill, natural eminence or elevated piece of land'

i prep. 'to'

-i suffix

iarll nm. 'earl, count'

iard¹ 'yard, court; industrial yard'

incline E 'mechanical incline for moving rocks, coal, etc'

inn E 'inn, Public House, tavern'

-iog¹ terr. suffix. '(land) belonging to, territory of'

-iog² adj. suffix

is 'below'

isaf adj. 'lower, lowest'

juxta Lat 'near'

kiln dialect *kill* see ***cylen*** OE

knap E see ***cnæpp*** OE

la see ***le*** Fr

lacu OE, *lake* ME drainage channel, side-channel of a river; water-course'

*****laec(c)***, ****læce*** OE 'a stream flowing through boggy land, a bog', ME *lache*, *leche* 'slow, sluggish stream'

lagher OE 'lower, lying lower down'

lake E 'pool, lake'

Glossary of Common Place-name Elements

land, *lond* OE, *land(e)* ME, 'land; a tract of land' and 'a strip of land in a common field'

lane, *lone, lanu* OE, 'a lane, a narrow road'

lang OE 'long'

lang ON 'long'

lāwerce OE 'a lark'

le, **la** Fr def.art.

lea E see **lēah** OE

lēah OE, 'a wood'; esp. 'clearing in a wood' (in Wales); later 'piece of open land, a meadow, a lea'

light E 'light, source of light, etc'

lime E, **līm** OE 'lime, limestone'

little see **lȳtel** OE

llaethog adj. 'abounding in milk; milk-like'

llafar adj. 'loud, resonant'

llan nf., *-nau, -noedd, llennydd* pl., originally 'clearing, open space' and piece of 'enclosed land' surviving in the last sense in compounds (*coedlan, perllan, gwinllan*) and later 'a piece of consecrated ground, churchyard, church' etc.

llandre see **llodre**

llannerch nmf., *llanerchau, -i*, etc. pl., 'a clearing, glade, oasis, pasture' etc.

lle[1] nm. 'locality; a specific place; residence; position'

llech[1] nf. 'slate; slab of stone; rock'

llechwedd nm. 'hillside, slope'

llety nm. 'lodging, home'

llidiart, *llidiard* nmf. 'gate'

llin[2] nm. and adj. 'flax; thread or cloth made of flax'

lliw[1] nm. 'colour, hue'

llodre nm. ?'place, location, building'

lluest nf. 'temporary dwelling, lodge, hut'

llwch[2], variant *llych* 'lake, pool, stagnant water'

llwm adj. 'bare'

llwyd adj., *llwydion* pl., 'grey; pale; muddy (of water); holy, blessed'

llwyn nm., *-au, -i, -ydd* pl., 'bush, plant', or coll. sense, 'grove, copse'. OBret *loin, loen*, Co **lon*, 'grove, thicket'

llydan adj., *lledan* adj.f., 'broad, wide; sturdy'

llyfn adj. 'level, smooth'

llyn nmf., *-noedd, -nau, -iau, -ydd* pl., 'lake, pool, pond, puddle' etc.

llys nmf., *-oedd, -au* pl., 'court, palace, manor-house, hall, imposing building, habitation of king, prince, nobleman, etc.; manorial seat of administration'

lôn[1] nf., *lonydd* pl., 'lane, by-road, road'

long see **lang** OE

lower see **lagher** OE

lȳtel OE 'little, small'

ma-, **-ma**, **-fa** nmf., *-au*, **mai**, *mei* pl., 'a plain, field; place, spot; ?small, flat piece of land'

mab nm., *meib(i)on* pl., 'boy, son, infant'

mǣd OE, dat. *–we*, 'meadow'

maen nm., dial. *mân*, **main**, *mein, meini* pl., and adj., 'stone, esp. one having some speciality or a particular use; large stone as used, e.g. in building, rock'

maenor nf., 'administrative unit', ?originally 'chief's residence', later associated with E *manor*

maer nm. 'administrative officer of court; steward'

maerdref nf. 'land adjacent to the court worked by unfree tenants supervised by the *maer biswail* (dung bailiff) to provide food, etc., for the court, demesne, home farm; hamlet attached to chief's court'

maerdy nm. 'farm supervised by **maer** or steward; farm, dairy farm'

(ge)mǣre OE 'boundary, border'

maes nm., *meysydd* pl., and adv., 'open country as opposed to woodland, expanse of open land, level land, plain, open field', later 'field'

mæþe OE 'mayweed'

mǣw OE, **mew** 'gull'

magwyr nf. 'wall; ruin'

xli

mai see *ma-*

major Lat 'greater'

*man*¹ nmf. 'particular place'

march nm., *meirch* pl., 'horse, stallion'; 'great, large' with extended sense 'strong, vigorous'

marl nm. 'marl'

mawr, *mor* adj. 'big, great, high'

May E, 'month of May'

mead, *meadow* see *mæd*

meisgyn nm. 'moth; weevil; an obnoxious larva'

mele ME (<ON *melr*) 'sand-bank, sand-dune'

melen see *melyn*

melin nf., *-au* pl., 'mill, water-mill'

melindref (*melin* + *tref*) nf. 'mill settlement, settlement owing suit to a mill'

mellt coll.n. '(flashes of) lightning'

melyn adj., *melen* adj.f., 'yellow; brown'

menyn see *ymenyn*, *menyn*

merch E, *merece* OE, 'wild celery, smallage'

mere OE 'lake, pool'

*merthyr*² nm. 'graveyard consecrated with the bones of a saint; martyr'

meudwy nm. 'hermit, anchorite'

mew E see *mæw* OE

middel OE 'middle'

middle see *middel* OE

mill see *myln*, *mylen* OE

minor Lat 'lesser, smaller'

*moel*¹ adj. 'bare', nf. 'bare mountain or hill', *moelydd* pl.

mommele ME 'mumble'

monk see *munuc* OE

mons nom., *montem* acc.

mont Fr 'mount, hill'

moor see *mōr* OE

mōr OE, 'a moor', earlier 'barren waste-land'

mor see *mawr*

*môr*¹ nm. 'sea, ocean'

morfa nmf. '(sea) marsh, salt-marsh, land (*or* marsh) by the sea-shore' later 'wet, marshy land', sometimes applied to inland locations for 'moor'

mount E 'a hill, a rise'

mountain ME, E 'mountain, lofty hill'

mūl OE 'a mule'

munuc OE 'a monk'

mwyndy nm. 'building used for processing ore or coal'

myln, *mylen* OE 'a mill'

*mynach*¹, *manach* nm., *-od*, *-iaid*, *mynaich*, etc pl., 'monk, sometimes also a friar'

mynachlog, *manachlog* nf. 'monastery'

mynwent nf. 'graveyard, cemetery'

mynydd nm., *-oedd*, *-au* pl., 'mountain, (large) hill' with extended sense 'exposed area, esp. a heath'

mystwyr colloquial *mystwr*, nm. 'monastery'

nant nf., earlier nm., *nentydd*, poet. *naint* pl., earlier 'valley, ravine, glen'

new ME, E see OE *nīwe*

newydd adj. 'new'

-ni suffix

nīwe OE 'new'

norð OE, *north* E 'north, northern'

nudd nmf. 'mist, haze'

o prep. 'from'

oak see *āc* OE

obry adv. 'down below, underneath, beneath'

ochr nmf. 'side; side of object or place; slope, (hill or mountain) side'

odyn nf. 'kiln; (lime-)kiln'

ofer, *ufer* OE, 'a slope, a hill, a flat-topped ridge'

-og adj. suffix

olau n.pl. (*ôl* nm.) 'path, paths'

old see *āld*, *eald* OE

on E prep. 'on, adjoining (a river, etc)'

Glossary of Common Place-name Elements

onnen nf., ***onn***, *ynn* pl., 'ash-tree'

orceard OE 'orchard'

-os dim. pl. suffix

oxa OE 'ox'

pabell see *pebyll*

pandy nm. 'fulling-mill'

**panog* (*pân²* 'cotton-grass' + *-og*) 'abundance of cotton-grass'

panos, *pannos* (*pân²* + *-os*)

pant nm. 'hollow, depression, valley'

panwaun (*pân²* 'cotton-grass, bog-cotton', *gwaun*) 'bog-cotton moor, marshy ground, peat bog'

parc nm., *-iau* pl., 'enclosed land, field, paddocks', later 'recreation area' and 'housing estate'

parc AF see *park* ME, E

park ME, E, *parc* AF 'an enclosed tract of land for beasts of the chase', later 'recreation area' and 'housing estate'

parsel nmf., ***parseli*** pl., 'parcel, division'

pebyll variant of *pabell* nmf. 'tent, (temporary) dwelling'

pedwar adj., *pedair* adj.f., 'four'

pen¹ nm., ***pennau*** pl., 'a head, height, hill; chief, supreme' and 'end of'. It is not always easy to distinguish these senses; and 'head'

pennardd (*pen¹* + *ardd¹*) nf. 'promontory, hillside'

pentref, *pentre* nm. 'chief farm, chief settlement' later 'village'

perai nm. 'pear-tree, perry'

perllan nf. 'orchard'

person² nm. 'parson, rector; clergyman'

perth nf., *perthi* pl., 'wood' later 'bush, hedge'

pia late variant of *pi²* nmf. 'magpie'

pīl OE, *pile* 'pile, pointed stick, stake'

pill E see *pyll* OE

pioden (dim. of *pi¹*) nf., *piod* pl., 'magpie'

pistyll nm., *-au* pl., 'spout, well'; occasionally 'rill, stream'

place E 'place; street'

plas nm. 'mansion, hall'

pleasant E 'agreeable, pleasant'

poeth adj. 'hot, burning; burnt'

pont nf. 'bridge'

pontbren, *pompren* nmf., ***pontprenni*** *-ni* pl., '(wooden) foot-bridge'

port ME, ModE 'town, often a market town; port'

portman (*port*, *man*) ME 'inhabitant or burgess of a town or port'

porth² nm. 'gate; door, porch'

porth³ nmf. 'harbour, haven'

pound see *pund* OE

**powndffald* (*pownd²*, *ffald*) nm. 'pound, animal pound'

pridd nm. 'soil, earth; (potter's) clay, mud or clay as building-material'

pryf nm., *-ed* pl., 'insect, fly; larva, maggot, earthworm'

prysg, *prys* nm. 'copse, grove'

pund OE 'a pound, enclosure'

pwll nm., *pyllau* pl., 'deep hole or shaft, a pit; pool, pond, a pool in a river' and occasionally 'stream, ditch'

pyll OE, 'tidal creek, pill, stream'

pynnau pl., *pwn* nm. 'load, burden'

pytt E 'pit'

quaker E 'member of Society of Friends'

`*r* see *y*, *yr*

ræw, *rāw* OE 'a row, row of houses'

ranny E dialect 'shrew mouse: field-mouse; any long-nosed thing'

ráth Ir 'a fort'

raven see *hræfn* OE

repaire Fr 'retreat'

rhaca nmf. 'a rake'

rhawdd see **rhodd**

rhedyn n.pl. 'ferns, bracken'

rhedynog adj. 'having ferns'

rhingyll nm. 'court official; ringild; bailiff'

rhisg, *rhisgl* nm., *rhisg(l)au* pl., '(piece of) bark'

rhiw W nf., *-(i)au* pl., 'slope, ascent, hill'

rhodd, **rhawdd* ?'noisy' as in *adrodd* vb. 'to utter, to speak'

rhos² '(upland) moor, heath(land)'

rhudd adj. 'red, ruddy, brown'

rhwmp¹ nm. '(large) auger'

rhwng prep. 'between'

rhyd nf., *-(i)au* pl., 'ford'

river E 'river'

rock see **rokke** ME

rokke ME 'a rock, crag'

***rydding** 'a clearing'

saddler E 'maker or dealer in saddles'

Saeson see **Sais**

sain, saint (< E *saint*) nm. 'saint, holy person'

Sais, pl. *Saeson*, 'Englishman'

salt OE 'salt'

sanctuary E 'holy place; place of refuge'

sand E 'sand; tract of sandy ground'

sandig OE 'sandy'

sandy E see **sandig** OE

sant, *san*, etc. nm.; *saint* pl., 'saint, holy person'

sarn nmf. 'causeway, stepping-stones, path, road'

sart 'assart' (not in GPC)

scelf OE 'shelf, terrace'

seintwar, *sentwar*, *seintwal* nf. 'sanctuary, refuge'

seofon OE 'seven'

seven see **seofon** OE

shelf see **scelf** OE

side OE 'side, the long part; land alongside, beside'

sign nf. 'sign (usually of the Zodiac)'

sister n., **sisters** pl., OE *sweoster*

siwt nm. 'gutter(ing); ?'water-course, shoot'

sker ON 'a rock'

skot ON 'projectile; projecting'

slade E, **slæd** OE 'valley; low flat valley'

soflyn variant **sowlyn, solwyn* > *solwyn, solfyn, sofl* pl., 'stubble'

spelter E 'alloy of zinc and copper, alloy of zinc and lead'

splott OE 'a spot, a plot of land'

spring OE 'a spring, well'

square E 'houses arranged in a square, group of houses'

stabl¹ nf. 'stable (for horses, etc)'

stæniht, stānig OE 'stony, rocky'

stalun ME (< OFr *estalon*) 'stallion'

sticil, sticill nf. 'stile'

stōw OE, 'a place, a place of assembly, a holy place', sometimes duplicating W **llan**

stubble E 'stubble'

sūð OE 'south'

sūðer OE 'southern'

super Lat 'above, over (a river, etc)'

swan OE, E 'swan, genus *cygnus*'

swfr nm. 'noise, din, murmur, a rustling'

swllt nm. 'shilling'

sych¹ adj. 'dry, arid, dried up'

tai see **tŷ**

tair see **tri**

tal, *tâl* nm. 'forehead, front, end' and in topographical sense 'end, brow of a hill'

***tam-** Br ?'flowing'

tan¹, *dan* prep. 'under, below, underneath'

tân¹ nm. 'fire, conflagration'

tarren dial. *tarran* nf. 'knoll, rock, tump; prominent rock, crag', locally 'piece of poor ground (amidst good)'

teg adj. 'fair, fine, beautiful'

Glossary of Common Place-name Elements

-teu see **-tou**

thistleboon E (OE *thistel* 'thistle', ?*boon* 'a blessing, a gift') 'feudal due for weeding fields'

thorn OE 'a thorn; thorn-tree'

three see **threō** OE

threō OE 'three'

throp ME (OE *thorp, throp*) 'outlying farm'

tir nm. 'land, ground, territory'

tirion[1] adj. 'gentle, mild; pleasant'

tlotyn, *tlodyn* nm. 'pauper'

tomen nf. 'dunghill, muck-heap; mound, hillock'

ton[2] nm., *tonnau* pl., 'lay-land' and nf., 'skin, surface'. Compounded in *gw(y)ndwn*, 'unploughed land'. Cf. Cornish *ton* 'lea-land'

-ton see **tūn** OE

toot ME 'look-out'

top E 'top, above; topmost'

tor nm. 'break, gap; heap'

–tou or **-teu** suffix

town see **tūn**

traean nmf. 'a third, third part'

traeth[1] nm. 'beach, (sea)shore'

traethen nf. '(small) beach, strand; sandbank'

trallwng, *trallwn* nm. 'dirty pool, boggy spot (on road, etc)'

tramway E 'tramroad; railway for trams'

transh, *trensh* 'trench; dyke, bulwark; 'a way cut through a wood by a stream'

tref nf., *-i*, *-ydd*, *-oedd* pl., 'house, dwellingplace, homestead', later 'hamlet, township' and 'town'.

trench E; OFr, ME *trenche*, 'a woodland road with clearings on either side to make the route safe for travellers'

trēow OE 'a tree'

tri, variant *try-*, fem. **tair**, 'three'

troed nmf. 'foot, base'

trum, *drum* nmf., *drumau* pl., '(crest of) mountain or hill, peak, ridge'

trwyn nm. 'nose, snout'

tūn OE, **-ton** ME, **town** 'an enclosure, a farmstead, an estate' later 'a village, town', etc.

twll[1] nm., *tyllau* pl., 'hole, aperture, hollow'

twmpath nm. 'hillock, knoll, mound'

twrch gen.sg. and pl. *tyrch,* nm. 'hog, (wild) boar'

twyn nm., *twyni* pl., 'hill, hillock, tump, knoll, rising; (sand-)dune'

tŷ nm., *tai* pl., 'house, building'

tyddyn, **tyn** nm., 'smallholding, small farm', earlier ? 'building'

tyle [< ?Ir *tulach,* 'hill, knoll'] nm., 'slope, ascent, hill'

tyn see **tyddyn**

tywyll adj. 'dark'

uchaf adj., 'highest; higher (of two)'

uchel adj. and nm. 'high, tall'

up E 'up, upper, higher'

upon prep. 'on, upon'

upper ME 'upper, higher'

vale E 'valley, vale'

valley ME (*valey* AF) 'valley'

village E 'small settlement, village'

ville Fr, E 'town, settlement'

wæter OE 'water'

wall pl. **walls** see OE **weall**

Wallia Lat 'Wales'

water E see OE **wæter**

way E, *weg* OE

weall OE, *wealles, walles* pl., 'wall'

weir, wer OE 'dam, weir'

well E, *wælle, wella, wielle* OE 'a well, a spring, a stream'

Welsh E 'Welsh people, Welsh language'

wermod, *wermwd* nmf. and pl. 'wormwood'

west OE 'west, western'

-wg suffix

wharf E see **hwearf** OE

white E see ***hwit*** OE

wīc OE 'a dwelling, a building or collection of buildings for social purposes, a farm, a dairy farm' and pl. ***wīcum***, 'a hamlet, a village'

wild E 'uncultivated, desolate'

winsh, *wins* nmf. 'winch; well-wheel'

wood E see ***wudu*** OE

wudu OE, E 'a wood'

-*wy*^{1} r.n. suffix; 'bending, turning'

-*wy*^{2} terr. suffix '(land) belonging to, territory of'

wyrm OE 'snake, serpent; maggot; earthworm'

y, yr,* `*r def.art. 'the'

yard see ***geard*** OE

ych*^{1}** nm. ***ychen pl., 'ox'

-*ydd*^{1} territorial suffix, '(land) belonging to, territory of'

-*ydd*^{3} noun suffix

ymenyn, menyn nm. 'butter'

yn, yng prep. 'in'

-*yn* suffix

ynys nf., *-oedd* pl., 'island; river-meadow'

***ysgol*^{1}** nf. 'school'

ysgubor nf., ***ysgubor(i)au*** pl., 'barn, granary'

ystrad nm., 'vale, valley bottom, river-valley; wider part of a valley'

ystyllen, *styllen* nf. 'plank, board, shelf'

Aberafan to Avan Vale

Aberdare church. Engraved by William Woolnorth from a drawing by John Preston Neale for the *Beauties of England and Wales*. (courtesy of Keith H. Edwards and Frank Hartles)

Aberafan (Aberavon) SS 762901
Neath Port Talbot
'mouth of the (r.) Afan': ***aber***, rn. *Afan Aven* c.1160, *Aber Auyn* c.1400, *Aber Avon* c.1538, *Avon* 1541, *Aberavan* 1549, *aber afan* c.1566
The n. of a medieval borough described in many sources simply as Afan, Avan etc, displaced later by the fuller form Aberafan and anglicised as Aberavon. The rn. Afan occurs as *Auene* c.1150, *Avena* c.1161, *Avan*, 1443 but its meaning is uncertain. It may be identical to a pers.n. Afan found in Llanafan Fawr, Breconshire, related to Breton Avan and perhaps Ir *abann* 'river'. Modern E sources spell the pn. with *–avon*, probably under the influence of ***afon*** 'river' and knowledge of the various rs. Avon in England. Local W-speakers call it 'Byrafan' [bər'avan]; cf. 'Byrdær' [bər'dɛːr] for Aberdâr (Aberdare) and 'Byrtŵe' [bər'tuːɛ] for Abertawe (Swansea). Aberafan often appears in 19th-20th cent sources as the W-language counterpart to Port Talbot though it is now regarded as an area within the modern town. Its once wider geographical application is attested by Aberavon Sands (SS 742899) and Aberavon Moors (SS 752908). The r. rises at Bwlch yr Afan (SS 917955) above Blaenafan

(***blaen***) fm. (now covered by Blaengwynfi) recorded as *Blaineavene* 1208 and *Blaenavan* 1574. See also also Afan Wallia and Cwmafan.

Aberaman SO 014013
Rhondda Cynon Taf (Aberdare)
'confluence of the (rs.) Aman (and Cynon)': ***aber***, rn. *Aman*
Aberaman 1623, *Aberamman* 1649
The rn. is *Amman* 1203 and may derive from earlier Amanw containing the el. ***banw*** nm. 'pig or young pig', probably alluding to the way in which the r. is thought to root through the ground like the animal (CVPN 18). There are similar names elsewhere in Wales, notably Banw (Banwy in late sources), Montgomeryshire, and Cwm-twrch (q.v.). Aberdare also has Nant-yr-hwch (***hwch*** 'sow'). The rn. occurs also in Blaenaman near its source (***blaen***) (see Brynaman-isaf) and Cwmaman (q.v.) the n. of its valley (***cwm***), and in the n. of two former farms Aberaman Isaf (***isaf***) and Aberaman Uchaf (***uchaf***). Treaman (***tref***) is a relatively modern n. recorded in the 1851 census in ref. to a colliery and railway station.

Aberavon see **Aberafan**

Aberbargod (Aberbargoed) SO 154001
Caerphilly (Bedwellte Monmouthshire)
'confluence of the (r.) Bargod (and Rhymni): ***aber***, rn. *Bargod*
Abergutt 1563, *Aber Bargoed* c.1700, *Aberbargod* 1729
Historical mentions refer to the bridge over the r. Bargod Rhymni as *pounte aber Bargod* 1709, *Abyrbargoed bridge* 1714 (***pont***, ***bridge***) and *Bargod Bridge* 1729. For the rn. see Bargoed.

Abercannaid (Abercanaid) SO 058036
Merthyr Tudful
'confluence of (stream) Cannaid (and Taf)': ***aber***, rn. *Cannaid*
Aber kanneyt 1449, *Abercanaid* 1541
The rn. is also found in Blaencannaid (SO 035047) recorded as *terre blaen kaneyt* 1449, *Blaen Cannayd* 1661 (***blaen***) and thought to contain the el. found in *cannu* 'to whiten, to bleach', possibly in the sense of a r. which is white through turbulence. Cwmcannaid is *Cwmcanaid* 1541, 'valley of (r.) Cannaid' (***cwm***) with a mill recorded as *Melingan(n)od* 1783, *Melin-caned* 1833 (***melin***).

Aber-carn ST 215950
Caerphilly (Mynyddislwyn, Monmouthshire)
'confluence of (stream) Carn (and Ebwy)': ***aber***, rn. *Carn*
Habercarne 1535, *Abercarne* 1543, *Abercarn, neu Abergwyddon, fel y gelwid y lle gynt* 1871
The n. properly applies to the point where the stream Nant Carn, flowing through Cwm Carn, meets the r. Ebwy (Ebbw) about a mile south of the village in what is now called Cwm-carn. This was the location of an ancient chp. which gave its n. to *Chapel Br.* railway station and *Abercarn Fm.* 1836. The geographical distinction between Abergwyddon and Aber-carn became blurred in the early 19th cent witnessed by *Abercarn House* 1813 (ST 217957) and *Aber-carn-uchaf* 1879-80 (see High Meadow) above Abergwyddon (q.v.), and the nascent settlement at Abergwyddon had already acquired the n. *Abercarne village* in 1841. The transfer of n. was evidently reinforced by its use in describing the coal and coke works of Abercarn Colliery Company and the nearby railway station. Nant Carn (***nant***, ***carn***) is recorded as *Nantgarne* 1667 and gives its n. to *Glyncarne* and (water grist mill) *Carnes Mill* 1630.

Abercregan SS 849966
Neath Port Talbot (Glyncorrwg)
'confluence of (Nant) Cregan (and Afan)': ***aber***, rn. *Cregan*
Aber Cregan 1570, *Abercregan* c.1700
The r. rises at Blaen Cregan recorded as *Blain Cragan* c.1200 (***blaen***). The meaning of Cregan is uncertain because early historic forms are rare but it may be compared with the rn. Cregan, Denbighshire. R.J. Thomas (EANC 59) suggests that both rns. might contain *creg* as a fem. of *cryg* 'hoarse, harsh, raucous', with a suffix **–*an***. The sense may be 'noisy river'.

Abercwmboi ST 025999
Rhondda Cynon Taf (Llanwynno)
'confluence of the (r.) Cynfoi (and Cynon)': *aber*, rn. *Cynfoi*
Aberconwaye Yssa 1541, *Ab(er)ken' Voye* 1547, *Aber Convoy Ycha*, ~ *Yssa* 1638, *Abercwmvoy* 1720, *Abercwmboy* 1789, 1877
Cynfoi may be identical to a pers.n. found as *conuiu, conuoe, conboe* c.1145. The r. rises on Craig Abercwmboi above Blaencwmboi (*craig, blaen*). From the early 18th cent the rn. was influenced by *cwm* and this in turn prompted the re-interpretations Cwm Boi for the valley and the recent Glenboi (q.v.). Two farms are distinguished in historical records as 'upper' and 'lower' (*uchaf, isaf*). Abercwmboi has displaced Cap-coch (q.v.).

Abercynffig (Aberkenfig) SS 894835
Bridgend (Newcastle)
'confluence of the (stream) Cynffig (and Llynfi)': *aber*, rn. *Cynffig*
Aberkenfyg 1591, *Aberkenfigg* c.1598, *Abercunfig* 1785, *Abercynffig* 1878
Nant Cynffig is identical in meaning to the r. at Kenfig (q.v.). Otherwise recorded as *Aberlyfny* c.1700, the village developed near Ton-du Ironworks in the early 19th cent and is shown as *Aber Llunfy* on an OS map 1833. Aberllynfi seems to be no longer current and the area is covered by Abercynffig. The r. Llynfi occurs as *Leveni* c.1168, *Thleweny* 1314, *Lleueny* c.1538, and has two tributaries Llynfi Fechan and Llynfi Fawr recorded as *Llyffny Vechan* 1570, *Lhynfi Vawr*, ~ *Fach* c.1700 distinguished as 'small' and 'great' (*bechan, mawr*). It probably means 'smooth one' with *llyfn*, found also in Llynfell, Breconshire and Glamorgan (see Cwmllynfell).

Abercynon ST 082948
Rhondda Cynon Taf (Llanwynno)
'confluence of the (r.) Cynon (and Taf)': *aber*, rn. *Cynon*
Abercynon 1893
Formerly called Navigation from Navigation House (built 1791) recorded as *the Navigation Counting House* 1797, near the canal locks, used by officials of the Glamorganshire Canal (opened in 1792). This was later a hotel. The Taff Vale Railway Company chose Navigation for the first n. of their station but changed it in 1846 to Aberdare Junction (CVPN 19-20), itself dropped in 1897. The village apparently continued to be known as Navigation until 1893 when residents of the town formally adopted the n. Abercynon in preference to other suggestions of Cynonvale (considered too English) and Abertafachynon. The last was the n. of a former fm. (ST 085952) recorded as *Abertaffacynon* 1814, *Abertaff a Cynon* 1861, ('junction of the Taf and Cynon') and later as Aber-taf. Most of the village lies within the old hamlet called Taf a Cynon (q.v.). The n. Navigation survived in local use and as that of the school for several years after 1893.

Aberdare, Aberdâr SO 005025
Rhondda Cynon Taf
'confluence of the (rs.) Dâr (and Cynon)': *aber*, rn. *Dâr*
Aberdar 1203, *Aberdaar* 1349, *Abyrthare* 1450, *Aberdare* c.1530, *aber daer* c.1566
Dâr is recorded as *Dare* 1541 and in *Pulthadar* 1256 (*pwll*). The rn. may contain the initial el. found in *derwen* and *deri* meaning 'oak river' perhaps from the former presence of oak-trees near its course. The same el. is found in rns. in England such as Dart and Derwent. Oak woods are mentioned in the area in the early 19th cent. The modern form with *-dare* rhyming with E 'dare' [dɛ:r] is an attempt to represent local W dialect rather than being an anglicised pron. of *-dâr* [dɑ:r] as sometimes supposed.

Aberddawan see **Aberthaw**

Aberdulais SS 773996
Neath Port Talbot (Cadoxton-juxta-Neath)
'confluence of the (r.) Dulais (and Nedd)': *aber*, rn. *Dulais*
Tir Ab(er)dylais 1621, *Aberdylais* 1667, (fulling-mill) *Melin Aberdyleys* 1666, *Aberdulas* 1740
Dulais meaning 'dark stream' (*du, glais*) a common rn. in Wales, sometimes found as

Dulas. The r. might be one shaded by trees or one with dark waters flowing over coal measures.

Aber-fan SO 070002
Merthyr Tudful
'confluence of the (stream) Fan (and Taf)': *aber*, rn. *Fan*
Teyr Aber-van 1536, *Aber y van* 1623, *Aberfan* 1783
The r. is *Nant Aber-fan* 1881 and rises on the northern end of a hill Cefn y Fan (***cefn***) at the south-west side of the village recorded in the n. of a tmt. *tir Keven y van* 1630 (***tir***), *Cefn y fan* 1783. Early sps. have not been found though it may contain ***ban**[1]*, ***fan*** 'summit, peak'. The village is named from two former farms distinguished as ***mawr*** and ***bach**[1]* and was developed from the 1870s between Pant-glas and the Red Cow Inn near Perthigleision fm. and Perthigleision Pit. A former chp. (ST 071980) above the village is *Capel Fan* 1876 and *Capel y Fan* 1900 (***capel***) identified by Thomas Davies (TVD I, 28) with *Capell y kyndynvan* 1623, *Cappell Dunvan* 1630, and *kyndynvaen* late 18th cent – of uncertain meaning – but it is difficult to reconcile these forms with Capel (y) Fan and the identification is unproven.

Abergarw SS 909849
Bridgend (Llangeinwyr)
'confluence of the (stream) Garw (and r. Ogwr)': *aber*, rn. *Garw*
Abergarw 1631, *Abergarrow* 1754, *Abergârw Farm*, *~ issa* 1767
Garw is thought to have ***garw*** 'wild, rough' as in Nantgarw (q.v.) near Taff's Well. The r. rises near Blaengarw (q.v.) and has a tributary Garw Fechan recorded as *Blaen Garw Fechan* 1711 (***bechan*** 'small, lesser').

Abergarwed SN 816023
Neath Port Talbot (Cadoxton-juxta-Neath)
'confluence of (stream) Garwed (and Nedd)': *aber*, rn. *Garwed*
Aber Garved 1541, *Abergared* 1698, *Abergarwedd* 1833
Garwed is recorded as *Garwed Brook* 1877 and rises above Blaengarwed in Rheola Forest (SN 814037). The stream also gives its n. to Ynysarwed fm. (SN 812018) recorded as *Innys Arwed* 1646, *Ynysarwed* 1656 (***ynys***) and a former ho. Ton-garwed (SN 818035) (***ton**[2]*) next to a second stream about a mile further up Cwm Nedd. Garwed contains ***garw*** (cf. Abergarw) and suffix *–ed*[1].

Aber-gwawr SO 011016
Rhondda Cynon Taf (Aberdare)
'confluence of the (stream) Gwawr (and Cynon)': *aber*, rn. *Gwawr*
Abergwarne 1541, *Tir Abergwawr* c.1612, *Abergwawr* 1814
Gwawr is recorded as *Gwawre* 1541. The stream rises near Blaen-gwawr (q.v.) and has been interpreted as *gwawr* nmf. 'dawn, sunrise' because the river flows east 'to greet the dawn' but *gwawr* is also used in the sense 'brightness; colour, bloom' and occurs as a pers.n. notably as that of Gwawr, a daughter of Brychan, the legendary king of Brycheiniog.

Abergwrelych SN 889065
Neath Port Talbot (Glyncorrwg)
'confluence of (r.) Gwrelych (and Nedd)': *aber*, rn. *Gwrelych*
(place) *Abergrewlich* 1638, *Abergwrelych* 1643, *Abergwrelich* 1692, (ho.) *Aber-gwerlech* 1833
Gwrelych, recorded as (water) *Wrelec* 1203, *Wrelech* 1253, and *Gwrelich* 1578, is found also in Ystumwrelych (lost) which is *Estunwrelech* 1253, located in Cwmgwrelych (***cwm***), and Blaengwrelych recorded as *Blaen Gwrelach* 1799 (***blaen***). The r. rises in Llyn Fawr (SN 9104), 'the great pool' (***llyn***, ***mawr***). The rn. may contain *gwre* 'mite, worm', and *llych* 'water, stream', a variant of ***llwch**[2]* 'lake, pool, stagnant water'. For the first el., cf. Cwm Gwreinyn, Montgomeryshire, with *gwreinyn* 'insect, maggot, grub'. See further Gwynedd Pierce in ADG[2], 8.

Abergwyddon ST 217950
Caerphilly (Mynyddislwyn Monmouthshire)
'confluence of (stream) Gwyddon (and Ebwy)': *aber*, rn. *Gwyddon*
Abergwiddon 1709, *Abergwyddon* 1733, *Abergwython* 1758

Gwyddon is recorded as *Nant Widdon* 1710, *Nant Gwyddon* 1813, in *Wythom's mill* 1570, and Glangwyddon which is *Glanwythow* 1661, possibly *gwiddon¹*, *gwyddon¹* 'giantess, female monster; witch', perhaps in the sense of 'dangerous, powerful, treacherous'. The village developed in the early 19th cent and was displaced as a pn. by Aber-carn (q.v.) before 1880.

Abergwynfi   SS 893961
Neath Port Talbot (Glyncorrwg)
'confluence of the (stream) Gwynfi (and Afan)': ***aber***, rn. *Gwynfi*
Aber Gwyn Viewe 1570, *Abergwnfyw* 1601, *Aber-gwynfy* 1833
Gwynfi is thought to be a pers.n. *Gwynfyw*, and a late natural development with dissimilation, i.e. (-fyw > -fy, -fi) partly to avoid repetition of –w- in Gwyn- in order to ease pron. Named from a fm. near the Tunnel Hotel close to the confluence of Nant Gwynfi with the r. Afan. The mountain Mynydd Abergwynfi (SS 889975) (***mynydd***) is immediately to the north. As far as the village is concerned, Abergwynfi is a misnomer since it is located *above* Blaengwynfi and was developed between Avon Colliery and Tre-shenkin Colliery in the 1890s.

Aberkenfig see **Abercynffig**

Aberllechau see **Wattstown**

Aberllynfi see **Abercynffig**

Aber-nant   SO 008032
Rhondda Cynon Taf (Aberdare)
'confluence of the stream': ***aber***, ***nant***
Abernaunte y Wennalt 1541, *Tyr Aber Nant y Wenallte* 1632, *Abernant* 1811
The stream is earlier Nant y Wenallt recalled in a fm.n. Aber-nant-y-wenallt which stood near Nant y Wenallt and Cynon. The n. was adopted in its truncated form for Abernant House (on the site of Aberdare Hospital) and Abernant Iron Works 1800. The stream rises at SO 016052 in an area identifiable with *terre blayn nant ewenallt* 1449 near Blaen-nant and is also recalled in *Tyre nant y wenallt* 1558. Y Wenallt is 'white (or fair) wooded-slope' (***y***, ***gwen***, ***allt***). There were two other farms in the area called Aber-nant-y-groes and Aber-nant-y-groes Isaf (***isaf***) recorded as *Abernaunte dy Groyes* 1541, *Abernant y grose* 1582, and *Abernant Y Groes Isha* 1840. Nant y Groes joined the r. Cynon at Tir Founder near Cwm-bach Station and may be named after a wayside cross (***croes***).

Aberogwr see **Ogmore-by-Sea**

Aberpennar see **Mountain Ash**

Aberpergwm   SN 8605, 8606
Neath Port Talbot (Cadoxton-juxta-Neath)
'confluence of the (stream) Pergwm (and Nedd)': ***aber***, rn. *Pergwm*
(grange) *Aber Pergn'* 1296, *Abergergum* 1443, *Aberpergwm* late 15th cent, *Aber Pergom* c.1538
Pergwm may be a compound of *pêr* adj. 'sweet' and ***cwm*** perhaps describing a r. in a fertile valley. The n. is found also in Blaenpergwm (SN 8507) which is *blayne pergome* early 16th cent, *Blaenpergum* 1733 (***blaen***), and in (land of) *Pergom* 1375. The location of a chp. recorded late 16th cent and 1702 (VNeath 191; LLR III, 200) and a grange. An identical rn. may be found in Aberpergwm (recorded 1782) and Penpergwm (SO 326100) at Llangatwg, Monmouthshire.

Abertawe see **Swansea**

Aberthaw, **Aberddawan**   ST 0266, 0366
Vale of Glamorgan (Penmark, St Athan)
'mouth of the (r.) Ddawan (Thaw)': ***aber***, rn. *Ddawan*
Abrerthawe c.1262, *Aberthau* 1307, *le havyn de Aberthawyn'* 1479, (haven) *Aberthaw alias Aberdaon* 1584, *Aberthawan* c.1598, *aber ðawen* 1606, *Aberddaw* 1742, *Aberddawan* 1888
Ddawan is *nadauan* c.1145, *Nadhauan* early 13th cent, *Thawan Ryver* c.1538, *Ddawon* c.1670 but its meaning is uncertain unless it contains the same root as *naddu* vb. 'to cut (with a sharp instrument)' applied to a r. perceived as cutting through the landscape. Naddawan became Ddawan [ˈðauan] through loss of unstressed *Na-* and this form

(and Aberddawan) was retained by W-speakers in the Vale. The form Aberthaw with loss of the unstressed final syllable -*an* (cf. Llandough/ Llandocha) developed at an early date and the pn. is now generally pronounced by E-speakers as if it contained E 'thaw' [θɔː]; see EANC 64-5. Aberthaw was a notable harbour, described as a seaport in 1349, flanked by the two small hts. of East Aberthaw (ST 034667) and West Aberthaw (ST 024668) which are *Westhawe* and *Eastthawe* in 1426. The haven was otherwise known as *Cowbrygge water* 1479 because the r. was partly navigable for small boats as far as Cowbridge (q.v.).

Aberthin ST 008752
Vale of Glamorgan (Llanblethian)
'confluence of (r.) Berthin (and Ddawan)': *aber*, lost rn. *Berthin*
ebirthun, aber epyrthun c.1145, *Aberberthynne* 1445, *Byrthin* 1570, *the Burthin* 1623, *Aberthyn* 1706
The meaning of the rn. Berthin (earlier Ebirthun) is uncertain but is probably identical to Berthin, Monmouthshire, recorded in *Aberthin, Eberthyn* 13th cent, etc and as (brook) *Berthin* 1753. The pn. seems to have developed from Aberebirthin or Aberebirthun > Abereberthin > Abérthin with loss of the first unstressed syllable –er- and contraction; see EANC 198-9. There may also have been a colloquial variant Y Berthin comparable with pns. such as Y Bermo for Aber-maw (Barmouth), Merionethshire. Many local E-speakers have shifted the stress from the second syllable of Aberthin to the first syllable as if it were 'Aber-thin' ['abɛrθɪn].

Abertridwr ST 120893
Caerphilly (Eglwysilan)
'confluence of three streams': *aber, tri, dŵr*
Abertreedwr 1708, *Abertridwr* 1736, *Tir Abertridwr* otherwise *Ynys y Turch* 1776, *the Aber* 1783
Referring to Nant Ilan (flowing out of Ffynnon Ilan), Nant Cwm-parc and Nant Cwmceffyl (*cwm, ceffyl* nm. 'horse'). The combined stream is known as Nant yr Aber below the village. The general area was known as *Cwm-yr-aber*

1875-8. The 1776 variant is 'river-meadow of the boar' (*ynys*, def.art. *y, twrch*).

Abertyswg SO 130055
Caerphilly (Bedwellte Monmouthshire)
'confluence of the (r.) Tyswg (and Rhymni)': *aber*, rn. *Tyswg*
Abertowsowe 1570, *Aber Towssoge* 1583, *Tyr Abertisuge* 1606, *Aber twssog* 1630, *Abertysswg* 1814
Tyswg is *Tysswg* 1694 and *Nant y tysswg* 1813 (*nant*). A few sps. seem to suggest that it was earlier *tywysog* nm., variant *twysog*, 'prince, lord', alluding perhaps to its attractive and noble nature. Tywysog, at Henllan, Denbighshire, has several similar historical forms dating from 1334 (PNBangor).

Adamsdown ST 193765
Cardiff (Roath)
'Adam's hill': pers.n. *Adam*, ME, E **down**
Adamsdowne 1401, 1541, *Adamesdowne, Adams downe farme* 1702
Nearby land is known as *Adamcroftes* 1401 and *Adamescrofte* 1492 (E *croft*). The area is relatively flat but **down** sometimes described small hills and raised areas. The n. is taken from a former fm., on the site of Adamsdown Square, pulled down c.1875. Reputedly named after Adam Kyngot who is mentioned in a Cardiff municipal charter 1331 but the pers.n. was common among E settlers. The W form given as Waunadda (*gwaun*, pers.n. *Adda* 'Adam') in EnWales 118 has no identifiable historical basis.

Afan, Afon see **Aberafan**

Afan Wallia
'Welsh Afan': rn. *Afan*, **Wallia**
(fee) *Avene* 1261, *Aveneslonde* 1326, *Aven Wallia* 1401, *Avene Walsch* 1415, *Avon Wallia* 1541, *Avan Wallia* 1627
Afan Wallia was that part of the cantref of Gwrinydd north of the r. Afan outside the borough of Afan (see Aberafan) and subject to Welsh law in the Middle Ages. Known also as Rhwng Nedd ac Afan and recorded as *rrwng nedd ac aven* 1543 and *Rwngnedh ac Avan* 1559

from its position 'between' (*rhwng*) the rs. Nedd (Neath) and Afan.

Allt-wen SN 727033
Neath Port Talbot (Cilybebyll)
'white (*or* fair) wooded-slope': *allt*, *gwen*
Alltewen 1493, *Alt Wenn* 1541, *Yr Allt Wen* 1610, *Alltwen* 1650, *Gallt wen* 1729
Referring to its location on slopes below Rhos which is *the Rose* 1615 (*y*, *rhos*²). Three farms distinguished as Allt-wen-*isaf*, ~ -*uchaf* and ~ -*ganol*, 'lower' (*isaf*, *uchaf*, *canol*) are recorded 19th cent. There is another Allt-wen (SS 579960) near Gowerton recorded as *Alte-wen* 1583, *Galltwen* 1754, *Altwen* 1764 and *Alltwen* 1852, and cf. Wenallt (with els. reversed). Some historical forms for both pns. have *G-* for *gallt*, a later development based on the assumption that *allt* is a len.

Alltycewri (Alltygawrddu) ST 056808
Rhondda Cynon Taf (Llantrisant)
'wooded-slope at ?': *allt*, ?
Galthe Caurde c.1538; *Alltekarthey*, *Allte Carthe* 1541, *Alltgawrddy* c.1612, *Alltgawrddu* 1767, *Allt-y-Cewri* 1833, *Allt-y-Cawri* 1885
The n. refers to a late medieval ho. Some historic forms favour *cawrdy* as second el., a compound of *cawr* nm. 'giant, hero' and *tŷ*, with regular len. (t > d), but the sps. are generally late and –*ddy* found in many forms would be irregular. They are also at odds with sps. for 1541 which favour an unrecorded el. **carddy*, perhaps composed of *cardd* nm. 'prisoner, slave' and *tŷ* 'house'. That seems to indicate the meaning 'prison' but they are otherwise uncorroborated. The modern form has been influenced by *cewri*, pl. of *cawr*. The former 'popish chapell' *Allt Gawredi* recorded here c.1700 by the scholar Edward Lhuyd is recorded as *Ruins of Alltscourddy* 1811.

Allt-y-grug SN 7507
Neath Port Talbot (Llan-giwg)
'wooded-slope bearing heather': *allt*, *y*, *grug*
Alltgreege 1585, *Allt greeg*, *Alltgreeg* 1650, *Parcell Allt y Grigg* 1670, *Tyr Altgreeg* 1729, (mtn.) *Allt y Greeg* 1799, *Gallt-y-cryg* 1835

Describing a slope characterised by a mixture of woodland and heather.

Aman see **Aberaman**

Angelton, Tre'rannell SS 898822
Bridgend (Newcastle)
'settlement of (man called) Ariannell (*or* Arannell): *tref*, pers.n. Ar(i)annell
Treranell 1518; *treranol* 1585, *Treanell* 1591, *Tre Angel* 1618, *Tre yr Annel* 1638, *Angelston* 1785, *Angelton* 1799, *Angleton, Angelton farm* 1846
Ar(i)annell may have the sense 'shining' comparable with *ariannell*, *arannell*, dim. of *arian* 'silver, money', found in rns. in Glamorgan and elsewhere. Historic forms of Tre'rannell suggest that Ar- in Ar(i)annell was associated with the def.art. *yr* (**Yrannell* > *Yr Annell*). When *Tre*- was prefixed to this, the affixed form `*r* of the def.art. was employed after the vowel in *Tre*- to produce the modern Tre'rannell. Anglicisation has reversed qualifier and generic and substituted E –*ton* for *Tre*-. The evidence is a little contradictory but the present E pron. is probably best represented by the form *Angleton* 1846 ['aŋgltən] with the sound -ngg- probably displacing an earlier ['aŋltən] with -ng-. It is also likely that Angleton was sometimes influenced as a written form by E *angel* (a messenger of God). The unfamiliarity of Tre'rannell as a pn. must account for forms such as *Danielston* 1703 and *Tre Daniel* 1716 which misassociate –*annell* with the pers.n. Daniel. The n. was borne by a fm. destroyed by expansion of the A4063, but survives in the ns. Angleton Road and Angleton House.

Argoed SO 177999
Caerphilly (Bedwellte Monmouthshire)
'(place) opposite the wood; woodland': *argoed*
Argoyd Serowy 1455, *argoed y hogol* 1546, *the Argoed* 1688, *Argoed Vawr* 1756, *Argoed*, ~ *house*, ~ *canol*, ~ *isaf* 1813
Near r. Sirhywi (q.v.). The village developed near coalworkings in the mid 19th cent. The form with *y(r) hogol* is otherwise uncorroborated and unexplained. There is a word *hogol* in Carmarthenshire with the particular sense

'rut, wheel rut', a variant of *hogl, hongl¹* nmf. 'ramshackle or dilapidated edifice, shed' etc (GPC) but it is difficult to reconcile these meanings with ***argoed***.

Argoed Afan SS 820947
Neath Port Talbot (Llangynwyd)
'woodland near (r.) Afan': ***argoed***, rn. *Afan*
Argoed Avan 1541, *Argoed Avon* 1550, *argoed afan* late 16th cent
For the rn., see Aberafan. Glamorgan also has Argoed Isha (***isaf***), Argoed Ganol (***canol***) and Argoed Uchaf (SS 993795) (***uchaf***) in Llansanwyr recorded as *Argoed* in 1721.

As Fach see **Nash**

As Fawr see **Monknash**

Atlantic Wharf, **Glanfa Iwerydd** ST 190754
Cardiff
n. of ocean, E ***wharf***, ***glanfa¹*** nf. 'landing-place, quay', *Môr Iwerydd* 'the Atlantic Ocean': ***môr***, *Iwerydd*
The ns. translate each other and are modern applications to housing and the surrounding retail area developed since 1990 along the docks feeder and East Bute Dock southwards to Cardiff County Hall and National Assembly. Môr Iwerydd is apparently a late form of Môr (y) Werydd recorded from the 16th cent (GPC).

Avan Vale see **Aberafan** and **Cwmafan**

Bae Caerdydd to Byeastwood

Entrance to Barry Docks c.1900. (courtesy of Glamorgan Archives ref. DCOMC/30/3/43)

Bae Caerdydd see **Cardiff Bay**

Baedan, Aberbaiden   SS 855844
Neath Port Talbot (Llangynwyd)
'(place near r.) Baedan': rn. *Baedan Baydan* 1541, 1600, *Aber Baydan* 1633, *Aberbaydan* 1664
The rn. is *Baidan* c.1118, *Baithan* c.1165, *Baythan* c.1246, probably describing a stream likened to a boar which rushes and roots containing *baedd* and suffix *–an*. The variation –d-/-dd- has parallels in historic forms of rs. Bidno and Honddu (DPNW 32, 197-8). Animals are commonly found in rns., eg. Twrch 'boar', Banw 'young pig', and Hwch 'sow'. Baeddan is also a pers.n. (EANC 37-8). The rn. survived in Cwrt Aberbaedan recorded as *Court Aberbaydan* 1664 (*aber*, *cwrt¹*); a chapel-of-ease Capel Baedan, so spelt 1703, and as *Baiden Chapel* 1757 (*capel*); the mountain Mynydd Baedan (SS 8685, 8785) recorded as *montem Baiban* (sic) 1203 and *mynyth Baydan* 1623 (*mynydd*); and in the n. of an administrative division Traean Baedan (*traean* 'a third') alias Lower Llangynwyd in Llangynwyd p. The chp. was located on Mynydd Baedan and was in ruins before the end of the 18th cent (HLlangynwyd 18).

Baglan SS 753922
Neath Port Talbot
(ch. or place of) Baglan: pers.n. *Baglan Bagelan* 1199, c.1262, (*llys*) *lan Vaglan* 15th cent, *Baglan* 1541, *p. maglan* c.1566
One of a number of pers.ns. such as Ceidio and Gwytherin, in Denbighshire, and Llywel, in Breconshire, which stand alone without a preceding generic such as **llan** or **merthyr**. The disused ch. in the churchyard of the modern St Catherine's is dedicated to a saint Baglan, possibly identical to the saint commemorated in Brittany and at Llanfaglan, Caernarfonshire. According to very late legends, Baglan was one of the eight sons of an Ithel Hael of Brittany and was a disciple of the saints Illtud and Cadog. The antiquarian Edward Lhuyd c.1700 records another story that St Illtud (see Llantwit Major) gave Baglan a staff (*bagl* 'staff, crozier' and suffix -*an*) with a brass head which was preserved here 'till of late years' as a sacred relic to cure the sick' (Par III, 27). Legends of this sort are common but as a n. Baglan might also describe a person who had a badly curved or twisted back. It is also worth adding that there is a stream Nant Baglan here, recorded as *Nant Baglan* 1570 (**nant**) and in *Blaen Baglan* c.1700 (**blaen**). That might simply mean 'stream in (the p of) Baglan' but 'curved, twisted' could also describe the course of the stream. If this is the case, then the dedication (absent in early historical sources) to Baglan is false and was prompted by the rn. Local W dialect used the form 'Baclan' recorded in a 19th cent poetic triplet (triban) (VNeath 201). The c.1566 sp. may be an example of the variation *m*- and *b*- sometimes found in historical sources. Both letters in W share the len. f [v] and it is fairly common to find sps. such as *Bachynlleth* for Machynlleth, Montgomeryshire, and *Bathafarn* for Mathafarn, Denbighshire (DPNW 304).

Balaclava SN 704004
Swansea (Llansamlet)
Balaclava 1871
Named from the battle in the Crimean War at Balaklava, 1854, best known for the disastrous charge of the Light Brigade commemorated in the poetry of Lord Tennyson. Cf. Waterloo (below) and Sebastopol, Monmouthshire. A common street and inn n. with examples in Cardiff, Dowlais and Swansea (St Thomas).

Banwen SN 856097
Neath Port Talbot (Cadoxton-juxta-Neath)
'the bog-cotton moor': (**y**) **panwaun**
Panwen Byrdhin 1695, *Panwaun Byrddyn* 1799, (moorland) *Banwen Perddyn*, *Tafarn-y-banwen* 1832, *Banwen* 1919
Stress on *Ban*- encouraged shortening of -*waun* to -*wen* and association with **gwen**; cf. historic forms of Hirwaun. The n. was transferred to an inn Tafarn y Banwen (*tafarn* nf. 'tavern, inn') (SN 858101) demolished in 1937 leaving its n. in that of a bungalow (Blaencwm 15) and a row of houses on the west side of the moorland Banwen Pyrddin (SN 864095). This contains the rn. Peurddin recorded as *peurdin* c.1150, *pyrthyn* 1503, *Perthin* 1690, *Byrddyn Brook* 1799, *Purddin*, *Pyrddin* 1813. **Panwaun** is also found in the ns. of several hills in this area such as that recorded in the ho.n. *Pen-waun-marchog* 1878 (SS 874080) in an area now largely destroyed by opencast mining, the lost *Panwen Gwayn Llwyd* 1769 (in Cadoxton-juxta-Neath) (**llwyd**), Banwen (SN 677010) near Clydach, and Banwen Torybetol (SS 8299) recorded as *Pan wen tor y bedal* 1799, *Banwen Tor-y-Betol* 1833 qualified by Torybedol. The latter is *Torbethel* c.1200 meaning 'gap (or heap) shaped like a horse-shoe' (**tor**, def.art. **y**, *pedol* nf.) possibly once describing the cairn (SS 841999) at the eastern end of the moor or the cairn on Carn Caca.

Bargoed ST 150999
Caerphilly
'(settlement near r.) Bargod': rn. *Bargod Bargoed* 1886
The r. Bargod Rhymni is *Bargau Remni* c.1150-3 containing the el. *bargod*[1] nm. 'eaves, edge'. The qualifier (see Rhymni) serves to distinguish it from Bargod Taf recorded as *Berkehu Taf* c.1150-3 and *River Bargoed Taf* 1799, a tributary of the r. Taf, on the other side of the watershed, recalled in the valley Cwm

Bargod (ST 0999) (*cwm*) and *Blaen Vargod* 1757 (*blaen*). Both tributaries rise closely together on Gelli-gaer Common and the 'eaves' might refer to the steep edges of the common. The industrial settlement developed in the mid 19th cent near the bridge Pont Aberbargoed (see Aberbargoed) at the junction of Rhymni and Bargod Rhymni and around Ffos-las. Initially known as Charlestown (also the n. of an area now absorbed into Blackwood), Bargoed was adopted after the n. was given to the station on the Rhymney Railway. The pn. has clearly been influenced by the common el. *coed* found in several local pns. such as Pen-y-coed (ST 169987) and Hengoed (ST 1595). Bargoed is generally pronounced by local people with a long -o- [o:] but in a 19th cent triban (a poetic triplet) it is rhymed with the short -o- [ɔ] in *hynod* and *briod* (Trib 205).

Barry, **Y Barri**   ST 116680
Vale of Glamorgan
'?hill brook': ?*bar*², suffix *–en* or later suffix *-i*
Barri c.1185, 1307, *Barry* c.1187, (ch. of) *Sancti Nicholai de Barri* 1254, *Barrey* c.1538
The n. is probably drawn from that of a small stream known as *Barrey Brooke* c.1538 and *the Barrie* 1586 rising on the Buttrills above the town and flowing down to the harbour called *Aberbarrey* c.1538 (*aber*), (port of) *Barrye* 1541 and *Barry* ('a drie haven') 1561/2. Both pn. and rn. may derive from an earlier form *Barren* which became *Barre* and *Barri* (cf. Rhos Sulien > Rhosili), possibly under the influence of nearby Sully and Porthkerry (EANC 104-5). The suffix *-en* could be that found in Hafren (the W n. for the r. Severn) or a dim. If this argument is acceptable, then the pn. was later transferred to the island Barry Island/Ynys y Barri (ST 118669), in Penmark p., recorded as *insulam, nomine Barren*, (ad) *Barrenam insulam* c.1200, *Insula Barry* 1479, and *le Ilande of Barry* 1547. The matter has, however, been complicated by historical refs. to a St Barrog, called *Sancti Barroci* by Gerald of Wales c.1191 who states that the saint drowned and was buried on the shore of Barry (*corpus Barruci in littore Barrensi*). This must be the 'fair little chapel of St. Barrok', a place of pilgrimage, recorded on the island by the antiquarian John Leland c.1538. The similarity of the pers.n. Barrog and the rn. and pn. Barri/Barry may, however, be coincidental. Gerald also assures us that his family *de Barri* tooks its n. from Barry/Y Barri, not the other way around, which indicates that the pn. dates from before the date of his birth c.1146. The modern form Y Barri retains the def.art. *y* like Y Bala, Merionethshire, and Y Borth, Cardiganshire, probably through long usage or perhaps from a contraction of Aberbarri > *Abarri, Y Barri comparable with Aberthin, Y Berthin (< Aberberthin).

Barry Island, **Ynys y Barri** see **Barry**

Beaupre, **Y Bewpyr** Old Beaupre ST 009720
Vale of Glamorgan (St Hilary)
'pleasant retreat': Fr *beu*, *beau*, Fr *repaire*
Bewerpere 1376, *Beaupre, Beaupire* c.1511, *the Bewpyre* c.1535
The pn. developed from an intermediate form 'Bewerper' with the *–re-* of *repaire* reversed by metathesis as *–er-* and later lost. The modern form Beaupre is a re-interpretation based on the supposition that the pn. contains Fr *pré* 'meadow'. Generally pronounced 'byooper' ['bju:pɛr] by local E-speakers in similar fashion to the identical pns. Bewper, Surrey and Kent. The form *ll. fair or bewpyr* c.1566 probably refers to St Mary Church about a mile south-west of Old Beaupre across the r. Thaw/Ddawan which marks the boundary between the ps. of St Mary Church and St Hilary. This stands for ModW Llanfair o'r Bewpyr in the sense of 'St Mary Church near Y Bewpyr' and it is worth noting that St Hilary is similarly recorded as *sain tilari y bewpur* c.1550. The historian Dafydd Morganwg 1874 (HMorg 470) says that Old Beaupre was also known as *Maes Esyllt* (*maes*, pers.n. *Esyllt*) but there is no good evidence for this. Old Beaupre was a ho. built by Richard Basset 1586. The qualifier Old seems to be a late adoption to distinguish it from New Beaupre formerly known as Maerdy Newydd (*maerdy*, *newydd*).

Beddau ST 060849
Rhondda Cynon Taf (Llantrisant)
'graves': **bedd** pl. *beddau*
Beddau 1875
Locally pronounced 'Bedda' ['beɪða] by local E-speakers with W dialect –a for –au [aɨ]. The village developed from about 1860 near a ho. recorded as *Heol-y-beddan* (sic) 1833 on the road (**heol**) running north-south through the village to *Croesyrheol-y-Beddau* 1875, properly Croes Heolybeddau 'crossroads of Heolybeddau' (**croes**). It is popularly explained as a battlefield or, more plausibly, a burial place for felons hanged at the crossroads. Beddau fm. in Eglwysilan (lost under Bondfield Park housing estate) is recorded as *the Bedda* 1783 and *Bedda* 1795. Beddau has been confused with *Y Betha* 1769 on the south side of the old part of Llantrisant near Ysticyll-y-beddau (ST 04658325), a group of hos. near the road leading to Llanharan, recorded as *Heol Stycil y Badda* 1861 and *Sticyl y Beddau* 1877 (**sticil, sticill** nf. 'stile').

Bedlinog SO 094012
Merthyr Tudful
?'house near (stream called) Llwynog': **bod¹**, rn. *Llwynog*
Bodloynog alias Tir Coli 1688, *Bodleinog* 1793, *Fodlinog* 1828, (hos.) *Beddyllwynog, Bedllwynog, ~ -fach* 1833, *Bedlinog* 1841, *Cwmfelin neu Bedlinog* 1877
The pn. is also recalled in *Gwayne Vedlinog* 1604 (**gwaun**). The stream Nant y Llwynog rises near Blaenllwynau (SO 102022) which is *Blaen Lleinau* 1799 and *Blaenllwynog* 1813 (**blaen**). The rn. has *llwynog* 'a fox' and may belong to a group of rns. which bear the names of animals from some fancied description of their behaviour. If Twrch 'boar' and Hwch 'sow' are likened to the rushing and rooting of wild pigs, then Llwynog may have been imagined as quiet and stealthy like a fox. If this is the case, then the pn. was confused with *bedlwynog* possessing the general sense of 'area of birch-groves' (**bedlwyn** and the adj. suffix **-og**). A few sps. also suggest association with **bedd** 'a grave'. The alternative n. Cwmfelin is now confined to the group of hos. immediately south of Bedlinog. *Tir Coli* 1688 refers to Tir Coly also recorded as *Tyr Coli* 1799 and in two fm.ns. *Coly-isaf* (SO 097018) and *Coly-uchaf* (SS 093021) 1833 (**isaf, uchaf**). *coly* is a variant of **col** nm. and coll.n. 'beard of corn, chaff; spike' etc but the precise sense here is unclear.

Bedwas ST 170887
Caerphilly (Monmouthshire)
'(place with) numerous birch-trees': **bedw**, **–os**
Bedewas c.1102 (1330), 1254, *Bedewes* 1448, *Bedwas* 1578, 1833
The suffix **–os** is often found with plant-ns., generally signifying an abundance of them; cf. Rhigos and Gurnos. The variation *–os, -as* and *–es* is common (DPNW 26) and probably arose because *–os* was unstressed causing the vowel *o* to become indistinct. This is reflected in modern pron. ['bɛdwəs].

Bedwellte (Bedwellty) SO 166003
Caerphilly (Monmouthshire)
'dwelling of (man called) Mellte': **bod¹**, pers.n. *Mellte*
Bedewellty 1431, *Bedwellte* 1437, 1747, *Bedwellde* 1447, *bod wellde* c.1560, *Bedwelldy* 1778
Probably deriving from unrecorded *Bodfelltau, Bodfellte*. The pn. appears to show the same development of *Bod-* to *Bed-* as in Bedwas and the variation of *-f-* and *-w-* found in words such as *cafod/cawod* 'shower'. The ch. is dedicated to Sannan in c.1566 and there is a well Ffynnon Sant Sannan (SO 168002) (**ffynnon**) possibly the saint recorded in Llansannan, Denbighshire. For Mellte, see also Ystradfellte.

Befecse Befecse-fawr SS 593944
Swansea (Loughor)
Uncertain
Bevexey, sometimes called Tir y don 1650, *Veddexe* 1743, *Beddexe alias Veddexe* 1744, *Tyr yr Eydon alias Bevexy Vawr, Bevexey* 1764, *Bedd Hecse-fach, ~ -fawr* 1832, *Feddexefawr, -fach* 1841, *Vexa Vawr Farm* 1875, *Bevexe-fawr, ~ -fâch* 1884
The n. is taken from two hos. Bevexe-fawr (SS 593943) and Bevexe-fach (SS 592949), distinguished as 'great' (**mawr**) and 'little'

(*bach*¹). A number of historic forms suggest the first el. may be ***bedd*** grave'. *Tyr yr Eydon* is ModW *Tir yr Eidion*, 'land of the bullocks': ***tir, yr, eid(i)on***.

Began¹ ST 228834
Cardiff (St Mellons Monmouthshire)
'clearing of (man called) Began': ?pers.n. *Began*, OE ***lēah***
Beganesleye 1314, *Bekanslegh* 1320, *Beckanslegh* 1403, *Beggam* 1535, *Began* 1578, (*Lisvane or*) *Began Mill* 1720, *Began*, ~ *Weir* 1887
Loss of a final, unstressed E el. is found in the Marches of Wales (DPNW 28, 142-3) and is generally a product of W influence since W-speakers regularly stress the penultimate syllable and a final unstressed syllable can be lost. Loss of –*ley* here, however, is a little unusual because 'Begansley' has also lost its possessive `s as in the case of Began². Began has been explained as Celtic, partly because a pers.n. Beccan ('small man') is recorded in the Irish Annals 7th cent, but Celtic –c- generally develops into –ch- [χ] in W. It is more likely to be an E pers.n. since Began is confined to the Cardiff area and the Vale in earlier records where there were E settlers in the Middle Ages. It may well be the secondary n. or epithet of, for example, *Griffin Began* c.1230, the qualifier in (land called) *Beggan's land* (at Pyle and Kenfig) 1724, and perhaps in *Began row* (Newton Nottage) 1784.

Began² (Beggan) ST 148747
Vale of Glamorgan (Leckwith)
'settlement of (man called) Began': pers.n. *Began*, lost OE ***tūn***
Baganeston 1254, *Beganeston'* c.1348, *Beganston* 1559, *the Beagan* 1675, *Began bach*, ~ *crwn* 1678, *Beganstone* 1699, *Began* 1799
A former manor. The same pers.n. may be found in Began¹. The second el. was lost before the mid 18th cent.

Beggars Pound ST 016683
Vale of Glamorgan (St Athan)
'a poor or ill-kept animal pound': E ***beggar, pound***
Begans pound 1590, *Beggars Pound* 1703, *Beggars Pond* 1841, *Beggars Bound* 1885
The first el. is common in fns. in England, often carrying the sense 'worthless'. This is highly likely too in the case of Beggar's Bush, a n. applied to a place at Tyn-y-caeau fm. (ST 007737), at Llanblethian, and to a mound near Cwrtydefaid (SS 802855). There are identical ns. elsewhere; there is a *Beggarsbush* at Pendine, Carmarthenshire, recorded in 1699 and Beggar's Bush (SO 262642) at Evenjobb, Radnorshire, in 1698. The expression 'to go home by Beggar's Bush' meant 'going to ruin' (www.beggarsbush.org.uk). Beggar is not likely to be the first el. in Beggarswell (at Merthyr Dyfan) which has very different historic forms (see PNDPH 135-6).

Berllan-gollen ST 198867
Caerphilly (Rhydri, Bedwas)
'(the) hazel-tree orchard': (***y***), ***perllan***, ***collen*** (ho.) *Berllangollen* 1871, *Perllan Gollan*, *Berllan Gollan* 1881, *Berllan-gollen* 1885
The ht. developed around Ebenezer Independent chp. near Rhydri. There is a small fm., a short distance north-westwards, recorded as *Ty-berllan* 1833, *Ty'n y Berllan* 1861, *Tyn-y-berllan* 1885, meaning 'house of the orchard' (***tŷ***) or 'smallholding of the orchard' (***tyn***).

Berry SS 471878
Swansea (Llanddewi/Penrhys)
Probably '(place) at the fort': OE ***burh*** dat. *byrig*
Berry 14th cent, *the Berrie* 1641, *Byrry, the wester Berry House, Easterne Berry* 1632, *Burry* 1799, *Bery Hall* 1826
The n. refers to a small prehistoric 'camp' (SS 471882) a little to the north. Similar forms survive for Bury (SO 489122) near Monmouth as *the Berry* 1665, *Bury Farm* 1831.

Berth-lwyd ST 097960
Merthyr Tudful (Llanfabon)
'grey bush': (***y***), ***perth***, ***llwyd***
Berth Lloide, ~ *Lloyde* 1541, *y berth lwyd* c.1612, *Tir y Berth Loyd* 1662, *Berthlwyd* 1812, (hos.) *Berthllwyd-fawr*, ~ -*fach* 1833, *y Berthlwyd* 1860
A common ho.n. with further examples in Llantwit Fardre (*Berthlloyde* 1541) and Loughor

(*Berthloyd* 1650, *Berthllwyd* 1764). Local habitants are said to have interpreted it as *aberth* nmf. 'sacrifice, offering' and **llwyd** meaning 'holy sacrifice' and taken it to be a ref. to early religious worship (StAbercynon 77). Berthlwyd was a t. in Llanfabon p and leaves its n. in Craig Berth-lwyd (ST 093961) recorded as *Craig y Berth Loyd* 1702, *Craig y berthlwyd* 1841 and *Graig Berthlwyd* 1852 (*craig*) and Pentwyn Berth-lwyd (ST 100962); cf. Pentwyn below.

Betws SS 899867
Bridgend
'house of prayer, chapel, chapel-of-ease': *betws*[1]
Bettus 1578, *the Bethous* 1688, *Bettws Gwayr* (with chp.) *Bettws bach alias Bettws Rys ap aren* 1697 (late 18th cent), *Bettws* 1799
This is also *capellam in nemore ex orientali parte Leueni* c.1168, 'chapel in the wood on the east side of Llynfi'. Sometimes qualified by Tir Iarll, the lp. in which it lay. Betws was probably once a chapel-of-ease of Llangeinwyr (q.v.). The form for 1697 is contained in a copy of notes made by the antiquarian Edward Lhuyd taken from a continuation of a lost manuscript of the research of Rice Merrick. Gwair was reputed to have been Gwair ab Aron, once lord of Betws, and Rhys was presumably his brother, but nothing has been found to confirm this. Betws is also recorded as *ll. ysbyttel* c.1566 but this too has not been properly explained. The historian Dafydd Morganwg 1874 (HMorg 222) uses the form *Llanyspyddel* but he was probably drawing on a related source. If it is genuine, then it may be a late borrowing *ysbytel from ME *spitel* 'hospital or religious house'.

Bewpyr see **Beaupre**

Birchgrove[1], **Llwyn-bedw** ST 168779
Cardiff (Llanisien/Whitchurch)
'grove of birch-trees': **birch**, **grove**, **llwyn**, **bedw**
Birch Grove 1831, *Birchgrove* 1880
The n. of a Cardiff suburb, developed from the 1890s around Llwynfedw Road and Birchgrove Road and railway station, taken from a private ho. The n. could originate with an unrecorded Llwyn-y-bedw, 'the birch grove' (with def. art. **y**), or Llwyn-y-fedw (with **bedw** as a nf. meaning 'birch wood'); a number of former hos. in the area have or had both W and E forms.

Birchgrove[2] ST 026915
Rhondda Cynon Taf (Llanwynno)
Birch Grove villa 1895, *Birchgrove Street* 1900, *Birchgrove* 1910
Deriving from the n. of a street constructed in the late 19th cent on hill-slopes below former woodland. The nucleus of the development was America-fach, 'little America', recorded as *America-fâch* and similar forms 1873-81, 'little America' (**bach**[1]), with an *America Place* 1881 but dropped from maps before 1900. Transferred names of this sort tend to be mocking, often for small or isolated places, but here the industrial village was probably likened to the 'land of opportunity'.

Birchgrove[3], **Gellifedw** SS 705985
Swansea (Llansamlet)
Birchgrove 1775, *Birch Grove* 1798, (fm.) *Tir y Bedw or Birchgrove* 1808, *Birch-grove* 1832
The 1808 sp. suggests an original Tir y Bedw 'the land with birch-trees' (**tir**, **y**, **bedw**) but unhistoric Gellifedw (**celli**, **bedw**) is in use. The village developed in the 19th cent. near several coal-mines notably Birchgrove Colliery (c.1845-1932).

Bishopston, Llandeilo Ferwallt SS 578894
Swansea
'bishop's settlement': OE **biscop**, **tūn**; 'church of (St) Teilo', 'church of Merwallt', **llan**, pers.n. *Teilo*, pers.n. *Merwallt*
Lann Merguall, (*cum*) *mergualdo illius ecclesie principe*, (monastery of) *sancti cinuuri, id est lannberugall* c.1145, (ch. of) *Sancti Teliaui de lannmergualt* c.1170, *Villa Episcopi in Guer* c.1230, *Bisschopiston' in Gower* 13th cent, *ll.deilo ar ferwallt* c.1566, *Bishopston* 1670, *Llandilo vairwallt* 1697
The E pn. refers to the bishops of Llandaf and is often found with the qualifier 'in Gower' to distinguish it from other pns. such as Bishton, Monmouthshire, found in some earlier sources as

Bishopston. Bishopston also has a few contracted forms such as *Bishton infra Gowre* 1535 and *Bison* 1764; cf. *Bolston* for Bonvilston (below). The current W n. Llandeilo Ferwallt appears to have displaced an earlier Llanferwallt. Merwallt was presumably the ch. officer or patron (*principe*) specified in the first ref. above. Bishopston has also been identified with the 'church of St Cynnwr (*or* Cynfwr)' largely on the strength of the ref. above and with *Porthtulon* in the Book of Llandaf c.1145 but see Caswell.

Blackmill, Melin Ifan Ddu SS 934867
Bridgend (Llandyfodwg)
'dark mill': E *black, mill*; 'mill belonging to Ifan the dark (or swarthy), *melin*, pers.n. *Ifan, du* (mill) *Melin Jeuan du* 1579, *Blackmill* c.1670, *Melin Evan ddu* 1729, *Melin-du* 1833
The E form and a small number of W forms misattribute the darkness to the mill rather than the person. Little appears to be known of Ifan Ddu but his n. is also found in that of a hill *Mynydd Evan Du* 1650, *Mynydd Ieuan duy* 1672 (*mynydd*) and (ho.) Dolau Ifan Ddu (*dolau* 'water-meadows') recorded as *Tolyfonddu* 1813, *Dola-Evanddu* 1826, and *Dolauevan-ddu* 1841 north of Blackmill (SS 935873). There was also a *Tir Jevan du* 1653, *Tir Evan Du* (in Coety) 1789 (*tir*) and Ton Ithel Ddu (*ton*²) reputed to be the home of Ithel, king of Morgannwg (HTonyrefail 53, 85), but this is unproven. We also have a 'red (*or* brown) Ifan' in Hendre Ifan Goch (SS 973884) about three miles away up Cwm Ogwr Fach recorded as *Hendre Evan Goch* 1683, *Hendre Evan Goch* 1785, *Hendregoch* 1813 (*hendref, coch*).

Blackpill, Dulais SS 618905
Swansea (Oystermouth/Sketty)
'black pill (or stream)': OE *blæc, pyll*; 'black (or dark) stream', *du* 'black, dark', *glais dubleis* c.1145, (brook) *Dilas* 1597, *Blakepulle* c.1168, (watermill) *la Blakepull* 1319, *the Blacke Pyll* 1504, (r.) *Blackepill* 1650, *Black Pill* 1729
pyll, pill is generally applied to small streams flowing through marshland into tidal creeks and the sea so that Black Pill may have referred specifically to the short stretch of Clyne River where it reaches Swansea Bay. Dulais by contrast would describe a stream in shadow flowing through a narrow, wooded valley or over coal measures. Mines of sea-coal (mineral coal) are recorded in this area in 1319 and there were several small collieries in and around the Clyne valley until the 1950s.

Blackweir, Cored-ddu ST 175777
Cardiff
'dark weir': E *black, weir*; *cored, du Corad Ddu, the Black Wares* 1769, *Black Wears* 1771, *Black Wear* 1811, *Black-weir* 1833
The n. might apply to a weir overhung by trees or one composed of dark stones. Named from an old salmon-weir on the r. Taf near the former Blackweir Farm (west of Nazareth House ST 176775). Later evidence for the W form seems to be lacking though a modern ho. has taken the n. Llys y Gored Ddu (*llys*). The ref. for 1769 shows that here *cored* is a nf., though it can also be a nm.

Blackwood, Coed-duon ST 174969
Caerphilly (Bedwellte Monmouthshire)
'black (or dark) wood': E *black, wood*; 'black trees': *coed, duon*
Blackwood, Coed-duon 1822, *Black Wood, vulgarly ... Tremoggridge* 1824, *Coed dion* 1847, (village) *Blackwood* 1851, *Coedduon (Blackwood)* 1883
Named from a wood on the south-west side of the town. Developed as a model settlement from 1820 by John Hodder Moggridge (1771-1834), an E landowner and social reformer who published an article in The Oriental Herald and Colonial Review in 1829 describing his scheme for the provision of progressive housing for 'the Labouring Classes of Society, in the Hills of Monmouthshire'. Thomas Morgan 1887 also cites the form *Moggridgeton* (OPN 15) but this is so far unsubstantiated. *Tremoggridge* has *tref* 'town'. Moggridge also founded Ynys-ddu (q.v.).

Blaenau Morgannwg
'uplands of Morgannwg': *blaen* pl. *blaenau*, pn. **Morgannwg**
blaenau Morgannwg late 15th cent, *Blayne, which in English wee call mountaines, Blaineu* c.1670

In contrast to the Vale of Glamorgan, Bro Morgannwg (q.v.). See also Glamorgan, Morgannwg.

Blaencaerau　　　　　　　　SS 862948
Bridgend (Llangynwyd)
'upper part of Caerau', *blaen*, (*y*), pn. **Caerau**
Blaen-y-Caira 1780, *Blaencaerau* 1813, (ho.) *Blaen-caerau* 1833, *Blaencaera* 1841
Located above Caerau (q.v.). Named from Blaencaerau fm. (SS 870947).

Blaenclydach　　　　　　　SS 985928
Rhondda Cynon Taf (Ystradyfodwg)
'headwaters of the (r.) Clydach': *blaen*, rn. *Clydach*
Blaen Cladach 1547, ~ *Cladache* 1550, (mountain ground) *Hendre Tydyr, otherwise Blaen Clydach* 1705, (mess.) *Blaen Clydach* 1736
Named from the fm. (approx. SS 970928) immediately above Clydach Vale (q.v.).

Blaen-cwm (Blaen-y-cwm)　　SS 920988
Rhondda Cynon Taf (Ystradyfodwg)
'head of the valley': *blaen*, *y*, *cwm*
Blaen-y-cwm 1833, 1964, *Blaenycwm* 1875, *Blaencwm* 1978
The valley is Cwm Selsig. Cf. Blaen-y-cwm (ST 213899) near Machen, recorded as *Blaen-y-cwm* 1879 and Blaen-y-cwm in Merthyr Tudful recorded as *Blaen y cwm* 1864. The nucleus of the village was *Long Row* above the Dunraven Arms and *Ty-uchaf* 'upper house' (*tŷ*, *uchaf*) recorded in 1877. OS maps since the 1970s have dropped hyphens and the def.art. *y* but the main road in the village is still Blaen-y-cwm Road. Colloquial loss of an unstressed def.art. is fairly common in Glamorgan and Monmouthshire.

Blaendulais see **Seven Sisters**

Blaenegel　　　　　　　　　SN 7209
Neath Port Talbot (Llan-giwg)
'headwaters of the (r.) Egel': *blaen*, rn. *Egel*
Blaenegl 1578, *Parcell Blaen Egle* 1670, *Blaen Egel* 1717, 1807, *Blaenegal* 1748, *Blanegal* 1764, *Blaenegil* 1776, *Blaen-hegyl-fach*, ~ *-fawr* 1832

There is also a ref. to a *Iohannis Blaneaighel* who granted the ch. of Pen-maen (in Gower) to the Commandery of the Knights of St John of Jerusalem, of Slebech, Pembrokeshire, in 1231-2. The rn. is generally recorded as *Egle, Eggle* etc. over the period 1556-1700 and occurs frequently in local dialect form as *Egal*. Gwynedd Pierce (ADG², 12; PNGlam 20-1) suggests that it is *egel* 'sowbread' (cyclamen hederifolium), a tuberous plant which grows wild in hedgerows and was used as fodder for pigs. This is typically found in southern Europe and is said to have been introduced to Britain before 1597 (BRC); clearly it is older. *egel* seems to occur only in late literary sources so it is especially intriguing that one ho-n. recorded as *Bogel Egel* 1764, *Bogel-hegyl* 1832 and *Bogel-egel* 1878-1953 combines the el. with *bogail¹*, *bogel* which has a number of meanings including 'navel, boss (of a shield), nave of a wheel', sometimes used as a topographical description for 'a hillock' as in Cornish (CPNE 19), and significantly 'sowbread' when combined with *daear* 'earth' in *bogel y ddaear* (GPC). The doubling of the two els. *bogail¹*, *bogel* and *egel* clearly needs further investigation but it confirms the association with the plant. Bogel-egel is now Rhyd-yr-egel (SN 724090) 'ford of Egel' (*rhyd*, *yr*). Blaenegel was also a **parsel** found mainly in south-east Wales to describe a subdivision of a p.) of Llan-giwg. Fforchegel is *Fforch-Egell* 1717, *Forch Egel* 1764 and *Fforch-hegyl* 1832 meaning 'fork of Egel' (*fforch*) since it lies between two branches of the r.

Blaengarw　　　　　　　　SS 901929
Bridgend (Llangeinwyr)
'headwaters of the (r.) Garw': *blaen*, rn. *Garw*
Blayne Garro 1541, *Blayne Garo* 1582, *blaen garw* 1630, *Blaengarw* 1813
The rn. has *garw* adj. 'rough, rugged' which in pns. usually applies to the nature of the landscape but it is evidently applied here to mean 'river with rough waters' possibly in contrast to the 'smooth' (*llyfn*) r. Llynfi (see Blaenllynfi). There are two rs. here: Garw (or Garw Fawr) recorded as *Garwe* late 12th cent, *Garewe* 1207, *Garoo* 1531, *Garrowe-vaure*

1589, *Garw* 1631 and Garw Fechan recorded as *Garrowe-vechan* 1589 distinguished as 'great' and 'small' (***mawr***, ***bechan***). Garw joins the Ogmore/Ogwr at Abergarw (*Abergarw* 1631). For the valley see Cwm Garw. The mill (***melin***) Melin-arw (SS 915877) is recorded as (mill) *Garrowe* 1535 and *Melinarw* 1833.

Blaen-gwawr   SO 009018
Rhondda Cynon Taf (Aberdare)
'headwaters of (r.) Gwawr': ***blaen***, rn. *Gwawr*
blayne gwawr 1592, *Blaen Gwawr* 1659, *Blaengwawr* 1682
For the rn., see Aber-gwawr. The n. is taken directly from Blaengwawr Colliery below Blaengwawr fm. (SO 002016). A (lost) *blane Gwawr* in Eglwysilan is mentioned in 1795, possibly near Glawnant (ST 117918).

Blaen-gwrach   SN 868053
Neath Port Talbot (Glyncorrwg)
'headwaters of the (r.) Gwrach': ***blaen***, rn. *Gwrach*
Bleinwrach 1208, *Blaen Gwrache* 1574, *Blaengwrach* 1664, (fm.) *Blaen-gwrach-fawr* 1833, *Parcell Blaen Gwrach* 1670
The r. is *Wrack* c.1200 (1358), *Gwrach* 1541, containing *gwrach* nf. 'hag, witch', either as a n. derived from a local tradition of a witch inhabiting its banks or a ref. to its nature, perhaps one which can be both mysterious and dangerous. Blaen-gwrach evidently once applied to the area (SN 0387) where its tributaries rise, now obscured by forestry and opencast mining and was the n. of a former administrative division (***parsel***) and a chp. – probably Capel Bach (***capel***, ***bach***[1]) – mentioned in 1595-7 (VNeath 91, 124-5, 127). The rn. also occurs in Cwmgwrach (q.v.).

Blaengwynfi   SS 891965
Neath Port Talbot (Glyncorrwg)
'headwaters of the Gwynfi': ***blaen***, rn. *Gwynfi*
Blaengwynfiw 1670, *Blangwynfyw* 1699, *Blaengwnfy* 1813, *Blaen-gwynfy* 1833
For the rn., see Abergwynfi. The village is named from a former fm. and developed between Corrwg Rhondda Colliery and Afan Colliery at the end of the 19th cent.

Blaenhonddan, Blaenhonddan Farm
SN 753005
Neath Port Talbot (Cadoxton-juxta-Neath)
'headwaters of the (r.) Honddan': ***blaen***, rn. *Honddan*
the parcell of Blaenhouthen 1566, *Blaen Hothney* 1609, *Blaen honddan* 1638, *Blaen-honddan*, *Blânhonddau*, *Honddau* c.1700, *Blaenhonddan* 1705
Early sps. of Honddan are lacking but it is possible that an original Hoddnant > Honddant > Honddan with reversal of -ddn- and -ndd- by metathesis and loss of –t. There are similarities to the development of the rn. Hondon, a tributary of Bachawy, Radnorshire, recorded as *Hotenant* 1397, *Hothnant* 1608 and *Hondant* 1624. Both ns. appear to have *hawdd* adj. 'easy; prosperous, pleasant' and ***nant*** 'stream' earlier 'valley'. Metathesis is found also in earlier forms of Honddu, Breconshire, and an identical rn. recalled in Llanthony, Monmouthshire, with the same first el. and suffix –*ni* (DPNW 197-8). R.J. Thomas (EANC 149-154, however, queries whether these rns. contain *hawdd* since he did not think that it applies very well to rapid streams. The rn. may, however, be placatory or euphemistic. In the case of Honddan (and Hondon) the rn. may actually be taken from the valley and it is worth noting that Hoddnant (*Hodnant* c.1200, *Odnante* c.1670) at Llantwit Major is annotated in Lat as *uallis prospera* 'prosperous vale' c.1200.

Blaenllechau   ST 001974
Rhondda Cynon Taf (Llanwynno)
'headwaters of (r.) Llechau': ***blaen***, rn. *Llechau*
(ho.) *Blaenllecha* 1814, *Blaen-llecha* 1833
The village is named from a fm. in Llanwynno and developed after the sinking of a colliery pit by D. Davies, esq., Blaen-gwawr, 1862 (see also Ferndale). Llechau may have referred to a small tributary of Rhondda Fach which it meets (ST 007962) below the village and fm. but the matter has been complicated by the existence of a larger tributary, now called Nant y Llechau,

'stream flowing over flat slabs or stones' (***llech***[1] pl. ***llechau***), which joins Rhondda Fach about two miles further downstream near a former fm. Aberllechau (ST 021938) in Wattstown (q.v.). This rn. is also recalled in *Tir Kevan llecha* 1633 which must be either Cefnllechau Uchaf (ST 018950) (*Kevan Llecha* 1751) or Cefnllechau Isaf (approx. ST 013943) (*Cefn-llechan* 1833), and a former alternative n. of Pen-yr-heol (ST 016950) recorded as *Pen tyir hewl lecha* 1633 and *Blaen Llecha alias Penhewl Ucha* 1833. Cefn Llechau must have been the adjoining hill (***cefn***). The local pron. *Blaenllecha* is confirmed in a triban (Trib 470). Cf. Blaenllechau (?SN 7302), in Cilybebyll, found as *Tyr Blaen Llech* 1729, *Blaenlleche* 1816 with a stream *Lecha* 1610.

Blaenogwr   approx. ST 939927
Bridgend (Llandyfodwg)
'headwaters of (r.) Ogwr': ***blaen***, rn. **Ogwr**
Blaen ogur 1576, *Blaine Ogwr* 1703, *Blaenogwr* 1767, *Blaen Ogwr* 1785
For the rn., see Ogmore. The fm. was removed by the growth of Price Town (q.v.) c.1898, its n. surviving in Blaenogwr Hotel. A former fm. Blaenogwr Uchaf (ST 933942) is *Blaen Ogwr ycha* 1682, *Blaenogwr Uchaf* 1826.

Blaenrhondda   SN 928997
Rhondda Cynon Taf (Ystradyfodwg)
'headwaters of (r.) Rhondda': ***blaen***, rn. **Rhondda**
blaen Ronthe 1479, *Tir blaen Rhothni* 1552, *Blaen Ronthey* 1666, *Blaen-rhondda* 1833, *Blaen-y-Rhondda* 1875
An industrial village which developed below Blaenrhondda Colliery, sunk 1868-9, near a former fm. (SN 921006).

Blaenrhymni   SO 1110
Caerphilly (Gelli-gaer, Merthyr Tudful)
'headwaters of (r.) Rhymni': ***blaen***, rn. **Rhymni**
blayn Rompny 1432, *Blayne Rompeney* 1570, *Blaen Rhymni* 1861, (area) *Blaen Rhymney* 1891
For the rn. see Rhymni. An area extending into Llangynidr, Breconshire, and Bedwellte.

Blaen-y-cwm see **Blaen-cwm**

Blue Anchor   SS 551951
Swansea (Llanrhidian)
'(place near inn called) Blue Anchor', E ***blue***, E ***anchor***
Blue Anchor 1832, 1841
Named from a public ho. recorded in 1802. The n. is fairly common, occurring mainly at ports and near navigable rs. Examples in Glamorgan include former inns in St Mary Street, Cardiff, in Loughor and Cadoxton-juxta-Neath. Swansea had a Blue Anchor Lane 1746 linking Wind Street to the Strand. The Blue Anchor at Aberthaw is named, according to the inn's website, from blue marl or mud which coated the anchors of vessels that stopped at the port. Blue Anchor in Preston, Lancashire, has been explained as referring to an *anker*, 'a Dutch measure or barrel that held about ten gallons' (and 'a small barrel' in EDD), painted blue and used as the inn-sign, but no instances of *anker* have been recorded in Glamorgan.

Bondfield Park   ST 147869
Caerphilly (Eglwysilan)
'housing estate named from Margaret Bondfield': surname *Bondfield*, E ***park***
One of several housing estates in Caerphilly named after politicians (see Lansbury Park and Churchill Park). Margaret Bondfield (1873-1953) was a Labour MP prominent in the women's suffrage movement. The estate developed from the late 1950s around crossroads where there was a ho. Y Beddau meaning 'the graves' (***y***, ***bedd*** pl. *beddau*) recorded as *Tir y Betha* 1767, *the Bedda* 1783, and *Beddau fm.* 1875; cf. Beddau (q.v.). The reason for the n. is uncertain but various mounds and minor earthworks appear here on late 19th-early 20th cent plans.

Bont-faen see **Cowbridge**

Bonvilston, **Tresimwn**   ST 065740
Vale of Glamorgan
'settlement of (family called) Bonville': OE ***tūn***, locative n. and surname *Bonville*, and 'settlement of (man called) Simwn(t)', ***tref***, pers.n. *Simwn(t)*

(ch. of) *Bonevill'*, *Bonevilestune* late 12th cent, *Boleuileston'* c.1180, *Bonevileston* 1254, *Bolstone village, Gal: Tresi[mon]* c.1538, *Bonvilstone ... for shortnes of speech, Bolson* 1591, *tre simwnt* c.1566, *Bolstone, Tresymon* c.1670, *Tresymwnd* 1740, *Bonvilston or Tre Simwn* 1833

Members of the de Bonville family such as Roger de Bonauilla occur in Glamorgan from the mid 12th cent, possibly taking their surname from Bonneville-sur-Touques, in Normandy (PNDPH 12-3). The W n. seems to be first recorded in the itinerary of the antiquarian John Leland c.1538 and may refer to Simon de Bonville who occurs c.1230-62. The contracted forms *Bolston, Boulston*, etc are common in historical sources from the mid 16th cent down to the early 19th cent, cf. *Coston* for Cosmeston, *Colston* for Colwinston and *Flimston* for Flemingston (q.v.), but most local people now pronounce the pn. in its fuller form. The 'old town' (*Veteris Ville* 13th cent) and 'old castle' (*Vetus Castrum* 1308) on the west side of Bonvilston appear to refer to Y Gaer (ST 064747) meaning 'the fort' (*y*, *caer*). The antiquarian Iolo Morganwg c.1797 said that there was an alternative W n. *Llwyn Mar* but there seems to be no evidence to confirm this.

Bon-y-maen SS 678952
Swansea (Llansamlet)
'base of the stone': **bôn**, *y*, **maen**
Boneymaen c.1583, *Bone y mane* 1650, *Bonmaen* 1799, *Bon-y-maen* 1832
Probably referring to a standing stone of uncertain age (SS 678952). There was an identical pn. (at about SO 061083) in Merthyr Tudful recorded as *terre bon meyne* 1449 (***tir***), *Bon y maen* 1540, *Bone y mane* 1757, *Bon-y-maen* 1833, probably recalled in Rocky Road.

Boverton, Trebefered SS 982684
Vale of Glamorgan (Llantwit Major)
'settlement belonging to Bouvier': pers.n. *Bouvier*, OE **tūn**, **tref**
Bovyareston 1296, *Bonyerton* 1322, *Boverton* 1330, *Bovierton* 1349, *Bovyarton* 1375, *Boverton alias Berton* 1559, *Bevertone* 1560, *Trebefered Ox-Town* 1756, *Tref Beferad, Trebefred* c.1800

Bouvier has not been identified. Antiquarians were plainly aware that it was also an occupational n. for a herdsman (Fr *bouvier*, Low Lat *bovārius* formed from *bōs*, gen. *bovis*, 'ox'), hence the spurious *Ox-Town* and attempts to identify Boverton with Roman *Bovium* (see Cowbridge). The W n. occurs only in late sources and is evidently derived from Boverton but its form and development are unusual. W-speakers have reversed the qualifier and generic and substituted **tref** for **-ton** but -befered is difficult to explain satisfactorily on the available evidence. The final –d may perhaps be a voiced recollection of the -t in -ton (Boverton > **tref** + Bovert- > *Trebofert, *Treboferd). The next step, if we accept this suggestion, must have been intrusion of epenthetic -e- > Trebofered, Trebefered to ease pron. after –r-, and shift of stress to –fer-.

Brackla SS 924798
Bridgend (Coychurch)
?'land broken up for cultivation': OE **brēc**, **bræc**, or 'land bearing brushwood': OE **bræc**, with **land**
Brackla 1783, *Bragland Hill* 1833, *Brackla Hill* 1885
The pn. is also recorded in (lane) *hewl y Blackla* (sic) 1702, (lane) *Heol y Bragland* 1833, *Brackla Lane* 1841. Sps. are late but the first suggestion may be compared with Breckland, Norfolk. The pn. has lost terminal -nd as in the case of Yackla (probably with OE *gēac* 'cuckoo') at Wenvoe. Heol y Brackla (*heol*, *y*), otherwise Brackla Street or Lane, runs eastwards from Nolton Street, originally as far as the south slopes of Brackla Hill (SS 920803). *Bragle* appears on current OS maps as the W form of this pn. but there seems to be no historic evidence for it. Local W dialect would generally favour a spoken form matching 'Brackla', i.e. *Bracla. The area was developed for housing from the late 1970s. See also Bragdy (SS 927815).

Bragdy SS 927815
Bridgend (Coety)
'(the) brewery': (*y*), **bracty**
y Bracty 1768, *Brack Ty* 1851, *Bragdy* 1877

Brackla (q.v.) is less than a mile away but the similarity is probably coincidental. Bragdy (SN 664029), in Llangyfelach, is *Malt House* 1877.

Breigam see **Ton-breigam**

Bridgend, **Pen-y-bont ar Ogwr** SS 905798
Bridgend
'(place at) the end of the bridge': E ***bridge***, ***end***; '(place at) the end of the bridge on (the r.) Ogwr', ***pen***[1], ***y***, ***pont***, ***ar***, rn. **Ogwr**
Bryggen Eynde 1444, *Brugeende juxta Coytyf* 1452, *Brygend* 1542, *Brigend* 1547, *Bridgend* 1584, *Penbowt* 1586, (*o*) *benn y bont* late 16th cent, *Pennebont* 1612, (*tua*) *Phen-pont-ar-ogwyr* 1778, *Penybont* 1801, *Bridgend, otherwise Penybont ar Ogwr* 1840
For the rn., see Ogmore. John Leland, antiquarian and scholar, c.1538 calls it *Penbont (ende of the bridge)* and *Pennebont* but his *Pont Newith on Ogor*, which has also been identified with Bridgend, probably refers to New Inn Bridge (SS 891784) a mile downstream.

Bristol Channel, **Môr Hafren**
'sea-channel leading to Bristol', pn. Bristol, E ***channel***; 'sea of (r.) Severn', ***môr***[1], rn. **Hafren**
ymor hafren c.1145, *the Severn Se* c.1538, *the sea of Sevarne* 1559, *De Canael van Brostu* 1584, *The seaverne sea* 1614, *Bristoll Channel* 1724, *The Severn or Channell of Bristoll* 1785, *Môr Hafren* 1820
The broad marine channel leading towards Bristol earlier known as the Severn Sea matched by Môr Hafren where the r. Severn / Hafren (CDEPN 88, 537-8) meets the open sea. Bristol Channel now refers to the sea west of Flatholm and Steepholm as far as Gower and Ilfracombe, Devon. Bristol Channel does not appear to have been in widespread use among E-speakers before the middle of the 18th cent. The n. may have referred originally to the sea channel running through the sea-bank known as the English Grounds recorded as *The Channell betweene the groundes* c.1595.

Britannia[1] ST 158984
Caerphilly (Bedwellte Monmouthshire)
'Britain': RB *Britannia*
Britannia Terrace 1919
The n. is drawn directly from the Britannia Colliery (ST 157980) sunk in 1910-12 which recalls *Britannia Cottage* (approx. ST 157979) recorded in 1879 next to the Brecon & Merthyr Railway mineral line. This may have been the location of the Britannia public ho. recorded in this area in 1841. 'Britannia' was typically applied to public hos., public buildings and industrial works, often as a nationalistic or entrepreneurial conceit. The settlement developed north of Gilfach Quarry but remained little more than a small group of hos. down to the late 1960s.

Britannia[2] ST 032909
Rhondda Cynon Taf (Llantrisant)
'Britain': RB *Britannia*
Britannia 1868, 1905
As Britannia[1]. Probably named from the Britannia Inn recorded 1861.

Brithdir SO 151020
Caerphilly (Gelli-gaer)
'land or soil of medium quality or of variegated character': ***brith***[1], ***tir***
le brithe tire 1556, *Cap. brathtcare* 1578, *Brîth tir chapple*, (chp.) *Brithdîr* c.1658, *Brithdir hamlett* 1670, *Capel Brithdir* 1729
brith[1] refers typically to land 'marked with different colours, speckled (often with stones)' with the extended sense of 'poor land'. A number of historic forms also have the def. art. ***y*** but this is now generally dropped. A very common pn., cf. Brithdir (SS 717977) near Skewen on the south slopes of Mynydd Drumau recorded as *Brithtir* 1813, *Brith-dir* 1830, Brithdir, Merionethshire (DPNW 47) and Brithdir, Montgomeryshire (PNMont 35-6). The chp. (SO 138025), roofless in 1878, on the hill Cefn y Brithdir (***cefn***) is ruinous. The village railway station initially bore the n. George Inn but changed to Brithdir 1882.

Briton Ferry, Llansawel SS 737942
Neath Port Talbot
'ferry at Briton': E *ferry*, pn. Briton 'bridge settlement': *brycg, tūn*; 'church of (St) Sawyl', *llan*, pers.n. *Sawyl* later *Sawel*, ?*Isawel*
Ponte 1208, 1254, *Brigeton*' 1208, *la Bruttone* 1314, *Briggetune* 1338, (ferry at) *Britton* 1349, *Llansawyl* late 15th cent, *Britan Fery, caullid in Walsche Llanisauël* c.1538, *Britton Ferry* 1566, *ll. isawel* c.1566, *Lan y Shawel, or Brittain Ferry* 1767
Ferry is a later addition to Briton. The ferry, recorded in 1307, was across the r. Neath / Nedd but several writers have remarked that there is no record of a bridge here. Gerald of Wales, in his itinerary 1188, noted only quicksands at the mouth of the r. Any bridge must have crossed a minor stream, perhaps that which descends from Cwmnantyrarllwys and Ynysmaerdy, flowing westwards into Briton Ferry where it is culverted. *Ponte* (Lat *pons*, Fr *pont*) 1208 has been identified with Llandeilo Tal-y-bont but *Brigeton* appears in the same source and favours Briton Ferry. The W n. is identical to Llansawel, Carmarthenshire. William of Worcester in his travels in 1479 records 'a ferry with a boat that goes to Swansea' at *villam Lanysawelle*.

Britwn see **Burton**

Brocastle, Brocastell SS 936771
Bridgend/Vale of Glamorgan (Ewenni)
?'broad castle': ME *brode, castle*
Brocastell 1565, *Brocastle* 1607, *Broe Castle* 1648, *Broadcastle* c.1670, *Brocastle, ~ Barn* 1813
Many forms favour *bro* 'region, land' as in Bro Morgannwg (the Vale of Glamorgan) and *castell* with the collective sense of 'area, district around a castle' but it is difficult to think of similar examples and it is possible that Brocastle and Brocastell derive from E 'broad castle' as the c.1670 sp. suggests. There seems to be no evidence of a castle here but *castle* was sometimes used fancifully for a locality thought to resemble a castle.

Brofeisgyn (Brofiscin) see **Meisgyn**

Brombil SS 790876
Neath Port Talbot (Margam)
'hill having broom': OE *brōm, hyll*
Brombell 1540, *the Brombylle* 1541, *Bromehill* 1551, *Brombill, Forest Brombille* 1588, *the Brembill* 1628, *Brembill, ~ mawr* 1683, *Cwm-y-Brombill* 1749, *Brombel Cross* 1729, (mountain) *Mynydd Brombill* 1799
The letter –b- has intruded in the same way as OE *bremel* > ModE *bramble* and also accounts for the loss of –h- in *hyll*. Brombil at Pyle beneath Pen Castell hillfort (SS 846826) is recorded in (land) *Erw yr Brombill* (in Kenfig) and *Gweyne y Brombylly* (in Stormy Fechan) 1518 (*erw, gwaun*).

Broughton SS 921709
Vale of Glamorgan (Wick)
'settlement by a brook': OE *brōc, tūn*
Broughton 1501, 1638, *Brychton in Wick* 1757, *Brufton* 1774, *Brychdwn* 1888
On Nash Brook, and identical in meaning to Broughton (SS 4193, at Llangennith) which is *Broughton* late 16th cent. The W form Brychdwn is poorly-evidenced and the 1757 ref. raises the possibility that it has replaced Brychton; both forms retain the ME aspirate -gh- as -ch-. Local E-speakers pronounce Broughton as 'Bruffton' ['brʌftən *or* 'brʌftʌn] as in the case of Broughton (SS 419928) at Llangennith.

Bryn[1] SS 525933
Swansea (Llanrhidian)
'hill': *bryn*
Bryn 1799, 1832, *Brynyrallt* 1813
Taken from a ho. Bryn-yr-allt, 'hill of the wooded-slope': *bryn, yr, allt*. Rallt (*Allt* 1841) is on the north side of Bryn and has been identified with Gower's Load but this is recorded separately as *Gowers Load* 1832, and *Gowersload* 1841. This has E *lode, load* derived from OE *(ge)lād* 'an artificial channel, a canalised river'.

Bryn[2] ST 168953
Caerphilly (Mynyddislwyn Monmouthshire)
Bryn 1813, *The Bryn* 1833
'hill': *bryn*

On the south slopes of a hill crossed by Rhymney Valley Ridgeway, known as Crown Lane in the middle of the village, running north towards Blackwood. 'Crown' refers to the Crown Hotel, a n. possibly inspired in part by its topographical location.

Bryn[3]   SS 814923
Neath Port Talbot (Margam)
'hill': *bryn*
Bryn 1852
The village developed after the opening of Bryn Navigation Colliery 1841 (closed 1963) which took its n. either from Bryn-gurnos (SS 810921) or more probably Bryn-troed-y-garn (SS 819924) (StTaibach 59). The first is *Bryngurnos* 1813 and *Bryn-gyrnos* 1833, probably 'hill in hillocky area' with *gurnos* (cf. Gurnos). The second is *Bryntrotgam isaf* 1813, *Bryn-troedgam* 1833, *Bryn-troed-y-garn* 1877 (*isaf*); a former neighbouring fm. is recorded as *Bryntrotgam uchaf* 1813, *Bryn-troedgam-uchaf* 1833, *Bryntroed-y-garn-uchaf* 1877 (*uchaf*). One of these is *y Bryn Troidgam* 1633. Both pns. appear to contain *troed* 'foot' and *cam*[2] 'bent, crooked' with ref. to the shape of the hill. Later forms show the influence of *carn*, *(y) garn*, 'the cairn'.

Bryn[4]   SN 921056
Rhondda Cynon Taf (Rhigos, Ystradyfodwg)
'hill': *bryn*
Bryn 1841, 1877
A hill on the south side of Rhigos, also recalled in the road Heol y Bryn, 'the hill road' (*heol, y*).

Brynafel   SS 553906
Swansea (Ilston)
?'apple-tree hill': *bryn,* ?*afall*
Brinavell 1583, *Brinaval, Brynavell* 1697, *Brinavel* 1764, *Bryn-avel* 1832, *Bryn-afal* 1878
The second el. is very uncertain and *afall* is offered on the assumption that E-speakers have substituted –l for W –ll [ł] and that forms with –*avell* represent a recorded W dialect variation *afell*[1] of *afall*. It is also possible that –*avel(l)* represents the pers.n. found in Llangatwg Feibion Afel, Monmouthshire (PNGwent 129-30) though this is very uncommon. Late forms with -*afal* suggest association with *afal* nm. 'an apple', plausibly alluding to its shape. An identical pn. at St Fagans is recorded as *Tyr Bryn Avell* 1664 and *Bryn Avell* 1670.

Brynaman-isaf   SN 707133
Neath Port Talbot (Llan-giwg)
Lower Bryn-amman 1898, *Brynaman Isaf* 1901
'lower Brynaman': pn. Brynaman, *isaf*
Brynaman (SN 713143), Carmarthenshire, 'hill near (r.) Aman': *bryn*, rn. *Aman*, is taken from a fm. (*Bryn-amman* 1831) near the bridge over the r. Aman (SN 713138) for which cf. Aberaman The village was earlier known as Y Gwter-fawr recorded as *Guter vawr* 1805, (hillside) *Gwtter-fawr* 1831, *Gutter Vawr* 1862, *y Gwterfawr* 1872, *Brynaman, neu'r Gwtter Fawr* 1874, meaning 'the great gutter': *y*, *cwter, mawr*. Brynaman-isaf began as a scattered settlement associated with coal-workings across the valley from Brynaman. Y Gwter-fawr was apparently dropped in favour of Brynaman in 1864 when the Swansea Vale Railway Station was built (CAS VI, 83-4; HBryn 10, 37).

Brynawel   ST 200912
Caerphilly (Mynyddislwyn Monmouthshire)
Bryn-awel 1922
'breezy hill': *bryn, awel*
Apparently a modern n. since it is not on OS maps before 1922. The settlement was partly prompted by the opening of the nearby Nine Mile Point Colliery 1902-5 and lies below Craig y Trwyn (*craig* 'rock, cliff'). The hill was evidently known as Y Trwyn, 'the nose' (*y, trwyn*) used to describe its shape; the 'top of the nose' is Pen y Trwyn (ST 195917) (*pen*[1]).

Brynbryddan   SS 776925
Neath Port Talbot (Michaelston-super-Avon)
'hill near (?r.) Bryddan': *bryn*, ?rn. *Bryddan Brynbruthan* 1759, *Brynbruthin* 1813, *Brynbryddain* 1830, *Bryn Bryddan Cottages* 1917, *Brynbryddan* 1940
The second el. is uncertain, possibly *brydd* adj. and nm., 'weak, feeble' and dim. suffix –*an* referring to the small stream in Cwm Bychan (*cwm*).

The cottages appear to have displaced a small fm. recorded as simply *Bryn* in 1841 and 1901, located on a hill on the west side of Cwmafan.

Bryncae see **Bryn-y-cae**

Bryncethin   SS 913844
Bridgend (St Brides Minor)
'dark hill': ***bryn***, ***cethin***
Bryn Kethyn 1631, *Brynn Kythin* 1680, *Brin Cethin* 1714, *Bryncethin Issa* 1717, *Bryncethin Isha* 1727, *Bryn Cethin Ucha* 1845
The pn. contrasts with Bryn-coch (q.v.), less than half-a-mile away. Three refs. apply to farms distinguished as 'lower' (*isaf*) and 'upper' (*uchaf*). Only Bryncethin-uchaf survives. The hill is a small rise immediately north of the village which developed from the late 19th cent near brickworks and small collieries.

Bryn-coch[1]   SS 743997
Neath Port Talbot (Cadoxton-juxta-Neath)
'red hill': ***bryn***, ***coch***
Brincoch 1729, *Bryncoch*, *Felinbryncoch*, *Pontbryncoch* 1813, *Bryn-coch* 1832
From a fm. (SS 740007) perhaps notable for its autumn colours or the colour of its soil or rock. Located downstream of Fforest-gôch 'red forest' (***fforest***). The village developed along the Neath road in the mid 19th cent near an old iron furnace, Wernfraith Colliery and Dyffryn Main Colliery.

Bryn-coch[2]   SS 911838
Bridgend (St Brides Minor)
Bryn-coch 1750, *Bryncoch* 1813, *Brincoch* 1845
As Bryn-coch[1]. Located below Bryncethin (q.v.).

Bryndulais see **Seven Sisters**

Bryngolau   ST 001881
Rhondda Cynon Taf (Llantrisant)
'bright hill': ***bryn***, ***golau***
Bryn Golau 1965
Describing light-coloured soil or a hill which was open and clear of vegetation. The n. of a housing estate possibly taken from a private ho. recorded in 1917. Development began between the World Wars and expanded after 1945, on a hill west of Tonyrefail. The hill is also recalled in a nearby estate Ty'n-y-bryn deriving its n. from a ho. *Ty yn y bryn* 1841, *Ty'n-y-bryn* 1884, 'smallholding at the hill' (***tyn***, ***y***, ***bryn***).

Bryn-gwyn   ST 149862
Caerphilly (Eglwysilan)
'white *or* fair hill': ***bryn***, ***gwyn***
Bryngwyn 1939
Probably a ref. to pale limestone outcrops; note Nant-y-calch (ST 160152) recorded as *Nant Calch* 1833, 'the limestone stream': ***nant***, ***y***, ***calch*** nm. 'lime, chalk'. An adjoining stream recorded as *Nant Ddu* 1875-81 takes its n. from a 'black *or* dark hill', ***bryn***, ***du***. The n. referred in 1939 to a single road but was applied during the 1960s to nearby housing development.

Brynheulog   SS 853946
Bridgend (Llangynwyd)
'sunny hill': ***bryn***, ***heulog***[1]
Brynheulog 1962
Apparently a new n. for a housing estate developed in the late 1940s on southward-facing slopes above Caerau. This is also the n. of a street (SS 900848) in Brynmenyn.

Brynhill   Great Brynhill ST 110704
Vale of Glamorgan (Merthyr Dyfan)
?'burnt hill': ME ***brende***, *brente*, E ***hill***
Le Bridehill 1566, *Brind Hill* late 16th cent, *Brine Hill* early 17th cent, *Brinhill Farme* 1674, *Brynhill* 1720
Influenced at an early date by ***bryn*** 'hill'. The n. refers to the area next to Great Brynhill (ST 110704) and Little Brynhill (ST 116700) recorded as *Little Brinhill* 1786, *Great Brinhill* 1844, *Brynhill fawr*, *Brynhill fach* 1811 (***mawr***, ***bach***[1]). See PNDPH 137.

Brynhyfryd[1]   SS 892800
Bridgend (Newcastle)
'pleasant hill': ***bryn***, ***hyfryd***
Brynhyfryd 1965
A new n. adopted for a housing estate on hill-slopes developed after World War II; cf. Brynhyfryd[2, 3].

Brynhyfryd²   SS 739951
Neath Port Talbot (Briton Ferry)
'pleasant hill': *bryn, hyfryd*
Cf. Mount Pleasant. A housing estate developed mainly during the 1930s on a hill above Briton Ferry north of *Brynhyfryd Road* 1921.

Brynhyfryd³   SS 655956
Swansea (St John's)
'pleasant hill': *bryn, hyfryd*
Brynhyfryd 1868, (ho.) *Bryn-hyfryd* 1879
As Brynhyfryd¹,²; cf. Mount Pleasant less than two miles away and Pleasant Row. An area of housing around Llangyfelach Road named from the ho. The n. is recalled in Brynhyfryd (formerly John) Street. Brynhyfryd has displaced *Eaton Town* recorded in 1868-1913 which was the area between Sydney Street and Penfilia Road, a n. surviving in Eaton Road. The n. may commemorate Henry Knight Eaton (1820-83), a timber merchant at Pontlase in 1854 and 1861, who took holy orders in 1865.

Brynmenyn   SS 902847
Bridgend (St Brides Minor)
'butter hill': *bryn, ymenyn* variant *menyn*
Bryn (..) Menyn 1541, *bryn y menyn* 1630, *Bryn y menyn* 1767, *Bryn menyn* 1813, *Brynmenyn* 1833
Probably in the sense of 'hill bearing rich land (capable of producing butter)' perhaps with the elliptical sense of 'fertile, fruitful place'; cf. Brynymenyn (Llantwit Fardre) recorded as *Brynner menin* c.1700 and *Bryn y Menin* 1729 and Buttrills (Merthyr Dyfan) recorded as *The Buttrill* 1601, *The Butter Hills* 1777, *Butterhills* 1784, *Buttrells* 1858 'butter hills' (OE *butere*). There is a Butterhill, at St Ishmaels, Pembrokeshire (PNPemb 634).

Brynmill   SS 635923
Swansea (St John's)
'mill near the hill': *bryn*, E *mill*
(2 corn mills) *Brynmelles* 1400, (water-mill) *Brynmyll'* 1433, *Bryn mill* 1641, (3 mills) *the Brynn mills* 1650, *Brin Mill* 1786, *Bryn Mills* 1803, *Bryn Mill* 1813
Three mills were recorded here in 1650 but later sources mention only *the Lower Brinmill* 1745 (SS 634920. Near Mumbles Road) and *Upper Brinmill* 1749 (SS 633925. Near Park Place). The third mill may be the former Green Mill (Gower 47: 67-73; 50: 22). The main stream which powered the mills is *Bryn-mill water or Dauid's ditch* 1651 identified in a survey 1764 with that which rises near the Cocket (SS 617941) flowing southwards through Sketty to the sea (SS 635918). Brynmill has been also been identified with *Breymiskeyl* 1256 and *Brynnemiskil* 1319 but these clearly refer to lands later recorded as *Bryn y Miskill* 1669, *Brynmiskill* 1764, and *Bryn Miskin* 1799. This was probably near Pant-gwyn (SS 623927) which is further west in Sketty, possibly at or near a former ho. Bryn (SS 622923) near Bryn-newydd, both lying close to a small stream flowing from Carn-glas southwards over Sketty Green to Mumbles Road. This n. appears to mean 'hill of the mussels' with ME *muskil* or more likely its W loan-word *misgl* npl. (*mishgil* in local dialect) a word not recorded in literary sources until the 17th cent. The pn. may refer to natural deposits of shells in local rocks rather than edible molluscs.

Brynna   SS 986832
Rhondda Cynon Taf (Llanharan/Peterston-super-montem)
'hills': *bryn* pl. *bryniau*, dialect *brynna*
(common) *Brynau Gwynon* 1813, *Brynau-gwynon* 1833, *Brynna Coal & Steel Co. Limited, Brynna Colliery* 1875, *Brynna Gwynion* 1906, *Brynna* 1908
The full n. meaning 'white *or* fair hills', with *gwyn* pl. *gwynion*, variant *gwynon*, referred originally to an open area of rough pasture west of Brynna village. The n. has been revived for the modern development Brynnau Gwynion (SS 978825). The village itself developed from c.1884 around the Eagle Inn (SS 986832) and St Peter's ch. after the opening of Brynau-gwynion Colliery.

Brynsadler   ST 029807
Rhondda Cynon Taf (Llantrisant)
'saddler's *or* Sadler's hill': *bryn*, E *saddler* or surname *Sadler*

Brynsadler 1863, *Bryn Sadler* 1868, *Bryn Saddler* 1874

Brynsadler is alleged to have been named from a John Sadler, alderman of London, who is reputed to have obtained a sub-lease of land here in the reign of Henry VIII, later acquiring a wrought-iron works (PNIG 34). A John Sadler, draper, was certainly an alderman for Farringdon Within ward, London, 1542-6 but there seems to be no way of connecting him with Brynsadler. The surname Sadler occurs in Llantrisant in 1717 and 1778.

Bryn-teg ST 060841
Rhondda Cynon Taf (Llantrisant)
'fair hill': **bryn**, **teg**
Brynteg 1895, 1964
A housing estate developed from the 1960s named from Bryn-teg House (ST 054839). The *Brynteg Arms* is recorded in 1875. A nearby ho. on Brynteg Lane is *Mount Pleasant* 1900.

Bryntirion[1] SS 886802
Bridgend (Newcastle)
'gentle hill': **bryn**, **tirion**[1]
Bryntirion 1875, *Bryn-tirion* 1885
Mainly post World War II housing named from a ho. (SS 885799) on the road to Laleston.

Bryntirion[2] ST 066966
Rhondda Cynon Taf (Llanwynno)
'gentle hill': **bryn**, **tirion**[1]
Bryntirion 1962
Apparently named from a ho. on Main Road. A housing estate developed from the 1950s on hill-slopes around the site of Pentwyn Colliery.

Bryn-y-cae (Bryncae) SS 993825
Rhondda Cynon Taf (Llanharan)
'hill with an enclosure': **bryn**, **y**, **cae**
Tye bryn y kae 1670, *Brin y Ca* 1783, *Brynycae fach, Brynycae fawr* 1813, *Bryn-y-cae* 1841
The n. of post World War II housing taken from a former fm. Bryn-y-cae (SS 998825) earlier known as Bryn-y-cae-fawr (**mawr** 'great') in contrast to Bryn-y-cae-fach recorded as *Ty hyw* (sic) 1841, *Ty-hunt* 1884, 'far house' (**tŷ**, **hwnt**) now largely occupied by housing known as Dolau (q.v.). The def.art. **y** was dropped on OS maps c.1970, presumably reflecting local usage.

Brysgedwyn see **Prysgedwyn**

Burry, Byrri SS 455901
Swansea (Llangennith)
rn. *Byrri*
(r.) *Borry* 1318, (fulling mill of) *Burry* 1323, (r.) *Byrri Auon* early 14th cent, *Byrry* 1641, *Borre, Burie* early 16th cent, *Bury alias Stenbrige* 16th cent, *Burrey* 1562, *Burries* ~ , *Burrys Head* 1583, *Burrey water* c.1670, *Burry Barr* [in sea], *Burrieshed* 1399

Burry and Burry Green (q.v.) lie close to a stream Burry, now called Burry Pill on OS maps, but the pill (OE **pyll**) is properly that part of the stream where it crosses marshes and sands to join the r. Loughor/Llwchwr. The rn. could contain **bwr** adj. 'fat, strong, big' with a suffix –**i** but it is a little difficult applying that sense to this rn. A similar rn. probably survives in Cwmburry (SN 379126) recorded as *Cwmbwrry* 1696 and *Cwmburry* 1766 at Llandyfaelog, Carmarthenshire (**cwm**). Charles suggested OE **byrig** dat. of **burh** 'fortified place, fort', and there is indeed a prehistoric fort (and chp.) on the small rocky island Burry Holms (SS 400925) at the end of the Gower peninsula but this is more than two miles from the r. Burry; any fort is more likely to be that on North Hill Tor (SS 45309381). Burry Holms itself has been identified with an island *Boring Holmi* recorded in the 9th cent saga of Ragnar Lodbrok, a semi-fictional Danish warrior, but this must be discarded because early sources refer to Burry Holms as simply *(the) Holm(e)s*. The chp. is *St. Kenyth atte Holmes* 1398, and the island is *Le Holm in Gowerland*, *Insula Holmys* 1478, *the Holmes* 1583, with ON **holmr** 'island'. Sps. lend little support to the alternative suggestion by the scholar Phillimore that it has ON berg, i.e. OE **beorg** 'hill, tumulus' applied to the sand-dunes or 'burrows' at the *r.* mouth. This is certainly an appropriate n. for the area stretching from Broughton Burrows (SS 4192) to Whiteford Point (SS 4496) but not to the area where Burry Pill reaches tidal water. About two miles north of this point, the pill forms a deep, broad channel extending towards the Carmarthenshire shore, suitable for shipping, and notable enough to have displaced Loughor/Llwchwr as the n. of the estuary for many years. This is specifically *Burrey a creeke* (for Llanelli) 1566, *Burra flu:* 1578, *arme of the sea called Burrye* 1609; that part serving the port of Llanelli is also described as *creek of North Burry* 1636. The n. for the estuary Burry Inlet has been dropped on recent OS maps but is retained in the pn. Burry Port, Carmarthenshire, recorded as *Berry Port* 1833, *Burry Port* 1841, which developed near docks constructed in the early 19th cent.

Burry Green SS 461914
Swansea (Llangennith)
'open land near (r.) Burry': rn. **Burry/Byrri**, E *green*
Buries greene 1650, *Burygreen* 1720, *Burry's Green* 1730, *Burry Green* 1872
Referring to a triangular area of land on the south side of the Llangennith-Swansea road.

Burton, **Britwn** ST 034676
Vale of Glamorgan (Penmark)
'bridge settlement': OE **brycg**, **tūn**
Bretton 1575, *Burton* 1578-81, *Britton* 1601, *Berton, -town* c.1670, *a'r Britwn* 19th cent, *Ponte Britoun* c.1538, *Burton Bridge* 1602
The cymricised form has the def.art. *y* now generally dropped and has substituted *–twn* for *tūn*; cf. Cortwn for Corntown (q.v.). Located next to Kenson River. This may also be *le Britton* 1503. B.G. Charles (NCPN 156) mislocated *Britton'* c.1348 and *Britton super Elly* 1535 here (see Drope). The sp. for c.1538 has **pont** 'bridge'.

Butetown ST 189748
Cardiff (St John and St Mary's)
'settlement named from (Marquess of) Bute': personal title *Bute*, E *town*
Bute Town 1853, *Butetown* 1855, *Bute Street, Bute crescent, Bute docks* 1875, *Tref Bute* 1867
From the second Marquess of Bute; a n. given to the commercial area which developed on his land here after the opening of the Bute West Dock 1839. Earlier sources simply call it the *Docks* and *y Docks* 1855 (**y**). The form *Tref Bute* does not seem to have become established and Tre-biwt (EnWales 118) has no historical basis. See also Cardiff Bay.

Bute Town SO 104091
Caerphilly (Gelligaer)
'settlement near Bute Iron Works': personal title *Bute*, E **town**
Bute Town 1832, 1884, *New Town* 1841, *Newtown* 1875, *Drenewydd* 1878
From the Bute Iron Works established in 1825, united in 1837 with the nearby, older Union Iron Works (established in 1800-2) to form the Rhymney Iron Company (EHOSW 121; MMF 63-4). The settlement was initially called New Town (MethC 20) and Y Drenewydd, 'the new town' (**y**, **tref**, **newydd**) (MCPP 20). Cf. Newtown (Ebbw Vale) recorded as *y Drenewydd* 1895.

Bwlch-y-cwm ST 144837
Cardiff (Eglwysilan)
'pass of the valley': **bwlch**, **y**, **cwm**
Pwlch y Cwm 1790, *Bwlch-y-cwm* 1833, *Bwlch y Cwm* 1841
The valley Cwm Nofydd is recorded as *Cumnovyth* 1541, *Cwm Novith* 1718, *Cwm Novidd* 1783, 'valley of (stream) Nofydd' (shown as Nant Cwmnofydd on OS maps) with a ho. *Blaenofydd* 1841, *Blaen-Nofydd* 1885 (**blaen**). The pass refers to the area where the road Rhiwbina Hill forks to lead on to Waunwaelod Way and Heol Pen-bryn which link Cardiff, Caerphilly, Cwm and Cwm Nant y Fforest. Nofydd is recorded as *arannouid* c.1145 but other forms are rare before the 19th cent and the meaning is uncertain. It is just possible that it has been associated with the rare nm. *nofydd* 'swimmer'.

Bwlwarcau, Y SS 831862
Bridgend (Llangynwyd)
'bulwarks': **y**, **bwlwarc** pl. **bwlwarcau**
(entrenchment) *Bwlwarka* c.1700, *Foelwarcau* 1833, *Bwlwarcau* 1876

The n. applies to a prehistoric enclosure. ***bwlwarc*** occurs also in Y Bwlwarc (SS 520982) and Bwlwarc y Gwair, at Llanelli, Carmarthenshire, and derives from E *bulwark* found, for example, in The Bulwark (SS 443929) at Llanmadog described as *the old fort upon Lanmadock Downe* 1615 and *The Bulwark* 1830, and The Bulwarks (ST 082664) at Porthkerry. Isaac Hamon (of Bishopston) in 1697 refers to the *old large forte or bulwarke* on Cilifor Top (SS 503922) in Llanrhidian.

Byeastwood SS 929817
Bridgend (Coety)
?'wood to the east (of Coety)': E prep. ***by***, ***east***, ***wood*** *y Biestwood* 1661, *Bestwood* c.1700, 1739, *Byestwood* 1746, *Bestwood Village* 1841, *Byeastwood* 1845, *Beast Wood, By-East-Wood* 1871

Pns. of this nature are not uncommon and the usual sense is that of proximity to a specific place such as the unlocated land called *Byssowthlake* 1541 (in Wenvoe) meaning 'by the south stream' (ME ***lake***), Bysouth (Penrice), Bythorn (Huntingdonshire) '(place) by the thorn-bush', and Bygrave (Hertfordshire) '(place) by the ditch' (see DEPN). There are some doubts with this explanation here since there is no identifiable 'east wood' but it is supported by the occurrence of an adjoining Byeaston (SS 928817) – no longer found on OS maps. This is *Byeaston* 1757, *Beeston* 1813, *Byaston* 1799 and *Byeston* 1833 meaning 'settlement to the east (of Coety)' with ME ***-ton*** (OE ***tūn***).

Byrri see **Burry**

Cadle to Cyntwell

Cardiff in 1841, looking south from the castle, from an engraving by J.H. Lekeux.

Cadle SS 624970
Swansea (Llangyfelach)
?'place of battle, battle-site': *cadle*
Cadele 1319, *Gaddele* 1322, *Caddley* 1549, *Cadley* 1563, *le Cadle* 1604, *Dyffrin Cadle* 1725, *Mynydd Cadley* 1754, *Cadle Vawr*, ~ *Ycha*, ~ *Vach*, ~ *Yssha*, *Cevin Cadley* 1811
The precise sense is uncertain. It could arguably be an area where soldiers gathered or simply an area that was in dispute. Identified by Thomas Morgan (OPN 129) and others with a battle in 1136 in which Hywel ap Maredudd, a lord of Brycheiniog, fought against local English settlers. Gerald of Wales (in 1188), however, simply located this battle near Loughor. Some sps. seem to have been associated with E pns. containing -*ley* (*lēah*). Other cited forms have *cefn*, *dyffryn*, *melin* and *mynydd*.

Cadoxton, Tregatwg ST 128691
Vale of Glamorgan
'Cadog's settlement': pers.n. *Cadog* variant *Catwg*, OE *tūn*, *tref*
Caddokeston 1254, *Kadogestona*, *Caddokestona* 1263, *Caddockeston* c.1291, *Cadoxston* 1535, *Cadokkystowne* 1541, *Cadoxton* 1578, *Cadoxton east Barry* 1662, *Tregattwg* c.1795, *Tregatwg* 1892

Catwg is the usual form in south-east Wales for Cadog. Tregatwg appears to be a late translation of the E n. and there are doubts on the authenticity of the form for c.1795 taken from the work of Iolo Morganwg, well-known for his ability to invent and embroider pns. Iolo also seems to be the source of a spurious form *Llangattwg wrth Farri* 'church of Catwg near Barry' c.1800 (*llan*).

Cadoxton-juxta-Neath, Llangatwg
SS 755985
Neath Port Talbot
'Cadog's settlement near Neath': pers.n. *Cadog* variant *Catwg*, ME *-ton*, Lat *juxta*, pn. **Neath**; 'church dedicated to Cadog', *llan*, pers. n.
(chp. *de*) *Sancto Caddoco* c.1205, (vicarage of) *Sancti Caddoci* 1254, *Caddokston* 13th cent, *Catoukston* 1433, *St. Cadock next Neath* 1559, *Cadoxtone by Nethe* 1561, *Langatock* 1543, *Langattoge juxta Nethe* 1556, *ll. gattwc glyneð* c.1566, *Llangattwg* 1578
Cf. Cadoxton. The W n. is now generally plain Llangatwg, occasionally qualified by Glyn-nedd (see Glyn-neath) and Nedd. The late appearance of –juxta-Neath suggests that the E n. was qualified by the town of Neath rather than the r. According to his reputed Life c.1200, Cadog was son of Gwynllyw, a prince of Gwent, and Gwladys daughter of Brychan Brycheiniog. The p. possessed a spring *Pistỳl Catuc* c.1200 (*pistyll*). Cadog is also recalled in Ffynnon Gatwg recorded as *Fynon Gattuke* 1518, *ffynon Gattug* 1595, 'well dedicated to Catwg' (*ffynnon*), near Bridgend.

Cae-draw
SO 049059
Merthyr Tudful
'far enclosure': *cae*, *draw*
Cae draw 1763, *Cae Draw* 1826, *Caedraw* 1852
A very common fn. An industrial settlement developed in the 1830s.

Caegarw
SO 047995
Rhondda Cynon Taf (Aberdare)
'rough enclosure': *cae*, *garw*
Caegarw Cottage 1871, *Caegarw* 1881

An area of housing partly on the former Dyffryn estate extending down slopes from Mountain Ash cemetery to the r. Cynon, developed in the late 19th cent. Called *Allen's Town* in 1851 and *Allenstown* 1874 after a landowner I.H. Allen. The n. was dropped c.1874 but is recalled in Allen Street in the village (CVPN 38).

Cae-mawr
SS 661979
Swansea
'large enclosure': *cae*, *mawr*
Caemawr fields 1891, *Cae-mawr* 1899
The n. probably once referred to a field abutting on Cae-mawr Road on the south where the first hos. appeared c.1870. Much of the northern part of the field is now part of Morriston Park.

Caenewydd
SN 708120
Neath Port Talbot (Llan-giwg)
'new enclosure': *cae*, *newydd*
Cae-newydd 1877
Possibly *y Kae Newydd* 1624 but the fn. is very common. On late 19th cent maps the n. applies to an oval area of pasture north of the Great Western Railway (Gwauncaegurwen Branch) which suggests that it was a relatively recent enclosure out of the moorland Gwaun Caegurwen.

Cae-pant-tywyll
SO 046066
Merthyr Tudful
'enclosure at the dark hollow' : *cae*, *pant*, *tywyll*
Caepantywyll 1852, *Cae-pant-tywyll* 1875
The n. referred in 1875 to the area next to Tydfil's Well but has shifted a little to the east. Local pron. is roughly ['kɑː pant 'tiuːil]

Cae Pantydugoed
SN 696014
Swansea (Llangyfelach)
'enclosure at Pantydugoed': *cae*, pn. *Pantydugoed* (wooded area) *Cae Pant-y-dugoed* 1879
Pantydugoed is 'hollow at the black wood' (*pant*, *y*, *du* qualifying *coed*, *goed*). Housing appeared on Pontardawe Road in the 1890s near Ynyspenllwch Graigola Colliery, gradually extending with the development of colliery works. Very little of the woodland survives.

Caeraca (Caeracca) SO 068090
Merthyr Tudful
'the rake enclosure': *cae*, *rhaca*
terre kaye racka 1449, *kay racka* 1561, *Kae Racca* 1757, *Cae Raca* 1864, (fm.) *Cae'r-acca* 1876, *Cae Racca* 1901
Perhaps an enclosure which needed to be raked regularly to remove stones and weeds. The n. might also describe an enclosure marked by rocks with the appearance of having been made by a rake or rocky outcrops bearing a resemblance to a rake. The n. applied to a ho. (SO 069089) and housing development took place here shortly before 1919. *Caeraca* had been applied to the area around Edward Street before 1908. The second el. also seems to be found in Graig-y-rhaca (ST 1989), Monmouthshire, recorded as *Creyge Rackawn* 1570, *Craig y raccha* 1630, *Graig yr Racka* 1841 and *Craig-rhaca* 1885 (*craig*, *y*).

Caerau[1] ST 134753
Cardiff
'(the) forts': *caer* pl. *caerau*
la Kayre 13th cent, *Kair* c.1291, *Kayr cum capella* c.1348, *Kayre* 1386, *Caire paroche* c.1538, *Kaere* c.1566, *Kayrey* 1578, *Cayra* 1720, *Caerau* 1833
Named from a prehistoric multivallate hill-fort and castle ring around the ch. Pronounced roughly 'Caira' ['kairə, 'kaira]. The pn. attracted the attention of antiquarians such as Iolo Morganwg who gives it the unsubstantiated alternative n. *Llanweirydd*. Dafydd Morganwg (HMorg 229) adds that it refers to a Roman fortress but there is no evidence for this. Some sources show that a def.art. has been lost, a supposition borne out by a local 19th cent triban (Trib 43).

Caerau[2] SS 854942
Bridgend (Llangynwyd)
'(the) forts': *caer* pl. *caerau*
Kaire c.1700, *Caerau* 1899
As Caerau[1] but there do not appear to be any forts here unless it is a fanciful description for the cairns on Mynydd y Caerau (SS 8794, 8894). This is *Mynydd y Cayra* c.1700, *Mynydd Caerau* 1832. The village developed from c.1893 below Caerau Colliery in the area known as Blaencaerau, 'uplands at Caerau'. Blaencaerau (q.v.) now refers specifically to a housing estate.

Caerdydd see **Cardiff**

Cae'r-eithin (Caer-eithin) SS 636962
Swansea (Llangyfelach)
'the gorse enclosure': *cae*, *yr*, *eithin*
Kaer ythin 1625, *Caeyrithin* 1813, *Cae-yr-eithin* 1830, *Cae'r-eithin* 1879
Named from a former fm. developed for housing from the 1930s. *eithin* may perhaps be a re-interpretation of a pers.n. *Aeddan* found in Penllwynaeddan which was the n. of two hos. in the 19th cent west of Carmarthen Road in the area of Fforest-fach (Pierce in Abertawe 94-95), meaning 'hill at Llwynaeddan', *pen*[1]. Llwynaeddan or 'Aeddan's grove' (*llwyn*) probably once extended eastwards to include Cae'r-eithin.

Caerffili see **Caerphilly**

Cae'r-hendy SS 776912
Neath Port Talbot (Margam)
'enclosure near the old house': *cae*, *yr*, *hen*, *tŷ*
Cae'r-hendy 1877-8, *Caerhendy* 1884
The 'old house' is apparently unidentified.

Caerphilly, **Caerffili** ST 156868
Caerphilly (Eglwysilan)
'Ffili's fort': *caer*, pers.n. *Ffili*
(castle) *Kaerfili* 1271, *caer fili* c.1275, *Kaerfilli* 1296, *Kayrfilli alias Kairfily* 1307, *Kaerphilli*, --*y* 1349, (*castell*) *Caerfili* c.1400, *Caerffyllye* 1541, *Carphilly* 1670, *Caerphilly* 1729, *Caerphili* 1778
The modern form Caerphilly is irregular but is now the established E n. of the town and local authority. The actual fort may be the Roman auxiliary fort in a corner of the grounds of the medieval castle begun by Gilbert de Clare, lord of Glamorgan, in 1268. Attempts have been made to identify Ffili here as a saint (cf. the ch. dedication to Fili at Philleigh, Cornwall) but the evidence is very flimsy. The antiquarian nonsense associated with this pn. is gathered together by Dafydd Morganwg (HMorg 248). According to this,

Caerphilly was variously said to contain the n. of a Roman military officer, to have been named from Julius Agricola who reputedly built the castle in the time of the emperor Domitian, and to refer to a Roman lady Philis who established the castle of 'Caer Philis'. Caerphilly lay in the old p. of Eglwysilan but possessed its own chp. dedicated to Martin/Marthin, recorded as *chappell Martin* 1586 and *St. Martins in Eglwysilan* 1712. Caerphilly Mountain / Mynydd Caerffili is *Monydd Carphilly* 1773 (**mynydd**).

Caerwigau ST 060758
Vale of Glamorgan (Pendeulwyn)
'fort near ?woods': *caer*, ?*gwig¹* pl. *gwigau* len. *wigau*, or pers.n. *Gwigau
Kaerwigau late 12th cent, (vill, ch. of) *Carwigan* c.1205, *Karewygeu* 1376, *Karwigen* 1567, *Carwigen* 1607, *Kaerwyge* c.1670, *Cae Wigga ucha* 1684, *Caerwiga Ycha*, ~ *Genol* 1795, *Cae'r-wigau-ganol*, ~ *-isaf* 1833
A few late sources associate **caer** with *Cae'r* (*cae, y, yr* affixed as `r). The second el. is less certain and *gwigau* is seemingly at odds with historic forms possessing terminal *–en* and *-an*. These would have to explained as scribal slips for *–eu, -au*. Whatever the case, it does not rule out some other el. such as a pers.n. and it is worth drawing comparison with Llandough² (q.v.) containing a pers.n. *Dochan* (with loss of *–n*) and Llandough¹ (q.v.) probably containing *Dochou*, later *Dochau, -a, -e*. In this context, it is also significant that there is mention in the Life of St Cadog c.1100 of *Atrium Cair guicou, cum uilla Ecclus Silid* (VSB 120), 'hall of *Cair guicou* with the homestead of *Ecclus Silid*'. The latter has been identified with Llanilid (q.v.) on the assumption that this stands for ModW *Eglwys Ilid* (**eglwys**, pers.n. Ilid). Llanilid later came into the possession of St Cadog's ch. at Llancarfan. This then became the basis for identifying *Cair guicou* with a location (SN 989813) in Llanilid named as *Blakeberege* and *Blakeburhe* in two 13th cent charters (Morgannwg 50: 45, 56). It is significant, however, that Caerwigau lies in the p. of Pendeulwyn whose ch. is also dedicated to Cadog. Both *gwigau* and a postulated pers.n. *Gwigau* would be regular developments from an earlier *guicou, Guicou*; cf. the common pl. terminal *–au* < MW *-eu*, < OW *–ou* (GPC *-(i)au*). Conclusive evidence for the specific location of *Ecclus Silid* is clearly lacking but the ref. to a priest of *Kaerwigan* c.1190 and a ch. in c.1205 indicates that Caerwigau once possessed its own ch., plausibly dedicated to a St Silid. No ch. has been located but T.J. Hopkins (VGS 1: 84, 85) notes a field *Ddwar capel* in the p. tithe apportionment c.1840, possibly representing *Y Ddwyar Capel*, 'the two acres at the chapel' (*y, dwy, erw*); he also records the discovery of a cross here c.1850. A moated enclosure (ST 05677546) and deserted settlement (ST 060755) have been found here.

Candleston, Tregantllo SS 871772
Bridgend (Merthyr Mawr)
'settlement belonging to Cantelo(w)': surname *Cantelo(w)*, ME *–ton* (OE **tūn**), **tref**
Cantlowstoune 1545, *Tre gawntyilo* c.1550, *Tregantelow* 1559, *Candleston* 1611, *Cantloston otherwise Tregantlow* c.1635, *Tregantelo* c.1659, *Cantlestone otherwise Treganthloe* 1753, *Tregawntlo, Tregawnllo* c.1800, *Treganllo* 1903
Early members included William de Cantalo 1128, Richard de Cantelou and his brother Elyas c. The castle here is late medieval (MSM 408). It is possible that the family is related to that of Cantelo or Cantilupe who held land at Calne, Wiltshire, and in Herefordshire. The origin of the surname is uncertain and it need not be related to the Fr surname Chanteloup or Canteloup (PNGlam 197-8). Tregantllo has reversal of qualifier and generic to follow W practice, and is both the official and current local W form. The suggestion (SLBM 164) that the pn. means 'meadow land along the Cant' with ON *ló*, 'low-lying meadow along a stream or water-course' as in Oslo (Norway) coupled with a reputed lost n. of Candleston Brook, is very doubtful.

Canton, Treganna ST 166765
Cardiff (Llandaf)
'settlement of ?(man called) Canna *or* Cana': ?*Canna* or OE *Cana*, ME *–ton* (OE **tūn**), **tref**
(mill of) *cānet'* (= *Canneton*?) late 12th cent, *Canetune* c.1230, *Kanetone* 13th cent, *Canton*

1535, *Cauntowne* 1640, *Caunton Hamlett* 1670, *Cantwn* 1874, *Treganna* 1900
For *Canna* see **Llan-gan**. *Cana* is found in Great Canfield, Essex. The main objection to the suggested meaning is the proximity of Pontcanna (q.v. for a fuller discussion). There seems to be no early historical evidence to corroborate Treganna, and both *Canton* and *Cantwn* appear in W literary sources. Iolo Morganwg seems to have invented the spurious form *Maes Milan* (IoloMor 22) c.1800.

Cap-coch　　　　　　　　　　SO 023000
'red hat': *cap*, *coch*
Capcoch 1861, *y Capcoch* 1872
Taken from a public ho. recorded as *Capcoch Inn* in 1865 variously said to be named from a publican who kept a tavern here c.1600 and wore a red cap when cockfighting took place (HMA 116) and from a prize fighter. The same n. appears to have applied to a former inn near New Bridge (SO 891784) over the r. Ogwr near Bridgend. This inn was a reputed haunt of a legendary criminal who wore a red liberty cap which he had brought over from revolutionary France (ASG 10-12). Such tales almost certainly draw on popular mythology An inn sign may well have borne an image of a man in a red cap – possibly a malevolent one – or that of a bird with a 'red hat' such as the redpoll. Cf. Cap-glas (SO 297188) meaning 'blue cap' (*glas*), at Llandeilo Bertholau, Monmouthshire. This may recall a former inn since there are several instances of 'Blue Cap' in England. Local residents petitioned the Postmaster-General and local authorities in 1905 to change the n. of the village from Cap-coch to Abercwmboi (q.v.), a n. already in occasional use. The n. continued to appear on OS maps for several years afterwards and as the n. of the school.

Capel Bach see **Blaen-gwrach**

Capel Baedan see **Baedan**

Capel Cwrtybetws see **Cwrtybetws**

Capel Cynydd see **Burry**

Capel Gwladus　　　　　　　　ST 125992
Caerphilly (Gelli-gaer)
'chapel dedicated to Gwladus': *capel*, pers.n. *Gwladus*
Egluswladus 1281, *Egloswladus* 1314, *Eglesowladus* 1401, *Eglosgwladys* 1541, *Capel glodus* 1578, (former chp., 'nowe used as a house') *cappel gwladis* 1584, *Ruins of Capel Gwladis* 1833
Earlier forms have *eglwys* 'church'. Gwladus was a reputed daughter of the legendary Brychan, traditional founder of Brycheiniog, and wife of the saint Gwynllyw, eponym of Gwynllŵg (the cantref extending along the eastern side of the r. Rhymni). She is also recalled in Fforest Gwladys (ST 126991) which was part of Gelli-gaer Common. The chp. ruins are mentioned by Dafydd Morganwg in 1874 (HMorg 297) and were rediscovered in 1906 when Gelligaer Urban District Council was surveying the area in order to establish a cemetery. They are now marked by a modern memorial.

Capel Ifan y Bedyddiwr　　　　ST 015885
Rhondda Cynon Taf (Llantrisant)
'chapel dedicated to John the Baptist': *capel*, pers.n. *Ifan*, *y*, *bedyddiwr*
(ruined chp.) *Cappel Ivan y Bedyddwr* c.1700, *St. Johns Chap* 1799, *St. Johns* 1833, *Capel, Capel-bâch* 1875
The n. was taken up by St John's Baptist ch. and survives in the street n. Capel Ifan.

Capel Llanilltern　　　　　　ST 095799
Cardiff (St Fagans)
'chapel called Llanilltern': *capel*, pn. *Llanilltern*
Laniltern 13th cent, *Lanultern* 1351, *llanellterne* c.1558, *Chappell Llanellturne* 1652, *Capel Llanilltyrne* 1664, (chp.) *Lanilterne* 1703, *Capel Llaniltern* 1833
Llanillteyrn, later Llanilltern, is 'church dedicated to (St) Illteyrn', *llan*, pers.n. *Illteyrn*. *capel* is prefixed in many sources from the mid 17th cent to indicate that it was a chapel-of-ease to St Fagans. Richards (ETG 187) says that it was previously Ellteyrn but no sps. have been found to prove this apart

from *St. Elldeyrn's Church* 1880 though there was certainly a variation *ill, ell* as in the pers.n. *Illtud, Elltud* in Llanelltud, Llanilltud, Merionethshire.

Capel Mair o Ben-y-graig see **Crug** (Margam)

Capel Tal-y-garn ST 026802
Rhondda Cynon Taf (Llantrisant)
'chapel at Tal-y-garn': *capel,* pn. *Tal-y-garn* (chp.) *Tallygaran* 1596, *Cappel Tallygarne* 1685, *Cappel Tal y Garn* 1695, *Taly garn Chapel* 1813, *St. Ann's Chapel (Capel Tal-y-garn)* 1899
An ancient, probably medieval, chp. located in the lp. of Tal-y-garn. The chp. stood in an enclosure within the fm. Crofft y Betws, 'croft of the prayer-house' (*crofft, y, betws¹*) and was granted by Sir Leoline Jenkins (1625-85) or his executors to Jesus College, Oxford. G.T. Clark (1809-98) – the architect, ironmaster and antiquarian – built a new ch. here dedicated to St Ann near Tal-y-garn House (ST 032800) when he bought the manor of Tal-y-garn in 1865. The manor is recorded as *Talgarn* 1429, *Tallegarn* 1536, *Talagarne Francklan* 1523, *Talygarne* 1580, (ho.) *Tal y Garn Vawr* 1799, meaning 'end of the cairn' (*capel, tâl², y, carn*) allegedly referring to an unlocated Carn Wen 'the white cairn' (*carn, gwen*) according to H.C. Jones (PNIG 37). *Francklan* seems to be otherwise unattested but appears to be a pers.n.

Capel Trisaint SS 842855
Neath Port Talbot (Margam)
'chapel dedicated to three saints': *capel, tri, sant* variant *saint*
(chp.) *Trisent* 1554, *Caple Tryssent* 1681, *Capple Trissent* 1713, *Capel Trisant* 1876
Cf. Llantrisant. The saints were probably Philip, James and Michael. James is confirmed by the existence of a well *Ffynnon Iago* 1876, 'James's well' (*ffynnon, Iago*) between the farms Ffynnon Iago-fawr (SS 848851) and Ffynnon Iago-fach (*mawr, bach¹*). There is some disagreement with regard to the location of the chp. The OS 1:2,500 map 1876 shows *Capel Trisant (Remains of)* at SS 84258550. Capel Trisaint may, however, be identical to the chp. and grange belonging to Margam abbey at or near the fm. Hafodheulog (SS 841846) recorded as *Havodhaloc* 12th cent, *Haudhaloc* c.1200, and *Hauothalok* 1261. The precise meaning of this n. is uncertain; the second el. may be *halog* adj. 'dirty, soiled' containing *hâl* 'dung' or an otherwise unrecorded **halog* containing *hâl³* nf. 'moor, moorland'. The last would favour 'summer-dwelling in moorland'. Very late forms of the pn. contain *heulog¹* 'sunny' which may be conscious re-interpretations with the intention of disassociating the n. from the disagreeable associations of *halog*. Capel Trisaint lay in the Middle Division of Trisaint in Margam p recorded as *Trissant Margam* 1547 and *Treesaint hamlet* 1670.

Capel y Brithdir see **Brithdir**

Capel y Creunant see **Creunant**

Cardiff, Caerdydd ST 181764
'fort by the (r.) Taf': *caer, Tyf* gen.sg. of **Taf**
Kard' c.1102, *Kairdi* c.1126, *Kaerdif* c.1135, *Kardif* 1148, *Kayrdif* 1156, *Caerdif* 1184, *Cardif' in Wallia* 1220, (o) *Gaer Dyf* c.1400, *Kaerdiff* 1421, *Cairdif, Cairtaphe* c.1538, *Cardythe* 1555, *Caerdidd* 1668, (p.ch. of) *Sancte Marie de Kardi* 1107 (1300), (chs. of) *Jeuan fedyðiwr, mair o gaer dyð* c.1566, *Taui urbis* early 12th cent, *aquam Thaph de Kaerdif castrum* c.1191
Tyf derives from Brit **Tam-i* by –i affection (PNGlam 125-7). In later sources Caerdyf is displaced by a colloquial pron. Caerdydd stressed on the second syllable in which dd [ð] substitutes for f [v]. The anglicised form Cardiff – widely pronounced ['kɛːrdɪf] – derives directly from Caerdyf. A number of antiquarians failed to recognise the development of the pn. and supposed that Caerdydd derived from *Caer Didi* containing the n. of a legendary giant (HMorg 230). The Roman fort at Cardiff has been identified with *Tamion* (variants *Tanisom, Taimon*) listed in the Ravenna Cosmography early 8cent between *Isca Augusta* (Caerleon on r. Usk) and *Aventio* (on the r. Ewenni) (PNRB 444-5).

Cardiff Bay, **Bae Caerdydd**   ST 193784
Cardiff
A modern n. for the area next to the former harbour around the Red Dragon Centre and National Assembly, partly displacing Butetown (q.v.) and the Docks (see Tiger Bay).

Cardiff West Moors   ST 180748
Cardiff (Llandaf)
'west moors near Cardiff': pn. **Cardiff**, E *west*, **moor** pl. *moors*
Westmor 1325, 1348, *Le Westmore* 1541, *the West Moore* 1672
'West' in contrast to East Moors (q.v.). The n. once applied to an area extending into Cardiff and Roath but is now applied to housing and a leisure and retail area on the west side of Cardiff Bay.

Carnetown, **Parcnewydd**   ST 078946
Rhondda Cynon Taf (Llanwynno)
'settlement named from Carne (family)': surname *Carne*, E *town*; 'new park', **parc**, **newydd**
Parc-newydd 1833, *Parc Newydd* 1842-50, *Carnstown* 1876, *Carnetown* 1893
Recalling the Carne family of Dimlands and St Donats. *Carnstown* is applied in 1876 and 1884 to a former row of hos. (ST 079937) near what is now a road Grovers Field between the main Taff Vale Railway and the former Llancaiach Branch Railway (constructed 1841). The modified sp. *Carnetown* was transferred to newer hos. built in the 1890s next to St Donat's ch. during the lifetime of J.D.V. Nicholl-Carne (1854-1905), owner of the Parcnewydd estate (MCPP 21-23). The original Carnstown is otherwise recorded as *Stormstown* in 1856 lying next to Stormstown (railway) Junction. Storm is presumably a surname but its significance here is uncertain. The park included the wooded slopes leading up to Pen-y-parc (ST 073935), 'top of the park' (**pen**, **y**, **parc**).

Carn-glas   SS 625935
Swansea
?'green hill shaped like a hoof': **carn**, **glas**
Karneglas 1319, *Carne Glase* 1594, (place) *y Carne glase*, (mess.) *Carne Glaes* 1669, *Carn Glase* 1764, *Garn-lâs* 1879
Taken from two former farms (SS 621935, 622932). **carn** generally means 'cairn, barrow, heap' but there is as yet no evidence of one here. When used as a nm. it means 'a hoof, a foot' and is probably employed here in a topographical sense. Forms such *Garnlas* 1852 and *Gârn-lâs* 1879 may be hypercorrections based on the supposition that the place-name contains **carn** as a nf.

Carn-lwyd see **Garnllwyd**

Casllwchwr see **Loughor**

Castell-ar-Alun see **Castle-upon-Alun**

Castellau   ST 051865
Rhondda Cynon Taf (Llantrisant)
'castles': **castell** pl. *cestyllau, cystylle*
The Hyghest ~ , The Lowest Krestulle 1541, *Kystille* 1584, *Tire David ap Treharne alias Tire Kystylle* 1630, *Kestelle hamlett* 1670, *Cystelle* c.1700, *Castella* 1727, *Castella fach, ~ House, Pentref Castella ganol, Castellau* 1833
The reason for the use of the pl. is unclear. Castellau is shown on the OS in 1875 as the site of a single castle and there are no castles at Castellau-ganol (ST 043872), Castellau-uchaf (ST 040876) and Castellau-fach (ST 046867) – with qualifiers **canol**, **uchaf** and **isaf**. It is possible that the n. developed as an extension in pl. form from the castle (**castell**) to neighbouring farms and the two administrative divisions (**parseli**) of Castellau Uchaf and Castellau Isaf. Pentre (ST 042875) is *Pentref* 1884 with **pentref** 'chief farm' (rather than 'village').

Castell Coch   SS 131826
Cardiff (Whitchurch)
'red (*or* brown) castle': **castell**, **coch**
Rubeocastro 1307, *Red Castle upon Taf above Tonn Gwenglais* 1591, *the redd Castle* c.1598, *Castelle Gogh* c.1538, *Cast: coch* 1578, *Castle Coch* c.1580, *kastell Koch* 1606

Matched by Lat *castrum* and *rubeus* and named from 'a high rok of red stone or soile' according to the antiquarian John Leland c.1538. Restoration of the medieval castle was begun by William Burges for the third Marquess of Bute in 1875. There is another Castell Coch (SS 852887) in Llangynwyd, recorded as (antiquity) *Castell-coch* 1833.

Castell Meredydd ST 225888
Caerphilly (Machen)
'Maredudd's castle': *castell*, pers.n. *Maredudd* variant *Meredydd*
Castell 1833, *Castell Meredydd* 1879
The castle lay in the lp. of Cyfoeth Meredydd and both names may refer to Maredudd ap Gruffudd of Caerleon, a minor lord of part of Gwynllŵg, mid 13th cent. He has also been identified with a Meredydd Gethin (BWGwent 372) reputedly one of eight sons of the Lord Rhys (d. 1197), prince of Deheubarth. In c.1217 it was acquired by Morgan ap Hywel (alias Morgan of Caerleon) and is described as the castle of Machen (*Machein*) in 1236. Cyfoeth Meredydd is *Kevoeth M(er)edith* 1379, *Covythmeredyth* 1406, *Kyuoethmeredith* 1513 probably 'land, possession of Maredudd' with *cyfoeth* nm. also recorded in Cyfoethybrenin, Cardiganshire, recorded as *Kyvoeth y brenin* 1550, *Kyvoeth y brenin* 1657, 'the king's land', with *y* and **brenin**.

Castell Morgraig ST 160844
Caerphilly (Eglwysilan/Llanisien)
'castle at Morgraig': *castell*, pn. *Morgraig*
(castle) *Mavrgraige* c.1670, *Castle Morgrig* 1831, (antiquity) *Castell Mor-graig* 1833
Morgraig is 'large rock, large cliff' (**mawr** variant *mor*, **craig**) referring to the western end of the ridge Craig Llanisien; see also Thornhill. The castle was at the southern edge of the lp. of Senghennydd overlooking the lowland area of Cibwr and Cardiff and may have been built by the mid 13th cent (MSM 199).

Castell-nedd see **Neath**

Castellymynach ST 082812
Cardiff (Pen-tyrch)
'the monk's castle': *castell, y, mynach*[1] variant *manach*
Castelle Menach c.1538, *Castell Menyth* 1541, *Cast: meneche* 1578, *Kestyll y Menych* 1550, *Castle Menyghe* 17th cent, *Castlemenich* 1623, *Castell Meneich* c.1800, *Castellymynach* 1811
The n. of a ho. drawn into the spread of Creigiau during the 1980s. The def.art. is probably intrusive and historical forms before c.1800 with *Menych*, *Menyghe*, etc generally favour a pl. *menych, meneich, myneich*. There is no evidence of any connection with monks and the castle probably refers to the late medieval ho. It is possible that –mynach recalls a lost rn. since there are examples of rs. Mynach in Cardiganshire and Merionethshire (and cf. Ystrad Mynach). Castellmynach lies close to the upper reaches of the stream Nant Coslech which rises near a well (SS 076813) and pool next to Tynant Road, west of the ho., flowing southwards past the former Castell-y-mynach Mill to the r. Ely. Castellymynach gives its n. to Castell ht. recorded as *Castle Hamlet* 1825.

Castle Ditches SS 959675
Vale of Glamorgan (Llantwit Major)
'(area adjoining) castle ditches': E **castle**, E **ditch** pl. *ditches the Castell Dychys* 1541, *Castle Ditches* 1633
The n. applies to a bank defining the eastern side of what appears to be a prehistoric fort projecting between the stream Afon Col-huw and the sea.

Castle Park ST 159869
Caerphilly (Eglwysilan)
Castle Park 1981
An area of housing which developed from the 1960s around a recreation park south-east of Caerphilly castle.

Castleton ST 023684
Vale of Glamorgan (St Athan)
'settlement with a castle': ME *castel, -ton*

Castelton 1350, *Castell Towne* 1530, *Castleton, Castelletoun* c.1538, *Castell towne* 1567, *Castleton in St. Athan* 1556-8
Located near East Orchard castle.

Castle-upon-Alun, Castell-ar-Alun
SS 911747
Vale of Glamorgan (St Brides Major)
'castle on (r.) Alun': E *castle* matched by *castell*, prep. *on*, *ar*, rn. *Alun*
Olde Castle upon Alem 1584, *Ould Castle* 1637, *Old Castle-upon-Alun* 1683, *Old-Castle-upon-Allem* 1716, *Castell Rulam* 1754, *Castell ar alain* c.1800, *Castell yr Allum* 1852.
Earlier Oldcastle, i.e. 'old (i.e. abandoned) castle', which appears to be the qualifier in the names of Payn and Peter 'of Old Castle': *Payn de ueteri castello, ~ veteri Castro* c.1144, (Peter de) *Veteri Castello* c.1235: Lat *vetus* gen. *veteris* 'old', *castellum*. The qualifier 'upon-Alun' was added later, perhaps to distinguish it from Oldcastle at Bridgend, and 'Old' itself is dropped on OS maps in the 1960s, presumably because there is no 'New Castle upon Alun'. The r. is *Alun* before 1148, (*rivulum*) *Alune* c.1227, *Alein* c.1538, *Alen* 1586. The meaning is uncertain though 'meandering' has been suggested. It must be related to the rns. Alun (Flintshire), Alne (Yorkshire), and Ellen (Cumberland) and the Celtic pers.n. *Alauna*. Local pron. apparently includes 'Alem' which may explain some sps. such as *Allam*, and *Alum* perhaps reflecting colloquial variation of *n* and *m*, though this generally occurs before *p* and *b*. Some sps. such as *Alein* may have misreadings and miscopyings of –*m*. Oldcastle Down (St Brides Major) near the castle is *Ould Castle Downe* 1631.

Castle View SS 909806
Bridgend (Coety)
Castle View 1983
A ref. to the castle in Newcastle (q.v.). The n. was coined in the 1970s for a housing estate developed since the late 1960s and has displaced the older Caefatri (Caevatry) recorded as *Cae Vattry* 1785, *Cavatry* 1799, *Caefatre* 1813,

Cae-fatry 1877, *Caeffatri* 1940, possibly 'factory enclosure': *cae*, *ffatri* nf. 'factory, mill'.

Caswell SS 589877
Swansea (Bishopston)
'cress stream': OE *cærse*, *wælle*
Carswell 1650, (close of land) *Carswell hope* 1675, *Caswel Bay* 1729, (ht.) *Caswell Bay* 1813, *Caswell*, (bay) ~ *Bay* 1832
Identifiable with Llandeilo Porth Tulon (ETG 141) recorded as *Porth Tvlon*, *portum dulon* c.1145, *Lann Teiliau portulon* c.1170, meaning 'church of (St) Teilo at Porth Tulon', *llan*, pers.n. *Teilo*; the qualifier has *porth*³ 'harbour' (= Caswell Bay) and possibly a pers.n. *Tulon*. A former chp., now ruinous. The plant is probably watercress which thrives in wet alkaline soils.

Cathays ST 180779
Cardiff (St John's)
'enclosures frequented by cats': E *cat* 'cat, wild cat', ME *hay* 'a fence, an enclosure'
Kate Haye 1699, *Cathays* 1716, *Cat Hays* 1759
Animal ns. are common in pns. and fns., eg. Pwll-y-gath (recalled in Pwll-y-gath Street, at Kenfig Hill) is recorded as *Pwll y Gath* 1751, *Catspit farm* 1814 and *Pwll-cath* 1833, meaning the 'cat's pit' (*pwll, y, cath*). Recorded instances of Cathays are very late and the precise significance of the n. remains uncertain. Its late occurrence probably rules out the OE pers.n. *Catta* or Scand pers.n. *Káti* found in pns. such as in Catton, Norfolk, as the first el. The n. applied to an area around Greyfriars Road (ST 183767) but was extended to the civic area Cathays Park (ST 182770) and later to an area of housing stretching from Cathays Terrace to Crwys Road.

Cefn Cefn Gelli-gaer ST 110704
Caerphilly/Merthyr Tudful (Gelli-gaer)
'ridge (in Gelligaer)': *cefn*
Gavely Keven hamlett 1670, *Keven* 1783, (common) *Cefn Gellygar* 1799, (mountain) *Cefn Gelli-gaer* 1813
The first sp. has *gafael*¹ 'holding of heritable land, tenement', with *y*.

Cefn Bryn SS 4890, 5089
Swansea (Llanrhidian/Nicholaston/Penrhys/Reynoldston)
'hill ridge': *cefn*, *bryn*
(mountain) Kevenbrin c.1230, (commons) Keven brynne 1583, (waste) Keven brynn 1650, (hill) Keven Bryn 1729, (common) Cefn Bryn 1799, Cefn y Bryn 1814
A long, narrow sandstone ridge and area of common extending from Reynoldston to Pen-maen, Gower. Described as a place for cutting turf c.1684.

Cefnbychan SS 544951
Swansea (Llanrhidian)
'small ridge': *cefn*, *bychan*
Kevenbychan 1650, Ceuen bechan 1665, Penclauth or Kevenbuchan 1688, Cefnbuchan 1813, Cefnbychan 1828
A small hill and ht. between Crofty and Blue Anchor; see Pen-clawdd. A common pn. and topographical n. with further examples in Merthyr Tudful and Pen-tyrch.

Cefncoedycymer SO 033079
Merthyr Tudful (Faenor, Breconshire)
'ridge near Coedycymer': *cefn*, pn. *Coedycymer*
Cefncoedcymmer, Cefncoedcymer uchaf 1814, Cefncoedcymmer 1873, Cefn-coed-y-cymmer or Cefn-coed (the latter its postal name) 1868, Cefn-coed-y-cymer 1872
The qualifier Coedycymer is 'wood at the confluence' (*coed*, *y*, *cymer¹*) recorded as Coed y Cummer 1725, Coed y Cymmar 1776, Coed y Cymer 1813. The confluence is *ychimer* 1128 (c.1170) and *cymer* c.1145, referring to the meeting-point of rs. Taf Fawr and Taf Fechan. The village - now part of Merthyr Tudful - occupies a ridge between the rs. extending north towards Cefn Cilsanws (SN 0209), and developed as an industrial settlement near Cyfarthfa ironworks. Known colloquially as *y Cefen* in 1824.

Cefncribwr SS 856827
Bridgend (Tythegston)
'ridge likened to a comb': *cefn*, *cribwr*

La Rigge c.1200, (wood) La Rugge 1303, la Rugge que vocatur Keven Cribour 1360, Kevencribor 14th cent (16th cent), (common) Rugg 1668, Kevenkrybor 1591, Kevencribor 1632, (common) Cefn Cribor 1749, (ht.) Cefncribwr 1813
cribwr can mean not only a 'wool-comber', i.e. the person who combs wool, but also the instrument and that is the likeliest explanation here. *cefn* is matched by ME *rugge* (OE *hrycg*) with the Fr def.art. *la*, seen in early sps. Cribwr is also recorded in the n. of a castle *Castellum Kibur* late 12th cent and *Castell Kribor* early 16th cent, its remains recalled in the 'old walls' of Lletygribwr (*llety*) mentioned by the antiquarian Rice Merrick (Merrick 105) or perhaps the so-called 'British encampment' on the west end of the ridge near Penycastell (SS 844826) which was identified by the antiquarian Siôn Dafydd Rhys with a legendary giant *Cribawr* (APNW 190). Sps. such as *Keven* represent local dialect *cefen* for *cefn*. The ridge extends from the vicinity of the ho. Ty-cribwr (SS 867826) which is *Tycribwr* 1813 to Penycastell (*tŷ*).

Cefn Cross, Cefn-y-groes SS 864826
Bridgend (Laleston)
'crossroads at Cefncribwr': pn., E *cross*; 'ridge at the crossroads', *cefn*, *y*, *croes*
Cefn Cross 1899
It is also possible that there was a cross here since there are several standing stones (SS 873826, 874826) in the area. A ht. which developed from the late 19th cent at crossroads on the east side of Cefncribwr. The W form appears to be a recent adoption.

Cefn Fforest ST 162977
Caerphilly (Bedwellte Monmouthshire)
'(the) forest ridge': *cefn*, (*y*), *fforest*
(ho.) Cefn-y-Fforest 1833, Cefn-y-fforest 1901, Cefn Fforest 1871, Cefn-fforest 1922
fforest often means 'hunting preserve' as with E *forest* but here the meaning may be 'woodland'. There are now no major woods in the area but Pen-y-coed, 'top of the wood' (*pen¹*, *y*, *coed*) lies a little to the north and Argoed, 'woodland' (*argoed*) about two miles further away.

Cefn-glas SS 892806
Bridgend (Newcastle)
'green ridge': *cefn*, *glas*
Keven Glase 1758, (ho.) *Cefnglas* 1852, (hill) *Cefn-glâs* 1877
A housing estate named from a small hill and identical in meaning to Cefn-glas (ST 078970) in Merthyr Tudful recorded as (ho.) *Cefn glas* 1783, *Ceven glaes* 1795 on the east slopes of the hill Cefn Glas.

Cefn Gwrhyd SN 7207, 7208
Neath Port Talbot (Llan-giwg)
?'ridge with a gap (in its middle)': *cefn*, *gwryd¹*, *gwrhyd*
Keven Gwryd 1628, *Cefn Gerwydd* 1799, *Cefn y Gerwydd* 1831, *Cefn Gwrhyd* 1878
gwryd¹ is used in a topographical sense probably for a small gap or dip in a ridge. Cefn Gwryd is a long ridge with two slight summits and a shallow depression between them. There are two hos. Gwrhyd-isaf (SN 738085) and Gwrhyd-uchaf (SN 736090) recorded as *tir y Gwrid ycha* 1728, *Tyr y Gwrid Yssha alias Tuy yn y Pant alias Pistill Gwin*, *Y Gwrid Yssha*, *Tyr y Gwrid Ycha alias Tuy yn y Pant* 1764, *Gwryd isha*, ~ *ucha* 1841 (**tir**, **isaf**, **tŷ**, **pant**, **pistyll**, **gwyn**, **uchaf**).

Cefnhengoed¹ ST 147957
Caerphilly (Gelli-gaer)
'ridge near Hengoed': *cefn*, pn. **Hengoed**
Keven hengoyde 1434, *Tire Ceven Hengoed* 1697, *y keven, hengoed* 1697 (late 18th cent), *Cefn-hengoed* 1750, *Ceven hengoed* 1807, *Cefn Hengoed* 1813
The village developed in the 19th cent above Hengoed (q.v.) along Cefn Road on a ridge between Nant Cylla and the r. Rhymni.

Cefnhengoed² SS 683954
Swansea (Llansamlet)
'ridge near the old dwelling': *cefn*, *hen*, *bod¹*
Keven Henvod c.1583, *Keven henvod* 1650, *Cefn-henfod* 1830, *Ceven Henfod* 1841, *Cefn Hengoed* 1881
bod¹ is an uncommon el. in pns. in south Wales and its unfamiliarity may partly account for misassociation with the far more common *coed*, len. –goed, from the late 19th cent.

Cefn Hirgoed SS 9283, 9382, 9482
Bridgend (Coety)
'ridge at long wood': *cefn*, *hir*, *coed*
Keven hiregoed 1592, *Keven Hirgott* 1641, (common, park) *Keven Hirgoed*, *Kevenhirgoed* c.1670, *Cefn Hirgoed* 1775
Little woodland now survives in the area.

Cefnmabli ST 223840
Caerphilly (Michaelston-y-fedw, Llanfedw)
'ridge of Mabli': *cefn*, pers.n. *Mabli*
Kenvabley 1507, *Kevynmableye* 1541, *Kevenmably* c.1580, *Keuen Mableie* 1586, *Kevanmably Park* 1702, *Cefn Mabley* 1799, (o) *gefn mabli* late 16ent
Traditionally associated with 'Mable', heiress of Robert Fitzhamon, the Norman who conquered Glamorgan. She was said to have married Robert the Consul (earl of Gloucester), son of Henry I, and to have died 1157 (CardV 113; HMON V, 21). Historical evidence is, however, late and the pers.n. common. The n. of a former mansion, later a hospital, thought to lie on the site of an older structure lying on the eastern edge of a low ridge. An identical n. (ST 001800) recorded as *Cefn-mably* 1876 in Llanhari may be a transferred n. as in the case of nearby Rhiwperra (ST 000800).

Cefn Onn ST 1885
mtn. Caerphilly (Rhydri)
'the ash-trees ridge': *y*, *cefn*, *onn*
y Kefen onne 1443, (forest) *Keven on* 1467, *Kevennon* 1541, *fforest keven Onn* 1570, *Cefn-onn* 1885
Still largely wooded. Local W pron. is recorded as 'Cefan-onn' in 1885 with characteristic intrusive vowel –a–; cf. Cefnpennar.

Cefn-parc SS 721966
Neath Port Talbot (Cadoxton-juxta-Neath)
'(recreational) park near Cefn': pn. *Cefn*, **parc** (road) *Cefn Parc* 1940, (hos.) *Cefn Parc* 1965
Housing developed along and around Pen-yr-alley Avenue in the 1930s. The park appears on OS maps from c.1940. Named in part from a former fm. Cefn (SS 717963) recorded as *Cefn* 1832, *Cefen* 1841, *Cefn Farm* 1878, which lay on

a small ridge *Cefn* 1813, now part of the site occupied by the oil refinery.

Cefnpennar SO 037006
Rhondda Cynon Taf (Aberdare)
'ridge by (r.) Pennar': ***cefn***, rn. *Pennar* (hill) *Penar* c.1538, *Keven Pennarth* 1541, (hos.) *Keven Penare yssa, ~ ycha* 1582, (mess.) *Tyr Keven Pennar ycha* 1604, *(syddyn) Keven Pennarth, ~ isha* c.1612, (lands) *hewl Keven Pennar* 1681, *(adre'n) Nghefan Penar* 1839, *Cefnpennaruchaf, -isaf* 1814, *Cwmpennar* 1831
For the rn., see Cwmpennar and Mountain Ash / Aberpennar. The 1839 sp. contains a local dialect form *cefan* for ***cefn***.

Cefn Rhigos SN 915069
Rhondda Cynon Taf (Ystradyfodwg)
'ridge at Rhigos', ***cefn***, **(y)** and pn. **Rhigos** (waste ground) *Keven y Rigos* 1666, (land) *Ceven y Rigoes* 1667, *Cefn Rhydgroes* 1833, *Cefnrhigos Gate* 1852, *Cefn Rhigos* 1899
Cefn Rhigos (SN 915068) developed after World War II around crossroads above Rhigos (q.v.). The 1833 form misassociates the pn. with **rhyd** and **croes** as if it were 'ford at a cross'.

Cefnstylle SS 570962
Swansea (Loughor)
'ridge likened to a ?plank': ***cefn***, ?***ystyllen***, *styllen* (mess.) *Kevenystlle, otherwise Berthllwyd* 1738, *Kevenystle* (at *Berth Llwyd*) 1739. *Kevenstylle* 1764, *Kefenstulle* 1775, *Cefn-stelle* 1832, *Cefenstylle* 1841
ystyllen may be used figuratively for a ledge of rock since Cefnstylle lies on a small steep-sided ridge; cf. Shelf (q.v.). It could also refer to the availability of building timber. Comparable pns. might include Ffosceibr (***ceibr*** 'rafter, beam'), Nant Tynyplancau (*planc¹* pl. *-au* 'planks') and Pantynenbren (***nenbren*** 'roof-beam') discussed by Gwynedd Pierce (PNGlam 148). Loss of –*n* is possible (see Llandough) and occurs in cymricised forms of E pns. such as Brackla. Deric John (PNSW: Lliw Valley) suggests that the second el. may be a contracted form of *pistyllau* 'spouts, wells' (***pistyll***) but ***ystyllen***

is more compelling. Berthlwyd Uchaf lies immediately north-west of Cefn Stylle and is probably *Berthloyd* 1650 and *Berth Llwyd* 1764, Berthlwyd Isaf (SS 564961) is *Berth-lwyd-isaf* 1830, 1879, meaning 'grey bush', **(y)**, ***perth***, ***llwyd*** qualified by ***uchaf*** and ***isaf***.

Cefn-y-groes see **Cefn Cross**

Cefnyrhendy ST 041815
Rhondda Cynon Taf (Llantrisant)
'ridge near (ho. called) Hendy': ***cefn***, ***yr***, pn. **Hendy**
(hill) *Cefn-yr-hendy* 1833, *Cefn yr Hendy* 1919, *Cefnyrhendy* 1962
A housing estate built after World War II on a hill Cefn yr Hendy; see Hendy.

Cegyrwen see **Gwauncaegurwen**

Celliwlybion see **Cillibion**

Cendon see **Kendon**

Cerrigllwydion SS 792947
Neath Port Talbot (Michaelston-super-Afan)
'grey rocks': ***carreg*** pl. *cerrig*, ***llwyd*** pl. *llwydion*
Cerrigllwydon 1852, *Cerig Llwydion* 1899, *Cerrig Llwydion* 1964
Shown on OS maps as *Gareg-lwyd* 1878 and 1884 with the sing. ***llwyd***. A small industrial settlement which developed in the mid 19th cent on a slope once covered with grey stones used to build the village (W.J. Llewellyn in TAMDHS 1930).

Chatham ST 216890
Caerphilly (Machen Monmouthshire)
Transferred n.
Chatham 1878
A small ht., now regarded as part of Machen, which developed around Chatham Villa and Chatham Place (earlier Chatham Row) built c.1850 (MachenR 27) near brickworks and Bovil Colliery. Rainers Row here was named from a James Rainer, 'a groom and native of Kent', who lived in nearby Draethen.

Cheriton SS 451932
Swansea
'church settlement': OE *cirice*, *tūn*
Cheriton 1387, *Cheriton'* 1394, *Cheryngton'* 1472, *Cheryton* 1535, *Cherytowne* 1580, *Chiriton* 1601, *Cheritone* 1691
A common pn. in England and note Cheriton, Pembrokeshire (PNPemb 738). There appears to have been a local onomastic explanation that it was 'a corruption of Cherrytown, ... from its abundance of cherries' (OPN 128).

Churchill Park ST 151880
Caerphilly (Eglwysilan)
'housing estate named from (Winston) Churchill', surname *Churchill*, E *park*
Developed during the 1970s, named from Winston Churchill, British Prime Minister, 1940-45, 1951-55. E *park* is applied to other Caerphilly housing estates such as Hendredenny Park, Lansbury Park and Virginia Park.

Church Village, **Pentre'r Eglwys** ST 085864
Rhondda Cynon Taf (Llantwit Faerdre)
'village at the church': E *church*, *village*; *pentref*, *yr*, *eglwys*
Church Village 1890, *Church Village Sta.* c.1898, *Pentre'r Eglwys* 1908, *Pentre Eglwys* 1941
Developed in the late 19th cent near Dyffryn Dowlais fm. around Cross Inn (ST 086859) south-east of Llantwit Fardre ch. on what is now St Illtyd Road leading towards Efail Isaf. The n. is drawn directly from the halt or station on the former Llantrisant & Taff Vale Junction Railway but ultimately from the area immediately around the ch. which was sometimes described as the Village (*Village* 1814). Upper Church Village (ST 081865) has effectively displaced the n. Llantwit Fardre/ Llanilltud Faerdref since the 1960s.

Cibwr (Kibbor)
Cardiff
Uncertain
Kybor c.1126, (forest) *Kibur* c.1176, *Kiburg'* c.1190, (land) *Kyburgh* 1295, *Kybur*, *Kibor* 1307, *Kibour* 1349, *Kebore in comitatu Kardiffe* 1476, *Kibworth* c.1538, (castle) *Kibwr* 1606

The n. of a former administrative commote covering most of north Cardiff, apparently taking its n. from high ground on its northern edge and specifically from Craig Cibwr, 'cliff, rock' (*craig*) which was at the west end of the ridge Cefn Onn near Castell Morgraig (ST 160843). This is *Kreic Kybor* 1443 and *craig Kybor* 1653. Cibwr is of uncertain meaning though it seems to occur also in the n. of hos. called *Kibor Issa* 1740, 'lower' (*isaf*), in Mynyddislwyn, Monmouthshire, and *Kibbor Vawr* 1791 (*mawr* 'great') in Llantrisant, Glamorgan. Historic forms appear to rule out any semantic connection with Ceibwr, a rn. at Moylegrove, Pembrokeshire (PNPemb 6: ?*caib* 'pickaxe, mattock' and suffix *-wr*) and *ceibr* in Penrhiw-ceibr (q.v.). Paterson (AC 1921, 78-79) identified *Kibwr* castle with an earthwork or fort (ST 152827) at the southern end of Y Wenallt (hill) but it could be that at Twmpath (ST 153822), near Clos y Bryn, recorded as a circular antiquity 1876 and castle mound 1940 on OS maps. His suggestion of a Scand origin with ON *borg* 'a fortified place' etc., and *kip* 'a jutting point, a pointed hill', fails to match the evidence.

Cilâ see **Killay**

Cilfái see **Kilvey**

Cil-ffriw (Cilfrew) SN 770004
Neath Port Talbot (Cadoxton-juxta-Neath)
'nook at the promontory': *cil¹*, *ffriw*
(*o*) *Gil Ffriw* late 16th cent, (*o*) *gil ffriw* early 17th cent, *kil y ffryw* 1600, *Tyr isha Kylfriu* 1686, *Kilfrew* 1733, (ho.) *Cil-y-ffriw* 1832, *Cilfriw* 1875-81
A n. taken from a fm. (SN 773006) on a slope above Ty-draw Brook. Some sps. have the def.art. *y* but this is probably intrusive. *ffriw* 'snout' is used figuratively.

Cil-frwch see **Kilvrough**

Cilfynydd ST 087923
Rhondda Cynon Taf (Eglwysilan/Llanfabon)
'mountain with a nook': *cil¹* as qualifier, *mynydd*

Kylvuwch 1729, *Gilfynith* 1740, *Kylvunich* (= *Kylvunith*) 1754, *Gilfynydd* 1763, *Kilfonydd* 1766, *Cilfynidd* 1813, *Cilfynydd* 1900
Taken from a ho. located immediately above the village in a small valley. Developed by the Albion Colliery and known initially as Albion Town. Villagers objected to the n. and Lady Llanover (1802-96) - a prominent figure in W literary and cultural circles - wrote to the Postmaster General arguing for the retention of Cilfynydd (PNIG 34). The village was located near a ho. Ynyscaedudwg recorded as *Annesaber Kadyduye* 1541, *yronys Codidug* 1783, and *Ynis Cae Dudwg* 1852 removed during construction of the Albion Colliery (HWG IV, 1850-2). The full form translates as 'raised ground in a watermeadow at the confluence of Nant Caedudwg (and Taf)' (***ynys***, ***aber***). Caedudwg has not been satisfactorily explained. The rn. does not contain ***cae*** and an unrecorded pers.n. Dudwg (as StAbercynon 78) or the authenticated pers.n. Tudwg (see Tythegston).

Cilhendre SN 730026
Neath Port Talbot (Cadoxton-juxta-Neath)
'nook at the winter dwelling': ***cil¹***, (***yr***), ***hendref***
A very recent n. taken from the ho.ns. recorded as *Cil yr Hendre Fach* 1771, *Kyl yr Hendre Vach* 1791, *Cilyrhendrefawr* and *Cilyrhendre fach* 1813, *Cil-yr-hêndre-fawr*, ~ *-ganol*, ~ *-fach* 1830, (***mawr***, ***canol***, ***bach¹***). The location of the ***hendref*** may have been at or near Twyn-yr-henlle (SN 728025) recorded as *Twynhenle ucha* and *Twynhenle isha* 1852, *Twŷn-yr-henllan* 1878, *Twyn-yr-henlle* 1898. This appears to mean 'hillock at the old place' (***twyn***, ***yr***, ***hen***, ***lle¹***) but early forms have not been identified.

Cil-lan (Cil-y-llan) approx. SS 582939
Swansea (Llanrhidian)
?'bank in a nook': ***cil¹*** as qualifier, ?***glan***
Kellan 1630, *Killan mawr* 1630, *Kyll y lan* 1650, *Kill llan vach* 1661, *Kyl-llan* 1672, *Killan Vach*, ~ *Vawr* 1764, *Killan-fach*, *Killanfawr* 1813
The n. survives in anglicised form in the ho.ns. Killan-fawr (SS 584942) and Killan-fach (ST 585939), and Killan Road. The two hos. lie either side of a road leading west from Swansea through Dunvant up a low ridge between Clyne River and an unnamed tributary. It is possible that the second el. is ***llan*** 'church' and indeed Cil-lan has been identified as the location of a ch. at *culalan*, *Cula-lan* 1118/9 in the Book of Llandaf (LL). The evidence, however, is ambiguous and there is, as yet, no proof of a ch. here.

Cillibion SS 517913
Swansea (Llanrhidian)
?'grove in a wet area': ***celli***, ?***gwlybion***
Kynthy libian 1339, *Kellylybyan* 1535, (man.) *Kelly lybyon* 1558, *Killyleibion* 1583, *Kelly lybion* 1650, *Kellybyon* 1682, *Gellylybion* 1697, *Kellibion* 1764, *Killibion* 1799, *Cil-ibion* 1832
?***gwlybion*** may be used as a coll.n. and is comparable with ***hirion*** pl. of ***hir*** in Gellihirion near Upper Boat (PNGlam 40-42). Modern forms appear to be contractions, i.e. Celliwlybion, Cellilybion > Cellibion, Cillibion. A former grange in the p. of Llanrhidian.

Cilmaen-gwyn (Cilymaengwyn) SN 742061
Neath Port Talbot (Llan-giwg)
'nook near the white stone': ***cil¹***, (***y***), ***maen***, ***gwyn***
Kyllymaen gwyn 1567, *Kilymaen Gwyn* 1603, *Killmangwin* 1650, *Kilmaen Gwyn Genol*, *Cillmaen Gwyn Ysha* 1729, *Kilmangwin Ycha*, ~ *Bach* 1764, (ho.) *Cil-y-maengwyn Isaf* 1832, *Cilmangwyn Genol* 1841, *Cilmaengwyn-isaf*, ~ *-uchaf* 1884
No 'white stone' seems to have been identified. The village is named from fms. distinguished as 'lower', 'middle' and 'upper' (***isaf***, ***cenol***, ***canol***, ***uchaf***). Cilymaengwyn Isaf is at SS 743066 in 1832, Cilymaengwynuchaf is at SS 742072

Cilonnen SS 547935
Swansea (Llanrhidian)
?'Gwynnen's nook': ***cil¹***, ?pers.n. Gwynnen
Kilcionen 1323, *Kilwannan* 1400, *Kilwnen* 1650, *Cillonen* 1665, *Kilwnnen*, ~ *vaugh* 1679, *Great Killionen* 1681, *Keelonen Vawr*, *Kilonnen Vach* 1764, *Kill-onen*, ~ *-fawr* 1832
The pers.n. is found in Llanwnnen, Cardiganshire. Later forms show that it was gradually displaced by ***onnen*** 'ash-tree' though forms such as *Kilwnen* still occur in 1841.

Cilybebyll SN 743046
Neath Port Talbot
'nook of the shelter': *cil¹*, *y*, *pebyll*
Killebebit 1254, *Kilbebill* after 1129 (1468), *Kilthibebilth* 1281, *Kelthibebul* 13th cent, *Kilthibebil* 1314, (ch. of) *St. Thomas the Martyr, Cilybebyll* 1528, *Kille-y-bebyll* 1536, *Kyllybybellth* 1541, *kil y bebyll* c.1566, *Kilybebill p[ar]ish Upp. Hamlett, Lower Hamlett* 1670
Some early forms suggest the first el. may have been associated with *celli* 'grove, copse' which occurs locally in Gelligeiros (*ceirios* 'cherries') and Gelli-nudd (q.v.). In common usage, *pebyll* was later wrongly assumed to be a pl. on the lines of *cragen*/*cregyn* 'shell', *castell*/*cestyll*, and a new sg. *pabell* was adopted. The p. was divided into Upper Hamlet or Cilybebyll Uchaf and Lower Hamlet or Cilybebyll Isaf recorded as *Killebebyll Ycha* and *Kellybebill ysha* 1650 (*uchaf, isaf*). Cilybebyll Fechan (*bechan*) was a fm. (SS 744054) north of the village.

Cimla SS 761963
Neath Port Talbot (Llantwit-juxta-Neath)
'common': *cimle* variant *cimla*
Kymne Kenol 1560, (waste ground) *Kevensayson otherwise called Kimne Kenol* 1612, (lands) *tyr y kymley* 1666, (mess.) *Tyr un yr Cymla* 1681, *Keven Saison or Kinney Kenol* 1707, *the Kimle* 1842
Earlier forms are qualified by *cenol* 'middle'. Gwynedd Pierce (PNGlam 42-43; ADG¹, 25) demonstrates that *cymfei, cymfai* is the likely source for a number of similar pns. in Glamorgan. Examples include *Landaffe Cimtha or Common* 1709 in Llandaf and *Kimdda bach* 1783 at Whitchurch. Llantrisant Common is *Kinme Lantressent* c.1670. Other recorded variants include *cymdda, cymfa* and may be compared with *simne, simdde, simla* etc. (derived from E *chimney* with colloquial E 'chimley, chimbley'). Cefnsaeson, 'Englishman's ridge' (*cefn, Saeson*) survives in the ho.ns. Cefnsaeson Fawr (SS 777964) (*mawr*) and Cefnsaeson Fach (SS 778962) (*bach¹*) and that of a secondary school. The pn. is recorded as *Kenensefhon, Renenseshon* (defective forms) c.1291, *Keven-sayson* 1359, and *Keven y Sayson* 1645. A ho. (SS 759959) recorded as *Cimneyglo* 1813, *Cimble-glo* 1832 (*glo*), *Cymmle Farm* 1878 and *Tir-y-Cimla* 1899, now lies under modern housing.

City SS 989783
Vale of Glamorgan (Llansanwyr)
E *city*
City 1813, 1841
Possibly a facetious n. for an unremarkable place comparable with City Dulas, Anglesey (DPNW 131), Moelfre City (SO 1175), Radnorshire, and City (SO 2189) near Ceri, Montgomeryshire. The public ho. here is the *City Inn* 1875 probably deriving from the pn. City (SS 900862), in Betws, was also the n. of several hos. recorded as *City Isaf* 1783, *City Fm.* 1813, (hos.) *City issa, ~ Genol, ~ ucha* 1841, *City y Betws* 1857 and *City-ganol* 1877 and was the location of a Nonconformist meeting-ho. recorded as *the Citty* 1740 and *y Siti* 1872. The chp. is probably 'the newly built house at Bettws' recorded in 1727. Betws also has a ho. known as Kensington (SS 904860) recorded as *Kingsington* 1833 and *Kensington* 1877.

Clas (Clase) SS 657978
Swansea (Llangyfelach)
'(the) monastic community': (*y*), *clas*
the Clayes 1536, *Clase Langevelach* 1583, *Clase Llangevelach* 1648, *Parcell Clase* 1650, *Parcell y Clase* 1670, *Classe* 1706, (ho.) *Clâs* 1832
An uncommon but widespread pn. el. found, for example, in Clas Garmon, Radnorshire (PNRad 43) and Clas, Montgomeryshire (PNMont 58), often assumed to be evidence of early religious communities but a *clas* also sometimes described a secular community. Local W dialect may account for sps. with *-ase, -ays*. The p. of Llangyfelach had several divisions which included *Parsel y Clas* (*parsel*) composed of Clas Uchaf (*uchaf*) and ~ Isaf (*isaf*); see also Mawr (q.v.). Clas was also the n. of a manor belonging to the bishops of St David's. Clasemont is the n. of a former ho. built c.1775 by Sir John Morris (see Morriston) recorded as *Clasemont* 1783, *Clasmont* and *Glasemont* 1782 (HGower 127-8; Gower 45: 17), with fashionable use of Fr *mont* 'hill'.

Clawdd-coch ST 055777
Vale of Glamorgan (Pendeulwyn)
'red (*or* brown) ditch (*or* bank)': *clawdd*, *coch*
Clauth Gogh, *Clawdd coch* 1595, *y Clawth coch* 1599, *Clawdd-coch* 1833
The ditch may be the very small stream which runs westwards to the the pond on the south side of the crossroads and towards Nant Tredodridge.

Clemenston, **Treglement** SS 924736
Vale of Glamorgan (St Andrews Minor)
'Clement's settlement or farm': pers.n. *Clement*, *tūn*
Clemestona 13th cent, *Clemenstoun* 1544, *Clemenston* 1568, *Clemenstowne* 1586, *Clemens Town* 1729, *Clemonstone* 1799, (*o*) *dre Glement* late 16th cent
Note also Little Clemenston (in Llampha, St Brides Major) recorded in 1767 and as *Clemenston vach farm* (in St Brides Major) 1845.

Clevis SS 839776
Bridgend (Newton Nottage)
'cliffs': E *cliff* pl. *cliffs*
Clevis 1777
Describing the low cliffs between Newton Point and the mouth of the r. Ogmore. *Clevis* may be another example of voicing f as v – a characteristic of the E dialect in the Vale and Gower. It is possible that Clevis is the lost *merthir gliuis* named in a grant by Cadwgan son of Owain c.935 copied into the Book of Llandaf c.1145. The boundaries of Merthyr Mawr are described as extending in length from Merthyr Glywys to the r. Ogmore/Ogwr and it is worth noting that Clevis lies close to the p. boundary with Merthyr Mawr. Clevis could be explained then as simply a re-interpretation but Merthyr Glywys, meaning 'graveyard containing the bones of Glywys' (***merthyr***, pers.n. *Glywys*), implies the existence of a ch. and none has, as yet, been identified.

Clun see **Clyne** Swansea

Clun-du SS 665980
Swansea (Llangyfelach)
'black meadow or moor': *clun*², *du*
Clyndee 1764, *Hên-clun-du* 1832, *Clynddu*, *Clyndee*, *Clyndee*, *Clyndu* 1852, *Clyn-du* 1876
Dark perhaps from the colour of its rock or soil. Coal was mined here in Clyn-du Level Colliery 1876.

Clwydyfagwyr SO 020070
Merthyr Tudful
'gate in the wall': *clwyd*, *y*, *magwyr*
Clwydfagwr 1841, *Clwydvagwr* 1852, *Clwyd-y-fagwyr* 1856
magwyr sometimes describes ruins and is best known from its occurrence in Magor, properly Magwyr, Monmouthshire (PNGwent 146-7). The n. earlier applied to a small scatter of hos. (SO 023065) and a former tramway next to part of Winch-fawr Road but neither the gate, wall nor ruins can be identified in 19th cent sources. Much of the area is former moorland, heavily marked by ironstone workings.

Clydach SN 691013
Swansea (Llangyfelach)
'(place on r.) Clydach': rn. *Clydach*
(mill of) *Cleudach* 1402, *Clydach Mill* 1650, *Clydach* 1691, *Lower Clydach*, *Aberclydach* c.1700, *Cledach B.* [R.] 1729, (brook) *Clydach Isha* 1755, *Cwm Clydach*, *Aber Clydach*, (brook) *Clydach Yssha* 1764
Also a ho. (SN 692012). The village is located near the r. Clydach Isaf (*isaf*) and its junction with Tawe (at SS 689012). The r. Clydach Uchaf (*uchaf*) in Llan-giwg is *Higher Clydach* c.1700, *Upper Clydach R* 1799 (found also in *Pont Cledach* 1729). Clydach is a fairly common rn. in Glamorgan. Apart from Clydach Vale (q.v.), examples include:
(1) Clydach (> Neath SS 734969) near Neath abbey: *Cloeda*, *Cloada* c.1129, *Cleudach* c.1208, *Cleydache* 1562, *Cledoch that runneth by Kelebebilch* 1586
(2) Clydach (Clydach Uchaf) (> Neath SN 828027) near Resolfen: *Cludach* 1289 (1336), *Cledaugh, which joineth [Neth] beneath the Resonlaie* 1586, *Higher Clydach* c.1700, *Cledach R.* 1799, *Aberclaudac* c.1200, *Aber-cleudach* 1246.
(3) Clydach (Clydach Isaf or Melincourt Brook) (> Neath SN 817023): *Cleudachcumkake* c.1200,

Cleodocumchach 1208, *Cleudach'comkake* 1329, *Abercleudaccumkac* c.1246, *Melynglydach* c.1700. The hill on the west is Carn Caca (SN 830006) recorded as *Carn Caca* 1877 and the valley Cwm Caca is *Cwm Cacca* 1666. W *caca* 'ordure, excrement' is used for muddy streams or those which were open sewers.

(4) Nant Clydach (>Taf SO 082929), in Llanwynno: *Klidach*, *Klydach* 1580, *Cledwed* c.1670, *Cledach R.* 1729, *Clydach* 1738, also in *Aber Clydach* 1633, *Cwm-clydach* 1833.

Sps. of most of these rns. suggest derivation from Cloudach and Cleudach which later developed into Clīdach, Clītach (prons. which are still heard) and Clydach. The precise meaning is uncertain but the suffix *-ach* is thought to be Ir and occurs in other rns. in south Wales such as Bradach (see Llanbradach) which prompts the suggestion that Clydach itself is Ir. The first el. in Clydach can be traced back to a Celt root **kleu-* found in W *clau* 'swift, ready' (and 'true, sincere, conspicuous') and Ir *cláidigh*, variant *clóidigh*, which occurs in several rns. in Ireland such as Clady and, more pertinently Cladagh/An Chlóldeach, co. Fermanagh. Both appear to mean 'the washing river' (www.placenamesni.org) or 'the swiftly-flowing one'. The absence of Clydach as a rn. in north and mid Wales is notable and its equivalent there is almost certainly Clywedog, a rn. customarily explained as deriving from *clywed* 'listen' and suffix *-og* with the contradictory suggestion that it means 'a noisy river'.

Clydach Vale, **Cwm Clydach** SS 976930
Rhondda Cynon Taf (Llantrisant/Ystradyfodwg)
'valley of (r.) Clydach': rn. *Clydach*, E **vale**, **cwm**
Dyffryn Clydach 1639, *Dyffryn Klydach* 1642, (ho.) *Cwm Clydach* 1799, *Clydach Vale* 1878
As Clydach. The valley is **dyffryn** in earlier sources typically meaning a large valley; **cwm** is generally a 'small valley'. The rn. is recorded as *Cleudac* before 1147, *Cledaugh* c.1538, and reaches the r. Rhondda Fawr at SS 994926. The n. is drawn directly from Clydach Vale Colliery, known as the Cambrian Colliery before 1900, south of the village. Cwm Clydach Colliery was at the eastern end of the village south of Blaenclydach.

Clyne[1], **Clun** SN 802007
Neath Port Talbot (Llantwit-juxta-Neath)
'the meadow, the moor': **clun**[2]
(tmt.) *Clyn y castell ycha* 1562, *o'r Clun eithinog* late 16th cent, *yklyn* 1611, *Parcell y Clyn* 1670, *Clynne (Upper Division)* 1728, *Clun* 1833, *Clyne (Glyn)* 1840
The n. of a medieval division or **parsel** of Llantwit-juxta-Neath. The village developed before 1914 on the north side of the Vale of Neath railway and Resolven tinplate works. **clun** is sometimes confused with **glyn** as in Glyn-Gwilym Isaf (SN 826014) in the same p. recorded as *Clŷn Gwillim ycha,* (mess.) *Tŷr y Clŷn* 1693, (mess.) *Clyn Gwillim Ucha* 1773, *Glyn-gwilim* 1833.

Clyne[2], **Clun** SS 607909
Swansea (Oystermouth)
'meadow, moor': **clun**[2]
(wood) *Clun* 1306, *la Clun* 1319, *Clune forest* 1369, (forest) *Clynne* 1400, *Fforest de Clyne* 1583, *the Forrest of Clyn and Clyn moor* 1650, *Clyne Farm* 1779, *Cline,* (moor) ~ *Moor* 1813, *Clyn* 1831
The n. survives in Clyne Common (SS 5990), Clyne Wood (SS 612913) and Clyne River which enters Swansea Bay at Black Pill (q.v.).

Cnap-llwyd SS 660965
Swansea (Llangyfelach)
'grey knap': **cnap**[1], **llwyd**
Cnapllwyd 1756, *Knapllwyd* 1764, *Cnap-llwyd* 1832
Named from a former fm. (approx. SS 659965) but the n. was applied to the area centred on the ruins of Morris Castle (SS 659964) in 1881. The first el. alternates with *cnwff* 'hillock, bump' in early forms of Cnap-coch (Llansamlet) recorded as *Y Knwffecoch* c.1583, *Knape Coch* 1650, *Knwffe Coch* 1764, *Cnap Coch* 1852 (**coch**), a n. displaced by Pentre-chwyth.

Coalbrook SN 590001
Swansea (Llandeilo Tal-y-bont)
'(place by) Coal Brook': E **coal**, **brook**

(brook) *Coal Brook* 1764, *Coalbrook* 1785 (1811), 1877
The Coal Brook flows eastwards to Afon Lliw. Several old coal pits are shown on the OS 1:2,500 plan in 1877 near the ht. Coal Brook, at Kenfig, recorded as *Colebrooke* 1503 and *Colbrocke* 1633 is probably identical in meaning.

Cockett, Cocyd   SS 630948
Swansea
?'(the) hill': E def.art. *the*, *cocket*
le Cockett 1583, *the Cockett* 1650, *Cocked* 1670, *the Gocet* 1683, *Cocket* 1764, *Cockit* 1799, (ht.) *Cwm-cockit*, (fm.) *Cockit Farm* 1833
Probably identical in meaning to Cocket-ganol, ~ -isaf and ~ -uchaf three hos. in Pen-tyrch recorded as *y Cocked* 1607, *Y Gockett* 1683 and *Gockid Isa*, ~ *Ycha* 1825 qualified as 'lower' and 'upper' (*isaf*, *uchaf*) and a hill called Cockit (SO 158280) near Llan-gors, Breconshire, recorded as *the Cockett* 1755 and *the Cockit* 1773-8. All refer to prominent locations which favour a hypothetical E noun formed from the adj. *cocked* with the particular meaning of 'raised up, turned up' as perhaps in *cockit-hat* 'a hat with the brim turned up' (EDD I, 683) or less likely a dim. of *cock* (note 'haycock' etc.). A few forms appear to show the influence of the W suffix – *ed* or *–yd*. Similar pns. refer to inns or buildings next to old highways which has prompted the suggestion that there is a connection with E *cocket*, a type of seal, used in the specific sense of 'a customs house' (DPNW 92). This seems to be the case with Chepstow, Monmouthshire, which formerly possessed an inn *Le Gocquet* 1677 reputedly re-named 'The Grouse'.

Coedarhydyglyn (Coedriglan)   ST 105751
Vale of Glamorgan
'wood of (family called) ?Raglan': *coed*, surname ?*Raglan*
Reglines Wood 1540, *Ragling* 1572, *Raglande* 1591, (park disparked) *Riglin* c.1670, *Riglyn* c.1700, *Coedriglan* 1758, *Coed Ryglyn* 1767, *Coedrhygland* 1799, *Coedyrhaglan* 1811
See further PNDPH 251-3 and PNGlam 43-44. The surname occurs as that of Sir John Raglan of Carnllwyd and Llantwit Raleigh, alive in 1521 (LimbPat 275). *coed* replaced E *wood* before 1597/8 although it may have been in use among W-speakers for a much longer period. Intermediate sps. show the development to *Coed Ryglyn*, *Coedrhygland* probably through popular association with *rhyg* 'rye' and *glan*. The modern form Coedarhydyglyn, seemingly 'wood along the valley' with *ar hyd* 'along, throughout' and *glyn*, is a re-interpretation. The def.art. *y* found in forms such *Coedyrhaglan* is typically found prefixed to non-W surnames in Glamorgan; cf. Cwrtyrala.

Coed-duon see **Blackwood**

Coedely, Coedelái   ST 018857
Rhondda Cynon Taf (Llantrisant)
'wood near (r.) Elái': *coed*, rn. **Ely**, **Elái**
Coed y lay 1764, *Coydylai* 1784, (ho.) *Coed y Lay* 1799, *Coed Ely* 1833
Several sps. show association of unstressed E- in Elái with the def.art. *y*. See Ely.

Coed-ffranc   SS 7194
Neath Port Talbot (Cadoxton-juxta-Neath)
'wood of the ?Frenchman *or* mercenary': *coed*, ?*ffranc*[1]
(*montem de*) *Coitfranc* 1289 (1336), *Coyd* ~ , *Coid ffranck* 1566, *Forest Coidfrank* 1578, *Coitfranke forrest* 1586, *Côdffranke* c.1700
The n. could refer to some unidentified Norman invader or simply a wood held by Norman Frenchmen. There is some support for AF influence in the area in the n. of a former chp. (in what is now Jersey Marine SS 710940). This was dedicated to St Margaret probably Margaret of Antioch whose feast day coincided with the date of a fair at nearby Neath. The dedication was uncommon at that time in Wales. The chp. of St Margaret is first recorded in 1289 and is *St. Margaret of Coydffranke* 1505, *Capel Verad* 1729 and *Capel St. Marg.* 1833 (VNeath 88-90). There was also a well dedicated to her in Kilvey recorded in the n. of land *Tir Ffynnon varred* 1650 and *Tyr y ffunnon Vared* 1764 (*ffynnon*, *Mared*, *Fared*). The W n. of Crymlyn Bog, which lies between Coed-ffranc and Kilvey, appears to be Gwern Fare (see Crymlyn[2]). The early form

Coitfranc appears to rule out *ffranc²* 'free, frank' (borrowed from E *frank*) which is not attested in literary sources before the 16th cent. *ffranc²* is however, likely to be the second el. in Heol Ffrainc (Llantrisant Monmouthshire) and Heol Ffranc (Llanhiledd, Monmouthshire) in the sense 'free road, road lacking tolls'.

Coedhirwaun SS 821844
Neath Port Talbot (Margam)
'wood near Hirwaun': *coed*, ho.n. *Hirwaun* (woodland) *Coed Hirwaun* 1876
The ho. Hirwaun (SS 818851) is recorded as *Hirwaine* 1633, *Hirwain* 1814 and *Hirwaun* 1831, 'long moor', *hir*, *gwaun*; cf. Hirwaun. There is now very little moorland around the fm. The area was developed for housing during the 1990s.

Coedmachen see **St Bride's-super-Ely**

Coed Morgannwg SN 8701
'wood in Glamorgan/Morgannwg': *coed*, pn. **Morgannwg**
A modern n. for forestry in central Glamorgan crossed by the recreational Coed Morgannwg Way/Llwybr Coed Morgannwg.

Coed-pen-maen ST 077908
Rhondda Cynon Taf (Eglwysilan)
'wood at Pen-maen': *coed*, pn. *Pen-maen*
Coed penmain common 1833, *Coedpenmain* 1841, *Coedpenmaen* 1872, *Coed-pen-main* 1885
Pen-maen is 'stone hill': *pen¹*, *maen*. Its rocky nature is testified by several quarries marked on earlier OS maps, and is unlikely to refer to Y Garreg Siglo alias the Rocking Stone (ST 081901) as H.C. Jones (PNIG 34) thought. The stone lay at the southern edge of the former Coedpen-maen Common (south of Coedpen-maen) and leaves its n. in (ho.) *Rockingstone* 1875 and Rockingstone Terrace. The village developed from the mid 19th cent north of Coedpen-maen Foundry.

Coed-y-brain ST 144898
Caerphilly (Eglwysilan)
'the crows' wood': *coed*, *y*, *brain*

Coad y Brain 1783, *Coed-y-brain* 1833
Part of Llanbradach and the n. of a school recalling a former fm. and woodland, some of which remains on the hill-slopes west of the village. There is another Coed-y-brain (SO 159009) near Bargoed recorded as *Coed-y-bran* 1833, (ho.) *Coed-y-brain* 1878-79 and in *Capelcoedybrain* 1817 but modern forms are deceptive since it is earlier (forest) *coet breint* 1499 and *Coedybraint* 1815 with *braint* nmf. 'privilege, freedom; dignity, honour'.

Coed-y-cwm ST 077928
Rhondda Cynon Taf (Llanwynno)
'wood belonging to or near Y Cwm': *coed*, pn. *Y Cwm*
A modern housing estate built during the 1970s below a wood Coed y Cwm (*Coed y Cwm* 1900). Located above a former fm. Cwm (ST 080929) meaning 'the valley' (*y*, *cwm*) recorded in 1833 and the wooded valley of the r. Clydach.

Coedygores approx. ST 203803
Cardiff (Llanedern)
'wood on the waste land': *coed*, *y*, *gores²*, *gorest*
Koyde y Gorres 1618, *Coed-y-gorest* 1673, *Coed y Gorras* 1703, *Coydagorst* 1724, *Koyd Gorass* 1744, *Coedegores* 1769, *Coedygors* 1811, *Coed-y-gores* 1833
See further Pierce in PNGlam 44-45. It is plainly not 'the gorse wood' (as CR V, 356). The n. survives as that of a street in Llanedern housing estate.

Coedymwstwr SS 940810
Bridgend (Coychurch/Pen-coed)
'wood of the ?monastic cell': *coed*, *y*, *mwstwyr*, *mystwr*
Coide Muster c.1538, *Coedmustur* 1613, *Coedmuster* 1629, (wood) *Koed Must* c.1670, *Coed Mwstwr, Coedymwstwr* 1711, *Coide y Mwstwr* 1796, *Coed Mwstwr* 1833
See further Gwynedd Pierce in Nomina 23 (2000) and PNGlam 46-47. *mwstwr* is a colloquial form of obsolete **mystwyr** a word borrowed ultimately from Lat *monasterium*. The Lat word is also the origin of Breton *moustoer* and E *minster* 'church' but here it may signify an

early Christian cell. Pierce notes a well *Funnon-y-Munalog* meaning 'well of the monastery' (**ffynnon**, **y**, **mynachlog**) in a field *Cae'r funnon* 1778 and other examples of ***mystwyr*** elsewhere in Wales.

Coetra-hen (Coytrahen) SS 890855
Bridgend (Betws)
'old woodland-dwelling': ***coetref***, **hen**
Coetter Hen 1541, *Coytrefhen*, *Coytrehen*, *Coedtrefhen* 1682, *Goytre hên* 1725, *Coytrahen* 1806, (ht.) *Pont Goytrehen*, (ho.) *Goytrehen* 1813, *Goetre-hên* 1877
The sps. with *–tra-* represent local dialect and may be compared with local pron. of the pl. suffix *-au* as *–a*. The village developed in the 19th cent on the west side of Afon Llynfi opposite Coytrahên House (SS 895853). *coetref* is erroneously shown as Godra Bryn (SS 896870) on current maps as if it contains ***godre*** nm. 'foot, bottom'. This is *Goetrebryn* 1833, *Goedrabryn*, *Gottrabryn* 1841 (***bryn***).

Coety (Coity) SS 922815
Bridgend
'black or dark wood': (***y***), **coed**, **duf**
Coitif c.1178, *Coytyf* 1199, *Coytif* 1254, *Coity* 1411, *y coetv* c.1500, *Coydtyff* 1535, *y koyty* c.1566, *Coytdy* c.1670, *Coitie*, *Coytie* 1702
The meeting of -d and d- produces the -tt-, -t- sound. Later sps. seem to show association with ***tŷ*** 'house' (DPNW 94). The lp. was divided into two smaller manors recorded as *Coiti Anglia* 1598, *English Coytie otherwise Coitie Anglia* 1601 and (man.) *Coyty Wallia* 17th cent, sometimes distinguished as *Anglica*, *Anglia* 'English', and *Wallica*, **Wallia** 'Welsh'. The area or commote around Coety is variously recorded as *Coetfesland* 1460, *Comm. Coytif*, *Com. Coitif*, (area) *Ter Coite*, (lp.) *Tercoite* c.1538 by John Leland (***tir***). Cf. Coety Green (SS 425910) at Llangennith recorded as *Coytygreene* 1642 and *Coyty Green* 1764.

Cog ST 163687
Vale of Glamorgan (Sully)
?'swelling' or 'hollow': ?***cawg***
Cogge 1541, *Cog* 1578, *Cogg* 1632, *The Cogg* 1846 *cawg* 'dish, bowl' may be used figuratively for the high ground on which the ht. lies or in the opposite sense for a hollow perhaps in ref. to the valley of Sully Brook flowing past Cog Bridge fm. (ST 164093) recorded as *Cokbryge* 1455, *Cole Brydge* 1541, *Cogbridge* late 16th cent, and over Cog Moors. Cf. Cogan.

Cogan ST 175725
Vale of Glamorgan
?'bowl-shaped hollow': ?***cawg***, dim. suff. *–an*
(*Emma de*) *Cogan* c.1145, *Cogan* c.1151, 1254, *Coggan* 1577, *Cogan Vach* c.1678, *Little Cogan* 1693
Or perhaps *cawg* in its opposite sense 'swelling' (PNDPH 30-35) but the first suits the topography. Paterson suggested ODan *kog* 'piece of marshland (lately reclaimed)' (AC 1921, 77) but it is inappropriate here though that might suit Cogan (ST 287841), at Pen-carn, Monmouthshire (PNGwent 72-73). Cogan Pill is recorded as *Crokonpile* 1479, *Cogan Pylle* 1492, *Cogan Pill* 1529, *Cogans Pyll* 1537, with OE ***pyll*** 'tidal creek, pool, stream', common along the Bristol Channel.

Colcot, **Colcoed** ST 109694
Vale of Glamorgan (Merthyr Dyfan)
?'(char)coal shelter' or 'cold shelter': ***col*** or ***cald*** and OE ***cot***
Colcote 1541, *Colcott (Colcock)* c.1575, *Colkot* 1601, *Colcoed* 1745, *Colcot* 1763, *Calcot House* 1777, *Coldcott* 1798, *Cold Cot* 1833
The evidence tends to favour the first explanation and there are mentions of coal-pits (for burning charcoal) in the area of Cold Knap (q.v.) (PNDPH 137-8). *col* is also likely to be the first el. in the n. of a small stream Cold Brook on the east side of Barry which gives its n. to a ho. Coldbrook-fawr (ST 135701) (***mawr***) and the former Coldbrook-fach (***bach[1]***) recorded as *Colebroke* 1541, *Collbrooke* 1664, *Coal Brooke* 1754, *Coldbrook* 1763 (PNDPH 214-5). Early historic forms of Colcot lack –d- which tends to weigh against the proposed alternative meaning 'cold shelter' but this cannot be completely ruled out. Loss of –d- occurs, for example, in pns. such as Calcot, in Flintshire (FPN 42) and some

historic forms of Caldicot, Monmouthshire (DPNW 66) where 'cold shelter' is a more likely explanation. The cymricised form *Colcoed* shows the influence of **coed**. Another (lost) Colcot is attested in (pasture called) *the Colcott att Slad* 1546 and (tmt.) *the Colcott at Slad* 1745, which lay at Slade in Oxwich, near *Cold-comfort* 1832 (at approx. SS474866).

Cold Knap   ST 103661
Vale of Glamorgan (Barry)
'cold hill-top or 'hill-top near charcoal pits': E **cold**, E **knap**
Colde Knapp 1622, *Coal Knap* 1762, *Cold Knap* 1809, *The Knap* 1811
Cold Knap Farm occurs as *The Coale* 1622, *The Cold Ffarme* mid 17th cent, *The Cole Farm* 1705, *Ye Coal Ffarm* 1789. Pierce notes *coal-pits*, i.e. 'charcoal pits', near the fm. 1762 on an estate map in Glamorgan Archives (PNDPH 7-8; PNGlam 47-48). Cold Knap also gives its n. to The Knap housing estate (ST 102665) in Barry named from the headland.

Colwinston, Tregolwyn   SS 940754
Vale of Glamorgan
'settlement of (man called) Colwine': OE pers.n. *Colewine*, **tūn**; **tref**
(ch. of) *Sti. Michaelis de Colvestone* 1141, *Colwinestune* c.1144, *Colwinestuna* c.1155, *Colwinestone* c.1170, *Coluenston* 1362, *Colwynstow'* 1480, *Colston* 1545, *Colwinston* 1564, *tref golwyn* c.1566, *Tregollwin alias Collwinstown* 1726, *Tregolwyn* 1863
The W form has reversed generic and qualifier, substituted **tref** for **tūn** and apparently associated the pers.n. with *colwyn* 'whelp, puppy', typically found in rns. Note in particular Colwyn Bay, Denbighshire (DPNW 95). The contracted form *Colston* is paralleled in other pns. in this area, eg. *Bolston* for Bonvilston, *Flimston* for Flemingston and *Berton* for Boverton.

Cored-ddu see **Blackweir**

Corlannau   SS 770908
Neath Port Talbot (Aberafan)
'folds, pens': **corlan** pl. **corlannau**

Corlenna 1814, *Corlanna Houses* 1841, *Corlana, -lanna* 1852, *Corlanau* 1876
Presumably in ref. to folds or enclosures on or adjoining the hill Mynydd Dinas.

Cornelly, Corneli North Cornelly   SS 821815
Bridgend (Pyle)
?'clearing frequented by cranes or herons': OE **corn**, OE **lēah**
Corneli c.1170, *Cornely* 13th cent, *Cornhely* 1208, *Corneli Boreali, ~ Australi* 13th cent, *Cornely Ychan, North Cornellye* [?alias] *Ycha* 1541, *Cornelly Waelod* 1591, *Northe-, Southecornelye* 1597, *North ~ , South Cornely* 1799
The pn. is more easily explained as E than W and there are similarities to Corley (*Cornelie* 1086), Warwickshire. OE *Cornelēah* (with middle *–e-* indicating the possessive) generally develops in England to Cornley or Corley ['kɔrnli:, 'kɔrli:] with loss of *–e-*. Its survival in Cornelly/Corneli may be attributed to W-speakers placing stress on the penultimate syllable, i.e. Cornéli [korn'eli:]. Cornelly is about a mile from Kenfig Pool, notable for its wildlife and birds. The pn. must have inspired the dedication of the former chp. of North Cornelly to Cornelius (pope and martyr, d. 253). The chp. of South Cornelly (SS 820804) was Tŷ Capel (now demolished) meaning 'chapel house' (**tŷ, capel**). Lat sources employ *borealis* and *australis* for 'north' and 'south'. The 1541 forms stand for Corneli Ychan, 'little Cornelly' (**bychan** len. *fychan, ychan*), probably referring to North Cornelly. *Cornelly Waelod* (**gwaelod** 'bottom') may refer to South Cornelly on lower ground. The area around North and South Cornelly is notable for its 'downs' (OE **dūn**) latinised as *duna* recorded as (land) *Caruelden* c.1160, *Corneldune* 13th cent, *Cornelisdon'* c.1218, (pasture) *Duna de Cornely* late 13th cent.

Corntown, Cortwn   SS 918774
Vale of Glamorgan (Ewenni)
? 'hill shaped like a crown, round hill': OE **corun**, OE **dūn**
(*Alexander de*) *Corendune* c.1135, *Corendon* c.1214, (*William de*) *Corundone* c.1227, *Corndun* 1262, *Corntoun, Coryndown* 1459,

Corn-, Cornedon 1473, *Cornton* 1573, *Cornetowne* 1631, *Cortowne* 1653, (*Ffynnon vair*) *yng Hortwn* c.1700, *Corntown* 1767, *Cortown* 1841, *Cortwn* 1867
Cf. Corringdon, Devon, recorded as *Correndon* 1284, *Corndon* 1288 (PNGlam 49-50). Sps. with *Corn-* suggest that *corun* could also have been associated with *corn* 'horn, point' for a pointed hill, found, for example, in Corn Gafallt (Llanwrthwl), Breconshire. The W n. is Cortwn ['kɔrtʊn] as Gwynedd Pierce states – not Corntwn (as GazWPN, WATU and OS maps) – and this is confirmed in a triban which rhymes the pn. with *Nortwn* (= Norton) (ADG², 24). The sp. c.1700 stands for Ffynnon Fair yng Nghortwn or '(St) Mary's well in Cortwn' (*ffynnon, Mair, Fair, yn, yng*).

Corrwg　　　　　　SN 8701, 8901, SS 8596
Neath Port Talbot (Glyncorrwg)
?'dwarf (r.)': *cor*, suffix *-wg*
Corroc Vaur, ~ Vechan 1503, *Corrug Broke* c.1538, *corrwge vawre, ~ veghan* 1575, *Corrwg R, ~ Vuchan R.* 1729
cor is found also in *corrach* 'dwarf, pygmy', *corrafon, corbwll* 'puddle', *cornant* 'small stream' etc, suggesting that the r. was regarded as small in comparison with the r. Afan which it joins near Cymer. Corrwg Fechan (*bechan*) rises on the hill Twyn Corrwg Fechan (SN 884024) recorded as *Twyn Corwg-fechan* 1877 (*twyn*) and Corrwg otherwise Corrwg Fawr (*mawr*), on Gwaun Blaencorrwg (*gwaun*) above the ho. Blaencorrwg (*blaen*) (SN 888002) recorded as *Blaen-corwg* 1833. Corrwg also occurs in the n. of two hos. Corrwg-fawr (ST 055759) recorded as *Corrwg, ~ Vach, ~ vawr* 1784 and Corrwg-fach in Pendeulwyn.

Cortwn see **Corntown**

Coryton　　　　　　　　　ST 144812
Cardiff (Whitchurch)
'settlement named from Cory': surname *Cory*, E *–ton*
From Coryton House (formerly at ST 142811), 'the old home of Sir James Herbert Cory (1857-1933) of the renowned family of shipowners' and Member of Parliament of Cardiff 1915-23. The ho. is recorded 1900 and the n. was transferred before 1969 to housing between Pendwyallt Road and Northern Avenue, largely constructed in the 1960s.

Cosmeston　　　　　　　ST 182695
Vale of Glamorgan (Lavernock)
'settlement of (man called) Constantine': pers.n. *Constantine*, **tūn**
(fee of Gilbert de Costantin in) *Constantinestun* c.1262, *Costyneston* 1314, *Costenton* 1266, *Costinton* 1307, *Costmeston* 1492, *Cosmeston* 1320, *Cosmaston, or Lavernock Church* 1762, *Coston* c.1503, 1799
Cf. Cosheston, Pembrokeshire (PNPemb 686). Clark (Cartae II, 655) identified him as one of the very early AN settlers in Glamorgan and a Robert de Constantino held a fee of William, earl of Gloucester in 1166 (NGG 52). It has been argued that the pn. contains the W pers.n. *Cystennin* (derived like Constantine from Lat Constantinus) on the basis of forms such as *Costyneston* but this is unlikely because loss of -n- in -nst- is also found in E Christian pers.ns. such as Constance, Constantine, etc. as Gwynedd Pierce shows (PNDPH 43-47). Forms containing *Cosmes-, Cosmaston* probably developed by way of an intermediate and unrecorded *Costymston* followed by loss of unstressed -y- and -t- in -ston (as in the spoken form of Christmas). Some sps. also suggest a by-form *Costinton* which may account for the contracted form *Coston* recorded in several sources from c.1500 down to the nineteenth cent. Constantine was fairly common as a secular n. and occurs in a lost *Constantoneswalle* 1426 and *Constantine Walles* c.1659 (**weall**) recorded by the antiquarian Rice Merrick c.1580 as lying in 'the Manour of Constantyne Waules & Fflemyngstone' on the west bank of the r. Thaw. Cosmeston earlier applied to the area of Cosmeston Medieval Village but was transferred to part of Lower Penarth and particularly to the housing constructed on the site of the South Wales Portland Cement and Lime Works in the 1980s.

Cottrell, Cotrel ST 076747
Vale of Glamorgan (St Nicholas)
'(house of family called) Cottrel(l)': surname *Cottrel(l)*
Tyrecoterel 1374, *Court Cottrell* 1574, *(or) gotrel* late 16th cent, *The Cottrell* 1596, *Y Kottrell* c.1670, *y Cottrell* 1680, *Cotterell* 1697, *Cottrell Court* c.1700
The surname is first recorded in that of Roger Cottrel c.1320 (PNDPH 279-80) and is fairly common in England but very little is known of this particular family. The first cited form probably contains *tir* 'land'. A number of forms have the def.art. *y*, characteristically prefixed to non-W surnames in Glamorgan pns. This might also help explain use of the E def.art. *the* in other sources. There appears to be no evidence to confirm the form *Ty'n y Llwyn* cited by Iolo Morganwg in c.1797.

Court Colman see **Cwrt Colman**

Courtyrala see **Cwrtyrala**

Cowbridge, (Y) Bont-faen SS 994746
Vale of Glamorgan
'cow bridge: OE *cū* 'cow', *brycg* 'bridge'; 'the stone bridge', *y*, *pont*, *maen*
Covbruge c.1262, *Coubrugg* 1289 (1336), *Coubrigg* 1296, *Coubrugge* 1307, *Cowbrygge walled toune* 1479, *Kowbrygge* 1484, *Cowbridge* 1578, *Pont vayn, (bridge) Ponte Vain, alias Cowbridge, of stone* c.1538, *Cowbridge called Pont-vaen, which is to saye Stonbridge* 1559, *y bont faen* c.1566
The reputed meaning is indicated in an onomastic tale of a cow which became trapped by the horns under the arch of an early bridge. The cow had to be killed on the spot and there was a tradition that the bridge had two points resembling a cow's horns. The proper meaning may simply be 'bridge over which cows may be driven' and, by implication, a strong bridge, described in 1706 as 'the Great stonebridge'. The most important bridge in Cowbridge is undoubtedly that where the ancient road or portway running between Cardiff and Swansea crosses over the r. Thaw at the eastern end of the medieval borough adjoining the site of the former East Gate. This must be the 'cow bridge' of Cowbridge and the 'stone bridge' of Y Bont-faen. This assumption would appear to be contradicted in a survey 1630 which mentions 'the port way near a mearstone and a stone bridge commonly called Cowe-bridge north west of the ... Burrough'. The only bridge of any consequence in this area lay near Darren Farm and Darren Hill (SS 988749) over a very small tributary of the Thaw, a short distance west of the former West Gate. This north-western bridge appears to be that recorded by Hopkin-James as *pont-y-fywch* 1701, drawing on notes made in c.1659. He also records land called *saith erw pont y bych* 1724 in Cowbridge (OCow 5, 46, 120) as well as *Pont y Vuch* 1765 and *Pont-y-Fywch* 1791 meaning 'the cow's bridge' (***pont***, *y*, *buwch*). The simplest explanation is that the survey 1630 has misassociated the stone 'cow bridge' at the East Gate with Pont y Fuwch near the West Gate because of their identical meanings. Cowbridge has been identified with the Roman 'Bomium' which occurs in the Antonine Itinerary (3rd cent) as *BOMIO*. The discovery of Roman pottery, tiles and a bathhouse at Cowbridge (RFWM 304) confirms the existence of a Roman settlement here. What is especially intriguing is that two bricks bearing the letters BOV were found near Whitton crossroads on the site of a Roman villa (ST 081713) – roughly six miles south-east of Cowbridge – which has prompted the suggestion that *Bomium* should be read as **Bovium* (PNRB 273). This would be a latinised form of Brit **bou-* 'cow' and **io-* meaning 'cow-place'. It is little wonder that some historians have suggested a semantic link between *Bovium* and *Cowbridge* and assumed that they refer to the same place. This remains unproven, however, and the documentary gap of one thousand years cannot be ignored.

Coychurch, Llangrallo SS 938796
Bridgend
'church in area called Y Coed': pn. *Y Coed*, OE *cirice*; 'church of (St) Crallo': ***llan***, pers.n. *Crallo Thotchirch, Totchirch'* 1200, *Cohytchirche* 1247, *Coychurch'* 1254, *Coytechurche* c.1291, *Koytcherch*

1376, *Langrathle* 1541, *Llangrallo* 1555, *Coychurch alias Langrallo* 1661
'church near a wood' according to Charles (NCPN 133) but hybrid pns. are not very common in Glamorgan and it is better explained as describing its location in an area called Y Coed, 'the wood': *y*, *coed*. There are other *coed* pns. in the immediate area, notably Coety and Pen-coed (q.v.). St Crallo was reputedly a nephew of St Illtud, but nothing certain is known about him (ETG 179-80). Edward Lhuyd c.1700 recorded a well Ffynnon Grallo and a St Crallo's Day (8 August) (Par III, 14). OS maps 1875-1964 show a 'St Crallo's College' on the south side of the ch. but there seems to be no reliable historical evidence for this.

Coytrahen see **Coetra-hen**

Craig-berth-lwyd ST 093960
Rhondda Cynon Taf (Llanfabon)
'cliff near Y Berthlwyd': *craig*, pn. Y Berthlwyd
Craig y Berth Loyd 1702, *Craig y berthlwyd* 1841, *Graig Berthlwyd* 1852, *Craigyberthlwyd* 1872, *Craig-berth-lŵyd* 1884
Y Berthlwyd is 'the grey bush': *y*, *perth*, *llwyd*. The n. is borne by several former hos. called *Berthllwyd* and *Berth llwyd fach* 1813, and *Berthllwyd-fawr*, *Berthllwyd-ganol* and *Berthllwyd-fach* (now Hen Berthlwyd ST 103958) 1833 (*bach¹*, *mawr*, *hen*). Earlier forms include *y berth lwyd* c.1612, *Tir y Berth Loyd* 1662 and *berthloid* 1730. Cf. Pentwyn Berthlŵyd.

Craig-cefn-parc SN 677027
Swansea (Llangyfelach)
'cliff near Cefn-parc': *craig*, pn. Cefn-parc
Graig Cefn y Park 1803, *Graigcefnpark*, *Craig cefn Park* 1852, (area) *Craig-cefn-parc* 1884
Cefn-parc (SN 674036) is 'ridge near an enclosure', *cefn*, *parc*, recorded as *Keven y Park* 1610, *Cefnparc* 1813, *Cefn-parc* 1830, and lies on the eastern edge of a ridge extending southwards from an unnamed hill (SN 676051). There seems to be no evidence for *parc* in its common sense of 'enclosed area

reserved for beasts of the chase' and it more likely held domestic animals.

Craig-gelli-nudd SN 737044
Neath Port Talbot (Cilybebyll)
'cliff at Y Gelli-nudd': *craig*, pn. (**Y**) **Gelli-nudd**
Craig y Gellynudd, *Craig Gellunudd* 1841, *Craig-gelli-nedd* 1878
Gelli-nudd (q.v.) lies immediately to the south.

Craig Trebanos SN 711033
Neath Port Talbot (Llangyfelach)
'cliff near Trebannos': *craig*, pn. **Trebanos**
Craig Trebannoes, *Graig y Trebannoes* 1764, *Graig Trebannos* 1803, *Craigtrebanos* 1872
Adjoining Trebanos (q.v.). The ht. developed in the 19th cent near coal-levels driven into the cliffs.

Craigybwldan SS 604946
Swansea
'rock (*or* cliff) of (man called) ?Bwldan: *craig*, *y*, ?surname ?*Bwldan*
Grayg boulden 1583, *Graige y bwlden* 1650, *Graig ŷ Buldan* c.1718, *Graig y bulden* 1754, *Craig y Bulden* 1764, (ho.) *Craig-y-bwldan* 1832
Gwynedd Pierce (ADG¹ 25; PNGlam 50-51) notes a Nicholas *Bulden* mentioned in the will of Philip Mansel of Llanddewi (Gower) 1553. The W def.art. was sometimes placed before unfamiliar, especially E, surnames, by W-speakers; cf. Coedarhydyglyn (q.v.). The presumed surname is found also in the unlocated pn. recorded as *Attelholdene* 1433, *Alte Buldan* 1583, *Alkt Boulden* 1585, *Alt Buldan* 1590 (with *allt* 'wooded slope'), known to have lain in the lp. of Gower.

Craig y Capel (Margam) see **Crug**

Craig-y-duke SN 711027
Neath Port Talbot (Llangyfelach)
'Duke's crag or cliff': *craig*, *y*, E *duke*
Craig-y-Duke 1878, *Craig y Duke* 1947
The ref. is to the Duke of Beaufort, lord of Gower. The lock on the Swansea Canal here is *Dukes Lock* 1813.

Craigyrhaca see **Graigyrhaca**

Creigiau ST 081814
Cardiff (Pentyrch)
'the rocks': *creigiau*
Creiga 1650, *the Creige* 1670, *Y Criga* 1693, *Y Creige* 1746, *Craigau* 1833
Named from a ho. The wooded hill on the east side of Creigiau is *Craig-ffynnon-dwym* 1833 (*twym* 'warm') which has been identified with a castle *Crege Castelle* (*on the top of an hille*) recorded by the antiquarian John Leland c.1538. Leland states that it was located a quarter of a mile from Castell-y-mynach. There are no traces of a castle there, however, and it may actually have been located at the earthwork (ST 084825) near Graig though this is nearly a mile from Castell-y-mynach. Early sps. suggest that the n. was pronounced 'Creiga' ['krəiga] with the plural ending –a (-au) widely found in south-east Wales. Local pron. is now generally 'Craiga' [kraiga], apparently reflected in the form *Craigau* 1831, but some older inhabitants also describe the village as 'Creega' ['kri:ga], a form probably reflected in the 1693 sp.

Creunant (Crynant) SN 794048
Neath Port Talbot (Cadoxton-juxta-Neath)
?'blood-coloured stream': *crau*[1], *nant*
Croynaunt 1296, *Creynaunt* 1316, *Capel Krenant* 1578, (chps.) *Cappell y crynant yssa, crynant ycha* late 16th cent (1697), *Chappell Krenaunt* 1586, *Croynant* 1662, (chp.) *Creynant* c.1700, *Crynant* 1703
Possibly alluding to the colour of the water, perhaps a stream flowing over sandstone or iron ore deposits (EANC 135-6; VNeath 332). The first el. could also be *crau*[2] meaning a 'pigsty; place of defence, stockade' but it is difficult relating this to the present landscape. Capel y Creunant Uchaf has been identified with Henllan Isaf (SN 801076) (HSeven 27). *Croynant* attempts to represent local pron. ['kroinant].

Croeserw SS 867954
Neath Port Talbot (Llangynwyd)
'acre shaped like a leg': *coes*, *erw*
(land) *Coeserowe* c.1557, *Koeserw* 1697 (late 18th cent), *Cors Erw* 1813, *Croes-erw* 1833, *Coeserw* 1841, *Croeserw* 1875
From some fancied resemblance in shape; *coes* occurs in a similar sense in Penegoes, Montgomeryshire (DPNW 364-5; PNMont 144). Later re-interpreted as 'acre of the cross' (*croes*, *erw*) from some supposed religious cross (PNIG 43). Named from a ho. (SS 865958), the village developed near several small coal-mines from c.1910 and expanded southwards after 1945. The 1813 form appears to favour *cors* 'marsh' but this is misleading.

Croes-pen-maen ST 196986
Caerphilly (Mynyddislwyn, Monmouthshire)
'crossroads near Pen-maen': *croes*, pn. **Pen-maen**
le Crosse pen Maine 1627, *Crose pen maine* 1691, *Croes pen'r maine* 1718, *Croes penmaen* 1813, *Croes Penmaen* 1833
At the junction of the road climbing up from Cwm Ebwy towards Pen-maen (q.v.) with an ancient ridgeway running north from Mynyddislwyn along the watershed between the Ebwy and Sirhywi valleys.

Croes Cwrlwys see **Culverhouse Cross**

Crofty SS 527950
Swansea (Llanrhidian)
'crofts': *crofft* pl. *crofftau* or perhaps 'house with a croft': *crofft*, *tŷ* 'house'
(land at) *Crofte* 1583, 1764, *Craftee* 1625, *Croffle* 1716, *Crofty* 1770, *Croffty* 1813
The pl. -au may have been reduced to –e by local W-speakers and –y by E-speakers. Contrast Crofftau (Llantwit Major) recorded as *Crofta* 1784 which has Gwentian dialect –a for -au.

Cross Inn ST 054828
Rhondda Cynon Taf (Llantrisant)
'(place near the public house called) Cross Inn'
Cross Inn 1851
From the 'Cross Inn' public ho. (ST 054828) at crossroads (E *cross*). Identical in meaning to Cross Inn (SO 027718) at Llancarfan recorded as *Cross-inn* 1786 and *Cross Inn* 1811.

Crosskeys ST 220921
Caerphilly (Risca, Monmouthshire)
'(place near the public house called) Cross Keys'
the Cross Keys 1859, (inn and village) *Cross Keys*, *y Cross Keys*, *(yn) Cross Keys* 1871
This is also likely to be the location of *the Cross Keys Inn* 1822. The n. was first applied to hos. north of the inn, later to the industrial village which developed in the late 19th cent. Osborne and Hobbs (PNWG 24) reject any association with the former ch. dedication to St Peter (with his sign of the crossed keys) at Risca (OPN 169) because the dedication was apparently changed to Michael in 1773 'long before Crosskeys was built'. That argument, however, does not necessarily hold true for the inn. The n. was chosen for the station on the Western Valleys line 1869.

Crug (Craig y Capel) approx. SS 801865
Neath Port Talbot (Margam)
'hillock or mound': ***crug***
Cryke, Cryke Woode 1543, (chp.) *Crickferme* 1554, *Cricke, ~ Trissent* 1562, (wood) *Krycke* c.1670, *Craig y Cappel* 1820, *Grykys myll* (belonging to Margam abbey) 1535
The 1820 spelling confuses it with ***craig*** probably through misassociating the pn. with the wooded slopes known as Graig Fawr north-west of Margam abbey. The actual hillock may be the hill north of the abbey around Crugwyllt-fawr (SS 798870) and Crugwyllt-fach collectively recorded as *Y Grygwallt* 1633, *Grigwalt farm* 1775, *Cricwallt* 1813, *Grigwallt* 1841 (***crug***, *gwallt* 'hair', figuratively for 'leafy mound'?). The chp. mentioned in 1820 may be *Hen Eglwys* ('old church', ***hen***, ***eglwys***) shown on the OS 1:2,500 in 1877 on the slopes of Craig y Capel above the abbey pool (SS 803864). Evans (StTaibach 95) also identifies it Capel Mair *o ben y graig* 1697 (late 18th cent). *Grykys myll* 1535 is thought to have lain on the east side of the pool. Crug lay in Trisaint, the middle ht. of Margam (see Capel Trisaint).

Crugau SN 834036
Neath Port Talbot (Cadoxton-juxta-Neath)
'rocks, cliffs': ***creigiau***
Criga 1666, 1766 *Creyge* 1669, *Creiga* 1820, *Craigau* 1833, *Crugau* 1879
Local dialect approximated to *Criga* (also recorded in 1814) with the typical pl. ending *–a* found in south-east Wales for standard pl. *–iau*, *-au*; reduction of *-ei-* to *-i-* has led to association with *crug(i)au* (sing. ***crug***) 'hillocks, knolls'; local pron. is 'Criga' ['krɪga].

Crwys see **Three Crosses**

Crymlyn[1] (Crumlin) ST 212983
Caerphilly (Mynyddislwyn, Monmouthshire)
'curved pool': ***crwm***, ***llyn***
(land) *rhyw Crymlin*, (~) *Tyr dann rhyw Crymlin* 1630, *Crumlyn's bridge* 1631 (c.1800), *Pont Grymlyn* 1710, *Crumlin bridge* 1626-7, *Crumlin* 1833
Presumably referring to a pool or a bend in the r. Ebwy. Misinterpreted as 'the bend in the valley' or 'the crooked valley' (PNWG 26) on the assumption that it contains ***glyn***. Rhiw (*Rhiw* 1630) is an industrial village named from a fm. (ST 206985) recorded as 1880 on a slope (***rhiw***) above Crymlyn.

Crymlyn[2] SS 704964
Neath Port Talbot (Cadoxton-juxta-Neath/Llansamlet)
'curved pool': ***crwm***, ***llyn***
Crimelyn 1203, (r.) *Cremelyn* c.1168 (1334), (brook) *Cremlin, --e* c.1538, (causey) *Crymlyne* 1587, (brook of) *Crymlin* 1650, *Krymlyn* c.1670, *Crimlin Burrows* 1758, (mess.) *Tir Pont Crimlin* 1762, (ho.) *Crumlin, ~ Morass, ~ Burrows* 1799, (ht.) *Crymlyn* 1832
The earlier n. of the bog (SS 6994) was probably Gwern Fare (< Gwern Fared) recorded as (lands) *Gwern vare* 1650, (moor or fen) *Gwern vawr, or Crymlyn poole, Gwaun F'ar, Gwern vare* 1705, (bog) *Wern Fyr* 1830, meaning 'Mared's alder-tree marsh' (***gwern***, *Mared*) suggesting a link with Capel Fared alias St Margaret's Chapel (SS 704940), in Coed-ffranc (q.v.). Loss of the final consonant -d must be colloquial. Phillips (VNeath 90n. and 201) supposed that forms such as *Gwern vare* stood for *Gwern Fâr* which he interpreted as 'The Moor of Wrath or

Contention' (*bâr* 'anger; affliction' and 'greed') or 'a corruption of "Gwern Fair", the Moor of the Virgin Mary'. Late forms such as *Gwern-Fair* 1771 certainly show association with *Mair* 'Mary' and *Wern Fyr* 1830 with *byr* adj. 'short, small'. The bog occupies the site of a prehistoric lake formed behind the sands of Crymlyn Burrows; see Pwll Cynan.

Crynant see **Creunant**

Culverhouse Cross, **Croes y Cwrlwys**
ST 119747
Cardiff (Michaelston-super-Ely/St Fagans)
'crossroads near Culverhouse': pn. *Culverhouse*, E *cross*; *croes*, *y*
(fm.) *Culverhowse* c.1535, *Culver House* 1636, *Culverhouse* 1654-5, *Curlass* 1729, *Cwrlws* 1764, (fm.) *Cwrlwys* 1776, *Culverhouse Crossroads* 1865 Gwynedd Pierce (PNGlam 51-53) shows that the n. refers to the crossroads recorded as *The Crossway* late 17th cent and *Croesheol* 1762 (*croes*, *heol*) and that Culverhouse/Y Cwrlwys refers to a former fm. (near Llanover Road) meaning 'pigeon-house, dove-cot' with OE *culfre* 'pigeon', E **house**. The W form shows reversal of -l-r- as -r-l- and loss of the unstressed penultimate syllable; *-house* has become *-ws* in the manner of other loans from E, eg. *storws* < *storehouse*, *tanws* < *tanhouse*. Sps. which have *–wys* may represent a development from *-ws*, perhaps on the analogy of **eglwys** often pronounced 'eglws' ['ɛglu:s]. The def.art. *y* is now generally dropped but it is recorded in fns. *bedair Erw'r Cwrlwys, Dwy Erw'r Cwrlwys* 1786 (1814) (*pedair*, *dwy*, *erw*, *y* affixed as `r).

Cwar, (**Y**) (The Quar)   SO 045068
Merthyr Tudful
'the quarry': (*y*), *cwar*¹
The Quar 1921-2
The n. referred between about 1921 and 1958 to a street now called Well Street which OS maps call *Quarry Street* 1875 and 1900, no doubt in ref. to one of several former quarries in the area. Locally 'The Quar' [ðə kwɔ:]. A fn. *Cae yr quar*, for Cae'r Cwar, is recorded elsewhere in the p. in 1763. The substitution of E Qu- for Cw- is also found in Quarr Clydach (SN 6801) near Clydach recorded as *Cwar* 1831, *Chwâr-Clydach* 1879 and *Quarr-Clydach* 1899.

Cwarelau (Quarella)   SS 903808
Bridgend (Coety)
'quarries': *cwarel*¹ pl. *cwarelau*
(tmt.) *Ty y quarella* 1758, (ht.) *Chwarelau* 1833, *Quarrella* 1841, *Quarella* 1885
*cwarel*¹ 'quarry, mine' also occurs in (ho.) *Chwarel y Cae-yr-eglwys* 1833 near Parc Fm (*Parc Garw* 1833). The first ref. stands for Ty'r Cwarelau with *tŷ* 'house' and *y* affixed as `r. Sandstone was quarried here reputedly from the 15th cent (Bridgend 65, 136). The n. survives in Quarella Road.

Cwm¹   SS 802941
Neath Port Talbot (Margam)
'valley': *cwm*
Cwm 1780, 1833
Named from a ho.

Cwm²   ST 056686
Vale of Glamorgan (Pen-marc)
'valley': *cwm*.
(ho.) *Kum* 1785, *Cwm* 1841
The n. of a former t. Cwm Cottages adjoin a small dingle and a stream running from Sufton towards Pen-marc village.

Cwmafan (Cwmavon)   SS 779921
Neath Port Talbot (Michaelston-super-Afan)
'valley of the (r.) Afan': *cwm*, rn. *Afan*
Combe Avon Works 1831, *Cwm Avon Tin Works* 1832, *Cwmavon, Cwmafan* 1851, *Cwm Avon* 1875, *Cwmafan* 1874
See Aberafan. The pn. has effectively replaced Michaelston-super-Afan, Llanfihangel Ynys Afan (q.v.). Avan Vale is an ecclesiastical p. formed in 1901. Avon or Avon Vale Colliery is recorded here in 1871.

Cwmaman   ST 004996
Rhondda Cynon Taf (Aberdare)
'valley of the (r.) Aman': *cwm*, rn. *Aman*

Cwm-Amman Farm (Y Llaethdy), Cwm Amman House 1778, *Cwm Aman* 1836, *Cwm Amman Colliery (Shepherd's Pit)* 1849, *Cwmaman* 1851
See Aberaman. The r. has two main headwaters found in *Blaenaman Fach, ~ Fawr* 1799 (**blaen**) with a confluence at Fforchaman 'fork of the Aman' (**fforch**). Cwmaman Colliery or Shepherd's Pit was named from the owner and there was a Shepherd's Arms here opened 1850 (CVPN 45-46). Cwmaman is also the n. of the valley in which Brynaman and Ammanford, Carmarthenshire, are located, recorded as *Cwmamman* 1757, *Cwmaman* 1743 (1856).

Cwm-bach SO 024019
Rhondda Cynon Taf (Aberdare)
'little valley': *cwm*, *bach¹*
Cwmbach 1788, 1833, *Cwm-bach* 1844
The n. is taken from a fm. in the valley Nant y Groes, 'valley or stream of the cross' (*nant*, *y*, *croes*). The village covers the area of Ynyscynon, 'water-meadow of (r.) Cynon' (**ynys**), Pantygerddinen, 'hollow of the rowan tree' (*pant*, *y*, *cerddinen*) and Werfa 'shaded place' (*gŵer*, *-fa*). Sps. include *ynys Kynon* 1632, *Ynys Cynon* 1831, *Tir Werva* 16th cent and *Wyrfa* 1831. The village developed after the construction of the Aberdare Canal 1812 and sinking of coal-pits 1837-50 (CVPN 46-48; HMorg 59, 203). There is another Cwm-bach (ST 109935) in Llanfabon found as *Cumbach* 1783 adjoining the valley of a stream Nant Cae-dudwg.

Cwm Bargod see **Bargoed**

Cwmbwrla SS 653944
Swansea
'valley of (stream called) Bwrla': *cwm*, rn. *Bwrla*
(brook) *Cwm Burla* 1641, (lands) *Cwm burla* 1650, (bridge at) *Comborla* 1656, *Cwmbwrla* c.1718
The stream is recorded as *Burlakesbroc* c.1170 (c.1300), *Burlakysbrok* 1306, *Burlock's brooke* 1689, *Nant Cwm Bwrla* 1752, *Nant Bwrla* 1764, and in the n. *Borlakesland* 1231-2. The rn. apparently means 'borough stream' (OE **burh, lacu**) (NCPN 164; PNGlam 57-8). Bwrla (now culverted) marked part of the boundary of the old borough of Swansea. Many historic sps. show that OE **brōc** 'brook' was added unnecessarily to the n. possibly through misassociating **lacu** with ME, E **lake** 'pool, lake'. The loss of *-k-* during the 17th cent is a little unexpected and it is possible that Bwrla developed through an intermediate form such as *Burlais* (recorded 1879) and *Bwrlais* under the influence of **glais** 'stream'. A similar rn., recorded as *Bulluchesbruhe* c.1165, marking the boundary of the former borough of Kenfig, now survives only in the n. of a bridge Pont Bwrlac (SS 805835) (*Pont-y-bwrlac* 1833) on the road running from Mawdlam to Margam.

Cwm Cadlan SN 9509
Rhondda Cynon Taf (Penderyn Breconshire)
'valley of (stream called) Cadlan': *cwm*, rn. *Cadlan*
Cwm Cadelan 14th cent, *Cwm Cadlan* 1885
The rn. is *Kadlan* 1448 found also in Blaencadlan recorded as *Blaengatland* 1813, *Blaen-cadlan* 1832 (**blaen**). This may have *cadlan* nf. 'battlefield, battle' used for a 'battling, destructive stream' or *cad¹* nf. 'battle, struggle' and **glan** 'river-bank, edge'. That suggests a r. forcing its course between high banks. Cf. the rn. Cadnant with **nant** (EANC 110). The ho. Esgair-y-gadlan (SN 962101) is *Esgargatland* 1814 (**esgair**).

Cwm-carn ST 219935
Caerphilly (Mynyddislwyn Monmouthshire)
'valley of the (stream) Carn': *cwm*, rn. *Carn*
Cwm Carn 1709, 1801
Nant Carn has **carn** 'a cairn' with ref. presumably to some feature near its source (ST 255980) on Mynydd Maen (see Aber-carn).

Cwmcerdinen SN 636066
Swansea (Llangyfelach)
'valley of the mountain-ash': *cwm*, *cerddinen*
The n. seems to be a recent adoption referring to the area around Blaen-gerdinen (SN 637074) recorded as *Blaen Gardinen* 1764, *Blaen-cerddinen* 1831 (**blaen**) and in the ho.ns.

Gerdinen-fawr, ~ -isaf and ~ -ganol recorded as *Gardinen Yssha* 1764, *Cerddinen-ganol* 1831, *Gerdenen-vaur, ~ -isa, ~ -vaur* 1841, *Gerdinen-isaf, ~ -ganol, ~ -uchaf* 1876 (***mawr, isaf, canol***). Cerdinen refers to a location recorded as *y gerdinen* 1607 and *Gerdinen* 1650.

Cwmcidi Cwmcidi Fm. ST 093679
Vale of Glamorgan (Pen-marc)
'valley of the (r.) Cydi (or Cedi)': ***cwm***, rn. *Cydi Cymmyoucyti* c.1100, (ch.) *Cumkedi* 1254, *Cumkydy* c.1348, *Come Kydy, Kiddey mouth* c.1538, (ch.) *Come kidie* 1586, *Combekydy, -kedy* 1596, (place) *Cwmkiddy* 1747, *Cwm y ci du* 1763, *Cwm Cidy* 1833
The rn. may be identical in meaning to a pers.n. Cydi, Cedi containing *cad* 'battle, army, host' with suffix *–i* (PNDPH 201-2, for a full discussion). Cedi certainly occurs in Caebitra Brook, Montgomeryshire, with ***brōc*** (PNMont 42-43). The first spelling cited above (in 'The Life of St. Cadog') favours *cymau* 'valleys' pl. of ***cwm***, probably referring to the small valleys Cwm Cidi and that of Nant Talwg (see Cwm Talwg). Cadoxton (q.v.) is about two miles to the east.

Cwm Clydach (Neath Port Talbot) see **Clydach**

Cwm Clydach see **Clydach Vale** (Rhondda Cynon Taf)

Cwmcorrwg ST 179997
Caerphilly (Bedwellte Monmouthshire)
'valley of Corrwg': ***cwm***, ?lost rn. or pers.n. *Corrwg*
Cwm careg 1813, *Cwm-corrwg* 1833, *Cwm Corwg* 1841
Sps. are very late but there is an obvious similarity with the rn. found in Glyncorrwg (q.v.), the ho.ns. Corrwg-fach (ST 056757) and Corrwg-fawr at Pendeulwyn, and with Melin-gorrwg (ST 101875) at Upper Boat recorded as *Melin Gorrug* 1708, *Melin gwrwg* 1813, *Melin-gorwg* 1885 (***melin***). Cwmcorrwg seems to have referred to a stretch of the Sirhywi valley since the bridge (***pont***) over the r. is recorded as *Pont Cwm-corrwg* 1879.

Cwm Cothi ST 0998
valley Merthyr Tudful (Gelli-gaer)
'valley of (stream called) Cothi': ***cwm***, rn. *Cothi* (valley) *Cwm Cyddy*, (ho.) *Ty-cyddy* 1833, (ho.) *Carncothy* 1841, (~) *Cwmcothi* 1864, (valley) *Cwm Cothi*, (stream) *Nant Cothi*, (ho.) *Cwmcothi* 1884
The rn. is also recorded in *Nant-cothi* 1864. Sps. are late but comparison may be made with Cwmcothi (Caeo) and r. Cothi, Carmarthenshire, thought to contain the el. *coth-* as in *cothi* 'throw out' and *ysgothi* 'clean, purge, squirt', suitable for a sweeping, fast r. or stream (EANC 134-5).

Cwmdare, Cwmdâr SN 982033
Rhondda Cynon Taf (Aberdare)
'valley of the (r.) Dâr': ***cwm***, rn. *Dâr*
Tir Kwmdaer 1638, *Cwmm daer* c.1612, *Cwmdare* 1680, *Blaen Cwm daer* 1725, *Cwmdare Vechan* 1771, *Cwmdare now Tyr y Bwllva* 1778, *Cwm Dare* 1833, *Cwmdare (Cwm-dâr)* 1840
For the rn. see Aberdare. The industrial settlement developed around a colliery of the Powell Duffryn Steam Coal Co. recorded 1871. There is another Cwmdâr (*Cwmdare* 1845) and stream Nant Dâr above Cwm-parc (SN 9495).

Cwm Darran see **Darran Valley**

Cwmdonkin SS 640932
Swansea
'valley of ?': ***cwm***, ?pers.n. or surname
Cwmdonkin 1850, *Cwm Donkin* 1856, *Cwmdonkin Park* 1879, *Cwmdonkin Terrace* 1899
Cwmdonkin seems to be first recorded in 1850 in connection with the construction of a reservoir. The park, best known for its associations with the poet Dylan Thomas, opened as People's New Park in 1874 on land partly occupied by the reservoir and land bought from the Ffynhonnau estate. Cwmdonkin Terrace, north of Uplands House and on the east side of the park, was built in the 1880s. The first el. is clearly ***cwm*** but the suggestion

(Abertawe 91) that the remainder is a pers.n. or a recorded local surname such as that of a harbourmaster Dunkin in 1823 is now thought doubtful because refs. to the n. have not been found in earlier records. If Cwmdonkin is a late coining, then it could commemorate General Sir Rufane Shaw Donkin (1773-1841) and his wife Lady Anna Maria Donkin (1785-1855), who are known to have visited the notable Vivian family at nearby Singleton in 1838. Donkin had seen service in various parts of the British Empire and was noted in later life for his literary and parliamentary interests. Swansea Council has adopted the form Parc Cwmdoncyn for Cwmdonkin Park. If the pn. is older than the evidence suggests, then it is worth noting similarities in late forms of a ho.n. Tirdwyncyn (SS 635985), about three miles to the north in Llangyfelach p. This is recorded as *Tere Dynchan* 1594, *Tyrdwncyn* 1689, *Tirdunkin* 1700, *Tir-dyncyn* 1830, and *Tir Donkin* 1852. The second el. is also unexplained but we can probably disregard *twyncyn* 'hillock' because this this would not lenite to *dwyncyn* after the first el. *tir* which is a nm.

Cwm-dows ST 202967
Caerphilly (Mynyddislwyn, Monmouthshire)
?'deep valley': *cwm*, ?*dwys*
Cwm Dowse 1813, *Cwm Dows* 1821, *Cwmdws* 1841, *Cwmdows* 1857, *Cwm-dows* 1879
dwys has a variety of meanings including 'intense, earnest' and 'deep, profound' though the last two definitions are generally used for the profundity of meditation and silence. The n. is taken from the valley which stretches northwards towards Oakdale. The village developed in the mid 19th cent near Cwm-dows Colliery.

Cwm-du[1] SS 8790
Bridgend (Llangynwyd)
'dark valley': *cwm*, *du*
Ycome Dee, Le Cum Dde 1541. *Cwmdy Hamlett* 1702, *Cumdy Hamlett* 1723, (ho.) *Comdee* 1799, *Cwmdu* 1813, *Cwm-du* 1833
The valley is that of Nant Cwm-du beginning above Blaen-Cwmdu (SS 877920). Identical in meaning to Cwm-du[2]. There was another Cwm-du (approx. SO 051018) near Aber-fan recorded as *Cwm du* 1783. The forms for 1541 contain the def.arts. Fr *le* and W *y* absent in later forms.

Cwm-du[2] SS 646948
Swansea
'dark, gloomy valley': *cwm*, *du*
Cwm-ddu 1830, 1879, *Cwmdu* 1852
Also recalled in translation in *Blackvale Works (Copper)* 1879 referring to the valley of Bwrla Brook (see Cwmbwrla).

Cwmdulais SN 613034
Swansea (Llandeilo Tal-y-bont/Llangyfelach)
'valley of (r.) Dulais': *cwm*, rn. *Dulais*
Combedeueleys 1306, *Cwm Dylais* 1638, (waste) *Cwm ddylais* 1650, *Cwmdylais* 1782
For the rn. see Pontarddulais. A small group of hos. taking its n. from the valley Cwm Dulais and two fms. Cwmdulais Isaf and Cwmdulais Uchaf recorded as *Cwm Dylaies issa, ~ ucha* 1621, 'lower' and 'upper' (*isaf, uchaf*).

Cwmdŵr SN 684008
Swansea (Llangyfelach)
'water valley': *cwm*, *dŵr*
Cwmdwr 1841, *Cwm-dŵr* 1884
Possibly in the sense of 'watery valley, valley prone to floods'. A late 19th cent industrial village named from a ho. (SN 684008) near an unnamed stream above Bwllfa.

Cwmfelin[1] SS 862899
Bridgend (Llangynwyd)
'valley of the mill': *cwm*, (*y*), *melin*
Cwmfelin 1813, *Cwm Felin* 1833, *Cwm-felin* 1884
H.C. Jones (PNIG 39) records mill ruins.

Cwmfelin[2] SO 094008
Merthyr Tudful (Gelli-gaer)
'valley of the mill': *cwm*, (*y*), *melin*
Cwm y felin 1841, *Cwmyfelin* 1861, *Cwm-felin* 1875
The mill is shown as *Melinbeddllwynog* 1813, *Melin Bedllwynog* 1833, i.e. 'mill at Bedlinog'; see Bedlinog.

Cwmfelin-fach[1]　　　　　SS 675990
Swansea (Llangyfelach)
'valley of the little mill': ***cwm**, (**y**)*, ***melin**, **bach***[1]
Cwm-felin-fâch 1879
The n. was applied in 1876-9 to two rows of hos. near a small stream that enters the r. Tawe. There appears to be no equivalent Melin Fawr or 'great mill'.

Cwmfelin-fach[2]　　　　　ST 184918
Caerphilly (Mynyddislwyn Monmouthshire)
'valley of the little mill': ***cwm**, (**y**), **melin**, **bach***[1]
Cwm felin fach 1813, *Cwm-felin-fach* 1833, *Cwm-felin-fâch* 1885
Referring to the small valley of Nant y Draenog on its north side. *Melin* ('mill') (ST 183915) is recorded on OS maps 1833-1901. The village was largely built for workers at Nine Mile Point Colliery 1900-10 named from a former station (ST 204910) and junction (near Dyffryn, Wattsville) nine miles from Newport on the Tredegar Tramway (later a mineral railway).

Cwm Garw　　　　　SS 9089, 9188
Bridgend (Llangeinwyr)
'valley of (r.) Garw': ***cwm***, rn. *Garw*
Glyn Garu 1261, *Cwm Garw* 1783, 1833
For the rn., see Blaengarw. The valley was earlier Glyn Garw (***glyn***). Garw Valley is the community council.

Cwmgelli　　　　　ST 174982
Caerphilly (Bedwellte Monmouthshire)
'(the) grove valley': ***cwm**, (**y**), **celli**, gelli*
(hos.) *Cwm y Gelly, Cwmgelly* 1841, (valley) *Cwm Gelli*, (wood) *Coed y Gelli* 1879
The village developed near coal-mines above Blackwood and around an episcopal chp. erected in 1841. ***celli*** is also recalled in a ho.n. (Y) Gellidywyll (ST 177982), 'the dark grove', with ***tywyll***.

Cwm-glas　　　　　ST 152914
Caerphilly (Llanfabon)
'green valley': ***cwm**, **glas***[1]
A new n. for a school and a housing estate developed from the mid 1960s as a northern extension of Llanbradach near a ho. Tarrenymwrthwl which is *Taren-y-morthwyl* 1873-7, *Taran-y-mwrthwl* 1922, 'the hammer rock' (***tarren**, **y**, **morthwyl*** nm. 'hammer, mallet'), below the wooded hill Coed y Darren (***coed***). Cwm-glas also has a street Pant Glas, 'green hollow' (***pant***).

Cwm-gors　　　　　SN 704105
Neath Port Talbot (Llan-giwg)
'valley of the marsh': ***cwm**, (**y**), **cors***
Cwm y Gorse 1621, *Cwmgors* 1767, (valley) *Cwm y gors* 1815, *Cwm-y-gors* 1831, (fm.) *Tyddyn-cwm-y-gors* 1883
The n. of the marsh was formerly Cors Feisach recorded as *Korsse vysaghe* 1576-7, *Cors Visagh* 1609 which is obscure. A former colliery village which developed after the opening of a mine c.1880 by the Cwmgorse Colliery Co. Ltd. The unstressed def.art. ***y*** has been lost by syncope.

Cwm-gwrach　　　　　SN 867052
Neath Port Talbot (Llantwit-juxta-Neath)
'valley of (stream called) Gwrach': ***cwm***, rn. *Gwrach*
Cwmgwrach 1841, *Cwm Gwrâch* 1876
For the rn., see Blaen-gwrach. This is also recalled in *Glynwrack* c.1200 (1358). The village developed from the mid 19th cent near the Venallt (Patent Fuel) Works which closed shortly before 1899.

Cwm-gwyn　　　　　SS 631935
Swansea
'white *or* fair valley': ***cwm**, **gwyn***
(ho.) *Cwmgwyn* 1813, *Cwm-gwyn* 1884
From a former ho. (SS 631933) on Glan-mor Road near the dingle and stream leading down to Sketty.

Cwm-hwnt　　　　　SN 915054
Rhondda Cynon Taf (Ystradyfodwg)
'far, yonder valley': ***cwm**, **hwnt***
(village) *Cwmhwnt or Rhygos* 1846, *Cwm Hwnt* 1852, *Cwm-hwnt* 1899
Referring to the upper part of the valley of Nant Gwrelych. The ht. developed around the

Plough Inn and is shown as *Rhyd-groes* on OS maps 1833-91, a n. which properly applies to Rhigos (q.v.).

Cwmllynfell SN 746129
Neath Port Talbot (Llan-giwg)
'valley of the (r.) Llynfell': ***cwm***, rn. *Llynfell Cwmllynfell* 1690, *Cwmllynvell* 1754, *Cwm llynfell* 1792, *Cwmllynfell* 1807
Llynfell (> Twrch SN 754116) is *Lleueneth* 1203, *Llyvenell* 1562, *Llynfell* 1610, (r.) *Llyfnell* 1610, (place) *Rydd ar duorth yn aber llyfnell*, (rivulet) *Llyfnell* 1665. The rn. contains **llyfn** 'even, smooth' and dim. suffix **-ell**. There was an identical rn. in Llansamlet recorded as (r.) *Nant llynvell* 1605. The metathesis (inversion) -fn- > -nf- is also found in the rn. Llynfi. The village developed in the late 19th and early 20th cent near anthracite coal-mines. *Rydd ar duorth* stands for Rhyd ar Dwrch, 'ford on (r.) Twrch' (**rhyd**, **ar**, rn. **Twrch**).

Cwmnantyrodyn ST 185953
Caerphilly (Mynyddislwyn Monmouthshire)
'valley of Nant yr Odyn': ***cwm***, rn. *Nant yr Odyn Cwm-nant yr Odyn* 1752, *Cwm nant odyn* 1813, *Cwm Nantodyn* 1833, *Cwm-nant-yr-odyn* 1886
The rn. is 'stream at the lime-kiln': **nant**, **yr**, **odyn**. The valley is below the junction of two small streams rising on the hill (ST 1994) north of Mynyddislwyn.

Cwmogwr see **Ogmore Vale**

Cwm Ogwr Fach SS 9586
valley Bridgend (Coychurch/Llandyfodwg)
'valley of (r.) Ogwr Fach': ***cwm***, rn. *Ogwr Fach Ogwr-fâch Valley* 1875-7, *Cwm Ogwr Fach* 1900
The rn. is 'little Ogwr' in contrast to the larger r. Ogwr (see Ogmore Vale and Glynogwr) recorded as *ogor vechan* 1553, *Ogwrfach R* 1799, *Ogwr-fach* 1833 (**bach**[1], **bechan**) and in *Blayne oggur vachan* 1521 and *Blaen Ogwr Vychan* 1631 (**blaen**). Earlier sources show that the r. was generally Ogwr *Fechan* with **bechan**, *fechan*, later Ogwr Fach.

Cwm Ogwr Fawr SS 9391
Bridgend (Llandyfodwg/Llangeinwyr)
'valley of (r.) Ogwr Fawr': ***cwm***, rn. *Ogwr Fawr Cwm Ogwr-fawr* 1875
Qualified by **mawr**, *fawr*, 'big, greater' (see Cwm Ogwr Fach).

Cwm-parc SS 949960
Rhondda Cynon Taf (Ystradyfodwg)
'valley containing enclosed land': ***cwm***, **parc** *Cwmpark* 1875, *Cwmparc* 1876, (valley) *Cwm Parc*, (chp.) *Park Chapel* 1877, *Cwm-parc* 1900
parc has several meanings including 'game-park' but there are no obvious traces of one here and the sense is likelier to be 'enclosed land' in contrast to the open land of adjoining hills. The former coal village developed in the mid 19th cent near the Parc Colliery (*Park Colliery* 1875) located near Parc Uchaf (SS 938958) and Parc Isaf recorded as (fms.) *Parc uchaf, ~ newydd* 1813 and *Parc Ucha, Parc-isa* 1833 (**uchaf**, **isaf**). Parc Uchaf is *Park Ycha, otherwise Park Cwm Brechinog* in 1793 probably for Parc Cwmbrycheiniog or Parc Cwmbrecheiniog. The n. is no longer current but is first recorded as *Parke Combregynoke* in 1541 and incorporates the n. of a ht. recorded as *Combreheynok* in 1316 (with similar forms down to c.1405). The first el. is clearly 'valley' (***cwm***) but the second part is less certain. The obvious comparison is with Brycheiniog, anglicised as Brecknock, 'land of (man called) Brychan' (DPNW 45), but it may actually contain **brech**, dim. suffix **–an** and a second suffix **-iog**[2], with the collective sense 'speckled' or 'variegated valley' perhaps describing an area notable for scattered rocks or patchy vegetation.

Cwmpennar SO 042000
Rhondda Cynon Taf (Aberdare)
'valley of (r.) Pennar': ***cwm***, rn. *Pennar* (ho.) *Cwmpennar* 1799, *Cwm-pennar* 1877
For the rn., see Cefnpennar and Mountain Ash / Aberpennar. The village developed in the mid 19th cent near Lower Dyffryn Colliery.

Cwmrhydyceirw   SS 668992
Swansea (Clas, Llangyfelach)
'valley of the deer', ***cwm***, ***rhyd***, ***y***, ***ceirw***
(brook) *Cwm rhyd y Carw* 1764, *Cwmrhydycwrw* 1832, *Cwmrhidycwrw* 1841, *Cwm-rhyd-y-cwrw* 1877, *Cwmrhydyceirw* 1886, *Cwm-rhyd-y-ceirw* 1900
Most historic forms suggest that this was earlier Cwmrhydycwrw or 'valley of the beer ford' and that the final el. was *cwrw* nm. 'beer, ale'. This has prompted the suggestion that it was a ford over which beer was carried or where water was taken for brewing (Elfen 43) but it could as easily be a fanciful description of the colour of foaming, muddied water passing over the shallows as Deric John argues (John SPN). The apparent change of *cwrw* to ***ceirw***, generally attributed to the sensitivities of the temperance movement, is plainly of long standing as the 1764 form (*carw*) shows.

Cwm Sychbant   SS 842902
Bridgend (Llangynwyd)
'valley near Sychbant': ***cwm***, ho.n. *Sychbant*
Cwm Sychbant 1876
The ho. is recorded as *Ysych Bant* 1541, *Sychpant* 1723, *Sych-pant* 1833, *Sychbant* 1876, meaning 'dry hollow': ***sych***[1], ***pant***, *bant*.

Cwmsyfiog   SO 152023
Caerphilly (Bedwellte Monmouthshire)
'valley of (stream called) Syfiog': ***cwm*** and rn. *Syfiog*
Cwm Syfiwg Lands 1814, *Cwmsyfiwc* 1858, *Cwmsyfiog* 1859, *Cwm-syfiog* 1885
The r. is *Nante seveeocke* 1588 and rises at Mountain Lodge (SO 142055) - probably the location of (mess.) *Tyre Blayne Shyviewegha* 1585 and *Blaine Sevewge issha* 1594 (***tir***, ***blaen***, ***uchaf***, ***isaf***). The rn. may have an unrecorded adj. *syfiog*, containing the el. *syfi* 'strawberries' and suffix *-iog*[2], meaning '(r. with water) resembling juice', i.e. a r. with dense, coloured water as *syfi* contains the Brit el. *seu- 'juice', found also in other words such as *sudd* 'juice' and *sugno* 'to suck'. The alternative explanation is that Syfiog means 'area characterised by (wild) strawberries',

perhaps a fanciful description of a fertile valley, and that this was transferred to the r. A *Nant Siviwr* is also recorded in this p. in 1694 but has not been precisely located. *Cwm Sibwc* (the valley), *Aber y Sibwc* (ho.n.) and *Cwm-y-Sibwc* (the village) in 1833 (in what is now New Tredegar) are unmatched and are likely to be false.

Cwm Taf see **Taff Vale**

Cwm Talwg   ST 105684
Vale of Glamorgan (Barry/Merthyr Dyfan/Porthceri)
'valley of Talwg': ***cwm***, false rn. *Talwg*
The stream Nant Talwg is recorded in 1879 but this derives from a misinterpretation of Rhytalwg, Rhytalog, a regular colloquial development (–t- < –d + h-) from Rhydhalog meaning a 'muddy ford' (***rhyd***, *halog*). Cf. Rhytalog, Flintshire (DPNW 423, PNF 172). Local examples include Rhydhalog (ST 023795) near Brynsadler. The ford (SS 099986) is recorded in (field) *Rhyd Hay Lock* early 19th cent., *Redhollocke Lane or Redhallock Waye* 1662, *Reedhallock Lane* 1762, *Retalog Lane* 1778-9 (PNGlam 56-57; PNDPH 140-1). The stream is properly Cidi recalled in Cwmcidi (q.v.). Cwm Talwg was adopted as the n. of a housing estate developed from the late 1960s.

Cwm Tawe see **Swansea Valley**

Cwm-twrch Uchaf   SN 760109
Neath Port Talbot (Llan-giwg)
'upper Cwm-twrch': pn. Cwm-twrch, ***uchaf***
Tyr Kum Twrch 1697, (valley) *Cwm Twrch* 1831, *Cwmtwrch* 1841, *Cwm-twrch* 1883, *Lower Cwm-twrch* 1901, *Upper ~* , *Lower Cwm-twrch* 1906, *Cwm-twrch Uchaf*, *~ Isaf* 1972
In contrast to Cwm-twrch Isaf (SN 766102) with ***isaf*** 'lower', in Breconshire (now Powys). Both villages are located in Cwm Twrch, 'valley of (r.) Twrch' with ***cwm*** and rn. recorded as *Turch* c.1170, *Tourthe* 1203, *Twrch* 1516, *Turch or Torch* 1586 meaning a 'boar', probably an allusion to its perceived aggressive, erratic nature. Also recalled in *Abertwrch* 1573 (***aber***)

and (ho.) *Craig-twrch* 1831 (**craig**). Twrch is the n. of a tributary of the r. Neath/Nedd recalled in Blaen-twrch (SN 815003) recorded as (tmt.) *Blane Twrch* 1719, (ho.) *Blaen-twrch* 1833 (**blaen**).

Cwm-y-glo (Cwm Glo)　　　　　　SO 0305
Merthyr Tudful
'the coal valley': ***cwm***, (***y***), ***glo***
Tir Cwmyglo 1540, *Cwmyglo* 1727, *Cwm y Glô* 1747, *Cwm y Gloe*, *Cwm y Glo Issa*, *~ Ucha* 1757
Cwm-y-glo referred to a scattered industrial settlement, with numerous small coal diggings and drifts; little remains but the n. survives in the n. of the valley Cwm Glo and Cwmglo Road, Heolgerrig. An identical n. Cwm-y-glo (SS 592943) at Dunvant is recorded as *Cwm y Glo* 1760, *Cwm-y-glo* 1830, *Cwm-glo* 1898.

Cwm yr Argoed　　　　　　SN 8703
Neath Port Talbot (Cadoxton-juxta-Neath/Glyncorrwg)
'valley ~, stream at Yr Argoed': ***cwm***, pn.
(valley) *Cwm yr Argoed*, (stream) *nant yr Argoed* 1877
The ho. Argoed (SN 869044) is recorded as *Yr-argoed* 1833, *Argoed* 1877 meaning 'the woodland, the forest': ***yr***, ***argoed***, and lies in the middle of the modern Rheola Forest but there was extensive woodland here before afforestation.

Cwrt Colman (Court Colman) SS 8881, 8882
Bridgend (Newcastle)
'monastic grange of (man called) Colman', ***cwrt¹***, pers.n. *Colman*
Court Colman 1336, (grange) *Court Colman* 1535, *Courte Colman* 1548, *Courtecollman* 1590/1, *Courtecolman* 1719, *Cwrt Coleman* 1833
The pers.n. derives from Ir *Colmán*, the n. of several saints in Ireland one of whom is recorded as a saint in Capel Colman and Llangolman, Pembrokeshire (PNPemb 83, 352-3). Colman here may be a secular person since there seems to be no evidence of a ch. or chp., simply a grange belonging to Margam abbey. Colman and related pers.ns. such as Calum can be traced back to derivatives of Lat *columba* 'a dove'. The perceived similarity must explain the false form *Gwrt Colomen* (HTonyrefail 58) with *colomen* nf. 'pigeon, dove'.

Cwrt-isaf see **Meles**

Cwrt-sart　　　　　　SS 743954
Neath Port Talbot (Briton Ferry)
'monastic grange on the assart': ***cwrt¹***, ***sart***
Sarc c.1291, *Curt sart*, *Co(u)rt Sart* 1535, *Court Sarte* 1587, *Courtsart Houses* 1794, *Cwrt-sarth* 1830
sart is probably a local W loan from from E *assart* 'cleared land'. Nicholl (NGG 108) identified the assart with land given in exchange by Neath abbey to Gilbert de Clare, lord of Glamorgan, in 1289 (*partem terrarum suarum de Assarto*). This is probably also (land of late Gilbert de Clare) called *Lassarte* known to have been in the Neath area 1296 with Fr *la* 'the'.

Cwrtybetws　　　　　　SS 723956
Neath Port Talbot (Cadoxton-juxta-Neath)
'the chapel grange': ***cwrt¹***, ***y***, ***betws¹***
Curtbedhowse 1535, *Courtte Pethouse*, *Court bethouse* 1566, *cappell court y bettus*, *Cwrt y Bettws* late 16th cent, *Cwrtybettws* 1813
A former grange of Neath abbey surviving as an oratory till the late 16th cent or later and a chapel-of-ease in the p. of Cadoxton-juxta-Neath (Coed-ffranc). Phillips (VNeath 66) suggests this was an early Norman bede-house but pn. evidence is far too late to warrant such speculation.

Cwrtycarnau　　　　　　SN 578005
Swansea (Llandeilo Tal-y-bont)
'grange at the cairns': ***cwrt¹***, ***y***, ***carn*** pl. ***carnau***
(chp. of) *Sancti Michaelis de Carnu* early 12th cent (1334), *Co(u)rte Carney*, *Co(u)rt Carny* 1535, *Carney grange* 1576, *Capel Courty Carny* 1729, *Court Carne* 1730, *Cwrtcarne* 1813, *Cwrt-y-carne*, *Capel-y-cwrt* 1832
A grange granted to Neath abbey by Henry de Vilers before 1184 - also called *Loghor* (NGG 116) from its location by the r. Llwchwr – near the site of the chp. (***capel***) described by Rice Merrick c.1580 as 'an old chapel, lately decayed, but now repaired'. There was an

identical ho.n. (ST 078813), in Pen-tyrch recorded as *Cwrt y Carna* 1825, *Cwrtycarnau* 1841 and *Cwrt-y-carnau* 1877-1964 which may be identified with *Court Carne Mawr* 1683.

Cwrtydefaid SS 801852
Neath Port Talbot (Margam)
'the sheep's grange': **cwrt**¹, **y**, **defaid**
Courte y Devaied 1633, *Court y Deved* 1729, *Court y Defaid farm* 1747, *Cwrtydefaid* 1813
A former grange of Margam abbey. This is also likely to be *Sheepes Courte* 1633. The apparent absence of earlier sps. is unexplained and the matter has been complicated by refs. to other 'sheep's granges' belonging to the abbey. Llangewydd Grange (SS 869814) in particular, at Laleston, is recorded as *Shepesgrange* 1543, *Sheppes grainge or ferme baghe* 1562, *Langewith, alias Farme bichan, alias Shepes grange* 1623, *Court y Devyd* 1702, and *Llangewydd Cwrt* 1813 – a n. transferred to Llangewydd Court Farm (SS 871814). ME *grange* in the specific sense 'farm' is confirmed by the sps. for 1562 and 1623, 'little farm' (*fferm*, **bach**¹, **bychan**).

Cwrt-y-fil ST 180703
Vale of Glamorgan (Penarth)
?'court (*or* grange) at the field': **cwrt**¹, **y**, ?**field** E
Courtyvill, *Court-y-Vil* c.1700, *Court y Vil* 1766, *Courtfield* 1780, *Court a Vele* 1792, *Cwrtyfel* 1811, *Cwrt-y-fil* 1833, *Court y veil* 1841
Fully discussed by Gwynedd Pierce (PNDPH 162-4; PNGlam 58-60). Its history is obscure but it may be the site of *Canon Courte* 1540-1, *Cannon Court* 1663. E **field** is sometimes found in Glamorgan as *vill(e)* with voicing of f as v, a characteristic of the speech of Somerset and north Devon, and evidence of a link in dialect. Remains of walls in a private garden may have been part of a grange belonging to St Augustine's abbey, Bristol.

Cwrtyrala (Courtyrala) ST 142734
Vale of Glamorgan (Michaelston-le-Pit)
'Raleigh's grange': **cwrt**¹, surname *Raleigh*
Raleyscort 1429, *Raylis courte* 1480, *Court y Rayle* c.1659, *Court Rayle* c.1670, *Court Raley* 1669, *Court y Lara* 1763, *Court yr Ala* 1765, *Cwrt yr ala* 1811, *Court-yr-alla ... corrupted from Court-yr-raleigh, it having been long a seat of the Raleighs of Nettlecombe* 1860
The surname, variant Rawley, may be taken from Raleigh, Devon. The Glamorgan branch of the family inherited Wrinston, Michaelston-le-Pit and Llantwit Raleigh by marriage of Simon de Ralegh (of Nettlescombe, Somerset, died c.1284) with Joanna de Reigny after 1262 (PNDPH 153-4; PNGlam 60-61). A certain Joan de Ralegh held a mess. and water corn mill in Michaelston in 1307 with an unidentified holding *Rallesclyf* 1307 (E **cliff**). The modern form with the def.art. **yr** may be a product of misdivision of *Raleigh* (*yr Ala*) and -*ala* influenced by W *alai* 'alley, passage'. Forms such as *Court yr Elerch* 1765 suggest association with *elyrch* 'swans'. Iolo Morganwg uses the form *Court yr Alaw* 1796, misassociating it with *alaw*¹ 'lily, water lily' or *alaw*² 'music, air, tune'. Sps. with *Lara* in the diary of William Thomas (DWT) may stand for a colloquial inversion of *Rala*.

Cyfarthfa Cyfarthfa Castle SO 041074
Merthyr Tudful
'place of barking': **cyfarth**¹, **ma**, **-fa**
Cyfartha Iron Works 1799, *Cyfarthfa Park*, ~ *Castle* 1833
Wilkins in 1867 thought it appropriate 'as the woody nature of the place made it a safe resort for fitchoes [polecats] and the like' and as a place of sport (HMerth 147). Cyfarthfa also has the extended sense of 'place where an animal might stand when chased across its land and challenges the dogs barking around it' or 'a gathering place for hounds' and even 'battleground' (ADG², 29). The same word appears in *torri cyfarth* 'retreat and flee' and *rhoddi cyfarth* 'stand and fight'. Identical pns. occurs in Modrydd in Breconshire, Cwmllyfnant in Cardiganshire, and Llanelltyd, Merionethshire. Cyfarthfa is best known for the ironworks established in 1765 which came into the possession of Richard Crawshay 1794 and for the castle built by William Crawshay 1824-5, later a school and a museum.

Cymdda SS 904831
Bridgend (St Brides Minor)
'common land': *cymdda*
Cymdda 1871
A road and area of housing deriving their n. from a ho. (SS 902830) which adjoined former pasture, some unenclosed, recalled in *Ty'n y Cimdda* and *Pen y Cimdda* 1841. Llantrisant Common is *y Cymdda* 1866. See Cimla.

Cymer[1] (Cymer Afan) SS 860961
Neath Port Talbot (Glyncorrwg)
'(the) confluence': (*y*), *cymer*[1]
the Cymmer 1637, (ho.) *Cymmerglyncorrwg* 1799, *-corwg* 1813, *Cymmer* 1832, *Cymmar glyn Corwg* 1849, *y Cymer* 1872, *y Cymar* 1892
The confluence of Corrwg and Afan, and distinguished in some sources by its location in Glyncorrwg. The sps. with *–ar* represent local dialect. Note also Cymer Dwy Ogwr (SS 934868), in Llangeinwyr, recorded as *Kymmer doy ogor* 1557, *Cummerdwy-Ôgwr* 1767, *Cymar Dwy Ogwr* 1785 from its location at the junction of the two (*dwy*) rivers Ogwr Fawr and Ogwr Fach.

Cymer[2] ST 025908
Rhondda Cynon Taf (Llantrisant/Llanwynno)
'(the) confluence': (*y*), *cymer*[1]
Tyrecomer 1541, *Tyr y kymer* 1580, *Kymer dwy rhoddne* c.1624, *Cymmer* 1738/9, *the Cymmer* 1789, *Cymmer Rhondda* 1833, *y Cymar* 1867
Referring to the confluence of Rhondda Fawr and Rhondda Fechan (SO 024915), hence the forms for c.1624 and 1787 standing for Cymer Dwy Rhondda with *dwy* 'two' referring to the rs. *Cymar* 1867 represents local pron. The bridge (*pont*) is *Pont Kemmer* c.1538, *P[ont] y Cumar* c.1700, and *Ponty Cymmar* 1799; cf. Pontycymer (q.v.). The settlement developed a little downstream on the south side of the former Cymmer Colliery around an Independent chp. recorded as *meeting house of Cymmer* and *Cwrdd-y-cymmer* 1833 (*cwrdd* nm. 'a meeting').

Cymin, Y see **Kymin, The**

Cyncoed ST 191801
Cardiff (Llanedern)
'ridge covered with trees': *cefn*, *coed*
Kevencoyte 1450, *Kenkoed*, *Kencoed* 1650, *Kevan-coyd* 1702, *Kevencoyd* 1703, *King coed* 1778, *Kevencoed Issa* 1782, (hos.) *Cefn-coed*, *~ Uchaf*, *~ -fach* 1833
The n. survived in that of several fms. (distinguished as **uchaf**, **isaf**, **bach**[1], **mawr**) and in Heol y Cyncoed (**heol**) alias Cyncoed Lane, now Cyncoed Road, recorded as *Heol-y-King-Coed* 1702, *Hewl y Cencôd* 1726, *Keven Koyd Lane* 1730. Identical in meaning to Kingcoed (SO 4305) at Llandenni, Monmouthshire (PNGwent 84). The contraction *Cen-* occurs in some sps. of Cefn-coed, at Llantrisant, (*Ken coyde* 1563, *Keven coyd* 1576), Cefncoed, at Cilybebyll, (*Kencoed* 1729), Cenfaes, at Cadoxton-juxta-Neath, (*Keven Vase* 1769, *Cenfaes* 1841) (**maes**) and Gendros (q.v.).

Cynffig see **Kenfig**

Cynon
Rhondda Cynon Taf (Aberdare, Llanwynno)
rn.
Cavan (= *Canan*) 1307, *Kenon* c.1538, *Kenan* 1541, *Cunno(n)* 1612, *Cynon* 1691
Earlier *Cynan* found also as a pers.n. The form *Cynon* occurs from the 16th cent with 'rounding' of the second vowel, a characteristic occasionally found in late forms of Nant Cynon, a tributary of the r. Afan (EANC 62). Cwmcynon is recorded in *Cwmcynon forge* 17th cent and *Cwm Cynon* 1801 (**cwm**), Pontcynon (**pont**), a ht. Glyncynon (in Llanwynno) which is *Glin Kynon* c.1670 (**glyn**), and *fforrest Glyn-Cynon* c.1670 (**fforest**). Ynyscynon (SO 0102), takes its n. from a ho. *ynys Kynon* 1632, *Tir Ynys Cynon* 1666 (**ynys**). Nant Cynon is found also in Blaencynon (not current) recorded as *Bleinkenan*, *Blaikinen* late 12th

cent, *Blankunen* early 13th cent, *Blaen Kynan* 1633 (**blaen**).

Cynonville SS 825952
Neath Port Talbot (Llangynwyd)
'settlement by (r.) Cynon': rn. **Cynon**, E *ville*
Cynonafan 1918, 1940-1, *Cynonville* 1962
ville has displaced the rn. Afan (q.v.). The first hos. were built from c.1913 by the former Cynon Colliery Co near the r. Afan as part of an intended – but uncompleted – garden village. The change of n. to Cynonville took place after 1947. The colliery takes its n. from Nant Cynon (EANC 62) and cf. r. Cynon (in Aberdare and Llanwynno).

Cyntwell ST 124753
Cardiff (Caerau)
'sanctuary': **seintwar** variant *seintwal*
the Sintwar (or Sanctuary) 1749, *the Sanctuary in Cayra* 1766, *Saint well* 1833, *Cintwell* 1841, 1866, *Saintwell* 1879-80, 1900-1
The colloquial form has *seintwal* with the variation -r, -l also found in *cornel* from E *corner*, etc. (ADG², 31). Taken from a ho. on Cowbridge Road and transferred to a row of hos. near Caerau Arms (later the Culverhouse) public ho. The anglicised spelling with *Cynt-* [sɪnt] was adopted before 1919 and *-well* is likely to be a product of association with E **well**. Identical in meaning to Saintwalls (SS 542951), at Llanrhidian, which is *Seintwar* 1641, *St Wall* 1764, *Saint Wall* 1790, and *Saintwalls* 1879.

Danescourt to Dynfant

Dinas, Rhondda. The landlord of the Gwaunadda Arms and a few of his regulars c.1920.

Ddorop see **Drope**

Ddraenen see **Thornhill**

Danescourt ST 139790
Cardiff (Radur)
A housing estate developed from the 1980s around St John's p. ch. and Danescourt Way. Its n. is a part-compound of the modern housename *Danes*brook 1926 and Radyr *Court* Farm: E *brook*, Radur (q.v.), E *court*.

Dan-y-graig SS 675933
Swansea (St Thomas Swansea/Llansamlet)
'(place) under the cliff': *tan¹*, *dan*, def.art *y*, *craig* Danygraig 1626, Dan y graig 1686, Tanygraig 1813, (fm.) *Dan-y-graig-fawr*, ~ *-fach* 1879
On slopes of Kilvey Hill, ultimately named from hos. Dan-y-graig Fawr, ~ Fach, ~ Genol (*mawr*, *bach¹*, *canol*). Tan-y-graig 1813 refers to Dan-y-graig Fach. The n. contrasts with Pen-y-graig recorded as *Pen-y-graig-isaf* 1832 (SS 682938) (*isaf*) and *Pen-y-graig-uchaf* (*uchaf*) (SS 676938) which was higher up the hill near

Pentre-graig 1830, *Pentre'r-graig* 1884 (**pentref**, *y* affixed as `*r*). Other examples of Dan-y-graig are recorded at Llangyfelach, Llanwynno, Margam and Rhisga.

Dare Valley see **Cwmdare**

Darran Valley, **Cwm Darran** SO 1103, 1202
Caerphilly
'valley of (Cwm) Darran': pn., **valley**, **cwm**
Darran Valley C(ommunity) 1987
Cwm Darran is recalled in the woodland Parc Cwm Darran (SO 118034) taken from the former Darren Colliery (*Darran Pit* 1878) just below Deri (q.v.). The colliery itself draws its n. from the rocks Tarren yr Ysgwydd-gwyn (SO 12913) meaning 'rock near Yr Ysgwydd-gwyn' (**tarren** dialect *tarran*). Ysgwydd-gwyn is *Uskoydgwyn* 1476, *Ysgwythgwyn* 1639, *Ysgwyddgwyn* 1700, meaning 'white shoulder': *ysgwydd* nm. 'shoulder' used figuratively for a projecting hill and **gwyn**.

Darren-las, Y (Darranlas)　　　　ST 046988
Rhondda Cynon Taf (Llanwynno)
'the blue or green rocky hill': *y*, **tarren**, **glas**[1], *las*
Darren Laes 1703, *Daren las* 1782, *Tarran las* 1804, *Tarenlas* 1814, *Darrenlas* 1851
glas[1] is employed in its common sense 'green, verdant' or may refer to bluebells (CVPN 51). The area developed from the late 19th cent along Llanwonno Road and around Conybeare Street below Craig Darren-las. The dialect form *tarran* is common in Glamorgan and Monmouthshire. *Laes* 1703 probably reflects local dialect; cf. Aberdare.

Ddawan, Thaw see **Aberthaw, Aberddawan**

Ddorop see **Drope**

Ddraenen see **Thornhill**

Denscombe　　　　ST 152867
Caerphilly (Eglwysilan)
Denscombe 1970
An area of housing around Claude Road built in the late 1960s largely on former allotment gardens. The origin of the n. is uncertain. A Mr Denscombe served as secretary of the local Prisoners of War Committee in 1916.

Deri　　　　SO 127017
Caerphilly (Gelli-gaer)
'(the) oak-trees': (*y*), **deri**
y Deri 1872, *Deri* 1875
Probably *Derie* 1744. Deri seems to have referred earlier to the area on the east side of the Rhymney Railway around the Horse & Greyhound Inn and post office, extending northwards to Tabernacle Particular Baptist chp. (SO 128018). The pn. is taken directly from a former fm. Deri Newydd recorded as *Teere y dery newith* 1680, *Derry-newydd* 1833, and *Y Derinewydd* 1872 (**newydd**). This fm. is reputed to have once been called Ysgwydd-gwyn, a n. which certainly applied to a ht. of Gelligaer and to two hos. Ysgwydd-gwyn Isaf (SO 125009) and Ysgwydd-gwyn Uchaf (**isaf**, **uchaf**). Ysgwydd-gwyn also referred to that part of Deri west of the railway, giving its n. to the Calvinistic Methodist chp. and the National School known as *Cwm Ysgwydd-gwyn School* in 1878. The village owed its growth to the former Deri Colliery (SO 127024). Deri is a common pn. el. found, for example at Whitchurch (*Dery* 1674, *the Derry* 1680, *Deri* 1811) and in Llan-giwg (*Tyr y Ddery* 1754, *Y Dderry* 1764).

Derwen　　　　SS 912823
Bridgend (Coety)
'oak-tree': **derwen**
Derwan 1871, (ho.) *Derwen* 1877
Possibly *Derwaun uchaf* 1841 with **uchaf** 'upper' to distinguish it from (Y) Dderwen Gopa (SS 930834) recorded as *Derwen Goppa* 1752, *Derwen Coppa* 1813, *Derwen Gopa* 1833, qualified by *copa*, *cop*[1] nmf. 'top, summit'. The precise sense is unclear. Derwen was a ho.n. extended to cover a small group of semi-agricultural dwellings in the 19th cent on the west side of the former Glamorgan County Asylum (now a prison) and later to a small housing estate.

Dimlands SS 955685
Vale of Glamorgan (Llantwit Major)
'lands belonging to (man called) Deme':?pers.n. *Deme*, *land*
(field) *Demelonde* 1495, *the Dymland* 1623, *The Dimlands* 1685, *Dimlands* 1813
The occurrence of a John *Deme* in Llantwit Major in 1495 seems to rule out an alternative meaning of 'tithe lands': ?**dime*, *deme* ME 'tenth, tithe', *land* OE.

Dinas ST 010917
Rhondda Cynon Taf (Llantrisant)
'fortress, stronghold': ***dinas***
(hill) *Dynas* c.1670, 1679, *the Ddinas* 1771, *Dinas Ucha, ~ Icha* 1831, (ho.) *Dinas* 1833, (tmt.) *Kraige y dynas* 1589, (mess.) *craig y dinas* 1621
Taken from Mynydd Dinas probably referring to the fortress-like appearance of the hill, sharply defined by cliffs and rocky slopes, recorded as *Dinas Rocks* 1811 and *Mynydd Dinas* 1833. Dinas developed in the 19th cent near Dinas Middle Pit (ST 007918) and Dinas-isaf Pit (ST 010913) in Graig-ddu but the n. was used down to the end of the cent for a scatter of industrial dwellings and settlements extending from what is now regarded as part of Pen-y-graig (q.v.) to Dinas proper. The westerly area developed after the entrepreneur Walter Coffin sank his first pit c.1812 on lands of Dinas Uchaf fm. (approx. ST 002914) which is probably *Y Dinas ycha* alias *Y Dinas mwya* 1810 (***uchaf***, ***mwyaf*** adj. 'biggest, greatest') near Ysgol yr Eos Primary School, Pen-y-graig.

Dinas-isaf see **Edmondstown**

Dinas Powys ST 153713
Vale of Glamorgan (St Andrews Major)
'fortress in Powys': ***dinas***, pn. *Powys*
Dinaspowis c.1195, *Denaspoys* 12th cent, *Dinaspois* 1243 (13th cent), *Dinas Powis* c.1262, *Dynaspowis* 1307, *Denyspowys* c.1376, *Dynaspowes* 1437, *Dinas Powys* 1606, *Dinas-powis* 1833, (ch. of) *St. Andrew, Dynaspowys* 1376
The n. of a former hundred, castle and manor taken ultimately from a fortified settlement (ST 149721) dating from the Iron Age down to the medieval period. The qualifier Powys may be identical in meaning to that of the ancient kingdom of Powys, derived from Lat *pagēnses* 'country people', but the precise significance here is not settled (PNDPH 216-221; WB 14 and 389). A number of antiquarian sources beginning with Rice Merrick late 16th cent derive Dinas from *Denis*, a reputed daughter of Bleddyn ap Cynfyn, prince of Powys. The explanation is fanciful but must be based on sps. with *Den(n)ys-/Denis-*, which may be products of E influence substituting a short vowel [ɪ, ɛ] for [iː].

Dolau ST 001827
Rhondda Cynon Taf (Llanharan)
'water-meadows': ***dolau***
Dolau 1900
Note also *the little Dolee* 1653 in the same p. The hos. developed south of Llanharan along the Bridgend road between the stream Ewenni Fach and the northern edge of Bryn-y-cae-fach (see Bryn-y-cae above) near Bryn-y-cae otherwise Llanharan Colliery (closed 1922).

Dowlais SO 065077
Merthyr Tudful
'dark stream': ***duf***, ***glais***
(place) *Dowlass* 1665, *Dowlais Furnace* 1767, *Dowlesh* 1824, *Dowlais, ~ Iron Works* 1833, *Dowlais, ~ Iron Works* 1891
Named from a small stream running south through Dowlais and 'dark' either because it runs over coal measures or because parts of it were shaded. The rn. contains the form ***duf*** rather than the more common ***du*** (see Dulais), and is found in various forms such as Diflas, Diwlas in other parts of Wales as well as Dowlais. Glamorgan also has (1) Dowlais (Llanedern) recorded as *Dowlais* 1650, *Nant Dulas* 1833 (2) Dowlais, a tributary of Nant Myddlyn (ST 073836, Llantwit Fardre) recorded as (r.) *Dyveleis* 1561, in (*syddyn*) *dyffryn dowles* c.1612, (r.) *Dowlis* c.1700, and (brook) *Dowlays* 1713. The village developed around the Dowlais ironworks near a common or waste called *Tyle Dowlass*, (place) *Tyle Dowlais* 1748 (***tyle***).

PLACE-NAMES OF GLAMORGAN

Dowlais Top SO 073080
Merthyr Tudful
'(place) above Dowlais': E *top*, pn. **Dowlais**
Top of Dowlais 1852, *Dowlais Top* 1882
Named from its elevated position above Dowlais. Cf. *Top of Twynyrodyn* 1852 for part of Twynyrodyn (q.v.).

Downs ST 107745
Vale of Glamorgan (St Georges/St Nicholas)
'hills, downs': E *down* pl. *downs*
Downs 1880
Probably named from St Lythan's Downs which extend southwards, recorded as *St. Lythans Down* 1811-14, 1833; cf. Downs (ST 166696), in St Andrews Major, found as *the Downe* 1576, *the Downs* 1648, and *Downs* 1763, also *the Downes* (in Llanblethian) 1659.

Draethen ST 220873
Caerphilly (Rhyd-gwern, Machen)
'(the small) sand-bank': (*y*), *traethen*
(grist mill) *Velyn Bagh* otherwise *Drathen* 1541, *Draythen* 1648, *Melyn y Draythen* 1659, *Draythan Farm* 1783, *Traethen* 1811, *Draythen Gate House* 1845, *Draethen* 1859, 1875
This el. generally refers to a marine location but the related word *traeth*[1] 'beach, shore' occurs locally in a pn. recorded as *trayth maghan* 1467 and *Trayth'* 1506, and in fns. *the Great Trathe* and *the Litle Trathe* 1621 which were part of lands belonging to the ho. Plas Machen (ST 235876) just across the r. Rhymni from Draethen. Clearly both *traeth*[1] and *traethen* could be used for inland sandbanks and mudbanks around rivers. The first ref. probably refers to Melin y Draethen 1659 and may be the 'little mill' (*melin, bach*[1]) recorded in 1677.

Drenewydd yn Notais see **Newton Nottage**

Drope, Y Ddorop ST 108758
Vale of Glamorgan (St Georges)
?'secondary settlement, outlying farm': ME *throp le Thrope, Thorpe* 1540, *the Drope* 1746, *Ddrop* 1762, *Throp* 1763, *the Ddrop* 1764, *y Drope* 1677, *Drope* 1799, *Y Ddorop* 1933

This el. and the development from thr- to dr- occur in Devon and Gloucestershire (NCPN 157; PNDPH 253-5). Often found with a qualifier as in Freystrop (PNPemb 588), Pembrokeshire, and in two lost pns. *Hensthorpe* 1495 and *Gregory drope* 1528 in the Llantwit Major area. Drope is probably the location of *Britton thorpe* c.1659 and *Brytton Throps* c.1670. *Britton*, etc. is 'settlement at a bridge' (*brycg, tūn*) (cf. Briton Ferry) referring to a bridge over a small stream recorded as *Nant y Drope* 1879 (*nant, y*). See further St Bride's-super-Ely, the p. immediately north of the r. Ely. The W form is recorded as *Y Ddorop* [ə 'ðɔroːp] in 1933 but older forms favour *Y Ddrop* or *Y Ddrop* with the def.art. *y* matching E *the*. If *Y Ddorop* is a genuine form then the first vowel –o– between Dd- and -r- must be epenthetic to ease pron.

Dulais
Neath Port Talbot (Cadoxton-juxta-Neath)
'dark stream': *du, glais*
(r.) *Deles, Dalyes* 1541, (r.) *Dyueleys* 1289 (1336), *Dulyshe flu:* 1578, *the Dulesse* 1586, (r.) *Dulas* 1612, *Dylais Ycha, ~ Issa* 1769-74, (village) *Dylas* 1840
The n. of a t. (and r.) extending from a location above Seven Sisters and Creunant to Aberdulais (SS 773996). Historic forms occasionally have *sh* [ʃ] for *s* found elsewhere in Glamorgan, eg. *Glan Dwllaish* (in St Fagans) 1786 (1814). Glyndulais Isaf, ~ Uchaf are recorded in *Glyndeueleys* 1289 (1468), *Glyndewles, Glyndewlysse* 1541, *Glyndylais ycha, ~ yssa* 1670, and parcel of *Glyn Diles* 1741 (*glyn, uchaf*).

Dulais rn. (> Loughor SN 587039) see **Pontarddulais**

Dulais see **Blackpill**

Dunraven, Dwnrhefn SS 888727
Vale of Glamorgan (St Brides Major)
Uncertain
Donreuyn c.1270, *Donreven* 1361, *Dunreven* 1441, *Dunraven in Wales* 1500, *Dwn Refn*, or *Donn Refn a phen Bre Dwn Refn* late 16th cent, (lp.) *Downe Raven* 1631, *Donreeven* 1693, *Twyn*

68

yr Rivan 1765, *Y Dwnryfan, (y) Dindryfan* c.1800, *Dindryvan ... the circular fortress* 1807
Nearly all sources before the late 18th cent have *Don-, Dun-* and *Dwn-*, and the form *Dindryfan* c.1800 is probably an invention of Iolo Morganwg based on a supposition that the first el. is *din* referring to the prehistoric promontory fort here. The latter appears on OS maps from 1878 as *Din-maen* meaning 'stone fort' but the authenticity of this form is in great doubt. The middle –d- could be intrusive with parallels in the pers.n. Cyndrig < Cyn(w)rig and Gendros (q.v.) but *Din-* is otherwise unmatched except in sources which are known to draw on Iolo. This invalidates the suggestion that *Dindryfan* means 'the triangular fortress' or 'the circular fortress' by Malkin and 'the fort of Tryfan' with a conjectural pers.n. (PNIG 39). The collective evidence is ambiguous but the second el. at least appears to be non-W, perhaps the OE pers.n. Hræfn or *hræfn* 'a raven'. That raises the possibility that *Dun-* is also non-W representing perhaps OE *dūn*, the whole pn. meaning 'hill of (man called) Hræfn' or 'raven's hill'. The word order is Celtic, however, and this would have to be explained as a product of later W influence. The alternative explanation is that the pn. is a hybrid of OIr *dún* 'fort' and the ON pers.n. Hrafn. Examples of Ir-ON compound pns. are found in other parts of Britain and Ireland, particularly in northern England, and there are ON pns. along this coast such as Sker and Tusker Rock (q.v.), and note in particular Roath which appears to be of Ir origin.

Dunvant, Dynfant SS 590938
Swansea
'deep valley': ***dwfn***, ***nant***
(brook) *Dovenant, Divernant* 1650, (mess.) *Dyffnant* 1652, *Dynvant, Dyfnant* 1764, *Dyvnant* 1736-65, *Dunvant* 1833, (ho.) *Cwm-y-dwfn'ant* 1832, *Dunfant* 1841, *Dynfant* 1875
nant probably has its less common meaning 'valley' (ADG¹, 45) because the unnamed stream here, a tributary of Clyne River (see Blackpill), is small and shallow. The reversal of -f- [v] and –n- may be E influence but instances are known where it is a W development; cf. Aberllynfi. The nucleus (SS 593938) of the village was near the station but it now includes the housing estate west of Dunvant Inn constructed around Fairwood Road and Killan (Cil-lan) Road after World War I and the estate centred on Ash Grove (SS 598933) towards Killay.

Dwnrhefn see **Dunraven**

Dyffryn[1] ST 094720
Vale of Glamorgan (St Lythans)
'valley, glen': ***dyffryn***
Dyffryn Golych ?15th cent, 1818, *Deffryn Golywch* 1596, *Y Dyffryn Goluch* c.1780, *Y Dyffryn Olwg* c.1785, *Dyffryn* 1762, *Dyffryn House* 1799, *Dyffryn golwg* 1833
Earlier *Dyffryn Golych* with a rn. *Golych* recorded as *gulich* c.1145, *Gulich* c.1200, *Gulych, Golich, Golith* 12-14th cent, possibly composed of dim. prefix *go-, guo-* (*gwo-*) and an unidentified *-lich, -lych*, perhaps connected with **llwch**[2]. The stress on the first syllable in *Golych* does not favour *gwlych* 'liquid, moisture' in which –w- is a semi-vowel. Later forms suggest association with *golwch, gwolwch* 'worship, prayer' encouraged by the 18th-19th cent cult of druidism. Dyffryn House was alternatively *Columbar* 1596, *Collumbar* 1758, possibly derived from Lat *columbarium* 'pigeon-house, culverhouse' (PNDPH 263-6). Dyffryn Golych has been misidentified with Worleton which is an alternative n. for Doghill (ST 093720) recorded as *Worletton* c.1291, *Worleton* 1332, *Urleton* 1539, *Worlton* 1540 meaning possibly 'settlement near a (stone) circle' or 'on a round hill': ?OE *hwerfel, hwyrfel*, ***tūn***, comparable with Whorlton, North Yorkshire, where nearby Whorlton Hill is 'a hill with a rounded top' (PNDPH 281-3). Doghill is recorded as *Doghill* 1540 (*dog*, ***hill***).

Dyffryn[2] (Dyffryn Clydach) SS 738999
Neath Port Talbot (Cadoxton-juxta-Neath)
'valley (of the r. Clydach)': ***dyffryn***, rn. **Clydach**
(*parsel*) *diffryn Clydach* 1635, *Duffryn* 1643, *Dyffryn* 1754, *Dyffrin Clydach* c.1700; *Dyffryn Clydach Division* 1792

A 19th cent industrial development ultimately named from the valley. The division (***parsel***) became a separate p. in 1873 after the building of the ch. of St. Matthew 1871 (VNeath 95). Dyffryn House is at SS 735996. Dyffryn Clydach is the now n. of the Community Council.

Dyffryn³ (Duffryn)   SS 836957
Neath Port Talbot (Llangynwyd)
'valley': ***dyffryn***
Dyffryn 1910-41, *Duffryn* 1962
In Cwmafan. Named directly from Dyffryn Rhondda Colliery (SS 844957) (***dyffryn***) sunk some time before 1899 by the Duffryn Rhondda Colliery Co. The western part of the village was largely constructed before 1918 around the former Tŷ Isaf fm.; the eastern part was developed from the late 1920s south of the railway and mine.

Dyffryn⁴   SS 851937
Bridgend (Llangynwyd)
'valley': ***dyffryn***
Dyffryn 1877
Named from a former fm. Dyffryn Llynfi (SS 852940) described as *Duffrynllunfy* 1813, *Dyffryn llynfy* 1833, *Dyffyn-llynfi* 1884, on the south side of the village, located in the valley of the r. Llynfi recorded as *Dyffrye' Llyffan* 1541 and *Diffrin. Lleueny* c.1538. The rn. distinguishes the fm. from *Duffryn Coegnant* 1852, *Dyffryn-coegnant* 1884 (SS 856933) near the stream Coegnant and a former fm. *Dyffryn Madog* 1833 recalled in a street-n. (SS 848922) at Twmpath-mawr: Coegnant probably means either a stream hidden by vegetation or rocks or one which sometimes ran dry (EANC 56) (*coeg* 'empty, worthless; blind', ***nant***).

Dyffryn Cellwen   SN 852100
Neath Port Talbot (Cadoxton-juxta-Neath)
'valley of the (r.) Cellwen': ***dyffryn***, rn. *Cellwen*
Dyffryn Cellwen 1909
The rn. is *Nant y Kellvayne* 1610, *Nant Cellwen* 1876. An early 20th cent colliery village near Blaen-Nantcellwen (SN 852094) recorded as *Blaen-nant-cellwn* 1832, *Blaen-nant-cellwen* 1876-8, 'upland, headwaters of the stream Cellwen' (***blaen***, ***nant***). Cellwen, earlier Cellfaen, appears to be *cellt*, *cell* 'flint' and ***maen***, possibly a ref. to the nature of local geology or a specific boulder.

Dynfant see **Dunvant**

Eaglebush to Ewenni

Ewenni Priory, from *Wales Illustrated* by Henry Gastineau (1830).

Eaglesbush, Llwynerydd SS 749958
Neath Port Talbot (Llantwit-juxta-Neath)
E *eagle*, *bush*; *llwyn*, *erydd*²
Eagles Bushe 1636, *Eagles Bush* 1646, *Eglosbush* 1682, *Eagle's Bush* 1701, *Llwyneryr* c.1770
Probably a fanciful n., once applying to a former ho., cottage and foundry. The n. survives in Eaglesbush Close in Pencaerau. The evidence for Llwynerydd is late but this may reflect the bias of surviving sources and the form is supported by (cottage and salt marsh called) *Morva-Llwyn-Erydd* 1809 and (marsh) *Morva Llwyn Erydd, otherwise Eaglesbush Marsh* 1856 (***morfa***).

East Aberthaw (ST 034667) see **Aberthaw**

East Barry see **Cadoxton**

Eastbrook ST 161716
Vale of Glamorgan (St Andrews Major)
'east brook': OE *ēast*, *brōc*
Estbroke 1479, *Eastbroke* 1565-6, *Eastbrook* late 16th cent, *Ysbrook* 1763, *Ishbrook* c.1766, *East-brook* 1833, *Nishbrook* 1839
The brook joins the Cadoxton River (possibly the 'west brook') near Dinas Powys. Gwynedd Pierce suggests (PNDPH 221-2) that the 1763 spelling shows loss of *-t-* in the combination

–*stb*- as in the case of Gwesbyr (< *Westbury*), Flintshire (DPNW 182-3, PNF 89-90). This could be due to W influence which probably also explains the apparent substitution of the short vowel i [ɪ] for the long î [iː] and contributed to the development of -sh- [ʃ] from -s-; the *N*- in *Nishbrook* may be wrong-division of the prep. *yn* 'in' or E prep. *in*. The development of this pn. may be compared with that of Yniston (ST 162745, in Leckwith) 'east farm or settlement' (E *east*, –*ton*) which possesses historic forms such as *Eston* late 15cent, *Easton* 1660-85, *Nishtown* 1745, *Nishton* 1840, *Yniston* 1876 (PNDPH 60).

East Moors ST 201760
Cardiff (Roath)
'moors lying eastwards (of Cardiff)': E *east*, *moor* pl. *moors*
Estmore c.1202, *the Eastmore* 1595, *Cardiff East Moors* 1833
A low-lying area extending along the Severn estuary eastwards from near the r. Taf towards r. Rhymni, most of it now occupied by industry, docks and housing (Splott, Adamsdown and Pengam). Cf. Cardiff West Moors.

East Orchard ST 028680
Vale of Glamorgan (St Athan)
'east orchard': OE *ēast*, OE *orceard*
Orchard 1208, *Est Orchard* 1317, *Estnorchard* 1411, *East Orchard* 1679, *Norchardberkeroles* 1369, *Norchet(e)* c.1538, *Norchurche* 1600-7, (castle) *Castletone ewest orchard* c.1700
The 1369 ref. recalls the n. of Laurence Berkeroles to whom the manor was granted. West Orchard was the n. of a manor in St. Athan recorded as *Westorchard* 1427, *West Orchard* 1456, *Westorchard* 1525, *West Orchyard* 1673. East Orchard possesses ruins of a castle and chp.

East Side SS 902864
Bridgend (Betws)
'eastern side (of Betws)': E *east*, *side*
East Side, West Side 1964

One half of a housing estate built in the 1960s and 1970s on the east side of Betws Road south of Betws opposite West View.

East Town or Prior's Town SS 428914
Swansea (Llangennith)
'eastern settlement': E *east*, *town*
Easton vel Priuston 1583, (manor) *Priorston*, *Priorstown otherwise East Town* 1642, *Priorstone otherwise East Town of Llangennith* 1786
In contrast to West Town in the west part of Llangennith (NCPN 121) found as *the Weste Towne of Langenethe* 1549, *westown Langennith* 1764 and *Western-town* 1832. The fm. once belonged to the priory of Llangennith (WGOW III, 29).

East Village see **Cowbridge**

Edmondstown, Dinas-isaf ST 007903
Rhondda Cynon Taf (Llantrisant)
'settlement named from Edmondes': surname *Edmondes*, E *town*; 'lower stronghold': *dinas*, *isaf*
Edmondstown 1879, (mess.) *llwyn Jevan eos otherwise dinas issa* 1709, (ho.) *Dinas-isa* 1833
The village developed from c.1879 near Dinas-isaf Colliery (SO 006903) on land belonging to Dinas-isaf fm. (ST 008901) which belonged to the Revd. Thomas Edmondes (1806-92). Edmondes was vicar of Llanblethian and Cowbridge and Welsh St Donats 1835-83 and inherited estates in Llanwynno, Ystradyfodwg and Llantrisant (MCPP 26-29). Dinas-isaf is 'lower' in contrast to Dinas Uchaf (formerly ST 003912) (*uchaf*) which is *Ddinas Ucha* 1731, *Dinas-uchaf* 1874. The variant Llwyn Ieuan Eos is 'grove of Ieuan the nightingale' (*llwyn*, pers.n. *Ieuan*, *eos*). Ieuan Eos was a member of local gentry. His father Dafydd ab Ieuan and grandson Thomas ap Dafydd ab Ieuan Eos are known to have held Gelli-fawr, in Ystradyfodwg, in 1540 and 1570. The cliff above Pen-y-graig and Williamstown is *Graig-yr-eos* 1874, 'the nightingale's cliff' (*craig*).

Edwardsville ST 087967
Merthyr Tudful
'settlement of Edwards': surname *Edwards*, E *ville*
Edwardsville 1898
The village developed during the 1890s next to the Great Western Hotel (recorded 1879), owned by a businessman Edmund Edwards (1851-1926), near Quakers Yard station (MCPP 30-32).

Efail-fach SS 787954
Neath Port Talbot (Baglan, Llantwit-juxta-Neath, Michaelston-super-Afan)
'(the) little smithy': (*yr*), *gefail, bach¹*
Esail [= *Efail*] *Vach* 1799, *Evel Vach, Evil Vach* 1841, *Efal Fach* 1852, *Gefail-fâch* 1878
The W def.art. is not used by E-speakers but has local testimony (TAMDHS 1930, 61) and occurs in the n. of bridge here *Pont-yr-efail-fach* 1830 (*pont*).

Efail-isaf ST 084845
Rhondda Cynon Taf (Llantwit Fardre)
'(the) lower smithy': (*yr*), *gefail, isaf*
Evel 1729, *Evelisaf* 1799, 1833, (village) *Eval Isa* 1841, *Efail-isaf* 1876
The smithy, shown on OS maps 1876 and 1885, became the focus for a small village before 1841. Known to some local inhabitants as 'Efail Isha' with colloquial –sh- [ʃ] for –s-. Presumably there was once a nearby Efail Uchaf or 'upper smithy' (*uchaf*).

Eglwys Brewys ST 005692
Vale of Glamorgan
'church of ?Brewys': *eglwys*, pers.n. ?*Brewys*
Egelespriwes 1254, *Eglesprywes* c.1291, *Egluspirwys* 1443, *Eglisprues* 1492, *Egloisbrus* 1386, *Eglowys Brewys* 1535, *Eglwys-Brewis* c.1535, *eglwys boywys* c.1566, *Eglwysbrowis* 1762
Not necessarily a saint, cf. Eglwysilan. Later forms seem to favour a conjectural pers.n. perhaps composed of *braw* 'terror, fright' and suffix *–ys* (ETG 211) though this does not fit very well with forms such as *-priwes, -prywes, -prues*. Unfamiliarity with Brewys probably explains the unreliable identification of Eglwys Brewys with St Brice or Brise (latinised *Bri(c)tius*), a 5th cent disciple of St Martin of Tours. Brewys has also been interpreted as a W form of the surname Breos (variants Braose, Brehuse, etc) on the basis of a proven family connection of the Breos family with the adjoining p. of Llan-maes (Merrick 57, 72) and a conjecture that a member of the same family established the ch. in Eglwys Brewys. The best that can be said for this argument is that the various forms of Breos may have influenced a few late forms of the pn.

Eglwysilan ST 106889
Caerphilly/Rhondda Cynon Taf
'church of Ilan': *eglwys*, pers.n. *Ilan*
merthir ~, Merthir ilan c.1170, *Eglisulan* 1254, *Eglwys Ilan, Egloysilan* 1535, *Eglois Elan* 1541, *eglwys ilan* c.1566, *Eglyssylian* 1578, *Eglwysilan* 1729, *Eglwys Shilan* 1762
Earlier sps. show that *eglwys* has displaced *merthyr*. No saint Ilan seems to be recorded. *Eglwyshilan* is the usual spelling in the diary of local man William Thomas 1762-95 (DWT) showing colloquial -sh- [ʃ] as in *isha* for *isaf* 'lower'. Mynydd Eglwysilan (ST 1092, 1192, 1292) is *Cefn Eglwysilan* 1831 and *Mynydd Eglwysilan* 1833 (*mynydd, cefn*).

Eglwys Newydd see **Whitchurch**

Eglwys Nynnid SS 803847
Neath Port Talbot (Margam)
'church of Nynnid': *eglwys*, pers.n. *Nynnid*
Egloose Nunney 1543, *Eglwys nynnid* c.1550, *Egglois Nynnid* 1633, *Eglwsnunyd* 1746, *Eglwysnynydd* 1799, *Eglwys Nynyd* 1832, *Eglwys-nunydd* 1877
The pers.n. has also been identified in Hendre Nynnid, Denbighshire, and Llanddewi Ystradenni, Radnorshire (EANC 173). It is generally supposed to be fem. because Nonn, mother of St David, is recorded as *Nonita* and because a fem. RB pers.n. *Nonnita* could produce the W form Nynnid. Melville Richards, however, has shown (AC 1969, 144-5) that Nynnid may also be a masc. pers.n. which has developed from a distinct base **Nwnn, *Nynn*

or *Nonn*. Eglwys Nynnid does not refer to 'nuns' (as GPNG 11). The site is now largely occupied by hos., the n. surviving in that of a street Eglwys Nunydd and a reservoir.

Elliots Town, **Tref Elliot**　　　　SO 146029
Caerphilly (Bedwellte Monmouthshire)
'settlement named from Elliot': surname *Elliot*, E **town**, **tref**
Elliotstown 1891, *Elliot's Town* 1901, (*yn*) *Nhre Elliot* 1913
Sir George Elliot (1815-93) was a director of Powell Duffryn Co. from 1863 (chairman 1886-8); the community developed after the opening of the west shaft of Elliot Colliery 1883 (MCPP 33-39). Caerphilly County Borough uses the W form Tref Eliot.

Ely, **Trelái**　　　　　　　　　ST 140764
Cardiff
'(settlement by r.) Ely', 'settlement (or farm) by (r.) Elái': *Ely*/*Elái*, **tref**
(bridge at) *Eley* 1531, (village) *Ely* 1761, *Trelai or Ely* 1833, *Ealy hamlett* 1670, (*o*) *dref lai* 1601
The rn. is recorded as *Eley* c.1126, *Ely* 1146, *Elei* c.1150, *Elay* late 12th cent, *Eleewater alias Eleebrygge* 1479, *Ley River, of sum in Englisch caullid Ele* c.1538, (r.) *Lay* 1559, *afon Lai* 1778, probably derived from Brit **Ele(z)i* < **Elegiió-* containing an el. **Eleg-* thought to occur in l'Ellé Brittany (OBret *Elegium*). Elái is stressed on the –*a*- and this is confirmed by *Y Lai*, the form used by W-speakers in Llantrisant p. c.1890 (HTonyrefail 27) and in a 19th cent triban (Trib 215). Historic forms show that W-speakers also knew the r. as plain *Lai*, hence Morfa Lai, recorded as *Eleymore* 1535 and *Morva Lei* 1514, for the former marshy area near the estuary (**moor**, **morfa**). Ely was a ho. (*Ely Farm* 1833) and small village next to Ely Bridge alias Pont Lai or Pont ar Lai recorded as *Pont Lay … caullid yn Englisch Ele Bridg* c.1538; *Pont ar Lay* 1612 (**pont**, **ar**). The rn. is also recorded in *Dyffryn Lay* 1662, in Llantrisant; Lan-y-lai Fawr (ST 080759) (*Lhan Elài* c.1700, *Lanlay* 1714) (**mawr**) in Peterston-super-Ely; and Lanelay Hall (ST 031828) (*tire glan y Laie* c.1612, *Glan y Lay* 1739, *Lanelay* 1833) (**glan**) in Llantrisant.

Coedely or Coedelái (ST 0185) 'wood by the (r.) Ely' (***coed***), between Llantrisant and Tonyrefail, is named from a fm. known as *Coydylai* 1784 and *Coedylay* 1811 on the western side of the r.

Energlyn　　　　　　　　　　ST 147881
Caerphilly (Eglwysilan)
'mouth of the valley': **genau**, **yr**, **glyn**
Generglyn 1525, *Tyre Generglyn* 1541, *genau'rglyn* 1591, *Energlin* 1696, *Energlyn* 1729, *Norglyn* 1763, *Eneu yr Glyn* 1782, *Energlin, or Geneu'r Glyn* 1815
Named from a ho. (ST 146881) near the opening to the narrow valley of Nant yr Aber. The modern form with *E-* is a lenited form probably caused by a prep. such as *i* 'to' and *o* 'from'. Otherwise identical to Genau'r-glyn, Cardiganshire, recorded as *Genneyrglyn* 1246, *Geneuerglyn* 1282.

Evanstown　　　　　　　　　SS 978895
Bridgend (Llandyfodwg)
'settlement named from Evans': surname *Evans*:, E **town**
Evanstown 1880
Evan Evans (c.1810-86) established the Six Bells public ho. at Penyrheolgerrig, Merthyr Tudful, and opened the Six Bells level in Cwmdafolog in 1862 (MCPP 40-43). The village developed from c.1880 and was initially regarded as part of Gilfach Goch. There is no connection with Christmas Evans (1766-1838), the well-known Baptist preacher (as PNIG 35).

Ewenni (Ewenny)　　　　　　SS 907771
Vale of Glamorgan
'(place at r.) Ewenni': rn. *Ewenni*
(priory) *Ewenny* c.1134, (r.) *the ewenni* c.1144, (~) *Euenhi* c.1145, (~) *Eweny* c.1160, (vill) *ewenni*, *Ewennith* c.1191, *Eweny* 1254, *Euweny* 14th cent, *Weny Bridge*, (r.) *Wenny*, ~ *Priory* c.1538, *y wêni* c.1566, *the Wenny* 1762, (ch. of) *Sancti Michaelis de Eweni* 1141-4
Identifiable with *Aventio* in the Ravenna Cosmography 7th cent. This probably derives from Brit **Auentios* containing a pre-Celtic el. possibly meaning 'spring, water-course' (Nomina 6, 38) as in the rns. l'Avance (France

and Switzerland) and Avenza (Italy), thought to derive from Aventia, possibly a goddess and protector of wells and springs (EANC 142-3; PNRB 260-1). Dafydd Morganwg (HMorg 14) and other antiquarians misidentified the first el. as *ewyn* 'foam, froth'. Also known locally as *Y Wenni* as well as *Ewenni* [ɛˈwɛniː] by W-speakers. The location of a priory established by Maurice de Londres 1141 and subject to Gloucester abbey. Generally pronounced 'yu wenny' [juːˈwɛniː] by E-speakers. Ewenni Down is (waste) *Ewennies Down* 1605.

Faenor to Furzehill

Fleur-de-lis. The High Street, looking northwards c.1935.

Faenor (Vaynor) SO 049104
Merthyr Tudful (Breconshire)
'administrative unit': **maenor**
Veynor, Mangon 1373, (p.) *Gwinaw* 1387-8, *Vaynor Weyno* 1401, (*parochia*) *Sci. Gwynoci* 1481, *Vaynor Wyno* 1488, *Mannor Wyno* 1522, *Vaynor* 1560, *Vaenor* 1798, *Faenor* 1832
Earlier sources qualify **maenor** with Gwynno to whom the ch. is dedicated. The precise sense is unclear but it may be 'administrative division associated with a ch. dedicated to Gwynno', i.e. the comparison may be with the ch. and, by implication, its settlement. Gwynno is also dedicated at Llanwynno (q.v.). The unfamiliarity of his n. must account for the scribal error *Mangon* 1373 and the false dedications of the ch. to Gwendolen and Gwenffrewi. Early forms such as *Vaynor Weyno* (= Faenor Wynno in ModW) have initial len. M- > F- which was probably caused by preps. such as *i* 'to' and *o* 'from'. The pn. is occasionally found with a prefixed def.art. but modern practice omits it. *Vaynor* is poor spelling which survives on OS maps and in administrative use.

Faerdre (Vardre) SN 689017
Swansea (Llangyfelach)
'(the) farm (*or* settlement) administered by the *maer*': (*y*), **maerdref**
Vairdre 1322, *le Vayrdreve* 1408, *Evayrdre egha, Evairdre yssa* 1546, (ho.) *Tuy yn Vard[r]e* 1764, *Fardre* 1832, *y Fardre* 1908

The *maer* was a seignorial officer of the administrative division Parsel Rhyndwyclydach in the commote or manor of Gower Supra Boscus alias Gŵyr Uwch Coed. Cf. Llantwit Fardre. The n. may have become attached first to the area under his jurisdiction and then specifically to the two fms. qualified as 'upper' and 'lower' (***uchaf***, ***isaf***) in 1546.

Fagwr SN 674028
Swansea (Llangyfelach)
'(place surrounded by a) wall': (***y***), ***magwyr***
Fagwyr 1876-9
The n. now applies to housing which developed along Cadwgan Road in the 19th cent and to nearby houses built around a house Fagwyr-isaf (***isaf***) recorded as *Fagwrisaf* 1813, *Fagwyr-isaf* 1876-9. The nearby hos. Fagwyr-uchaf (SN 673029) and Fagwyr-ganol are *Fagwruchaf* 1813 and *Fagwyr-ganol* 1876-9 distinguished as 'upper' (***uchaf***) and 'middle' (***canol***). One of these is *the Vagwr* 1727, *the Fagwr* 1740. An otherwise unlocated Fagwyr-wen is recorded as *Vago' wen* 1650, *Bagwr Wen* 1754, *Vagorwen* 1764 (***gwen***) with Pantybaban (SN 681022). Cf. Magor alias Magwyr, Monmouthshire (DPNW 309).

Fairoak ST 178995
Caerphilly (Bedwellte)
'fair *or* fine oak-tree': E ***fair***, ***oak***.
Fare Oak 1841, *Fairoak* 1879
A group of hos. initially known as Fairoak, later distinguished as Grwyne Terrace and Woodland Terrace (an indirect ref. to Argoed above). Fairoak/Derwen-deg (approx. ST 187789), at Roath, is *Fair Oak* 1771, *Dderwen deg* c.1784, and *Derwen-deg* 1833 (***derwen***, ***teg***).

Fairwater, Tyllgoed ST 139775
Cardiff (Llandaf)
'beautiful stream': E ***fair***, ***water***; 'the pierced wood, the wood with a gap', ***y***, ***twll***[1], ***coed***
bella aqua c.1300, *Farrewater* 1431, *Feyrwater* 1530, *Fairwater* 1582, *Tvll Coit; estrat agcr, idest tollcoit; uillam Strat hancr* c.1145, *Tilthecoit, Tilcoyth* c.1538, *Tilcot* 1578
The meaning of Fairwater is confirmed by the Lat form c.1300. The n. applies to a small tributary of the r. Ely/Elái rising west of Waterhall (formerly at ST 136785). Tyllgoed could mean 'a wood full of holes' or 'trees pierced by holes' but *Tyll-* is also known to have described rivers and streams which cut a path, as in this case, through woodland. The pn. is comparable with Fforest y Tyllgoed (in Llangynwyd) recorded as *Fforest Tyllgoed* 1580, (mtn. land) *Fforest y tilcoed otherwise Nant y fforest* 1729, *Forrest y Tillcoid* 1815, *Tyllgoed* 1623 (***fforest***, ***nant***). *Strat hancr, estrat agcr* c.1145 is probably 'valley-floor of the hermit' (***ystrad***, ***ancr***[1] 'anchorite, hermit').

Fairwood SS 569930
Swansea (Ilston)
'beautiful wood': E ***fair***, ***wood***
Ffairewood, (forest of) *Ffairwood al's Ffairwood moor* 1583, (ho.) *Fairwood* 1736, *Fairwood's Moor* 1764
Located around Fairwood Cottage (SS 569930) now known as Redcroft and taken indirectly from a wood and Fairwood Common (SS 568934). The 'fair wood' is also recalled in Fairwood Corner (SS 568926) recorded as *Llwynteg* 1813, *Llwyn-teg* 1833 meaning 'fair grove' (***llwyn***, ***teg***), and *Fairwood* 1799. A ho. known as Fairwood in this area bore the alternative and former n. Bryn-hir recorded as *Brynnhere* 1594, 'long hill' (***bryn***, ***hir***). Fairwood Common (SS 5691), is still largely unenclosed, partly occupied by Swansea Airport.

Fan, Y (Van) ST 16638665
Caerphilly (Bedwas)
?'peak, point, beacon': ***y***, ***ban***[1]
(place) *Vanne* c.1538, *the Vann* 1552, (park) *Vann, the Vanne* 1578, *or fann* 1600, *Y Fan* c.1800
Referring to Castell y Fan, a small isolated hill (ST 16738688) (***castell***). Also recorded in a 19th cent triban (Trib no.572).

Fanhalog ST 048943
Rhondda Cynon Taf (Llanwynno)
'(the place) abounding in broom': (***y***), ***banhadlog*** variant *banhalog*

Vanhaddloge 1633, *Vennallog* 1770, *Vanhalog* 1783, *Fanhalog* 1814, *Fynachlog* 1833, *Vanhaulog* 1841, *Y Fanhaulog* 1888

Fully analysed by Gwynedd Pierce (PNGlam 72-74; Morgannwg 45: 69-79). Some late forms give the misleading impression that the pn. contains **man**, len. *fan*, and **heulog**[1], 'sunny place'. The n. was also confused by some historians with *y fynachlog*, 'the monastery' (**mynachlog**), a form appearing on the OS map in 1833. The association with monks may have been prompted by the perceived similarity of the names and the existence of Mynachdy (about a mile to the north), 'monk's house' (**mynach**[1], **tŷ**). Refs. to a Capel y Fanhalog (**capel**) have also been mistakenly located at the site of Fanhalog fm. (ST 04839430) and taken as further proof of ancient ecclesiastical associations but Pierce shows that the 'Capel' was a nearby Nonconformist chp. (ST 05109472), first recorded in 1786. This was replaced by a chp. known as Bethel in 1876 and the older building was converted into two hos. (now a single dwelling). There is also evidence of a chp. in the n. of a nearby ho, Buarth-y-capel otherwise Buarth-capel (ST 053945) recorded as *Buarth y Cappell* 1766, *buarth Chapel* 1782, *Buarth y Capel* 1826, meaning 'the chapel yard' (**capel**, **y**, **buarth**), but this has not been found in earlier records.

Farteg Hill, Y Farteg   SN 777077
Neath Port Talbot (Cilybebyll)
'hill called Y Farteg': **y**, pn. *Farteg*, E **hill**; 'large fair (hill)': **march**, **teg**
(**mynydd**) *Craig y Farteg* 1868, *Farteg Hill* 1878-1984

Craig y Farteg seems to have applied specifically to the northern slopes of the hill (despite the 1868 ref.), otherwise recorded as *Graig Varteg* 1799 and *Craig-y-farteg* 1831, and to several hos. Farteg-isaf, Farteg-uchaf, Farteg-fach and the lost Farteg-fawr recorded as *Varteg Issa* and *varteg Ycha* 1783, *Varteg Vacchan* 1541 and *Vargdeck Vaur* 1528 (**isaf**, **uchaf**, **bach**[1], **bechan**, **mawr**). Y Farteg probably once referred specifically to the hill. Identical names include Farteg (Varteg) (SO 2605), Monmouthshire, and Farteg Fach and Farteg Isaf at Margam in ref. to hills, and Marteg which is a rn. in Radnorshire. The current OS Explorer has the irregular form *Varteg Hill*.

Felinarw   SS 915877
Bridgend (Llangeinwyr)
'(the) mill by the (r.) Garw': (**y**), **melin**, rn. *Garw*
Felinarw 1813, *Melinarw* 1833, *Rough Mill Village* 1841, *Felin Arw (Corn)* 1876

For the rn. see Blaen-garw. The valley (**cwm**) immediately around it is *Cwmfelyn Arw* 1799, *Cwm-felin-Arw* 1885, *Cwm Felin-arw* 1919 and is now described as Cwm-y-felin. The n. was displaced in the 1920s by Llangeinor (see Llangeinwyr), a n. which properly applies to the p. and area around the p.ch.

Felindre[1]   SN 638027
Swansea (Llangyfelach)
'(the) settlement with a mill': (**y**), **melindref**
Velendre 1319, *Velyndre* 1512, *y velindre*, (water-mill) *Y Velindrey* 1596, *Velindre* 1650, *Velindra* 1729, *Felindre* 1813

The mill was on the r. Lliw. A common pn.; cf. Felindre (ST 143803), in Whitchurch, which has similar sps. including *Velindre* 1748, *Felindra* 1788, *Velindra* 1790. *Felindra* [veˈlɪndra] was evidently the local form; it is located near Melin Gruffudd (q.v.).

Felindre[2]   SS 971813
Vale of Glamorgan (Llanilid)
Felindre 1813, 1876, *Velindra* 1852
As Felindre[1], with a mill on r. Ewenni Fach. Also recalled in *Hevle y velindre* (in Coychurch) 1580 (**heol**, **y**). Possibly identical to Milton recorded as *Milton* 1645, c.1700 (E **mill**, **-ton**) and *Milton otherwise Brin Curin* 1688. The latter is properly Bryncwtyn (SS 966809) (in Pencoed p.) recorded as *Bryn Cuttin* 1560-1, *Bryncuttyn* 1600, *Bryn Cutting* 1714, *Brincwtyn* 1833. Possibly 'hill shaped like a little tail' with **bryn** and perhaps **cwtyn** a dim. of **cwt**[1] nmf. 'tail; rump', referring to the (low) hill on which the fm. is located or the narrow projection of land between Afon Ewenni (Fawr) and Ewenni Fach.

Felindre³ (Velindre)   SS 769904
Neath Port Talbot (Aberafan/Margam)
Velinder 1541, *Velindre* 1561, (land) *tir yn y velindre* 1604, *Velindra* 1753, *Felindre* 1785
As Felindre[1, 2]. The dialect form *Felindra* is testified in a 19th cent triban (TAMDHS 1932-3, 103; Trib 118). There was apparently once a dam opposite Carmarthen Row (obliterated by the M4).

Felin-wyllt see **Wild Mill**

Ferndale, Glynrhedynog   SS 999968
Rhondda Cynon Taf (Ystradyfodwg)
'valley having ferns': E *fern, dale*; *glyn, rhedynog*
(village) *Ferndale, Ferndale Colliery* 1877, *Glynrhedynog* 1900
The use of Glynrhedynog as the official W n. of the village is recent and many W-language sources down to the mid 20th cent use the E form Ferndale. The origin of both pns. is complex. The coal-owner David Davis (d. 1866), of Blaen-gwawr, is said to have bought a disused level near Blaenllechau (q.v.), raising the first coal in 1862 (LlUF). This pit, known as Blaenllechau (later Ferndale) Colliery, lay on the east side of Afon Rhondda Fach close to Blaenllechau fm. (SS 006966). Glynrhedynog first appears in the n. of Glynrhedynog Inn/Hotel (now demolished) located in Blaenllechau village north of the colliery. The collective evidence suggests that the inn was constructed c.1862 in the area where the first temporary dwellings were built for coal workers. There is no proof, however, that this fledgling settlement ever bore the n. Glynrhedynog. Later sources suggest that it was already known as Blaenllechau and that this n. was taken directly from the colliery. The actual village of Ferndale beyond the r. was laid out about 1865-6 and the two names were used interchangeably for a period. The reason for the choice of an E n. in an area which was largely W-speaking at that time is unclear. The likeliest explanation is that Glynrhedynog was an informal description of a part of the valley of Afon Rhondda Fach and that the n. was transferred to the inn, then in translation as Ferndale to the colliery and to the subsequent village. It is worth noting that a ho. Rhyd-y-glyn, 'the valley ford' (*rhyd, y, glyn*) is shown on the OS plan 1877 next to the railway and near the r. The form Ferndale may have been given to the colliery simply because some mine-owners tended to favour E rather than W ns. In 1900 it was stated that David Davis chose the n. without consulting anyone. If Glynrhedynog was actually in local use, then it may not have been formally applied to the new village because of the risk of confusion with Glynrhedynog Inn in Blaenllechau and perhaps because of the disagreeable associations of inns and public hos. The antiquarian and poet Glanffrwd certainly detested the E n. and was using the form *y Glynrhedynog* for the general area in 1888. Dislike of the n. may also explain why the former Welsh Independent chp. in Ferndale chose the n. Trerhondda. The statement in 1911 that the village was named Glynrhedynog by Charles Davis, 'a well-known linguist', from one of three fms. owned by the coal company, is unsubstantiated and there seems to be no evidence that the company ever held a fm. with this n. (see SalemN).

Fernhill¹   ST 033993
Rhondda Cynon Taf (Aberdare, Mountain Ash)
'hill notable for ferns': E *fern, hill*
Fernhill 1975
The n. of a housing estate developed from late 1960s on the site of a fm. Abercwmboi-isaf and slopes known as Pymtheg Erw ('fifteen acres': *pymtheg, erw*).

Fernhill²   SS 426883
Swansea (Rhosili)
'hill notable for ferns': E *fern, hill*
Vernhulle 1306, *Vernhull* 1400, *Vernell, alias Verne Hill* 1583, (manor) *Vernhill* 1650, *ffernhills* 1681, (hill) *Fern-hill, Fern-hill top* 1832
As Fernhill¹ with voicing of f > v in some sps. also seen in historic forms of Fernel (SS 576974) at Loughor recorded as *Vernel, Vernel Yssha, Vernhill ycha* 1764, *Vernal* 1803 and *Fernel* 1884, and in many pns. in south-west England,

eg. Vernham Dean, in Hampshire. *Fern-hill* 1832 is a hill at SS 432888. Recorded 1306 with Furzehill (q.v.) and Pilton (*Pyltoune*) (West Pilton SS 438871, East Pilton SS 439872).

Fernlea ST 239913
Caerphilly (Rhisga)
E *fern*, *lea* 'meadow'
Fernlea 1965
A modern n. for housing built in the 1950s and 1960s near Cwm-y-nant.

Ffontygari (Font-y-gary) ST 051662
Vale of Glamorgan (Pen-marc)
?'well of Tygari': ?*ffynnon*, later E *font*, ?pers.n. *Tygari*
Fundygari 1587, *Funtgare* 1578, *Fontigary* 1599, *Funtigarye* 1603, *Fountegarye* 1622, *Fondigary* 1784, *Fontigery* 1831, *Font-y-gary* 1833
Gwynedd Pierce (PNDPH 184-6) cautiously suggests that it may be a contracted form of *Ffynnon Tygari*. The pers.n. is unrecorded but may be composed of the honorific prefix *ty-* and the authenticated pers.n. *Cari*. The identification here of a service-tree or *ceri*, *cerïen* (see Porthceri) is probably coincidental since historic forms almost universally have the forms *–gari*, *-gary*, etc.

Fforchaman SS 995996
Rhondda Cynon Taf (Aberdare)
'fork or meeting place (of the two streams called) Aman': *fforch*, rn. *Aman*
(tmt.) *Forgh Aman* 1541, (*syddyn*) *Tir fforch amann* c.1612, *tire fforch Amman* 1666, *Fforchamman Hamlet* 1778, *Fforchamman* 1814
For the rn. see Aberaman and CVPN 55. The n. is no longer current but referred to the area between Nant Aman Fach and Nant Aman Fawr (*nant*, *bach¹*, *mawr*).

Fforddygyfraith SS 868842
Bridgend (Llangynwyd)
?'the lawful, customary road', *ffordd*, *y*, *cyfraith* (ht.) *Fforddcyfraith* 1813, *Fforddygyfraith* 1841, (road) *Ffordd-y-gyfraith* 1876
The n. of a small ht. laid out along the road Ffordd y Gyfraith running north from Cefn Cross past Baiden Farm. South of Fforddygyfraith the road is shown as Law Street. It seems to have been a road of considerable local importance, possibly a customary road used by manorial tenants passing to and from their holdings and common pasture. With its continuations, the road linked Laleston and the main Cardiff-Swansea turnpike to a ridgeway running north towards Twmpath Diwlith (SS 830888). Ffordd Gyfraith, in Ystradgynlais, Breconshire, is recorded as *Fordd Gyverraith* 1571.

Fforest¹ ST 136806
Cardiff (Whitchurch)
'woodland': *fforest*
the Forrest of Whittchurch 1699, *Fforest* 1811, 1886
There are a number of *fforest* pns. in the valley of the r. Taf. Most undoubtedly refer to woods rather than *forest/fforest* in the sense of 'unenclosed area for hunting' etc. Only small areas of woodland survive around Fforest but there are more extensive woods (partly plantation) further up the valley around Tongwynlais, Gwaelod-y-garth and Tr fforest.

Fforest² SO 0800
Merthyr Tudful
'forest, unenclosed woodland': *fforest*
Forest Hamlet 1540, *Forest hamlett* 1670
The n. applies to an area described in 1843 as 'a mountainous and partially wooded district between two branches of the r. Tâf' (LewisTD I). The hill is *Keven y fforest* 1725, *Cefnyfforest* 1763, (mtn.) *Cefn Forest*, *Lower Cefn Forest*, *Cefn Fforest* 1831. There was an ancient chp. Capel y Fforest or Forest Chapel (SO 082005) recorded as *Capel* 1833 (*capel*) ruinous in 1908. Recollection of a ch. (*llan*) may survive in a ho.n. *Tirylan* 1833, now Tir-lan (SO 096992). Capel y Fforest is alleged to have been built in the time of Elizabeth I and pulled down after 1650 (HMerth 80-81).

Fforest-fach SS 620964
Swansea (Llangyfelach)
'little forest': *fforest*, *bach*¹
(lp.) *Forestvachan* 1508, *Forrest Baghan* 1529, *Forrest Vach* 1764, *Fforest-fach* 1832

Early forms have *bachan* as a variant of **bechan**. Comparable with Fforest (Llansamlet) on the east side of the r. Tawe recorded in fm.ns. *Forrest vychan als' Forrest yssa* (in Kilvey) 1650, *fforest* 1707, *Forest ycha* 1716, *Forrest Llansamlet* 1729, (hos.) *Fforest-uchaf, ~ -isaf* 1832 (***isaf, uchaf***). Fforest Uchaf is at SS 676983. Fforest-fach was re-applied to a large amorphous area of housing, retail and light industrial estates extending from late 19th cent ribbon development on Pontarddulais Road and Carmarthen Road towards the Swansea-Carmarthen railway.

Fforest-goch SN 741017
Neath Port Talbot (Cilybebyll)
'red (or brown) forest': ***fforest, coch***
Forest Goch 1666, *Forest goch* 1814, *Fforest-goch* 1830
Probably from its vegetation. The n. was extended from the ho. to include the area around Tynydderwen and a colliery. An identical pn. is recorded as *Forest Goh* in the lp. of Tir Iarll in 1541.

Fforest Gwladys (ST 126991) see **Capel Gwladus**

Ffwl-y-mwn see **Fonmon**

Ffynnon Taf see **Taff's Well**

Flat Holm [Ynys Echni] ST 222647
Cardiff
'flat island': ON ***flatr***, ON ***holmr***
ynys Echni c.1145, *insula Echni que modo Holma uocatur* c.1200, *Platam Holmam, insula Platta Holma* 12th cent, *Flotholm* 1375, *the Floteholmes* 1387, *Insula Flatholm* 1478, *Flatholmes* 1541, *The flatt Holmes* 1596, *The Flat Holme and the Steepe* 1612, *Les Holmes* 1358, *the Holmes* 1567, *The Holmes, being a certain island in the Severn called the fflatteholmes* 1653
Ekwall (DEPN) and Watts (CDEPN) identify the first el. as ON *floti* 'fleet' on the basis of forms such as *Flotholm* and a ref. in the Anglo-Saxon Chronicle describing how a Scandinavian fleet retreated to the island in 918 after their attacks on Somerset. One version of the chronicle, however, names the island as *iglande æt Bradan Relice* and another as Steepholm (*æt*) *Steapan Relice*. Whichever island is meant, there is an obvious contrasting of low, level Flatholm with high, prominent Steep Holm. The latter is independently recorded as *Stepholm* c.1195, *Stipholmes* 1374, Steep Holme 1417, and *the Holmes, an iland* early 17th cent, containing OE **stīepe* 'steep'. If the forms with *Plat(t)a* are latinisations of *flatr* (> ME, E *flat*) – perhaps under the influence of AN *plat* 'flat' – then they support the suggested meaning. It is also worth noting that *Bradan Relice* may be translated as 'the broad graveyard': OE *brād*, dat. *brādan*, and OIr *reilic*. Remains of early and medieval Christian graves have been found on the island. The identification of Flatholm with Ynys Echni rests on a description of the boundaries of Llandaf diocese in the Book of Llandaf (GlamLM 263-5). The meaning of Echni is obscure and attempts to associate the pn. with a saint Echnus, possibly St Éogan of Ardstraw, are simply guesswork. The religious associations of Flatholm may help explain why Gytha, mother of King Harold, stayed here in 1067 before departing for St Omer after the Norman conquest of England.

Flemingston, Trefflemin ST 017700
Vale of Glamorgan
'Fleming's farm': surname *Fleming*, OE ***tūn***; ***tref***
(*ecclesia*) *de Villa Flandr'* 1254, (~) *villa Fflandrensi, Fflemyngston* 13th cent, *Flemyngeston* 1360, *Flemingston* 1425, *Flemston, Flemyston* 1541, *Flymston* 1549, *Treflemig, alias Flemingeston, and shortely Flemston* c.1538, (a) *Threfflemin* 1820
Traditionally named from Sir John Fleming, one of the reputed 'twelve knights' who are reputed by antiquarians to have conquered Glamorgan in the 12th cent but the Fleming family can be traced no further back than c.1200 in Glamorgan. Flemingston appears in contracted form as *Flemston, Flimston(e)*, etc. from the mid 16th cent, mainly in local sources (NCPN 6), but is now generally pronounced in full. Flemingston is also recorded as *Flemingstone or St. Michael on the Hill*

1851 and as *'Llanfihangel-y-twyn*, St. Michael's church-on-the-hill' (referring to the ch. dedication to St Michael/Mihangel) and the uncorroborated *Llanelwan* and *Ton Gwenynwg* deriving from Iolo Morganwg (IoloMor 22).

Fleur-de-lis, Trelyn　　　　　　ST 155967
Caerphilly (Mynyddislwyn)
fleur-de-lis the iris or lily flower ; 'settlement at a pool': *tref*, *llyn*
Flower-de-luce 1833, *Flourdeluce* 1841, *Flower de lis* 1846, *Flowerdeluce* 1851, *Fluer de lis* 1859, *Fleur de Lis or Trelyn* 1869, *Fleur-de-Lys* 1901, *Trelyn* 1839, 1871
Almost certainly derived from an inn-name recorded c.1831 (PNWG 32) and brewery. The n. probably recalls the fleurs-de-lis in the arms of the Duke of Beaufort who were prominent local landowners. It has been suggested (CardV 132) that it was coined by Huguenot refugees who allegedly established the spelter works below New Inn but no evidence has been produced to support this statement. The likelihood of Huguenots using such an emblem is very unlikely in view of their mistreatment by the kings of France. The W n. is also recorded in the house name *Upper Tre-lyn* 1880 (ST 164965). No pool is shown on 19th cent maps.

Fochriw　　　　　　　　　　　SO 104054
Caerphilly (Gelli-gaer)
?'bulging slope, slope or hill which bulges like a cheek': (*y*), *boch* 'cheek, jaw', *rhiw*
Bohrukarn c.1170, *y vougryw garn* c.1700, (ho.) *Llwynau Iago or Dan y Ffoc-rhiw*, (?rock) *Ffoc-rhiw Gelli-gaer* 1833, *Vochryw* 1860, *y Fochriw* 1867
The n. applied to the area around Mynydd Fochriw but was transferred to the village which developed on its north-east slopes after coal-pits were sunk 1855-63. Earlier sps. evidently contain *carn* 'cairn, barrow', applying to some such feature on Mynydd Fochriw which has Arthurian associations (APNW 190).

Fonmon, Ffwl-y-mwn　　　　　ST 047675
Vale of Glamorgan (Pen-marc)
Transferred n.?

Funnemunne 1290, *Foumonnue* 1436, *Ffonmon* 1450, *Fonmon* c.1535, *Fonmone* c.1538, *Funmun* 1575, (*o*) *gastell ffwnmwn* c.1564, *funmwn* c.1659, *ffu[n]Mon commonly called ffulmon* c.1598, *ffun y moon* 17th cent, *Foonmoon* c.1670, *Ffonmon commonly called Ffulmon* 1596, *Full Moone* 1678, *Fulymun* 1693, *Faulmont ... vulgarly pronounced ... Fulmun* 1803
A problematic pn., fully analysed by Gwynedd Pierce (PNDPH 176-184), because although historic forms are plentiful, they are generally late and vary considerably. One explanation, which can be traced back at least as far as Iolo Morganwg c.1800, is that it derives from Faumont 'beech-tree hill' with Fr *fou, fau* and **mont**. Iolo was drawing on a rare printed publication 1713 relating to the St John family who were associated with Fonmon from c.1436 (possibly from the late 14th cent) down to the 17th cent. The n. is not, however, particularly appropriate here unless it is a transferred n., perhaps from some place in France. Pierce tends to favour an original Valmont, the n. of a barony in Normandy. This would require unvoicing of original *V-* to the current *F-* [f] of Fonmon and Ff- of Ffwl-y-mwn on its transfer to Wales. This seems unlikely in view of the local (and opposite) tendency to voice E *f* as *v*. In addition to this, there are inconsistencies with recorded forms: none have -a- to favour Val-, Fal- and none have -t to favour -mont. The -l- seen in some forms could perhaps preserve -l- of the Fr def.art **le** (*fou-le-mont*) or the final -l of Fal-, Val- but it is absent in historic forms before the late 16th cent and may be intrusive owing to the relative difficulty of pronouncing the closely-spaced consonants *n, m, n*. Despite these problems, a transferred n. remains the best option and further research may resolve them. A few late sps. appear to show popular association with 'full moon', commonly found in inn-names.

Font-y-gary see **Ffontygari**

Forest Farm see **Fforest** (Whitchurch)

Forge-uchaf see **Upper Forge**

Foundry Town SO 002023
Rhondda Cynon Taf (Aberdare)
'settlement with a foundry': E *foundry*, *town*
Foundry Town 1861
Named from the Dare Foundry (iron and brass) in Elizabeth Street behind Sion Wesleyan chp. (CVPN 54). The foundry disappears from maps between 1885 and 1900.

Fountain SS 882834
Bridgend (Newcastle)
(village near) the Fountain public house: E *fountain*
Fountain public-house 1852, *Fountain Arms (P.H.)* 1877, *Fountain* 1899
The original Fountain public ho. adjoined Fountain Cottages. The n. was dropped before 1899 when the Talbot Arms appears on the south side of the junction of Ty-cribwr Hill and Fountain Road near Fountain railway crossing. This re-adopted the n. *Fountain Inn* after World War II. No current W n.

Foxhole SS 664941
Swansea (Llansamlet)
E *foxhole*
the Fox Hoole 1644, *Foxhole* 1739, *y Foxhole* 1758
A village which developed at the terminus of the First Swansea or Llansamlet Canal which extended to collieries at Gwernllwynwydd. Williams (HLlansamlet 240) attributes the pn. to the occurrence of fox-holes in the r. bank but it may simply describe a place in a secluded location like a fox-hole. There is a Foxhole Bay (SS 3872), ~ Slade (SS 438858) at Pennard.

Frampton Great Frampton SS 973702
Vale of Glamorgan (Llantwit Major)
'settlement or farm of Franca': OE pers.n. *Franca*, **tūn**
Frank(e)ton 1492, *Franketon*, *Fra(n)keton Well* 1495, *Frampton* 1541, *ffraunton* 1663, *Upper ~* , *Great Frampton* 1682, *Great Franton* 1766, *Great ~* , *Little Francton* 1799, *Great ~* , *Little Frampton* 1833
The pn. also occurs in *Frawntons Close* and *Frowntyns Weye* 1541, and (land) *the Framptons*. Frampton has developed from reduced forms such as *ffraunton*, *Frawnton* with an intrusive *–p-*. Cf. Frankton, in Warwickshire, and Shropshire (NCPN 151-2). See also Coed-ffranc.

Frederick Place SS 700971
Swansea (Llansamlet)
'place commemorating (man called) Frederick': pers.n. *Frederick*, **place**
Frederick Place 1878
Referring to Frederick Arthur Aylwin (1823-1868), a prominent local industrialist, whose family lived at Brynawel House on the south side of the road Frederick Place. This formerly linked Lon-las with Tai'r-ysgol and Peniel Green. Current maps show the area as part of Llwynbrwydrau.

Furzehill SS 547906
Swansea (Ilston)
'hill covered with furze': OE *fyrs*, **hyll**
Forshulle 1306, *Vorsehull* 1400, *Vorshill* 1400, *Furzhill* 1624, *Furze Hill* 1650, *Furzehill* 1813
A ref. to the vegetation (NCPN 118); furze (and gorse) is widespread in the Gower peninsula and there is a Furzeland fm. (SS 542911) recorded as *Furzeland* 1801, *Furze-land* 1813, a little to the north-west. Some historic sps. have voicing of *f* as *v*; cf. Fernhill above.

Gabalfa to Gyfeillion

Gelli, Rhondda. The Eastern Colliery opened in 1877 and closed in 1937.

Gabalfa ST 159786
Cardiff (Llandaf)
'ferry': ***ceubalfa***
Coupalva ... idest penn yporth, Coupalva penniporth c.1145, *Gabalva ucha* 1528, *Cabalua Yessa* 1542, *Gabalva* 1584, *Cabalva* 1650, *Gybalva hamlett* 1670, *Gabalfa* 1762
Cf. Cabalfa, Radnorshire (PNRad 37). The development *-eu-* > *-a-* is colloquial (ADG², 39) and len. *C-* > *G-* is probably caused by a prep. such as *i* 'to' or *o* 'from'. The ferry over the r. Taf appears to have been below the weir near the former Gabalfa House which is identifiable with Gabalfa Uchaf (***uchaf***) in older sources. The former ho. Little Gabalfa (ST 166784) is probably Gabalfa Isaf (***isaf***). Early refs. link Gabalfa with a lost pn. that would have produced ModW 'Pen-y-porth' meaning 'top (or end) of the entrance' (***pen¹***, ***y***, ***porth²***) but the precise significance of this is unclear.

Gadlys¹ SN 998028
Rhondda Cynon Taf (Aberdare)
'(the) court-yard, enclosure': (***y***), ***cadlys***
Y Gadlys 1631, *Tir y gadlys ycha*, ~ *yssa* 1632, *Gadles* 1666, *Gadlas isha*, ~ *ycha* 1788, *Gadlys* 1833
The earlier sense may have been 'defensive place' as Deric John suggests (CVPN 57-58) and it is worth noting in this respect that the

former ho. Gadlys Uchaf is also recorded as *Gadlas Ycha formerly Tyr y dadley* 1778, 'land of disputes, disputed land' (*tir, y, dadl* pl. *dadlau*). That suggests **cadlys** might have sometimes meant 'disputed house or tenement'. The pn. is so common, however, that it may have meant little more than 'house with a yard' and 'farmyard, court-yard' as in the case of the local form *cadlas* found in Anglesey and Caernarfonshire. There are identical pns. at Baglan, Llandyfodwg (SS 952879) and Llangynwyd (SS 860879).

Gadlys[2] SS 981697
Vale of Glamorgan (Llan-maes)
'(the) court-yard, enclosure': (*y*), **cadlys**
Gadlys Meadow 1800, *Gadllys* 1813, *Gadlas* 1878
Cf. Gadlys (Aberdare).

Galon Uchaf SO 053082
Merthyr Tudful
?'little hazel-tree': ?*collen, bechan*, later **uchaf**
Tyre (?Ca)llon Vchan 1690, *Tyr Calon Vechan* 1727, *Calon Echa* 1729, *the Collen* 1775, *Callon Ucha* 1779, *Galon Ucha* 1784, *Collen ycha* 1795, (mess.) *Callon ycha* 1816, *Galon-uchaf* 1832
From a fm.n. (SN 053082). Gwynedd Pierce (ADG[2] 40; PNGlam 78-9) tends to favour **collen** possibly in the broader sense 'young tree, sapling', on the basis of some early forms. The second el. **bechan**, *fechan* (variants *echan, ychan*) 'small, lesser' was later displaced by **uchaf** (though there is no contrasting Galon Fawr or Galon Isaf). The len. (*c > g*) seen in later sps. could be attributed to a lost def.art. *y* or more likely the effect of a prep. such as *i* 'to' or *o* 'from'. Pierce suggests *Calon, Galon* may have developed from a colloquial form *collan* but found it difficult to account for -ll- > -l-. This cannot be attributed to E influence since the change occurs before the area became anglicised. Most historic forms actually favour *calon* nf. 'heart', perhaps in the sense 'centre, central (place)', but it is difficult to think of comparable pns. Attempts have been made to connect it with *galon* pl. of *gâl* 'enemy' giving rise to antiquarian stories of battles in the hills north of Merthyr Tudful and individuals such as 'Hychan', a reputed brother of Tudful, and 'Ucha', a reputed officer of Ifor Bach. Popular etymology interprets the pn. as composed of *cae, lôn*[1], *uchaf*, with the sense of 'field of the upper lane'.

Garnllwyd (Carn-lwyd) ST 057713
Vale of Glamorgan (Llancarfan)
'brown or grey cairn': **carn, llwyd**
Carne Lloide 1441, *Carnlloyd* 1519, *Carnllued* c.1538, *Carnelloide* 1541, *Carn Lloyd* c.1670, *Garn llwyd* c.1700, *Y Garn Llwyd* c.1785, *Garn-llwyd* 1833
A former manor. Other sps. and a full discussion are given by Gwynedd Pierce (PNDPH 78-80). Identical in meaning to Garn-lwyd (SN 725074, in Llan-giwg) recorded as *y Garn Loyd* 1506; Garn-llwyd (Cwm-du) *Ygarne Lloide* 1541, *Garnllwyd* 1845; and Garn-llwyd (Gelli-gaer) *Tuy and Tir y Garn Lloyd* 1786 (*tŷ, tir*).

Garn-swllt SN 627087
Swansea (Llangyfelach)
'shilling cairn': **carn, swllt**
(lands) *Carn y swllt* 1650, *Carne Swlt* 1764, (hill) *Carn Swllt* 1831, *Garnswllt* 1851
The precise sense is uncertain; it might describe a cairn shaped like a shilling, one where treasure was found, or perhaps one where payments were habitually made. The name was gradually transferred from the hill to the village which developed in the early 20th cent north of Efail y Garn (SN 625089) which is *Evely-garn* 1841, *Efail y Garn* 1878-9 meaning 'smithy at the cairn' (*gefail*) near Garn-swllt Colliery. Cf. Crug y Swllt (Tavernspite) (*crug*), co. Pembroke.

Garth[1] ST 095940
Rhondda Cynon Taf (Llanfabon)
'mountain ridge, promontory': (*y*), **garth**[1]
(tmts.) *Tyre Ygarllrth, Tyrergallrth'* 1541, *Y Karth* 1546, *le Karth* 1550, *Garth Hamlett* 1670, (lands) *Tir y Garth* 1708, *Garth, Garth Vach, ~ Isha* 1783, (hos.) *Garth, Garthfach* 1833
Referring to the hill recorded as *Cefn Garth* 1833 immediately west of Garth Hall (ST 096941) above Abercynon. The refs. for 1541 and 1708 stand for 'the Garth land' (*tir, y*).

Garth²   SS 864903
Bridgend (Maes-teg, Llangynwyd)
'(the) mountain ridge, promontory': (*y*), *garth¹* Ygarthe 1541, *the Garth* 1588, *y garth* 1630, (hill) *Garth* 1813, (ho.) *Garth* 1833
Named from the hill Garth (SS 8790) east of Maesteg. Also the n. of a former fm. (SS 856897) described as *Tred y Rhyw Garth* 1799 and *Troedyrhiw* 1813 which gave its n. to the railway station (*Troed-y-rhiw Garth* 1877) in Cwmfelin now known as Garth; cf. Troed-y-rhiw.

Garth³   SO 064095
Merthyr Tudful
'(the) mountain ridge, promontory': (*y*), *garth¹* *Garth Hamlett* 1670, (ho.) *The Garth* 1766, *Garth, ~ Hamlet* 1795, *Upper Garth* 1799, (hos.) *Garth, Blaen-y-garth* 1833
The hilly district between Merthyr and Dowlais. Upper Garth was at approx. SO 064078.

Garth⁴   ST 1182, 1282
Cardiff (Pen-tyrch)
'(the) mountain ridge, promontory': *garth¹* *Garthe* 1623, *the Garth* 1675, *ye Garth* 1729, (hill) *Lower Garth* 1799, *Garth Fawr, ~ Fach* 1825, (hill) *Garth Hill*, (ho.) *Garth-fawr* 1833, *Garth Pen Tyrch* c.1800
In ref. to Mynydd y Garth otherwise Garth Hill (ST 1083) (**mynydd**). This appears as *Arthors buttes hill* on Saxton's map of 1580, with similar forms on derivative maps of Glamorgan 1610-1729, but this may be a reinterpretation of Garth. If reliable then it may refer to Bronze Age cairns on the top of the hill with some fancied likeness to E *butts* 'heaps; archery butts' etc, and the legendary Arthur. The hill possessed a beacon recorded in 1638.

Garthgynyd   SO 0901
Merthyr Tudful (Gelli-gaer)
'ridge where fuel was gathered': *garth¹*, *cynnud* *Garth kenyd* 1527, *Teer garthe kened* 1543, *Teer y Karth Kynyd* 1566, *Garth Gynid hamlett* 1670, *Garthgynyd* 1760, *Carthgynyd Hamlet* 1783, (ho.) *Garth-gynydd* 1833
The second el. is unlikely to be the pers.n. *Cynidr* with loss of –r in colloquial use (cf. Llangynidr, Breconshire: PNBre 106-7) because of the absence of –r in historic sps. The ridge lies between the rivers Rhymni and Bargod Taf. The fm. Garth-gynydd (sic) is at SO 098013.

Garthmaelog Garth Uchaf   ST 023830
Rhondda Cynon Taf (Llanharan)
'ridge of (man called) Maelog': *garth¹*, pers.n. *Maelog*
Cartmaylog c.1262, (forest) *Corthmaylok* 1281, (wood) *Carthmaylok* 1314, *Karthmayllok* 1375, (forest) *Carthmaylocke* 1541, (~) *Garth Mayloge* 1574, *fforest of Arthmaylogg* c.1598, (mess. and land) *garth maylog* 1765, (heath lands) *Fforest Garthmailog* 1745 (1800)
The pn. survives in Garth Uchaf and Garth Isaf (ST 023828) (**uchaf, isaf**) but was formerly the n. of a ht. in Llanharan and an extensive forest represented in part by the woods centred on the hill Mynydd Garthmaelwg (q.v.). The pn. may be the location of a battle *Gueith Gartmailauc* recorded under the year 722 in the Welsh chronicles.

Garth Place   ST 188873
Caerphilly (Rhydri t.; Bedwas)
'place near Garth': pn. *Garth*, E **place**
Garth Place 1892
Named from its proximity to Garth fm. (ST 184875) recorded as *Garth Fm.* 1813 meaning 'mountain ridge, promontory' (*garth¹*) located on a northern projection of Mynydd Rudry. The ht. originated with four rows of hos. constructed in the 1890s near Rudry Colliery and an older brickworks.

Garw see **Blaengarw** (Llangeinwyr)

Garw Forest and **Garw Valley** see **Nant-garw**

Gelli   ST 975948
Rhondda (Ystradyfodwg)
'grove, copse': **celli**
Kelligaled 1671, *Tyir gellygaled* 1633 CL 4.1264, (ho.) *Gelli, Gelligaled, Gellidawel* 1813, *Gelli*, (ho.) *Gelli-galed*, (ht) *Gelli-dawel* 1884-5, *Gelli Ystradyfodwg* 1892

Formerly the n. of three fms. Gelli (ST 975947), Gelligaled and Gellidawel with **caled** 'rough, hard' and *tawel* 'quiet, calm'. Len. C- > G- may be caused by an unrecorded def. art. *y* or a common prep. such as *i* 'to' and *o* 'from'.

Gelli-deg SO 031071
Merthyr Tudful
'fair wood': ***celli***, ***teg***
Gelly deaye hamlett 1670, *Gellideg* 1752, *Gellidêg* 1776, *Gelli deg Hamlet* 1783, *Gelli-deg* 1832
Len. of ***celli*** suggests a lost def.art. *y* recorded in a 17th cent triban (Trib 16). The village developed in the 19th cent north of ironstone pits and coalworkings. Cf. Gelli-deg (SS 779983, at Llantwit-juxta-Neath) recorded as *Ygelly Dege* 1541 and *Y Gelly degg* 1584.

Gellifaelog SO 061077
Merthyr Tudful
'grove of (man called) Maelog': ***celli***, pers.n. *Maelog*
kellyvaylock 1426, *Tir Gellifaelog* 1541, *Gellivailog* 1743, *Gellivaylog* 1757, *Gellifailog* 1783
The pers.n. (cf. Garthmaelog) was fairly common and there is no proven connection with the saint commemorated in Llandyfaelog in Anglesey, Monmouthshire and Breconshire. The n. is taken from a former fm. (approx. SO 058077).

Gellifedw see **Birchgrove**[2]

Gelligaer ST 135968
Caerphilly
'(the) grove at the fort': (***y***), ***celli***, ***caer***
Kelligaer 1254, *Kilthegayr* 1281, *Kylthygayr* 1307, *Kilthigair* 1349, *Kellygaer* 1487, *Kellygare* c.1557, *y gelli gaer* c.1566, *Gelly Gare* 1670, *Gellygaer* 1676
The pn. may refer to the Iron Age fort on the hill Buarth-y-gaer immediately east of the village (ADG[2], 42) recorded as *Gaer Castell* 1833 and *Twyn Castell or Caer Castell* 1875 (**twyn**, **castell**) or the Roman auxiliary fort on the north-west side of the village (ST 134970) recorded as *Gaer Fawr* 1875 (ETG 22). Local pron. is now [gɛliːˈgɛːr, gɛθliːˈgɛːr] rhyming with E 'dare' [dɛːr] but is *Gelligâr* in a W-language source 1750 (WP) which tends to favour a former pron. [ˈgeɬiːgaːr] rhyming with E 'car' [kaːr]. It is possible that ***celli*** had a variant *cylli* in Glamorgan since most recorded sps. before the 16th cent have *Kilth-* , *Kylth-* as in the case of Gelli-garn (q.v.) and another Gelligaer (in Neath) found as *Kiltikar* c.1208 (1336), *Kelly Gaer* 1541 and *Kellygare* 1587.

Gelli-garn SS 9578, 9678
Vale of Glamorgan (St Mary Hill)
'grove at the cairn': ***celli***, ***carn***
(land, fee) *Kilticar*, (mill of) *Kiltecar* c.1208, *Kilthekarn* 1254, *Killecarne* c.1291, (ch.) *beate Marie juxta Kilthecarn* 13th cent, *Kyllygarne* 1560, *Kellygarne* c.1670, *Gelligarn* 1813
Lenition C- > G- is probably caused by a prep. such as *i* 'to' and *o* 'from'. Modern maps apply the n. to the south slopes of St Mary Hill Down and a ho. (SS 957783) at the western end of what is now described as St Mary Hill (village) but this is properly Gelli-garn and St Mary Hill should refer to the area around the ch. of St Mary (SS 957793) 0.5 miles to the north-west on the north side of St Mary Hill Down. The transfer of the n. to the modern village took place between 1833 and the appearance of the OS 1:2,500 map 1877. Gelli-garn was the location of a grange of Neath abbey, recorded in the ref. for c.1291 and in 1535, which was probably at St Mary Hill Court (SS 957783) recorded as *Cwrt* 1833, *Court* 1841 (**cwrt**[1]). The mill may have been at Tŷ-candy (SS 949791) recorded as *Ty candy*, *Ty kandy* 1661, *Tycandy Farm* 1767 meaning 'house at the fulling-mill' (*candy*) on the r. Ewenni.

Gelli Gawrdaf see **Allt-y-cewri**

Gelli-groes ST 176947
Caerphilly (Mynyddislwyn Monmouthshire)
'grove at crossroads': ***celli***, ***croes***
Kellygrose c.1541, *kellee grose* 1692, *Gellygros* 1813, *Gellygroes* 1819, *Gelli-groes Farm* 1833
Named from the fm. (ST 177948). The crossroads are apparently those east of Capel

Silo (erected 1813) on Heol Ddu meaning 'dark road' (***heol***, ***du***).

Gelli-gron SN 715048
Neath Port Talbot (Llang-giwg and Llangyfelach)
'round grove': ***celli***, ***cron***
Gelli gronn 1649, Kelligron 1717, Melyn y Gelly Gron 1733, Gelligron Mill 1801, Gelli-gron, Felin-gelli-gron 1833
From a fm. located near woodland 1884. The mill (SN 714052) (***melin***) lay in Llangyfelach p. (Mawr hamlet). Identical in meaning to Gelli-gron (ST 007887) at Llantrisant recorded as y gelli gron 1580, Celligronn 1673, (ho.) Gelhi gron c.1700, Gelli-gron 1833.

Gelli-haf ST 159957
Caerphilly (Bedwellte Monmouthshire)
'summer grove': ***celli***, ***haf***
Gelly have 1740, Gellyhave Colliery 1813, Kelly haf 1832, Gellihâve 1833, Gelli-hâf, ~ Farm 1880
The len. C- > G- is probably caused by preps. such as ***i*** 'to' and ***o*** 'from' rather than use of the def.art. ***y***. The n. of two former hos. on slopes facing south and southwestwards.

Gelli-nudd SN 737041
Neath Port Talbot (Cilybebyll)
?'misty grove': ***celli***, ?***nudd*** 'mist, haze'
Kelly Nydd 1541, Gellynydd 1814, Gelli-nudd 1832, Gellunydd Farm 1841
The second el. could also be ***nydd***[1] nm. 'spin, twist' and adj. 'twisted', perhaps a former n. for the stream now known as Nant Gelli-nudd (Nant Gelli-nedd on OS maps). See also Craig Gelli-nudd.

Gelliwion ST 056890
Rhondda Cynon Taf (Llantrisant)
'Gwion's grove': ***celli***, pers.n. *Gwion*
(wood) Kellywyon 1541, (syddyn) kelli wion c.1612, Kellywyon hamlett 1670, Gelli Wyon c.1700, Collywyon fawr, Cellywyon genol, ~ isha 1768, Gelliwion 1811, Gelli-hwyon 1833
One of the five administrative hamlets (with Castellau, Traean, Brofeisgyn and Llantrisant Town) of Llantrisant p. though most historic forms apply to a single ho. (ST 056890). The c.1612 form has *syddyn* nm. 'tenement, dwelling-place'.

Gendros SS 635953
Swansea
'(the) moor on a ridge': (***y***), ***cefn***, ***rhos***[2]
Genros 1714, Cen-ros, Genrose 1735, Genros 1766, Gendros 1832, Genrhos 1845
Gwynedd Pierce (PNGlam 82-83) shows that -d- is intrusive as in the pron. 'Pendryn' for *Penr(h)yn* and 'Cyndrig' (anglicised *Kendrick*) from *Cynwrig*. For the contraction Cen- in place of Cefn-, cf. Cyncoed. Gendros fm. lay on a low ridge followed by Middle Road.

Georgetown SO 043066
Merthyr Tudful
'settlement named from George (Crawshay)': pers.n. *George*, E ***town***
George Town 1839, George Town, Georgetown 1851
Built at the same time as the adjoining Williamstown in first half of 19th cent respectively named from George Crawshay (1794-1873) and William Crawshay (1788-1867), sons of William Crawshay I (1764-1834). *Georgetown* occurs from the 1820s and *Williamstown* c.1840 according to Eyers (MCPP 44-48). Georgetown (SO 1408) (*George town* 1871), built from c.1860, at Tredegar, may be named from Samuel George Homfray (1831-1894) (son of a managing director of Tredegar Ironworks) or perhaps his son and namesake (1855-1908).

Giants Grave SS 737949
Neath Port Talbot (Briton Ferry)
'(site of a) giant's grave', E ***giant***, E ***grave***
the Giants Grave 1797, Giants Grave Coal Wharf c.1798, Giant's Grave 1830
Probably named from prehistoric stones recorded in William Weston Young's *Guide* 1835 (referring to some date after 1797) and or the stone recorded by E. Humphreys in *Reminiscences* (1898) identifiable with *Erect Druidical Stone* on the OS map 1830 near Cwrt-sart. This required twelve horses to move it to the grounds of Woodside House,

Baglan, in 1883. Similar prehistoric stones and grave-mounds are often associated with heroes and giants. The Giants Grave Pill or r. creek is recalled in Pill Terrace. Giant's Grave is also recorded as the n. of a public ho. at Aberdare 1841.

Gibbonsdown   ST 122694
Vale of Glamorgan (Cadoxton-juxta-Barry)
'hill of Gibbon': surname *Gibbon*, E **down**
Gibbons Down 1743, *Gibbonston* 1765, *Gibbon's Down* 1783, *Gibbonsdown* 1811, *Gibbin's Down farm* 1852, *Gibon's town* 1868
See Pierce (PNDPH 26) for further sps. Named from a fm. (approx. ST 121693) built over after c.1970. The surname is fairly common in Glamorgan; John Gibbon held a tmt. *Gybbons Lande* in St Andrews Major in 1541.

Gileston, Silstwn   ST 018670
Vale of Glamorgan
'Joel's settlement or farm': pers.n. *Joel*, **tūn**
Juleston 13th cent, *Jeoliston* 1350, (John Joell of) *Joelstone* 1362-3, *Jeleston* 1425, (John Gyles of) *Gyles Towne* 1530, *Gilston* 1578, *Siltwn* 1590-1, *Gyllston some tyme called Joyleston* c.1598, *Silstwn* 19th cent
William Juel occurs 1262 and a certain Thomas Joel (d. 1350) later held the manor but little is known of the family. Joel was clearly associated with and eventually displaced by the distinct pers.n. Giles. *Gileston* and similar variations had become established by about 1530 and misled the antiquarian John Leland c.1538 who claims that a certain Giles, 'a gentilman of an auncient house', was lord of *Gilestown*. The ch. dedication to St Giles, recorded in the 17th cent, derives from the pn. There is no reliable evidence that it was ever dedicated to St Mabon. The W form has substituted *Sils-*; cf. *Siôn* for John, *Sincyn*, *Siencyn* for Jenkin.

Gilfach (Gilfach Fargoed)   ST 152983
Caerphilly (Gelli-gaer)
'corner, nook': *cilfach*
Gilfach 1900
The village developed during the late 19th cent and occupies a site adjoining a tramway running from a former colliery recorded as *Cilfach Colliery* 1878, *Gilfach Colliery* 1900, apparently drawn from the n. of the ho. Gilfach Fargoed Fach (ST 144987) recorded as *Cilfach bargoed* 1813, *Gilfach-fargoed Fach* 1878 (**bach**¹). The n. also applied to Gilfach Fargoed Fawr (**mawr**) (ST 147993) and other hos. in the immediate area collectively recorded as *Kylvach y Vargod* 1481, *Kylvach Vargoyd* 1541, *Tyre Kilvache vargoed* 1629, *Kilvach bargoed* 1632, *Kilvach Bargod* 1729. For the rn. Bargod Rhymni see Bargod. Gilfach Fargoed survives as the n. of the railway station.

Gilfach-goch   SS 981893
Rhondda Cynon Taf (Llandyfodwg/Llantrisant)
'(the) red nook': (**y**), **cilfach**, **coch**
tire y gilvach cogh 1553, *Kilvach goz* 1592, (mtn. ground) *Gilvach Goch* 1710, *Gilfachgoch* 1784
The colour probably refers to the red-brown of local vegetation (cf. Wenallt) or soil. This seems better than a derivation from 'a heap of red cinders ... a memento of the ironworks that stood there in olden times' suggested by Dafydd Morganwg 1874 (HMorg 386) and others. Gilfach Garden Village (SS 982882), immediately south of Gilfach Goch, developed from just before World War I, and is named from a former fm. Gilfach (at SS 983884) recorded thus 1813 and 1833. Gilfach-goch (SN 760093), near Ystalyfera, is *Tir y Gilvach Goch* 1548, *Y Gilvach Goch* 1764, *Gilfach-gôch* 1878-9.

Glais   SN 702005
Swansea (Cadoxton-juxta-Neath/Llansamlet)
'(the) stream': (**y**), **glais**
(stream) *Gleys* 1184 (1334), *Aber Gleys* 1203, (brook) *Glaisse* 1650, *Glaish* 1743-4, *Glais* 1832, *the Glais* 1845, (r.) *Clais* c.1700, (brook) *Claish* 1686
From Nant Glais which flows down from Mynydd y Drumau through Cwmcyrnach. Late sps. suggest association with *clais* nm. 'groove, rut' – a very good description of the course of this stream – but all early forms have G-. Some late forms such as *Claish* show that it was often pronounced with the aspirate 'sh' [ʃ] found widely in south Wales after -i.

Glamorgan, Morgannwg
'land of Morgan': *gwlad*, pers.n. *Morgan*, terr. suffix *-wg*
Morgannuc c.1100, *morcannuc, morcanhuc, gulatmorcant* c.1145, *Glammorgan* before 1147 *Wlatmorgan'* 1230, *Morgannok* c.1316, *Glamorgan and Morganok* 1322
Both names earlier applied to the area extending from the r. Tawe to the r. Rhymni but were transferred to the county formed 1536-43 which included the formerly distinct lp. of Gower / Gŵyr. The antiquarian Rice Merrick c.1580 describes historic Morgannwg as that area between the rs. Ely and Ogmore 'beneath the common Portway' (the main road running west from Cardiff through Cowbridge towards Bridgend) and says that people who lived north of the road called the southerners 'Gwŷr Gwladforgan' or 'Men of Glamorgan' (BG 4). Other historical sources, however, make no such distinction. The southern area is properly Bro Morgannwg or Y Fro, translated as Vale of Glamorgan (q.v.) in contrast to Blaenau Morgannwg (q.v.). Morgan is reputed to be either the 8th cent Morgan ab Athrwys, king of Glywysing, or Morgan ab Owain alias Morgan Hen (died 974). Morgannwg corresponded in whole or part with the kingdom of Glywysing (q.v.).

Glan-bad see **Upper Boat**

Glandŵr see **Landore**

Glanfa Iwerydd see **Atlantic Wharf**

Glan-lliw   SN 611004
Swansea (Penderi ht.; Llangyfelach)
'bank of (r.) Lliw': *glan*, rn. *Lliw*
Glan Llyw 1644, *~ alias y Tyr Bach, Llanlluw alias Bach y Greyddin Ycha* 1764, *Glan lliw ycha* 1790, *Lanlliw* 1813, *Glan-lliw* 1830, *Glan-lliw, ~ -fâch* 1884
For the rn. see Pont-lliw. The n. of a housing estate developed around a ho. The Poplars from the 1960s. Bachygwreiddyn-uchaf (*uchaf*) refers to a ho. (SN 614004) later recorded as *Glan-lliw* 1877 and *Glan-Lliw* 1898- 1959. Bachygwreiddyn-isaf (SN 606002) is recorded as *Bachygwreiddyn isaf* 1813, now plain Bachygwreiddyn. The two hos. are undifferentiated as *Bagh Gwreythyn* 1478, (place) *Bagh Egwrythyne* 1555, *Bach y greyddin* 1583, *Bach y Gwreiddin* 1699, *Bach-y-gwreiddyn* 1792 meaning 'bend of the root' (*bach*[2], *y*, *gwreiddyn* nm. 'root (of a plant, etc)'). There is a notable bend in the r. Lliw between Pont-lliw and Bachygwreiddyn.

Glan-y-llyn   ST 120842
Rhondda Cynon Taf (Eglwysilan)
'bank of the pool': *glan*, *y*, *llyn*
Glan y Llyn 1868, *Glan-y-llyn* 1875
There is no pool here now though it was presumably in the r. Taf. It is unlikely to have been the small boggy pool on the east side of the village above the former canal lock. This was probably caused by construction of the Glamorganshire Canal.

Glan-y-nant   ST 151973
Caerphilly (Gelli-gaer)
'bank of the stream': *glan*, *y*, *nant*
Glan-y-nant 1920
The stream is Nant y Cascade. Largely industrial housing constructed shortly before World War I between Pengam Foundry and Rhos Colliery.

Glebeland   SO 048062
Merthyr Tudful
'piece of land serving as part of a clergyman's benefice': *glebe*, *land*
Glebland 1820, *Glebe land* 1852, *y Glebeland* 1861
Edmunds (THPM 72) 1864 states that the p. priest of Merthyr Tudful had a living worth £1,700 yearly of which the greater part came from Glebeland.

Glenboi   ST 034991
Rhondda Cynon Taf (Aberdare)
Glenboi 1995
A misinterpretation of the rn. Cwmboi, properly Cynfoi (see Abercwmboi), substituting ModE *glen* for the perceived *cwm*. The n. of housing

built in the 1980s (on part of Abercwmboi-isaf fm.).

Glyncastell (Glyn Castle) SN 836026
Neath Port Talbot (Llantwit-juxta-Neath)
'valley of the castle': *glyn*, (*y*), *castell*
Glyn y castell yssa 1548, *glynncastle issa* 1585, *Clyn y castell ycha* 1562, *Glyn Castell* 1587, (ruinous castle) *Clyn y Castle* late 16th cent, *Glyncastle, Clyn Castle farme* 1722, *Tyr Pen y Gwyn antiently called Glyncastell* 1777, *Glyncastle farm* 1798
The anglicised form has substituted E *castle* in late sources. The first el. presumably applies to the valley of the stream Clydach but might also have displaced *clun*² 'meadow' etc. found also in Clun (Clyne), about two miles down the Vale of Neath. Two properties are distinguished as 'lower' (*isaf*) and 'upper' (*uchaf*).

Glyn-coch ST 076923
Rhondda Cynon Taf (Llanwynno)
'red valley': *glyn*, *coch*
Glyncoch 1738, 1841, *Clyn Coch* 1782, (fm.) *Glyn-coch* 1833
Probably alluding to the red-brown of local vegetation (cf. Gilfach-goch). Taken from a former fm. (near Craig-yr-hesg School) itself referring to the valley of Nant Clydach. The village developed from the 1950s around the ho. Greenmeadow.

Glyncorrwg SS 874991
Neath Port Talbot
'valley of the (r.) Corrwg': *glyn*, rn. *Corrwg*
(place) *Corrok* 1376, *Glyncorrog* 1519, *Glyncorock, -corrock* c.1528, *Glin Corrug* c.1538, *Glyncorrwg* 1559, *Glyncorruck, Glyn-corwk* 1574, *Glyncorrwg Parish, Parcell Glyncorrwg* 1670
See Corrwg and cf. Cwmcorrwg. Located at the meeting point of Corrwg Fechan with Afon Corrwg.

Glyncynon see **Cynon**

Glyndulais Isaf, ~ Uchaf see **Dulais**

Glyn-fach ST 026908
Rhondda Cynon Taf (Llantrisant)
?'little valley': *glyn*, *bach*¹
Glyn 1833, *Glynn fach* 1841, (wood) *Coed Glyn-fâch, Glyn-fâch Colliery* 1874
There are some doubts with this explanation because historic forms are very late and it is recorded as *Bryn fach* 1811, probably in error. *glyn* is a nm. but the len. f- for b- shows that it was regarded here as a nf. Examples do occur elsewhere such as Glynfechan (Llansanffraid Glynceiriog), Denbighshire, where it is a nf. but they are uncommon. Confusion with *clun*² (cf. Glyn-llan) can be ruled out because that too is a nm. The second el. could be *bach*² 'nook, angle, bend' after a lost def.art. This el. can be both a nm. and nf. which raises the possibility that Glyn-fach was earlier Glyn-y-fach with len. bach > fach. That might refer to a twist in the course of the stream here or a bend in the adjoining r. Rhondda but further evidence is needed. The village developed on the west side of the colliery from the late 19th cent below the ho. Glyn-fach (ST 028906) which adjoined a small stream.

Glyn-gaer ST 140970
Caerphilly (Gelli-gaer)
'valley of the fort', *glyn*, (*y*), *caer*
(ho.) *Glyngair* 1841, *Glyn-gaer* 1877, *Glyngaer* 1909
Referring to the Roman fort at Gelli-gaer. The ho. (ST 142966) is called *Potteries* 1832, a n. surviving in Pottery Road. The village developed from about 1910 around Oxford Street, Glyn-gaer Road and Glyn Gaer School. The valley is that of Nant Cylla.

Glyn-llan SS 942871
Bridgend (Llandyfodwg)
'(the) church meadow': *clun*², (*y*), *llan*
Klyn y llan 1650, *Glynn y Llann* 1764, *Clyn y llann* 1785, *Glyn-y-llan* 1841, *Glynllan* 1845
Probably a meadow belonging to the ch. of Llandyfodwg. Later forms show association with *glyn* 'narrow valley' and loss of the unstressed def.art. *y*. A small area of housing developed from c.1960 near Glyn-llan fm.

Glynllwchwr SN 5904, 5905
Swansea (*parsel* of Llandeilo Tal-y-bont)
'valley of (r.) Llwchwr': *glyn*, rn. *Llwchwr*
Glynlozchorne 1306, *Glynlvgnewre* 1535, *Glinlochor* c.1580, *Glyn Llychwr* 1682, *Parcell Glyn Lougher* 1670, *Glyn Loughor, ~ Yssha* 1764, *Llyn-llwchr* 1778
For the rn. see Loughor. The rn. is also found in Ynysllwchwr (approx. SN 619088), another *parsel* or t. of Loughor p., recorded as *Ynes Lochor* 1559, *Ynis loughour* 1650, *Parcell ynis Lloughor* 1670, *Ynis Loughor* 1764, and *Ynys-llwchwr* 1832 (*ynys*).

Glyn-nedd (Glynneath) SN 882053
Neath Port Talbot (Cadoxton-juxta-Neath)
'valley of the (r.) Nedd': *glyn*, rn. *Nedd Glynneth'* 1281, *Clynneth* c.1291, *Glynneth, Glinneth* 1314, (valley) *Glyn Nedd* late 15th cent, *Glyne nethe* 1603, *glynnedd* 1600-7, *Glynneath* 1735
See **Neath**, **Nedd**. In the Vale of Neath (*The vale of Neath* 1819). The n. also described the three *parseli* or sub-divisions in the p. of Cadoxton known as Parsel Glyn-nedd Genol, ~ Uchaf, and ~ Isaf (*cenol, uchaf, isaf*) recorded as *Glyn Neath ucha* 1593, *parcell of Neath Ycha, Neath Yssa* 1644, *Parcel Glyn Neath yssa, ~ Genol, Glyn Neath ycha* 1670 (*parsel*).

Glynogwr SS 956872
Bridgend (Llandyfodwg)
'valley of the (r.) Ogwr': *glyn*, rn. *Ogwr*
(land) *Glynnogor* 1295, *Glinogor alias Glenogor* 1296, *Glynogor* 1303, *Glynnogour* 1349, *Glynogur* 1531, *Glinogwr, Angl[icised] Llanevodok* c.1700, (park) *Clennok^r, Glynnog^r* 1440, *Meanaur Glyn Ogour* c.1538, *maenor glynn ogwr* before 1564
For the rn. see Ogmore, Ogwr. The n. also applied to the lp. of Glynogwr (covering Llangeinwyr and Llandyfodwg) and has displaced the p. n. Llandyfodwg. This is recorded as *Landewodoc* c.1261, *Landyvodduck* 13th cent, *Landevodouc* 1429, *Landevodog* 1532, *ll. dyfodwc* c.1566, *Llandyvoduck* 1670, *Llandyfodog* 1799, *Llandyfodwg or Eglwys Glyn Ogwr* 1833, meaning 'church of (St) Tyfodwg':

llan, Tyfodwg. Tyfodwg is also one of the three saints dedicated at Llantrisant.

Glynrhedynog see **Ferndale**

Glynrhondda see **Rhondda**

Glyn-taf ST 087893
Rhondda Cynon Taf (Eglwysilan)
'valley of the (r.) Taf': *glyn*, rn. *Taf*
(forest of) *Glintaf, Glyntaf* 1307, *Glyntaf* 1426, *Glyn Tâf* 1758, *Glyntaff Hamlet* 1783, *Glyn Taff* 1831
The n. seems to have described the narrower part of the valley between Pontypridd and Tongwynlais. The n. also applied to a ht. or division of Eglwysilan p. but became attached to the industrial village which developed in the 19th cent near the Taff Vale Iron Works, becoming a separate p. in 1848. Identical in meaning to Glyn-taf on the opposite side of the r. (in Llantwit Fardre) found as (forest of) *Glyntaf* 1281, *Glyntaff* 1541, *fforrest Glyntave* (in manor of Clun) 1670 (*fforest*).

Glywysing
Gliuising c.1100, *gleuissic, gleuissicg* c.1145
'land of (man called) Glywys': pers.n. *Glywys*, suffix *–ing*
Charters dating to the 7th-9th cent copied into the Book of Llandaf 12th cent show that the kings of Glywysing held an area extending from the r. Tywi to the lower Wye – roughly equivalent to the area held by the kings of Gwent (*Ventia*) in the 6th cent. The n. itself, however, probably once applied to a smaller area and was displaced by Gwlad Forgan alias Morgannwg (see Glamorgan) stretching from the r. Tawe to Rhymni or to Usk. Gwent proper described the area east of the r. Usk. Little is known of Glywys save that the Life of St Cadog – of dubious reliability – composed c.1100 states that he was grandfather of St Cadog and father of Gwrai or Gwrin (see Gwrinydd). This places him in the 5th cent. The pers.n. is also found in Merthyr Glywys which seems to have been at or near Clevis (q.v.).

Gnoll, Y Gnol SS 761972
Neath Port Talbot (Llantwit-juxta-Neath)
'hillock', later 'hill-top, knoll', E *knoll* (OE *cnol*); *y, cnol*
La Knolle 1332, *Le Knolle, Tyre Ygnoll, Knollys Lande* 1541, *Gnoll* 1666, *ye Gnol* 1720, *The Knoll* 1729, *Gnoll Castle* 1741, *y Gnoll* 1878
Gnoll is undoubtedly an E pn. but it is worth noting that historic forms in earlier sources have *Kn-* and that the variation Kn-/Gn- in E pns. elsewhere and in general vocabulary is uncommon. The frequency of forms with Gn- suggests that the form *Gnol(l)* has been influenced by the cymricised form (in which the consonant G- is sounded). OE *cnol*, ME *knoll* was borrowed in W as a nm. *cnol* but the evidence here suggests that the pn. was taken to be a nf. in which *Cnol* lenites to *Gnol* after the def.art. Note in particular the form *Tyre Ygnoll* standing for ModW *Tir y Gnol*, 'land at (or belonging to) the Knoll/Gnol' (*tir*) and (brook called) *nant y gnoll* c.1700 (*nant*). Gnoll Road (recorded 1877), now Gnoll Avenue and Gnoll Drive, is recorded in *Penhewl y Gnol* 1684 (*pen¹, heol*) and as *Heol y Gnol* 1685. See PNGlam 84-5.

Godreaman SO 012006
Rhondda Cynon Taf (Aberdare)
'edge of a hill near (r.) Aman': *godre, Aman*
Godreaman 1871
For the rn. see Aberaman. The area developed near Fforchneol Arms from the late 19th cent but *Godreaman* was not applied on OS maps until c.1919.

Godre'r-graig SN 752067
Neath Port Talbot (Llan-giwg)
'edge of the rock or cliff': *godre, yr, craig*
Godre'r-graig 1877
Adjoining a rocky hillside Graig Arw recorded as *Craig-garw* 1831, *Graigarw* 1841, 'rough cliff' (*garw*) between Godre'r-graig and Ystalyfera.

Goetre (Goytre) SS 785896
Neath Port Talbot (Margam)
'settlement in woodland': *coetref*
the Goytre 1633, *Goytre* 1810, *Goetre* 1876

Len. C- > G- may have been prompted by a def.art. *y* not recorded in historic forms or by a prep. such as *i* and *o*. The village developed near coal workings from the early 20th cent and was named from a fm. in Margam p. A common pn. with other examples at Radur (Goitre-fawr ST 116805: *Coytre* 1541, *syddyn y Goytre* c.1612) (*syddyn*), St Mellons (Goitre ST 239822: *the Goytre* 1676) and Swansea (Goetre Fawr SS 598934: *Goytre* 1583, *the Goytre* 1650, *Goytre-bella, ~ -fawr, ~ -fach* 1832) (*pellaf* 'furthermost', *mawr, bach¹*).

Gorfynydd see **Gwrinydd**

Gorseinon SS 589987
Swansea (Llandeilo Tal-y-bont/Llangyfelach)
'Einon's marsh': *cors*, pers.n. *Ein(i)on*
Corse Inon 1691, *Gorse Eynon* 1720, *Cors-Eynon* 1750, *Croes-Eynon* 1751, *Nydfych vach, otherwise Corse Eynon* 1776, *Cross Inon* 1729, *Ty yn y Coedman, Ty yr helig all generally called Gorseynon Fawr* 1820, *Gorseinon* 1851
Len. of C- as G- may be attributed to the effect of preps. such as *i* 'to' and *o* 'from'. Some sps. show association with *croes* and E *cross*. The pers.n. is very common and there is no good reason for identifying it with Einion ab Owain, grandson of Hywel Dda. As a pn. Gorseinon originally applied to what is now Penlle'r-gaer. The modern village developed around a railway station at Rhydymaerdy, opened in 1867, later known as Gorseinon Station. Gorseinon Garden Village (SS 596977) was begun shortly before World War I on part of Stafford Common.

Gower, Gŵyr
?'curved, bent (promontory)': *gŵyr¹*
Guohir, Guhir, Guyr 8th cent, *Goer* c.1100, *patria Guhir* c.1145, *Guoher, Guhir* c.1170, *Guher* 12th cent, *Gohir* 1220, *Gwhyr* c.1400, *cantref guyr* early 13th cent, *Gower* 13th cent, *Guwer* 1305, *Gouwer* c.1329, *Gowerslond* 1398, *Anglicane Gowerie* 1331, *Gower Anglashrie* 1400, *English Gower* 1508, *the Sher' of Gower* 1520, *Welschery of Gower* 1532, *Gouher supra boscus* 1466, (manor) *Gower-supra-Boscos* 1710, (commotes) *Couthceyd*

et Iscoid 1325, (manor) *Westgower* 1469, *Gower Wallicana or Welsh Gower ... commonly called Parcel Iscoyd and sometimes west Gower* 1764, *Browyr* 1828

Gower is now generally used to refer to the peninsula known to W-speakers as Bro Gŵyr (***bro***) but applies in early records to the whole of the ancient cantref extending from Worm's Head to Black Mountain. The precise meaning of Gower, Gŵyr is uncertain though the suggestion that it is related to *gŵyr* 'curved, bent' – referring either to the perceived shape of the cantref or the promontory – makes very good sense. It is also clear, however, that Gower, Gŵyr was earlier *Gwhyr* with two distinct syllables and the function of the original -*h*- has not been satisfactorily explained but cf. Gwrhai (q.v.).

Gowerton, Tregŵyr   SS 589962
Swansea (Loughor)
'settlement in Gower': pn. **Gower**, E ***town***; ***tref***, pn. **Gŵyr**
Gower Road 1852, 1891, *Gowerton* 1886, *Tregwyr* 1896

An industrial village and an ecclesiastical p. from 1882 which developed near Gower Road Station, established on the Swansea-Llanelli railway 1852. Its n. apparently changed to Gowerton 1885 at the request of the p. council owing to post straying to Gower Road, Sketty; GowerH 102-3: at the proposal of Thomas Jones, a colliery manager). The W form is said to have been suggested by D.E. Williams, former headmaster of Gowerton Council School, in 1934 but it is clearly older. Its late appearance, however, is evident in the absence of expected len. of -g- which is regularly dropped after ***tref*** as a nf. Located near a former ho. Ffosfelen (approx. SS 588964). Historic forms such as *Foes-y-velyn* 1799, *Foesyfelin* 1813 favour the meaning 'the mill ditch' (***ffos***, ***y***, ***melin***) from its location near Melin Trafle. Later recorded as *Ffos-felan* 1830, *Ffosfelin* 1841, and *Ffosfelen* 1851-76. The final el. was re-interpreted as ***melen*** and attributed to yellow-stained water seeping through coal and shale seams into nearby marshy ground.

Goytre see **Goetre**

Graig   ST 067896
Rhondda Cynon Taf (Llantwit Fardre)
'(the) cliff': (***y***), ***craig***
(wooded area) *Graig*, ~ *y Fforest* 1833, *the Graig* 1854, (hill) *Graig* 1875, *y Graig* 1906
Part of Pontypridd which developed below a rocky slope south of Pontypridd. The len. (C > G) is caused by the def.art. before the nf. ***craig***.

Graigfelen   SN 685016
Swansea (Rhyndwyglydach ht., Llangyfelach)
'(the) yellow (*or* brown) cliff or rock': (***y***), ***craig***, ***melen***
Ty dan y Graig Velan, Graig Velan 1823, *Graigfelen* 1841, *Graig-felen Farm*, ~ *House* 1879
Named from a steep, wooded slope with a rocky crest west of the village. An area of housing developed partly on Graigfelen fm. from the 1950s.

Graig Ola   SN 711014
hill Swansea (Ynysymwn ht., Cadoxton-juxta-Neath)
?'light, fair cliff': ***craig***, ***golau***
(hill) *Craig-oleu* 1830, *Graigola colliery* 1865, *Craig-ola*, *Craig-ola Collieries* 1879
There is some doubt with this explanation since the slope faces north-west away from the sun. The modern form with -*ola* is also unexpected since local W dialect is typically -*ole* ['ɔlɛ]. Sps. are, however, late and it is possible that -*ola* reflects the dialect of workers moving here from areas further east. Graigola was transferred as a n. to a colliery opened by the Clydach Merthyr Co. in 1863 (known as the Graig Merthyr and Graigola Co Ltd in 1885). The south-west end of the hill is Craig y Pâl (*Craig-y-pâl* 1879) with ***pâl***[2] nm. 'post, pale' and there is a ho. Craig-y-perchyll (SS 716013) on the east side of the hill, recorded as *Graigyperchyll* 1813, *Graigyporchell* 1841, with ***porchell*** nm. 'young pig' or its pl. ***perchyll***.

Graig Pen-llin (Graig Penllyn)   SS 977776
Vale of Glamorgan (Penllyn)
'cliff near Pen-llin': ***craig***, pn. **Pen-llin**

(hill, rocks) *Craig Penlline* 1833, (village) *Craig Pen-llin*, (wood) *Coed y Graig*, (ho.) *Pen-y-graig* 1877-8
Referring to the rocky slopes around the village of Pen-llin (q.v.).

Graig Trewyddfa SS 666972
Swansea (Llangyfelach)
'cliff at Trewyddfa', *craig*, pn. *Trewyddfa*
Craig Trewyddva 1735, *Craig-Trewyddfa* 1751, *Trewyddva fforrest otherwise Graig Trewyddva* 1754, (hill) *Craig Trewyddfa* 1876, *Graig-Trewyddfa* 1899
For the pn. see Trewyddfa Fach. An area of housing which developed on slopes above r. Tawe near former tinplate, copper and brick works industrial sites. Recorded in earlier sources as *fforrest Treoyddeva* 1556, *fforrest Trewiddva* 1686, 'forest of Trewyddfa' (*fforest*) a n. later recalled in Forest Copper Works

Graig-wen ST 068904
Rhondda Cynon Taf (Llanwynno)
'(the) white cliff': (*y*), *craig*, *gwen*
Tyre Ygrayc Wen 1541, *y graig wen* early 17th cent, *Tir y Graigwen* 1682, (ho.) *Graigwen* 1697, *Graig-wen* 1741
The n. has been transferred from an adjoining steep slope, formerly wooded, bisected by Pantygraigwen Road. Also the n. of a ho. (ST 063911), above Pen-y-graig-wen. Cf. Graig-wen (ST 133894), in Eglwysilan, recorded as *Graige Wen* 1675, *Craicwen* 1783, *Craig-wen* 1885.

Graigyrhaca (Graig-y-rhacca) ST 194890
Caerphilly (Machen Monmouthshire)
'cliff of the rake': *craig*, *y*, *rhaca*
Creyge Rackawn 1570, *Craig y raccha* 1630, *Craigŷrracca* 1767, *Craigracka* 1813, *Craigrhacca* 1833, *Craig-y-rhaca* 1900
'rake' may be through some fancied resemblance between the rocks and the prongs of a rake (cf. *crib* in Cefncribwr) or because the slope was thought to resemble the furrows made by a large rake (cf. also Caeracca). The n. has been transferred from a ho. on the south side of the housing estate.

Grangetown ST 177752
Cardiff (Llandaf)
'settlement near the grange': E *grange*, *town*
Grangetown 1868, *Grange Town* 1872
Developed as a suburb of Cardiff from the late 1860s. The n. recalls a tithe barn and fm. which belonged to Margam abbey located on the West Moors recorded as *More grange, Moregraunge* 1329, *More Grange* 1535, *Grange de More* 1537, *le grange moore in Llandaff* 17th cent. The bishop's barn (*bercariam*) is recorded c.1200. The form Trelluest shown on railway signs (and in EnWales 119) is false and a mistranslation; *tref* answers to 'town' but *lluest* typically means 'temporary dwelling' not a grange.

Great Heath see **Heath**

Greendown ST 062725
Vale of Glamorgan (Bonvilston)
'green hill': OE *grēne*, *dūn*
(grange) *Grenedona* c.1161, *Greyndon* 1485, (grange) *Grene Downe* 1535, (fm.) *Grynedons, otherwise Grynedowne* 1549, *The Greyndowne, The Eastern Grindon* 1614, *Grindown* 1782, *Greendown* 1785, (ho.) *Green down* 1833, *o'r Grindwn* 1867
Some sps. and particularly that for 1867 suggest a cymricised form *Y Grindwn* with def.art. *y*.

Green Uchaf SS 921720
Vale of Glamorgan (Wick)
'upper green': E *green*, *uchaf*
Green-uchaf 1878
In contrast to Green Isaf which is *Green Ishah* 1767, *Green Isha* 1785, *Green-isaf* 1878 (*isaf*) on the east side of Wick village. The word order of both pns. is W which hints that **green** may have entered the local language. Note, for example, Lock's Common (SS 806775), at Porthcawl, which possessed the W form Gryn-y-locs – since it is located near a channel in marine rocks recorded as *Gwter-gryn-y-locs* in 1877 (*cwter*) – and a lost fn. *Gren y velin* 1589, at Marshfield, 'the mill green' (*y*, *melin*).

Griffithsmoor, Morfa Gruffudd
Cardiff (Roath)
'moor of (man called) Gruffudd': pers.n. *Gruffudd*, OE **mōr**, **morfa**
Mora Griff 1307, *Gruffesmor* 1314, *Griffithesmore* 1349, *Griffithsmore* 1401, *Griffith More* (in) *Kybor* 1550, (manor) *Griffithe More* 1567
A lost n. which referred to lands mainly west of Cardiff-Newport road, extending to Rumney bridge, identified (CR II, 29; V, 374) with a former fm. Pengam (ST 211776); cf. East Moors. The identity of Gruffudd is uncertain. The antiquarian Rice Merrick (BG 54-5) states that William, earl of Gloucester, granted a meadow near the r. Rhymni (*Romney*) to Ifor Bach called *Morva Yvor* (Morfa Ifor) and *Morva Ryffidd* to his son Gruffudd. This is unconfirmed but part of *Gryffythmore* is certainly described in 1541 as lying between *Evour More* and the causeway (*le caucey*) leading from Rumney to Cardiff. The pers.n. has also been linked with Gruffudd ap Rhys, last W lord of Senghennydd c.1262.

Groes SS 790870
Neath Port Talbot (Margam)
'(the) crossroads': (*y*), *croes*
Brombell Cross 1754, *Cross y Brombil* 1794, (hill) *Y Groes*, *Croes-y-brombil* 1833, *Groes* 1871
The former meeting-point of the old main road running through Margam to Port Talbot and a lane running north to Brombil (q.v.). The former ht. was largely destroyed by the construction of the M4 motorway. Nearby Groes-wen (approx. SS 774888), a former monastic grange, is *Whitecrosse* 1535, *Whyte crosse grange* 1537, *Whittcrosse* c.1670, *White Cross* 1689, *Crôswen* 1705, *Crosswen* 1772, *Grosewen* 1773, (fm.) *Groes-wen*: 'the white cross (or crossroads)' (*y*), *croes*, *gwen*. It is possible that there was once a wayside cross here, perhaps at the junction of Dyffryn Road with the main road through Tai-bach (StTaibach 21-23). The part-anglicised form *Crosswen* gave its n. to a colliery recorded in the 18th cent.

Groes-faen ST 069810
Rhondda Cynon Taf (Llantrisant and Pen-tyrch)
'the stone cross': (*y*), *croes*, *maen*
Croyse Vane 1541, *Croyse Vaen* 1570, (syddyn) *y groes vaen* c.1612, *y groes faen* 1630, *Y Groes-Vane* 1636, *Grosvane* 1650, *Croesfaen* 1825, *Croes-faen* 1833
Referring to a standing stone at the crossroads (ST 071809) on the boundary between Llantrisant and Pen-tyrch ps. Gwynedd Pierce (ADG², 49) notes that this is confirmed by a ref. to *Harston* 1492 which is likely to be OE *hār* 'grey, covered with lichen' and *stān* 'stone, rock' in the sense of ModE hoar-stone, a boundary stone. The base of a cross used to be located in the porch of the modern St David's ch. in Groes-faen. Sps. such as *Gros(e)* and *-vane* point to dialect 'grôs' [gro:s] and pron. of *-faen* is confirmed locally as 'Cross-vane'; cf. *–vane* [veɪn] in *Lisvane* (*Llys-faen*). Church Cottage (next to St David's) is located on the site of Groes-faen fm.

Groes-wen ST 126869
Caerphilly (Eglwysilan)
'(the) white cross', (*y*), *croes*, *gwen*
Cross Wen 1741, *Groesewen* 1748, *Cross Wen in Eglwys Shilan* 1762, (tmt.) *Tir y Grose Wen* 1764, *White Cross* 1748, *Croes Wen* 1786 (1814), *y Groeswen* 1841
Recalled in the Whitecross Inn public ho. The significance of the pn. is uncertain but the OS 1:2,500 map 1875-77 shows fms. called Ysgubor-wen (ST 119869) 'white barn' (*ysgubor*) and Ffynnon-wen (ST 117867) 'white well' (*ffynnon*) adjoining a stream Nant y Ffynnon-wen. Ffynnon-wen presumably lay at the head of the stream on Mynydd Meio and may be translated as 'holy spring, holy well' but the frequency of 'white' in this area may be a ref. to limestone rocks. The home of an Independent meeting-ho. recorded from 1741-2, probably identifiable with *Penygros Wen* 1744. Pen-y-groes applied in 1885 and earlier sources to a fm. (ST 122689) at the

junction of Eglwysilan and Groeswen Roads but was transferred before 1900 as a n. to a distinct fm. and a couple of hos. recorded as *Groes* (ST 119872) in 1885 half-a-mile west of the village.

Grovesend, Pengelli SN 591008
Swansea (Pryscedwyn ht.; Llandeilo Tal-y-bont)
'end of the grove': E *grove*, E *end*; *pen¹*, (*y*), *celli*
Penygelli 1585, *Pen y gelly* 1639, *Pen-y-gelli* 1832, *Pengelly* 1841, *Pengelli, Pengelliddrain uchaf, ~ issaf* 1845, *Grovesend* 1813, *Groves-end* 1832
Deric John (PNBont 44, 57) shows that Grovesend is a translation of Pengelli (SN 588004), earlier Penygelli, and is taken from the fm. Pen-y-gelli-ddrain Uchaf, 'upper Penygelli-ddrain (end of the thorn-grove)': *draen¹*, *drain*, *uchaf*. The ho. Pen-y-gelli-ddrain Isaf has been known as *Tyrisha* (SN 594007), i.e. Tir-isaf meaning 'lower land' (*tir*, *isaf*), from c.1930. It was recorded as *Pen-y-gelli-gilion* in 1879 and 1898 (*cil¹* pl. *cilion* 'corners, nooks') and *Pen-gelli-ddrain Isaf* 1907-1921 (*isaf*). The census 1841 also has a *Pengelliforch* 'end of the forked grove' (*fforch*). The village developed during the 19th cent near Grovesend Pit.

Gurnos SO 0407
Merthyr Tudful
?'(the) area with a hillocky appearance', (*y*), *curn*, cyrn, *-os*
Tir y Gyrnos 1541, *gyrnos* 1630, *y Girnos*, (watergrist mill) *Melyn y Girnos, Coyd y Girnos* 1716, *the Gurnos* 1769, *Gyrnos* 1783, *Melin y Gyrnos* c.1800, *a'r Gurnos* 1874
-os can be used both as a dim. suffix and, more appropriately here, in a collective sense for an abundance of something, particularly plants such as *bedwos* (*bedw*), *brwynos* (*brwyn* 'rushes') and *grugos* (*grug*) (ADG², 50). Cf. Bedwas. The def.art. *y* accounts for the len. G- and is perpetuated (in translation) in 'the Gurnos' among E-speakers. In Glamorgan, *gurnos*

occurs in the n. of a (tmt.) *Tir nant y gurnos alias Coed y ffalde* (in Llan-giwg) 1610 (Coed-ffaldau SN 744116) (*ffald* pl. *ffaldau*) and in Gurnos (near Gowerton) which is *Gurnose* 1650, *Gurnoss* 1764, *Gurnos* 1813, *Cyrnos* 1832; see also PNGlam 88-89. The pn. is also recorded in Gwenddwr, Breconshire.

Gwaelod-y-garth ST 115839
Cardiff (Garth ht., Pen-tyrch)
'bottom of Y Garth': *gwaelod*, hill-name *Y Garth Gwailod ~ , Gwaelod y Garth* 1841, (mansion) *Gwaelod y garth* 1858, *Gwaelod-y-garth* 1875
Referring to (Y) Garth⁴ otherwise Garth Hill. The village developed after the establishment of the Pen-tyrch Ironworks in the 1740s and associated coal and iron mining. Identical in meaning to Gwaelod-y-garth, a former ht. of Merthyr Tudful, recorded as *Gwaylod garth* 1426, (lands) *Tire Gwailod y Garth* 1712, *Gwailod y Garth* 1757, *Gwaelod y garth, ~ vach* 1783, *Gwailod y Garth, gwailod y Garth Isha* 1795. The n. survives in Gwaelodygarth Road (SO 051070).

Gwauncaegurwen SN 703119
Neath Port Talbot (Llan-giwg)
'moor in Cegyrwen': *gwaun*, pn. *Caegurwen*
Gwayn Kegerwen 1574, *Gwayne Kegerwen* 1607, (commons) *Gwayn cae gerwen, Gwaun Kegerwen* 1610, (common) *Gwayn Kygerwen* 1681, (moor) *Gwain cae Gerwen* 1799
Caegurwen was a manor and *parsel* in Llangyfelach hundred, recorded as *Kegerwyn* 1356, *Cregurwen* 1558, *Cogurwen* 16th cent, *Caegyrwen* 1597, *Kegerwen* 1607, *Parcell Kagerwen* 1670. Deric John (John SPN) has suggested that *ceger* (and *cecer*) is the Glamorgan form of *cegyr*, thought to be a variant of *cegid¹* 'hemlock', and *gwen*, i.e. 'white hemlock'. *cegyr* probably occurs in the rn. Cegir, Montgomeryshire, at Abercegir and the lost *Nant Kegir* 1638 in Llansbyddyd, Breconshire. He adds that Gwauncaegurwen is known locally as Y Waun, 'the moor' (*y*, *gwaun*).

Gwaun-leision SN 701125
Neath Port Talbot (Llan-giwg)
'moor of (man called) Lleision': *gwaun*, pers.n. and pers.n. or surname *Lleision*
Gwaen Leyson 1841, *Gwaun-leision* 1877
Lleision is generally found as *Leision* in later historical sources and gave rise to the surname Leyshon and similar forms (WS 145-6). The nucleus of Gwaun-leision was a small group of hos. on the edge of moorland in the late 19th cent, developing in tandem with the growth of coal-workings between Garnant and Gwauncaegurwen. An identical n. *Gwayn Leyson* is recorded at Baglan in 1793. *Lleision* is also found in Gwernleyshon fm. (ST 236865), at Llanfedw, near Draethen, recorded as *Gwernleyson* 1795, *Gwernlyson* 1841 and *Gwern-glesyn* 1833 (*gwern*).

Gwaun Treoda ST 162796
Cardiff (Whitchurch)
'heath at Treoda': *gwaun*, pn. *Treoda*
Treoda (in *Landaff*) 1459, *Treodda* 1529, (heath) *Tre Oda* 1650, (common) *Wain Troda* 1702, *Wayntreoda* 1703, *Court Odda otherwise called Waen yr Odda* 1782, *Gwaen Trodau* c.1800, *Gwaendu-rhoda* 1833, (fm.) *Gwayn Troda* 1858, (ho.) *Treoda Castle* 1868
Otherwise Whitchurch Common. Treoda has been identified with a former castle mound (ST 291808) near the site of the old ch. (see Whitchurch). The first el. appears to be *tref* 'settlement' (earlier 'farm') perhaps with an E pers.n. *Oda*. The lack of obvious meaning explains the ingenuity of the local tale interpreting it as 'the horse trots' (*trotian, trotan* 'to trot') recounting how a local 'Lady Godiva' was compelled to ride around Waun Treoda as far as Waun Ddyfal (= The Little Heath; see Heath). The area is sometimes referred to as The Philog but this properly applies to the main road running from Merthyr Road to the common and once referred to a ho. recorded as *Ffillocks* 1754, *fillog* 1782, *Tyr y Fillog* 1824, *Phillog* 1852 of uncertain meaning possibly taken from a small stream Nant y Ffilog, now partly culverted.

Gwawr see **Aber-gwawr, Blaen-gwawr**

Gwenlais SN 6101
Swansea (Llandeilo Tal-y-bont)
'white stream': *gwyn* later alternating with fem. *gwen, glais*
Plas Gwilais 1569, *Gwynles* 1621, (ho.) *Gwinlais* 1650, *Parcell of Gwinleys* 1670, *Gwynlais* 1692, *Gwenllays* 1697, (parcel) *Gwilless* 1742, *Gwyn lais, Gwinlais Ycha, ~ Vach, Gwin Lais vawr* 1764, (hos.) *Gwenlais-fawr, ~ -fach, ~ -uchaf* 1830
The rn. is also recalled in Abergwenlais (SN 615012) recorded as *Abergwynlais* 1690, *Abergwenlais* 1830. Cf. Tongwynlais. The form found in *Plas Gwilais* represents local dialect and Deric John (PNBont 44) notes the local pron. *Y Wilash, Y Wilesh* recorded for Pentregwenlais (at Llandybïe), Carmarthenshire (*Pentregwenlais* 1760). The –sh [ʃ] in these forms is a common substitution for -s (after –i-) in south Wales; cf. Glais (q.v.). Gwenlais is the n. of several hos. as well as a ht. and division (*parsel*) of Llandeilo Tal-y-bont.

Gwern-y-steeple ST 077755
Vale of Glamorgan (Pendeulwyn)
?'alder marsh notable for its stubbly appearance': *gwern, y,* E ?*stubble*
Gwerne Stubil 1718, *Gwern Stiple* 1784, *Gwern y Steeple* 1795, *Gwern-y-Steeple Cottages* 1900
The *y* is apparently intrusive and the second el. may have been influenced by E *steeple* 'church-tower'. The nucleus of the ht. was two pairs of hos. built in the 1890s.

Gwrach see **Blaen-gwrach, Cwmgwrach**

Gwrhai (Gwrhay) ST 183995
Caerphilly (Mynyddislwyn)
?'twisted' or 'slanting': ?*gwyrai, gw(y)rhai*
Gwrhai 1739, *Gwarhai isaf* 1813, *Gwrhai-fawr, ~ -fâch* 1836, *Gwrhay, Gwrhay-fach* 1871
gwyrai 'saw-set, saw-rest' is composed of *gŵyr* 'askew, slanting' and suffix *-ai* with the meaning 'twisted' describing the stream Nant Gwrhay (*Gwrhay* 1886), which flows down to the r. Sirhywi, or 'slanting' with an appropriate topographical application. The

pn. is unlikely to contain the pers.n. *Gwrai* because of the persistence of *–h-* in historic forms (see Gwrinydd) indicating stress on the second syllable. The n. applies to a ht. which developed near Gwrhay Colliery in 19th cent. close to the point where a stream Nant Gwrhay meets Afon Sirhywi. Also the n. of two hos. Gwrhay Fawr (SO 190000) and Gwrhay Fach (ST 184993) (**mawr, bach**¹).

Gwrinydd (Gorfynydd)
'land of (man called) Gwrin': pers.n. *Gwrin*, territorial suffix *–ydd¹*
guorinid, cantref ... wurhinit c.1145, *Wrenid* c.1170, *Gurinid* c.1100 (1200), *Gur(neth)* c.1210, *Guorinid* c.1236, *Goronid'* c.1239, *Gronyd* 1254, *Gronyth* c.1348, *Groneth* 1433, *Grouneth* 1443, *Cantref Goruenith* c.1538, *Groneath* 1673
The n. of a cantref which extended from near Cowbridge to the r. Ogmore/Ogwr in the early Middle Ages. The cantref later covered the commotes and lps. of Afan, Coety, Glynogwr, Tir Iarll, Margam, Nedd, Newcastle and Ogwr, and gaves its n. to a deanery known in modified form as Groneath. Associated in later sources with *gor-* 'over-, sur-' and **mynydd** to produce Gorfynydd, etc with the implied sense 'mountainous'. It is possible that Neath (q.v.) influenced some written forms of the pn. with *-neth, -neath*. A familiar form of the pers.n, viz. Gwrai, is recorded as *Gurai* in the 12th cent. Cf. Llyswyrny. Cadog's grandfather was Glywys who gave his n. to Glywysing and Gwynllyw recalled in Gwynllŵg (see PNGwent 217-8).

Gwynfi see **Abergwynfi**, **Blaengwynfi**

Gyfeillion   ST 053910
Rhondda Cynon Taf (Llanwynno)
?'(the) two facing rock slopes': (*y*) **cyfeilltion*
Gyfeillon 1864, 1874, 1965, *Gyfeillion* 1962
cyfeilltion is a postulated compound of the prefix *cyf-* and a dual pl. *eilltion* of **allt** 'slope'. The prefix is used, among other things, in W to express the existence of two things in close proximity and to emphasise a relationship (PNGlam 91-92). If this interpretation is correct then the pn. could have been affected by *cyfaillt* nm., *cyfeill(i)on*, 'friend, fellow'.

Hafod to Horton

Hirwaun. The Lamb & Flag on Brecon Road c.1900. (courtesy of Rhondda Cynon Taf Libraries)

Hafod SS 659946
Swansea
'summer dwelling': *hafod*
the Havod 1641, Havod 1651, Hafod village 1841, Hafod Gate [TG] 1845, Hafod Works 1879
A fm.n., later copperworks (*Upr. Bank Works* 1813) developed by the Vivian family. John Vivian settled in Swansea c.1800 and in 1810 land was leased in the names of his two sons John Henry Vivian and Richard Hussey Vivian from the Duke of Beaufort and Lord Jersey and copperworks were established on the site. The first urban development was known as Vivianstown and Trevivian (*tref*), co-existing with Hafod, but neither n. became firmly established. The n. survives in Vivian Street.

Hafod-ddreiniog ST 0491
Rhondda Cynon Taf (Llanwynno)
'thorny summer-dwelling: *hafod, dreiniog*
havod Treinogg 1657, *Havertreeneg Hamlett* 1670, *Havod Treniog* 1672, *Hâvoddryniog (Hâvod-dreiniog)* 1840, (ht.) *Hafod-ddriniog* 1841
The southern part of Llanwynno covering the northern part of Pontypridd extending to Trehafod (q.v.). The first el. is found in several fms. Hafod (*Hafod* 1777, *Hafod faur* 1841), Hafod Ganol (*Hafod Genol* 1841), Hafod Uchaf

(*Hafod Ucha* 1841, *Hafod-uchaf* 1875) and Hafod Isaf (*Hafod-isaf* 1833) (***mawr, cenol, uchaf, isaf***) near the junction of Nant Hafod and Rhondda.

Hafod-y-porth SS 801899
Neath Port Talbot (Margam)
'summer dwelling near the gate': ***hafod, y, porth***² (*de*) *Hauoto Portarii* 1261, *Hauotporth* 1336, *Porth Auoth'* 1339, *Havotporth* 1470, *Havodporthe* 1535, *Hauodaport chappell* 1586, (manor) *Hawood y Porth alias Havod y Porth* 1547
The first ref. contains Lat *portarius* which may be translated as 'portreeve' or 'gate-keeper' and strengthens the supposition that ***porth***² has displaced E *portreeve* 'chief officer of a town or borough', presumably of the medieval borough of Aberafan, about a mile from Hafod fm. If so, then this is also likely to be the place recorded as *Portreveshavot* in 1314. This was a grange and chp. of Margam abbey, later called simply Hafod (*Havod Mergam* 1758). A nearby field is recorded as *Maes y Court* 1702 (***maes, y, cwrt***¹). Margam abbey also possessed other granges containing ***hafod***: (1) Hafodwgan (SS 846866) recorded as *Handugan, Kavodduga* c.1291, *Havothduga* 1336, *Havod y Dyga* 1527, *Hafod Digoed* 1814, with a pers.n. *Gwgan* (ADG², 53) and (2) Hafodheulog (SS 841847) recorded as *Havodhaloc* late 12th cent, (chp.) *Haudhaloc* c.1200, *Hauothalok* 1261, *Havothalok* 1336, *Hevedhaloc* 1207, qualified by **halog* containing *hâl* 'moor, moorland' (PNGlam 93-4) influenced in late sources by ***heulog***¹ 'sunny'.

Hafodyrynys ST 228989
Caerphilly (Mynyddislwyn)
'summer-dwelling at the river-meadow': ***hafod, yr, ynys***
Hafod Yrynys 1534, *Hafod ar enys* 1541, *Havod yr Ynis* 1582, *Havod yr Enys* 1619, *Hafod-yr-ynys* 1707, *Havodyrynys* 1813, *Hafodyrynys* 1833
A former grange of Llantarnam abbey. An identical n. is recorded in Merthyr Tudful as *Tir Hafod yr Ynys* 1540, *havod yr ynnis* 1670.

Hanover Square SS 677950
Swansea (Llansamlet Lower, Llansamlet)
Transferred n. *Hanover*, E ***square***

Hanover 1841, *Hanover Square* 1879
Originally a small group of hos. shown, but not named, on OS drawings 1813, near the Jersey Arms on Bon-y-maen Road. The n. is presumably a transfer from the well-known fashionable Hanover Square, London; there is a London Terrace on Jersey Road.

Hardings Down SS 437906
Swansea (Llangennith)
'hill of (man called) Harden': pers.n. or surname *Harden*, E ***down***
Hardens downe 1608, *Harding downe* 1633, (hill) *Hardens Downe* 1764, *Harding Down* 1830
Later associated with the more common surname Harding (recorded at Marcross and Wick 1670).

Haregrove (Horgrove) SS 860812
Bridgend (Tythegston Higher ht.; Tythegston)
?'muddy grove': OE ***horu, grāf(a)***
Horegrove c.1218, *Boregrove* c.1291, *Horegravam, Horgrave* 13th cent, *Horgroue* 1336, *Horgro* 1535, *Horgro alias Horgrove* 1543, *Horgrove* 1590-1, 1833, *Haregrove* 1966
OS maps have *Horgrove* down to 1965 but the current OS Explorer map calls the fm. here *Hare Grove* as if it refers to the animal. The reason for the change of spelling is uncertain unless Horgrove was felt to be too reminiscent of E 'whore'. Historic forms show that we can certainly reject 'grey grove' with OE *hār* 'grey' as in Hargrave, Cheshire, and other counties, because historic forms for these places have *Har-*. The W form – apparently no longer current – was probably *Horgro* or *Orgro* as suggested by some historic forms; it is *Orgro* in a 19th cent triban (Trib 457).

Hawthorn ST 094876
Rhondda Cynon Taf (Eglwysilan)
'(place at the) hawthorn': E ***hawthorn***
(ho.) *Hawthorn* 1868, (ht.) *White Hawthorn, Hawthorn Cottage* 1875, *White Hawthorn* 1956, (village) *Hawthorn* 1958-9
Presumably a ref. to white hawthorn. The general area was also known as *Taff Vale* 1868, probably a translation of Dyffryn Taf (*Dyffryn Taf* 1811); cf. Taff Vale.

Heath, Y Waun ST 1779
Cardiff
'(the) heath': E *heath*; 'the heath', *y*, *gwaun*
(heaths) *Muchel Heth' et Litel Heth'* 1340, *the Heaths called ... Mynydd Bychan, Y-wayn-ddyval, and Tre Oda* 1650, (common) *Mynith bychan* 1703, *Mynydd Bychan* 1765, *Cardiff Heath* 1766, (fms.) *Mynydd-bychan, Heath Farm* 1833, *Great and Little Heaths, or Mwynydd Buchan and Wain Dyval* 1801, *waynddyfal* c.1670, *Waun-ddyval Common* 1784, *Wain Ddyfal* 1789, *the Little Heath* 1737, *Great and Little Heath* 1801
The Heath once described a large common extending from the boundary of St John's p. to a point near Llanisien, enclosed by awards in 1802 and 1809. The n. now applies to a smaller area of housing and park land near the University Hospital of Wales, taking its n. directly from the Heath estate and fm. W-speakers now generally describe the Heath as Mynydd Bychan (as well as Y Waun, *gwaun*) although the n. properly applies to the Great Heath. Mynydd Bychan generally translates as 'little mountain' (*mynydd, bychan*) but 'mountain, hill' is clearly inappropriate here and it is likely that *mynydd* is used in a similar sense to 'heath', i.e. 'open, exposed pasture', an elevated area used for the grazing of animals, and subsequently 'common land' – a meaning authenticated in Pembrokeshire and other parts of west Wales. The Great Heath was the site of a gibbet and gallows recorded in 1778 and a race-course in 1765 and 1811. Little Heath lay further south and east, extending as far as Albany Road in Roath where it is recorded as *Le Hethe* 1541. The W n. Y Waun Ddyfal means 'the wild moor' (*y, gwaun*) with *dyfal* a variant of *dywal* 'savage, fierce', probably because of its wild vegetation or exposure to the wind, etc. It is also notable that forms for Y Waun Ddyfal appear later than those of Little Heath and it is just possible that the n. alludes to the site of executions near what is now the junction of Richmond Road and Crwys Road. Two Roman Catholic priests, Philip Evans and John Lloyd were executed here in 1679 (Gwynedd Pierce in Y Gadwyn LXIV (4), 11-14). For Whitchurch Common see Gwaun Treoda.

Hendre SS 940819
Bridgend (Coety)
'old (*or* former) winter-dwelling, permanent residence': *hendref*
Hendre 1751, *Hendrewen* 1799, *Hendre Village* 1841
This may be the same place as *Yr Hendre* 1720 and perhaps Hendrebedran in the same p. recorded as *hendrebedran* 1592 and *Hendre Beddrem* 1640 possibly containing a pers.n. *Pedran* which R.J. Thomas (EANC 82) also identifies in r. Pedran, in Pembrokeshire, Caerbedran, in Breconshire, and †*Lodrepedran'*, Cardiganshire.

Hendredenni Hendredenny Hall ST 136878
Caerphilly (ht. Eglwysilan)
'winter dwelling of (man called) Tenni': *hendref*, pers.n. *Tenni*
Hendredeni 1307, *Hendredenny* 1374, *Tyre Henrye Dennye* 1541, (mess.) *Hendre denny* 1700
The pers.n. is found in Llandenni (*Mathenni*) Monmouthshire (ETG 142). Hendredenni gives its n. to Hendredenny Park (ST 135877), a housing estate built on the site of Hendredenny Hall in the 1970s. Hendredenny Park (*park*) appears as the n. of a housing estate on OS maps from 1981.

Hendreforgan SS 982882
Rhondda Cynon Taf (Llandyfodwg)
'winter dwelling of (man called) Morgan': *hendref*, pers.n. *Morgan*
Hendre vorgan 1553, *Hendreforgan* 1813, *Hendre Forgan* 1833
Taken from a ho. (SS 981880) on the south side of the ht. The first el. is also found in Hendre Ifan Goch (SS 973884), a ho. less than a mile to the west, recorded as *Hendre Evan Goch* 1683 and 1767. Neither Morgan nor Ifan Goch ('the red': *coch*) have been identified. Hendreforgan properly applies to the post World War II housing estate (SS 988884) between Heol y Mynydd and Heol y Bryn but as a n. it has been gradually extended to include Gilfach Garden Village (see Gilfach Goch) on some maps. Hendreforgan (SS 748111, in Llan-giwg) is recorded as *Hendre Morgan* 1671, *Hendre vorgan* 1716, *Hendre-forgan* 1831.

Hendy　　　　　　　　　　ST 043815
Rhondda Cynon Taf (Llantrisant)
'old house': **hen**, *tŷ*
(ho.) *Hendu* 1811, *Hendy* 1824, 1876
A housing estate built around a former ho. as an extension to Cefnyrhendy (q.v.) from the late 1990s.

Hengoed　　　　　　　　　ST 152950
Caerphilly (ht. Gelligaer)
'old wood, old trees': **hen**, *coed*
(tmt.) *Hengoed* 1434, *Henecoyde* 1542, *Hengoyd* 1555, (ht.) *Hengoed* 1783, *Hengoed Lodge* 1813
An industrial village which developed at the end of the 19th cent near Hengoed Colliery, Hengoed Hall (*Hengott* 1670) and an early Nonconformist chp. further up the slopes of Cefn Hengoed (q.v.). Many pns. and ho.ns. suggest that there were once extensive woods in the area.

Henllys　　　　　　Old Henllys SS 593944
Swansea (Llanddewi)
'old manor-house': **hen**, *llys*
Hentles 1306, (*villa de*) *Hentels* 1396, (free chp.) *Hontles* 1440, (free chp.) *Henllys* 1535, *Henlles in Goer* 1566, *Hentlis* 1650, (manor) *Hentllys alias Cylvrooth* 1680, *Hênllish* 1688, *Henllys, alias Henlys* 1738, (hos.) *New ~* , *Old Henllys* 1799
Described in 1697 as the manor ho. of the lp. of *Hênlhiske* 1697. For the 1680 spelling see Kilvrough.

Hensol　　　　　　　　　　ST 048785
Vale of Glamorgan (Pendeulwyn)
'old ?': **hen** and uncertain el.
Hensol 1429, 1799, *Hensol castle, ~ Park, ~ Mill* 1833, (tmt.) *Hensoll* 1556, *Hensel* 1729
The second el. could be *sofl* with a variant ?*sol*, 'stubble' (see Resolfen) but it is difficult to suggest a convincing meaning with **hen**. Historical sps. do not support *Hen Sail* (as PNIG 17) with *sail* nf. 'foundation'.

Henstaff　　　　　　　　　ST 080801
Vale of Glamorgan (Peterston-super-Ely)
'old stable': **hen**, *stabl¹*

Henstab late 16th cent, 1744, *Henstapp* 1600, *Henstaffe* 1607, *henstable* c.1625, *Henstaff* 1764
The –l of *stabl¹* is lost in the same way as posib < posibl, peryg < perygl and the change from –b to –ff is paralleled in the colloquial *cwnstaff* for *cwnstabl* 'constable' in Dyfed (ADG², 55).

Heolgerrig　　　　　　　　SO 031059
Merthyr Tudful
'stony road': (*yr*), **heol**, *cerrig*
Hewl Gerrig, Pen hewl Gerrig 1757, *Heol Gerrig, Pen yr heol gerrig* 1783, *Pynerheol Graig* 1799, *Penrheolgarreg* 1833, *Heol y cerrig* 1855, *Pen-yr-heol-gerig* 1889
The ht. is properly Penyrheolgerrig from a former fm. meaning 'top of the stony road' (*pen¹*) and developed near iron ore and coal works during the 19th cent along Heol Gerrig which crosses Mynydd Aberdâr. Heolgerrig was adopted as a n. for housing constructed in the 1950s and 1960s. Penyrheolgerrig is now generally applied to the most westerly part of the ht.

Heol-laethog　　　　　　　SS 930846
Bridgend (St Brides Minor)
?'milky street (*or* road)': (*yr*), **heol**, *llaethog*
Rheol Llaethog 1813, *Hewlaethog* 1841, *Heol-laethog* 1877
Perhaps one which is muddy or creamy in appearance from local limestone in this area. The n. applies to the ht. which had developed along the road Heol Laethog running south from Blackmill over Cefncarfan Road. Cf. Heol-y-cyw. Local pron. 'Hewl' for 'Heol' is supported by the 1841 form.

Heol-las　　　　　　　　　SS 698985
Swansea (Llansamlet Higher ht., Llansamlet)
'green way': **heol**, *glas¹*
Tir yr heol lâs 1760, *Heol Lase* 1783, *Heol-las* 1832, *Heol Las Rowe* 1841
A road bordered by trees and woods, possibly in the specific sense of 'abandoned road (overgrown by plants)' or perhaps 'unmetalled road' referring to what was once a narrow lane running through the village. Identical ns. in Glamorgan are recorded in Coety, Llantrisant,

Merthyr Tudful, Pyle and Swansea (*Heol Lase* 1735). Not all refer to insignificant roads. Heol Las (SS 9171), for example, refers to what was once an important local road linking the St Brides Major-Wick road (B47265) to Marcross running through Monknash and Cwrtymynach (SS 914715), and marks part of the western edge of the p. of Wick. This is *yr hewlase* 1767, *Heol-lâs* 1878.

Heolwermwd SO 0406
Merthyr Tudful
'road where wormwood grows': ***heol***, ***y***, ***wermod***, wermwd
Howell Wermont hamlett 1670, *Heolchwormwd* 1752, *Howel wormed hamlet* 1766, *Heolwormwood*, *Heolwermood* 1851
The second el. is also found in Llwynywermod, Carmarthenshire (***llwyn***). Wormwood was used as a weed inhibitor and insect repellant but is best known for its use in absinthe and vermouth, and in beer (in place of hops).

Heol-y-cyw SS 945843
Bridgend (Coychurch)
'the chick's road': ***heol***, ***y***, ***cyw***
(lane) *Heol-y-cyw* 1877
The n. may be disparaging for a narrow or rough rural lane fit only for a chicken or small animal. The road runs southwards from a mill Felin Rhaglan (SS 947847) (***melin***). Shown as *Capel* 1833 from the Independent chp. next to the road. ***heol*** occurs in several ns. locally, cf. Heol-laethog. Note also Cockstreet (SS 426920) (*Cockstreet* 1781) on a lane leading north from Llangenydd to Broughton Bay, in Gower, explained as a ref. to gaming and cockfighting.

Heol-y-mynydd SS 882750
Vale of Glamorgan (St Brides Major)
'the mountain road': ***heol***, ***y***, ***mynydd***
tir heol y mynydd, Hewly Mynydd 1799, *Heolymynydd* 1813, *Heol-y-Mynydd* 1833
The n. now applies to the road and adjoining hos. between Groes fm. (SS 879746) and Cnwc (SS 883751) but may once have applied to its continuation – now only a track – proceeding northeastwards over Beacons Down and Ogmore Down to Rhiwforgan and the B4265 leading to Ewenni.

Hernston (Heronston) SS 910782
Bridgend (Coety)
'Henry's settlement or farm': pers.n. Henry, OE ***tūn***
(*Thomas de*) *Henruston* 1303, *Henrieston* c.1316, *Herstone* 1598, *Heryston* c.1541, *Herston* 1638, *Hernston* 1783, *Heronston* 1833, *Hernstone* 1841
Henry has not been positively identified. Late sps. and current pron. have been influenced by *heron* (the bird) and is reflected in the n. Heronston Hotel.

Higher End see **St Athan**

Highlight, Uchelola ST 099696
Vale of Glamorgan (Merthyr Dyfan)
'high path (*or* paths)': E ***high***, ***light***; ***uchel***, ***olau***
Hukheloeu 1254, *Highanwole* 1291, *Zolyuwole* 1374, *Yoghanolley* 1541, *Ycholey, -lley* 1566, *Uchelole* 1600, *Ycher Oley or Highlight* 1653, *Highlight* c.1598, *High-light* 1661
The n. of a former chp. which stood near the fm. Highlight, now largely lost under housing. The second el. in Uchelola was re-interpreted as ***golau*** 'light' with the inference that it refers to lights used in medieval churches, etc. but Gwynedd Pierce (PNDPH 311-2; PNGlam 209-11) argues in favour of ModW ***olau*** (MW *oleu*) 'track(s)'; cf. Rheola. The n. would have referred to the minor road which passes from Port Road West (ST 105694) over a small hill towards Lidmore (SS 093703). There is a comparative example in Uchel-oleu (SS 907783) between Ewenni and Bridgend, shown as *The Parc* 1941 and 1971 but recorded as *Echelloley* 1611, *Ychelola* 1799, *Highlight* 1846, *Uchel Oleu* 1908, and two former fms. above Cwm Ogwr Fach recorded as *Uchel oleu* 1813, *Uchel-olaf-uchaf* (at SS 973846), ~ -*isaf* 1833 (***uchaf***, ***isaf***).

High Meadows, Aber-carn-uchaf ST 219960
Caerphilly (Mynyddislwyn)
'(housing estate near) High Meadow': E ***high***, ***meadows***; 'upper Aber-carn': pn. *Aber-carn*, ***uchaf***

(ho.) *High Meadow* 1813, 1840, *Abercarn Uchaf* 1859, *Aber-carn-uchaf* 1879-80
The n. of a housing estate begun in the 1950s on slopes above the Ebwy valley recorded as *High Meadow* 1962 and *High Meadows* from c.1974. The pn. derives from that of a ho., probably named by Richard Crawshay (1739-1810) the ironmaster, who gave it to his daughter Charlotte, wife of the industrialist Benjamin Hall (1778-1817). The ho.n. fell out of use, re-appearing on OS maps as *Highmeadow House* in 1962, and was later demolished. Aber-carn-uchaf is 'upper' in relationship to Abercarn House which was itself a misnomer (see Aber-carn). It is possible that the n. was given by Hall's son Benjamin (1802-67), 1st Baron Llanover, or his wife Lady Llanover (1802-96), enthusiastic supporters of the W language and culture.

Hirfynydd　　　　　　　　SN 8205, 8206
mountain Neath Port Talbot (Cadoxton-juxta-Neath)
'long mountain': **hir, mynydd**
hiir vynidd c.1700, *Long Mountain* 1799, *Cefn Hir Fynydd* 1832, *Hir-fynydd* 1884
Long Mountain in 1799 seems to have been a purely map form with no widespread currency.

Hirwaun　　　　　　　　　SN 957056
Rhondda Cynon Taf (Aberdare)
'long moor': **hir, gwaun**
Hyrweunworgan 1203, *Hyrwenworgan* 1253, *-wurgan* 1256, *Hirwen (long whit) Urgan* c.1538, *Hirweyne* 1541, (moor) *Herwenorgan* 1591, (common land) *Hîrwain wrgan in english Gwrgans lond medow* c.1659, (common) *Hirwayn Wrgan, Hirwain Furnace* 1799
The moor is south-west of Hirwaun and Pen-y-waun 'top of the moor' (**pen¹**). The n. was formerly qualified by a pers.n. *Gwrgan(t)*, lenited as *Wrgan*, who was identified by antiquarians with the father of Iestyn ap Gwrgant, lord of Morgannwg 11th cent. Iestyn reputedly seized power in Morgannwg in 1081. Deric John (CVPN 64-5) also suggests Gwrgant, bishop of Llandaf c.1148. The village developed near Hirwaun Ironworks established by John Maybery of Brecon in 1757 on that part of the common in Breconshire. Hirwaun (SS 932838) at Coety is *Hirwaun* 1649, *Hirwen* 1653, *Hirwayne* 1661.

Hollybush　　　　　　　　　SO 164033
Caerphilly (Bedwellte Monmouthshire)
(place near the public ho. called) Holly Bush: **holly, bush**
Hollybush 1861, *Holly Bush* 1901
Probably named from an inn recorded in 1851 or directly from Hollybush Colliery opened c.1860. Most development took place after 1868. There seems to be no evidence that Hollybush was ever known as Llwyncelyn though **llwyn** 'bush' is found in nearby Llwynarfon (SO 160035) and Llwyn-bach (SO 163031). There is another Hollybush (ST 234842) in Michaelston-y-fedw Monmouthshire a few miles to the south, recorded as *Llwyn-Celyn* 1751 and *Hollybush* 1887, and Hollybush alias Llwyncelyn (ST 017744) at Llanblethian which is *Llwyn-celyn* 1877-1947, *Holly-bush Farm* 1951.

Hollybush Estate　　　　　　ST 143810
Cardiff (Whitchurch)
housing estate (near the public ho. called) Holly Bush: **holly, bush, estate**
(ho.) *Holly Bush* 1841, *Hollybush* 1852, *Hollybush Inn* 1875
A housing estate which developed from the 1930s and named from the inn. No W n. has been formally adopted though its W equivalent Llwyncelyn was the n. of a late 19th cent ho. near Gerddi Tŷ Celyn and **celyn¹** is recalled in the modern road-ns. Lôn y Celyn and Heol Pantycelyn.

Hopkinstown, Trehopcyn　　ST 062904
Rhondda Cynon Taf (Llantrisant)
'settlement named from Hopkins': surname *Hopkin*, E **town; tref**, cymricised *Hopcyn*
Hopkin's town 1866, *Hopkin's Town, Tref Hopkin* 1874, *Hopkinstown* 1875, *Trehopcyn* 1895, *Trehopkin* 1896
Evan Hopkin (1798-1869) was owner of the Tŷ Mawr estate on which the first hos. were built

in the late 1840s after the opening of Tŷ Mawr Colliery (MCPP 51).

Horton SS 474859
Swansea (Penrice)
'muddy farm': OE *horu*, *tūn*
la Hortone 13th cent, *Horton* 1319, *Horeton*' 1394, *Hurton* 1435, *Hortone* 1583

A common pn. in England. Located in a small hollow. Charles (NCPN 128) suggests this may be *Hornblauton* c. 1250 in Cartae II, 571, but there is nothing comparable in other historic sps.

Ilston to Is Caeach

The ruined chapel, Ilston valley, Parkmill c.1904.

Ilston, **Llanilltud** SS 556904
Swansea
'settlement associated with (St) Illtud', pers.n. *Illtud*, OE *tūn*; 'church of (St) Illtud in Gower', *llan*
Lann Jldut, (ch. of) *sancti Ilduti* 1129 (c.1170), (ch. of) *Sancti Yltiuti Vanik* 1232, (~) *Sci' Illtuti de Illiston* 1482, *Iltwiteston* 1319, *Iltutiston* 1400, *Illiston* 1482, *Ilston* 1487, *Llanylltyd* 1697
Elwyn Davies uses the form *Llanilltud Gŵyr* (GazWPN) and Dafydd Morganwg has *Llanilltud Browyr* (*Bro Gŵyr*) (HMorg 304) in ref. to its location in Gower /Gŵyr (q.v.), but neither form seem to be authenticated elsewhere and W publications often use the E form. What evidence there is, suggests that it was plain Llanilltud with an isolated example in 1232 of what appears to stand for ModW Llanilltud Fynach with *mynach*[1], variant *manach*, 'monk'. Illtud is also dedicated locally at Oxwich and Bishopston.

Incline Top SO 050069
Merthyr Tudful
'(place at) top of the incline': E *incline*, E *top*
Incline Top 1914
Named from a former coal-incline running down to Penydarren Ironworks shown on the OS 1:2,500 map 1882. Cf. Dowlais Top.

Is Caeach see **Senghennydd**

Jersey Marine

Jersey Marine c.1900. (Courtesy of West Glamorgan Archive Service)

Jersey Marine SS 710940
Neath Port Talbot (Coed-ffranc ht.; Cadoxton-juxta-Neath)
'(place near) Jersey Marine (hotel)'
Jersey Marine station 1894, *Jersey Marine* 1897
Near the Tennant Canal and named from the 5th earl of Jersey who inherited Baron Vernon II's estates in the Swansea-Neath area 1814. The canal was developed across Jersey's land in 1824. Jersey Marine hotel (SS 715936) is recorded in 1865 is on the south side of Briton Ferry Road station on the Swansea & Neath Low Level Railway. Urban development largely began after the opening of Jersey Marine station in 1894 on the Rhondda & Swansea Bay Railway. Jersey Road (in Llansamlet) was earlier Pentregaseg, 'mare's village': **pentref**, lost *y*, ***caseg***; see also Coed-ffranc and Pentre'r-gaseg.

Kendon to The Kymin

Kenfig Hill c.1910.

Kendon, Cendon ST 199987
Caerphilly (Mynyddislwyn, Monmouthshire)
?'unploughed land shaped like a ridge': ?*cefn*, ?*ton*²
Cendon 1831, *Kendon Colliery* 1833, (valley) *Cwm Kendon, Kendon, Kendon-fâch* 1879
Ken- may stand for the contracted *Cen-, Cyn-* of *cefn* as in Cyncoed (ST 191977) recorded as *Kingcoed* 1813 and *Cincoed* 1886 and Cyncoed (q.v.) with *coed*. The len. d < t could be the effect of a lost def.art. *y* since *ton*² is both a nf. and nm. as in the case of Cefn-y-don (at Hirwaun) for which Deric John (CVPN 40-1) offers the meaning 'the layland ridge'. It is possible, however, that *cefn* is the qualifier; cf. *cefndir* (*cefn, tir*) 'upland, ridge; butt of ploughed land'. This suggestion receives support from an unlocated place with a prefixed def.art. recorded as *y kevendon* 1606 and *y Kendon* 1750 in Ystradyfodwg. Another Cefndon (SS 768983) near Neath is simply *Kendon* 1734, *Cefndon* 1790, and *Cendon* 1873. Kendon now applies to a post-World War I housing estate but the nucleus was a small group of hos. a little to the east built in the late 19th cent associated with Kendon Colliery (formerly at ST 202987, 203988) which was itself named from Kendon fm. and the valley Cwm Kendon.

Kenfig, Cynffig SS 803815
Bridgend
'(place near r.) Cynffig', rn. *Cynffig*

109

Chenefeg c.1158, (r.) *Chenefec* c.1161, (water of) *Kenefeg* c.1176, (territory) *Kenefec, Kennefeg'* 1184, *Kenfeg* c.1405, *Kenfigg, -e* 1535, *Kenfike ... a smaul broke*, (former borough) *Kenfik* c.1538, *the Kensike or Colbrooke riuer* 1586, *Kenfigg, otherwise Pyll* 1594, *Kynffig* 1704, *Configge Hamlett* 1670
From the rn. Afon Cynffig which rises at Rhyd Blaen-y-cwm (SS 834879) on Mynydd Margam flowing through Cwm Cynffig (SS 8386) which is *Cumkenefeg* 1299 (**cwm**). There is an identical n. Nant Cynffig (or Kenfig) which rises on Cwm-ffôs (SS 864833) only two miles east of Afon Cynffig (see Aberkenfig). This is unlikely to be a coincidence and tends to favour a territorial n. transferred to the rs., possibly containing a pers.n. *Cynffig* found as *Cinfic, Conficc* c.1145. Gray (BCKenfig 34) says that Kenfig Pool (*Kenfege Pole* 1541) was originally a marsh and that the ancient town stood on flat ground at the head of the swamp near the castle and r.: 'and so the true name is Cen-y-ffig, the head of the swamp', in the mistaken belief that *cen* was identical to **pen**[1] 'head, top'. Kenfig was a borough, possessing a market, castle, a ch. dedicated to St James and a chp. of St Thomas, both recorded c.1178, but suffered from the spreading sands of Kenfig Burrows or Twyni Cynffig (SS 7881, 7981) (**burrow, twyn**) recorded as *Cunfig burus* 1740. *Pyll* 1594 properly refers to Pyle (q.v.).

Kenfig Hill, Mynyddcynffig SS 837829
Bridgend (Pyle and Kenfig)
'hill, mountain near Kenfig/Cynffig': pn. **Kenfig**, OE *hyll*; **mynydd**, pn. **Cynffig**
Mynydd Kenfig 1841, *Kenfig Hill* 1851, 1876, *Mynydd Cynffig* 1872
A largely 19th and 20th cent village which developed in the p. of Pyle and Kenfig on the western slopes of the ridge or hill of Cefn Cribwr in association with coal workings and limestone quarries. The hill may also be *Kenffigs Downe* 1665 and *Kenfig down* 1694 (E **down**).

Kibbor see **Cibwr**

Killay, Cilâ SS 603929
Swansea (Swansea Higher)
?'enclosure with a kiln': E **kiln** dialect *kill*, **hay**
Kyllar 1554, *Kyllan* 1574, *Kellaie* 1625, *Keela* 1650, *kylhay* 1697 (late 18th cent), *Killay* 1764
Killay refers in early sources to the area along Gower Road leading towards several fms. in Bishopston p. (see Upper Killay). Cf. *Killhays* 1728, a lost fn. in Llanblethian. The first el. is frequently found in minor pns. and fn.s. as *kill* as in *Kill Houses* 1675, in Bishopston, and *Kill Park* 1669, at Paviland. For **hay**, cf. Cathays, also stressed on the second syllable. There is little support in historic forms for a derivation from *ciliau* (**cil**[1]) 'nooks' which would generally be *cile* in local W dialect. Cilâ is poorly evidenced and indeed *Killay* is found in W-language sources in 1877 and 1916.

Kilvey, Cilfái SS 6793
Swansea
?'places in a nook': **cil**[1], **mai**
Kylvey 1311, *Kilvey in Wales* 1320, (chp. of St Thomas the Martyr) *in Kylvei* 1340, (manor and forest of) *Kilvey* 1369, *Kilvay* c.1598, *Trekilvay* 1697, *Kilvey Hill* 1799, *Cilfay Hill* 1832
Apparently **cil**[1] as qualifier with –*fai* a lenited form of **mai**, pl. or dual form of **ma** 'field, place', found elsewhere in pns. such as Brechfa, Carmarthenshire, and Gwyrfai, Caernarfonshire (see DPNW 45, 184, and Pen-y-fai). The n. may refer to the small confined valley on the south side of Kilvey Hill (SS 672940) with a stream running into Tawe between Foxhole (q.v.) and St Thomas. Conclusive evidence is, however, lacking. The W form is stressed on the second syllable as shown by 'Nid llai yng Nghilfái' and 'Cilfái drum o'r clwyfau draw' late 15th cent in the poetry of Lewys Glyn Cothi; see also Paviland and St Thomas Swansea. *Trekilvay* 1697 (**tref**) is otherwise unauthenticated.

Kilvrough, Cil-frwch SS 560895
Swansea (Pennard)
?'badger's nook': ?**cil**[1], ?**broch**[1]
Kilvroch in Goer 1302, *Kilvron* (?*Kilvrou*) 1319, *Kylvroch' in Gouweria* 1367, *Kylbrogh'* 1396,

Kylvorogh 1534, *Killvrough* 1583, *Kilefrwch* 1687, *Cilfrwch* 1703, *Kilyfrwch* 1770
This is unlikely to contain *broch²* 'foam; rage, tumult' which is better suited to a mountain stream. Local E pron. is 'Kilvroo' ['kɪlvru:] The OS 1:63,360 map 1832 applies *Kilvrough* to what is now Kilvrough Manor and *The Farm* to Kilvrough Farm.

Kittle SS 574893
Swansea (Bishopston/Pennard)
'kite hill': OE *cȳta*, OE **hyll**
Kutehulle 1319, *Kitehull* 1360, *Kytehull* 1400, *Kythull* 1469, *Kettehulle* 1508, *Kittle* 1650, *Kettlehill* 1768, *Kittlehill* 1727, *Kittle Green* 1799, (hos.) *Kittle, Great Kittle, Kittle-hill* 1832
A hill where birds of prey are found. Charles (NCPN 116, 126) misidentified the first two forms with Kittlehill (SS 460928), a n. of identical meaning, in Cheriton; this is *Kittlehill* 1757, *Kittle* 1799 and 1832. There are similar pns. elsewhere in Glamorgan, eg. *Higher Kittle and the Middle Kittle* (in Llancarfan) 1709 and Kittle (in Penrice) near Kittle Top (SS 491889) recorded as *the Kittill'* 1518, *Kithille* 1533, (land) *Kittle-grownd* 1625, *Kittle-hill* 1722.

Knap, The see **Cold Knap**

Knelston, Llan y Tair Mair SS 468889
Swansea
'settlement of (man called) Knoyl': pers.n. *Knoyl*, OE *tūn*; 'church dedicated to three Marys': **llan**, **y**, **tair**, *Mair*
(fee of) *Cnoyl* c.1291, *Knoylestoune* 1306, *Knoyliston in Goheria* 1367, *Knowlston* 1556, *Knolston* 1578, *Knoylston* 1583, *Knelston* 1602, *Llan y Tayr Mayre* late 16th cent

Nothing certain is known of Knoyl. The pers.n. is clumsily re-interpreted as 'know well' in a late 16th cent source and identified with an Adam de Bien Savoire, reputed to have lived in the early 14th cent (Cartae VI, 2353). This is unsubstantiated. The W n. is unusual but according to one tradition, Anne, daughter of the Virgin Mary, was married three times and had three daughters called Mair (E Mary). The existence of a St Mary's well and refs. to a chp. of St Anne seem to confirm this association (Gower 21, 59-60). The less likely explanation is that the three Mary's refer to the Virgin Mary, Mary Magdalene and Mary of Bethany or the Virgin and her reputed sisters, wives of Cleopas and Salome. The ch. was reputedly dedicated to St Taurin (d. c.410) probably through confusion with Llangennith and it was later credited to St Maurice. The priory there was annexed to the monastery of St Taurin d'Evreux, in Normandy. The form *Nelston* 1575 shows that initial K- was dropped in common speech before the late 16th cent.

The Kymin, Y Cymin ST 190715
Vale of Glamorgan (Penarth)
'the common': **y**, *cymin*
Kimming farm c.1700, *ye Kemmin* 1730, *Kiming* 1799, *the Kymin Cottage* 1808, *Cymmyn* 1811
The origin of this pn. is uncertain but the evidence, albeit late, tends to favour *cymin* ['kəmɪn] (not in GPC) as a local form of **cwmin³** borrowed from ME *cumin, comin* 'unenclosed land held in common'. *Cymin* appears to have been current in Gwent (see further PNGlam 61-62; PNDPH 164) and cf. The Kymin (SO 5212), at Monmouth, recorded as *Kymin* c.1790, *the Kymin* 1860.

Laleston to Lunnon

St Cenydd's church, Llangennith, c.1910.

Laleston, Trelales SS 875798
Bridgend
'settlement of Lageles': a family n. *Lageles*: OE *tūn*; *tref*
Lagelest' c.1170, *Lathelestune* c.1180, *Lageleston* 1205, *Lawelestone* 1265, *Laliston* 1535, *Laleston* 1574, *Lawson, -ston* 1591, *Lalaston* 1755, *tre lalis* c.1566, *Trelales* 1698, *Trelalas* 1763
A Walter de Lageles occurs mid/late 12th cent. Late sources claim that Lales was a Saracen from the Holy Land brought over from the Crusades by Richard Grenville III, lord of Neath, to build castles, and Thomas Morgan (OPN 137) claimed that Laleston is 'A translation of the Welsh *Trelalys*, the town of Lales', in honour of Lales who, he claimed, built Neath and Margam abbeys. The core of this preposterous tale may lie in a misinterpretation of the gift by Walter de Lageles of *Lachelesland* c.1240 and the grant by Thomas Lageles of all his land in *Lagelestun* 13th cent to Margam abbey. The W n. derives from Laleston, reversing generic and qualifier and replacing *-ton* with *Tre-*. W influence may also account for the preservation of the -es- of Laleston. An unstressed middle syllable was generally lost in E pns., probably accounting for historic forms such as *Lawston* first recorded in 1469. Generally pronounced ['lalɛstən].

Trelalas is a dialect form and is confirmed in a local W triban in which it is rhymed with *safas* and *feddylias* (Trib 2).

Lamby ST 223779
Cardiff
?'long farm': ON *lang*, *býr*
Langby 1401, 1457, *Lamby* 1814
There are some doubts with this explanation (NCPN 240-1) because the evidence is late but Lamby's location near the Severn estuary is significant. In Wales, Scand pns. are typically found in coastal areas and have survived through usage by E-speakers familiar with the sea coast. There is no longer a settlement here, simply a reclaimed refuse tip and an area of light industry.

Landimore, Llandimôr SS 465930
Swansea
?'church dedicated to Tyfor': *llan*, ?pers.n. *Tyfor Landimor* c.1260, *Llandymor* c.1291, *Landymor* 1306, *Landymore* 1319, *Landymour* 1469, *Llandimor* 1558, 1865, *ll. di mwr* c.1566, *Landimore, Llandre moore* 1583, *Landremore* 1697
Tyfor is composed of the honorific prefix *ty-* with the pers.n. *Môr*, preserved in an archaic form *Tymor* possibly attributable to E influence. The first part of Landimore has been misidentified with *llandre* found in Llandremor (Pontarddulais) (EANC 82; PNBont 49-50) and derived from *llodre*, of uncertain meaning but related to Ir *láthair, láthreach* 'place, site, building'. Past sps. of Landimore and Llandremor are, however, quite different and there is no trace of -r- in sps. of Landimore before 1583 and it would be difficult to explain its loss. The pn. has also been misinterpreted as 'the Church of the Sea' (WGOW II, 131) (*glan, y, môr*) but the persistence of *-d-* in past and present sps. is left unexplained.

Landore, Glandŵr SS 660959
Swansea (Llangyfelach)
'bank of the water': *glan, dŵr*
Tyr-glandwr 1686, *Tyr Glandwr alias Tyr y bont* 1764, *Landŵr* 1772, *Landore* 1780, *the Landore*

coal-pit 1842, *Glandwr* 1846, *Llandore* 1860, (a) *Phont Glandwr* 1874, *Glandŵr* 19th cent
Apparently named from an old fm. and land (*tir*) near the r. Tawe. This may also be *Dourlan* 1319 with els. reversed. The anglicised form derives from a len. Lan- < Glan- probably caused by a prep. such as *i* or *o*.

Langland SS 604876
Swansea (Oystermouth)
'long piece of land': E *long*, E *land*
Longeland 1650, *Longlands* 1803, *Longland, ~ bay* 1813, *Langland* 1852, *Longland, ~ Farm, ~ Bay* 1878-80, *Langland Farm, ~ Bay, Bay Hotel* 1898
Forms with *Lang-* seem to first appear in *Langland Cottage* 1841 but may be compared with Langlon, at Ewenni, which is *Langlon Farm* 1766, *Longland* 1826. Longland is a common pn. and fn. el. in Glamorgan with examples in Bishopston, Bonvilston and Lavernock.

Lansbury Park ST 163873
Caerphilly
'housing estate commemorating (George) Lansbury: surname *Lansbury*, **park**
Lansbury Park 1970
Developed from about 1970 and named from George Lansbury (1859-1940), a prominent English Labour MP. His political opposite is found in Churchill Park (q.v.). Several streets also bear the ns. of British politicians.

Lavernock, Larnog ST 184681
Vale of Glamorgan
'lark's hillock': OE *lāwerce*, OE *cnocc*
(*Willelmo de*) *Lawern'* 1234, (*Roberto de*) *Lawernak, Lawernach* 13th cent, *Lavermarke* 1401, *Lavernock* 1426, c.1536, *Lavernoge* 1603, *laurnock* 1584, *Rhaes Larnog* c.1780, *Llanfyrnog* 1809, *Llywernog* 1799, *Lafernock* 1865
The first el. is thought to occur in Laverstock, Wiltshire, Laverstoke, Hampshire, and Laverton, Gloucestershire, and Somerset. The hillock may be Lavernock Point recorded as *Llauerock poynt* 1578, (*the Pennarth and*) *the Lauerocke pointes* 1586 (Pierce in PNDPH 39-43; PNGlam 102-2). The pn. has been the subject

of unwarranted speculation. Matthews, for example, favoured a Norman corruption of 'Llanwernog, the church by the alder-trees' or 'Llanfrynach, the church of Saint Brynach' (CR V, 383) though the ch. is dedicated to Lawrence (Sain Lawrens c.1566). Sps. with Llan- occur from 1610 but are uncommon even after that date and are clearly attempts to link the pn. with llan. Dafydd Morganwg (HMorg 305) and others derived it from Llywernog, i.e. llywern 'fox' and coll. suffix -og, 'place of foxes', comparable with the rn. Llewyrnog, Cardiganshire. There is, however, little evidence for Llyw- in early sps. and Pierce rejects this explanation, partly on the basis of the local W spoken form ['larnɔg] and the E form ['lɑː(r)nɔk] indicated by sps. such as Llarnog early 19th cent, Laurnock 1584, Larnog, etc. Rhaes c.1780 is glossed 'a cliff, a rock' but is not recorded in GPC and may be an invention of Iolo Morganwg.

Leach Castle (Liege Castle)   ST 055732
Vale of Glamorgan (Llancarfan)
'castle near ?a boggy stream': *laec(c)*, *læce* OE, E *castle*
Lachecastel 1376, Lyche Castell 1541, Leche Castell 1567, Lechecastell 1582, Leach Castle, Leachcastle c.1598, Leech Castle 1657, Liege Castle c.1700, Castell Moel, in English Leech Castle 1697, castle moel in English lech castle c.1700
This may also be Leche in Walis 1107 granted by Robert Fitzhamon to Tewkesbury abbey. OE *laec(c)*, *læce* 'a stream flowing through boggy land, a bog', a fairly common el. in England, found as ME lache and leche 'slow, sluggish stream'. The stream must be Nant Whitwell flowing through the fm. Cf. Leechmere (q.v.). The actual castle is Castell Moel (ST 053734) above the fm. and is specifically described as Castle Moyle 1676, Castle Mayle 1718, Y Castell Moel c.1800 with the likely sense 'bare, exposed castle' (*castell, moel¹*) perhaps one lacking walls or in a location open to the weather. Liege is uncommon in historic forms and is a product of popular association with the common E noun liege. No examples have been noted before c.1700 and only one between that date and the appearance of the OS drawings in 1811. The OS drops the form c.1970.

Leason, Treleision   SS 484925
Swansea (Llanrhidian)
'Lleision's settlement or farm': pers.n. Lleision, OE *tūn; tref*
Leysanteston' 1304, Leissaneston 1319, Leyshanston 1396, Leisonston' 1472, Leistoune 1584, Leyston or Leisheston 1632, Leaston, alias Leisonston 1697, Leason 1813, Treleison 1641
Leason is a contraction. Lleision, found as Leisan, Leyson, Leyshon, etc., is common in the Gower surveys, eg. Leyson Pryce 1584 (GOW 165). The W form has *tref* 'farm, settlement'.

Leckwith, Lecwydd   ST 157744
Cardiff/Vale of Glamorgan
'(place of) Heligwydd': pers.n. Heligwydd, or perhaps 'willow-trees': *helyg¹* (sing. *helygen*), *gwŷdd*
Lecwithe c.1179, Leocwtha c.1180, Lequid 1185, Lecquid c.1239, Leecwith 1281, Lequyth alias Lecwitthe, Lekwythe 1307, Lycuyth 1450, Leckwith 1561, Lleckwlth 1700, Lleccwydd, Llechwydd c.1795, Llanvihangel Legwydd 1789, (bridge) Pont Lecwith c.1538, Lecwydd 1871
Gwynedd Pierce (PNDPH 49-52) prefers the pers.n. which also occurs as *heliguid* and *Elecuid* in a pn. recorded on the boundary of Mathern (, Monmouthshire), and in *fynnaun elichguid* c.1145 (**ffynnon**). Unvoicing of -*g*- between a vowel and -*w*- is found in other pns. and in the pers.n. Tecwyn (< Tegwyn). Initial *(H)e-* must have been lost early but there are documented parallels, eg. (r.) Leri < Eleri, Cardiganshire, Lái < Elái (see Glanelái), and Liddon < Eliddon (see St Lythans). Heligwydd could be the n. of a saint with the pers.n. standing independently like Baglan (q.v.). Long associated by many scholars with **llechwedd** 'slope', an error encouraged by the location of its ch. and village on a ridge, but this would require -ch- > -c- [k] by the mid 12th cent and the development of –dd [ð] to –th [θ]. Evidence favouring -ch- [χ] is not found before c.1700.

Leechmere SS 943710
Vale of Glamorgan (Llantwit Major)
?'boundary defined by a stream in boggy land':
OE *lǣc(c)*, *lǣce*, OE ?*(ge)mǣre*
Lechemere, *Lytyll Lachemere* 1541, *Leachmore farm* 1675, *Lechmere* 1764, *Leechmoor* 1813, 1964, *Leachmore House* 1841, *Llech-mawr* 1851, *Leechmere* 1971
Several sps. appear to favour E *mere* 'a lake' but there is no lake here apart from a very small pool at Pwllhelyg (ST 952713) and Leechmere lies near the meeting point of five ps. A small stream runs eastwards from near Leechmere to Pwllhelyg where it turns northwards. From this point it is known as *Leechmoor Brook* 1878 down its junction with Sutton Brook. The first el. is also likely to occur in Leach Castle (q.v.) in Llancarfan. The 1851 form taken from the census gives the misleading impression that the pn. contains *llech¹* and *mawr*, 'big slab of rock'.

Lewistown SS 933883
Bridgend (Llangeinwyr)
'settlement named from Lewis': surname *Lewis*, *town*
Lewistown 1915
Named from Sir William Thomas Lewis (1837-1914), Baron Merthyr of Senghenydd, head of the Lewis Merthyr Consolidated Collieries Ltd., and developed after the sinking of the Rhondda Main Colliery (SS 936888) 1912 (MCPP 52-56). The first hos. took the n. *Pentrebailey Terrace* (1914) from their proximity to the fm. Pentrebeili. Pentrebeili is *Pentrêbaili* 1767, *Pentrebaily* 1826 and *Pentre-beili* 1875, probably with the sense 'chief farm with a yard' (*pentref*, *beili* 'farm-yard, farm').

Limeslade SS 622872
Swansea (Oystermouth)
'shallow valley in area of limestone': E lime, *slade*
(bay) *Lime-slade* 1832, *Limeslade Bay* 1878
The modern village developed around the ho. recorded as *Plunch* 1878-1951, perhaps with E dial. *planch* 'a floor, a plank' but further evidence is required. Slade (SS 4885) at Oxwich is recorded as *Slade alias Limeslade* 1671 and *Slade alias Lymeslade* 1691.

Lisbon SS 652961
Swansea (Llangyfelach)
Transferred n. *Lisbon*
Pentre Lisbon, *Lisbon* 1841, *Lisbon* 1881
Presumably named from the capital city of Portugal. Swansea had trading links with Portugal. The n. might also commemorate the Lisbon earthquake of 1755. *Pentre* is *pentref* 'village'.

Lisvane, **Llys-faen** ST 191830
Cardiff
'stone court, palace built of stone': *llys*, *maen*
(chp.) *Lisfeni* (?= *Lisfein*) c.1180, *Lysfayn* 1392, *Lucyvayn* 1450, *llysvayen* 1558, *llys faen* c.1566, *Llysvaine* 1589, *Llisvaen* 1654, *Lisvane* 1670, *Llisvane* 1754, *Llysvaen* 1769
Evidently a building of importance, perhaps a court of the lords of Cibwr which covered much of the Cardiff area (CR II, 10; V, 384). E-speakers have replaced Ll- [ɬ] with L- [l] and rhyme Lisvane with E 'vane' [veɪn] as in the case of Llanmaes and Pentrebaen (Pentrebane). This pron. is probably a substitution and approximation for a 'narrow' long ǣ. E scribes had difficulties finding suitable ways of representing ǣ, often using forms such as *kay* for *cae* (PNGlam 150-1).

Litchard, **Llidiard** SS 909816
Bridgend (Coety Higher ht., Coety)
'gate': *llidiart*, *llidiard*
Lydeard 1452, *Cay yr lidiat* 1598, *Kae yr llydiard* 1636, *Llyddiart* 1720, *Lydiart* 1793, *Lydiat farm* c.1798, *Lytchad* 1831, *Llidiart* 1833
The n. derives ultimately from OE *hlidgeat* with a similar meaning and especially 'gate in a wall through which to drive animals to prevent their wandering from their pasture' and 'boundary gate'. Historic forms suggest that the cluster –idi- in Llidiart developed colloquially into [–idʒ-] as in [dʒɛŋɡɪd] for *diengyd* and [sɡɪdza, sɡɪdzɛ] for `sgidia, `sgidie (*esgidiau* 'shoes, boots'). This is borne out by forms such as *Llidjad penclawdd* and *Llidjad pen*

yr heol 1762 at Glan-lliw and *Llediad y Park* 1785 for Llidiard-y-parc alias the Mountain Gate, in Llangyfelach. E scribes represented this with – tch- [tʃ] (ADG¹, 61). The pn. is not likely to be E since most sps. have -*r*- found also in other W borrowings from E such as *fflodiart, ffodiard* nf. 'flood-gate'. Litchard Hill Road – formerly Coity Road – is locally known as Bryn Llidiart, taken from hos. recorded as *Litchard Hill* 1919.

Little Heath see **Heath**

Little Reynoldston　　　　　　SS 488892
Swansea (Reynoldston)
'lesser Reynoldston': E *little*, pn. **Reynoldston**
Little Reynoldston 1841, 1898
The n. came to prominence in the late 19th cent applying to housing development along the road to Reynoldston.

Llampha, Llanffa　　　　　　SS 923756
Vale of Glamorgan (Ewenni)
'church dedicated to (St.) Tyfai': *llan*, pers.n. *Tyfai*
(ch. of) *Sti. Michaelis de Huggemora* 1138, (chp.) *Ugemor Lanfey* 1141, *Landenei* c.1144, *Landefei* c.1148, *lan tiuei* c.1150, *Landefey* 1317, *Lanfey* 1411, *ll.ffai* c.1566, *Lanffay* 1600, *Lanphe* 1648, *Old Lamphey* 17th cent, *Llampha* 1673, 1833, *Lampha* 1831
From an original Llandyfái. > Llanfái This has the honorific *ty*- 'thy' as in Tyfodwg, Tyfaelog, Tysilio (ADG², 58) prefixed to a pers.n. *Mai* probably found in Caer Fai (Pembrokeshire) and Castéllmai (Caernarfonshire) (EANC 31-2). The development is complex; firstly, unstressed –*dy*- was lost, then stress on -*fái* encouraged unvoicing -*f*- as -*ff*- (and -*ph*-), and the dipthong -*ai* was reduced to -*a*. The form Llampha reflects a further step in which -*nff*- has become confused with colloquial -*mff*- (-*mph*-) – comparable with *Llanbedr* > *Llambed(r)*. Identical in form to Lamphey, Pembrokeshire, and Foy, Herefordshire, recorded as *lann timoi* c.1145, *Lann tiuoi* early 13th cent (HerPNs 98). Llampha Court is *Court Lamphey* 17th cent and *Court Lamfey*) 1754: (*cwrt¹*).

Llanbethery, Llanbydderi　　　ST 038697
Vale of Glamorgan
?'stream called Bydderi': ?*nant*, ?rn. *Bydderi Landebither', Llandebethery* 13th cent, *Llanbethery* 1322, *Lambithery* 1622, *Lambetherie* 1657, *Lanbethery* c.1670, *Lanbeddery* 1764, *Llanbederyes More* 1541, *Lanbydderi Moor* mid 17th cent
Stressed on the penultimate by both E and W-speakers. The first el. would appear to be *llan* 'church' which regularly demands len. so that the second el. would seem to be one with radical *p*-, i.e. an unrecorded and unexplained *Pydderi*, but there are instances where len. has not taken place – usually attributable to E influence (see Llanblethian). Early sources fail to mention a ch. here and it is possible that *Llan*- has displaced an earlier and unrecorded *nant* as in the case of Llancarfan. This would favour a rn. possibly containing the rare *buddair, byd(d)air* 'bird of prey' and 'bittern' (with suffix –*i*), an el. also suggested for Llanybydder, Carmarthenshire. That might describe a r. where the bittern was found or perhaps be a comparison with its characteristic 'booming' sound. This seems likelier than *bydderi* nm. 'deafness' used as a collective term for 'people afflected with deafness' (see PNDPH 83-85). The conjectural rn. could have applied to the stream on the north side of the village running through Pant y Coed or that on the south; both streams are tributaries of the r. Thaw/Ddawan.

Llanblethian, Llanfleiddan　　SS 986738
Vale of Glamorgan
?'church of Bleddian (*or* Bleiddian)': *llan*, pers.n. *Ble(i)ddian*
Landblec'h c.1170, *Land-, Lanbleth'* c.1180, *Lamblethyam* 1205, *Landbledian* 1234, *Lanblithan, Llanblidan* 1248, *Lanblethian* 1254, *Lanblethyan alias Lamblethian* 1307, *Thlaublethian* 1330, *Castrum Landblothyan,* ~ *Landblythian* 1479, *Llanblevion* c.1528, *Seynt Flethyans* 1541, *Lanbleithian* c.1598, *Llanblevyan* 1601, *Lanblythyan* 1653
The regular form would be Llanbleddian or Llanfleiddian with len. -*b*- to -*f*- [v] though this

is absent in the great majority of historic forms. Most of our sources before 1500 are, however, E and may not be reliable representations of what W-speakers called the place; note in particular *Lanvlethyan* c.1670. It is also worth noting that irregular unlenited pns. are found elsewhere in the Vale, eg. Llan-maes and Llanmihangel. An alternative interpretation is that the first el. of Llanblethian is not **llan** but some other el. such as **nant** as in the case of Llancarfan. As yet, no evidence has been produced to support this argument and there is no evidence that the main stream in the village Factory Brook was ever called Ble(i)ddian. The supposition that the pn. contains the n. of a saint is seemingly borne out by refs. to the p. as *Seynt Flethyans* 1541 and *St. Blithians* 1783 and the ch. dedication to Bleiddian recorded in 1849 though it is also given as John. Such doubts did not trouble some antiquarians who were keen to establish the saint's authenticity. Dafydd Morganwg, for example, in 1874 was adamant that 'Bleiddian (*Lupus*)', was a colleague of St Garmon, and that he established the ch. here (HMorg 336). No doubt Dafydd was aware that St Lupus of Troyes (d. 479) is traditionally said to have accompanied St Germanus of Auxerre to Britain in 428 and that *blaidd* and Lat *lupus* both mean 'wolf'. Any connection between Llanblethian and St Lupus can be safely rejected although Ble(i)ddian is perfectly feasible as a pers.n. or rn. Iolo Morganwg uses the form *Llanfleiddan Fawr* 1799 with **mawr**, *fawr* possibly through association with St Lythans (q.v.).

Llanbradach ST 148901
Caerphilly (Llanfabon)
'bank of (r.) Bradach': **glan**, rn. *Bradach Lanbrad(a)gh* 1597, *Llanbradach* 1616, *Lanbradach* 1632, *Llanbradoch*, ~ *Mill* 1729, *Lanbradach*, ~ *Isha* 1783, (ho.) *Lanbradach* (= Llanbradach Uchaf) 1799, (ho.) *Llanbradach-isaf* 1833
The stream, now called Nant Llanbradach, is a little to the north of the modern village. *Blaenbradoch* 1617 and *Blayn Bradach* c.1670 (**blaen**), probably now Llanbradach Fawr (ST 137925), confirm the existence of the form Bradach. The first el. cannot be **llan** since this requires len. (p > b). The rn. is likely to contain *brad* nmf. 'treachery, betrayal, deceit' with a suffix **-ach**, i.e. a 'treacherous stream, stream which floods destructively' as in Y Bradnant, Montgomeryshire (see further EANC 3-4).

Llancadle, Llancatal ST 036683
Vale of Glamorgan (Llancarfan)
?'church of Cadell (*or* Cadel)': **llan**, pers.n. *Cadell* (or *Cadel*)
Lancedel 1114, (Walkelin of) *Landcadhele* c.1180, *Llancathell* 1541, *Llancadl* 1578, *Llancadell* 1582, *Llancadle* 1597, *Lankadle, Lancadle* c.1598, *Llancaddle* 1788, *Landcaddle* 1831
The location of a former chp. with remains still visible in 1853 (CBS 380, n.2). The absence of len. (c > g) expected after **llan** raises some doubt over this interpetation (PNDPH 85-8) but there are exceptions in areas where E influence was strong; cf. Llan-maes and Llanmihangel. The form Llancatal reflects local W dialect which characteristically unvoices -d- as –t and –al appears to be a substitution for E –el before its reduction to -l. E-speakers now generally rhyme the pn. with E 'ladle' ['lankeɪdl]. Iolo Morganwg c.1785 unjustifiably connected Llancadle with Cadell Deyrnllwg, reputed founder of the kingdom of Powys, and uses the form *Llangadell* which is unmatched elsewhere. Llancadle has been identified with *Talcatlan* and *Talcathlan* (VSB 126-8) and *Lanhoitlan*, variant *Lanhoitlon* – all in the Life of St Cadog c.1100 – where a certain *Catlon* is reputed to have granted an *agrum* (probably 'share') of land. The evidence is far too weak to support identification with Llancadle.

Llancaeach (Llancaiach) ST 113963
Caerphilly
'bank of the (r.) Caeach': **glan**, *Caeach*
(*o*) *Lan Kaeach* 1575, *Lankayach* 1613, *Glancayach issa* 1619, (ho.) *Glancayach* 1663, 1831, *Lancayach* 1630, *Lan Caeach* 1681, *Lancayach ycha*, (lands) *Lancayach Park* 1702, (hos.) *Lanciaiach-fawr*, ~ *-fach, Gwern Caiach* 1833
The rn. is *Caayach* 1268, *Caagh* 1349, *Kayach, Kaihach* c.1538 and is found also in (water mill)

Mellin Kayats late 16th cent, *Cayach Mill* 1783, and *Blaen Cayach* early 17th cent (***melin***, ***blaen***). R.J. Thomas (EANC 5-6) says that *Cae-* is connected with ***cae*** and *cau*[1] 'to close, to enclose', etc and *-ach* as in Bradach (see Llanbradach) with a possible meaning '(r.) enclosing (area of land)'. The area around Llancaeach Fawr is largely enclosed between the rs. Caeach and Bargod Taf.

Llancarfan ST 051702
Vale of Glamorgan
'valley of the (r.) Carfan': ***nant***, *Carfan*
Lancaruan 1106, *Landcaruan* 1107, *Sancti Cadoci de Lankarvan* 1138, *nant carban*, (*abbate*) *carbani uallis*, (*Catoci*) *Lann Caruanie* c.1145, *Lancarban* c.1155, *Lantcarvan* c.1188, (*in*) *Carbana Valle, Nancarbenensis, Nautcharvan* 12th cent, *Nantcaruan, Nantcaruguan* early 13th cent, *Lanncarvan* c.1200, *Lankarvan* c.1291, *Llancarvan* 1535, *ll.karfan* c.1566
The first el. has been displaced by ***llan***; cf. Llangwnadl (< Nant Gwnadl), Caernarfonshire), and Llanthony (< Nant Hodni), Monmouthshire. The rn. may derive from *carfan* 'row, ridge', possibly referring to some sort of boundary, or perhaps a pers.n. *Carfan*. The pn. has long been understood as indicating 'valley of deer', apparently containing *carwan*, a pl. of ***carw*** 'deer, stag', but this is ruled out by early sps. containing *–b-* . The association is old, however, since one spelling *Nant Caruguan* (*Nant Carwan* in modern form) in the Life of St Cadog c.1200 is actually glossed as *vallis cervorum* 'valley of stags' in the same source. There are similar pns. elsewhere, eg. Cwmcarfan, in Monmouthshire (DPNW 109), and Cwmcarfan, in St Brides Minor, recorded as *Cwmcarvan Isha, Cevancarvan Ucha* 1845.

Llandaf (Llandaff) ST 154779
Cardiff
'church by the (r.) Taf': ***llan***, **Taf**
(*de*) *landauo*, (*apud*) *landauum* c.1126, (bishop of) *Landavensi* 1130, *Lann tam, eccluys Teliau olanntaf, eccluys lantam*, (*ecclesia*) *Landauia* c.1145, *ecclesie beati Thelyawy de Landaf* c.1260, *Landaph ecclesia sita super Taph fluvium* c.1191, *Llandaff* 1340, 1428, *Llan Daf* c.1400, *ll.daf* c.1566, *Llandaf* 1606
Llan-daf [ɬanˈdɑːv] with a hyphen, stressed on the second syllable, is the regular W form though Llandaf has current status. Llandaff is generally 'Landaff' [ˈlandaf] to E-speakers with stress on the first syllable. The cathedral bears several dedications: early sources such as those confirmed in the Book of Llandaf 12th cent attribute it to Teilo but it is thought that the ch. constructed by Bishop Urban in 1120 was dedicated to Peter, Dyfrig, and Oudoceus (Euddogwy), as well as Teilo (GCH III, 91) and Peter and Paul in 1428. There are also refs. to a chp. of St Andrew 1546 and shrines of Teilo, Dyfrig and Euddogwy in 1558.

Llandaf North ST 148793
Cardiff
'Llandaf north (of r. Taf)': pn. *Llandaf*, E ***north***
Llandaff Wharf 1811, *Llandaff-yard* 1840, *Llandaff Yard* 1904, *Llandaff North* 1906
A suburb which partly owes its development to its proximity to a former wharf and lock on the Glamorganshire Canal. Also recorded as *Yard Llandaf*, 'Llandaf Yard', with ***iard***[1] in a W literary source 1872 but it is difficult to know whether this n. was in widespread use. Llandaf North has been identified as the location of the chp. of *stuntaf* 1126 (in the Book of Llandaf 12th cent) and *brachium de Taf* c.1178. The first stands for Ystum-taf meaning 'bend of (r.) Taf' with *ystum* 'bend, curve'; the second has Lat *brachium* 'arm' used in a similar sense. The description suits the general area of Llandaf North but no trace of any ancient chp. has been found here (see also Whitchurch) and no other historical evidence has been found to support the identification. Cardiff Council has resurrected the n. in the form Ystum Taf.

Llandarcy SS 716954
Neath Port Talbot
Llandarcy 1940
There is no ancient ch. to justify the use of ***llan***. Named from William Knox D'Arcy (1849-1917), a director of the Anglo-Persian Oil Co. established in 1909. The site, between

Hen-barc fm. and cottage, was acquired in 1917 and developed from 1919 as an oil refinery; the village acquired the n. in 1921 (MCPP 57-9; VNeath 318). Pronounced 'Lan'darsi' [lan'dɑ:rsī] among local E-speakers.

Llanddewi [Llanddewi Gŵyr] SS 460890
Swansea
'church of (St) David': *llan*, *Dewi*
Landewi in Goer c.1211, *Landewy in Gower county* 1281, *Landewy* 1284, *Llandewy in Goheria* 1326, *Llandewye in Goyr* 1546, *Llanthewy* c.1554, *ll. ðewi* c.1566, *Llanddewye cast:* 1578, *Llanddewy* 1630
For the cantref see Gower, Gŵyr.

Llanddunwyd see **Welsh St Donats**

Llandeilo Ferwallt see **Bishopston**

Llandeilo Tal-y-bont SN 584029
Swansea
'church of (St) Teilo at Tal-y-bont': *llan*, *Teilo*, pn. *Tal-y-bont*
(uillam) sancti teliaui detalipont 1128 (c.1170), *lan Teliau talypont* c.1145, (p. of) *St. Thelyawy by Talabount* 1447, *Llandylo Talapont, Llandeilo Taleypont* 1535, *ll.deilo ben y bont* c.1566, *Llandilo talabont* 1578, *Llandeilo-tal-y-bont* 1832, *Llandilovach* 1712
Tal-y-bont is 'end of the bridge' (*tal, y, pont*) referring to the fee or manor recorded as *Talbund* c.1187, *Talbont* early 12th cent (1334), (*Turrym de*) *Talebont* 1319, *Talbont* 1322. The earlier bridge over the r. Llwchwr lay north of the ch. but it has left no ruins. Later sources also call it Llandeilo Fach with **bach**[1], perhaps distinguishing it from Llandeilo Fawr (**mawr**), Carmarthenshire, and other places called Llandeilo. It is sometimes difficult to separate this in historical sources from Llandeilo Abercywyn, Carmarthenshire, which also occurs as Llandeilo Fechan and ~ Fach.

Llandimôr see **Landimore**

Llandough[1], **Llandoche** (Llandochau'r Bont-faen) SS 995729
Vale of Glamorgan

'church of ?Dochou': *llan*, *Dochou* (or *Docheu*)
Landoch 1254, *Landochhe* c.1262, *Landoh* 1307, *Llandoghe* 1314, *Landogh'* 1317, *Landozwe* c.1348, *Landough* 1376, *Llandouhe*, (bridge) *Pont Landouhe* c.1538, *ll.doche* c.1566, *Llandough* 1578, *Landoughe iuxta Cowbridge* 1634, *Llandocho, Castell Llandocho* c.1700
There are obvious similarities with Llandough[2] and the two were sometimes confused. The church is dedicated in late sources to Dochdwy but evidence generally favours an original *Llandochou, -eu with loss of -ou, -eu under AN influence. Locally pronounced by E-speakers as 'lan duff' [lan'dʌf]. The association with Llandough[2] explains the occasional qualifier 'near Cowbridge' (Lat *iuxta*) and Y Bont-faen. *Llandochdwy'r Bontfaen* 1874 is an antiquarian form with no historical basis.

Llandough[2], **Llandocha** ST 167732
Vale of Glamorgan
'church of Dochan': *llan*, *Dochan*
Landohhan' c.1156, *Landocham* c.1180, *Landochan* c.1188, *Landoch* 1238, *Landoghe, Landuh* 1254, *Landogh* 13th cent, *Landocho* 1107 (1300), *Llandouch* 1561, *ll.doche fach* c.1566, *llandoghe upon eley* 1573, *Landoche juxta Cardif* c.1598, *Landoch-penarth* 1621, *Landock* 1661, *Landough* 1665, *Llandough* 1833
Early forms suggest original Llandochan with later loss of –n (cf. Barry and Rhosili. The modern form Llandochau in gazetteers (GazWPN, WATU) is probably a restoration through supposition that –a and –e are colloquial W for the literary pl. terminal –au. The unstressed –a and –e have been completely lost in the anglicised form Llandough, pronounced 'Landock' [lăn'dŏk]. The forms for c.1566 and *Llan Doche Vach* 1799 also suggests a variant Llandoche/Llandocha Fach with **bach**[1] 'little, lesser' but the reliability of both sources is questionable. The unfamiliarity of the pers.n. encouraged many historians to link Docha(n) with a number of distinct individuals and to associate him with several unreliable tales (see further PNDPH 111-5). Refs., for example, in the Book of Llandaf 12th cent to an abbot of *Docunni, Docguinni*, led some to identify him with an abbot of *Dochou* in the

same source c.1145 but this is very uncertain. The matter has been further complicated by confusion of Llandough² with Llandough¹ in original and secondary sources and by a ref. in the 'Life of St Cungar', written by the chronicler John Capgrave early 15th cent, which says that Cungarus (Cyngar) alias Docuinus established a monastery c.474 dedicated to the Blessed Trinity and endowed by Paulentus, a legendary king of Glamorgan. How much truth there is in all of this is difficult to say but it has given rise to the unauthenticated form *Llangyngar* cited by Iolo Morganwg and the supposition that the monastery was located here. Matthews (CR II, 34-5; V, 386) adds further confusion in stating that the ch. was dedicated to 'Oudoceus, the third Bishop of Llandaff' but Oudoceus – a latinised form of Euddogwy – is a distinct saint dedicated at Llandogo, Monmouthshire (DPNW 230). The ch. dedication (as with Llandough¹) is now credited to Dochdwy but this only seems to occur in very late sources.

Llandow, Llandŵ　　　　　　　　SS 943733
Vale of Glamorgan
'church of God': ***llan***, ***Dwyw*** (> *Duw*)
(Baldwin of) *Landu* c.1220, *Landou* 1254, *Landov* c.1291, *Landowe* 13th cent, *Landow* 1349, *ll. dwf* c.1566, *Llandow* 1578, *Landw* 1591, *Llandduw, neu Landwf (Y Drindod)* 1874
Cf. Llanddew, Breconshire (PNBre 93-4). The dedication to the Holy Trinity is sometimes associated with dedications to God such as Llanddwy, Cardiganshire (*Llandev* 1425, *LL.ddwy* c.1560, *Trinity Chapel* 1651) and Llandrindod (PNRad 68-9). Llandow has a Ffynnon y Drindod (SS 937737), 'the Trinity well' (***ffynnon***, ***y***, *trindod*), recorded in 1878.

Llandyfodwg see **Glynogwr**

Llanedern (Llanedeyrn)　　　　　ST 201800
Cardiff
'church of Edern': ***llan***, pers.n. *Edern*
(chp. of) *sancti Ederni* c.1180, *Lanneder* 1254, *Lanedarn* c.1291, *Lanedern* 13th cent, *Lanyderne* 1376, *llanedern* 1558, *ll. edyrn* c.1566, *Llanedarn* 1578, *Llanederne* 1654, *Lanedarne* 1799

The pers.n. is also found in Bodedern, Anglesey, and Edern, Caernarfonshire (DPNW 38, 136). The common sp. with *-deyrn* probably derives from association with the el. *teyrn* found in pers.ns such as Cyndeyrn. Sps. with *-edarn(e)* are likely to reflect local dialect. Now the n. of a housing estate constructed in the 1980s. The p.ch. (ST 220820) is more than a mile away near the r. Rhymni.

Llaneirwg see **St Mellons**

Llanelen　　　　　　　　　　　SS 516934
Swansea (Llanrhidian)
'church of Elen': ***llan***, pers.n. *Elen*
Lanhelen, Lanelyn 1319, *Lanheleyn* 1327, *Llanellen* 1640, *Llanelen* 1799, *Llanelan* 1832
Recent OS maps use the erroneous form *Llanallen*. The evidence for a ch. (at SS 511933) is archaeological since there are no specific mentions of a ch. in written sources. Ecclesiastical activity is said to have ceased here before 1231 (Gower 46) though J.D. Davies claims that the ch. was in use down to the 16th. There is an identical pn. (SO 3010) near Abergavenny in Monmouthshire (DPNW 237).

Llanfabon　　　　　　　　　　ST 107937
Caerphilly
'church of Mabon': ***llan***, pers.n. *Mabon*
Llanvabon 1457, *ll. fabon* c.1566, *Llanuabor* 1578, *Lanvabon* c.1598, 1799, *Llanfabon* 1833
Mabon is said to have been a 6th cent saint (HMorg 331) and has been identified with a reputed son of the legendary king Brychan who gives his n. to Brycheiniog (Brecknock) but the recorded historical forms are far too late for such supposition. The same pers.n. is found in Rhiwabon (otherwise Ruabon) (***rhiw***), Denbighshire (DPNW 427), and Manorafon (< Maenor Fabon) (***maenor***), Carmarthenshire; a Celtic god Maponos is recorded in Roman Gaul (ETG 158).

Llan-fach　　　　　　　　　　ST 220951
Caerphilly (Mynyddislwyn Monmouthshire)
'little bank': ***glan***, ***bach***¹

Lan fach 1841, (ho.) *Lan-fâch* 1901, *Lanfach* 1953, *Llanfach* 1962
Lan-fach earlier referred to a ho. (ST 220951) recorded as *Twyn-cae-singrug* in 1879 and 1886 from its location on a short ridge recorded as *Twyn Cae-singrûg* 1833, 'hillock at Cae Singrug' (*twyn*) and 'enclosure at the chaff-heap' (*cae, eisin*[1] 'chaff. bran', *crug*). The form *Llan-fach* is a late development based on the assumption that the pn. contains *llan* 'church' and that this refers to the chp. of Lady Llanover (for which, see Persondy). Llan-fach was transferred as a n. to a housing estate built after World War II. *glan* is found also in the nearby ho.n. Glan-Shôn (ST 225960) with the pers.n. *Siôn*.

Llan-faes see **Llanmaes**

Llanfair Fawr　　　　　　　　　ST 096791
Cardiff (St Fagans)
'greater church of (St) Mary': *llan*, pers.n. *Mair*, *mawr*
Lanuair c.1538, *Llanvayr* c.1670, *Llanver-vawr* 1729, *Lanvair Vawr* 1766, *Llanfair-fawr* 1833
Large in contrast to Llanfair Fach (ST 098792), 'little church of Mary', recorded as *Lanveir* (recorded with Trewern) c.1262, *Llanberbagh* 1541, (*syddyn*) *llan vayr vach* c.1612, *Lanvair vach* 1670 and *Lanfairfach* 1762 (*syddyn* nm. 'tenement, dwelling-place', *bach*[1]). The ch. was apparently demolished between 1840 and 1846 (ASFL 33). Earlier OS maps describe it as a monastery but there is no good evidence for this.

Llanfedw　　　　　　　　　　　　ST 2286
Caerphilly (Michaelston-y-fedw)
?'church in an area characterised by birch-trees', *llan*, *bedw*
Landivedon 1281, *Lanvedue* 1296, *Landevedu*, *Lanvedu* 1307, *Lanvedu in Sengh'* 1401, *Llanvedu* 1541, *Lanvedow* 1650, *Llanvedw* 1754, *Lan fedw, ~ Mill* 1833
Llanfedw was the Glamorgan part of the ecclesiastical p. of Michaelston-y-fedw alias Llanfihangel-y-fedw with its ch. in Monmouthshire. The qualifier does not become fixed to Llanfihangel until the mid 16th cent after the formation of the cos. of Glamorgan and Monmouthshire 1536-42. It is also worth noting that two sps. in 1281 and 1307 suggest a lost def.art. *y* raising the possibility that -y-fedw was in colloquial use for the general area on both sides of the r. or that the qualifier was transferred from Llan(y)fedw which was more wooded than the remainder of the p. Before 1536 the p. is generally found as plain Michaelston or Llanfihangel, sometimes distinguished as 'near Rhymni' (1415, 1535). The Monmouthshire part of the p. is also distinguished as *Lanuhangel in Wentlok* 1318 since it lay in the lp. of Gwynllŵg in contrast to Llanfedw in the lp. of Senghennydd (1401 ref.). The assumption that there once was a ch. in Llanfedw probably helps to explain why some historians thought that the pn. contained a pers.n. Dafydd Morganwg 1874 (HMorg 334), for example, calls it *Llanfedwy* and records a fanciful tale of Medwy, a missionary reputedly sent by King Lleurwg to Bishop Elidir in Rome in the 2nd cent. Medwy is said to have established a ch. on the west bank of the Rhymni – for which there is no evidence. The germ of the tale apparently lies in the statement in the Book of Llandaf, the writings of the Venerable Bede and other sources (LWS 60) that *Meduuinus* and *Eluanus* were messengers sent by Lucius, misidentified as a king of the Britons, to Pope Eleutherius (floruit c.180) (WB 322-3).

Llanfeuthin (Llanvithyn)　　　　ST 051713
Vale of Glamorgan (Llancarfan)
?'church of (St) Meuthin': ?*llan*, pers.n. *Meuthin*
(chp. of) *Sancti Meuthini* (at) *Lantmeuthin* c.1188, *Landmeuthin* before 1191, *Lanmeuthin* 1223, *Llanmythyn* 1535, *Lanvythyan* 1564, *Llanvithen* 1577, *Llanveithen, -vethewy* 1587, *Llanveithin* 17th cent, *Lanfeithyn* 1764, *Llanfeithyn* 1833, *Trewaithin* c.1658
The mention of the building of a chp. of St Meuthin at Margam abbey's grange (first ref.) suggests that the first el. is *llan* but, as Gwynedd Pierce shows (PNDPH 88-91), the -*t*- in this and other early forms are reminiscent of early sps.

of Llancarfan and there is a similar lack of len. (m > f). That raises the possibility that *nant* 'valley', later 'stream', was displaced by *llan*. The second el. *Meuthin*, variant *Meuthi*, latinised as *Meuthinus*, is an alternative form of the pers.n. *Tathan* (see St Athan), though not necessarily the same saint. Local dialect probably accounts for -eu- > -ei- > -i-. *Trewaithin* c.1658 seems to be unmatched and may be a false form created by Thomas Wilkins (d. 1699), rector of St Mary Church and antiquarian, by analogy with *uilla Tremguithen* recorded in the Life of St Cadog c.1100 near Llancarfan. The suggestion (LBS II, 17) that *Tremguithen* is Llanfeuthin is unreliable. Trevithyn (ST 057718) is a modern ho. (*tref*).

Llan-ffa see **Llampha**

Llanfihangel-ar-Elái see **Michaelston-super Ely**

Llanfihangel y Bont-faen see **Llanmihangel**

Llanfihangel-y-pwll see **Michaelston-le-Pit**

Llanforda approx. ST 208803
Cardiff (Llanedern)
?'church of ?': ?*llan*, rn. or perhaps pers.n. *Lanbordan* c.1178, 1236 (13th cent), *Lanvorda* 1392, 1450, *Lanvorda* c.1670
A former medieval chp. recorded as *Cappell Lanvordra* 1618 next to what is now Circle Way East, at Tŷ'r Capel which is found as (parcel of land) *Tyr-y-Capel* 1702, 'land belonging to the chapel' (*tir, y, capel*). Late forms suggest *llan* 'church' which gains support from the len. seen in forms such as *Lanvorda* with *v* (for W f) from radical *b* or *m*. Late forms are also similar to those for Llanforda, Shropshire, 'church at (r.) Morda', as Richards noted (ETG 171). Early forms with -*bordan* may appear to cast doubt on any etymological link but *b* sometimes alternates with *m* because they share len. *f* [v]; cf. *Bachynlleth* for Machynlleth (DPNW 304). There is a small unnamed stream north of the site of the chp.

Llanfrynach SS 980747
Vale of Glamorgan (Pen-llin)
'church of Brynach': *llan*, pers.n. *Brynach Llanburnokke* 1541, *Lanfrenach* c.1598, *Lanfrynach* 1662, *Lanfrynach alias Penlline* 1711, *Lanfranwch* 1762, *Llanfrynach* 1813, *St. Brynach's Church* 1878
Brynach may be Brynach Wyddel who reputedly married a daughter of the semi-legendary Brychan Brycheiniog recalled in Brecon and Brecknock/Brycheiniog (DPNW 45). Identical in meaning to Llanfrynach, Breconshire, and Llanfyrnach-ar-Daf, Pembrokeshire (ETG 172). Dafydd Morganwg 1871 (HMorg 140, 338) states that Llanfrynach was subordinate to Pen-llin. In actuality, St Brynach's is the original p. ch. of Llanfrynach-with-Penllyn and this is confirmed in 1662 and 1711. The smaller ch. (SS 974761) in Pen-llin may have originated as a chapel-of-ease. If this is the case, then earlier refs. to the ch. of Pen-llin properly apply to St Brynach's and would explain why there seem to be no refs. to Llanfrynach by n. before 1541.

Llanfugeilydd ?approx. SS 772891
Neath Port Talbot (Margam)
'shepherd's church': *llan, bugeilydd*
Lanvigelethe 1521, *Llangvegellyth* 1547, (chp.) *Llanvegelithe* 1554, *Lanvigelith* 1623, *Llanvigelithe* 1633
Perhaps a 'church serving sheep granges'. The n. of a grange of Margam abbey though the precise location is uncertain. The 1521 ref. places it near *the grene way* which has not been identified. This may also be (o) *gwrt llan figel* late 16th cent in a poem of Dafydd Benwyn. The pn. has nothing to do with Llangyfelach, a misunderstanding based on the rough similarity of spelling Evans (StTaibach 24) says that it was later called Maes y Court (*cwrt¹* 'grange') and suggests the n. refers to 'land attached to Court Ucha Farm, now demolished', i.e. before 1963. Maes y Cwrt barn was apparently on the site of the Mission Hall in Tai-bach. The grid ref. above applies to Maes-y-cwrt Terrace on Commercial Road.

Llan-gan, Llanganna SS 957776
Vale of Glamorgan
'church dedicated to (or belonging to) Canna': *llan*, pers.n. *Canna*
Landgenne 1254, *Lamgan* c.1291, *Langan* 13th cent, c.1348, *Langanne* 1431, *Llangan* 1535, *ll. gain* c.1566, *Llanganne* 1769, *Llangana* 1901
Early sps. favour the form *Canne*, later *Canna* in dialect, and *Can* by loss of unstressed *-n(n)e*, *-(n)a*. Llanganna is in current use among W-speakers. The ch. is dedicated to St Canna reputedly wife of St Sadwrn, and mother of St Crallo (see Coychurch). St Mary Hill possessed a Ffynnon Ganna, 'well of Canna'. The form Llanganna was used by Iolo Morganwg c.1800 and later sources.

Llangatwg see **Cadoxton-juxta-Neath**

Llangatwg ST 201823
Cardiff (Llanedern)
?'grove of Catwg': ?*llwyn*, pers.n. *Cadog* variant *Catwg*
Llwyn Cadyw farm 1776, (ho.) *Llangattwg* 1841, 1900, *Llwyngattwg* 1844, *Llan-cadw* 1882, *Llwyncadw* 1898
Catwg is the usual form of the pers.n. in south-east Wales; cf. Llangatwg Feibion Afel and Llangatwg Lingoed, in Monmouthshire (PNGwent 129-131; DPNW 254-6). Modern forms favour *llan* but it has probably displaced *llwyn*, prompted by association with St Catwg/Cadog. Llangatwg is said to have been the location of 'a dismantled chapel' (CR V) but there seems to be little evidence for this. The former fm. was on the north side of Bryngolau and survives as *Llangattock* on current maps.

Llangeinwyr (Llangeinor) SS 913874
Bridgend
'church dedicated to Ceinwyry': *llan*, pers.n. *Ceinwyry*
(chp. of) *Sancte Kehinwehir* c.1195, *Egluskeynor* c.1145, *Egleskeynwyr* 1258, *Egloiskeynor* 1314, *Lanconur* 1360, *Llanginwire* c.1538, *ll. geinwyr* 1590-1, *llann gainwyry* late 16th cent, *Langeinwir* 1602, (o) *Langeinwr* 1778, *Llangeinor* 1833

Ceinwyry is a compound of *gwyryf* 'virgin' and a pers.n. *Cain* (*cain* 'fine, fair') found as a variation of Ceinwen (with *gwen*); cf. Dwyn and Dwynwen, and Llwyncynhwyra (Talyllychau), Carmarthenshire (*llwyn*) (ETG 175). Cain or Ceinwen was a reputed daughter of Brychan Brycheiniog. All but one of the early forms have *eglwys* as the first el. rather than *llan*; cf. Llanwensan (below) and the displacement of *merthyr* by *llan* in pns. such as Llandegfedd, Monmouthshire, and Llangeler, Carmarthenshire. As a n., Llangeinwyr shifted after 1918 from the p.ch. (SS 924879) to the Garw valley to the area between Ty-nant (SS 967876) and Llwynyffynnon (SS 913871).

Llangennith, Llangynydd SS 428914
Swansea
'church of Cennydd (*or* Cynnydd)': *llan*, pers.n. *Cennydd, Cynnydd*
lann Cinith c.1170, (ch. of) *St. Kenetus* 1195, *Langenith* 1284, *Langenyth* 1300, (priory of) *sti' Kenedi de Lengneneght* 1400, *ecclesiam ville Sancti Keneth in Gowerland* 1478, *Langenyth'* 1535, *ll. gynyð* c.1566, *Llangenith* 1669, *Llangenydd* 1832
This is also likely to be *Landgenuth* in a grant of land by John Laheles 1189-1201 to Robert de Penrhys (*Penris*) rather than Llangewydd (q.v.). The same saint is dedicated at the nearby chp. on Burry Holms (SS 402926) recorded as the hermitage of *St. Kenyth atte Holmes* 1398, *Langenyth' apon' Seynt Kenyth' is hedde* 1472, *Sct' Kenetes chapel* 1578. The priory originated with a grant of the ch. by Henry (d. 1119), earl of Warwick, to the abbey of St Taurinus at Evreux, in Normandy. It was transferred to the care of Ewenni priory in 1400 and dissolved in 1441.

Llangewydd SS 869814
Bridgend (Laleston)
'church of Cewydd': *llan*, pers.n. *Cewydd*, earlier *Cewy*
Langewy c.1165, *Lantgewi* c.1192, *Landgewi* 1203, *Langhewi* 1218, *Langewey* 1314, *Langewy* c.1348, *Langewyth grange* 1547, (o) *Langewydd* 16th cent, *Court Langewith* 1814, *Llangewydd Cwrt* 1833

Cewydd is reputed in some pedigrees to be a son of Caw – though there appears to be no formal connection between them (ETG 178) – and to have been the W saintly equivalent of St Swithin. A former chp. and grange of Margam abbey in Laleston p. Llangewydd Court (SS 889808) has been adopted as the n. of a housing estate formerly considered part of Cefn-glas.

Llan-giwg SN 723056
Neath Port Talbot
'church of Ciog (*or* Ciwg)': *llan*, pers.n. *Ciog* variant *Ciwg*
Lan Cyok in Gower, Langoych, Langyuk 1284, *Langyok* 1299, *Llann Giwc* c.1400, (p. of) *St. Kewg in Gowersland* c.1530, *ll. giwg* c.1566, *Langewicke* 1577, *Llangiwick* 1617, *Llanguick* 1697
Early refs. generally favour the form Ciog. Pron. is generally 'Llan-giwg' [ɬan'giu:g] among W-speakers and 'Lan-giwic' (with an epenthetic –i- to ease pron.) [lan'giu:ɪk] among E-speakers. The regular form Llan-giwg is better represented in (waste called) *Kregg Llangewg* 1558 and *Graick Llangiwg* 1588. The pers.n. also occurs in Cwm-ciwg (SS 9883) at Coychurch recorded as *Cumtioch* 1208, *Comtyok* 1327, *Comkiwke* 1633, *Cwm-ciwc-uchaf, ~ -ganol, ~ -isaf* 1833 (*cwm, uchaf, canol, isaf*) and rn. Nant Ciwg (> Ewenni Fach SS 973823) with *nant*.

Llangrallo see **Coychurch**

Llangyfelach SS 647989
Swansea
'church of Cyfelach': *llan*, pers.n. *Cyfelach*
lanngeuelach c.1170, *Langamelach in regione Guhir* c.1090 (c.1200), *Langauelac* after 1200, *Langavelagh* 1284, *Langavelach in Goheria* 1290, *Langevelach* 1326, *ll. gyfelach* c.1566, *Llangefelach* 1832
The pn. is recorded in the poetry of Gwynfardd Brycheiniog 12th cent as *balchlann gefelach* (*balch* adj. 'proud, splendid') The ch. is dedicated to Dewi/David (Gower 31: 78-79) with the later addition of Cyfelach though there seems to be no evidence of a saint with this n. The statement that Cyfelach was a bishop of Llandaf is unreliable and probably arose through misinterpretation of a distinct *Cimeilliauc* (ModW *Cyfeiliog*) in the Book of Llandaf. Note also (mess.) *Kevenkevelach* (in Llangyfelach) 1699, literally 'ridge of Cyfelach' (*cefn*) probably an oblique description for 'ridge in Llangyfelach'; cf. Eisteddfa Gurig, Cardiganshire/Montgomeryshire (DPNW 140). Llangyfelach lay in the cantref of Gower/Gŵyr.

Llangynydd see **Llangennith**

†Llangynwalan
Swansea (Rhosili)
'church of Cynwalan': *llan*, pers.n. *Cynwalan*
Lann cingualan, podum Cyngualan c.1145, *Lann Cyngualan* 1119 (c.1170), *Lann cingualan* 1128 (c.1170)
Cynwalan may be a variant of *Cynwal*, with dim. suffix. *-an*. The n. of a chp. recorded in the Book of Llandaf 12th cent, perhaps at Pitton or at Rhosili, since 'the land of Cynwal' (*agrum cinguali*) was said to lie west of *Penn ibei inrosulgen* (see Paviland and Rhosili). It is possible that Cynwalan is identical to St Conval dedicated at Saint-Gonval (Penvenan, near Tréguier) and Saint-Conval (Hanvec, north of Chateaulin) in Brittany. A St Conval was also honoured in the diocese of Aberdeen on 28 September and was patron of a number of churches in Scotland (LWS 69-70).

Llangynwyd SS 857883
Bridgend
'church of Cynwyd (*or* Cynwydd)': *llan*, pers.n. *Cynwyd*
(chp. of) *Sancti Cunioth' de Leueni* c.1180, *Langenuth* late 12th cent, *Landgenud* 1254, *Langunyth* 1258, (chp. of) *Sancti Cuniti de Langunyth* 1331, *Langenoith* 1400, *Llangonoyd* 1535, *Llangynwid* 1559, *ll. gynwyd* c.1566, *Llangonwdfawr* c.1700, *Llangonoyd or Llangynwd* 1833
Cynwyd is variously described as a 6th cent saint and as Cynwyd Cynwydion, a son of Cynfelyn, in medieval pedigrees. His two reputed sons Cynan and Cadrod are said to be

recalled in the fm.ns. Bryncynan (SS 863877) and Maescadlawr (SS 866872) recorded as *Maesgadlloer* 1813 and *Maes-gadlawr* 1833. This unsubstantiated story seems to derive from T.C. Evans (HLlangynwyd 2). The same pers.n. occurs in Cynwyd, Merionethshire (DPNW 116).

Llanharan ST 002831
Rhondda Cynon Taf
'church of Aran (*or* Haran)': **llan**, pers.n. ?*Aran*, ?*Haran*
Lanharan c.1178, c.1598, *Llanharan* 1540, *Llangharran* 1541, *ll. haran* c.1566, *Llanharen* 1670, *Llanharran* 1831, (place) *Gwein Lanharan* 1563
Richards (ETG 186) suggested that -h- may be intrusive before the stressed vowel –a-. The ch. is dedicated to SS Julius and Aaron, allegedly martyred at Caerleon, perhaps mid 3rd cent. The present dedication to Aaron at least may have been prompted by its similarity to Aran/Haran.

Llanhari (Llanharry) ST 006804
Rhondda Cynon Taf
'church of Ari (*or* Hari)': **llan**, pers.n. ?*Ari*, ?*Hari*
Landhary 12th cent, *Lanhari* c.1178, 1254, *Lanhary* c.1262, *ll. hari* c.1566, *Llanharry* c.1541
For the variation Ari/Hari, cf. Llanharan. Possibly not a saint since the ch. is dedicated to Illtud. Doble (LWS 115-6, 133) recounts an onomastic tale in the 'Life of St Iltut' 12th cent of two robbers who steal Illtud's herd of swine, 'taking them from the *hara* where they were kept and driving them towards the woodlands'. They lose their way and at dawn find themselves back at the place from which they had started. At nightfall the robbers return to the pig-sty (Lat *hara* 'pen or coop for domestic animals') and make a second attempt to drive the pigs off to the distant mountain, with the same result: 'The patience of the King of Heaven being now exhausted, they were turned into stones, which are still called after them, and the site of the *hara* still bears the n. of Iltut'. Wade-Evans (WCO 135) located the reputed pig-sty at Llanharan ("where to our own time survived a place called Llecha, 'stones' "). If there is any basis to the tale, then the ch. dedication to Illtud would favour Llanhari, not Llanharan. Llechau fm. (ST 017807), on the eastern edge of the village, is recorded as *Llechfa* 1811, *Llecha* 1841, *Llechau* 1867 (**llech** pl. *llechau*).

Llanilid SS 977813
Rhondda Cynon Taf
'church of Ilid': **llan**, pers.n. *Ilid*
(*castellum de*) *Sancta Julitta* (ch.) *Sancto Ilith* c.1130 (1208), (chp. or ch. of) *sancta Ilith* c.1180, *Sancta Julita* late 12th cent, (ch. of) *Sancte Iulite* 1254, (parson of) *Sancto Tylith* early 13th cent, *Sancta Julitta* c.1348, *Llanilyd* 1564, *ll. ilid a chirig* c.1566, *Llanilid alias St. Julitts* 1710, *Lanhilid* 1764
Ilid was identified at an early date with Julitta (of Tarsus), who shared a feast day with her fellow martyr Ciricus (16 June) matched with St Curig in Wales; the two saints were then linked as a dual ch. dedication, probably in the late middle ages. Ilid may also be the person found in Lanillis (Léon) in Brittany. Several writers have been reluctant to accept Ilid as a pers.n. or saint: H.C. Jones (PNIG 36), for example, suggests that it referred to 'a geographical feature' and Fenn states that Julitta, as 'the Latin equivalent of Ilid, represents the n. of a district and not an individual' (VGS4: 119). Ilid (*Ilud*) is described as one of the many daughters of the semi-legendary Brychan Brycheiniog c.1200 and her local connection is confirmed by a mention in a manuscript of 'Llud daughter of Brychan, in Rhuthun in Gwlad Forgan' mid 13th cent (*Llud verch Vrachan yn Ruthun yGwlat Vorgant*). *Llud* is a scribal error for *Ilud*. Rhuthin or Ruthin was the n. of the lp. which included Llanharan, Llanilid and St Mary Hill.

Llanilltern see **Capel Llanilltern**

Llanilltud see **Ilston**

Llanilltud see **Llantwit-juxta-Neath**

Llanilltud Faerdref see **Llantwit Fardre**

Llanilltud Fawr see Llantwit Major

Llanisien (Llanishen)   ST 176818
Cardiff
'church of Nisien': *llan*, pers.n. *Nisien*
(ch. of) *sancti nisien, sancti Tussien* c.1170, (chp. of) *Sancti Dionisii de Kibur* c.1175, *Landyneys* 1317, (chp.) *St. Denis in Kybour* 1400, *Lanysan in Kybour* 1440, *Llan Isen* c.1538, *Llanyssen* 1557, *Lanisshan* 1578, *ll. nisen* 1590-1, *Lanissan* c.1659, *Lanishen* 1833
Nisien is almost certainly the same saint dedicated at Llanisien (Llanishen), Monmouthshire (DPNW 269). The n. is not a W corruption of the Lat pers.n. Dionysius as Green thought (NCDL 32, 34). Dionysius (probably St Denis the martyr, patron saint of France) is simply another example of the substitution of the n. of a continental saint for a lesser-known Celtic saint, a change often prompted by a perceived similarity of form and through the use of Lat in ecclesiastical and secular administration. The chp. recorded in c.1175 and 1400 has also been identified with the ch. at Lisvane which is dedicated to Denis but Llanisien possesses a Ffynnon Denis (in the Oval in the north part of Roath Park) near the ho. marked as *Capel Denis* on the OS map 1833 (approx. ST 183806). The well was associated with St Denis and resorted to for the cure of rheumatism and sore eyes (CR V, 368). Both names confirm the popular association with St Denis. Nisien (or 'Isien') is reputed to have been a disciple of St Illtud but this seems to be an error derived from a misunderstanding of the Breton Life of St Samson (of Dol) c.610 which records an abbot Isanus summoned by St Illtud to his monastery (at Llantwit Major). This Isan may be the saint of Llanisan-yn-Rhos (identified with St Ishmael's, Pembrokeshire) which occurs in the Book of Llandaf 12th cent as *lanyssan, lann isann* and similar sps. Early sps. of Llanisien, Glamorgan, show conclusively that the pn. does not include the pers.n. *Isan*. Later sps. such as *Lanisshan* 1578 and *Lanishan* 1758 reflect the local colloquial pron. with 'sh' [ʃ].

Llanmadog (Llanmadoc)   SS 441933
Swansea
'church of Madog': *llan*, pers.n. *Madog*
Landmadoch 1249, *Lanmadok* 1284, *Lanmadoc* 1300, *Lammaddok in Gouer* 1312, *Lanmadock* 1319, *Llanvadok* 1535, *Llanmadok* 1578, *Lanvadocke* 1624, *Llanmadock* 1813
Llanfadog would be the regular W form and the absence of len. (m > f) in many forms shows E influence as with Llan-maes and Llanmihangel. The ch. is now dedicated to Madog but Merrick attributed it to Cadog and Hamon to Illtud in 1697. The ch. at Nolton, Pembrokeshire, is also dedicated to a St Madog (PNPemb 620).

Llanmaes, Llan-faes   SS 980695
Vale of Glamorgan
'church in open country (as opposed to woodland)': *llan, maes*
(William de) *Lanmays* c.1239, *Lanmaes, Landmais* 1254, *Thlanmays* 1284, *Llammays* 1447, *Llanvays* 1535, *ll. faes* c.1566, *Llanmaies* 1578, *Llanvayes* 1601, *Lanmaes* 1605
Identical in meaning to Llan-faes, Anglesey and Breconshire (DPNW 241). The absence of len. in the modern E form is almost certainly a product of AN influence; cf. Llanmihangel. Some sps. suggest a further development to *Lamaes* with assimilation of –n- but this is not current. The ch. is dedicated to Catwg and possessed a wooden effigy of him c.1700. Llanmaes is reputed to have been anciently called *Llan Ffagan Fach* but the story may have originated through confusion with a ho. Llanmaes (ST 122768) at St Fagans recorded as *Lanvaise* 1637, *Lanvase* 1734, *Lanmâs* 1766, *Llanvas* 1841, *Llanfaes* 1880.

Llanmihangel, Llanfihangel y Bont-faen
SS 981718
Vale of Glamorgan
'church dedicated to (St) Michael the Archangel': *llan*, pers.n. *Mihangel*
Landmihangel 1254, (ch. of) *Sci' Michis' de Lennyhangell* c.1291, *Lanmyhangel* 1314, *Lanvyhangel* 1350, *Mechelstowe prope Cowbrugge* 1516, *Llanmyhangell* 1528, *Llanvehangle prope Cowbrige* 1530, *Llanvihangell otherwise*

Michellstone juxta Cowbridge 1626, *Lanmihangell* 1670, *Llanfihangel* 1833
The non-current Michaelston contains *Michael* with OE *stōw* 'holy place' (answering to **llan**) replaced by the more common ME *–ton* (OE *tūn*). Cf. Michaelston-le-pit. The present W form has the qualifier Y Bont-faen (see Cowbridge) but this appears to be a modern adoption. There is a second Llanmihangel/ Llanfihangel (SS 816829) near Pyle recorded as *St. Michael-super-Montem* c.1190, *St. Michael's Grange* 1685, *Llanmihangle* 1725 with a mill *Seynt Michelle is mylle* 1527 and *lannmihangells mille* 1691. This appears to have been a grange of Margam abbey.

Llanmorlais SS 529945
Swansea (Llanrhidian)
'bank of the (r.) Morlais': **glan**, rn. *Morlais Glanmorleis* 1617, *Lanmorlais* 1650, *Glan Morlesse* 1662, *Glanmorlais* 1715, *Llanmorlais* 1764, *Lan-morlas* 1832, (place) *Morlas* 1671
The rn. contains *mor* (**mawr**) 'big, great' and **glais**. The r. Morlais recorded as (r.) *Morlais* 1602 is not a particularly large stream (in contrast to Morlais (q.v.), near Merthyr Tydfil) and it is possible that it refers to its tidal stretch recorded as (*aper*) *morcleis* c.1145 and *Morlais, otherwise Salt House Pill* 1764, where it reaches the r. Loughor.

Llanquian ST 018743
Vale of Glamorgan (Llanblethian)
Uncertain
(chp. of) *sancti Iacobi de Lancoiuan* c.1178, *Llancovian* c.1262, *Lancovyan* 1314, *Lancovian* 1349, *Llanquian* 1549, *Lankoyan* 1574, *Languyan* 1576, *Lancwyan* c.1659, *Lancovian otherwise Lanquean* 1739, *Llangwyan* c.1800, *Llan-chwain* 1833, *Llan-Chwain*, ~ *-fâch*, ~ *Castle* 1877
The first el. appears to be **llan** 'church' but there seems to be only a single ref. to a chp. of St James, possibly at or near the small castle here. Melville Richards suggests (ETG 181) that **llan** may be combined with a pers.n. *Cwyfan* as in Llangwyfan, Anglesey, but an unrecorded and unexplained *Cofian* would be closer to older historic sps. Current pron. by W-speakers is 'Llan-chwian' [ɬan'χwiːan] and roughly 'Lankweeun' [lan'kwiːən] by E-speakers. What is notable is the absence of len. (g < c) in most historic forms. This could be attributed to E influence (see Llanmaes and Llanmihangel) but out of a sample of thirty-four historic forms taken from unrelated sources, only four have *-g-*, which suggests that Llan- may have displaced some other el. such as **nant**, cf. Llancarfan, in the sense of 'valley' rather than 'stream'. The only stream of any consequence here is Nant Aberthin (properly Berthin), authenticated from the 12th cent.

Llanrhidian SS 497919
Swansea
'church of ?Rhidian': **llan**, pers.n. ?*Rhidian Lanradien, Lanriden* c.1190, *Llanridian* 1230, *Lanrydyan* c.1291, *Landridian* 1185 (13th cent), *Lanridian* 1331, *Lanndrydian'* 1396, *ll. Riden* c.1566, *Llanridian Chapel, Llanrhidian,* ~ *Chapel* 1832
The ch. is dedicated to Rhidian but he is unattested as a saint and early sources associate it with Illtud. Sps. such as *Landridian* 1185 and *Llandrydian* 1774 have an intrusive -d- (after -n-), a characteristic of a number of historic forms of *Llan-* pns., especially in the Vale, and paralleled in pers.ns. such as *Cyn(w)rig* > *Cyndrig*, *Henry* > *Hendry*. Llanrhidian was a relatively large p. for the Gower peninsula requiring an additional chp. Llanyrnewydd (Llanenewyr) (SS 548948) in the upper part or higher division of the ecclesiastical p. sometimes known as Capel Llanrhidian.

Llanrhymni (Llanrumney) ST 224808
Cardiff (Llanedern)
'bank of the (r.) Rhymni': **glan**, rn. **Rhymni**
Lanrompney 1615, *Lanromney* 1621, *Lanrhumney* c.1659, *Lanrumney* 1729, ~ *house* 1764
H.C. Jones (PNIG 11) also records *Landrumney* (with intrusive –d-) on 17th cent gravestones; cf. some forms of Llanrhidian. The suburb developed from the late 1960s around the former Llanrumney Hall (ST 217811), Llanrumney Farm, and Mill Farm (ST214807) extending to Newport Road.

Llansamlet SS 685974
Swansea
'church of Samled': *llan*, pers.n. *Samled*
Lansamle c.1168 (1334), *Llansambled* 1535, *Lansamlet* 1556, *ll. siamled* c.1566, *Llansamled* 1578, *Lansamlett* c.1598, *Llansamlett* 1643
The ch. is said (HMorg 377) to be dedicated to Samled in the tract known as Bonedd y Saint 12th cent but the supposed saint does not appear in the text edited by Bartrum (EWGT 51-67) and the pers.n. is unexplained. Richards (ETG 196) also knew of no such saint. Lewys Glyn Cothi, however, seems to refer to one in a poem addressed to Dafydd ap Siôn of Llysnewydd (in Llansamlet) (GLGC², no.101.35-38). There was also a well Ffynnon Samlet (*ffynnon*) attested in a fn. *Cae Funnon Samlet* (*cae*) 1844 at Talycopa (SS 696966).

Llansanwyr (Llansannor) SS 993774
Vale of Glamorgan
'church of ?Senewyr': *llan*, pers.n. *Senewyr*
(ch. of) *sancte Senware de la Thawa* c.1180, *La Tawe* 1254, *La Thawe* 1296, *Thawe* 1401, *Llansannor alias Thawe* 1535, *Llansannoer* 1557, *Llansannure* 1670, *Lansannwr* 1799
The pers.n. occurs in Bonedd y Saint 12th cent as *Seneuyr*, son of Seithennin of Maes Gwyddno. Hopkin-James (OCow 137-40) identified the saint with Senara or Sennara (Bret *Azenora*) in the pn. Zennor, Cornwall, but this is unlikely due to the regular occurrence of -*wy*- (reduced to –*w*-, -*o*-) in Llansanwyr. The alternative n. *La Thawe* refers to the r. Thaw/Ddawan (see Aberthaw). The scholar Egerton Phillimore (OPemb III, 310) supposed that *La* derived from *llan* and ultimately from *nant* (with the rn.) in the same way as Nant Carfan > Llancarfan and traced it back to the forms *Nant Auan* and *Nantauan* in the Book of Llandaf c.1145. For the supposed development of *llan* to *La*-, *La*- he had to look for parallels in Cornwall, notably Lawhitton (< *Landuithon*), and to suppose that such names were influenced by the Fr def.art. *la*. There are, however, no recorded instances of any intermediate forms such as *Lan*-, *Llanddawan* and the forms *Nant Auan* and *Nantauan* are likely to be a copyist's errors for *Nadauan* (= Naddawan, Ddawan, Thaw).

Llansawel see **Briton Ferry**

Llantrisant ST 048834
Rhondda Cynon Taf
'church of the three saints', *llan*, (*y*), *tri*, *sant*
Llantrissen 1247, *Lantrissan* 1254, *Lantrissain* 1263, *Thlanatrissent* 1297, *Lantrissan in Morgan* 1345, ~ *in Meskyn* 1386, *Lantrussan* c.1405, *Llantrissent* 1535, *ll. y trissaint ymisgyn* c.1566, *LL. trisaint* 1606, *Llantrissant* 1833
Many early sources have the pl. *saint* but modern convention is to use the sing. form after a numeral. The three saints are Illtud, Gwynno and Tyfodwg – all dedicated in neighbouring ps. The unstressed -*y*- (shown in 1297 as –*a*- and in c.1566 as –*y*-) was lost between -*n* and *t*- in a similar fashion to Llanypumsaint > Llanpumpsaint, Carmarthenshire, 'church of (the) five saints' (DPNW 273). Earlier sps. substituting –*ent*, -*en* for –*aint*, also seen in many historic forms of Llantrisant, Monmouthshire (DPNW 282), probably reflect local dialect. Llantrisant lay in the hundred of Meisgyn and lp. of Morgannwg. Some antiquarian sources state that Llantrisant was earlier known as Llangawrdaf in honour of Cawrdaf, alleged founder of a seminary here (HMorg 380), but there is no reliable evidence for this.

Llantrithyd, Llantriddyd ST 044728
Vale of Glamorgan
?'stream called Rhirid': ?*nant*, pers.n. or rn. *Rhirid*
Landrirede c.1126, *Lanririth* 1254, *Lanririd* c.1262, *Lanryryd* c.1348, *Llanrithyd* 1535, *Llantrythed* 1548, *ll. triðid* c.1566, *Llantrydded* 1603, *Lantrithyd* 1708, *Nantririd* c.1545, *Nant Ririd* 1569
All early forms have *Lan*- which prompted many antiquarians and historians to suppose that the pn. was composed of *llan* coupled with the n. of a saint identified, among others, as Trynihid (VGS 1, 41), wife of St Illtud, recorded in the Life of St Illtud c.1145. Trynihid, however, is almost certainly a ghost n. drawn from historic

forms containing –*trythed*, -*trydded*, etc. The first el. is likelier to be **nant** in the sense 'valley' or the more common meaning 'stream' coupled with the pers.n. *Rhirid* used as a rn. Cf. Nant Carfan > Llancarfan (q.v.). The stream is now known as Nant Llantrithyd. If this argument is valid, then **nant** was displaced at a very early date by **llan** leaving no clear trace in recorded sps. until 1492. The pers.n. probably developed into *Rhiddid* to ease pron., a characteristic also witnessed in Tyddyn Rhirid > Tyddyn Rhiddyd, Caernarfonshire (ETG 199). A few late forms of Llantrithyd such as *Lloyntrithed* 1596, *Llwyn Ridit* c.1659, and *Llaynrhiddid* 1662 suggest further association with **llwyn** leading to occasional confusion with Llwynrhiddid (q.v.).

Llantwit see **Llantwit-juxta-Neath** (Neath Port Talbot)

Llantwit Fardre, **Llanilltud Faerdref**
ST 081865
Rhondda Cynon Taf
'church of (St) Illtud at the *maerdref*', **llan**, pers.n. *Illtud*, **maerdref**
(well) *fonte Sancti Ylthuti* late 12th cent, *Llanyllted*, *Llantwytt* 1541, *Llanilltyd Fairdre* c.1549, *Lantwit vayrdre* 1556, *ll. ylltyd or faer dref* c.1566, *y Blwyf Llanylltyd Vayrdre* c.1612, *Lantwit minor* 1675, *Lhan Illtud Vaerdref* c.1700, *Lantwit Fardra* 1762, *Llantwitt fardre* 1833, *Llanilltyd Faerdref* 1880, *Llanilltyd Fardre* 1892
The present spelling on OS maps *Fardre* reflects local pron. of -ae- as -â- [a:] (cf. Maerdy) and colloquial loss of –f [v]. 18th cent sps. also show local pron. of terminal –ef, -e as –*a* (also substituted for the pl. –au). The sps. with *-twit* etc are generally later than those for Llantwit Major (q.v.) and it is possible that the latter has influenced the later development of Llantwit Fardre. The first ref. is to St Illtud's well (Lat *fons*). The antiquarian Edward Lhuyd c.1700 mentions a 'faire spring', recorded as *Fynnon Illtid ar dŷr-y-ddi-Hewid*', 'Illtud's well on Dihewid land' (**ffynnon**). The former fm. Dihewid or Dyhewyd (ST 078857) is about a mile from the ch. Llantwit Fardre has been effectively displaced as a n. by Church Village (q.v.).

Llantwit-juxta-Neath, **Llanilltud** SS 763980
Neath Port Talbot
'church of (St) Illtud near Neath', **llan**, pers.n. *Illtud*, Lat **juxta**, pn. *Neath*
Laniltavit 1289 (1468), (p. of) *St. Illtud* 1535, *Llantwytt* 1535, *Saint Iltyde* 1546, *Lantoid* c.1549, *Llanyltude iuxta Neathe* 1562, *ll. elldyd fach* c.1566, *Lantwit iuxta Neathe* 1584, *llantwit by Neath* 1626, *Lantwitt Parish, ~ yssa* 1670, *Llanilltyd* 1769
The late appearance of the qualifier –juxta-Neath suggests that Neath refers to the town not the r. Modern sources (GazWPN, WATU) give the W n. as Llanilltud Nedd but most sources call it plain Llanilltud and an alternative form Llanilltud Fach (**bach**[1], *fach* 'little') seems to be based on a single instance in a list of ps. c.1566 which has a number of unreliable forms. It is possible that the person who compiled the list has confused it with Llantwit Fardre which is qualified by Latin *Minor* in 1675 and 1692.

Llantwit Major, **Llanilltud Fawr** SS 966687
Vale of Glamorgan
'greater Llantwit/Llanilltud': Lat **major**, **mawr**; 'church of (St) Illtud': **llan**, pers.n. *Illtud*
Llan Iltut c.1100, *Landiltuit* 1106, *Lannildut*, (*Catgen abbas*) *ilduti* c.1145, *sancti ilduti* c.1170, *Lantiltwit'* c.1200, *Laniltwit* c.1262, *Laniltut alias Lan Iltut* 1296, *Lantwyt* 1480, *Llanyltwydd*, -*twyt* 1535, *ll. ylldyd fawr* c.1566, *Lantwit Major* 1580
Illtud is also dedicated at Llantwit Fardre, Llantwit-juxta-Neath, Ilston, Newcastle and Llantrisant, and in Brittany, but little is known for certain about him (LWS 88-145). The sps. with -*twit*, -*twyt* etc. nearly all derive from E sources but they may nonetheless indicate a by-form *Illtwyd*, under the influence of Ir *Illtuaith*; cf. Llantood or Llantwyd, Pembrokeshire (PNPemb 88-9). 'Greater' draws comparison with Llantwit Fardre and Llantwit-juxta-Neath but neither Major nor Fawr seem to be in evidence before the 16th cent. The manor Llantwit Rawley is recorded as *Luntewyte* 1463, *Raley* (in p.) *Llantwit* 1525, *Raylee Lantwitt* 1567 and *Lantewitt Rawley* c.1598. The surname Raleigh, Rawley

also occurs in Cwrtyrala (q.v.). The family inherited the de Reigny lands - the manors of Wrinston, Michaelston-le-Pit and Llantwit Raleigh - by marriage of Joanna de Reigny with Simon de Raleigh (d. before 1287-8) (PNDPH 153-4). Part of Llantwit was granted by Robert Fitzhamon, Norman conqueror of Glamorgan, to Tewkesbury abbey 12th cent and became known as West Llantwit or Abbots Llantwit.

Llanwensan　　　　　　　　　　ST 079794
Vale of Glamorgan (Peterston-super-Ely)
'church of Gwensan': **llan**, pers.n. *Gwensan Egloiswensen* 1254, *Llanwensan* 1541, *Lanwensam* 1550, *y blwyf Llanwensant* c.1612, *Lanwenslan* 1698, *Lanwensol* 1774, *Lanwensan* 1833
llan has displaced an earlier **eglwys** (cf. Llangeinwyr) and an unrecorded pers.n. composed of **gwen** in the particular sense 'holy' and perhaps **sant** 'saint'. Loss of –*t* is notable in many historic forms of Llantrisant and sps. with –*m* reflect the variation also found in Llandinam < Llandinan, Montgomeryshire. Llanwensan seems to have been a chapel-of-ease to Peterston-super-Ely. Fragments of the ch. or chp. appear to be incorporated in Llanwensan-fawr farmhouse.

Llanwynno (Llanwonno)　　　ST 030955
Rhondda Cynon Taf
'church of (St) Gwynno': **llan**, pers.n. *Gwynno Lanwonno* 1450, (chp.) *Llanivonno* 1535, *Llan Wonni* c.1538, *ll. wno* c.1566, *Llanwunnyo* 1578, *lanwonno, llanwuno* c.1598, *Llanwynno* 1670, *Llanwunno* c.1700, *Llanwonno* 1787
Little is known of Gwynno save that he is dedicated at Llantrisant (with Illtud and Tyfodwg), Llanpumpsaint (with Gwyn, Gwynoro, Celynnin and Ceitho), in Carmarthenshire, and Faenor. The fm. Darwynno (ST 024962) recorded as *Tir Dar Wonno* 1570, *syddyn Tir daerwyno* c.1612, *Daer Wynno* 1638 and *Darwynno* 1833, has **dâr** 'oak-tree'. The association of saints with trees is rare in Wales and it is possible that 'Gwynno's oak' is used indirectly for a notable 'oak-tree in Llanwynno'. Sps. with *Daer* are probably attempts at representing the local pron. [dɛːr]; cf. Aberdare/Aberdâr. Glanffrwd (William Thomas, 1843-90) supposed that *Daer* is *daear* nf. 'earth, ground, land', hence his translation 'Gwynno's land' (HLlanwyno[1], 5-6). He also attempted to persuade the School Board not to use the irregular spelling *Llanwonno* but this persists on OS maps. St Gwynno Forest (ST 0396, 0496) is a modern n. for afforestation.

Llanyrnewydd　　　　　　　　SS 549948
Swansea (Llanrhidian)
'church of Enewyr': **llan**, pers.n. *Enewyr Lanyynewys* 1499, *Llan Enewir* 1536, *ll. ininewyr* c.1566, *Llannyenwere* 1578, *Llanynewer* 1587, *Llooneenewire* 1609, *Llaninewer* 1640, *Llangnewyr* 1697, *Llan y newyr Chapel, Llan y newir or Cwm y Nant* 1764, *Llan-newydd* 1851
A former chp-of-ease in Llanrhidian Higher, sometimes recorded as Llanrhidian Chapel, dedicated to Gwynour, an anglicised form of Gwynnwr, which is probably a supposition based on late forms such as *Llanweynour* 1733. Sps. such as this also led to identification with a Breton saint Gwynour. Llanyrnewydd was identified by Evans (LLRees 386n.) with *Lann conuur* and *lann cynuur* c.1145 in the Book of Llandaf (LL 144, 145), known to have been located in Gower, but the sps. are at odds with those cited above. Pierce (PNGlam 110-1; ADG[1], 68) suggested that the 1499 spelling is a miscopying of *Llanynewir*, a supposition strengthened by other sps. He also noted a saint Eneour in Brittany supporting the case for a related W pers.n. Enewyr. Llanenewyr developed firstly into *Llanynewyr*, probably through association of the first unstressed -*e*- with the def.art. *y*, and secondly into *Llanyrnewydd* through association of -*newyr* with **newydd** 'new'. The ho. Cwmnewydd (SS 550946) and the lost Berthynewyr are recorded as *Kwm Ynewyr* 1568, (lands) *Cwm y newir* and *Berth y newir* 1650, *Cwmynewir, Berthy Newir* 1764, *Coomynewydd* 1841, *Cwm-newydd* 1879 (**cwm, perth**), and refs. to *Capel Kae y newyn* and *y Newers field* in a description of the boundaries of Landimore 1602.

Llan y Tair Mair see **Knelston**

Llechryd SO 107094
Caerphilly (Bedwellte, Monmouthshire; Llangynidr, Breconshire)
'stone ford, ford having stone slabs': **llech**¹, **rhyd**
Llechred 1434, (mess.) *Lechryd* 1770-9, (fms.) *Upper and Lower Llechrydd* 1807
Formerly the site of two fms. Llechryd Isaf, ~ Uchaf (**isaf, uchaf**) near the point where the road running from Merthyr Tudful towards Tafarnau Bach crosses the r. Rhymni. The area is called *Rumney bridge* 1814 and *Rumney Bridge* 1832 (PNBre 113) and (*o*) *Bontlechryd* 1871.

Llety Brongu SS 882886
Bridgend (Betws)
'temporary dwelling of Brangu': **llety**, pers.n. *Brangu*
Llodre Brangye 1541, 1570, *Llodre Brangig* 1548, *Lletty Brongu* 1769, *Llette-Brankey* 1777, *Lletybrongu* 1873, *Llety-bron-gu* 1892
llety has displaced the less common **llodre** thought to be a cognate of Ir *lathrach* 'site or location of a ho. or ch., or similar edifice' (PNGlam 117-8). The pers.n. may be the same as *Brancu* on a monumental stone at Baglan dating c.1000. **llodre** is found elsewhere in Glamorgan as a former ho.n. Llodre-brith (approx. SS 617949, near Swansea) recorded as *Lodre Bryth* 1583, *Lodrebrith* 1714, *Llodrybryth* 1764, *Lletty-frith* 1830 and, less obviously, in Llandremôr (SN 616055, at Llandeilo Tal-y-bont) recorded as *Lladre Morte* 1559, *Llandre moore* 1583, *Llandremore* 1665.

Lletyharri SS 773905
Neath Port Talbot (Margam)
'temporary dwelling of (man called) Harri': **llety**, pers.n. *Harri*
Lletty Harry 1813, *Lletty-Harry* 1877
llety occurs in other pns. in the area such as Lletyllwyd (approx. SS 807946) recorded as *Lletty Lloyd* 1689, *Lletty-llwyd* 1877, **llwyd** or possibly a surname *Llwyd/Lloyd*, now under forestry.

Llidiard see **Litchard**

Lliw
rn. (Swansea)
'bright, brilliant (r.)': **lliw**¹
Lyv c.1187, *Liv* 1334, *Llyew* 1590-6, *Lhu* 1612, *Luw ycha, & Luw issa, Lugh the Greater* 1697, *Rivers Llyw and Llyw Ytha* 1764
lliw¹ 'colour, hue' has the extended sense of 'lustre, good or flourishing condition'. Lliw is also described as *Northyr Lyu* 1306 'northern Lliw', and *Llugh the greater* c.1700, distinguishing it from Lliw Eithaf, 'further Lliw' (*eithaf*), now called Afon Llan from its proximity to the village of Llangyfelach. The r. also gives its n. to Pont-lliw (q.v.). Lliw Eithaf is *Llugh the lesser* c.1700 and leaves its n. in Pont Llewitha/Llewitha Br. (SN 6196) recorded as (place) *Pont liw Eitha* 1720.

Llwchwr, Afon see **Loughor**

Llwydcoed SN 991047
Rhondda Cynon Taf (Aberdare)
'grey wood': **llwyd, coed**
lwytcoed c.1500, (forest of) *Lluid Coite* c.1538, *Lloyde Coyde* 1547, *Llwyd-goed Hamlet* 1755, *Llwydcoed* 1768, (*pentref*) *y Llwydcoed* 1874, (forest) *fforrest Llwyd Coed* 1666, *Forest y Llwyd coed* 1698
Perhaps 'grey, dimly lit woods' as Deric John suggests (see further CVPN 68-69). The industrial settlements developed near Llwydcoed fm. and ho., and ironworks recorded in 1815. Identical in meaning to the common Llwyd-coed in Llanfabon which is *Lludcoed* 1697, *Ludcoed* 1720, and (area) *Llwyd Coed* (at approx. ST 1092) 1833.

Llwyn-bedw see **Birchgrove**¹

Llwynbrwydrau SS 703972
Swansea (Llansamlet)
'grove of dispute': **llwyn, (y), brwydr**¹
Lloyn y Vroydyr c.1583, *Llwyn Vrwydir* 1650, *Lloyn vr Wydir* 1688, *Llwyn yr Wydir* 1764, *Llwynbrwydre* 1813, *Llwynbrwydrau* 1862, *Llwyn-brwydrau* 1884

Early forms clearly stand for what would now be regularly spelt as Llwyn-y-frwydr but the final el. has been displaced in later forms by its pl. *brwydrau*. It is notable that the n. referred to a ho. close to the boundary of Llansamlet with Cadoxton-juxta-Neath – possibly once lying in a disputed area. Cf. Llwynydadlau (lost, in Aberdare) recorded as *Lloyn Ydadele*, *Lloyn Dadle* 1541 and *llwyn y dadley* early 17th cent, *dadl* nmf. 'argument, dispute', pl. *dadlau*.

Llwyncelyn[1] ST 202854
Caerphilly (Lisvane, Llanfedw)
'holly grove': ***llwyn***, ***celyn***[1]
Tir llwyn kelyn 1703, (ho.) *Llwyn y celyn* 1811, (~) *Llwyn-celyn* 1833, *Holly Bush* 1841
Cf. Llwyncelyn[2-4]. The n. has been extended from a fm. to include hos. around the junction of Cefn-porth Road and Rudry Road. There are extensive woods in the surrounding area.

Llwyncelyn[2] (Bedwellte) see **Hollybush**

Llwyncelyn[3] ST 032911
Rhondda Cynon Taf (Llanwynno)
'holly grove': ***llwyn***, ***celyn***[1]
(ho.) *y lloyn kelyn* 1633, *Llwyncelyn* 1833, *Llwyncelyn House* 1874
Named from the fm. Llwyncelyn (ST 033917) which also gave its n. to a colliery recorded in 1871 (HMorg 61). The village developed as an easterly extension of Porth in the late 19th cent, eventually occupying the greater part of the area around Llwyncelyn House. There are identical pns. elsewhere in Glamorgan such as the former Llwyncelyn at Llanfabon recorded as *Lloyn Celyn* 1783, *Lloyn Kelyn* 1795, which leaves its n. in *Llwyncelyn Terrace* in Nelson; and *Llwyncelyn* at Merthyr Tudful recorded as *Tir Llwyncelyn* 1540, *Llwyn Kellin* 1757, *Llwyn y Celyn* 1783.

Llwyncelyn[4] SN 666021
Swansea (Llangyfelach)
'holly grove': ***llwyn***, ***celyn***[1]
Llwyn-celyn 1899

Cf. Llwyncelyn[1-3]. A late 19th cent development north of Rhydypandy near the hos. Llwyn Meurig and Llwyn-y-domen, 'Meurig's grove' and 'grove at the mound' (pers.n. *Meurig*; *y*, *tomen*).

Llwyneliddon see **St Lythans**

Llwynerydd see **Eaglesbush**

Llwyn-onn (Llwyn-on Village) SO 014114
Merthyr Tudful (Faenor Breconshire)
'ash grove': ***llwyn***, ***onn***
Tere llowyn on 1701, *Tire Llowyn on* 1756, (ho.) *Llwyn-on* 1832, *Llwyn-on Village* 1977
A small ht. constructed in the 1950s in association with Llwyn-onn Reservoir (SO 0011) by Cardiff County Borough and named from the ho. Early forms have *tir* 'land, (tenement of) land'.

Llwynrhiddid ST 0477
Vale of Glamorgan (Pendeulwyn)
'Rhirid's grove', ***llwyn***, pers.n. *Rhirid*
Loynririd 1314, *Lloyn Ridit* 1429, *Lloynrhythid* 1667, *Llwyn-rhuddid* 1833, *Llynrythed otherwise Lloyne Rethyd* 1564, *Lantrithed* 1580, *Llanrhiddid, Llaynrhiddid* 1662, *Lantryvett* late 16th cent
Rhirid is unidentified. For the variation Rhirid/Rhiddid see WS 183 and cf. Llantrithyd (q.v.). A former manor.

Llwyn-teg see **Fairwood**

Llwyn-y-bwch SS 484915
Swansea (Llanrhidian)
'the buck's pool': ***llyn***, ***y***, ***bwch***
Klyn de Bough, *Lin y bough* 1583, *Llynyboch, Llanyboch* 1602, *Landibuch* 1619, *Lleyn y bouch* 1650, *Llwyne Bwch* 1666, *Llyn y bough, otherwise Lan y bough* 1764
Historic forms show great uncertainty with regard to the first el. though *Klyn* is probably just a scribal error for *Llyn*. Other forms favour association with ***glan***, len. *lan*, and ***llwyn***. There are several small pools on a stream which flows westwards to Burry Pill. Described as a manor in 1583 and 1764.

Llwynypia SS 998939
Rhondda Cynon Taf (Ystradyfodwg)
'the magpie's grove': ***llwyn, y, pia***
Llwyn y Pia 1799, (hos.) *Llwyn Pia* 1813, *Llwynpia* 1814, (ho.) *Llwyd-pia* 1833
Originally referring to a fm. Identical ho.ns. are recorded on the borders of Llantrisant and Llantwit Fardre (ST 060884) as *Llwyn y Pia* 1768 and *Llwynypia* 1793, and the former Llwynypia (approx. ST 180788) recorded as *Llwynypia* 1833 and *Llwyn y pia* 1841, near Allensbank fm. (Cardiff), now lost to Cathays Cemetery. ***pia*** is a late form of *pi²*. The pl. ***piod*** is more common, found, for example, in Llwynpiod, Cardiganshire, Pentrepiod at Abercarn, Monmouthshire, and in Llangywer, Merionethshire. The village developed around a colliery opened in 1863.

Llychwr, Afon see **Loughor**

Llyn Fawr SN 917034
Rhondda Cynon Taf (Ystradyfodwg)
'big lake': ***llyn*** 'lake, pool', ***mawr***
Llyn fawr 1814, *Llyn-fawr* 1833
'big' in contrast to Llyn Fach (SN 9003) which is *Llyn fach* 1814, *Llyn-fach* 1833 (***bach¹*** 'small, lesser'). The lens. are unexpected since ***llyn*** is generally a nm. The rules are sometimes broken when the n. is taken directly from a ho. but that is not the case here.

Llystalybont approx. ST 171783
Cardiff
'court at the end of the bridge' or 'court in Tal-y-bont': ***llys, tal, y, pont***
Lisbonit c.1188, *Lestelebont* 1261, *Lestilbont* 1314, *Listelbont* 1326, *Listallapont* 1516, (grange) *Llistalabont* 1560, *Lystalabont in Kibor* 1564, *Listalybont* 1670, *Llys-tal-y-bont* 1833
There seems to be no evidence of any bridge in the immediate area and it is possible that Tal-y-bont referred to a wider area extending up river. It is interesting to note refs. in the Book of Llandaf to *talponescop* 1128, *talpon escop*, *Talpontescop* 1129 (c.1170) meaning '(area or place at) end of the bishop's bridge' (*esgob* nm 'bishop, prelate'). The precise location of this place is uncertain but the refs. seem to apply to a bridge close to Llandaf cathedral, probably at the old Llandaf bridge in Llandaf North.

Llyswyrny (Llysworney) SS 962741
Vale of Glamorgan
'court of Gwrinydd': ***llys***, n. of cantref *Gwrinydd*
(chp. of) *Liswini* c.1180, *Liswrony* 12th cent, *Llys ronwy yGwlat vorgan* c.1140 (c.1200), *Liswrinni* 1248, *Lyswryny* 1317, *Lyswronny, Lyswronnyth* 1474, *Llyswornneth* 1535, *Llesbroinuith (Scirpetum)* c.1538, *llys Ronyð* c.1566, *Lhes Broimith, or Skirpton* 1586, *Llisvroneth* c.1598, *llees y Vronydd* 1729, *Llisyfronydd* 1767, *Llisworney* 1833
This is likely to have been the administrative centre of the cantref Gwrinydd (q.v.), hence the form for c.1140 standing for ModW *yng Ngwlad Forgan*, 'in Glamorgan'. The sps. with -*wyrny,* -*worney* show shift of vowel -*wry*- > -*wyr*-, possibly under E influence. Many W sps. show association with the pers.n. *Goronwy* as in *llys Ronwy*; *brwynydd* based on *brwyn* 'rushes' translated by the antiquarian John Leland c.1538 as *scirpetum*, a form drawn from Lat *scirpus* 'rush, bulrush'; and *bronydd* based on *bron* 'breast, breast of a hill'. The last must explain *Llysyfronydd*, said by T.J. Hopkins (VGS II, 117-8), to have been the form used by W-speakers. Iolo Morganwg c.1800 uses the similar form *Llysvronudd* but his explanation of the pn. as derived from a certain 'Nudd Hael, the son of Senyll, of the college of Illtyd', can be safely rejected (see ETG 85; PNGlam 121-2).

Login SS 619948
Swansea
?'dirty brook': ***halog***, suffix *–yn*
Login 1837, 1879
Cf. Login (SN 1623) near Llanboidy, Carmarthenshire, recorded as *Loggin* 1684, *Login* 1843, in Llywel, Breconshire, and Ferwig, Cardiganshire. A small brook runs westwards and turns northwards near Waunarlwydd to join Afon Llan. The same el. probably occurs in Aberlogin (SS 510938), at Llanrhidian, which is *Aberloggin* 1665, *Aber-logwyn* 1830 and *Aber-login* 1878 (***aber***).

Long Acre SS 497867
Swansea (Oxwich)
E *long*, *acre*
Long Acre 1974
Apparently a modern n., possibly derived from a fn., fairly common in Gower, with examples recorded in Llanrhidian, Nicholaston and Reynoldston.

Lônlas SS 702972
Neath Port Talbot (Cadoxton-juxta=Neath)
'green lane': *lôn¹*, *glas¹*
(land) *Tir Llon Lase*, *Tir Lon Las* c.1583, *Tyr Llon Llase* 1764, *Lonlaes* 1841, *Lone Las* 1844, *Lon-lâs* 1884, *y Lonlas* 1908
A lane which was either unmetalled or defined by hedges and trees. Named from a fm. (formerly at SS 272974) which lay at the head of a small lane running east from the ht., near the modern Back Drive and Park Drive. Similar names include Heol-las (q.v.), Greenway (ST 223793) at St Mellons recorded as *Heoll lase* 1736 and *Greenway* 1811, and Greenway (ST 053742), at Llancarfan, recorded as *The Greene Way* 1631, *Greenway* 1676, *Heol Las* 1784 (**heol**).

Loughor, Casllwchwr SS 566981
Swansea
'castle on (r.) Llwchwr': ***castell***, rn. *Llwchwr* (r.) *Leuca*, *Leucaro* 1-4th cent (8-12th cent), (r.) *Luchur*, *lychur* c.1145, *Logherne* 1203, (r.) *Locher* c.1191, (grange) *Lochor* 1208, *Locghern* 1278, (water) *Lozcharne* 1306, (*chastell*) *Aber Llychwr* c.1400, *Lougher* 1459, *Lloughour* 1469, *Lochor* c.1538, *Loughor* 1775, *kastell llwchwr* c.1550, *Caslougher* 1691, *Câs Lychür* 1719, *Castel Loughour* 1583
castell has contracted to *Cas-* as with Casnewydd, the W n. of Newport, Monmouthshire (DPNW 347-8). Llwchwr derives from Brit *Leucarum* containing **leuco-* 'bright, shining, white' and suffix **-ara(a)*, probably with the sense 'shining (r.)'. *Leucarum* would normally produce ModW *Llugar* whereas ModW *Llwchwr* ought to derive from Brit **Luccarum*. For this reason, Jackson (JRS 38, 57) believed that *Llwchwr* and *Leucarum* could not refer to the same r. and dismissed the similarity as a coincidence but that is very unlikely, as Rivet and Smith argue (PNRB 389). It has to be emphasised that there are just two early sps., viz. *Leuca*, *Leucaro*, and it is quite possible that these are miscopyings for *Lucca*, *Luccaro*, or that there were variant forms of the rn. The other curiosity is the final *–n* found in sps. such as those for 1278, 1322, etc taken from E sources, for which there seems to be no obvious reason unless there was occasional administrative confusion with Laugharne (Lacharn), Carmarthenshire, though *–n* is an original el. in that pn. (DPNW 211). See also Glynllwchwr.

Lower Penarth see **Penarth** (Vale of Glamorgan)

Lower Porthkerry see **Porthceri** (Vale of Glamorgan)

Lower Sketty, Sgeti Isaf SS 617912
Swansea
'lower Sketty': pn. *Sketty/Sgeti*, E ***lower***, ***isaf***
Sketty Isha c.1720, *lower Sketty* 1764, *Lower Sketty* 1799, *Ysgettyisaf* 1872
The 'lower' or southern end of Sketty (q.v.). The name initially referred to a fm. and adjoining houses and was extended to the settlement which developed along Derwen Fawr Road after c.1880. Derwen-fawr ('great oak') was the name of a house opposite the fm. and later the site of the Bible College of Wales.

Lunnon SS 547897
Swansea (Ilston)
?'ash grove': ?*llwyn*, *onn*
Lunan 1322, *Lononn* 1385, *Lunon* 1402, *Lynon* 1432, *Laynon* c.1598, *Lunnon*, *Lonnon* 1650, *Llwynon* 1697, *Llwyn-on* 1832
The 1697 and 1832 sps. seem to favour this interpretation with substitution of L- for Ll- by E-speakers but the numerous sps. with *Lun-* are less supportive. This presumably explains why Melville Richards (WATU) places it under *Llan-non* as if were identical to Llan-non, in cos. Cardigan and Carmarthen, meaning 'church of (St) Non', but there is no evidence for *Llan-* (***llan***) or anglicised *Lan-* in historic sps.

Machen to Mynydd y Gwair

Merthyr Tudful. Looking north along the river Taf towards Cyfarthfa castle c.1830. (courtesy of Keith H. Edwards and Frank Hartles)

Machen ST 210891
Caerphilly (Monmouthshire)
'plain, open land of Cain (*or* Cein)': **ma-**, pers.n. *Cain*
Mahhayn c.1102 (1330), *Maihen* 1254, *Mahham*, *Magheyn* 1330, *Machan* 1392, *Machen* 1403, *Maghein* 1429, *Machain* 1447, (manors) *Diffren Maughan, Maughan Bedel* c.1568
See ETG 247. Machen is a 19th cent industrial development recorded as *Upper Machen (works of the Machen Iron and Tin Co., Machen Colliery, foundry etc)* 1859 and *Upper Machen* 1871, and the n. earlier applied to what is now Lower Machen (ST 227880) where the Rhymni valley widens a little. The pn. has generated unwarranted speculation, fuelled by Iolo Morganwg's fictitious *Meigan Cil Ceincoed* and Bradney's confusion (HMON V, 116) with a genuine pers.n. *Meugan*.

Maendy[1] (Maindy) ST 173782
Cardiff (St John's Cardiff)
'(the) house roofed by slates': (*y*), **maen**, **tŷ**
(*syddyn*) *y Maendy alias the Tyle howse* c.1612, *ye Maindy* 1729, *Maindu* 1767, (hos.) *Maendy, ~-bach* 1833
This interpretation is favoured by the first reference. Thatch was once used extensively in the lowland areas of Glamorgan so that a slate or tiled roof would have been distinctive.

This specific meaning is explicit also in the case of Maendy (ST 065815), Llantrisant, which is *Mandye alias Tylehowse* 1541.

Maendy[2]   ST 010764
Vale of Glamorgan (Llanblethian)
'(the) house roofed by slates' or perhaps '(the) stone house': (*y*), *maen*, *tŷ*
Y Maendy otherwise Tir y pwll 1612, *Y maendy* 1671, *Maindy* 1779, *Maendy* 1799, *Maendu* 1833
Taken from fm.ns. The alternative form in 1612 means 'land at the pit': *tir*, *y*, *pwll* probably referring to old limestone quarries here. There are identical pns. in other parts of Glamorgan at Gelligaer, Llandyfodwg, Peterston-super-Ely, and Pendeulwyn.

Maenor Crugmarchan see **St Bride's-super-Ely**

Maenor Glynogwr see **Glynogwr**

Maerdy   SS 974983
Rhondda Cynon Taf (Ystradyfodwg)
'steward's house': *maer*, *tŷ*
may dy 1580, *Tyir y Mardee* 1633, *Mardy* 1813, *Meardy* 1833, *Mairdy* 1845, *Maerdy* 1877
A former mining village which developed from the 1860s, taking its n. from a fm. in the manor of Penrhys. *Mardy* reflects local pron. A common ho.n. and pn. with identical examples in Gelligaer, Llanwynno, and Merthyr Tudful. Note also Maerdy Newydd (ST 049747) in Llancarfan and Maerdy otherwise Maerdy Rhys (approx. SN 714118), in Llan-giwg, recorded as *Maerdy Sr. Rees* 1681, *Maerdy Rhys* 1831, *Mardy Rys* 1852 with pers.n. *Rhys*.

Maescynon   SN 965056
Rhondda Cynon Taf (Penderyn Breconshire)
'field by (r.) Cynon': *maes*, rn. **Cynon**
Maescynon 1964
A housing estate built mainly after 1945 near a ho. Bryn-cynon (*bryn*).

Maesteg   SS 856910
Bridgend (Llangynwyd)
'fair open-field': *maes*, *teg*
Mates Take, Mays Tek Kenoll, Ymas Tege Ycha 1541, *maes tege issa* 1543, *Maesteg* 1657, *Maesteg ycha* 1647, *Maesteg Ucha* 1699, (forest in) *Gwaine y maes Teg* 1731, *Maesteg genol, ~ Isha* 1740, *Maes-têg Works* 1833
The pn. is stressed on *–teg* but Maesteg is the established modern form. According to Dafydd Morganwg 1874, a Thomas Jones of Abergavenny came here in 1798 to seek a place in which to build an ironworks and leased a coal level on the fm. Y Llwyni (see HMorg 363-4; HLlangynwyd 55-56) but there seems to have been little industrial development until work began on an iron furnace in 1826 and the opening of the tramway to Porth-cawl in 1828. The ironworks took its n. directly from a fm. Maes-teg Uchaf (SS85139130) (*uchaf*) around which the town developed. Maes-teg Isaf (approx. SS 862904) (*isaf*) was about half a mile below Maes-teg Uchaf. The town developed rapidly from c.1830 but the n. did not become fixed until it acquired its own Local Board of Health in 1858. Sometimes known as Llwyni from a ho. (approx. SS 859918) which stood on the north side of the town recorded as *Llwyney* 1773, *Llwynau* 1813, *y Llwyni* 1835, 'the groves' (*llwyni*).

Maes-y-coed (Maesycoed)   ST 067898
Rhondda Cynon Taf (Llantwit Fardre)
'field at the wood': *maes*, *y*, *coed*
Maesycoed 1879, (ho.) *Maes-y-coed* 1900
The ho. lies below *Gelliwion Wood* 1875 described as *Coed Lan-draw* 1900 from its location near the fms. Gelliwion (ST 055890) recorded as *Kellywyon* 1541, *kelli wion* c.1612, *Kellywyon hamlet* 1670, *Gelliwion* 1792, 'Gwion's grove': *celli*, pers.n. *Gwion*, and Lan-draw (ST 061896) recorded as *Llan* 1811 and *Lan-draw* 1875, presumably *lan draw* in the sense '(place) up and afar, up and distant' (*glan*, *draw*) with refs. to its location above Pontypridd.

Maesycwmer (Maesycwmmer) ST 155945
Caerphilly (Bedwas, Monmouthshire)
'field near the footbridge': *maes*, *y*, *cwmwr*

Maesycwmwr 1828, 1835, *Maes-y-Cymmer* 1868, *Maesycwmmwr* 1869, *Maescwmwr* 1903, *Maes-y-cwmmer* 1901
cwmwr is evidenced from the 17th cent but is rare in pns. Osborne and Hobbs (PNWG 48) say that the n. probably derives from the n. of a ho. recorded as *Maes-y-Cwmmer House* 1880 (ST 155948) built in 1826 by a minister of Hengoed Baptist chp. The ho. was approached by way of a footbridge.

Maes-y-dre SO 001027
Rhondda Cynon Taf (Aberdare)
'the town field': *maes, y, tref*
Maes-y-dre 1868, 1964
tref has lenited as *dref* with colloquial loss of -f. A part of central Aberdare defined by Hall Street, Gloucester Street and Canon Street.

Maesyffynnon see **Springfield**

Maindy see **Maendy** (Cardiff)

Man-moel SO 179038
Caerphilly (Mynyddislwyn Monmouthshire)
?(place or ch. associated with) Mab Moel: pers.n. *Mab Moel*
Ecclesia Mac moilo c.1100 (c.1200), *Mapinoil* (= *Mapmoil*) c.1102 (1330), (water-mill) *Melyn Van Hoell* 1570, (wastes, common of) *Mamm Howell* 1630, *Mamhoel* 1641, *Mamole* 1713, *Pentref Manmoel* 1813, *Pentremam heol* 1833, *Cefn Manmoel* 1833
Man-moel is a late form of Mab Moel 'son of Moel' (**mab**), probably a W adaptation of Ir Macmoil (*Macmoillus*) substituting **mab** for *mac* 'son' and ***moel¹*** for *mael* 'bald'. Macmoil is recorded c.1100 with St Finian (also an Ir pers.n.) as a disciple of St Cadog in the Life St Cadog c.1100 (DPNW 311). Cadog, Elli and Macmoil are said to have had altars at Cadog's ch. in Llancarfan (WB 602). Moel meaning 'the bald one' occurs in medieval W sources, often as a nickname. If this interpretation is correct, then Man-moel belongs to a group of pns. which consist of a pers.n. (usually a saint) standing alone, eg. Margam (q.v.). The modern form Man-moel may have developed from later sps. such as *Mamhole* (for *Mam-moel, Mamoel*) in which *–b-* has been assimilated and re-interpreted by popular etymology as 'bald, bare place' with ***man¹***, probably by ref. to Cefn Manmoel. A few 19th cent forms have **pentref** 'village', an el. surviving in the ho.n. *Tir-y-pentre* 1878 and Tir-y-pentre fm. (*tir, y*). Local pron. has *-ô-* [ō] for *-oe-* [oi].

Manselfield SS 591887
Swansea (Nicholaston)
pers.n. and surname: *Mansel,* **field**
Mauncellifeld 1400, *Maunsellfield* 1626, *Manselfield* 1632, *Mansellfild* 1666, *Mansel field* 1832
Named from a ho. (SS 589890) which belonged to the Mansel family which first appears in Gower in 1310. Manselfold (SS 474919), at Llanrhidian, is *Maunsel's fould* 1747, *Mansel's fold* 1764, *Mansel fold* 1832, *Manselfold* 1841 (E *fold*). Charles (NCPN 122) locates *Mauncellisfeld, -ysfeld* 1399 and *Mauncellysfeld* 1465 here but this is uncertain.

Manselton, Trefansel SS 654953
Swansea
'settlement named from Mansel': surname *Mansel,* **-ton**
(racecourse) *Manselton* 1887
An area of housing developed from the 1880s north of Courtenay Street and around Pwll-y-domen extending onto the short-lived Manselton racecourse from 1890. Named from the Mansel estate, Swansea (PNIG 52; WGOW IV, 421). The surname Mansel is found in other pns. in this area; see Manselfield. Trefansel is in use by Swansea Council and among W-speakers but its historical basis is uncertain.

Marcross, Marcroes SS 925693
Vale of Glamorgan
?'boundary cross': OE ***(ge)mære***, OE ***cros***
Marcros c.1155, *Marecros, -crosse* 12th cent, *Marecros* 1254, *Marescrosse* 1349, *markroes* c.1566, *Marcroes* 1578, *Marchros* 1636, *Marcross* 1799
Marcross ch. lies only 100 yards from a stream marking the p. boundary with Monknash and it is possible that Marcroes derives directly from the E form substituting **croes** 'cross' for

cros. The alternative explanation is that it is an anglicised form of Marchros 'stallion's promontory' containing **march** and **rhos**² (NCPN 144) referring perhaps to Nash Point. If Marchros is the original form, however, then –*ch*- [χ] has left no trace in early sps. though it is important to emphasise that most historic forms derive from E sources and may be re-interpretations. Other suggestions owe more to imagination than wisdom: Dafydd Morgannwg (HMorg 392), for example, and others favoured a translation of *Croes Marc* referring to a supposed cross or a corruption of *Mêr-groes* 'the cross on the sea shore'. The Burrows at Marcross are *Marecrosberwes* 1336 and *Martesborghes, Marecrosburwes* c.1291 with 'sand dunes, burrows' (OE *beorg*).

Margam SS 783875
pers.n. *Margan* variation *Margam*
(monks of) *Margan* c.1170, (~) *sancte Marie de Margan* 1148-83, (*abbas de*) *Morgan* 1208, (abbot, etc of) *B(ea)te Marie Virg(in)is de Morgan* 1535, *Morgan Abbay and village* c.1538, (late monastery) *Morgan' alias Margam* 1540, *margam* c.1566, *Margam* 1578, (*o*) *vargan* early 17th cent, (manors) *East Margam, West Margam* 1718
Probably another example of a saint's n. standing alone (cf. Baglan) rather than qualifying **llan** or **merthyr**. A saint Marcan is found paired with Briog in Cornwall and Brittany though there is no evidence to link him directly with Margam. The pers.n. was confused at an early date with Morgan in Morgannwg. This in turn led some antiquarians such as Rice Merrick late 16th cent to identify Morgan with Morgan son of Maglawn (sic), 'duke of Scotland' before the birth of Christ (BG 5) but Merrick drew on the untrustworthy Geoffrey of Monmouth (d. c.1155). Others such as Nicholls identified 'Morgan or Margan' as the source of the territorial title 'Lord of Glamorgan and Morgan' (NGG, xi and 150-1). The monastery was established by a colony of monks from Clairvaux in 1147 (BirchM). The village was originally centred on its ch. near Port Talbot railway station. Final -n has been influenced by initial M-; cf. Mawdlam.

Markham SO 167013
Caerphilly (Bedwellte Monmouthshire)
'(settlement near) Markham Colliery'
Markham Village 1919, *Markham* 1976
A village laid out in 1913-16 and named from Markham's Navigation Colliery north of r. Sirhywi 1912-85 owned originally by Markham's Steam Coal Co., itself named from the company chairman Sir Arthur Basil Markham (1866-1916), Liberal MP for Mansfield 1900 (MCPP 60-63). The colliery was sunk in 1910. The village developed near Berllan-llwyd recorded 1833 (SO 170011) 'grey orchard' (**perllan**, **llwyd**).

Mawdlam SS 806819
Bridgend (Pyle and Kenfig)
?'(ch. dedicated to St) Mary Magdalen':
*Mawdlen
church of Mawdelen 1580, (ch. of) *Maudlen* 1587, (p.) *Mawdlem in Kenfig* c.1598, (churchyard of) *Magdalen one of the Churches of the ... parish of Kinfigge and Pile* 1662, *Modlen* 1740, *Maudlam church* 1804, *Kenfig or Mawdlam* 1833
A local variant of Magdalen pronounced as E ['mɔ:dləm] and as W ['maudlam]. An old ch. in the p. was said to be dedicated to St Mary. Pns. such as the former chp. called The Maudlin, at Tenby, and another chp. in Haverfordwest, Pembrokeshire, have similar sps. (PNPemb 560, 649). Note also that the former Augustinian priory of St Mary Magdalene, in Maudlin Street, Bristol, is called simply *the Mawdlen* 1597.

Mawr centred on SN 6405
Swansea (Llangyfelach)
'big (*parsel*)': (**parsel**), **mawr**
Trayn Mawr in Gower 1314, *Parcell Mawre* 1670, *Parcel Mawr* 1756
The first recorded form has **traean** nmf. 'a third'. Llangyfelach was a very large p., divided into three divisions or **parseli**, viz. Clas, Mawr and Rhyndwyglydach, all of which possessed ts. or hts. distinguished as **isaf** 'lower' and **uchaf** 'higher'. Mawr was the largest **parsel** extending from Afon Lliw (at SN 6301) to the Carmarthenshire border. Identical in meaning

to Mawr, a township and *parsel* of Llan-giwg, recorded as *Parcell Mawr* 1650, *Parcell Mawre* 1670, (ht.) *Mawr* 1851. The n. survives as that of a community council.

Mayals SS 608902
Swansea (Oystermouth)
?'hills where mayweed grows': OE *mæþe*, OE *hyll*
Moys, Moyl c.1291, *Maieles* 1322, *le Mailles* 1399, *Meiles, Mayalls* 1650, *Mayles* 1739, *the Mayals* 1764, *Mayels* 1834
Possibly a ref. to the hill above Blackpill. There are considerable doubts with this explanation and it is tempting to find a duplicate for the lost Meles (q.v.) Sps. with *Mai-, May-*, however, tend to rule this out. The earliest hos. of the village developed on Mayals Green in the 19th cent. Major housing development took place after 1945.

Mayhill SS 647941
Swansea
?'hill pleasant in May' or 'hill where mayweed grows': E **May** or **mayweed**, **hill**
May Hill 1813, *May's Hill House* 1815, *Mayhill* 1879
Cf. Mayals. The n. of a housing estate initiated with the construction of 29 houses for an exhibition. A further 500 houses were planned in 1912 but further development was delayed until the 1920s. Named from a ho. (approx. SS 646937) near what is now Llewelyn Crescent.

Meisgyn (Miskin)
Uncertain
Meyskin 1243, *Meyskyn* 1268, (court of) *Meskyn* 1281, *Miskyn* 1307, *vro veisgynn* c.1450, *Kymwt Meisgyn* c.1400, (lp.) *Myskyn* 1447, *Comm. Meyskyn, Miskin Commote, or Glade Miskin, Misken* c.1538, *Meiscyn* mid 16th cent, *Misgin* 1631, *Miskin Hundred, ~ hamlett* 1670
Two main interpretations have been offered but neither can be accepted without further evidence. R.J. Thomas (ELlMeisgyn 184) suggested the pn. may contain **maes** and a pers.n. *Cyn(n)* containing a root el. which also appears as Cen- and -gen in pers.ns. Driessen (StC XXXIX), by contrast, connects the pn. with *meisgyn* which he interprets as 'an obnoxious larva' though it is 'moth, weevil' in GPC. That might be applicable to an area infested by these creatures such as the former common Gwaun Feisgyn (or Gwaun Miskin ST 0684) recorded as *Wayn Vyskin* 1588, *Gwayn Miskyn* c.1670. Meisgyn was the n. of a commote and hundred (covering seven ps.), and a ht. in Llantrisant. The lower part (*bro*) of the p. was Brofeisgyn around Brofeisgyn Fawr (ST 069816) and Brofeisgyn Fach recorded as *Vro Veisgynn* 1450, *Croviskin* (sic) 1578, *Broviskin* 1617, *Brofiscin-fawr, ~ -fach* 1833, *Miskin Vale* 1672.

Meles (Lower Court Farm), **Cwrt-isaf** SS 7689
Neath Port Talbot (Margam)
'sand-hills, sand-banks': ME **mele**
Mieles 1186, (*de*) *Melis* late 12th cent, (grange) *Melis* c.1220, (land of) *Meles* 1261, c.1291, *Meles of Avan* 1633, *Cwrt-isa* 1830, *Lower Court* 1876
ME **mele** is a borrowing from ON *melr* and is identical in meaning to Meols, Cheshire. Neither pn. can be regarded as proof of Scand settlement because both have the E pl. form with -s. Cwrt Isaf 'lower grange' (*cwrt¹, isaf*) and Lower Court refer to a monastic grange of Margam abbey. The n. of nearby Upper Court (*Cwrt* 1830) survives as Court (SS 766895). Meles is no longer current.

Melincryddan SS 749966
Neath Port Talbot (Llantwit-juxta-Neath)
'mill on (r.) Cryddan': **melin**, rn. *Cryddan*
(mill) *Credan* 1296, (grist mill) *Crathanysmyll* 1541, (place) *Creathan* 1638, *Melin Grythen, Melingrythan* 1647, *Crethans Mill* 1666, *Melin Crythan* 1688, *Melin-cryddan* 1830
The rn. is *Crudan Brooke* 1397, *Kryddan* c.1700, *Crythan Brook* 1666, possibly containing the el. in *cryddu* 'to shrink, lessen', perhaps 'because the brook was sluggish' (VNeath 329; EANC 61).

Melin-cwrt (Melincourt) SN 820019
Neath Port Talbot (Llantwit-juxta-Neath)
'(the) grange mill': **melin**, (**y**), **cwrt¹**

meline glidaghe 1598, (grist mill) *Melyn Glydach* 1604, *Court Mill* 1656, *Melinglydach* 1697 (late 18th cent), *Mellin y Court Furnace* 1718, *Melin y Cwrt* 1764, *Melyn y Court bridge* 1777, *Melincourt Furnace* 1831, *Melincwrt* 1867

cwrt¹ has been displaced in some sources by E *court*. Earlier known as Melin Glydach, 'mill on the (r.) Clydach'. Phillips (VNeath 223) suggested that the change of n. was a result of the transfer of manorial courts to the mill and inn in the 16th or 17th cent. The ht. developed around an ironworks recorded in 1718. Melincourt Brook was earlier known as Clydach Cwmcaca recorded as *Cleudachcumkake* c.1200 (1358). Cwm Caca meaning 'dung valley' (*cwm*, *caca*) is now applied only to its upper reaches but distinguishes the stream from Clydach Brook or Clydach Uchaf at Resolfen (Clydach q.v.).

Melin Gruffudd (Melingriffith)   ST 144803
Cardiff (Whitchurch)
'Gruffudd's mill': *melin*, pers.n. *Gruffudd*
Griffith Mill 1666, (grist mill) *Griffith's Mill* 1715, *Melyn Griffith* 1764, *Griffith Mill's Forge* 1767, *Melin Griffith* 1833, *~ Works* 1831
The pers.n. is anglicised as Griffith. The site of a water-mill adjoining the r. Taf which became the location of tinplate works in the 18th cent. The mill is also recalled in nearby Felindre (*melin*, *tref*). Melin Gruffudd may be the water-mill mentioned in Whitchurch (*Album Monasterium*) in 1296 and *Res Mylle* 1541 (possibly containing the pers.n. *Rhys*). There have been some highly conjectural identifications of Gruffudd (eg. OPN 140 and PNIG 11) despite the fact that our sources are late and that it is a very common pers.n..

Melin Ifan Ddu see **Blackmill**

Mellte
rn. (Neath Port Talbot)
'river which moves (*or* flashes) like lightning': *mellt*, suffix *–tou* or *-teu*
Meldou 1129 (c.1170), *Melltou* c.1145, *Mellte* 1482, 1503, *Melte, Melta* 1578, *Melltey* 1691

A n. appropriate to a fast, bright mountain r. also found in Ystradfellte, Breconshire (DPNW 504). Mellte also occurs as a pers.n.; see Bedwellte.

Merthyr Dyfan   ST 113697
Vale of Glamorgan
'graveyard containing the bones of Dyfan': *merthyr²*, pers.n. *Dyfan*
Mertherdevan 1254, *M'ther* (= *Merther* or *Marther*) c.1291, *Martheldouan* 13th cent, *Merthyr Dovan* c.1535, *Mertheldavan, Mertherdavan* 1541, *y merthyr dyfal* c.1566, *M. dyfan* 1591, *Merthir Dovan* 1670, *Merthyr Devan* 1729
Dyfan was once thought to have been a missionary with St Fagan to Britain in the 2nd cent but his true identity is unknown. Gwynedd Pierce (PNDPH 133-5) suggests that *Marthel-* may be a product of dissimilation *r-r* > *r-l* as in Marteltwy, Pembrokeshire (PNPemb 521-2).

Merthyr Glywys see **Clevis**

Merthyr Mawr   SS 883775
Bridgend
'graveyard containing the bones of Myfor': *merthyr²*, pers.n. *Myfor*
merthirmimor, merthir Miuor c.1145, (ch. of) *sancti teliawi de merthyr mymor* 1129 (c.1145), *Matthelemaur* 1146, *Merthirmouor* before 1199, *Merthurmaur* c.1262, *Marthelmaur* 1314, *M(er)thermaure* 1535, *merthyr mawr* c.1566
The same pers.n. is found in Llanofer (Llanover), Monmouthshire (ETG 194). Myfor was associated with *mawr* 'big, great' at an early date. For dissimilation *Marther-* > *Marthel-*, cf. Merthyr Dyfan. The ch. is dedicated to Teilo.

Merthyr Tudful (Merthyr Tydfil)   SO 0506
Merthyr Tudful
'graveyard containing the bones of Tudful': *merthyr²*, pers.n. *Tudful*
Merthir 1254, *Merthir in Morganno* 1295, *Merthyr* 1296, *M(er)thur Tudvyl* 1535, *Martyr Teduil* c.1538, *Merthure Tudvyle* 1547, *Merthertydvill* 1559, *Merthyr Tydfil* 1799

Plain Merthyr in earlier refs. Tudful contains the el. *tud* 'country, people' – also found in Tudno in Llandudno and Tudwal in Tudweiliog, Caernarfonshire – and is recorded in pedigrees dating from c.1130 where she is described as a daughter of the semi-legendary Brychan Brycheiniog. Misinterpretation of the pn. inspired a number of fanciful tales about her reputed martyrdom by pagans in 420 or 480 AD (HMorg 399-400). Intrigue was added to speculation when a stone tomb was found in the foundations of the old ch. in 1807 containing a large skeleton (reputedly one of three giant brothers) which was re-buried outside the walls of the new ch.

Merthyr Vale, Ynysowen   ST 076995
Merthyr Tudful
'valley near Merthyr Tudful': pn. **Merthyr**, E *vale*; 'river-meadow of (man called) Owen', *ynys*, pers.n. *Owen* variant of *Owain*
Tir Ynys Owen 1540, *Ynys Owen* 1630, *Tir Duffrin Tâf alias Tir Ynis Owen* 1750, *Ynysowen* 1813, *Ynys-owen* 1833, *Merthyr Vale* 1880, *Merthyr Vale, once named Ynysowen* 1894
Merthyr Vale is evidently a translation of Dyffryn Taf (*dyffryn*, rn. **Taf**) but the village is named directly from Merthyr Vale Colliery (approx. SO 073000), initially known as Taff Colliery which was sunk by John Nixon 1869-75, five miles below Merthyr Tudful. Merthyr Vale was first applied to housing which developed along Cardiff Road on the east side of the colliery but is now regarded as the E n. for the whole village including Ynysowen which properly applies to the area around and south of Station Square. Ynysowen was the n. of a former fm. (ST 076995).

Mewslade Bay   SS 4187
Swansea (Rhosili)
'shallow-valley frequented by gulls': ME, E *mew* (OE *mæw*), *slade* (*slæd*)
Newslade c.1600, (*Bottom called*) *Mewslade* 1632, (little creek) *Mew Slade* 1764, (ho.) *Mewslade* 1813, *Mewslade Bay*, (valley) *Mew Slade* 1879
Charles (NCPN 129) thought that the first el. is OE *nīwe* 'new' but historic forms – apart from the first cited ref. taken from a survey of Gower – generally have *Mew*-.

Michaelston-le-Pit, Llanfihangel-y-pwll
ST 151729
Vale of Glamorgan
'holy place (*or* church) dedicated to (St) Michael in the hollow': OE *stōw* later *–ton*, AF *le*, OE *pytt*; *llan*, pers.n. *Mihangel*, **y**, *pwll*
(ch. of) *Sancti Michaelis de Renny* 1254, *Michelstowe* c.1291, 1488, *Michaelstown* 1535, *Michelston le Pole* 1563, *Mighelston in le pitt* 1567, *Michellston the Pitt* c.1598, *Mychelstone in the Vale* c.1670, *Landmihangel* 13th cent, *ll. V'el or pwll* c.1566, *~ y pwll* 1606, *Llanianngle* 1578
The E form may well have displaced the W form despite the late appearance of the latter in records. OE *stōw* itself was replaced by ME *–ton* (*tūn*), probably in the early 16th cent; cf. Tythegston and for the use of *le*, cf. Hutton-le-Hole, North Yorkshire, 'Hutton in the hollow'. Located in the valley of a tributary of Cadoxton River. The area was held in the 13th-14th cent by the de Reigny family hence the 1254 form (see further PNDPH 146-152).

Michaelston-super-Avan, Llanfihangel Ynys Afan   SS 780920
Neath Port Talbot
'settlement of (St) Michael on (r.) Afan': *Michael*, ME *–ton* (OE *tūn*), Lat *super* 'over, on', rn. *Afan*; 'church of (St) Michael at Ynys Afan': *llan*, pers.n. *Mihangel*, pn.
Enys Abon 1519, *Seynt Mychel* c.1528, *Myazchaelstowne* 1535, *Lanmighangell' Ynys Avan'* 1537, *Llanuihengle, St. Michell super Avan* 1564, *ll. V'el ynys Afan* c.1566, *Enys-aven or Enys Avan* 1574, *Michaelchurch* 1578, *Sainte Michell upon Avan* 1580, *Ynisavan* c.1670, *Michaelstone super Avan* 1792, *Ynys-afon* 1832
Ynys Afan is 'river-meadow by (r.) Afan' (*ynys*). There is no evidence that *-ton* has displaced *stōw* as in the case of Michaelston-le-Pit. The paucity of early evidence means that we cannot be certain when Michaelston first came into common use and the n. alternates with Michaelchurch and similar forms in E records down to the mid 18th cent. Michaelston has

been identified with a grange (*de*) *Sancto Michaele super Montem* c.1190, 'grange of St Michael on the mountain', Lat **mons**, accusative *montem*, and a grange of *Mikael* c.1291 but the evidence is inconclusive. The pn. has been effectively displaced by Cwmafan.

Michaelston-super-Ely, Llanfihangel-ar-Elái   ST 119758
Cardiff
'settlement of (St) Michael on (r.) Ely': *Michael*, ME **–ton**, Lat **super** 'over, on', rn. *Ely*; 'church of (St) Michael on (r.) Ely': **llan**, *Mihangel*, **ar**, *Elái*
(ch. of) *Sancti Michaelis* 1254, (~) *Sancti Michaelis-super-Elie* 13th cent, (~) *S'ti Michael' sup' Elly* 1535, *Mihelstowe* 1369, *Mighelston upon Elye* 1549, *Mychelstowe super Elye* 1559, *ll. fihangel* c.1566, *Llânyhangle* 1578, *Lannihangell* 1638, *Michaelston Supr. Ely* 1799.
For the rn. see **Ely**, **Elái**. Two sps. suggest **–ton** may have displaced OE **stōw**; cf. Michaelston-le-Pit. The p.ch. (ST 115763) lies on the edge of suburban housing begun in the 1950s.

Middleton   SS 421878
Swansea (Rhosili)
'middle farm or settlement': E **middle**, ME **-ton**
Middleton 1673, 1689, *Middle Town* 1799, 1831
Midway between Rhosili and Pitton. The ho. Middleton (approx. ST 150688) at Sully is *Midleton* 1632, *Middleton* c.1700, *Middletown* 1833.

Millwood   SS 6595
Swansea
'wood by the mill', OE **myl(e)n**, **wudu**
Mullenwood 1232 (16th cent), *Millewode* 1399, *Mylwood* 1520, (lp.) *Mylwode* 1548, (manor *Millwood* 1614, *east and west Millwood* 1764
The first refs. record it with *Borlakestand* (see Cwmbwrla) in a late copy of a grant by John de Braose to the commandery of Slebech, Pembrokeshire. Located on the north side of the old town outside its north gate near the r. Tawe. St John's ch. (SS 65669374) and p. were said to be *at Mylwood* 1520 and in *Mylwode* 1548. Charles (NCPN 117) identified Millwood with *villa de Milwodesketty* 1396 but this was probably near Brynmill, at Sketty.

Milton and Bryncwtyn see **Felindre**[2]

Miskin[1], Meisgyn   ST 047809
Rhondda Cynon Taf (Llantrisant)
'(place in) Meisgyn': **Meisgyn**
Misken 1868
A largely modern village which developed from the 1860s near coal and iron workings. The n. is taken from the commote and ht. of Meisgyn (q.v.) and was formerly known as New Mill recorded in 1799, 1811 and as *Melin newydd* 1833 (**melin**, **newydd**). The change of n. may have been recommended by Gwilym Williams (1839-1906) who re-built and re-named Broviskin House as Miskin Manor (ST 056802) in 1864.

Miskin[2]   ST 051983
Rhondda Cynon Taf (Llanwynno)
?'(place near the public house called) Miskin'
Miskin 1875, *Miscyn* 1896
An industrial village which appeared c.1850-62 on two fms. Clun Gwyn and Ty'r-arlwydd (CVPN 73), probably taking its n. directly from *Miskin* public ho. 1871, *Miskin Inn* 1875 and indirectly from Miskin Higher division (of Meisgyn hundred) which included Llanwynno, Aberdare and Rhigos.

Moltwn see **Moulton**

Monknash, Yr As Fawr   SS 920705
Vale of Glamorgan
'(place) near the ash-tree of the monks': ME, E **monk**, OE **atten**, **æsc**; def.art. **yr**, cymricised *As*, **mawr**
Aissa c.1140, *Essam* c.1178, (grange) *del' Hesse* c.1250, *Asse* c.1291, *Monkenashe* 1535, *Nash, -e* 1542, *Nashe magna* 1578, *Mouncke Ashe or Ashe manour* c.1598, *P[lwyf]. Rarre* 1606, *Monken Ashe alias Magna Aish* 1607, *Great Nash* 1610, *Muncke Nashe* 1638, *Race vawor* 1670, *Monkston, or Rase Vawr* 1782, *Monknash* 1831
The final *-n* of **atten** has become fixed to the second el. in the same way as Nash (q.v.). The qualifier Monk- appears in the 16th cent

and alludes to its earlier existence as a grange of Neath abbey. Some sps. show that it was sometimes qualified with **great** and Lat *magna* to distinguish it from Nash (at Llyswyrny). The cymricised *As* (from *Ash*) is similarly qualified by **mawr**, *fawr*. The same p. also has West and East Monkton (SS 932709) and nearby Wick has Lower Monkton (SS 926710) (*tūn*). One of these is recorded as *Monketowne* 1535, *Mounton* 1548, *Monkton farme* 1602, *Mwncton* 1673, *Monkston* 1783, and a W form *Y Mwntwn* occurs in a triban recorded in the late 19th cent. Sps. such as *Mounton* and *Mwntwn* show assimilation of -k-, -c-; cf. Mounton, Pembrokeshire. The short form of Monknash also gives its n. to the headland Nash Point (SS 914683) recorded as *the Nash point* 1586, *Nashe poynt* 1645.

Moore Town　　　　　　　　SS 721975
Neath Port Talbot (Cadoxton-juxta-Neath)
'settlement named from Moore': surname *Moore*, E **town**
Mooretown 1886, *Moore Town* 1899
An area of housing which developed from the 1870s near Cwm-du Foundry, a small colliery and brickworks, taking its n. from a prominent local family. John Newall Moore (d. 1905) of Longford Court (Cwrt Rhydhir), Neath, coalowner, built Lon-las mission ch. (All Saints) here 1904.

Morfa Bank　　　　　　　　SS 767877
Neath Port Talbot
'sea-bank at Morfa', pn. *Morfa*, E **bank**
Morfa Bank 1940
Located near a former mud-bank (SS 760885) recorded as *Morfa newydd* 1813 and *Morfa-Newydd* 1885 meaning 'new sea-marsh' (*morfa*, *newydd*). There was a second mud-bank (now covered by the steelworks) a little to the south recorded as *Morfa-mawr* 1832 (SS 758884) (*mawr*). This gave its n. to *Morfa Colliery* 1885.

Morfa Glas　　　　　　　　SN 8706
Neath Port Talbot (Cadoxton-juxta-Neath)
'green, verdant moor': *morfa*, *glas*[1]
Morva glaes 1792, *Morfa Glas* 1845

Now the n. of a group of hos. described until some time after 1947 as Maesmarchog. The first el. meant 'sea-marsh' but later developed the sense 'wet, marshy area, marsh' since it is found in inland areas such as Morfa Arglwydd (at Trewyddfa, Llangyfelach) recorded as *Morva'r Arlwydd* 1650, *Morva'r Arllwydd or the Lord's Marsh* 1764 (**arglwydd**); Morfa Breigam at Pen-llin recorded as *Morva Brigam* 1766, *morfâ brigam* 1767; and Morfa Mawr at Llanblethian recorded as (lands) *y Morva Mawre* 1677, (land) *Morva Mawr* 1722 (**mawr**).

Morfa Gruffudd see **Griffithsmoor**

Morgannwg see **Glamorgan, Morgannwg**

Morganstown, Treforgan otherwise **Pentre-poeth**　　　　　　　　ST 127816
Cardiff (Radur)
'settlement named from Morgan': pers.n. *Morgan*, E **town**, W **tref**; 'burnt village' or 'village in area cleared by burning': **pentref, poeth**
Pentre 1845, *Pentrepoeth* 1850, *Pentrepoeth* 1854, *Treforgan* 1857, 1906, *Morganstown* 1861, *Morgan's town* 1866
See DPNW 329. Morganstown is apparently named from a Morgan Williams who was largely responsible for development known initially as Tynyberllan (1851 census) from the nearby fm. (IHCS 139). Pentre-poeth alternates with Treforgan in W written sources and both ns. seem to be current use. The adoption of Morganstown may have been reinforced by the occurrence of an Evan Morgan here described as seller of sundries in 1868 and blacksmith and grocer 1871. For Pentre-poeth cf. Pentre-poeth (q.v.) at Swansea. W **poeth** generally means 'hot, warm' but was also used in the sense 'burnt' and applied to areas cleared by burning or an area of industrial activity. That might refer to lime-burning in the area. The village developed after the opening of Bethel Calvinistic Methodist chp. in 1842. Cf. Treforgan (SN 7906) near Creunant and Morgantown (SO 046066) in Merthyr Tudful, recorded as *Morgan's Town* in 1851 and *Morgan Town* 1875 (MCPP 62-3).

Môr Hafren see **Bristol Channel**

Morlais　　　　　　　　　　　　SO 0409
Merthyr Tudful
'big stream': *mor, glais*
Kemeyrmorleys 1307, *Morles* 1287, *Castelle Morlleys, Morllays Castelle, Morlays riveret* c.1538, *Morleis* 1564, *Morlashe cast:* 1578, *Castle Morlays* 1757, (rivulet) *More Laish* 1775, *Castlemorlais* 1795, *Morlais Castle* 1799, *Castell Morlais* 1832
Cf. Llanmorlais and r. Morlais, near Llangennech, Carmarthenshire (*Morles* 1520, *Morleis* 1564) and other examples in Monmouthshire and Denbighshire/Shropshire. Morlais is the n. of a stream, which rises at SO 079120 above Twyn Pwll Morlais and flows across Merthyr Common down to meet the r. Taf in Merthyr Tudful. Presumably the n. shifted westwards to the castle (SO 047097) which is located near Taf Fechan. The 1307 refs. contains *cymer¹* (cf. Cefncoedycymer).

Mornington Meadows　　　　　ST 167879
Caerphilly (Eglwysilan)
A housing estate which developed during the 1970s and 1980s on meadows on the east side of Porset Brook but the origin of this n. is obscure. There seems to be no connection with the earls of Mornington and it is in sharp contrast to its W street-names.

Morriston, Treforys　　　　　　SS 666984
Swansea (Llangyfelach)
'settlement named from Morris': surname *Morris*, E *-ton*; *tref, Morys*
Morriston 1780, *Morris Town* 1789, *Treforus* 1832, *Treforys* 1854, *Treforis* 1867, *Treforris* 1874
The pn. recalls the Morris family of Clasemont which had interests in copper works, brass mills and collieries and was probably given by Sir John Morris (1745-1819). Morris initiated a company housing scheme in 1768 (Malkin II, 499). This included a ho. for workers on Craig Trewyddfa called Morris Castle (*Castlemorris* 1792, *Morris Castle* 1813) built c.1750 (MCPP 64-67; HMorg 357). The main settlement Morriston developed after 1779. Morris arranged for William Edwards (the bridge builder at Pontypridd) to plan the new settlement but the hos. were built by the lessees; by 1796 there were 141 hos. here. The 'castle' was in ruins in 1899.

Morristown　　　　　　　　　　ST 176710
Penarth
'settlement named from Morris': surname *Morris*, E *town*
Morristown 1887
Probably named from William Longhurst Morris JP who lived at Compton House in nearby Stanwell Road 1895. The nucleus was a row of hos. along Lavernock Road, developing after 1920 as a suburb of Penarth.

Moulton, Moltwn　　　　　　　ST 073701
Vale of Glamorgan (Llancarfan)
?'settlement of (man called) Mūl', 'mule settlement' or perhaps 'mill settlement': pers.n. *Mūl, mūl, myl(e)n* OE, *tūn* OE
Molton c.1535, (manor) *Molton alias Lydmerston* 1558, *Molton (& Lidmerston)* c.1659, (o) *Vowlton* c.1575, *Moulton* 1578, *Mowlton* 1587, *Moultown* 1785, *Moltwn* c.1797
Cf. Moulton, Cheshire and Lincolnshire for the first suggestion and Moulton, Northamptonshire, for the second. Charles (NCPN 155) preferred 'mill settlement (*or* farm)': OE *myl(e)n, tūn*, but his opinion was influenced through mislocating *Mylton alias Velindre* c.1670 here (see Felindre²). It cannot be ruled out entirely because the evidence is late (Pierce in PNDPH 92-4). *Lydmerston* etc properly refers to Lidmore (ST 092703) in the adjoining p. of Wenvoe. This may contain a surname (PNDPH 314) of uncertain origin.

Mountain Ash, Aberpennar　　　ST 0499
Rhondda Cynon Taf (Llanwynno)
'(place at the) Mountain Ash (public house)'; 'confluence of (r.) Pennar (and Cynon)': *aber*, rn. *Pennar*
Mountain Ash 1814, 1841, (lands) *Aberpennarthe* 1541, *Aber Pennarthe* 1570, *Aber Pennar alias Tire y Dyffryn* 1633, *Aber Penarth* 1638, *Aberpennar alias Dyffryn* 1693

See further Deric John (CVPN 24-26). The n. Mountain Ash was allegedly chosen in 1809 by John Bruce Pryce, owner of the Dyffryn estate on which it lay, and Dafydd Morgannwg in 1874 (HMorg 429) and others recount a tale of a certain David John Rhys requesting a lease of land for a public ho. and choosing *cerddinen* 'mountain ash' as its n. on seeing a nearby tree. The 'Mountain Ash' inn (in Commercial Street) first appears on record in 1814 but does not seem to have become firmly established as the n. of the adjoining settlement until after 1833. By 1852, there were 600 hos. here described collectively as *Mountain Ash Inn*. Aberpennar properly applies to the location where the r. Pennar joins the Cynon and was an alternative n. for the ho. Dyffryn. Aberpennar was not formally adopted as the W n. of the town until shortly before 1905 when the National Eisteddfod visited the town. Many writers with local connections such as Glanffrwd, William Bevan (HMA) and the Revd. John Davies (CofiantJD) used the form *Mountain Ash* in their publications, though writing in Welsh. The rn., recorded as *Pennar* 1720, has **pennardd** in ref. to the ridge at its head (see Cefnpennar). There is an identical rn. in Mynyddislwyn, Monmouthshire.

Mountain Hare SO 062060
Merthyr Tydfil
'(place at the) Mountain Hare (public house)'
Mountain Hare public ho. 1871, 1895
The former public ho. on Penheolferthyr is shown, but not named, on OS maps 1882-89. The n. was also applied in 1860 to a former ironstone mine. Mountain Air (SO 1509) near Ebbw Vale is also named from a former public ho. described in 1880 as the *Mountain Air Inn*, a re-interpretation. Both PHs were close to open hill land.

Mount Pleasant[1] ST 078986
Merthyr Tudful
'(place on a) fair hill'
E *mount*, *pleasant*
(ho.) *Mountpleasant* 1814, *Mount Pleasant* 1833
A very common n., sometimes with a religious connotation. The n. was transferred from a ho. and former fm. on Cardiff Road to adjoining hos., the former Mount Pleasant Hotel (recorded 1900) and a school. There is an identical n. at Troed-y-rhiw (SO 073021) which initially referred to a row of hos. later known as Lower Mount Pleasant, apparently taking its n. in translation from a ho. Plas Brynteg, 'fair-hill mansion' (***plas***, ***bryn***, ***teg***).

Mount Pleasant[2] SS 754966
Neath Port Talbot (Briton Ferry and Neath)
Mount Pleasant 1852, 1881
As Mount Pleasant[1]. A housing estate developed from the late 19th cent on hillslopes above Melincryddan and Neath and named from a house displaced by the former Ty-segur Reformatory School.

Mount Pleasant[3] ST 020917
Rhondda Cynon Taf (Ystradyfodwg)
(ho.) *Mount Pleasant* 1841, 1852
As Mount Pleasant[1, 2] The n. of a housing estate which developed from the 1880s taken from the ho. on Troed-y-rhiw Road. There was also a nearby ho. *Pleasant Hill* at what later became the junction of Cemetery Road and Mount Pleasant Road.

Mount Pleasant[4] SS 653932
Swansea
(ho.) *Mount Pleasant* 1799, (hos.) *Mount pleasant* 1849, *Mount Pleasant terrace* 1869
As Mount Pleasant[1-3.] The n. of housing built in the 1890s on the site of Mount Pleasant Quarry (recorded 1879) which lies west of the road Mount Pleasant. This ascends from De La Beche Street towards Terrace Road.

The Mumbles, Y Mwmbwls SS 619878
Swansea (Oystermouth)
Uncertain
Mummess c.1538, *Mommulls* 1549, *Mombles* 1562, *Mumbles poynt* 1578, *Mommells* 1583, *y Mwmlws* 1606, *Mumbles, The key of Mumbles, Mumble Clifft* 1650, *The Mumbles Point* 1729, *Mumbles Cliff, ~ beach* 1769, *Mumbles Head* 1803, *y Mumbles* 1820, *`r Mwmbwls* 1877

Melville Richards queried Lat *mamilla*, pl. *–ae*, 'teats, breasts', which would give Fr *mamelles*. This might produce forms such as *Mommells* by 'rounding' of the first vowel and it has an obvious topographical significance but the written evidence is inconclusive. Morgan suggested that it refers to 'the perpetual mumbling of the sea' (OPN 140), i.e. ME *mommele*. That would describe the noise of waves against the rocks. Both suggestions require an intrusive -b- comparable with ModE *thimble* (from OE *thȳmel*) and Brombil (q.v.) to produce modern Mumbles. Historic forms are far too late to accept a third suggestion by Charles (NCPN 125-6) that the second el. is OE *mull* (< ON *múli*) 'promontory' since there is no clear evidence of a full vowel in –les. According to a local man, Isaac Hamon (TCym 1965, I, 98) in 1697, the two islands were called *ye outer mumble* and *the midle mumble* (= Middle Head) and the nearby cliff was *the inner mumble*; collectively they were called Mumbles Head (**head**). W-speakers knew them as *ye tair twarchen*, i.e. Y Tair Tywarchen, meaning 'the three little clods (of turf)' (**tair**, *tywarchen* nf.), presumably from their fancied appearance.

Murch   ST 160711
Vale of Glamorgan (St Andrews Major)
'(place near fields of) wild celery, smallage': E ***merch***
The Merch 1601, *Merch, The Mearch* 1784, *The Mirch* 1693, *Merch* 1833
The n. of two fms. in St Andrews Major, one recorded as *Merch* 1833 (probably also *Merch-Mawr* 1783) (at about ST 161712) leaving its n. in that of a housing estate in Dinas Powys, the other near the railway station (ST 154709). Gwynedd Pierce (PNDPH 228) suggests the ns. may derive from field-ns. containing **merch**, 'wild celery, smallage' (*apium graveolens*), borrowed as W *mers*. Smallage was loosely applied to plants of the family *apiaceae*, typically found in wet, marshy areas.

Murton   SS 585890
Swansea (Bishopston)
'moor settlement (*or* farm)': OE ***mōr, tūn***
(manor) *Morton* 1299, (*villa de*) *Morton'* 1396, *Mooreton nunc vocat' Bishopston* 1583, *Moorton* 1704-7, *Mortown* 1650, *Murton* 1736, 1764
The moor presumably included Murton Green (*Mooreton green* 1675) between the ht. and Northway extending into Clyne Common. The antiquarian Rice Merrick (Merrick 117) identifies Murton with Gwern y lath (editor's spelling) but this properly applies to the area of Upper and Lower Wernllath (SS 589905) about a mile to the north also recorded as *Werne Llaeth*, *Gwern laeth* 1583, *Wen lath* 1596, *Wernllaeth* 1641, *Wernllâth* 1650. The first el. is clearly **gwern** probably in the sense 'place where alder-trees grow with the def.art. **y** and apparently *llaeth* 'milk'. The form *Wern-llaith* recorded in 1832 favours **llaith**[1] adj. 'damp, moist, wet' but it is at odds with earlier evidence.

Mwmbwls see **Mumbles**

Mwyndy   ST 055816
Rhondda Cynon Taf (Llantrisant)
'(the) mine-house, (the) mineral-house or store': (**y**), **mwyndy**
(tmt.) *Moyndey* 1541, (mess.) *mwyndaie* 1615, *y moyndy* 1623, (*syddyn*) *y Mwyndai bach*, (~) *y Mwyndai* c.1612, (ho. or fm.) *Mwyndy* 1831, *y Mwyndy* 1872
mwyndy alternates in some sources with its pl. *mwyndai*. The n. may actually refer to the Crown iron and lead mines in Clun park. Whatever the truth of that, Mwyndy Iron Ore Works were begun by D. Davies (Gallt Gawrdaf) 1855, later held by N.E. Vaughan, and by Mwyndy Iron Ore Co. from 1860.

Mynwent y Crynwyr see **Quakers Yard**

Mynachdy   ST 169787
Cardiff (Llandaf)
'monk's house, monastic grange': **mynach**[1], **tŷ**
Managhty 1657, (ho.) *Mynachdy* 1833
Probably *Manachdy* 1562 and *Monachty* 1673. A grange of Llantarnam abbey which has been identified with *Lann Menechi, uillam meneich* c.1145 in the Book of Llandaf but the evidence is inconclusive. There is an identical pn.

Mynachdy (ST 048951) in Llanwynno recorded as *Mynachdy* 1630, *manachty* 1633, *Manachdy* 1668, *Monachdu* 1750, *Mynachty* 1833.

Mynydd-bach　　　　　　　　SS 652975
Swansea (Llangyfelach)
'little mountain': ***mynydd, bach***[1]
(waste) *Mynydd bach* 1650, (common) *Mynidd Bach* 1799, *Mynydd Bach* 1813, *Mynydd-bach* 1832
A hill, former fm. and now a housing estate. The nucleus of the settlement was north-west of Mynydd-bach Common near an early Independent chp. 1762 (HMorg 151) (SS 648978) and 'Welcome Inn' but the focus shifted at the end of the 19th cent to the other side of the common along Llangyfelach Road.

Mynydd Bach y Cocs　　　　SS 558934
Swansea (Llanrhidian)
'little hill (or moor) characterised by shells of crustaceans' with ***mynydd, bach***[1], ***y***, ?***cocos***, *cocs*
Mynydd Bach 1702, *Little moor otherwise Mynndy Bach y Cocks* 1754, (common) *Mynidd bach* 1755, *Mynnydd Bach, otherwise Mynydd Bach y Cocks* 1764, *Mynydd-bach* 1832, *Mynydd-bach-y-cocs* 1879
The n. has been explained as referring to the route taken by Penclawdd cocklepickers to market in Swansea. The 'cockles', however, are more likely to be natural deposits of shells, distinguishing the hill from Mynydd Bach Rhosybishwel recorded as *Mynnydd Rhose y Bishwell* (in Loughor) 1764, *Mynydd Bach y Bishwell* 1854 (***rhos***[2], *biswail, biswel,* and *bishwel* and *pishwel* in local dial., nm. 'dung (of cattle, etc), urine, slurry') and Mynydd-bach-y-glo (q.v.). Bishwel is recalled in the ill-chosen n. Bishwell Park, Gowerton.

Mynydd-bach-y-glo　　　　　SS 613956
Swansea (Llangyfelach)
'little mountain notable for coal': ***mynydd, bach***[1], ***y, glo***
Mynyth Forrest Vach 1729, *Mynyth Vach* 1754, *Mynyddbach-y-glo* 1810, *Mynydd Bach y Glo* 1831
Cf. Mynydd-bach (q.v.) in the same p. The 1729 spelling indicates its proximity to Fforest-fach (q.v.). Once largely open hill-pasture, housing developed in the late 19th cent near Mynydd-bach-y-glo Colliery (closed before 1898). The qualifier distinguishes it from Mynydd Bach Rhosybishwel and Mynydd Bach y Cocs (q.v.).

Mynyddcynffig see **Kenfig Hill**

Mynydd Drumau　　　　　　SS 723995
Neath Port Talbot/Swansea (Cadoxton-juxta-Neath/Llansamlet)
'mountain near (places called) Drumau': ***mynydd***, ho.ns.
Mynydd Dryme c.1583, *Mynidd Drymey* c.1700, *Mynidd Drumma* 1799, *Mynydd Drumau* 1884
The pl. ***drumau*** (***trum, drum***) probably refers directly to several hos. and their individual locations since Mynydd Drumau is a single ridge between the watersheds of rs. Neath and Tawe. The ridge extends northwards from Drumau Road near Drumau House (on the east side of Birchgrove) to a point near Tir-abbey fm. (SN 726020). Drumau Farm (SS 706998) and Drumau House (SS 705994) are located on a low rise between the streams Nant y Cyrnach and Nant Brân extending eastwards to the mountain. Drymma Hall (SS 714979) and Drumau-fach (SS 713982) are on slopes at the southern end of the mountain. Drumau Farm, earlier Drumau-uchaf, is recorded as *Tir Ievan Jenkin Treharn* c.1583, *Tir Howell ap Ievan Jenkin* 1650, *Tir Howell ap Jevan Jenkin now called Trymme Ycha* 1688, *Drumau-uchaf* 1830 (***uchaf***). Ieuan ap Jenkin Trahaearn and his son Hywel ap Ieuan Jenkin appear to be unidentified. Drumau House is *Drumma Isha* 1799, *Drumau-isaf* 1830, *Drumma Ishaf* 1841 and *Drumau House* 1879 (***isaf***). Drumau House has also been identified with *Dreme in Kylvei* 1340 (see Kilvey), *Drymme* c.1583 and *Tir Drymme* 1650 but the evidence is inconclusive. Drymma Hall is *Mount Drymma* 1799 and *Drumau House* 1830.

Mynyddislwyn　　　　　　　ST 193939
Caerphilly (Monmouthshire)
'mountain below the grove': ***mynydd, is, llwyn***
Menedwiscleuyn 1102, *Munitistlun* 1254, *Menethestlyn* c.1291, *Menethistelon* 1330,

Monythustloyn 1479, *mynydh Ystloyn* 1600-7, *Mynyddisllwyn* 1640, *p. tydyr ap howel* c.1566, *Eggluis Tider Vab Hohele* c.1537, *Egglins Tider vap Hoell, otherwise called Fanum Theodori, or the church of Theodorus* 1586

Mynyddislwyn was also known, at least to antiquarians, as Plwyf Tudur ap Hywel and Eglwys Tudur ap Hywel, 'parish/church of Tudur ap Hywel', with **plwyf** and **eglwys** rendered as Lat *fanum*, 'a holy place, a temple', in one source. The ch. is now dedicated to Theodore or Tudor and the 16th cent refs. show that he was regarded as 'a son of Hywel'. He was also dubiously identified with Tudur, a son of Awstl Gloff, dedicated at Darowen, Montgomeryshire. The historian Bradney (HMON V, 134) suggests that Tudur may have been a vicar, citing a source which alleged that the ch. possessed an effigy of 'Sir Theodore Powell patron of the church' described as a 'stately statue gilded, a staff lying by it and a letter sealed up.' Whoever Tudur was, he is also recalled in the n. of a prehistoric mound Twyn Tudur, 'Tudur's hillock' (**twyn**) recorded as *Twyn Twdor* 1813, *Twyn Tudur* 1833, south of the p.ch.

Mynydd Marchywel　　SN 7603, 7604, 7704, 7705
Neath Port Talbot
'mountain of Marchywel': **mynydd**, pers.n. *Marchywel*
Kevenmarchowell 1506, *Keven March howell* 1512, *Marchhowell* 1601, (mtn.) *March Howell* c.1700, (mtn.) *Mynydd March Howel*, (fm.) *March Howel* 1814
mynydd has displaced **cefn** 'ridge'. Marchywel is probably a compound of **march** 'powerful, strong' and pers.n. *Hywel* variant *Howel*. The separation of these els. in many sps. suggests that the pn. may have been re-interpreted as 'Howel's horse'.

Mynydd y Gaer　　SS 9585, 9685
mtn. Bridgend (Coychurch)
'mountain with a fort': **mynydd**, **y**, **caer**
Mynydd y Gaer 1633, 1813, *Mynydd y gaer* 1664
There seems to be no fort nearer than Gaer (SS 972850) so spelt 1833, about a mile east of the main summit. The n. may, however, derive from some fancied resemblance of the prehistoric stones known as Mynwent y Milwyr (SS 953858), 'the soldiers' graveyard' (**mynwent**, **y**, *milwr* pl. *milwyr*) to ruinous walls of a fort. Cf. Mynydd y Gaer (SS 766936) recorded as *mynudh y Gaer, Mynudh Gaer* 1615, *Mynyd y Gare* c.1798, *Mynyddygaer* 1813, *Mynydd y Gaer* 1830, crowned with a prehistoric fort Buarth y Gaer, 'the fort enclosure' (**buarth** nm. 'fold or enclosure').

Mynydd y Gwair　　SN 6507
mtn. Llangyfelach
'mountain where hay is gathered': **mynydd**, **y**, **gwair**[1]
Mynydd gwair 1650, *Mynydd y Gwair* 1799, *Mynydd Gwair* 1811
Gwair might also be a pers.n. but the def.art. favours the suggested meaning. Maps for the period 1799-1831 show that the n. properly applies to the hill between the rivers Clydach Isaf and Afon Llan (SN 6705) but OS 1:2,500 maps (1877, 1917) moved the n. a mile northwestwards to its present location above what is now Upper Lliw Reservoir. Other OS maps apply the n. to the area immediately adjoining the ridgeway running southwards from a point near Penlle'rcastell (SN668097) past the hillock Tor Clawdd (SN668061) to the original location.

Nantgarw to Nurston

Nash Point, from *Wales Illustrated* by Henry Gastineau (1830).

Nantgarw ST 119852
Rhondda Cynon Taf (Eglwysilan)
'rough stream' or 'rough valley': ***nant, garw***
Nant Garro 1729, *Nantgarw* 1741, *Nant Garw* 1785, *i'r Nantgarw* 1818, (stream) *Nant Garw* 1833
The n. might describe the nature of the stream or the valley which is defined by rocky slopes on its south side (later transferred as a n. to the stream). The pn. was sometimes thought to contain ***carw*** 'deer, stag' because ***nant*** in the sense 'stream' is now generally a nf. requiring len. *c* to *g*. The village developed along Cardiff Road near the r. Taf but now includes post-War housing developments east of the A470 around Dyffryn Ffrwd. The village is shown as *Portobello* on Yates's map 1799 next to a toll bar but this seems to be an error (see Taff's Well) or may be an earlier, shortlived n. of the Cross Keys Inn at the junction of Cardiff Road and Caerphilly Road (PNIG 36).

Nant-y-cafn SN 810076
Neath Port Talbot (Cadoxton-juxta-Neath)
'stream in the trough': ***nant, y, cafn***
Naunte Ecavan 1541, *Nant y Cavan* 1703, (ho.) *Nant-y-cafn* 1832, (stream) *Nant y Cafn*, (ho.) *Nant-y-cafn-uchaf, Nant-y-cafn-isaf* 1884

149

'trough' describes the shape of the valley. The village developed after the opening of Dillwyn Colliery (SN 811072) in 1884 (closed 1966).

Nantyffyllon SS 850928
Bridgend (Llangynwyd)
?'small, puny stream': *nant, ffyrlling, ffyrlin(g)*
Naunte Ferlynge 1541, *Nant firlling* 1570, *forest Nant Firlloige* 1588, *nant ffyrllinge* 1630, (r.) *Nant ffirlling*, (brook) ~ *ffyrlhing* c.1700, *Nant-y-ffyrlon* 1833, (village) *Nant-y-ffyllon* 1884
ffyrlling is derived from ME *ferling* 'a farthing' and may be used in a transferred sense for something small or of little value (see further PNGlam 132). Later forms have an intrusive *y* after –t and obscuring of the final vowel, i.e. -*llin(g)*, -*lin(g)* > –*lon*, -*llon*. The n. of the village, recorded as *Nant y firlling row* 1841, is taken directly from Nantyffyllon fm. bought by the Cambrian Iron Co. in the 1830s.

Nant-y-moel SS 934928
Bridgend (Llangeinwyr)
'bare valley': *nant, y, moel¹*
nant moel c.1700, *Nantmoyl* 1703, *Nant Môle* 1767, *Nantymoel* 1813, *Nant-y-moel* 1833, (village) *Nant-moel*, (valley) *Cwm Nant Moel* 1877
The def.art. *y* is probably intrusive since it is not recorded before 1813 but it has given rise to the suggestion that the pn. contains Y Moel, 'the bald man'. Named directly from a fm. (formerly SS 931928). The valley is now called Cwm Nant-y-moel (*cwm*) and is heavily afforested. Cf. Nant- moel (Llangyfelach) near Cwm-gors recorded as *Nant moil* 1627, *nant Moel ycha* and *Nant Moel Is(a)* 1688, *nant mole* 1764. Nant-moel-uchaf is at SN 684075.

Nash, Yr As Fach Nash Manor SS 962729
Vale of Glamorgan
'(place) at the ash-tree': OE *atten*, OE *æsc*; 'little Nash': *yr*, pn. *Ash, bach¹*
(fee) *Aissa, Aissam* 1208, (ch.) *Fraxino*, c.1291, *lanasch' osmundi* late 14th cent, *le Nasshe* 1431, *Lytill Nash* 1448, *Parva Fraxina alias Lytell Nassh* 1499, *Osmond is Asshe* 1528, *the Assche* c.1538, *Nash p(ar)va* 1578, *yras fach* c.1566, *Race Vagh* 1670, *Race or Little Nash* 1765

Several forms have Lat *fraxinus* 'ash-tree' and *parva* 'little' in literary and administrative usage. E *little* is found in early sources but, unlike its equivalent *bach¹, fach*, it is uncommon after c.1700. The qualifiers distinguish it from Monknash (q.v.) otherwise Nash Magna. The def.art. *yr* is sometimes matched in sources by E *the* and Fr *le* down to the 16th cent. Nothing appears to be known of any Osmund: the OE pers.n. *Ōsmund* – also commonly found among Normans – is found in Osmaston, Derbyshire, and Osmington, Dorset. Nash is also found in Pembrokeshire, Monmouthshire and several E counties.

Nash Point see **Monknash**

Neath, Castell-nedd SS 755974
Neath Port Talbot
'(place by r.) Nedd': rn. *Nedd* anglicised *Neath*; 'castle by (r.) Nedd': *castell*, rn. *Nedd*
Nido 8-9th cent, (castle) *Nethe* c.1129, (ch. of Holy Trinity and St Mary of) *Neeth* c.1140, *Neth* c.1165, *Neht, Neyth* c.1291, *Neath* 1578, *Foresta de Neth alias Neth Forest* 1440, *aber Ned* c.1400, *kastell Nedd* 15th cent, (castle of) *Nedd* 1609, *kastell neð* c.1566, (bridge) *Ponte Castelle Nethe* c.1538, *Castell-nedd* 1778
Nido is an ablative case form of *Nidum* latinised from Brit *Nidā*, and applied to the Roman auxiliary fort here recorded in the Antonine Itinerary (PNRB 425; RFWM 265-7). The r. is specifically recorded as *ned, Ned* c.1145, *Neth*, c.1178, (*flumen*) *Ned, Nééd* c.1200, *Neath flu:* 1578, *Neath* 1612, with two tributaries Nedd Fawr and Nedd Fechan recorded as *Neth Vacchan* 1541, *Neath Vychan, ~ Vawre* c.1598. Nedd derives directly from Brit *Nidā*. The meaning is uncertain but the n. is clearly related to other rns., notably the r. Nidd, Yorkshire, and on the continent in Nidda (Germany) and Nied (France/Germany). Two main suggestions have been made for Neath and Nidd. The first is that they contain an OE root *n(e)id-* 'to flow, to stream' (Nomina 6, 39; ERN 17) meaning simply 'river' and the second is that it has a root *nei-* 'to be brilliant' (TPS 94, 94 and note). The evidence

has been reviewed by Breeze (NH 40, 365-8) who suggests that Nidd may actually contain a root *ni- meaning 'down' and observes that the river flows over limestone and disappears underground for part of its course. That provides a cogent etymology also for Neath/Nedd, the upper reaches of which flow over carboniferous limestone, and the r. Neden (or Nedern), co. Monmouth, but requires substantiation. The rn. is also recalled in Neathsland, recorded as *Nedeslonde* 1326, *Nethislond* 1512, *Neeth ultra* 1508, and *Nethe Citra* 1535. The n., now obsolete, is better known as Glyn-nedd (q.v.), and was subdivided into Neath Citra (Lat *citra* 'within') near the borough of Neath, and Neath Ultra (Lat *ultra* 'beyond, farther') further up the Vale of Neath or Glyn Nedd.

Neath Abbey, Y Fynachlog SS 737975
Neath Port Talbot (Cadoxton-juxta-Neath)
'(settlement near) Neath Abbey': pn., E ***abbey***; ***y, mynachlog***
Neath Abbey 1876, *Fynachlog* 1875, `*r Fynachlog* 1899
Named ultimately from the monastery founded by Richard de Granville 1130 for monks drawn from Savigny. Urbanisation took place in the 19th cent mainly in association with Neath Abbey Iron Works.

Nedd see **Neath**

Nelson ST 113955
Caerphilly (Llanfabon)
'(place named from) Lord Nelson Inn'
Nelson 1833, *the Nelson, Nelson's Arms* 1845, *Nelson Village* 1852
The Lord Nelson Inn is recorded next to the road leading from Caerphilly to Quakers Yard before 1825 and was formed by amalgamating three cottages located near waste land and a ho. Ffosygerddinen, 'ditch of the mountain-ash' (***ffos, y, cerddinen***). The pn. has been explained as commemorating a visit by Lord Nelson in 1803 (two years before the battle of Trafalgar). Nelson certainly undertook a tour of England and Wales in the company of Sir William and Lady Hamilton, visiting Wales between July and August 1802 and is reputed (in 1864) to have stayed at the Star Inn in Merthyr Tudful but there is no good evidence that he visited the Nelson area.

Newbridge, Trecelyn ST 209968
Caerphilly (Mynyddislwyn Monmouthshire)
'(place at the) new bridge': E ***new, bridge***; 'settlement near holly-trees', ***tref, celyn***[1]
Newbridge 1566, *Newbrige* 1576, (water grist mill) *Newbridge mill*, (ground) *Tir ynis y bont newyth* 1630, (bridge) *Pont newydd* 18th cent, *y Bontnewydd* 1839, *Capel Trecelyn, Pontnewydd* 1883, *Trecelyn* 1885
The location of a bridge over the r. Ebbw/Ebwy (ST 210970). Local W-speakers know the bridge as Y Bontnewydd (***y, pont, newydd***) and the adjoining area as Tir Ynys y Bont Newydd 'land near the river-meadow at the new bridge' (***tir, ynys***). Trecelyn first appears in 1883 and has been explained as a recollection of the Celynen Collieries, the first shaft of which was sunk in 1876. The absence of regular len. *c > g* provides further evidence for its late appearance; cf. Trecynon. *Celynen* meaning 'holly-tree' (***celynnen***) referred to a row of hos. (ST 219958) in the period 1833-1947 (later regarded as part of Aber-carn) and to a stream Nant Celynnen which appears to be that now known as Nant Hafod-fach. The tree species is also recalled in Holly Terrace and a ho.n. Ty-celyn (ST 211965) (***tŷ***), both recorded on OS maps from 1901.

Newcastle, Castellnewydd SS 902800
Bridgend
'(place at the) new castle': OE ***nīwe, castel***; 'the new castle', (***y***), ***castell, newydd***
(ch. of) *sancti Leonardi de Nouo castello* c.1178, (castle of) *Novi Castri* 1185, (ch. of) *Sancti Leonardi de Ruthelan* 1260, (*de*) *Novo Castello* 1107 (1300), *Castellum Novum* late 12th cent, (fee) *Newcastle in Penney* 1351, *Newecastell* 1411, *Newcastle Bridgend* 1747, *Castelle Newith* (c.1538), *Castellnewydd-pen-y-bont* 1778, *Y Cas Newydd pen y bont* c.1800, *Tre-newydd or Newcastle* 1833

The castle was apparently constructed before 1106 during the AN conquest and was evidently provided with its own ch. dedicated to St Leonard, possibly at or close to a pre-existing Rhuddlan meaning 'red bank (***rhudd***, ***glan***); cf. Rhuddlan, co. Flint (DPNW 417-8). The castle was 'new' in contrast to Oldcastle/ Hengastell (the presumed castle mound SS 90527950) recorded as *the Olde Castell* 1549, *Old Castle* 1729, *Old Castle-bridge-end* 1755, *Oldcastle* 1833, *Henecastelle* c.1538, *yr hen gastell* c.1566, and *Hengastell Pen y Bont* c.1800 (***hen***). The adjoining settlement Nolton (SS 905795) is recorded as *(de) Veteri Villa* 1199 (Lat *veterus* 'old'), *(villa) Noltown'* 1535, (chp.) *Nowlton* 1708, *Nolton* 1415, *Hen dref* 1778, meaning 'old settlement' (Lat *villa*, OE ***tūn***; ***tŷ***, ***hen***, ***tref***). The *N-* is from misdivided ME ***atten*** 'at the' attached to 'Olton' (cf. Nash) or perhaps W ***yn*** 'in' as in Yniston ('east farm') and *Nishbrook* (for Eastbrook). Little evidence for Hendre(f) has been found and the form may be purely literary. For *Penney* 1351 see Penyfái.

Newland SS 947774
Vale of Glamorgan (Colwinston)
?'newly-cleared land': E ***new***, ***land***
Newland 1570, 1645, *the Newland ffarme* 1697
Newland seems to have lacked a W n., emphasised by the existence of *Newland-fâch* 1878 (SS 954775), i.e. 'little Newland' (***bach***[1]), in the same p., and an area to the south near Brocastle Barn called *Tyle Newland* 1878, 'slope near Newland' (***tyle***). Another Newland, now lost, is recorded as *Niveland* 1208, *la Newelond* 1327, *Niwelande* 1336, *La Niwelonde*, in Cwm-ciwg, in the lp. of Coety. This probably lay near, and contrasted with, Hendir-uchaf (SS 976835) and nearby Hendir-isaf, 'upper old-land' and 'lower old-land' (***hen***, ***tir***, ***uchaf***, ***isaf***) in Coychurch Higher.

Newton[1] SS 604881
Swansea (Oystermouth)
'new settlement': E ***new***, ME ***-ton***
Newton 1626, 1650, *Newtown* 1738, *Newton-on-Mumbles* 1872
Possibly in comparison with Norton recorded 1574, 'north settlement' (E ***north***). There are identical pns. elsewhere in Glamorgan such as Newton (High Newton approx. SS 453884, now lost) recorded as *Newton* 1650 and *High Newton* 1832 and Newton (ST 002763), in Llanblethian, recorded as *Newton* 1541, *Welshe newton* 1578, *Welch Newton* 1729, *Newtown iuxta Cowbridge* 1627 (E ***Welsh***).

Newton[2] ST 238784
Cardiff (Rumney)
'new settlement': ME ***new***, ***-ton***
Neuton 1401, *Newton'* 1448, *Newton* 1793
Possibly a settlement on land newly reclaimed from the Wentlooge Levels; cf. Newton[1].

Newton Nottage, Drenewydd yn Notais SS 836774
Bridgend
'new settlement near Nottage': OE ***nīwe***, ***tūn***; 'the new settlement in Nottage': (***y***,) ***tref***, ***yn***, pn. *Nottage*
(p.) *Sancte Brigida juxta Novum Burgum* late 12th cent, *Nova Villa* 1208, *Neweton* 13th cent, *Newton Nottasshe* 1314, *Newton Nottage* 1525, *Newton Notes* c.1538, *y dre newyð ynottais* c.1566, *y Dref-newydd* 1778
See also Nottage. Drenewydd is also recorded in (land called) *Newton field or Caetrenewydd* 1862 and in the W n. for Newton Down (SS 8479), a hill a mile to the north, recorded as (common) *Newton's Downe* 1611, *Mynydd Trenowydd* c.1700, *mynydd y Drenewydd, Newton Down* c.1800 (***mynydd***, OE ***dūn***).

Newtown[1] ST 054985
Rhondda Cynon Taf (Llanwynno)
'new settlement': E ***new***, ***town***
Newtown 1871
A small former coal-mining village built on land of Troed-y-rhiw Forest and Fforest Uchaf (CVPN 74) near Fforest Level, later part of Navigation Colliery.

Newtown[2] ST 2191
Caerphilly (Mynyddislwyn Monmouthshire)
'new settlement': E *new*, *town*
Newtown 1874, 1901
An industrial village known alternatively 1875-1902 as North Risca which largely developed after the opening of the Risca New Mine by Watts, Ward & Co. in 1875. Located near Rock Vein and Black Vein Collieries operated from the 1840s by the Risca Iron and Coal Co.

Newtown[3] ST 192762
Cardiff
'new settlement': E *new*, *town*
New town 1849, *Newtown* 1852
The area adjoining the prison developed on part of Upper Splott fm. c.1850.

New Tredegar, Tredegar Newydd SO 142031
Caerphilly (Bedwellte Monmouthshire)
'(settlement near) New Tredegar Colliery: E *new*, pn. *Tredegar*
New Tredegar 1859, *Tredegar Newydd* 1865
A village developed on the site of fms. recorded as *Aber-y-sibwr* and *Cwm-y-sibwr* 1833 in the mid 19th cent near collieries. Initially known as White Rose from Whiterose Colliery opened 1857, a n. recalled in *White Rose* (station) 1869 and *Whiterose Terrace* 1878. The modern n. is taken directly from New Tredegar Colliery opened in 1858, which was itself new in contrast to Tredegar in the adjoining Sirhywi valley named from the Tredegar iron works established under a lease 1799 (PNGwent 203-4).

Nicholaston SS 520884
Swansea
'settlement of (man called) Nicholas': pers.n. *Nicholas*, OE *tūn*
Nicholastoune 1306, *Nicolaston'* 1396, *Nacleston* 1400, (ch. of) *Sancti Nicholai de Niclaston'* 1435, *Nicholaston* 1465, 1650, *Nycholaston* 1539, *niklas down* c.1566
The ch. is dedicated to St Nicholas but the person here is likely to be secular (WGOW IV, 396-7). In common with a number of E pns. in Gower, there seems to be no W n. apart from the cymricised form c.1566 which is of doubtful reliability.

Nolton see **Newcastle** (Bridgend)

North Cornelly see **Cornelly**

Northway SS 586893
Swansea (Bishopston)
'north way *or* road': E *north*, *way*
Northway 1675, *Norway* 1772, *North-way* 1832
In contrast to Oldway (q.v.), a little to the south on a lane running through Murton.

Norton SS 611887
Swansea (Oystermouth)
'north settlement': E *north*, ME *–ton*
Norton 1574, 1650, *Nortwn* 1821
Lying north of Oystermouth castle and north-east of Newton (q.v.). A common pn. Norton (SS 491865), at Oxwich, is *Morton* (sic) 1396, *Norton* c.1598, and Norton (SS 552890), at Pennard, is *Nortwn*, *Norton* 1650, *Norton* 1764 (north of Southgate).

Nottage, Notais SS 818781
Bridgend (Newton Nottage)
'pollard ash-tree': OE *hnot* 'close-cropped, pollard', *æsc*
Notasse 1272, *Nothasse* 1328, *le Nothasse* 1339, *Nothashe* 1351, *Notage* 1557, *Nottais* 1778, 1860
See also Newton Nottage. Nottage Court, formerly Tŷ Mawr, 'great house' (*tŷ*, *mawr*) was a grange of Margam abbey. Also the n. of a former fm. Nottage, at Newton, in Oystermouth, recorded as *Nottage* 1650, recalled in Nottage Road.

Nurston ST 054672
Vale of Glamorgan (Pen-marc)
'settlement of Nurse': pers.n. or surname *Nurse*, ME *–ton*
Nearston 1596, *Nerston* 1622, *Nearstone* 1784, *Nurston* 1810, *Nwrston* c.1797, *Myrstwn* 1856
Gwynedd Pierce (PNDPH 188-9) notes the pers.n. or surname *Nurse* (generally derived from OF *nurice* 'nurse') and suggests that an

original surname *Norris, Norreys* could have become *Nurs(e)-* by analogy and similarity of pron. Members of the family of le Norreis, Norreys, Norris occur in Glamorgan 12-14th cent though there seems to be no direct connection with Nurston. *Myrstwn* 1856 is a printing error for *Nyrstwn* which is the local W pron. in the 19th cent. Iolo Morganwg c.1797 records a *Capel Sinan* here but this appears to be fictitious. The chp. here is Salem Independent which opened in 1868.

Oakdale to Oystermouth

Oystermouth, looking towards the Mumbles c.1930.

Oakdale ST 185984
Caerphilly (Mynyddislwyn Monmouthshire)
'(place at colliery called) Oakdale'
Oakdale Colliery was opened in 1907 by Oakdale Navigation Collieries Ltd., a subsidiary of the Tredegar Iron & Coal Co. Ltd, and the village was established 1910-11 under a competition to design a village of 660 hos. (BWGwent 459-60). No W n. has been formally adopted though it has been described as 'glyn derwen or glyn deri' (www.oakdalevillage.net/placenames) (*glyn, derwen, deri*) but this lacks historical support. The village adjoins Rhiw Syr Dafydd (ST 182984) recorded as *Rhiw-Sir-David* 1833, *Rhiw Syr-Dafydd* 1879 and in the bridge (over r. Sirhywi) Pont Syr Dafydd recorded as *Pont Sir Davy* 1813 and *Pont Syr Dafydd* 1886 probably 'the Revd. Dafydd's slope' (*rhiw, syr* often 'reverend' as well as 'sir', pers.n. *Dafydd*). The same n. occurs in the place called *heol Sir David* 1546 (*heol*) on the west side of the r. in Bedwellte, probably taken from the road leading from the bridge up through Rock towards Bedwellte ch.

Ochrwyth ST 2389, 2489
Caerphilly (Machen, Monmouthshire)
?'unusual *or* sinister slope': *ochr* 'side (of a hill)', ?*chwith*
Ochr chwith, Ochorwyth 1851, *Ochrwyth* 1861, *Ochorwyth* 1875, *Ochrwith* 1879, *Ochr-chwith* 1883,1953, *Upper ~ , Lower Ochrwyth* 1964-5
The n. describes a scatter of hos. on hill-slopes above Rhisga divided into Upper and Lower Ochrwyth. *ochr* is fairly common in minor names

155

and is found locally in Ochor-ddu 'dark slope' (*du*, *ddu*) near Llanbradach which is recorded as *the ochor die* 1624 and *Ochor du* 1814. The second el. **chwith** generally means 'left, left-handed' with the added sense of 'strange, unusual, sinister' which might describe a dangerous or remarkable slope. The first meaning prompted Osborne and Hobbs to suggest (PNWG 56) that it might refer to the location of this place on the 'wrong side', i.e. on the left and northern side of Machen at some distance from the p.ch. Further evidence is clearly needed and we cannot completely rule out *chwyth* 'blast, breath' as in Pentre-chwyth (q.v.) perhaps with the sense 'windy *or* exposed slope'.

Ogmore, Ogwr SS 882763
Bridgend (St Brides Major)
'(place by r.) Ogwr': rn. **Ogmore**, **Ogwr**
Hoggemora 1148, (fee) *Ogmor* c.1160, c.1200, *Wuggemore* 1173, *Hoggomore*, *Oggemore* 1261, *Ogemor* 1281, (seaport) *Ogemore* 1349, (lp.) *Ogmore* 1441, *Ogmore castrum supermare* 1479, *Ogor*, ~*Castelle* c.1538, *kastell ogwr* c.1566, *Teraslogur [ithrafl Ogur]* 13th cent (16th cent), (castle) *Aber Ogwr* 1609, *Oggmoresland* 1411
Ogmore (SS 882769) derives its n. directly from a castle established in the 12th cent by William de Londres and ultimately from the rn. recorded as (r.) *Ocmur*, *ocuur* c.1145, *Ugemor'* 1207, *Uggemor* 1234, *Ogmorewater* 1479, *Ogwr* 1631, *River Ogmore or Ogwr* 1833. The first el. may be *og-* 'sharp, keen, fast' or, arguably better, *og-* 'burrow, rut', cf. the rn. Ogwen (with **banw** 'pig, young pig'), Caernarfonshire, but the second el. is obscure. The W form of the rn. appears to have developed from OW *Ocmur* > *Ogfwr* > *Ogwr*. Ogmore first appears in the 12th cent and is probably derived directly from OW *Ocmur*, a form which was already archaic locally in the 12th cent, current only in manuscripts, but must have been familiar to the earliest E settlers along the south side of the Bristol Channel in Somerset. It is also possible that *–more* was re-inforced by association of *-mur* with OE *mōr*, 'a moor', by E-speakers. The rn. is also found in Blaenogwr, Glynogwr and Cwmogwr (**blaen**, **glyn**, **cwm**). Ogmore

Forest (SS 9489) is modern forestry between r. Ogwr Fawr and Nant Iechyd in Llandyfodwg and should not be confused with (wood of) *Uggemore* c.1145 near Ogmore-by-Sea.

Ogmore-by-Sea, Aberogwr SS 867748
Vale of Glamorgan (St Brides Major)
'(place by r.) Ogmore, *by*, *sea*; '(place at) mouth of (r.) Ogwr': **aber**, rn. **Ogwr**
Ogmore-by-Sea 1964, *Aberogwr* 1970
A modern seaside village which developed from the late 19th cent on the south side of the mouth of the r. Ogmore/Ogwr around a ho. recorded as *Craig Er Eos* 1767, *Craigyrheos* 1813 OSD and *Craig-yr-eos* 1833 (SS 866750), 'the nightingale's cliff' (**craig**, **yr**, **eos**), located next to old limestone quarries. Aberogwr 'estuary of (r.) Ogwr' (**aber**) is a much older n. which earlier and additionally applies to the estuary and the area extending from the northern end of Ogmore-by-Sea upriver to Ogmore Castle (SS 882770) (see Ogmore). Ogmore-by-Sea became a ward of St Brides Major p. in 1920.

Ogmore Vale, Cwmogwr SS 932903
Bridgend (Llandyfodwg/Llangeinwyr)
'valley of (r.) Ogmore/Ogwr': rn. **Ogmore**, E **vale**; **cwm**, rn. **Ogwr**
Ogmore Vale, or *Tynewydd* 1875, *Ogmore Vale* 1881, *Cwmogwr* 1900
A late 19th cent pn., initially named Tynewydd from a fm. recorded as *Tŷnewudd farm* 1767, *Ty newith* 1785, *Ty-newydd* 1831, 'new house' (**tŷ**, **newydd**). W-speakers continued to know the village by this n. down to the 20th cent and generally applied *Cwmogwr* 1868 and *Cwm Ogwr* 1884 to the area and valley. See also Cwm Ogwr Fawr and Ogmore. Ogmore Valley is the community council.

Ogwr see **Blaenogwr**, **Ogmore/Ogwr**, **Ogmore Vale**, **Pen-y-bont ar Ogwr**

Olchfa SS 612931
Swansea
'(the) place for washing'; (**yr**), **golchfa**
(land) *Maen yr olchva* 1583, (close of land) *Y tyr wrth ryd erolchva* 1624, *Olchva* 1714, *Olchfa* 1813

Probably a place for washing sheep (ADG[1], 79) but popularly explained as one where cocklewomen washed their feet on the way to Swansea market (Morgannwg 32: 79). Nant yr Olchfa is a stream (**nant**), recorded as *the Olchva* 1744 and *Nant yr Olchfa* 1879, rising near Hendrefoilan (SS 606937) and flowing through Olchfa to Clyne River (Dulais). Other sps. cited refer to 'a stone, a rock' (**maen**) and 'a ford' (**rhyd**) pre-dating the bridge. Cf. *Twyn yr Olchfa* 1845 (**twyn**), at Cwm-du, Glamorgan, and Olchfa (SN 732275), at Llandovery, Carmarthenshire, recorded as *Olchfa* 1783, *Golchfa* 1831.

Oldcastle see **Newcastle** (Bridgend)

Oldwalls　　　　　　　　　　SS 488919
Swansea (Llanrhidian)
'old walls', ?'ruins': E *old*, **walls**
The Ould Walls 1631, *Olde Walls* 1697, *Ould walles* 1715, *Oldwalls* 1832
The significance of the n. is uncertain but there are two prehistoric stones (SS 48429197, 48689200) near the Greyhound Public House, which may have been interpreted as part of ancient ruins, and there are ruinous limekilns in the area.

Oldway　　　　　　　　　　SS 586886
Swansea (Bishopston)
'old way, old road': E *old*, E **way**
(fns.) *Oldway* 1675, 1697
A ht. which developed from the 1920s and especially after 1945 taking its n. directly from Old Way lane which runs south from Murton by Marmounthill to Pyle Road. Cf. Northway (q.v.).

Onllwyn　　　　　　　　　　SN 844103
Neath Port Talbot (Cadoxton-juxta-Neath)
'(the) ash-grove': (**yr**), **onn**, **llwyn**
The Onllwyn 1838, *Onllwyn* 1851, (fm.) *Onllwyn* 1883
Misinterpreted as (moorland) *Oerllwyn-isaf, ~ -uchaf* as if it contains *oer* 'cold' on the OS map 1832. An industrial village which appeared c.1840 near ironworks and after the expansion of anthracite coal mines. There is an identical n. (SN 998088) at Penderyn, Breconshire, recorded as *Onllwyn* 1802. The generic and qualifier are reversed in Llwyn-onn (q.v.).

Overton　　　　　　　　　　SS 461852
Swansea (Port Eynon)
'settlement on the flat-topped ridge': ME *over* (OE *ofer*), **-ton**
Overton 1788, 1830
Overton Mere, a small cove below Overton, is *Uvertown Mare* 1826 and *Overton mere* 1830.

Oxwich　　　　　　　　　　SS 500864
Swansea
'oxen farm': OE *oxa* gen.pl. *oxna*, OE *wīc*
Oxenwiche c.1187, *Oxenwych* c.1291, *Oxewyche* 1306, *Oxenwich* 1396, *Oxewiche* 1539, *Oxwyche alias Oxmynche* 1559, *Ogsmids* c.1566, *Oxwyche baye* 1562, *Oxwiche poynt* 1578, *Oxwich Point, Oxwiche Bay* 1799
Cf. Oxwick, Norfolk, and pns. such as Gatwick (OE *gāt* 'goat'), Surrey, and Shapwick (*scēap* 'sheep'), Somerset. The second el. has also been identified as ON *vīk* 'bay', but proven examples of this el. are rare in Wales. There does not seem to be a distinct W n. for Oxwich unless it is the obsolete Llwynarth (see Oystermouth). The form *Ogsmids* is taken from a source which contains several questionable forms but it bears comparison with forms in E sources such as *Oxmuch* 1583, *Oxmose, Oxmoche* early 16th cent and may be a cymricisation of an E variant of Oxwich. The *-ds* in *Ogsmids* may be an attempt at rendering E *-ch* [tʃ] and *-m-* in these forms probably derives from colloquial confusion of *-nw-* in *Oxenwich*. There is no reliable evidence for a reputed W form *Trenyni* given by Dafydd Morganwg 1874 (HMorg 432).

Oxwich Green　　　　　　　　SS 461852
Swansea (Oxwich)
'open pasture near Oxwich': pn. **Oxwich**, E *green*
Oxwich Green 1632, *Green* 1799
19th cent maps show a cluster of hos. in a roughly semicircular area, possibly once open, adjoining the road running from Ganderstreet

(*Ganderstreat* 1632) to Heronstreet (*Heringstreet* 1841, *Heronstreet* 1852) distinguished by E *gander* 'male goose' and *heron* the bird or *herring* the fish.

Oystermouth, Ystumllwynarth SS 615882
Swansea
'bend of grove ridge': **ystum**, **llwyn**, **garth**[1]
Ostrenuwe in Goer 1141, *Oestremue* c.1239, *Ostremew* 1287, *Ostrenmuth* c.1291, *Oystremuth'*, *Oistremutha* 1319, *Oystermouth in Gouweria* 1367, *Oystresmouth* 1370, *Oystermouth* (freq.) 1469-1832, *Est Wilthlunarde otherwise Ostermuthe* c.1538, *castell Ystum Llwynarth* c.1400, *ll. ystym llwynarth* c.1566, *Ystim lhoynarth* 1697
The location of Oystermouth on a low ridge (**garth**) next to the sweep of Swansea Bay provides topographical support but conclusive evidence is lacking. Ystumllwynarth has been associated with *Loyngarth* (in *Guyr*) recorded in the Historia Brittonum early 9th cent (HRB c.71) but this was probably located at Oxwich (LWS 100-1, 141) seven miles to the west. This gave rise to the supposition that Llwynarth may have applied to the district stretching from Oxwich to Oystermouth but there is no proof of this. AF sources associated Ystumllwynarth at an early date with ME and OFr *oistre* 'oyster' and OE *mūtha* 'mouth', typically 'river-mouth, estuary', later explained as 'from its abundance of oysters' (OPN 140; BPN 362). The association with oysters was reinforced in a number of later historical sources. Oysters were gathered here in 1697, oyster perches are mentioned in 1764 and there was a large oyster fishery at Mumbles in 1868. The unfamilarity of Ystumllwynarth must account for the forms *ynis dan lhwnarth* and *ystradlhwynarth* recorded by Isaac Hamon, of nearby Bishopston, in 1697, misassociating the pn. with **ynys** and **ystrad**. Iolo Morganwg c.1800 is responsible for the fictitious form *Caer Gwyrosydd*.

Palmerstown to Pyle

Porthcawl. The sea-front c.1957.

Palmerstown   ST 136694
Vale of Glamorgan (Cadoxton)
'settlement named from Palmer': surname *Palmer*, E ***town***.
Palmerstown 1889
A suburb of Barry developing from a nucleus of hos. around Palmer Street. Both are named from a local family.

Pant   SO 067087
Merthyr Tudful
'a hollow': ***pant***
Pant 1868, 1873
The n. of an area of housing taken from Pantysgallog (SO 065095) 'thistly hollow' (*ysgallog*) recorded as *terre pant yschalloke* 1449, *Pante Isgallok* 1555, *Pant yskallog* 1725, *Pant Scallog* 1757, *Pant ysgallog* 1783, *Pantscallog* 1852. The full form of the n. appears on maps 1900-1951 but *Pant* seems to have been in local use in 1868, certainly by 1873.

Pantcadifor   SO 063091
Merthyr Tudful
?'hollow of Cadifor': ***pant***, pers.n. ?*Cadifor* variants *Cedifor*, *Cydifor*
Pant Coed Ifor 1783, *Pant caedivore* 1784, *Pantcadifor* 1813, *Pant-coed-ifon* 1832, *Pantcoed Ivor Inn* 1873, *Pant-cadivor* 1875-7
Influenced in some sources by ***coed*** 'trees, wood', *cad* 'battle' and the pers.n. *Ifor* leading to the fanciful suggestion that this was the hollow where the hero Ifor Bach (d. c.1158), lord of Senghennydd, was once engaged in

battle. ***pant*** is found in the names of several former fms. in this area, including Pant (q.v.), Pantysgallog and Pantcerddinen (q.v.). Pantcadifor properly refers to the area next to crossroads at Pant cemetery (SO 062092).

Pantcerddinen　　　　　　　　SO 061090
Merthyr Tudful
'hollow with a mountain-ash', ***pant***, ***cerddinen***
Pantgardd Einon, *Pantgarddinon* 1852, *Pantygerdinen* 1873, *Pant-cerddinen* 1875-7
Earlier historical forms show loss of the def. art. ***y*** which explains the len. -gar-, -ger-. The first spelling shows misassociation with *gardd* 'garden' and pers.n. *Einion*. A housing estate named from a former fm. (SO 061091). Pantygerddinen, in Aberdare, is recorded as *Pant y Gerdinen* 1780, *Pant y Gardinian* 1824, *Pant y Gerddinen* 1844.

Pantlasau (Pont Lase)　　　　　SN 659000
Swansea (Llangyfelach)
?'hollow streams, streams in a hollow': ?***pant***, ?***glasau***
Pontlasse 1695, *Pantloose* c.1702, (place) *Ponlassey* 1720, *Pant y lasse* 1743, *Pant yr Echeldith Yssha alias Pant lassa Ycha alias Cawsey* 1764, *Pant-lasse* 1799, (mess.) *Pont y llasse* 1807, *Panllasse* 1813, (ht.) *Pant-lâsau*, (ho.) ~ *-isaf* 1832, *Pontlassie* 1926
Also the n. of fms. *Pantlasse Uchaf* 1838 (***uchaf***) and *Pant-lâsau-isaf* (SN 657996) 1832 (***isaf***). The first el. is presumably ***pant*** 'hollow' - a wet one, judging by mention of a causeway c.1702 and local testimony – which was sometimes misassociated with ***pont*** 'bridge'. The remainder is even less certain unless the pn. contains *glasau* as a contrived variant pl. of ***glais***, signifying a number of streams which could overflow. If this is the case, then *lasau* has len. gl- > l- which suggests ***pant*** is the qualifier; cf. *pantlawr* (***pant***, *llawr*) 'uneven or concave floor', *pantle* (***pant***, ***lle***[1]) 'hollow, place full of hollows'. The alternative form in 1764 appears to be an error since it refers to a distinct place Pant-yr-ehedydd (SN 667010) and is otherwise recorded as *Pant yr Ychedith Ycha* in the same source and as *Pent yr ychedidd* 1722. This is 'the lark's hollow' (***yr***, *ehedydd*, variant *echedydd*).

Pant-mawr　　　　　　　　　　ST 148816
Cardiff (Whitchurch)
'big hollow': ***pant***, ***mawr***
Pantemaure 1541, *Pant Maure* 1672, *Pant Mawr* 1701, *Pantmawr* 1795, *Pant-mawr* 1833
A n. taken from a former fm. (ST 148819) and assigned to a housing estate, largely constructed in the 1960s.

Pantside　　　　　　　　　　　ST 219978
Caerphilly (Mynyddislwyn Monmouthshire)
'(hos. at) side of Pant': pn. *Pant*, E ***side***
Pantside 1975
The n. of a housing estate which developed from the 1960s on hillside above Pant (recorded 1962-1965 on the OS) which itself takes its n. from a ho. *Pant* 1841 recalled in Pant Farm Road (ST 214969): ***pant*** 'a hollow' referring to its location next to the stream Nant Gawni. The latter is *Nant Gwrnai* 1833, *Nant Gawney* 1879 (with loss of –r-), also recalled in fns. *Sych Gawrney*, *Gwlyb Gawrney* and *Cae Blaen Gawrney* 18th cent., the ho.n. *Blaen gawnee* 1813, *Blaengawrney* 1841 (***nant***, ***sych***[1], ***gwlyb***, ***cae***, ***blaen***). The rn. may contain *gawr*[1] nmf. 'shout, cry, battle-cry' describing a noisy stream or the poorly-evidenced *gawr*[2] adj. 'grey' and a suffix –*nai* (EANC 25).

Pantyffynnon　　　　　　　　　SN 759073
Neath Port Talbot (Llan-giwg)
'hollow of the well': ***pant***, ***y***, ***ffynnon***
Tir Pant y Fynnon 1797, (ho.) *Pantyfynon* 1841, *Pant-y-ffynnon* 1877
Located close to an area called *Llygad y Ffynnon* 1877 (SN 755075), 'source of the well', with *llygad* 'eye, source of a stream'. The ht. adjoins a very small stream and the Swansea Canal.

Pant-y-fid　　　　　　　　　　SS 948880
Bridgend (Llandyfodwg)
'hollow at the hedge': ***pant***, ***y***, ***bid***
Pantevyd 1531, *Pant y vyd* 1607, *Pantyveed* or *Pantyvie* 1628, (fms.) *Pant-y-fid* 1884-5

The area where the valley Gadlys meets Nant Iechyd. The precise meaning of **bid** here is unclear but it may be used for 'hollow enclosed within a hedge' or in a broader sense for 'hollow characterised by dense hedges or bushes'. There is a notable stretch of woodland extending from Pant-y-fid down to a point below Gelli-fid Fach 'little Gelli-fid' (**bach**[1]) earlier *Gelli'r vide issa* 1619 (**isaf**). Gelli-fid, 'grove of the hedge', is *Gelli'r vide ycha* 1619, *Celli'r veed* 1767, *Kelly r Veed* 1785 (**celli, y, uchaf**).

Pant-y-graig-wen　　　　　　ST 063907
Rhondda Cynon Taf (Llanwynno)
'hollow at Y Graig-wen': **pant**, pn. *Y Graig-wen* (ho.) *Pant-y-graig-wen* 1874
An area of housing which developed along what is now Pantygraigwen Road from c.1880. Note also Pen-y-graig-wen.

Pantypyllau　　　　　　SS 928823
Bridgend (Coety)
'hollow of the pits': **pant, y, pyllau**
(ho.) *Pant-y-pyllau* 1899, (~) *Pantypwllau* 1914, (area) *Pant-y-pyllau* 1941
The ho. (later known as Rose Cottage) appears on OS maps from the late 19th cent and was located north-west of a prehistoric earthwork and a ho. *Pwllau* 1833, *Pylla* 1841, *Pyllau* 1899. Maps also show shallow pits north of Pant-y-pyllau – possibly evidence of diggings for iron ore – and the former site of an iron furnace (approx. SS 928827).

Pantyrawel　　　　　　SS 931879
Bridgend (Llangeinwyr)
Uncertain: **pant**, ?
pant nawell 1579, *Pant y nawell* 1632, *Pant-un-awel* 1650, *Pantynawel, Pant nawell* 1673, *Pantŷnawel Farm* 1767, *Pant Nawel* 1776, *Pant-y-nawl* 1833, *Pantyrawel* 1891, *Pant-yn-awel* 1899
The current form *Pant-yr-awel* 'the breeze hollow' (**pant, yr, awel**) is a re-interpretation. The likeliest explanation is that –*ynawel, -nawel* in historic forms represents *anawell* adj. '?clear, mature' or perhaps *nawell*[2] adj. '?bright, clear' (GPC). Both els. are, however, very poorly recorded in literary texts and there is doubt with regard to their precise meanings. The variation -*ll* [ɬ] and –*l* is found elsewhere in Glamorgan; cf. Pontsticill (below).

Pant-y-waun　　　　　　SO 094078
Caerphilly (Gelligaer)
'hollow of the moor': **pant, y, gwaun**
Pantywain c.1760, *Pant y wain* c.1772, (ho.) *Pant-y-waun* 1885
gwaun is also recalled in Twyn y Waun recorded as (hilly area) *Twyn y Waun* 1798, 1882 (**twyn**). A former coal and iron ore mining ht. largely removed in the 1960s by open-casting. Located a little north-east of the old fair Marchnad y Waun (*marchnad* nf. 'market'), once held near the Full Moon public ho.

Parc[1]　　　　　　Parc-mawr ST 110911
Caerphilly (Eglwysilan)
'enclosed land, park': **parc**
Y Park 1490, (tmt.) *Tere parke* 1525, *Parke Hamlett* 1670, *Park* 1744, (ho.) *Parc-fawr*, (~) *Ty'n-y-parc* 1833
parc is sometimes used to describe quite small fields but there is a cluster of **parc** names here which suggests that there may have been a large enclosure suitable for deer or other animals. These include Parcnewydd, Parc-mawr and the former Ty'n-y-parc – all within half-a-mile of each other – lying west and south of a stream Nant Cae'r-moel and east of a mountain road running north from Eglwysilan.

Y Parc[2]　　　　　　SS 850905
Bridgend (Maes-teg, Llangynwyd)
'the enclosure': **y, parc**
Y Parc 1962
The n. of a ho. estate constructed in the 1920s and 1930s between the former Park isolation hospital and the loop of the old Port Talbot & Garw mineral railway. The origin of the n. is uncertain but **parc** in the sense of 'enclosure, field' is found locally in *Waun-y-Park* 1857 (near Cwrtymwnws SS 851918).

Parc le Breos see **Parkmill**

Parcnewydd see **Carnetown**

Parc Tawe　　　　　　　　SS 658933
Swansea
'retail park by (r.) Tawe': *parc*, rn. **Tawe**
The n. of a retail area developed in the 1980s on the site west of Tawe Bridge on the site of former warehouses, flour mill, fuel works and mineral yards. The area was formerly known as The Island (1879-1938) because it was enclosed by the old North Dock and the New Cut of the r. Tawe.

Parc y Rhath see **Roath Park**

Parkmill　　　　　　　　SS 545891
Swansea (Ilston/Pen-maen)
'mill at (or belonging to) the park': AF *parc*, E *park*, E *mill*
Parke mill 1583, (2 mills) *the Parke mills* 1650, *Park mill* 1740
The park also gives its n. to Parc le Breos/Parc Brewys (SS 529895), west of Pennard Pill, recorded as (*silva de*) *Bruiz* 1230, *parcum de Breoz* 1306, *Parke brewes* 1547, *Park Brius* 1563, *Park brewis* 1578, *Park le Bruce or Parke Price* 1650, *Park* 1832. The le Breos family were lords of Gower 1203-1326. Part of the park boundary is described in 1650 as *the ould parke Ditche* 1650. Note also *Parc Cwm* (SS 537898) and *Park Woods* (SS 530902) so spelt 1832.

Paviland　　　　　　　　SS 446865
Swansea (Pen-maen detached)
'land belonging to Pen-y-fai': pn. *Pen-y-fai*, OE *land*
Penn ibei inrosulgen c.1145, *uillam penn iuei cum ecclesia* 1129 (c.1170), (grange) *Pauilond* c.1291, (*villa*) *Pavylond* 1396, *Pavilande* 1558, *Paviland* 1583
Paviland is a contracted form. Cf. Pen-y-fai. Paviland lay in the manor of Rhosili hence the first ref.

Pelenna, Afon　　　　　　SS 8106, 7895
Neath Port Talbot (Baglan, Michaelston)
Uncertain
Pelena 1877, *Pelena River* 1899
The rn. is recorded in the n. of a mill *Penlyney* 1541, *Pellyne mill* 1689, *Penllanna Mill* 1793, *Felin-penllena* 1830 (**melin**) and also gives its n. to the valley Cwm Pelenna, Pelenna Forest (SS 8198) and the area Blaenpelenna (SS 8197) recorded as *Blaen Pylinny* 1652, *Blaen Pylynne* 1653, *Blaen pell lenna* 1694, *Blaen-penllena* 1833 (***cwm, blaen***). It appears to contain the el. *pelen* nf. '(little) ball' with suffix *–a* possibly in the sense of a torrent which bounces over rocks and rolls through its valley but it is difficult to think of comparable rns. Most historic forms have *Pel-* [pel] which rule out comparison with Pellenni (not current) which referred to a wood identifiable with Monkswood (SO 3402) (PNGwent 153-4), at Llanbadog, Monmouthshire. The great majority of historic forms for this place have *Pell-* [peɫ]. Pellenni is obscure.

Penalltau (Penallta)　　　　ST 143953
Caerphilly (Gelligaer)
'top of the wooded slopes': ***pen***[1], ***allt*** pl. ***alltau***
penallte ygha 1562, *Pen Allt vgha* 1629, *Penallta isha* 1697, *Penalltau* 1772, (ho.) *Penalltau-fawr, ~ -isaf* 1833, *Penallta, ~ Isha, ~ Fawr* 1841
The n. seems to have referred specifically to the area around Penalltau-fawr (ST 137952) and Penalltau-isaf (ST 143952) above steep slopes over Ystrad Mynach and was transferred to Penallta Colliery (ST 139958). The dialect *-a* for standard *-au* has many parallels in south Wales, cf. Beddau.

Penarth　　　　　　　　ST 185715
Vale of Glamorgan
'top of the headland': ***pen***[1], ***garth***[1]
Pennard c.1165, *Pennard'* c.1190, *Pennarth* 1254, *Penharth* 1266, *Pennart* 13th cent, *Penarth* 1479, *Penarthe* 1535, (hill) *Penarth, ~ Pointe* c.1538, *the Pennarth baie, the Pennarth and the Lauerocke pointes* 1586, *Lower Penarth* 1762; *Pennarth Isha* 1766.

Fully analysed by Gwynedd Pierce (PNDPH 158-161). On the basis of historic sps. we can reject *arth* 'bear' as second el. though animal ns. are found elsewhere (see Pen-tyrch) combined with **pen**[1] in its sense of 'head' probably through some fancied resemblance to the shape of the headland. Penarth developed during the 19th cent as a fashionable resort and a dormitory town of Cardiff.

Pencaerau SS 747961
Neath Port Talbot (Neath)
'top (*or* hill) of the forts': **pen**[1], **caer** pl. **caerau**
Pencayra Farm 1799, *Pencire* or *Pencayra House* 1835, *Pencaira* 1841, *Pen-caerau* 1881
The n. is taken from a ho. on the Briton Ferry-Neath road but may have referred to the hill above Eaglesbush on which there are slight traces of a prehistoric fort.

Pen-clawdd SS 545957
Swansea (Llanrhidian)
'top of the ditch' or 'top of the bank': **pen**[1], **clawdd**
Penyclawdd 1650, *Pennclawdd* 1666, *Penclauth or Kevenbuchan* 1688, *Penclawdd* 1729, *Pen-clawdd* 1832
Referring either to a ditch or its upcast heap. The def.art. *y* found in 1650 seems to be intrusive since it is unmatched in other historic sps. The pn. may also be recorded in the n. of Nicholas de *Penclau*, a witness to a charter at Margam 1199. The ditch or bank has been associated with *'Pen Cae Clawdd,* an old camp on the Gaer mountain' (OPN 147); this is Pen-y-gaer (SS 536955). *Kevenbuchan* 1688 properly refers to Cefnbychan (SS 544950).

Pen-coed SS 961817
Bridgend (Coychurch)
'wooded hill' or 'end of the wood': **pen**[1], **coed**
Penkoyt c.1166, (wood) *Penkoyt* 1303, (wood of) *Pencoyd* 1415, c.1700, *Pencoit* c.1538, *Penkoyd* c.1598, *Pencoed* 1710
Pen-coed stands near to the eastern slopes of Cefn Hirgoed and north-east of Coedymwstwr. Pen-coed one of three hts. in Coychurch recorded as *traen Pencoed* 1639 (**traean**). There are identical pns. in Eglwysilan, Llanilid and St Fagans, and cf. Pen-coed, Monmouthshire (PNGwent 168).

Penderi SS 6199
Swansea (Llangyfelach)
'end of the oak-wood': **pen**[1], **deri**
Penderry 1565, *parcel of Penthery* 1322, *Parcell Penthery* 1621, *penddery* 1697 (late 18th cent), (ho.) *Pentherry vach* 1729, *Pentherry* 1764, (ho.) *Penderry Vawr* 1799, (hos.) *Pendery fawr,* ~ *fach* 1813
The len. *dderi* seen in many historic forms suggests a lost def.art. and that **deri** is a fem. coll.n. as well as a pl. of **dâr** nf. 'oak-tree'. Similar examples include (Y) Dderi-goch (SN562491) and Twr y Dderi near Lampeter, Cardiganshire. Penderi was a former **parsel** or division of Llangyfelach p. The n. also applies in irregular spelling to Penderry Community Council.

Penderyn SN 947088
Rhondda Cynon Taf (Breconshire)
'bird's head': **pen**[1], **aderyn** variant *ederyn*
Spemederm 1281, *Pennyderyn* 1291, *Penederyn* 1372, *Penderin* 1373, *Pennederyne* 1410, *Penderyn* 1448, *Penyderyn* 1461, *Penyderen* 1503, *Penhederyn* 1559
The simplest explanation is that the n. is taken from a topographical feature, probably the hill Moel Penderyn (SN 938087) recorded as *Penderyn-foel* 1892. The n. has also been interpreted as a ref. to animal sacrifice. Deric John (CVPN 76-8), for example, suggests that Penderyn was the n. of 'the totemistic tribal meeting place or territory' which was transferred to the p. and later to the settlement which grew around the ch. of St Cynog (SN 944085); cf. Pen-tyrch. Parallels have been drawn with pns. in England containing OE **hēafod** 'head' which occurs in the ns. of administrative hundreds taken from central meeting-places. Conclusive evidence is so far lacking in Wales.

Pendeulwyn (Pendoylan) ST 059766
Vale of Glamorgan
'head of the two groves': **pen**[1], **dau**, *deu* 'two', **llwyn**

(Gwrgan of) *Penduuelim* 1190, (Urban of) *Pendiuelin* c.1205, *Pendeuloin* 1254, *Pe[n]dyuelyn* 1317, *Pendyuylyn* 1401, *Pendoylvyn* 1508, *Pendeyloyn* 1535, *pen daylwyn* c.1566, *Pendaulwyn* 1764, *Pendoylon* 1799, *Pendoylan* 1885

This has also been identified with (mill of) *Pandelia* c.1129. Local pron. in 1959 was 'Pendeulan', probably for [pen'doilan, pen'doilən], according to T.J. Hopkins (VGS 1: 79), though this is not clearly reflected in historic forms. Hopkins adds that 'Pendeulan' was explained as meaning 'head, or end, of two churches', i.e. Pendeulwyn and Caerwigau, but the regular form in that case would be *Pendwylan*.

Pendre SS 908810
Bridgend (Coychurch)
'town end, top of the town': **pen**[1], **tref**
Pendre 1940
The n. appears with the construction of a housing estate in the 1930s north of Newtown, itself an area developed from the late 19th cent near the town cemetery.

Pendyrys ST 0096
Rhondda Cynon Taf (Llanwynno)
?'wild *or* rough hill': **pen**[1], **dyrys**
Pedyrrys isaf farm c.1778, *Pendyris Isha* 1841, *Penderys ucha* 1845, *Pendyrrisissa* 1852, *Pendyrys-isaf* 1885

No hill of this n. seems to be recorded in historical records and it is possible that it is used elliptically to mean '(place or area at the) top of Nant Dyrys'. Nant Dyrys, 'wild, rough stream' (**nant**) is a tributary of Rhondda Fechan (ST 007962). Pendyrys appears on late 19th cent maps in the n. of a ho. Pendyrys Isaf (ST 008967) (**isaf**) which is identifiable with *Nantdyrris* 1841, *Nant-dyrûs* 1759 and *Tyir nant dyrys ysha* 1633. Pendyrys Uchaf (**uchaf**) is presumably *Tyir y nant dyris ycha* in 1633. The n. was transferred to Pendyrys Colliery (ST 011958) and is so closely associated with nearby Tylorstown, that it is sometimes used as the W n. for this place. The n. also survives as that of a male voice choir and in street-ns.

Penfilia SS 654960
Swansea (Llangyfelach)
'head of the ?': **pen**[1], (**y**), ?rn.
Peneviller 1319, *Penvilar* 1332, *Penyvilar* 1611, *Penvilia* 1773, *Pen-y-fillia* 1832, *Penyvilia*, *Penvilia* 1841, *Penfilia* 1876, *Pen-filia* 1879

Penfilia lies near a stream (a tributary of Tawe) recorded as *Nant Rhyd y Vilast* 1641 and *Vilast* 1764. The first translates as 'stream at the ford of the greyhound-bitch': **nant**, **rhyd**, **y**, **mil(i)ast**, **fil(i)ast**. The last el. is feasible as a rn. and there may be some semantic relationship between -*filast* and –*filia* seen in late sps. but earlier historic forms of Penfilia consistently have -*viller*, -*vilar*, later -*vilia*, -*filia* and it is unlikely that –*filiast* > -*filar*, -*fila*, -*filia*. The best that can be suggested – if we accept a link – is that –*filiast* is a re-interpretation of an otherwise obscure rn.

Pengam[1] ST 158971
Caerphilly (Bedwellte Monmouthshire)
?'crooked hill': **pen**[1], **cam**[2]
(bridge) *Pont y manpengam* 1704, *Pont a Penpangam* 1729, *Pont y pen Pengam* 1753, *Pontar Pengam* c.1790, *Pont Aber Pengarn*, *Tir Pont Pengam* 1813, *Pontmaenpengam* 1851, *Pengam, or Pontaberpergam* 1860, (bridge) *Pont Aber Pengam, Pengam* 1867

C.J. Evans (GPNG 14) says that the ht. was formerly called *Pont-maen-pen-gam* which he explains as 'the bridge on the crooked rock, or the stone bridge on the River Pengam'. His first interpretation seemingly draws support from the forms for 1704 and 1851 but is unconvincing and a rn. is more likely – perhaps a lost n. for that which rises at a point (ST 140990) above Cascade House and meets Afon Rhymni just below the bridge Pont Aberpengam (ST 154971). Aberpengam, 'outflowing of Pengam' (**aber**) certainly indicates a stream and it is possible that forms such as *Pont a Penpangam* and *Pontar Pengam* are attempts at representing a compressed form of Pontaberpengam (cf. Pontarddulais). Pengam refers to urban development on both sides of r. Rhymni but the centre is on the Monmouthshire side around High Street and Commercial Street. The former Pengam Colliery and railway station (ST 150970) lay in Glamorgan.

Pengam[2] ST 215772
Cardiff (Roath)
?'crooked hill': *pen*[1], *cam*[2]
(mess.) *Pengam* 1695, 1702, *Pengam farm* 1852
Otherwise Pengam Green. perhaps referring to a small rise on which the fm. was situated. Pengam Moors is the area extending to the Severn estuary recorded as *Pengam Moors* 1779.

Pengarnddu see **Pen-y-garn-ddu**

Pengelli see **Grovesend**

Pengwern SS 534913
Swansea (Ilston)
?'hill distinguished by alder-trees': *pen*[1], *gwern*
Pengwerne 1578, *Pengwern* 1650
The n. presumably applies to the area immediately around Pengwern fm. (SS 535913) at Ilston or to Pengwern Common but is not obviously appropriate since the small hills and moors in this part of Gower are rocky and characterised by rough pasture and vegetation rather than the wet conditions where alder-trees are found; note Furzehill (SS 548907) and Furzeland (SS 542910) immediately south-east of Pengwern. Pengwern Moor (SS 5391) is so called in 1764 and as *Mynydd Pengwern* 1830 with **mynydd** in the extended meaning 'open, exposed pasture'.

Pen-hydd Pen-hydd-fawr SS 806931
Neath Port Talbot (Margam)
?'dark, gloomy hill': *pen*[1], *hudd* adj. 'dark, dusky, gloomy'
Pennudh late 12th cent, *Penhuth* 1235, *Pennuð* c.1241, *Pennuth* 1336, (chp.) *Penydd* 1697 (late 18th cent), *Penydd* 1728
Referring to the hill Mynydd Penhydd which casts a shadow over Pen-hydd-fawr. Later forms have probably been influenced by *hydd*[1] 'stag, hart'. Also the n. of hos. recorded as *Pennyth-ycha* 1572, *Pen-hydd-fawr*, ~ *-ganol* (SS 806933), ~ *-fâch* 1884 and *Pen-hydd-isa* 1832

(*uchaf, mawr, canol, bach*[1], *isaf*). Pen-hydd-waelod (SS 802920), recorded as *Penydd' Waylod* 1514 and *Penhyddwailod* 1852 (*gwaelod*), was a grange and chp. of Margam abbey.

Pen-iard (Penyard) SN 055068
Merthyr Tudful
?'top of the yard': *pen*[1], *iard*
Penyiard 1820, *Pen yard* 1841, *Penyard* 1873, *Pen-yard* 1875
The n. is said to have referred to a yard at Penydarren Ironworks (St MT 364) described in 1841 as *Penydarran yard*. A *Pen yard* is also recorded in 1841 near Cyfarthfa and Gelli-deg, at the Plymouth Ironworks and at Llwydcoed, Aberdare, 1875.

Peniel Green SS 696976
Swansea (Llansamlet)
'open space of land at Peniel': ?biblical *Peniel* or *Penuel*, E *green*
Penial Green 1879, *Peniel Green* 1895, *Peniel Green (Penhewlgreen)* 1905, *Peniel Green (Penhewl y Green)*, (o) *dir glas* 1908
Penuel or Peniel was the biblical city on the east side of the r. Jordan and was typically applied as a n. to a Nonconformist chp. The chp. is not identified and Peniel Green English Congregational was not established until 1885. The only other chp. shown on late 19th cent OS maps is Bethel Independent (SS 694974), a little to the south-west. The n. was evidently established before 1871 when Peniel Green School opened. The forms for 1905 and 1908 associate the pn. with *pen*[1], *hewl* (*heol*), E *green*, 'green space of land at the top of the road', but they are not confirmed in other sources.

Pen-lan SS 644961
Swansea (Llangyfelach)
'top of (the) slope': *pen*[1], (*y*), *glan*
Pen y lane 1795, *Penlan* 1797, *Penlann Farm* 1815
Named from fms. *Panllanmain, Penlan* 1813, *Pen-lan-fawr* (SS 646963), *Pen-lan-fach* (SS 648973) 1832, *Pen-lan-fawr* 1884 (*mawr, bach*[1]).

Penlle'r-brain see **Raven Hill**

Penlle'rfedwen SN 7211
Neath Port Talbot (Llan-giwg)
?'place on a hill marked by a birch-tree': *pen¹, lle¹, y, `r, bedwen, fedwen*
(hill) *Penlle Fedwen* 1811, (hill slopes) *Penlle'r-fedwen* 1883, 1962
The northern slopes of the hill Mynydd Uchaf.

Penlle'r-gaer SS 613988, 621988
Swansea (Llangyfelach)
?'place on a hill with a fort': *pen¹, ?lle¹, y, caer*
Penllergeer 1608, *Penlloyngare* 1632, *Penller gâr* 1650, *Penllergare* 1729, *Penllyrgaer* 1748, *Penllygaer* 1763, *Penllegaer* 1792, *Penlle'rgare* 1832
The second el. has been identified as *tyle* 'slope' as in Penlle'r-brain (see Raven Hill) though historic forms have no evidence of *-t-*. This is a modern village located partly on an area called *The Camp* in 1876 taking its n. from a former ho. Penlle'rgaer (approx. SS 623991). The pn. may be compared with Penlle'rbebyll (SN 634048) which possesses a small earthwork ('barrow' 1877) and Penlle'rcastell (see **Mynydd y Gwair**) which has traces of a medieval castle; both places are on hill summits. The village developed from the late 19th cent west of the crossing of Swansea Road and Gorseinon Road partly on Gorseinon Common and was initially known as *Gorseinon* 1884 and *Penlle'rgaer or Gorseinon* 1898.

Pen-llin (Penllyn) SS 973760
Vale of Glamorgan
'flax hill': *pen¹, llin²*
Pendelin' 1208, *Pendlin* 1254, *Penthlin* c.1262, *Penlyn* 1305, *Penthlyn* 1317, *Castrum Penthlyn* 1479, *Penllyne* 1535, *Penlline Castelle* c.1538, *Penlyne* 1560, *pen llin* c.1566, *Penllyn* 1578, *Penline* 1661, *Penlline* 1670
Located on a promontory stretching from Pen-llin village to Graig Penllyn (q.v.). *llin²* does not seem to occur in other major pns. with the exception of Ardd-lin (Arddleen), Montgomeryshire, where it qualifies *gardd*, meaning '(the) flax-garden'. The use of the form Penllyn on road-signs and modern maps and by the community council is based on the supposition that the pn. contains *llyn* and indeed a very small pool is shown on the OS map 1833. This is located on water meadows known as Pen-llyn Moor near the r. Thaw/ Ddawan and there are drainage ditches which suggest it may once have been larger. However, current pron. by local W-speakers and many sps. – including a poetic verse attributed to Iolo Morganwg in which *Pen-llin* is rhymed with *flin* (BroM 42) – indicate a mid [i] to long vowel [i:] rather than the short vowel in *llyn* [ɪ]. The pn. is generally pronounced [pen'lein] by E-speakers, probably through re-interpreting sps. such as *Penlline, Penline* and associating it with E *line* 'string' etc.

Pen-llwyn ST 176956
Caerphilly (Mynyddislwyn Monmouthshire)
'grove hill' or perhaps 'top of the grove': *pen¹, llwyn*
Penllwyn 1739, 1814, *Pen-llŵyn Row* 1879, (village) *Pen-llwyn* 1938
The hill may be that between Penllwyn-fawr (at what is now The Circle ST 173955) and Penllwyn-fach (ST 175963) recorded as *Pen Llwyn mawr, Pen Llwyn fach* 1813, *Penllwyn-fach*, (ho.) ~ *-fawr* 1833 (*mawr, bach¹*). The village developed from the late 19th cent near Tredegar Junction Station, Penllwyn Colliery and the former Mynyddislwyn Urban District Council offices.

Penllyn see **Pen-llin**

Pen-maen¹ SS 531887
Swansea
'stone headland': *pen¹, maen*
(villam de) *Penmain* c.1230, (ch. of) *Sancti Iohannis Baptiste de Penmaine* 1232, *Penmayn* 1306, *Penmayne* 1394, *Pen Mayne* 1535, *pen maen* c.1566, *Penmain* 1650, *Penmaen* c.1670
The ruins of the old ch. stand on the crest of a small hill close to sea-cliffs and to a chambered cairn (SS 532881), traces of a medieval ringwork and settlement. There are also rocky outcrops on the green (SS 532887) near the present ch.

Pen-maen² ST 181977
Caerphilly (Mynyddislwyn Monmouthshire)
'stone hill': *pen¹, maen*
(mill) *Melyne Penne Mayne* 1487 (1570), *Tir Penmayne* 1653, *Penmaine* 1707, *Tir pen maine* 1718, *Penmain* 1723, *Penmaen* 1813
Cf. Pen-maen¹. Located on a hill overlooking the r. Ebwy and Blackwood. The mill (*melin*) in the first spelling is also recorded in 1630; see also Croespen-maen and Mynydd Maen. Notable for a Congregational chp. established in 1691.

Pen-marc (Penmark) ST 057688
Vale of Glamorgan
?'stallion hill': *pen¹, ?march*
(*Alwardo de*) *Penmarc* c.1168, (lp.) *Penmarc'* c.1178, *Penmark* 1254, c.1785, *Penmarch* 13th cent, *Penmarke* 1335, *pen mark* c.1566, *Penmarck, sometyme called Pen March Howel* c.1670
There are some doubts with this explanation since early mentions are scarce and W sources such as that for c.1566 have *Penmark*, etc not *Pen-march* (see PNDPH 166-170). Replacement of W *ch* [ ] as *c* [k] is, however, possible in an area such as this where there was extensive E settlement in the Middle Ages; cf. perhaps Marcross. If this is the right interpretation then 'stallion hill' would refer to its fancied shape or perhaps a ref. to the practice of animal sacrifice (R.J. Thomas in AC 1934, 328-31, and cf. Penderyn). Iolo Morganwg c.1785 cites a tradition that a skull was found here, reputed to be that of St Mark. He also supplies the spurious form *Llanfark* as if it were 'Mark's church'. *Pen March Howel* c.1670 may be a result of confusion with Mynydd Marchywel.

Pennard SS 565887
Swansea
'promontory': *pennardd*
Pennard c.1187, *Pennart* c.1291, *Pennarth* 1316, *Pennarth, ~ poynt, ~ cast* 1578, (well of) *beate Marie de Pennard* 1320, *Pennarth'* 1396, *Pennarthe* 1508, *pen arth* c.1566, *Penard, Penards pill* 1650, *Penard or Pen-arth anciently* 1697, *Penard, ~ Castle* 1729, *Penard* 1830

Pennard village occupies a plateau above a small gorge but the actual promontory may have included the whole area extending from near the castle and former ch. (SS 545884) in Pennard Burrows (*Penard Burrows* 1830) to Pwll-du Head (SS 570864). There are some spelling similarities to Penarth, hence suggestions that it has *pen* and *garth*² 'enclosure' or *arth* 'bear', but most sps. in E sources suggest –*d* [d] < -*dd* [ð]. Dafydd Morganwg 1874 (HMorg 440) favoured *Penhardd*, with *hardd* 'beautiful' but there is no trace of -*h*- in historic sps.

Pennon ST 053694
Vale of Glamorgan (Llancarfan)
'hill bearing ash-trees': *pen¹, onn*
Pennon c.1100, 1541, *Penhou* c.1134, *Pennun* c.1137, *Pennum* 1146, *Pennune* before 1263, *Penhun* 1303, *Penon* c.1598, 1811, *Penone* c.1670
Despite the current OS map's form with a hyphen, the pn. is generally stressed on the first syllable; that might explain the -*u*- in some forms, possibly reflecting shift -*o*- [ō] to middle vowel [ə]. See PNDPH 96.

Penpedair-heol ST 141974
Caerphilly (Gelligaer)
'top of four roads': *pen¹, pedair, heol*
Pen peter heol 1839, *Penpedairheol* 1849, *Penpedair-heol* 1878
There is also a ref. to a ho. *Four Roads* here in the census 1841. OS maps 1878 and 1884 apply *Penpedair-heol* to an area extending along Hengoed Road which follows the ridge of a promontory between Nant Cylla and Afon Rhymni. There are identical pns. at Goetre (SO 335037), Monmouthshire, recorded as *Penpedairheol* 1833 and at Llangatwg, Breconshire, recorded as *Pen Peder heole* 1706 and *Pen-pedair-heol* 1832 (SO 221167).

Pen-prysg SS 963823
Bridgend (Coychurch)
?'hill characterised by brushwood': *pen¹, prysg*
Penyprisk 1700, *Pen y Prisk* 1740, *Penprisc* 1745, *Penbrysge* 1760, *Penprisk* 1799, *Penprysg* 1852
The second el. is also found in *prysgoed* (with *coed*) 'brushwood, brushes'. There was an

identical, lost n. recorded as *Penn iprisc, uillam penn iprisc idest, difrinn anouid* early 13th cent, *penn i prisc, Penniprisc* c.1170, north of Cardiff; *anouid* must refer to Nofydd, the stream which rises at Blaen-nofydd (ST 159845) and flows south through Rhiwbeina to Whitchurch Brook and the r. Taf.

Pen-rhiw ST 241909
Caerphilly (Rhisga)
'top of the slope': ***pen***¹, lost ***y***, ***rhiw***
Pen y rhue 1755, (hos.) *Pen-y-rhiw* 1883, 1953, *Penrhiw* 1965
Located at the top of a steep slope above r. Ebwy. The loss of an unstressed def.art. is fairly common in south Wales. An identical pn. (ST 208901), near Machen, is recorded as *Pen y riwe* 1629, *Pen-rhiw* 1885.

Penrhiw-ceibr (Penrhiwceiber) ST 058976
Rhondda Cynon Taf
?'place characterised by heavy timbers' or '(place at) top of slope where joists were cut or assembled': ***pen***¹, ***rhiw***, (***y***, affixed as '***r***), ***ceibr*** 'rafter, joist'
Penrewkeibir 1704, *Rhiw'r Kibier* 1740, *Rhyw Kibyr* 1771-81, *Penrhiwceibyr* 1784, *Pen rhiw'r ceibir* 1788, *Penrhiw ciber* 1814, *Penrhiw-ciber* 1833
Glanffrwd (1878-88) in his history of Llanwynno interpreted *ceibr* in the sense of thick, entwined branches through which a track had to be cut to permit traffic up the slopes of Glyn Cynon to the old farmhouse of Berthgelyn (= Perthgelyn). A likelier explanation is that ***ceibr*** is used in a collective sense and that the pn. refers to a place at the top of a slope characterised by heavy timbers or where joists were cut. Gwynedd Pierce (PNGlam 148-9) also notes nearby *Pantynenbren* 1841 and a wood *Coed Ffos-ceibr* (at Pendeulwyn) through which the stream Nant Tynyplancau flows (***pant***, ***nenbren*** 'roof-beam', ***coed***, ***ffos***, ***tyn***, *plancau* 'planks'). Penrhiw is a common compound in pns.: note Penrhiw Cradoc (ST 046980) recorded as *Pen Rhyw Gradock* 1703 and *Pen Rhyw Cradock* 1747 with pers.n. *Caradog*. The village developed after sinking of Penrikyber Colliery 1872-9.

Penrhiw-fawr SN 749108
Neath Port Talbot (Llan-giwg)
'top of Rhiw-fawr': ***pen***¹, ho.n. *Rhiw-fawr* (ho.) *Penhuefawr* 1841, *Pen-rhiw-fawr* 1878, 1947, (Sunday school) *Rhiw-fawr* 1878
Rhiw-fawr (SN 747109) means 'big slope': ***rhiw***, ***mawr***.

Penrhiw-fer ST 004900
Rhondda Cynon Taf (Llantrisant)
'top of the short slope': ***pen***¹, ***rhiw***, ***ber***
pen rewe ver 1580, *Pen Rhiw ver* 1666, *Pen rhuw ber* c.1700, *Penrewver* 1768, *Penrhiwfer* 1833
Named from a former fm. There is also mention of a fn. here recorded as *Riw ver* 1673. The village developed in the 19th cent near Penrhiwfer Colliery (Penrhiwfer Coal Co. 1871).

Penrhiwtyn SS 743958
Neath Port Talbot (Llantwit-juxta-Neath)
?'top of the slope notable for rushes (*or* trailing plants)': ***pen***¹, ***rhiw***, ***gwden*** variant *gwdyn*
Penny Ruttyng 1541, *Penn-ryw-wtting* 1558, *Penrowting* 1587, *Penrwtting* 1628, *Penroutinge* 1668, *Penrowtin* 1681, *Penrooting* 1688, *Penrowting issa*, *~ ucha* 1703, *Penriwtin* c.1800, *Penrhiwtyn* 1829, *Pen'rhwtyn* 1832
Local pron. 'Penrwtin' [pen'ru:tin] provides little clue to the meaning but the -t- in Penrhiwtyn is likely to be another example of unvoicing of -d- found in south-east Wales found notably in the pers.n. Catwg for Cadog. If so, it strengthens the case for ***gwden*** found in other plant-names such as *gwden y coed* 'old man's beard'. The -g in many historic forms is likely to be an inorganic addition. See further Gwynedd Pierce (ADG¹, 85).

Pen-rhys ST 002943
Rhondda Cynon Taf (Ystradyfodwg)
'hill of ?': ***pen***¹, ?
(chp. of) *Bte' Marie V(i)rginis de Penryce* 1535, *Penrise* c.1538, *Penruy* 1550, *Penrice* 1563, *Penrees* c.1598, *Penrees Ucha*, *~ Isha* 1799, *Pen Rhys ap Tewdwr, Pen-rhys-isaf* 1833, *Pen rees ycha*, *~ icha* 1841

Traditional explanations are similar to those for Penrice (q.v.). In this case it was the place where Rhys ap Tewdwr was reputedly killed and beheaded in battle with Robert Fitzhamon 1091 (hence the translation 'Rhys's head'). Thomas Wilkins, the antiquarian, c.1659 dates the battle to 1090 and says that it took place at *Brin y beddau*. It is also said that there was a 'Pen Syr Rhys, or the well of Sir Rhys's head' at Battle, Breconshire. This is all unfounded speculation but Pen-rhys was certainly the site of a well and a chp. containing a holy shrine of Mary in the late Middle Ages mentioned by the antiquarian John David Rhys (d. c.1609) and by the poet Gwilym Tew (floruit c.1470-80) in his *awdl* to *Wyry Fair Wen o Benrhys* ('Holy Virgin Mary of Penrhys'). The chp. became a place of pilgrimage built at a grange belonging to the abbey of Llantarnam and became the subject of a cycle of verse, mainly by Glamorgan bards including Lewis Morgannwg. Penrhys ht. was otherwise known as Home recorded as *Penrees als Holme hamlett* 1670 and in (mill) *Melin yr Om* 1833 (approx. SS 989946), presumably E *home*, employed in the sense of 'township in the middle of the p.' or t. containing the parish church'.

Penrice, Pen-rhys SS 493879
Swansea
'hill of ?': ***pen¹***, ?
(ch. of) *Sancti Andree de Penris* 1132, *Penrice* 1176, 1670, (*John de*) *Penris* before 1201, *Penres* 1282, *Penrys* 1347, *Penrees* 1394, *Penrise* c.1538, *Pen Rys* c.1566, *Penn Rrys* 1606, *Penryce Castle* 1607
Reputedly the location where Rhys ap Caradog ap Iestyn was captured by Normans and beheaded in 1099 (HMorg 441; WGOW 25-6) but this is an onomastic tale; cf. Pen-rhys (q.v.), Penrhys-fawr (SS 796955) and Penrhys-fach in Michaelston-super-Afan. It is worth noting that all of these places lie on or adjoin hills and that ***pen¹*** describes their locations. The second el. is more problematic. One possibility is that *-rhys* is the el. found in the pers.n. and in *rhysfa¹* 'attack, assault, rush' and *rhysedd* 'glory, splendour, pomp'. The precise sense remains unclear and there seem to be no close parallels in other parts of Wales.

Pensgynor (Penscynor) SS 767996
Neath Port Talbot (Cadoxton-juxta-Neath)
?'end of Cynfor's river-meadow': ***pen¹***, ?***ynys***, ?pers.n. *Cynfor*
Penscunor 1841, *Penisconnor* 1852, *Penisgynor Cottage* 1861, *Peniscynor* 1871
The n. is taken from a ho. and cottages and is poorly evidenced. The first el. is clearly ***pen¹*** but the remainder is uncertain. The pers.n. *Cynfor* is found in Llangynnwr, Carmarthenshire (DPNW 265) with assimilation of –f-. The third el. could also be the poorly recorded *cynor* nm. 'huntsman' or perhaps *cynnor* nmf. 'door-post; outer door, porch' as in Cynghordy, Carmarthenshire, but the latter would not make good sense with ***ynys***.

Pentre¹ SS 969960
Rhondda Cynon Taf (Ystradyfodwg)
'(the) farm or settlement' : (***y***), ***pentref***
Pentre 1757, 1841, *Tyr Rhiw maen Gwyn yssha alias Tyr y pentre* 1762, *Pentra* 1799, *Pentref* 1814, *Pentre'r Ystrad* 1833
pentref in the sense 'village' is inappropriate since the modern village takes its n. from a former fm. on the same site alternatively known as Tir Rhiw Maen-gwyn Isaf, 'land called lower white-stone slope' (***tir***, ***rhiw***, ***maen***, ***gwyn***, ***isaf***). The n. was applied in the early 19th cent firstly to the industrial settlement next to Nant y Pentre and later to Pentre Colliery begun by the Pentre Coal Co in 1864 on the south side of the village. Judging by the 1833 refs., the village was also distinguished by its proximity to Ystradyfodwg, a n. displaced as a pn. by Ton Pentre. The local dialect form was *Y Pentra* in 1839 (HTonyrefail 108).

Pentre² SS 655948
Swansea
'village, settlement': ***pentref***
(tmt. of land at) *Estill* 1570, 1634, *Pentrey still* 1799, *Pentrestill* 1813, *Pentre Estyll* 1851, *y Pentre* 1872, *Pentre* 1879
Earlier plain Estyll, literally 'planks': *estyll* pl. of *astell* nf. 'plank, board', possibly in the sense of a place or area in marshy land where planks might have been laid to enable access. Pentre

lies close to Burlais Brook (see Cwmbwrla). The alternative explanation is that *estyll* is used in a topographical sense for terraced hill-slopes adjoining the stream; cf. Cefnstylle and Shelf.

Pentre-bach[1] SO 065035
Merthyr Tudful
'little settlement': **pentref**, **bach**[1]
Pentre Bach 1729, *Tyr Pentrebach* 1757, *Pentra Bach* 1784, *Pentrebach* 1795, *Pentre-bach* 1833
The historian Charles Wilkins (HMerth 127) in 1867 says that it described a cluster of fms. and cottages 'long before' the iron works (SO 062041) were established here (in 1807) though in 1746 it applied to a specific ho. With industrial and urban re-development, the focus of the village shifted towards the area of housing (now simply a road) known as Taibach in 1841-c.1976 ('little houses': **tai**, **bach**[1]), Dyffryn (**dyffryn**) at Rhyd-fach and the Dyffryn Fawr Estate.

Pentre-bach[2] ST 088896
Rhondda Cynon Taf (Eglwysilan)
'little settlement': **pentref**, **bach**[1]
Pentrabach 1784, *Pentrefbach* 1813, *Pentrebach* 1852, *Pentre-bâch* 1875 OS 1:2,500
A small village which developed along the road running from Pontypridd towards Cardiff.

Pentre-bach[3] SN 601052
Swansea (Llandeilo Tal-y-bont)
'little settlement': **pentref**, **bach**[1]
Pentrebach 1821, 1844, *Pentre-bach* 1832
Cf. Pentre-bach[1, 2].

Pentre-baen (Pentrebane) ST 130779
Cardiff (St Fagans)
'ridge near Paen's house': **cefn**, **tref**, pers.n. *Paen*
Kentrebaine c.1538, *Keven Trebayne* 1570, (mess.) *Keven Tre Payne* 1595, (*syddyn*) *Keven Tre baen* c.1612, *Ceven tre baen* 1666, *Pentrebaen* 1564, *Pentrepayne* 1567, *Pentrebane* 1762
Named from a fm. (ST 120785). The pers.n. probably derives from AF *Pain*, *Payn(e)* found in Painscastle (Castell-paen), Radnorshire (DPNW 357) and locally perhaps in Pancross (Llanfeuthin) and Pains Wood (St Andrews Major). The ridge may be the small rise immediately north of the fm. The map spelling with *–bane* [beɪn] is an anglicisation of local dialect *ǣ* (PNDPH 94, 229-30; and see Lisvane). *Cefntre-* has become confused with **pentref** in late sources. For the contracted form c.1538, cf. Cyncoed. The identity of Paen or Payn(e) is uncertain though he was identified by H.C. Jones (PNIG 11) on very flimsy grounds with Sir Payne Turberville, reputedly custodian of the lp. of Glamorgan and Morgannwg after the AN conquest.

Pentre-chwyth SS 670951
Swansea (Llansamlet)
?'windy settlement: **pentref**, **chwyth** 'blast, breath'
Pentrechwith 1818, *Pentrewith* 1841, *Pentre-chwyth* 1881, *Pentrechwyth ... Grenfell Town* 1908
From its location on the exposed north slopes of Kilvey Hill; cf. Cold Blow, Pembrokeshire (DPNW 94). The qualifier could also perhaps be *chwith* 'strange, sinister' as in Ochrwyth (q.v.) though the precise meaning of the pn. would be unclear. Note also Gwernllwyn-chwith (approx. SS 697983), about 2 miles north-eastwards, recorded as *Wernlehauwith* 1626, *Wern Lloynwheeth* 1676, *Gwern llwyn whith* 1697 (late 18th cent), and *Gwern-llwyn-chwith* 1832 (**gwern**, **llwyn**). Popularly and mistakenly thought to derive from its habitation by eight (**wyth**) families. The alternative and later n. Grenfell Town recalls Pascoe St Leger Grenfell (1798-1879) (HLlan 239-40) who possessed interests in the copper trade and smelting in the Swansea Valley. The n. is recorded from 1879 but now applies specifically to hos. around the road linking Pentre-chwyth Road to Brokesby Road.

Pentreclwydau SN 849049
Neath Port Talbot (Cadoxton-juxta-Neath)
'settlement near (streams called) Clwyd': **pentref** and rns. *Clwyd* pl. *Clwydau*
Pentreclwyd 1814, *Pentre-clwyda* 1833, *Pentre-clwydau* 1877
Clwyd Fawr recorded as *Clwyd vawre* 1657 the 'greater Clwyd' (**mawr**) is the stream which rises above Craig Clwyd and passes through

the hamlet to the r. Nedd at Aberclwyd (*aber*) recorded as *Aber Clwyd* 1541. Clwyd Fechan recorded as *Clwyd vechan* 1657, the 'lesser Clwyd' (*bechan*), is now called Rheola Brook, rising near Craig Clwyd Fechan and flowing into Neath/Nedd about half-a-mile below Aberclwyd. The rns. Clwyd may be identical to Clwyd in Denbighshire and Flintshire signifying a r. named after a ford protected by a hurdle (*clwyd*) (DPNW 89; PNF 51).

Pentredŵr SS 693962
Swansea (Llansamlet)
'settlement by water': ***pentref***, ***dŵr***
Pentredwr 1709, *Pentre'r Dwr* 1758, *Pentre-dwr* 1832, *Pentre-dŵr* 1881
Probably in ref. to its location near Crymlyn Bog.

Pentreffynnon SS 728970
Neath Port Talbot (Cadoxton-juxta-Neath)
'settlement at the well': ***pentref***, ***ffynnon***
Pentre-ffynnon 1876-81, *Pentreffynnon* 1940
Several nearby springs are shown on the OS 1:2,500 map 1881.

Pentremeurig (Pentre Meyrick) SS 966757
Vale of Glamorgan (Pen-llyn)
'settlement *or* farm belonging to Meurig': ***pentref***, pers.n. *Meurig*
Pentre Meirig 1833, *Pentre Myric* 1841, *Pentre Meyrick* 1852
Anglicised as *Meyrick*, hence the OS map form. Meurig has not been identified.

Pentrepiod SO 199011
Caerphilly (Mynyddislwyn Monmouthshire)
'magpies' farm': ***pentref***, ***piod***
(ho.) *Pentref-piod* 1833, *Pentref-peod* 1836, *Pentrapeod Farm* 1901, *Pentrapeod* 1921
Perhaps a mocking description for a remote or deserted place. The form *Pentrapeod* which, first appears on OS maps in 1901, partly reflects local dialect with *Pentra* for *Pentre*. Identical in meaning to Pentre-piod (SO 267021), at Abersychan, recorded as *Pentref Piod* 1813, 1833.

Pentre-poeth see **Morganstown** (Cardiff)

Pentre-poeth SS 669986
Swansea (Llangyfelach)
'burnt village *or* farm': ***pentref***, ***poeth***
Pentrepoth 1764, *Pentre-poeth* 1832
poeth generally means 'hot' and might describe a settlement in a warm, sheltered location but it also seems to have developed the sense 'burnt'; cf. Tre-boeth. There are at least eight identical pns. in other parts of Wales. Pentre-poeth (SO 222848) at Llanfedw is recorded as *Pentrepoeth* 1721, *Pentra Poeth* 1795, *Pentre-poeth* 1833 and as *Twyn-yr-Hwch* 1841 and *Trwyn-yr-hwch* from 1875 on OS maps meaning 'the sow's nose' (***trwyn***, ***yr***, ***hwch***) probably from its location next to a wedge of land between the streams Nant Fawr and Nant Du.

Pentre'r Eglwys see **Church Village**

Pentre'rgaseg SS 676956
Swansea (Llansamlet)
'the mare's farm *or* settlement': ***pentref***, ***y***, ***caseg***
Pentre-gaseg 1830, *Pentregaseg* 1841, *Pentre'r-gaseg* 1879
Perhaps in the sense of 'settlement where horses are bred'.

Pentretân SN 623083
Swansea (Llandeilo Tal-y-bont)
'fire settlement, ?burnt settlement': ***pentref***, ***tân***
Pentretan 1890, *Pentre-tân* 1898
The pn. is not found on early OS maps or the census 1841. It now refers to an area around two hos. Ty-canol and Ty-draw (***tŷ***, ***canol***, ***draw***) next to former rough open pasture.

Pen-twyn[1] SO 104044
Caerphilly (Gelligaer)
'hillock top': ***pen***[1], ***twyn***
Pen y Twyn 1841, *Pen-tŵyn* 1880
One of the most common pns. in south Wales, often applied to single hos. The village developed along a road running up the side of Mynydd Fochriw to Gelligaer Common near a number of coal-pits, levels and quarries

immediately north of a ho. Ffynnonau-duon which is *Ffynnonau-dûon* 1833, *Fynonadyon* 1841: 'black, dark springs' (*ffynhonnau*, *duon*).

Pen-twyn[2]   SO 206005
Caerphilly (Mynyddislwyn Monmouthshire)
'hillock top': *pen*[1], *twyn*
Pentwyn 1813, 1833, *Pen-tŵyn* 1880
Cf. Pentwyn[1, 3].

Pen-twyn[3]   ST 206814
Cardiff (Llanedern)
'hillock top': *pen*[1], *twyn*
Pentwyn 1716, (ho.) *Pentwyn-isaf* 1833, *Pentoyn Farm* 1742, *Pen twyn* 1782
The n. of a Cardiff housing estate, with anglicised pron. 'Pent-wyn' [pɛnt wɪn] with even stress rather than [pɛnˈtʊɪn]. Drawn from the fm.n. Pentwyn-isaf known now as plain Pentwyn (ST 206813). The pn. is common in south Wales and local examples include (1) Pentwyn (St Georges-super-Ely) recorded as *Pentwyn Farm* 1808; (2) Pentwyn (St Mellons), Monmouthshire: *Pentwyn Farm* 1710, *Pen y Toyne* 1728, *Pentwyn* 1833; (3) Pentwyn (ST 098814 Pen-tyrch): *Pen y Toyne* 1677, *Pentwyn Evan Thomas* 1825, *Pentwyn* 1833; (4) Pentwyn (Upper Hamlet, Whitchurch) *Pentoin* 1788, *tir pentwyn* 1789.

Pentwynberth-lwyd   ST 101963
Merthyr Tudful (Llanfabon)
'hillock-top near Berthlwyd': *pen*[1], *twyn*, pn. **Berthlwyd**
Pentwyn Berthllwyd 1875
A small industrial village developed from the late 19th cent along Pentwyn Road above Berthllwyd expanding from the late 1970s to include an area formerly part of a ho. Ty-llwyd.

Pentwyn-mawr   ST 198964
Caerphilly (Mynyddislwyn Monmouthshire)
'big hillock-top': *pen*[1], *twyn*, *mawr*
Pentwyn mawr 1709, *Pentwyn Mawr* 1813, *Pentwyn-mawr* 1833
Distinguished from Pentwyn (ST 192969) recorded in 1833 and Pentwyn-isaf (ST 199972) which is *Pen-tŵyn-isaf* 1886 (*isaf*).

Pen-tyrch   ST 103817
Cardiff
?'(hill shaped like a) boar's head': *pen*[1]; *twrch* gen.sg. *tyrch*
penn tyrch 1129 (c.1170), *penntirch* c.1100 (c.1200), *Pentiry* 1254, *Pentirech* c.1262, *Pentirgh* 1281, *Pentirch* c.1348, 1668 *pen tyrch* c.1566, *Pentyrch* 1670
The n. could also mean 'hill of boars' since *tyrch* is also a pl. of *twrch* but, as Thomas Morgan noted, 'the similarity of the brow of Garth mountain … to a boar's head' (OPN 145) is striking. There are identical pns. in Carmarthenshire, Caernarfonshire, and Montgomeryshire and it has been suggested that they could refer to animal sacrifice (see Penarth and Penychen) but the topographical interpretation makes better sense here. Stress falls on the second syllable as confirmed in a late 19th cent triban (Trib 129).

Penyard see **Pen-iard** (Merthyr Tudful)

Pen-y-bont ar Ogwr see **Bridgend**

Pen y bryn[1]   ST 135962
Caerphilly (Gelligaer)
'top of the hill': *pen*[1], *y*, *bryn*
Penybryn Terrace 1919, *Pen-y-bryn* 1938
A housing estate which developed after World War I near the former Penalltau Colliery. Located on the site of a small fm. called Pen-yr-heol, 'top of the road' (*pen*[1], *yr*, *heol*) near a Roman road which runs northwards from Ystrad Mynach towards Gelligaer.

Pen-y-bryn[2]   SS 837846
Neath Port Talbot (Margam)
'top of the hill': *pen*[1], *y*, *bryn*
Pen y Bryn 1814, *Pen-y-bryn* 1833, *Penybryn* 1852
Pen-y-bryn-du (SS 832843) recorded in 1833 is on an adjoining rise also recalled in Bryn-du Uchaf (SS 834843) (*Brun-du* 1833, *Bryn-du-uchaf* 1876), Bryn-du Fawr (*Bryn-du-fawr* 1833) and Bryn-du Fach otherwise Bryn-du-isaf (SS 831839) (*Bryn-du-isaf* 1876, *Bryndu Fach* 1899) meaning 'black hill' (*du*, *uchaf*, *mawr*, *bach*[1], *isaf*).

Pen-y-cae[1] SS 907820
Bridgend (Coety)
'top of the field (*or* enclosure)': *pen*[1]*, y, cae*
(ho.) *Pen-y-cae* 1877
From a ho. (SS 903826) though the modern housing estate lies largely on what was formerly part of Pen-yr-allt, recorded as *Penyrallt* 1813 and *Pen-yr-allt* 1833, 'top of the wooded-slope', *pen*[1]*, yr, allt.*

Pen-y-cae[2] SS 775902
Neath Port Talbot (Margam)
'top of the field (*or* enclosure)': *pen*[1]*, y, cae*
Pen-y-cae 1877
Gwar-y-caeau (SS 775897) so spelt 1876 and as *Cwary caeau* 1833 is on a road on the south side of Pen-y-cae meaning 'above and behind the fields (*or* enclosures)', *gwar, y, caeau*. The 1833 spelling suggests association with *cwar*[1] 'quarry' but there is no such feature on OS maps.

Penychen
Rhondda Cynon Taf, Vale of Glamorgan
'oxen hill': *pen*[1]*, ychen*
pennichenn c.1145, *penichen, Penn echenn* c.1170, *Pennichen* c.1200, *Penheken* c.1236, *Penhechen* c.1239, *cantref Penychen* early 13th cent
The occurrence of *pen*[1] with animal names has led to the suggestion that some refer to totemistic cults (ETG 57); see also Penarth and Pen-tyrch. No specific hill of Penychen has so far been identfied. The n. referred to a cantref covering the commotes and lps. of Clown, Glynrhondda, Meisgyn, Rhuthin and Tal-y-fan, and at an earlier date the whole of Dinas Powys hundred. Penychen has also been identified with *Penn-Ohen, latina autem Caput dicitur Boum* ('written in Latin as ox head') which was the original home of St Paul Aurelian (6th cent) in his reputed 'Life' c.884. Paul was founder of the bishopric of Saint-Pol-de-Léon, in Brittany.

Penycoedcae ST 060877
Rhondda Cynon Taf (Llantwit Fardre)
'top of land enclosed by a hedge': *pen*[1]*, y, coedcae*
Pencoedca 1799, (hill) *Pen y Coed-cae,* (ho.) *Pen Coed-cae* 1833, *Pen-coedcae* 1875
Perhaps a specific ref. to the ho. Coedcae-du (ST 061869) recorded as *Coed-cae* 1833 and *Coedcae-du* 1875 meaning 'dark land enclosed by a hedge' (*du*). The village developed in the late 19th and early 20th cent near a coal-mine and quarries. Identical in meaning to Penycoedcae (at Merthyr Tudful) recorded as *Pen y Coed kae* 1757, *Pen y Coed Cae* 1783, *Pen y Coedca* 1795.

Penydarren SO 056072
Merthyr Tudful
'top of the rock': *pen*[1]*, y, tarren*
Pen y darren or otherwise Ton y ffald 1736, *Pen e Darren, Pen y darren* 1757, *Penydarran* 1788, *Pen y darren Iron Works* 1833
The n. applied to land and a tmt. earlier recorded as Ton-y-ffald including *tonnefalde* 1426 and *Tir Ton y Ffald* 1540, meaning 'layland at the fold' (*ton*[2]*, y, ffald*). The ht. developed around the Penydarren Ironworks. Identical pns. have been noted in Gelligaer, Llan-giwg and Llanwynno.

Pen-y-dre SN 694022
Swansea (Llangyfelach)
'top of the town': *pen*[1]*, y, tref*
(road) *Penydre* 1938, (hos.) *Penydre* 1961
A relatively recent n. for a small, mainly post-War II housing estate above Clydach and Faerdre.

Pen-y-fai SS 894820
Bridgend (Newcastle)
?'head (*or* end) of the plain': *pen*[1]*, y, ma-, mai*
(land) *Penuain, Penuei* late 12th cent, *Penvei* 1202, *Penuey* 1261, *Penvey* 1518, *Penyvai* 1591, *Penevay* 1638, *Penyvay* 1774, *Pen-y-fai* 1778
This interpretation suits the topography although the pn. also translates as 'chief plain' or 'hill of the plain'. The el. *mai, fai* is probably also found in Myddfai, Carmarthenshire, 'bowl-shaped flat place', with *mydd* 'vessel, large bowl' (DPNW 331). Comparable pns. have been identified elsewhere such as the unlocated †*Penn iuei, Penuei* c.1170, on the borders of Breconshire and Herefordshire, and

†*Penvey* 1214, probably in Carmarthenshire (EANC 31). See also Paviland.

Pen-y-garn ST 099822
Cardiff (Pen-tyrch)
'top of the cairn': ***pen***[1], ***y***, ***carn***
(*syddyn*) *tir pen y garn* c.1612, *Penygarn farm* 1803, *Pen-y-garn* 1833, *Penygarn* 1852
Named from a former fm. (ST 100821). The cairn may have been at nearby *Carreg* 1811 (***carreg*** 'a stone'). A common pn., identical to Pen-y-garn (ST 048876), near Llantrisant, which is *Penygarne* 1629, *Pen y garn* 1768, and Pen-y-garn (SN 721072), in Llan-giwg, recorded as *Penygarn* 1711 and *Pen-y-garn* 1884 near Carn Llwyd, 'grey (*or* holy) cairn' (***carn***, ***llwyd***). The first form has *syddyn* nm. 'tenement; dwelling-place'.

Pen-y-garn-ddu SO 074088
Merthyr Tudful
'top of the black cairn', ***pen***[1], ***y***, ***carn***, ***du***
Penygarnddu 1813, *Pen-y-garn-dû* 1832, *Pengarnddu* 1873, *Pen-y-garn-ddû* 1891
The form *Pengarnddu* on OS maps since c.1968 displays the tendency to lose an unstressed def. art; cf. Blaen-cwm (q.v.).

Pen-y-graig SS 998915
Rhondda Cynon Taf (Llantrisant, Ystradyfodwg)
'top of the rock': ***pen***[1], ***y***, ***craig***
(ho.) *Pen y graig* 1833, *Penygraig* 1845, ~ , *Penygraig Colliery* 1875, *Pen-y-graig* 1885
The ho. (SS 993911) also gave its n. to a colliery sunk in 1858. Identical pns. in Glamorgan include Pen-y-graig (Llandyfodwg) recorded as (cottage) *Ty pen y Craig* 1762 and Pen-y-graig (formerly ST 091935. Llanfabon) which is *Pen y Graige* 1783 and *Pen y Graig* 1784. The actual ht. occupies the site of a former ho. Ffrwdamos recorded as *Ffrwd damos* 1811, *Ffrwd-amws* 1833, *Frwd Amos* 1845, named from a stream Nant Ffrwdamws meaning 'horse stream' or figuratively for a 'stream which jumps and darts like a horse' (***ffrwd***, *amws* 'steed, horse'). The n. survives in the street names Ffrwd Amos Cottages and Amos Hill.

Pen-y-graig-wen ST 067908
Rhondda Cynon Taf (Llanwynno)
'top of Y Graig-wen': ***pen***[1], pn. *Y Graig-wen*
(ho.) *Pen y Graigwen* 1841, *Pengraig Wen* 1852, *Pen-y-graig-wen* 1874
See Graig-wen. The n. is also recorded in translation in the modern street names Whiterock Avenue, ~ Drive, ~ Close. The housing estate was largely built in the late 1960s and 1970s.

Pen-y-lan[1] (Penylan) ST 196787
Cardiff (Roath)
'top of the bank': ***pen***[1], ***y***, ***glan***
Pen-y-Lan 1702, (ho.) *Penylan* 1799, *Pen-y-lan* 1833
A ho.n. transferred to the suburb occupying the slopes between Roath and Cyncoed above Roath Brook/Nant y Rhath built mainly after World War I.

Pen-y-lan[2] SS 999768
Vale of Glamorgan (Llanblethian)
'top of the bank', ***pen***[1], ***y***, ***glan***
Penallan 1731, *Penylan* 1813, *Pen-y-lan* 1833
Located on a low hill on the edge of Llanblethian p. near Llansanwyr. A very common minor pn.; note Pen-y-lan (ST 139747, in Caerau) recorded as *Penyrlan* 1762, *Pen y lan* 1767, *Pen-y-lan* 1833, and Pen-y-lan (in Upper Hamlet, Whitchurch) which is *Penelan* 1541, *Pen y lan* 1699.

Penyrenglyn SS 944980
Rhondda Cynon Taf (Ystradyfodwg)
'top of the ?deep valley': ***pen***[2], ***yr***, *****englyn***
Pen-yr-englyn 1833, *Penrewglyn* 1841, *Penyrenglyn* 1869
englyn is a conjectural compound of the intensifying prefix *an-* and ***glyn*** 'a valley' and is unrelated to *englyn* nm. describing a stanza in poetry. The village is named from a former ho. and developed above Ynys-feio Colliery in the mid 19th cent.

Penyrheol[1] SS 921825
Bridgend (Coety)
'top of the road': ***pen***[1], ***yr***, ***heol***
Pen-yr-heol 1833, 1877, *Penyrheol* 1841

The road is Heol Spencer recorded 1841 which runs northwards from Coety to Bryncethin. The surname Spencer is recorded in St Athan, Llantwit Major and other parts of the Vale in 1670.

Penyrheol[2]   ST 140880
Caerphilly (Eglwysilan)
'top of the road': ***pen***, ***yr***, ***heol***
Pen yr heol 1767, *Pen-yr-heol* 1878
Located at the top of what is now St Cenydd Road where it meets the B4263 at Bowls Inn. There was a ho. a little to the north (approx. ST 138886) recorded as *Penyrheoldu* 1813 and nearby Penyrheol-las (ST 141897) is *pen r heol Lase* 1795, *Penyrheollas* 1813, *Pen-yr-heol-las* 1833, respectively on 'dark road' (***du***, ***ddu***), now Bowls Lane, and 'green road' (***glas***[1], ***las***). Heol Las is on the supposed line of the Roman road running north from Caerphilly to Gelligaer.

Penyrheol[3]   SS 722967
Neath Port Talbot (Cadoxton-juxta-Neath)
'top of the road': ***pen***[1], ***yr***, ***heol***
Penerhewl 1799, *Pen-yr-heol* 1830, (hos.) *Pen-yr-heol* 1918
The nucleus was a row of hos. developed from the late 1890s on Burrows Road a little to the north of a former smithy and ho. (SS 722964) recorded in 1830. Nearby Penyralley Avenue is named from a distinct place recorded as *Pen'r Alley* 1771, *Pen-yr-alley* 1830, 1919, *Pen-yr-aly* 1877-81, 'head of the narrow street' (***pen***[1], ***yr***, ***alai*** nf. 'narrow street, alley').

Penyrheol[4]   SS 585995
Swansea (Llandeilo Tal-y-bont)
'top of the road': ***pen***[1], ***yr***, ***heol***
Pen yr heol 1760, *Pen-'r-heol* 1830, *Pen-yr-heol* 1877, *Penrheol* 1901
Named from a ho. (SS 582998) at the junction of Llannant Road, Pencefnarda Road and Penyrheol Road. The ht. developed from the late 19th cent near several small collieries and now covers the area of Pencefnarda-uchaf recorded as *Pen-cefn-arda-uchaf* 1877 and Pencefnarda-isaf recorded as *Pen-cefn-arda*

1830 and *Pen-cefn-arda-isaf* 1877: 'top of the hill ridge' (***pen***[1], ***cefn***, ***ardd***[1] pl. ***arddau***, ***uchaf***, ***isaf***).

Penyrheol[5]   SS 620931
Swansea (Swansea)
'top of the road', ***pen***[1], ***yr***, ***heol***
Pen yr heol 1650, *Penyrheol, Penrheol* 1852, *Pen-yr-heol* 1879
On Gower Road near Sketty.

Penyrheolgerrig see **Heolgerrig**

Pen-y-waun   SN 977046
Rhondda Cynon Taf (Aberdare)
'top (*or* end) of the moorland': ***pen***[1], ***y***, ***gwaun***
Pen-y-waun 1833, *Pen-y-wain* 1841
See CVPN 75-6. The earliest cottages of the ht. were built on Gamlyn Isaf fm. on the top part of Gwaun Uchaf recorded as *Wain Ychaf* 1844, 'upper moor' (***uchaf***) recalled in Hirwaun. Identical pns. include Pen-y-waun (ST 124945, in Llanfabon) recorded as *Pen y wain* 1783, *Pen-waun* 1833 and there are other examples in Llan-giwg, Llangyfelach and Roath.

Pen-y-wern   SO 068084
Merthyr Tudful
'top of the alder-tree marsh': ***pen***[1], ***y***, ***gwern***
Penywern 1852, *Pen-y-wern* 1891
gwern is recalled in nearby Gwernllwyn Uchaf, ~ Isaf recorded as *Gwernllwyn uchaf*, ~ *isaf* 1814, 'upper' and 'lower' (***uchaf***, ***isaf***). The n. originally applied to the hos. of Upper and Lower Row, later including Barrack Row.

Persondy   ST 220955
Caerphilly (Mynyddislwyn Monmouthshire)
'parson's house', ***person***, ***tŷ***
(ho.) *Persondy* 1879, *the Persondy* 1886
A n. transferred from the ho. to a housing estate built in the 1950s. The ho. was built for the minister of the former ch. ('Lady Llanover's Church') built by Lord and Lady Llanover in 1853 serving as a chapel-of-ease to Mynyddislwyn (CofiantCE 49-50). Lord Llanover, who was keen to see that the W language was properly defended in the p., objected to the proposal by the vicar of

Mynyddislwyn that the ch. should provide E services. In 1863 Llanover appointed a Calvinistic Methodist minister to serve the ch. on condition that he should use the liturgy of the Church of England. The ch. is generally recorded as Presbyterian or Welsh Presbyterian reflecting its administration by the Presbyterian Church of Wales.

Pergwm see **Aberpergwm**

Perthgelyn (Perthcelyn)   ST 053975
Rhondda Cynon Taf (Llanwynno)
'holly bush': ***perth***, ***celyn***[1]
(fm.) *Llan-uchaf Perth-celyn* 1833, *Perthgelin, Berthcelyn* 1841, *Perthcelyn* 1842, *Perthgelyn* 1876
Named from a ho. (ST 053972). Forms alternate between *Perthgelyn* and *Perthcelyn* which reflects local dialect. The ho. bore the alternative n. recorded as *Lanuchaf* 1814 as well as that cited for 1833 probably containing ***glan***, *lan*, and ***uchaf*** in the general sense of 'upper slope (*or* bank)'.

Peterston-super-Ely, **Llanbedr-y-fro**
ST 083764
Vale of Glamorgan
'settlement of Peter on the (r.) Ely/Elái': pers.n. *Peter*, OE ***tūn***, Lat ***super***, rn. **Ely**; 'church of Peter in the Vale', ***llan***, pers.n. ***Pedr***, terr.n. *Y Fro*
(ch. of) *Sancti Petri* 1254, *Pet(er)ston* c.1291, *Peterston* c.1348, (ch. of) *S'ti Petri sup' Elly* 1535, *Llanpeder* c.1538, *Petirston super Eley* 1556, *Llanbeder y uro* 1578, *Peterston upon Ely* c.1598, *LL bedr y fro* 1606, *Peterston: ond yr enw Cymraeg yw Llanbedr-ar-y-fro* 1778, *llanbedrfro* 1818, *Peterston-sup*^r*.-Ely or Llanbad arfro* 1833
For *Y Fro* see Vale of Glamorgan. The ch. is dedicated to St Peter but Peterston is said to recall Peter le Sor, one of the reputed Norman conquerors of Glamorgan (HMorg 306). Peter allegedly built a castle here c.1100. Nothing of this can be substantiated though there was certainly a le Sore family at St Fagans mid-late 12th cent. If Llanbedr is the older n. then its absence in early sources is curious (contrast Peterston-super-montem), even allowing for their bias towards E and anglicised sps. This leaves open the possibility that a secular Peter has given rise to both the ch. dedication and the W pn. There are certainly instances in Glamorgan where a secular pers.n. has inspired ecclesiastical dedications, eg. Gileston (ETG 136).

Peterston-super-montem, **Llanbedr-ar-fynydd**   SS 994853
Rhondda Cynon Taf
'settlement of Peter on the mountain': pers.n. *Peter*: OE ***tūn***, Lat ***super***, ***mons***; 'church of (St) Peter on the mountain': ***llan***, pers.n. ***Pedr***, ***ar***, ***mynydd***
Lamped(er) in Cumtioch 1208, *Lampered* c.1291, *llambett ar Menedd, in English Lambete upon the hill* c.1598, *Lanbeder ar vynidd* 1637, *Peterston upin the Mountin* 1640, *Peterstone hill* 1672, *Peterston-super-montem or Capel Llanbad, Llambad fach* 1785, *Llanbedr-ar-Fynydd* 1874
This is probably also Llanbedr Uchaf recorded as *Llanbed-ucha* in a 19th cent triban (Trib 21). *Llanbad, Llambad* are colloquial forms exhibiting interchange of *n* and *m* before *b*, also recorded in historic forms for other places in Wales called Llanbedr, eg. Llanbedr Pont Steffan alias Lampeter, Cardiganshire, familiarly known as 'Llambed' (DPNW 209). Peterston appears to be a late translation and is generally qualified in earlier sources as 'upon the Mountain', 'upon the Hill' and similar forms. *Cumtioch* 1208 stands for *Cumcioch* which is Cwm Ciwg found as *Cwm-ciwc-uchaf, ~ -isaf, Felin Ciwc* 1833 (***cwm***, ***melin***) referring to the r. Ciwg, a tributary of Ewenni. The ch. ruins lie on the south slopes of Mynydd Maendy above the fms. Llanbad Fawr and Llanbad Fach distinguished as 'big' and 'little' (***mawr***, ***bach***[1]).

Phillip's Town   SO 145035
Caerphilly (Bedwellte Monmouthshire)
'settlement named from Phillips': surname *Phillips*, ***town***
Phillipstown 1908, *Phillip's Town* 1919

Part of New Tredegar, largely built by the Powell Duffryn Co., on land belonging to Cefnrhychdir and named from Nehemiah Phillips (1845-1929), colliery manager, county councillor and active Baptist preacher (MCPP 68); cf. Elliot's Town.

Picketston ST 001697
Vale of Glamorgan (Llan-maes)
'settlement of Picket': surname *Picket*, ME *–ton*
Pykkerston Weye 1541, *Peckstone* 1561, *Pyckedston* 1617, *Pickitston* 1626, *Picketston* c.1659, *Pickettstone* c.1670
A Walter Piket is connected with Llandough (Penarth) 13th cent; the surname may also occur in Picket (SS 931732) in St Andrews Major recorded as *Pickettshill* 1637 and *Picket hill farme* 1691 (PNDPH 232).

Pîl see **Pyle**

Pilton Green SS 4444871
Swansea (Penrhys)
'green near Pilton': pn. *Pilton*, E *green*
Pillton Green, *Easter Pilton Green* 1632, *Pilton Green* 1820
From its proximity to two hos. West and East Pilton (SS 440871) recorded as *Pyltoune* 1306, *Pylton'*, *Pilton'* 1332, *east ~*, *west Pilton* 1574 and *Wester ~*, *Easter Pilton* 1632. The second el. is ME *-ton* 'settlement' but the first is uncertain. OE *pyll*, E *pill* 'tidal creek, pool, stream' is unlikely because there is no stream of any significance here. There is a very small stream at Pylewell but this flows northeastwards to Monkland (SS 459878), Scurlage Castle and Knelston and is quite untypical of a *pill*. The main alternatives are an OE pers.n. *Pil(a)* as in Pilham, Lincolnshire, or more likely OE *pīl* 'pile, pointed stick, stake' (as Pyle q.v.) and *tūn*.

Pitcot SS 896744
Vale of Glamorgan
'cottage (*or* shelter) near a pit': OE *pytt*, OE *cot*
Pitcota c.1260, *Putcote* 1361, *Pyttcot* c.1598, *Putcoed*, *Pyttcoed* 1631, *Pittcott* 1635
Forms such as *Pitcoyd* 1586 and those for 1631 show association with *coed* 'trees, a wood'.

Pitton SS 427877
Swansea (Rhosili)
'settlement near a pit': OE *pytt*, *tūn*
(*villa de*) *Picton'* 1396, *Pytton* 1459, *Pitton* 1511, *~ otherwise Pilton* 1764, *Pitton*, *~ Cross* 1813, *Pitton*, *Great Pitton* 1832
The 1396 form is unmatched and is probably a scribal error for *Pitton'*. The ht. is in a hollow adjoining a small stream. A number of sources confuse Pitton with Pilton (see Pilton Green above), no doubt because of their close proximity and similar form.

Plas-marl SS 663964
Swansea (Llangyfelach)
'house (*or* place) where marl was made': *plas*, *(y) marl*
Place y Marl, *-e* 1764, *Plas y Marl* 1786, *Plase y marl* 1841, *Plas Marl*, *Plas-marl Pit* 1881
Two lime-kilns are recorded here in 1764 (SGOW 162). Old lime-kilns also appear on late 19th cent OS maps of the area. Marl was a mix of lime and sand or clay which could be burnt and refined for use in industry such as lime mortar and bricks and in agriculture for de-acidifying and fertilising soil.

† Poitevin Land (lost) ?SS 7981
Bridgend
'land held by (man or family called) Peitevin': pers.n. or family n. *Poitevin*, E *land*
(fee) *Peiteuin* c.1197, *Terra Peyteuin* late 12th cent, (land) *Peitevin* 1208, (fee) *Peittevin in territorio de Kenefeh* late 13th cent
A grange of the Cistercian monastery of Margam abbey apparently lost under the shifting sands of Kenfig Burrows. The same n. is found in Peutyn, Breconshire, recalled in several hos. Peutyn-du, Peutyn-glas and Peutyn-gwyn (SO 0331, 0431), one of which is recorded as *Peytevenescastel* 1373 and *Peytevenescastell* 1522 (PNBrec 129-30). It may be significant that Kirkstall abbey, Yorkshire – also a Cistercian ho. – was established on land of a William de Poitou in 1152.

Pontardawe SN 722041
Neath Port Talbot (Llan-giwg/Llangyfelach)
'bridge on (r.) Tawe': *pont*, *ar*, rn. **Tawe**

(tmt.) *Tir penybont ardawe* 1584, *Ty pen y bont ar y Tawey* 1675, *Pontardawey* 1711, *Pont ar Dawye* 1729, *Pontardawe* 1799, *Pont-ar-dawe* 1832
Early sps. suggest that it derives from a ho. either *Tŷ'r* ~ or *Tir Pen-y-bont*, 'land ~' or 'house near head of the bridge': *tir*, *tŷ*, *y*, `*r* (ETG 54; ADG², 82). Local pron. is represented in sps. for 1711 and 1729.

Pontarddulais　　　　　　　　SN 592036
Swansea (Llandeilo Tal-y-bont/Llanedi)
'bridge on (r.) Dulais': *pont*, *ar* displacing *aber*, rn. *Dulais*
(*Lanedi nigh*) *Brige end* 1550, *Pen y bont aber Duleis* 1550, *Ponte artheleys* 1557, (place) *Bridge end* 1589, *Penybont ar ddylays* c.1670, *Pontardilash* 1674, *Pont ar Ddylais* 1765, *Pontardulais* 1740, *Pont-ar-dulais* 1832
The old village (SN 587038) is located in Llanedi, Carmarthenshire, next to a bridge Y Bont Fawr (*mawr*) over Afon Llwchwr but Pontarddulais is now more prominently applied on maps to the large village on the eastern side of Llwchwr in Glamorgan extending along the Dulais valley and the road leading towards Swansea. Pontarddulais is now the favoured official form which is based on the supposition that the pn. contains the prep. *ar* 'on' which causes len. of Dulais to *-ddulais*. This is actually a contraction, as Deric John has shown (PNBont 18-23), of an earlier Pen-y-bont Aberdulais, '(place at the) end of the bridge in Aberdulais'; *aber* refers to the area around the confluence of Dulais and Llwchwr just below the bridge.

Pontbren-llwyd　　　　　　　　SN 950080
Rhondda Cynon Taf (Penderyn Breconshire)
'grey foot-bridge': *pontbren*, *llwyd*
Pontpren Llwyd 1799, *Pontprenllwyd* 1814, *Pont-pren-llwyd* 1833, *Pontbren*, *Pontbrenllwyd* 1852
pontbren is the usual form of *pompren* in Glamorgan. The n. refers to a small bridge adjoining a ford over Nant Cadlan below Penderyn. There is an identical pn. (SN 654003) near Llangyfelach recorded as *Pontprenllwyd* 1720, *Pont-bren-llwyd* 1830 and *Pontbren-llwyd* 1884 over Afon Llan.

Pontcanna　　　　　　　　ST 167773
Cardiff (Llandaf)
'bridge of Canna': *pont*, pers.n. or rn. *Canna*
bridge of Canne 1559, *Pontganne* 1690, *Pontganna* 1703, 1853, *Pont Canna* 1761
Canna could refer to a small stream, marking a ward boundary in 1880, traceable in property boundaries running south from the location of the former bridge near the junction of Mortimer Road and Cathedral Road and along the line of Wyndham Road and Wyndham Crescent to Cowbridge Road where its course is obscured by housing. The main objection to this suggestion is that this stream is not actually named Canna in historical sources. Such a n. might plausibly contain the el. found in *cannu* 'to whiten, to bleach' (see Abercannaid) but this would be more appropriate to a mountain stream white with foam than a small, meandering brook on the floodplain of the r. Taf. It is more likely that the n. simply describes a bridge belonging to or associated with the same person recalled in Canton (q.v.) – about a mile away – or that the n. is employed elliptically for 'bridge near Canton'.

Pontcynon　　　　　　　　ST 076957
Rhondda Cynon Taf (Llanwynno)
'bridge on (r.) Cynon': *pont*, rn. **Cynon**
Pontgynon 1750, *Pont-Cynnon alias Cynnon Bridge* 1758, *Pont Cynon* 1799, *Pont-cynon* 1833
See Cynon. Also the n. of a ho. north of the r.

Pontllan-fraith　　　　　　　　ST 180959
Caerphilly (Mynyddislwyn Monmouthshire)
'bridge by the speckled pool': *pont*, *llyn*, *braith*
tir penybont llynvraith 1492, *tre penbont* 1502, *Pont llynfraith* 1713, *Pont lanfraith* 1782, *Pont Llanfraith* 1813, *Pont llanvraith* 1814, *Pont Lanfraith* 1833
llyn is generally a nm. but it is clearly a nf. here; cf. Llyn Fawr (*mawr*). The bridge crosses the r. Sirhywi. The first sps. stand for *Tir Pen-y-bont* 'land at the end of the bridge' (*tir*, *pen*, *y*, *pont*). Later forms misassociate *llyn* with *llan* 'church'.

Pont-lliw SN 610012
Swansea (Llandeilo Tal-y-bont/Llangyfelach)
'bridge on (r.) Lliw': *pont*, rn. **Lliw**
(bridge) *Pont-llew* 1698, *Llue bridge, Llue vill and Mill* 1729, *Llew Bridge* 1792, *Pont-lliw* 1832
Pont-lliw developed around the bridge, a flour mill recorded as *Melin llyw* 1650 (**melin**) and along the Swansea to Pontarddulais road in the 19th cent, expanding with the construction of housing estates after 1950.

Pontlotyn (Pontlottyn) SO 116061
Caerphilly (Gelligaer)
?'wide bridge', *pont*, ?*llydan* or 'pauper's bridge', *tlotyn*
Pont Lydan 1729, 1754, *Pont lottyn* 1813, *Pont Lottin Farm* 1824, *Pont y lotyn* 1833, *Pontlotyn* 1851, *Pontlottyn* 1885
'wide bridge' is possible since local dialect typically unvoices -*d*- as –*t*-; cf. Brynllydan (Llantwit Fardre) recorded as *Bryn Llutan* 1776 as well as *y bryn Llydann* early 17th cent and *Bryn Llyddon* 1778, 'wide, broad hill' (**bryn**). It is, however, difficult to explain the change of vowel -*y*- [ə] to –*o*- [ɔ] and there are further doubts with this explanation since the second historic form *Pont Lydan* is taken from Thomas Kitchin's map 1754 which derives some of its pn. details from Bowen's map 1729 and may be repeating an inaccurate form. Later forms favour *tlotyn* but more evidence is needed. Dafydd Morganwg (HMorg 450) states that when the Bute ironworks were opened, two small villages were built here called Sodom and Gomorrah, the first applying to hos. built between Heol Ifan Wyn and the ironworks and the second to hos. on both sides of the road. Dafydd adds that the names were dropped c.1860 because an influx of Irish people led to them being associated with the evils of the biblical Sodom and Gomorrah (*Gomorah* 1857), a prejudice reinforced through association with the biblical Lot (DPNW 390). The two names remained in informal (and pejorative) use at least as late as 1918. Sodom and Gomorrah are also said to have been unofficial names for Ruspidge and Soudley, Gloucestershire. Similar pns. are recorded elsewhere, notably Sodom (in Caerwys), Flintshire (PNF 176).

Pontmorlais SO 052065
Merthyr Tudful
'bridge over (r.) Morlais': *pont*, rn. **Morlais**
Pontforlas 1799, *Pont morlais* 1820, *Pontmorlais* 1852
Sometimes lenited as Pontforlais. Two cottages here are recorded as *Ty Pont forlaish* 1779 (*tŷ*) with dialect –sh [ʃ] for –s.

Pontneddfechan (Pontneathvaughan)
SN 901076
Neath Port Talbot (Cadoxton-juxta-Neath/Ystradgynlais)
'bridge on Nedd Fechan': *pont*, rn. **Nedd, bechan**
Pont Neath Vechan 1617, *Pont Neath vychan* 1666, *Pont Nedd Fychan* 1765, *Pont neath vechan* 1782-5, *Pontneathvaughan* 1805, *Pont Neath Vaughan, or Pont ar Nedd Fechan, i.e. the Bridge over the lesser Neath* 1813, *Pontneath Vaughan* 1831, *Pontneddfechan* 1875
The village is partly in Breconshire, now Powys. Sps. with *Vuchan, vychan*, and *Fychan* show that **bechan** alternated with the masc. form **bychan**, *fychan*. Many E-only speakers pronounce the third el. 'vawn' [vɔːn] as if it were the surname Vaughan. This has probably arisen through re-interpretation of forms such as that for 1805 which is an anglicisation of *Pontneddfychan*. This tendency may have been reinforced through awareness that the surname Vaughan was an anglicisation of the epithet Fychan ('the lesser').

Pontprennau approx. ST 215823
Cardiff (Llanedern)
'footbridges': *pontbrenni*
Pontprenny 1735, *Pont preny, Pontbrenni Farm* 1767, *Pontprenay* 1782, *Pont y Prenny* 1788
Sps. with the variant pl. –*au* first appear in 1833. The bridges crossed Nant Pontprennau, a small tributary of Rhymni. The area is now a large housing estate begun in the late 1990s.

Pont-rhyd-y-cyff SS 868889
Bridgend (Betws/Llangynwyd)
'bridge at the ford near the stump': ***pont, rhyd, y, cyff***
Pontrhydycyff 1797, *Pont-rhydd-y-cyff* 1833, *Pontrhydycuff* 1841, *Pont Rhyd-y-cyff* 1884
A bridge over the r. Llynfi presumably replacing a ford identified by its location near a prominent tree stump.

Pont-rhyd-y-fen SS 795940
Neath Port Talbot (Baglan/Michaelston-super-Avan)
'bridge at the ford used by wagons': ***pont, rhyd, y, ben***[1]
Ryd y venn c.1470, (bridge) *Ponte Retheuenne, the forde of the Waine* c.1538, *Tir pont rydyven* 1601, (bridge) *Rydyfen* c.1670, (~) *Pont Rhyd y ven* 1714, *Tyr Pen Pont Rhyd y Ven* 1756, *Pontrhydefen* 1813, *Pont-rhyd-fen* 1832
See ADG², 82. The 1601 and 1756 sps. suggest a tmt. or holding of land (*tir*) near the bridge. The village developed around the Pontrhydyfen Ironworks and other metal works from 1824.

Pont-Shôn-Norton ST 083912
Rhondda Cynon Taf (Eglwysilan)
'Shôn Norton's bridge': ***pont***, pers.n. *Shôn* variant spelling of *Siôn*, surname *Norton*
Pont-shon-norton 1862, *Pont Shon Norton* 1868, *Pont-Shon-Norton* 1875, *Pontshonnorton* 1894
The bridge (approx. ST 084914) crossed the Glamorganshire Canal and was removed during the construction of the A483 dual carriageway. Shôn Norton does not seem to have been identified. The village developed along the Merthyr Tudful road in the mid 19th cent.

Pontsticill SO 055112
Merthyr Tudful (Faenor Breconshire)
'bridge at the stile': ***pont, sticill***
(mess.) *Tire pen Pont Stickill* c.1663, (land) *Tir y Nieadd alias Tir pen Pontstickill* 1694, *Pont Stickel* 1729, *Ponty Stikill* 1799, *Pont-y-stickyll, a bridge of one arch* 1807, *Pont-sticcill* 1832
Local pron. is [pɔnt 'stɪcīl, ~ stɪcl]. The bridge (SO 059115) crosses Taf Fechan but the n. has shifted up the hill to the area around the Butcher's Arms public ho.

Pontwalby SN 890066
Neath Port Talbot (Glyncorrwg/Llantwit-juxta-Neath/Ystradyfodwg)
'bridge of (person called) Walby': ***pont***, *Walby*
Pont Walby 1833, *Pontwalby* 1835, *Pontwalby, -whalby* 1841, *Pontwhalby* 1872
Reputedly named from a John Walbeof who drowned here (VNeath 349) in the r. Neath/Nedd. Walby, found elsewhere in south Wales, may derive from an AN pers.n Waldboeuf (SW 218). A John Waldboeuf held two fees in the adj. lp. of Brecknock in 1299 and a namesake was receiver of Hay and Huntington 1499-1501 and receiver of the lp. of Brecknock 1503 although there is no proof of any direct connection between these two men and Pontwalby. Walby has also been associated with the legendary Moll Walbee, almost certainly a ref. to Maud de St Valéry (c.1155-1210), Lady of Bramber and wife of William de Breos, lord of Brecknock. Maud – or Matilda – is known to have successfully defended Painscastle, in Radnorshire, against a W siege in 1196. John Leland the antiquarian gives her n. as *Malt Walbere* in c.1538. The bridge over the r. Neath is recorded in 1800.

Pont-y-clun (Pontyclun) ST 035813
Rhondda Cynon Taf (Llantrisant)
'bridge of (r.) Clun': ***pont, y***, rn. *Clun*
(wooden bridge) *Pont Gloun* c.1538, *Pont y Clown* c.1700, *Pont Llwyn, Pont y Llwyn R.* 1729, *Pont Clown* 1768, *Pont-clun* 1833, *Pontclown, ~ Vach* 1841, *Pontyclun* 1895, *Pont-y-clun* 1899
y [ə] may be intrusive, formed between *t* and *c* in rapid speech. The bridge (ST 036819) crosses the r. just above its junction with the r. Ely/Eláí. The village developed around Llantrisant railway station. Clun or Clown was the n. of the adjoining manor recorded as *Cloune* 1281, 1375, *Clune* c.1405, *Clonne* 1401, *ỳ Arglwyddiaeth Clwnn* c.1612, (park of) *Cloon(e), ~ Clon* c.1670, *Clunn (in Welsh Clown)* c.1700. The rn. is probably derived from a Brit rn. *Colaunā, of obscure meaning, and may be

identical to Clun, Shropshire (PNSHR I, 91-2), which has many similar historic sps. but is now pronounced [klʌn]. The form Pont-y-clun was adopted c.1894 under the mistaken supposition that the pn. contains *clun²* [kli:n] 'meadow'.

Pontycymer (Pontycymmer)　　SS 904914
Bridgend (Betws/Llangeinwyr)
'bridge at river confluence', ***pont***, ***y***, ***cymer¹***
Pont y Cymmer 1719, *Pontycymer* 1881, (bridge) *Pont y Cymmer*, (village) *Pont-y-cymmer* 1884
Located near Braichycymer (SS 903909) recorded as *Bray Ykynner* 1541, *Braighe y Kymer* 1589, *Braich-y-cymmer* 1786, close to the meeting point of r. Garw and Nant Gelli-wern next to the bridge (SS 904914). This has *braich* nf. 'arm' probably referring to the narrow hill between them. Identical in meaning to Pontycymer (ST 026914) in Llanwynno (see Cymer, Rhondda) and Pont y Cymer (ST 219917), a bridge over r. Ebbw/Ebwy at Crosskeys, recorded as *Pont y Cymmar* 1707, *Pontacymer* 1710 and *Pont y Cymmer* 1813.

Pont-y-gwaith　　ST 010940
Rhondda Cynon Taf (Llanwynno/
Ystradyfodwg)
'bridge at the works': ***pont***, ***y***, ***gwaith¹***
Pont y Gwaith 1729, *Pontygwaith* 1833, *Pont-y-Gwaith, Bridgend Inn* 1885
Ironworks are recorded here c.1850 by Dafydd Morganwg (HMorg 283). The historian Glanffrwd adds that Pontygwaith Inn was located where the Llanwynno-Ystradyfodwg road crossed the r. Rhondda. There was an identical pn. (ST 080976) near Quakers Yard recorded as *Pont y gwaith ... from an iron work formerly there* c.1700, *Pont y Gwaith* 1754, in ref. to an old ironworks, attributed to the activities of Anthony Morley temp. Elizabeth I.

Pontymister　　ST 239902
Caerphilly (Machen and Rhisga
Monmouthshire)
'bridge of the ?monastery': ***pont***, ***y***, ***?mystwyr***, *mystwr*
master myll 1581, *Pont y Maister* 1624, (bridge) *Pont y mistir* 1625, *Pont y Myster* 1630, *Maister bridge* 1635, *pont y Maister* 1671, *Pont y Mister* 1805, *Pontymeistyr* 1813, *Pont-y-Meistr* 1833, *Pontymister* 1859
Gwynedd Pierce (ADG¹, 88) suggests that this contains ***mystwyr*** as in Coedymwstwr. Pontymister fm. is thought to have been the location of a grange and water mill of Llantarnam abbey (ST 242898) recorded as *Maister Kanvawr* 1204 (possibly with a pers.n. *Cynfor*) and *Mayst'* (= *Mayster*) c.1291. The difficulty is that very few historic sps. show clear similarities with other pns. thought to contain this el.; most forms favour *maestir*, variant *meistir* 'open land, plain'. Pontymister, however, is not in open countryside but in a valley (of the r. Ebwy) and though the el. could apply to that area where the valley broadens (occupied by the modern industrial village of Rhisga), it is possible that *maestir* etc was substituted at an early date for the less familiar *mystwyr*. The n. has also been interpreted as '(iron)-master's bridge' with ***pont***, ***y*** and *meistr* 'master, lord', referring to an ironworks recorded here in 1806. This interpretation is reflected in forms such as those for 1813 and 1833.

Pontypandy　　ST 157887
Caerphilly (Eglwysilan)
'bridge at the fulling-mill': ***pont***, ***y***, ***pandy***
Pontypandu 1739, *Pontypandy* 1740, *Pont y Pandy* 1764, *Pont-y-pandy* 1833
On Nant yr Aber downstream of Pont y Gwindy recorded as *Ponty Gwindu* 1776, *Pont y Gwindy* 1781, *Pont-y-gwyndy* 1833, probably with *gwindy* nm. 'wine-house, wine-cellar'. Pandy-mawr (ST 161894) takes its n. from a ho. recorded as *Pandy-mawr* located a little above the former *Pandybach* 1833 (ST 165892) on the stream Nant y Bwch on the north side of the r. Rhymni (*mawr, bach¹*).

Pontypridd　　ST 072903
Rhondda Cynon Taf (Eglwysilan/Llantwit Fardre/Llantrisant/Llanwynno)
'bridge of the earthen house': ***pont***, (***y***), ***tŷ***, ***pridd***

Newbridge c.1598, *Newbridge* (in Llantrisant) 1773, (mess.) *Newbridge* (in Llanwynno) 1777, (bridge on r. Rhondda) *Pont Newith* c.1538, *Pont y Tŷ Pridd, Pont Newith* c.1700, *Pont y tu prydd* 1773, *Pontytypridd* 1818, *Bont-y-tŷ-pridd, a marchnad y Bontnewydd* 1819, *Newbridge, or Pont-y-Pridd* 1829, (village) *Newbridge*, (bridge) *Pont y Prydd* 1840

A ho. made of earth or clay, possibly coated with limewash. The original Pont y Ty-pridd crossed the r. Taf. This is confirmed in Edward Lhuyd's Parochialia c.1700 and in a petition to Glamorgan Quarter Sessions in 1753 which indicates that the ancient and common bridge of *Pont-y-ty-pridd* was out-of-repair. The precise location of the bridge on the r. Taf remains uncertain though it seems to have lain very close to the bridge built by William Edwards in 1756. We also know that the 'earthen house', recorded as *Ty pryth* in 1665, lay in Llanwynno p., north of Rhondda and west of Taf. This has been identified with a ho. shown in a painting by Richard Wilson c.1767 next to Edwards's bridge but this suggestion remains unproven. The New Bridge otherwise Pont Newydd (ST 071900), mentioned in earlier sources, crossed the Rhondda just upstream from its confluence with Taf and was one of two bridges mentioned in 1682 (with a Pont Rhondda near Gellifynaches-isaf). This new bridge gave its n. to a small settlement on both sides of Rhondda in Llantwit Fardre and Llanwynno ps. The construction of another new bridge over the r. Taf by William Edwards in 1746-57, however, meant that the n. Newbridge was gradually – but inconsistently – associated with the Edwards bridge over the Taf. Urban growth meant too that the settlement of Newbridge merged with Pontypridd, gradually extending beyond the original bridges into Llantrisant and Eglwysilan ps., and their names inevitably became confused and interchangeable. In 1841 – a year after the Taff Vale Railway reached the town – the railway company named their new station Newbridge probably because of its proximity to the old settlement next to the Rhondda. Clarity was not restored until the 1860s when Newbridge as a n. was dropped, apparently at the insistence of the postmaster, owing to confusion with Newbridge, Monmouthshire.

Pont-y-rhyl SS 905898
Bridgend (Betws/Llangeinwyr)
'bridge at Yr Hyl': ***pont***, hill-name *Yr Hyl*
Pont-y-rhyll 1877, *Pontyrhyl* 1882
Yr Hyl (SS 903902), recorded as *Rhyll* 1877, *Rhyl* 1899, is a hill immediately north of the ht. Coed yr Hyl (wood *Coed y Rhyll* 1877) was on its eastern side and is now part of Garw Fechan forestry.
Sps. are very late but tend to favour a local borrowing *hyl* from E ***hill***, probably with some specialist meaning; other pns. in the immediate area are all W. The n. is reminiscent of (Y) Rhyl, Flintshire, which contains ***hill*** prefixed with the def.art. *yr* (DPNW 422; PNF 171). The third el. could also be *rhyll*[2], a variant of *rhill* nf. 'order, range, row', which includes the meaning 'rift, cleft'. This sense is poorly recorded and it would require substitution of –l for –ll [ł] but cf. Pontsticill.

Pont-y-waun ST 220925
Caerphilly (Rhisga Monmouthshire)
'bridge at the moor': ***pont, y, gwaun***
(bridge) *Pont y waen* 1813, *Pont-waen* 1833, *Pontywain* 1871
Taken from a bridge over the Monmouthshire and Brecon Canal. The moor appears in Waunfawr (ST 224914) recalled in Waunfawr Road.

Port Eynon, Porth Einon SS 467853
Swansea
'cove of Einon': ***porth***[3] and ME ***port***, pers.n. *Ein(i)on Portheinan* c.1187, (Roger de) *Porteniaun* early 13th cent, *Portheynon* 1230, *Portheinon* c.1250, *Portenon in Wales* 1335, *Porteynon'* 1396, *Porthynon* 1433, *Port Inon* 1539, *porth einion* c.1566
Einion has not been satisfactorily identified and attempts to identify him with Einion ap Gollwyn and Einion ab Owain are antiquarian guesses. Einion ap Gollwyn (late 11th cent) was a member of a prominent family in Gwynedd who is reputed to have moved to Morgannwg and headed a dynasty in Senghennydd. The

second Einion was a grandson of Hywel Dda (d. 950), a king primarily connected with Dyfed. In 1562 *Portynon* is described as having a pier and common passage from Wales to Cornwall and Devon.

Porth ST 025912
Rhondda Cynon Taf (Llantrisant/Llanwynno/Ystradyfodwg)
?'(the) gateway', (*y*), ***porth***²
porte Kemes [= *porte Kemer*] c.1598, *Porth* 1782, *Porthycumma* 1813, *Porth* 1833
Named from Porth fm. otherwise known as Tir Hywel Fawr recorded as *Tyr Howell Vawr* 1827, *Porth otherwise Tyr Howell fawr farm* 1884 (***tir***, pers.n. Hywel, ***mawr***, *fawr*) near a ford (***rhyd***) recorded as *Rhyd y Porth* 1827. The earliest form has ***cymer***¹, describing its location at the confluence of rs. Rhondda Fawr and Rhondda Fach (see Cymer). The village developed near Pwll y Porth and Pwll y Glyn Fach collieries in the mid/late 19th cent.

Porth-cawl (Porthcawl) SS 817769
Bridgend
'sea-kale harbour': ***porth***³, ***cawl***
Porth Cawl 1617, *Port Call* 1628, (bay) *Portcawl Harb* 1799 Yates, *Porth Cawl Bay* 1819, (bay) *Pwll Cawl or Porth Cawl* 1825, *Porth-cawl Harbour* 1833, *Porthycawl* 1865
The first el. is generally a nf. and the absence of len. *gawl* has been taken to imply that the def. art. ***y*** has been lost from the pn., i.e. an original Porth-y-cawl (ETG 250), but ***porth***³ was also a nm. (see Porth). *Porth-y-cawl* was current in the Swansea area but no instances of this form have been found in early historical sps. and it is not current. Gwynedd Pierce (ADG², 48) notes the occurrence of ***cawl*** in Gowlog (near Llanfeuthin) and in the Cardiff street-n. Heol y Cawl (= Wharton Street) recorded as *Hewle y Cawle* 1682, *Heol-y-Cawl* 1819, *Broth Lane*, *Porridge Lane* 1610 and *Werton ~ , Worton Strete* 1549. ***cawl*** [kaul] now generally means 'dish of vegetables and meat, pottage' and 'broth' but its earlier meanings included 'cabbage, kale'. Sea-kale must have grown abundantly here and perhaps collected for food or cultivation.

The harbour is that described – but not named – by John Leland c.1538 as 'a station or haven for shippes' at Newton Nottage. The town developed after the construction of a tramway to the industrial area of Maesteg 1826-7 and new harbour works begun in 1827. E-speakers rhyme –cawl [kɔːl] with 'crawl'.

Porthceri (Porthkerry) ST 082666
Vale of Glamorgan
'harbour of (man called) Ceri' or 'harbour near service-trees': ***porth***³, pers.n. Ceri or ***ceri***
Porciri 1254, *Porthkery*, *Porthkire* 13th cent, *Porthkyry* c.1348, *Portkyry* 1401, *Porthkyrye* 1535, *Portkerry* c.1541, *porth kiric* c.1566, *Porthkerick* 1602, *Porthkerry* 1596, *Porth Kerig* 1763
The pers.n. Ceri, evidently with a variant Cyri, is thought to be a compound of the el. ***câr*** and a suffix *–i* or a transferred use of the tree-species ***ceri*** 'service-tree(s)' recorded in Welsh sources from the 12th cent. The use of tree-names in this way is parallelled in pers.ns such as Celyn and Celynnin (***celyn***¹ 'holly-trees'). The supposition that the pn. contains a pers.n. gave rise to a number of fanciful interpretations linking it to a reputed 'Ceri, one of the early Welsh princes', reputed to have founded 'Port Ceri for the benefit of sailors and as a harbour for them'. Porthceri has also been supposed to contain the pers.n. Curig, first recorded here in the c.1566 spelling, but this is at odds with earlier forms. It is also notable that sps. with -k, -ck which appear to support this pers.n. all date after 1566 (see further PNDPH 198-200). The alternative explanation is that Porthceri refers not to a pers.n but the service-tree (Sorbus domestica), a rare fruit-bearing plant, and it is especially interesting that a number of trees of this species were identified here and at Ffontygary (q.v.) in 1994. The larger trees at Porthceri have not been precisely dated (described by Hampton and Kay as 'a minimum of several hundred year's old: Watsonia 20 (1995), 379-84, perhaps no older than c.1500 so that we have no certain proof that *Sorbus domestica* was actually growing here when the pn. first appears in the written record.

The collective evidence, however, is sufficient to show that the tree is likely to be native to Britain. The discovery of another six service-trees at Lancaut, co. Gloucester, in 2014, has also prompted the suggestion that the service-tree is one of the 'Marvels of Britain' written into the Historia Brittonum 10th cent. This states that 'Near the river called Gwy (Guoy), apples are found on an ash-tree growing on a steep slope which is near the mouth of the river'. The service-tree has leaves resembling those of the mountain ash.

Portmead SS 634968
Swansea
'burgess meadow': *portman* ME, *mæd*
Portis'mede 1425, *Portman Meade* 1432, *Portmen Med* 1546, *Portte Meade* 1592, *Portmead* 1650, 1764
An area belonging to the burgesses of Swansea once extending from what is now Pentregethin Road (the old Carmarthen road) to Afon Llan, and Wig south-east of Raven Hill and Middle Road. The modern form is a compressed form with loss of unstressed –*man* and influence of *port* (see PNSW Lliw Valley). The first el. is found also in Portmanmoor, Roath, recorded as *Portmannis More* 1516, *portmanmore* 1526. Port Mead is a housing estate developed after World War II around (hos.) *Blaen-y-maes* 1852 and *Pwll-yr-hwyaid* 1879. The first form has *blaen* but this seems to be a substitution since it is *Pant-y-maes-isaf* 1830 (*isaf*). Pant-y-maes is 'hollow at the open-field' (*pant, y, maes*). Pwllyrhwyaid is 'the ducks' pool' (*pwll, yr, hwyaid*).

Portobello see **Taff's Well**

Port Talbot SS 765900
Neath Port Talbot (Aberafan/Margam)
'port commemorating Talbot': E *port*, surname *Talbot*
(dwelling ho.) *The Port Talbot* 1840, *Port Talbot* 1841, *Port Talbot Station* c.1850
Named from C.R.M. Talbot (1803-90) of Penrice Castle, builder of Margam Castle. Acts in 1834 and 1836 authorised the development of a new harbour at Aberafan (Aberavon) and the Aberavon Harbour Co. was re-named the Port Talbot Co. in 1840 in recognition of Talbot's co-operation (MCPP 69-72). The town is sometimes found in W-language sources as Aberafan (q.v.) because of its close proximity to the ancient borough. The gradual spread of the town during the 20cent southeastwards towards Port Talbot (now Parkway) Station (SS 766896) and Tai-bach and eastwards up the Afan valley led to the gradual adoption of Port Talbot in preference to the more specific n. Aberafan.

Port Tennant, Porth Tennant SS 680934
Swansea
'port named from Tennant' : E *port*, **porth**³ surname *Tennant*
Port Tennant 1826, *Porth Tennant* 1893
Named from George Tennant (1765-1832) who built Tennant's Canal (*Tennant's canal* 1817), opened in 1824, linking Glan-y-wern Canal (draining Crymlyn Bog) to the r. Tawe. Tennant took over wharfland near Swansea and expanded the port facilities. The n. was in use by the beginning of 1826 when contracts were invited for the constuction of houses (MCPP 73-6).

Powndffald (Poundffald) SS 566945
Swansea (Llanrhidian)
'pound for stray animals': **powndffald*
Poundfald 1661, *Punfald* 1713, *Poundffald*, (mess.) *Tir y Pwm Fald* 1730, *Pumfald* 1764, *Pumfallt* 1813, *Pumpffallt* 1833, (hos.) *Pound-ffald-isaf, ~ -uchaf* 1879
**powndffald* is probably a borrowing from E *poundfold* (OE *pundfald*) or perhaps a compound of W *pownd*² 'pound (for stray animals etc)' and *ffald*. The el. is found also in a lost fn. recorded as *kayr powndffald* 1615 (*cae, y* affixed as `*r*) in Loughor. Historic forms (1730, 1764) provide evidence of a variant form (Y) Pwm-ffald possibly influenced by *pum(p)* 'five'. The fold was incorporated into the structure of the inn (GGower 48).

Price Town SS 937921
Bridgend (Llandyfodwg)
'settlement named from Price': surname *Price*, E ***town***
Price Town 1891, *Pricetown* 1892
From Daniel Price (1837-93), traffic manager of the Ocean Merthyr collieries (later the Ocean Coal Co.) in the 1870s. Price set himself up as a builder 1883 to develop the area near the ho. Blaenogwr (q.v.), and the collieries recorded as *Wyndham Pit* and *Blaen-ogwr Colliery* 1877. The village was constructed in 1890 (MCPP 77-80).

Princetown SO 114100
Caerphilly (Bedwellte Monmouthshire)
'settlement commemorating the Prince of Wales': E ***town***
Princetown 1879
The n. might also be elliptical for 'settlement near the Prince of Wales Inn' recorded in 1880 with *Prince Farm* (now Old Prince Farm) (SO 111102). The n. probably commemorates Prince Albert (1819-1861).

Prior's Town see **East Town**

Prysg (Prisk) ST 015765
Vale of Glamorgan (Welsh St Donats)
'copse': ***prysg***
Y Pryske, *Priske* 1612, *Prisk* 1655, *Prysc* 1811, *Prisc* 1833, *y Prysg* 1892
A very common el. in Glamorgan and Monmouthshire, also found compounded in *prysgoed* (with ***coed***) and *prysgwydd*, npl. 'brushwood, bushes'. The same el. is found in Pen-y-prysg (q.v.).

Prysgedwyn (Brysgedwyn) SN 591025
Swansea (Llandeilo Tal-y-bont)
'copse of (man called) ?Cedwyn': ***prysg***, pers.n. *?Cedwyn*
Preskedwen 1559. *Priskedwen* c.1580, *Pryskedwin* 1650, 1764, *Briskedwyn* 1719, *Pentre Briskedwin* 1795
The variation with *B-* in late forms is probably len. caused by preps. such as ***i*** 'to' and ***o*** 'from'. *Cedwyn* occurs in Ynyscedwyn otherwise Ynysgedwyn (SN 784096) (***ynys***), Ystradgynlais, (PNBrec 154); –*kedwen* in two early forms of Prysgedwyn, however, is not matched in Ynyscedwyn and further evidence is required.

†**Pwll Cynan** (lost) approx SS 694945
Neath Port Talbot/Swansea (Cadoxton-juxta-Neath/Llansamlet)
'Cynan's pool': ***pwll***, pers.n. *Cynan*
(water) *Poncanum* c.1129, (*piscariam de sub*) *Ponthanan'* c.1187, *Pulkanan* c.1168, (water) *Pulkanan* c.1208, *Pulcanan* early 13th cent (1334), *pulle kynon* 1605, *the great Pool in Crumlyn Marsh called Pwll Kynnan* 1764, *Pwll cynan* 1830
One of the traditional limits of Morgannwg identified with Crymlyn Bog (see Crymlyn²). Reputedly the location where Cynan, a son of Rhys ap Tewdwr (d. 1093) king of Deheubarth, was killed according to the antiquarian Rice Merrick late 16th cent (BG 19). *Ponthanan'* has been misidentified as Pontantwn, Carmarthenshire (SDEA 66).

Pwlldu Head SS 5686, 5786
Swansea (Pennard)
'promontory near Pwll-du': pn. *Pwll-du*, E ***head***
Pwll dû head 1832
A late n. referring to the promontory in the pn. Pennard (q.v.). The easternmost promontory is Pwlldu Point (SS 574867) recorded as *Pool dy Point* 1807, *Pwlldu Point* 1813, *Powldy Point* 1831. Pwll-du (SS 574872) is recorded as *Pwlldy* 1659 (1675), *Pwll duy* 1764, *Pwlldu* 1813 and *Pwll-du* 1830 meaning 'black *or* dark pool' (***pwll***, ***du***) referring to the small bay. The waters may have been dark from the peaty mud of the stream (*Puldie river* 1650) descending Bishopston Valley.

Pwll-gwaun ST 065902
Rhondda Cynon Taf (Llantrisant)
?'pool (*or* pit) at the moor': ***pwll***, ***gwaun***
poolh gwayn 1623, *Y Pull gwayn* 1638, *Pwll Gwaine* 1737, *Pwllgwain* 1807, *Pwll-gwaun* 1833
From a former ho. (ST 067898). Probably a pool in r. Rhondda.

Pwll-helyg SS 952713
Vale of Glamorgan (Llantwit Major)
'pool with willow-trees': *pwll*, *helyg*[1]
Pwllhelygfach, ~ *-fawr* 1810, *Pwllhelyg Fach*, ~ *Fawr* 1833, *Pwllelig* 1852
The n. of two hos. Pwllhelyg-fach (SS 952713) and Pwllhelyg-fawr (formerly SS 955713) (*bach*[1], *mawr*). Pwllhelyg-fawr appears as *Pwll-helyg* on OS maps 1877-1964 but appears to have been removed during the development of the Llandow Trading Estate and car racing circuit. A small pool is shown on earlier OS maps next to the point where four lanes meet at the former Llandow Wick Road Halt on the railway running north from Llantwit Major towards Bridgend.

Pwll-mawr ST 223790
Cardiff (Rumney)
?'moor with a pool (*or* creek)': E *pool*, ?*moor* (tmt.) *Pull Moer* 1627, *Pwll Mawr* 1841, (area) *Pwll-mawr* 1882
Pull Moer and in particular the occurrence of *Poollmoores Batch* 1630-1 and *Pool Moor pill* 1738 in this area favour this interpretation and fit the low-lying, formerly marshy topography. The later forms suggest that the n. has been re-interpreted as *pwll* 'pool, pit' and *mawr*.

Pwll-y-glaw SS 792932
Neath Port Talbot (Michaelston-super-Afan)
?'the rain pit, pit where rain-water collects': *pwll*, *y*, ?*glaw*
Pwll-y-glew 1729, *Melin-pwll-y-glaw* 1755, *Felinpwllyglaw* 1813, *Pwll-y-glaw* 1832, *Pwllygwlaw* 1868, *Pwll-gwlaw* 1878
There were a number of old coal levels in and around the village and it is possible that the final el. is properly *glo* 'coal, charcoal'. Cf. Pwll-y-glo (Llanrhidian) recorded as *Powll egloe* 1594 with *glo* also recalled in Cwm-y-glo (*Cwm y Glo* 1764) (*cwm*). There was a mill (*melin*) here on the r. Afan.

Pwll-y-pant ST 152889
Caerphilly (Eglwysilan)
'pool at the hollow': *pwll*, *y*, *pant*
Pwll y Pant 1713, *Pwllypant* 1738, *Pwlly pant* 1784, *Pwll Pant* 1815, *Pwll-y-pant* 1833
Possibly referring to a river-pool in the Rhymni and the 'hollow' where the Caerphilly-Llanbradach road dips at the crossroads.

Pyle[1], **Y Pîl** SS 826824
Bridgend
?'(place at the) stake': ME *pile*
Pyle 1485 (1540), (manor) *Pittevin'* or *Pile* early 16th cent, *The Pile* 1536, *Pyll'* c.1536, *Pylle alias Pyle* 1543, *Peyell* 1547, *Pile* 1668, *y pil* c.1566, *y Pil* 1606, *Pyle Inn* 1799, *Pil*, *Y Pil* 1875
Charles (NCPN 139-40) cites Pile Lane, Dorset, Pile Hill, Surrey; and Pilemoor, Devon; cf. also Pilton and see Pilham, Pillaton and Pilley in CDEPN. The precise sense may be 'area defended by stakes'. The alternative OE *pyll* 'tidal creek, pill', generally found as *Pill*, *-pill* in Pembrokeshire, Monmouthshire and other parts of Glamorgan, is less likely. Sps. such as *Pyle*, *Pile* suggest a long first vowel which is supported by the W form [iː] rather than the short vowel [ɪ] found in other examples of Pill. Some forms have the E def.art. *the* and this is matched by W *y*. Pyle has been identified with *Pyll'* 1420, where Margam abbey held tithes, but the context suggests this is a lost location near what is now Port Talbot.

Pyle[2] SS 580882
Swansea (Bishopston)
Uncertain
Pyle 1878
Note also *Pile Fields* 1764 in the same p. We can safely reject OE *pyll* 'tidal creek, pill' since it is located on a small hill in Gower overlooking the sea. The nearest stream – which is not tidal – is a quarter mile to the west in the deeply-cut Bishopston Valley. Possibly identical in meaning to Pyle[1] but early refs. are lacking. The n. is applied on late 19th cent maps to a crossroads near a quarry and later to housing developed from the 1930s.

Quakers Yard to Quarella

Caerphilly Road, Quakers Yard.

Quakers Yard, Mynwent y Crynwyr
ST 097965
Rhondda Cynon Taf (Gelligaer/Merthyr Tudful)
'enclosure where Quakers are buried', : E *quaker*, *yard*; 'cemetery belonging to the Quakers', ***mynwent**, **y**, **crynwyr***
Quakers Yard 1799, *the Quakers' Yard* 1803, *Claddfa'r Crynwyr* 1821, *Mynwent y Crynwyr* 1836, (*i*) *Fonwent y Crynwyr* 1861
One W source has *claddfa* nf. 'cemetery, graveyard'. Named from a meeting-ho. of the Society of Friends or 'Quakers' who became established in the Merthyr Tudful area before 1656 at Blaencannaid Farm. They are said to have opened the burial ground in 1667 (HMorg 12, 331-2) although it is described in 1669 only as 'waled about and made redy' for burials. See also Clive Thomas (GuideHTV 10-11). The industrial village developed after the arrival of the Glamorganshire Canal 1791-8 when a lock or basin was constructed south of the cemetery.

Quar, The see **Cwar, Y**

Quarella see **Cwarelau**

Radur to Ruthin

Commercial Road, Resolven c.1910.

Radur (Radyr)   ST 133803
Cardiff
'oratory': *aradur*
uillam Arad[ur] c.1100 (c.1200), *Aradur* 1506, (*trwy'r*) *Adur* late 15th cent, *Rador* c.1291, *Radur* 1254, *Radur alias Le Radur* 1307, *Radour* 1322, *Errader* 1544, *yr adyr* c.1566, *Radyr ycha, ~ yssa*, 1666, *Radir* (= Radyr Court), *Radir-uchaf* (= Radyr Farm) 1833, *Higher ~ , the Lower Radyr* c.1659
aradur is derived from Lat *oratorium* (which also gives E *oratory* and Fr *oratoire*). Unstressed initial *A-* has become confused with the def.art. *y* [ə] > Y Radur (see ADG[1], 91), variant Radyr (with short *y*). The def.art. is also seen in *Rhyd y Radir* 1734 (a ford at ST 144792 in the r. Taf)

and it probably accounts for the AF def.art. *le* 1307 and E *the* in 1554, etc. Radur now refers specifically to the modern village (ST 133804). Radyr Farm (ST 130799) is *Higher Radyr* c.1659 and *Radir-uchaf* 1833 (***uchaf***). Radyr Court (probably *the Lower Radyr* c.1659) with the older p.ch. of St John the Baptist (ST 140791) is in the middle of Danescourt (q.v.) housing estate. Cf. The Rhadyr (sic) at Llanbadog, Monmouthshire, recorded as *Radour* 1552, (chp. of) *Radour* 1556-8 and *the Raddir* 1671.

Rallt   SS 525938
Swansea (Llanrhidian)
'the wooded slope': **yr**, ***allt***
the Ralt 1785, *Allt* 1841, *Rallt* 1879

The *r* of the def.art. *yr* has become fixed to *allt* in a similar manner to Rhewl[1, 2] (< Yr Hewl), Denbighshire (DPNW 410).

Raven Hill, Penlle'r-brain　　　　SS 632956
Swansea
'hill frequented by ravens': E *raven*, E *hill*; 'top of Tyle'r Brain': *pen*[1], pn. *Tyle'r Brain*
Pentyle y Brain 1600, *Pentylarbraene* 1611, *Pentylaur Brain* 1720, *Penllwynbrain* 1754, *Pentilabrain* 1764, *Penller Brain* 1799, *Penlle'r-brain* 1832, *Penlle Brain*, *Raven Hill* 1841
Tyle'r Brain is *Tyle'r brayn* 1650 meaning 'the crows' slope (*or* hill)', *tyle*, *y*, *brân* pl. *brain* and Raven Hill (SS 6395) must be a loose translation. Gwynedd Pierce (ADG[1], 77) notes a former fm. Ravenhill House, earlier called Penlle'r-brain House, and Ravenhill Park. Penlle'r-brain has been identified with *Crowewode* 1305, *Crowode* 1319 and *Keven coyd or Crowswood* 1650 (E *crow*, *wood*) but the last ref. favours a location south of Carmarthen Road including the Wig area and extending towards Cockett and the fms. recorded as *Cefn-coed*, ~ *East*, ~ *Wen* 1832, *Cefen Coid* 1841 meaning 'ridge with a wood' (*cefn*, *coed*).

Resolfen (Resolven)　　　　SN 828028
Neath Port Talbot (Llantwit-juxta-Neath)
?'stubble moor': *rhos*[2], *soflyn*
Rossauilin c.1204, *Roshaulyn* 1208, *Rhoshoulwyn* c.1291, *Rossulyn*, *Rosoulyn*, *Rouselyn* 1314, *Rosowlen* 1535, *Resolven* 1604, *Resolwen* 1681, (hill) *Solfen Hill* 1799, *Parcell Resolven* 1670, *Cappel Rhesolfen*, (mtn.) *Mynydd Rhesolfen* 1833, *Resolfen* 1879
There are some doubts with this explanation because all historic forms before the mid 16th cent have -*aulyn*, -*aulin* (for ModW -*awlyn*?) not -*auvlyn*, -*auvlin* (ModW -*awflyn*, -*awflin*, -*oflyn*, -*oflin*). The answer may lie in a variation -aw-/-af- found, for example, in *tawlod/taflod* 'loft'. That raises the possibility of a variant *sowlyn* (not recorded in GPC). Metathesis would account for *sowlyn/soflyn > solwyn/solfyn*. The development *Ros- > Rys- > Res-* with shift of vowel may have occurred through heavy stress on the second syllable. It has been objected that 'stubble' – typically associated with cereal crops and hay – is unlikely in connection with moorland but the n. could describe the appearance of a moor created by burning leaving stumps of plants. Some support for this suggestion may be found in the forms *Reeding or Soflen* 1591 with OE **rydding* 'clearing' (see Rhyding). The pn. applied earlier to a former medieval chp. and 'new grange' (*Nova Grangia* 1296) of Margam abbey near Tyn-y-cwm (SN 848022) on Mynydd Resolfen (*Resolven Mountain* 1947), now afforested.

Rest Bay　　　　SS 7978
Bridgend (Newton Nottage/Sker)
'bay near The Rest': ho.n., E *bay*
Rest Bay 1916
The Rest (SS 804784) was built in 1874-8 on land given by the Talbot family of Margam and was successor to an older convalescent home established in 1862 by Dr James Lewis, medical officer of Bridgend and Cowbridge Union and of Messrs Brogdens' Mines and Colliery Company on New Road (Porthcawl 83-4).

Reynoldston　　　　SS 481901
Swansea
'Regenweard's settlement (or farm)': OE pers.n. *Regenweard*, *tūn*
Renewardestoune 1306, *Reynewardeston'* 1396, *Reynoldston* 1400, *Reyndeston* 1465, *Raynalston* 1560, *Rinaldston* 1598, *Reynaldston* 1602, *Rinallston* 1609, *Rinoldston* 1641
The pers.n. was later replaced by the more familiar *Reynold* found, for example, in Reynalton, Pembrokeshire (NCPN 128). There is no evidence to connect Reynoldston with Reginald de Breos (as in OPN 150).

Rheola (Hirola)　　　　SN 840040
Neath Port Talbot (Cadoxton-juxta-Neath)
'long trackway': *hir*, *olau*
Hirrole 1296, *Hirolle* 1375, *Hyrola* 1375, *Hyrrole* 1541, *Hireoley* 1657, (mill) *Mellin Hire Oley* 1722, *Rheola in Glynedd* 1763, *Rheole* 1833
With dialect -*a* for -*au*, and inversion of *h* and *r* probably in part through association with *heol* 'path, road'. *olau* also occurs in Uchelolau, later re-interpreted as Highlight (q.v.). Rheola

Brook is properly Nant Clwyd Fechan (VNeath 191).

Rhigos (Rugos)　　　　　　　　SN 922059
Rhondda Cynon Taf (Ystradyfodwg)
'place with abundance of heather; heath': *y*, *grug*, *-os*
Rugois 1281, *Rugoys* 1314, *Rigois*, *Rigos* c.1538, *Erygos*, *Regoiz* 1580, *o'r ygos*, (*o*) *Regoes* 16th cent, *Clyn y Rigos* 1666, *Rhygos* 1793, *Rhydgroes* 1833
The suffix *-os*, is often found with plant-ns. indicating a place where they are particularly common (CVPN 43-44, 85-86; ADG², 51); cf. Bedwas, Gurnos. Local pron. *Rhicos* (VNeath 532n.) is confirmed in a triban (Trib 57) and *Ricos* 1857. Rhigos also referred in earlier sources to Cwm-hwnt (q.v.) but now applies to the village which developed from the 1920s around Maesygarreg and an earlier Independent chp. on the east side of a ho. Rhyd (recorded 1814) where Heol Pendarren which crosses the stream Nant Gwrangon. This may help explain why some late sources show misassociation with **rhyd** 'ford'.

Rhisga (Risca)　　　　ST 263911, 242902
Caerphilly (Monmouthshire)
?'place where bark is found or treated': **rhisg**, *rhisgl* pl. *rhisgau* '(piece of) bark'
(*Kadmor de*) *Risca* 1146, (chp.) *Risca* 1330, (p.) *Risca* 1476, *Ryscha* 1535, *Riska* 1540, *Riskey* 1559, *Risgaf* c.1566, *Riscae* 1591, *Rishka* 1695, *Rhisga* 1778
The precise meaning remains uncertain. Melville Richards suggests 'a wooden house with bark on the logs' which invites comparison with Hafodrisclawdd recorded as *Tyr havod Ryselog*, *Havod Rislogg* 1630, *Hafod-yr-ysclawdd* 1833 meaning 'summer-dwelling covered with bark' (**hafod**, *rhisglog* 'having bark'). Cf. also Rhisgog, at Llanbedr Dyffryn Clwyd and Llangollen, in Denbighshire, Aberedw, in Radnorshire, and Llanfyllin, in Montgomeryshire, all with similar historical forms, probably with the sense 'place where bark is found'. More pertinent are two lost rns., viz. Nant y Rhisga (in Eglwysilan) recorded in *Diffrin Risca* (**dyffryn**) and as (r.) *Riska*, *Risca* c.1538, *Risga* 1578, *Rishka* 1638, which appears to be the r. now called Nant yr Aber (ST 1388), and secondly (r.) *Risga* 1600 (in Llangynwyd) later recorded as *Nant Cwm-bâch* 1876 surviving in two ho.ns. as *Cwm-risca* 1833 (SS 879847), *Cwmyrisca*, *Cwm isha* 1841, and *Cwm-risca-isaf* 1876 (SS 881845). Other interpretations of Rhisga are etymologically unsound even if they raise legitimate concerns about the precise meaning of the pn. See further GLH 114, 42-45.

Rhiw　　　　　　　　　　　　ST 207985
Caerphilly (Mynyddislwyn Monmouthshire)
'(the) slope': **rhiw**
(ho.) *Rhew* 1841, *Rhiw* 1880
Rhiw may be short form of Rhiw Crymlyn recorded as *Rhew Crumlyn* 1841 since it is located on hill-slopes above the village of Crymlyn (q.v.). A nearby ho. (ST 204983) is *Penrhiw Crumlin* 1813, 'top of Crymlyn slope' (**pen**¹). Rhiw developed from the end of the 19th cent in association with industrial development at Crymlyn and nearby collieries and brick works.

Rhiwbeina (Rhiwbina)　　　　ST 155817
Cardiff (Whitchurch)
'slope of ?': **rhiw**, (**yr**), ?
Rubyney 1595, *Rywer beyney* 1602, *Riwrbyne* 1632, *Riwbina* 1699, *Rubina* 1685, *Rewbeine* 1748, (ho.) *Rhiwbina* 1833, (fm.) *Rhiwbeina* 1864
The n. is drawn from the fm. (ST 145827) north of the M4. The third el. *-b(e)ina* is obscure though it occurs also in an unlocated n. recorded as *Riwbine* 1597 at Llantrisant and in that of a tmt. *Tir Ribine otherwise Tyr Rheed y bine* 1755 and *Tyr Bine alias Tyr Rhydybine* 1784 in Llanfeugan, Breconshire. Sps. from W sources tend to favour the form Rhiwbeina [r̥uˈbeɪna] rather than [r̥uˈbiːna]. E-speakers pronounce the pn. [rʊˈbaɪna] rhyming it with 'china'. It is tempting to identify Rhiwbeina with *Riv Brein*, *Riubrein* c.1145, *riu brein* and *Riubrein* c.1170 in the Book of Llandaf but a boundary description indicates that this lay further west between Castell Coch (ST 131826) and Morgraig (ST 160843). This probably means 'slope frequented

by crows' (***rhiw***, ***brain***). Rhiwbina Garden Village was developed on part of the Pentwyn estate from 1913, expanding rapidly from 1920.

Rhiwceiliog SS 972843
Bridgend (Coychurch)
'(the) cockerel's slope': ***rhiw***, (***y***), ***ceiliog***
Tir Rhiwr Keilog 1621, *Rhiw r kilog* 1632, *Riwr kilog* 1633, *Riwciliog* 1771, *Rhiwrceiliog* 1813, *Rhiw ceiliog* 1833
The n. originally applied to a tmt. of 'land' (***tir***) located on the lane running north up slopes to the crossroads next to Zoar Calvinistic Methodist chp.

Rhiwperra (Ruperra) ST 220864
Caerphilly (Michaelston-y-fedw)
'(the) pear-tree slope': ***rhiw***, (***y***), ***perai***
Rewrparrye 1541, *rriw r perre* 1550, *Rhiw r perrai* 1561, *Rrywrperrey* 1572, *Ruperrey* 1578, *Ruerperrye, Ruerperre* 1586, (*o*) *Riw perai* 1605, *Riewperrey* 1633, *Ruperra* 1717
See ADG², 89. The modern map spelling with *Ru-* is an anglicisation; cf. *Ruabon* for Rhiwabon, Denbighshire (DPNW 427) and E pron. of Rhiwbeina. There was an identical pn. Rhiwperra (approx. ST 000800) – destroyed by construction of the M4 motorway – at Llanhari recorded thus 1833, as *Ruperra* 1841 and *Rhiwperra* 1875 but this may be a transferred n. since a nearby ho. is recorded as *Cefn Mabley* 1841, *Cefn-mably* 1875. See Cefnmabli.

Rhiwsaeson ST 070827
Rhondda Cynon Taf (Llantrisant)
'Englishmen's slope': ***rhiw***, ***Saeson***
Rew Saesson 1541, *Rhyw Saeson Ycha alias Y Kae lloyd* 1615, (*syddyn*) *Rhyw'r Saysonn* c.1612, *Rw Sayson ycha, ~ issa* c.1670, *Rhuw Seison*, (bridge) *Pont rhyw seyson* c.1700, *Rhyw Seison*, (water corn grist mill) *Mellin Rhyw Seson* 1737, *Rhiw Saeson Farm* 1833
The second el. has been explained as a ref. to the slaughter of the followers of Robert Fitzhamon, conqueror of Morgannwg, by Welshmen in the 12th cent and a reputed battle between Welsh and Saxons 873 but there is no reliable evidence for either suggestion. Rhiwsaeson (SN 9005), Montgomeryshire, is identical in meaning. **Saeson** is a fairly common el. in pns., note Rhydysaeson (Pendeulwyn) c.1659 recorded as *Ryd y Saisson* c.1659 (***rhyd***) and Cefnsaeson (SS 776964) near Neath recorded as *Kenensefhon* c.1291, *Keven-sayson* 1359 (***cefn***).

Rhondda SS 9597, 9795, 9992, ST 0291
Rhondda Cynon Taf (Llantrisant, Llanwynno, Ystradyfodwg)
'noisy (r.)': ****rhawdd***, suffix **–ni**
(r.) *Rotheni* late 12th cent, *Rotheni Maur* 1203, *Rotheny* 1297, (r.) *Rotheney* 1448, (water) *Rotheney Vehan*, (r.) *Rodeney, ~ Vaur* c.1538, *The greate Rodney and the little rodney* c.1598, (lp.) *Ruthny* c.1598, *Rhonddyvechan alias Tyr llyn Elvarch* 1711, *Pont Rhonda* 1729, *Rhondda R, Rhonddafechan R* 1799, (rs.) *Rhondda, ~ fawr, ~ fychan* 1833
****rhawdd*** is inferred from *adrodd* 'to relate, report' and *ymadrodd* 'saying'. Early sps. show that the rn. was *Rhoddni* or *Rhoddneu, Rhoddnei, Rhoddne*. From the 17th cent *-ddn-* produced *-ndd-* by reversing consonants (metathesis) and the suffix **–ni** was associated with the common pl. ending *–au*, generally found as *–a* in the dialect of most of Glamorgan. Modern Rhondda is essentially a string of industrial villages along the courses of rs. Rhondda Fawr and ~ Fechan, distinguished as 'great, greater' (***mawr***, *fawr*) and 'small, lesser' (***bach***¹, *bechan, fach, fechan*). Rhondda did not become fixed as a pn. until 1897 when Ystradyfodwg Urban District Council adopted the n. The r. Rhondda is also recorded in Blaenrhondda (q.v.) and Glynrhondda, the n. of a former commote in Penychen cantref, recorded as *Glinrotheni* c.1262, *Glenrotheny* 1268, *Glynrotheny* 1314, *Glinrotheney, The vale of Rotheney, Com. Glyn Rodeney* c.1538, *Glynronthie* 1559, *glyn Roðne* c.1566, *Glyn Ronddey* 1631 taking its n. from the 'narrow valley' (***glyn***).

Rhoose see **Rhws, Y**

Rhos SN 738031
Neath Port Talbot (Cilybebyll)
'(the) moorland': ***rhos***²

Ros 1523, *le Rose* 1529-30, *the Rose at Alltwen* 1615, *Roos* 1610, *Rhos* 1852, *Rhôs* 1877
The village developed along Plas Road and Neath Road in the late 19th cent near *Bryn-brych* 1832, 'speckled hill' (***bryn***, ***brych***) on a hill immediately east of Allt-wen and west of *Melin-y-rhos* (SS 747035) (***melin***). Major housing development after World War II occupies the area of Tir-bach Farm, 'little land' (***tir***, ***bach***¹).

Rhosili (Rhossili)　　　　　　　　SS 416880
Swansea
'Sulien's promontory (*or* moor)': ***rhos***², pers.n. *Sulien*
Penn ibei inrosulgen c.1145, *Rossili* c.1187, *Rossilly* 1230, *Ressely* c.1291, *Rossily* 1306, *Rossully* 1360, *Ros ssili* c.1566, *Rosilli*, *Rhosily* 1583, *Roosilly* 1742, *Rhos sili* 1832
Rhosili lies on the exposed north slopes of a promontory. The pn. is generally spelt and pronounced with *-ss-* though *s* is not regularly doubled in ModW. For loss of *–(e)n*, cf. Llandough², Llandocha < Llandochan. Rhosili Down (SS 4289) is *Rosylis downe* 1583, *Rossilly Downe* 1682 (E ***down***). Rhosili Bay is *Rosilly Bay* 1754, *Rhos Sili Bay* 1830.

Rhuthin (Ruthin)　　　　　　　　SS 969798
Vale of Glamorgan
'red bank': ***rhudd***, ***hin***²
Ruthun c.1200, *Ruthyn* 1281, *Ruthin* 1314, (*patria*) *Ruthyn* 1317, *Com. Meanour Ruthyn* c.1538, *Maenor Rythyn* 1559
A former commote or ***maenor***. The n. applies to a flattish hill extending westwards from the ho. Ruthin (*Rhythin* 1885) towards the fms. recorded as *Pant-rhythin-fawr*, *-fâch* 1885 and *Pant Rythen* 1537 where there is a sharp slope down to Afon Ewenni. The n. is also recorded in Graig y Ruthin (SS 974803) where the hill slopes northwards down towards Trallwm (SS 980803) and the M4. Identical in meaning to Rhuthun (Ruthin), Denbighshire (DPNW 427-8). Both pns. have been widely understood to be compounds of ***rhudd*** and ***din*** with the meaning 'red fort' but such a combination would regularly produce *rhuddin*, not *rhuthin*.

Rhwng Nedd ac Afan see **Afan Wallia**

Rhwng Nedd a Thawe
Neath Port Talbot
'(commote) between Neath and Tawe', (***cwmwd***), ***rhwng***, rn. **Nedd**, prep. ***a***, rn. **Tawe**, asp.mut. Thawe
Com. Rungneth a Thawe c.1538, *Rrwng nedd a thawy* mid 16th cent
Otherwise known simply as Nedd (see Neath). The commote included the ps. of Cadoxton-juxta-Neath and Cilybebyll in the cantref of Gwrinydd.

Rhwng Twrch a Chlydach　　　　SS 8100
Neath Port Talbot (Llantwit-juxta-Neath)
'(area) between Twrch and Clydach': ***rhwng***, rns. **Twrch**, prep. ***a***, *Clydach* asp.mut *Chlydach*
Between Twrch and Clydach 1601
An area between the r. Twrch rising (at SN 815003) above Clyne and either the stream known variously as Clydach Brook or Higher Clydach (*Higher Clydach* c.1700) or perhaps the stream Clydach Cwmcaca now known as Melin Court Brook (see Melin-cwrt). D.R. Phillips (VNeath 193-4) knew the first as Clydach Uchaf ('higher') and the second as Clydach Isaf ('lower'). See Clydach above.

Rhŵs (Rhoose)　　　　　　　　ST 061664
Vale of Glamorgan (Penmark and Porthceri)
'moorland, heath': ***rhos***²
Rhos in Penmark 1533-8, *Rhoose*, *Rouse* c.1541, *Plas Rws* c.1569, *Rowse* 1578, *Roose* 1595-6, (*o*)*r Hws* c.1613, *Roos* 1716, *Rooes* 1784
The modern map spelling Rhoose and standard W Y Rhŵs with [u:] are likely to be products of E influence and Gwynedd Pierce (PNDPH 203-5) drew a comparison in this respect with Roose, Pembrokeshire (PNPemb 570), where the E-language was widely spoken from the 12th cent. Some early sps. with *-oo-* may be attempts, however, at representing the long W *o* [o:] in script as in the case of *Roos* 1610 for

Rhos (q.v.) where there was little E influence before the 19th cent.

Rhyding (Rhydding) SS 749986
Neath Port Talbot (Cadoxton-juxta-Neath)
'a clearing, open place (in a wood)': OE **rydding*
Reeding 1591, *Rhyding* 1627, *Rheeding* 1666, *Reddinge* 1676, *Reading*, (fields) *Rheedingan issa, ~ ganol* 1768, *Rheeding Mill* 1795, *Rhedyn* 1830, *Rhydding* 1877-81
Possibly clearings made for agriculture by monks of Neath abbey. The area developed along Heol Pen-y-wern in the 19th cent near Rhydding Colliery but takes its n. from a ho. The 1830 sp. shows association with **rhedyn** 'ferns'. Cf. Rhyddings (SS 6493), a former fm. in Oystermouth, its n. preserved in Rhyddings Terrace (SS 637926), recorded as *les Redyngez de Sweynesey* 1402, *the Reeding* 1617, (lands) *the Riddinges* 1650, *Ryddings* 1735, *Rhydings* 1832.

Rhydfelen (Rhydyfelin) ST 091882
Rhondda Cynon Taf (Eglwysilan)
'yellow-brown ford': **rhyd**, *melen*, *felen*
Tir ynys y Ryd velen 1522, *Ennes Rede Vellen* 1541, *ynys ryd velyn* 1570, *tir rhyd velen* 1630, *Rhydfelen* 1839, 1877, *Rhyd-y-felin* 1885
Gwynedd Pierce (ADG[1], 95) suggests it may have been yellow-brown from the colour of the mud churned up by horses' hooves and carts. Cf. Rhyd-goch, 'reddish-brown ford' (*coch*) in Rhondda. The ford was near the footbridge (ST 088881) at the bottom of Dyffryn Road. Rhydyfelin is a late error meaning 'ford of the mill' (*y*, **melin**, *felin*). Identical pns. Rhydfelen are found in Llanina and Llannarth, Cardiganshire.

Rhydlafar ST 115799
Cardiff (St Fagans)
'loud, resonant ford': **rhyd**, *llafar*
Rethlauar c.1538, *Rydelaver, Rydelavar* 1570, *Rhyd Lafar* early 17th cent, (*syddyn*) *Rhydlavar* c.1612, *Redlaver* 1625, *Ridlaver* c.1670, *Felin Rhydlafer* 1833, *Rhyd-lafar* 1880
See Gwynedd Pierce (PNGlam 167-8; ADG[2], 84). The n. must have applied specifically to the ford since there is no evidence that the stream here (a tributary of Nant Dowlais) was ever called Llafar though there are examples of this as a rn. in Caernarfonshire and Merionethshire. It is simply *Nant Rhydlafar* in 1880 (**nant**). There is no substance to the claim (ASFL 7) that a King Lleurwg lived here and that he was called 'Lleufer Mawr' by the Venerable Bede. Lleurwg refers to Lucius, once thought to be a king of Britain, who allegedly wrote to Pope Eleutherius (floruit c.180) requesting that he be made a Christian. Another Rhydlafar is recorded in Llanrhymni or Marshfield, Monmouthshire, as *Rydlaver* 1621 and *Ridlavar* 1624.

Rhydri (Rudry) ST 193865
Caerphilly (Bedwas)
Uncertain
Rutheri 1254, *Rethery* 1281, *Rudri, Rudry* 1307, *Ruthry* 1352, *Rothery* 1375, *Reddery* 1476, *y Rydri* c.1566, *Rydry* c.1670, *Rudry* 1747, *Rhydri* 1848
Early sps. with *Ruth-, Reth-, Roth-* invite comparison with a rn. Rhuddan, Carmarthenshire, for which R.J. Thomas (EANC 85) suggested **rhydd** adj., *rhedegog* 'running, flowing', or **rhudd** 'red', in this case with suffix *-ri*. This may be –*ri* (*rhi*[1] nm. 'king, lord') found in pers.ns. such as Bleddri and Tudri. Historic forms show that *-dd-* has developed into *-d-* possibly through association with **rhyd** 'ford'. There is no stream called Rhydri here although it may have been a lost n. for that which lies immediately south of Rhydri ch., flowing down to the r. Rhymni at Draethen (ST 224874). The spelling *Rudry* represents current E pron. ['r ʌ dri:].

Rhydwaedlyd ST 160810
Cardiff (Whitchurch)
'? ford': **rhyd**, ?rn.
Ryddwathley, Ridd y Wathla 1702, *Rhydwathla* 1726, *Rydwathle* 1762, *Rhydywathle* 1795, *Rhydywyllty* 1811, *Rhydwathle* 1852, *Rhŷdwaedlyd* 1875
The modern form suggests 'bloody ford': **rhyd** and *gwaedlyd* adj. 'bloody' but the interpretation is at odds with earlier evidence. The ford is

near Rhiwbina station and Capel Beulah where the main road (Pant-bach Road and Heol y Deri) crosses a small brook running south from Mynydd Caerffili. This is *Rhŷd-waedlyd Brook* 1875. The ford was replaced by a bridge recorded as *Pont Rydwathle* 1777 and *Rhydwathla bridge* 1801. In a history of Beulah chp. in 1872 (HEAC II, 410) local Independents are said to have established a meeting place in a former smithy, called *Nantywathle*, known more often as *Rhydywathle* and by some as *Nantrhydgwaedle*. The authors of the history suggest that the n. is a corruption of *Gwaedle* and state that there was a battle here between the armies of Cromwell and Charles I, for which there is no evidence. This reputed 'Site of Battle' is shown on OS maps in 1875 around Ty'n-y-coed and Ty-gwyn (ST 161814). The chp.'s trust deed apparently names this place as *Nant-rhyd-Walter* but it is otherwise unauthenticated. The best that can be suggested on the available evidence is that the pn. may contain a rn., perhaps *Gwaethlai containing an el. such as *gwaethl* nm. 'debate, dispute, battle' and the common suffix *–ai* often found in rns. as *–e*, eg. Baddege, Dothïe, Hore, etc (EANC 22-33).

Rhyd-y-bedd   SO 064087
Merthyr Tudfull
'ford near the grave': **rhyd**, **y**, **bedd**
Tir Rhyd y Bedd 1540, *Ridd y bede* 1561, *Rhyd y Bedd* 1757, *Rydybedd* 1784
Named from a ho. (SO 064088) which stood next to Nant Morlais near what is now Pantysgallog Primary School. The area has been so markedly affected by industrial, urban and highway development that it is now difficult to identify the precise location of the ford. The area near Rhyd-y-bedd is recorded as *Cwm-rhy-bedd* 1833 (**cwm**).

Rhydyboithan   ST 130850
Caerphilly (Eglwysilan)
'ford of the ?': **rhyd**, **y**, ?
Ryddy Boydan 1670, (ht.) *Rhyd-y-boithen* 1723, *Rhydyboithan* 1767, *Rydboithan Hamlet* 1783, *Rydyboithan* 1784, *Rhandir Rhydyboethan* 1873
The pn. has been linked with *inis peithan* 1128 and *Ynis peithan* 1129 identified with a wood described in c.1145 as on the north side of Tongwynlais near Castell Coch. Peithan could contain *paith* nm. 'a desert, uninhabited' with a suffix *-an*, comparable with several rns. in Cardiganshire such as Paith, Peithnant and Peithyll. It is, however, difficult to reconcile *Peithan with historic forms of Rhydyboithan which generally have *–oith-*. Very late forms seem to have been influenced by **poeth** 'hot' with the extended sense 'fervent'. Historically a ht. making up most of the southern part of Eglwysilan extending from Tongwynlais to Hawthorn.

Rhyd-y-car   SO 048054
Merthyr Tudful
'the cart ford': **rhyd**, **y**, **car**¹
terre R...ekarre 1449, *Tir Rhyd y Car* 1541, *Ryd y Car* 1757, *Rhyd y Car* 1783
Over the r. Taf. The first ref. is from a defective manuscript and should probably read *terre Redekarre*, 'land of Rhyd-y-car' (Lat *terra*, gen. *terre*). There was another Rhyd-y-car, in Llan-giwg, recorded as *Red y Karr* 1549, *Ryd y Karr* 1557, and *Nant Rhyd y Kar* 1617 and other examples at Talgarth, in Breconshire, Llanedi, in Carmarthenshire, and elsewhere. There is a fm. Rhyd-y-ceir (SN 978639) near Llanwrthwl, Breconshire, containing the pl. **ceir** 'cars, carts'.

Rhydyfelin see **Rhydfelen** (Rhondda Cynon Taf)

Rhyd-y-fro   SN 714055
Neath Port Talbot (Llan-giwg)
'ford of the ?lowland': **rhyd**, **y**, ?**bro**
(place) *Gweyn Redvro* 1504, *Gwayn Ryde yvero* 1584, *Rhyd y Vro*, (water mill) *Melin Rhyd y Vro* 1615, *Rhyd y frô* 1707, *Rhydyfro* 1807, *Rhyd-y-fro* 1832
The third el. appears to be **bro** as in Bro Morgannwg (= Vale of Glamorgan) generally meaning 'vale, lowland' but that seems inappropriate here since the ht. is at a junction of the two narrow valleys of the rs. Egel and Higher Clydach, not in an open vale. It is possible that it has the alternative sense 'border, limit' but only two literary instances

for this meaning are cited in GPC. The first forms above have *gwaun* 'moorland'. The ford is probably that shown just above the Baran Road bridge in the r. Higher Clydach.

Rhyd-y-gwern ST 216884
Caerphilly (Machen Monmouthshire)
'ford near the alder-trees': *rhyd, y, gwern*
Ree(d) Gwerne 1488, Redegwerne 1501, Redwerne 1541, Reedgwern 1649, Reedygwerne 1658, Rhyd-gwern 1833, Rhŷd-y-gwern 1875
A number of historic forms show loss of the unstressed def.art., a common characteristic of pns. in Glamorgan. The ford crosses the r. Rhymni.

Rhyd-y-gwin SN 676037
Swansea (Llangyfelach)
'ford of the wine': *rhyd, y, gwin*
Rhyd-y-gwin, (well) Ffynnon Rhyd-y-gwin 1879
Probably a ford associated with the goods and produce taken across it or perhaps in ref. to dark reddish waters. Identical ns. occur at Cilgerran in Pembrokeshire and in Cardiganshire. No ford appears in the nearby r. Clydach Isaf but it may have been located at the the point (ST 677038) north-east of Pantycrwys Independent chp. where the road running up the valley crosses a very small stream. The 'well' (*ffynnon*) (ST 676039) is shown as 'spout' on the OS 1:2,500 map in 1898. The ht. developed during the 19th cent near small coal workings and quarries.

Rhydypandy SN 667022
Swansea (Llangyfelach)
'ford at the fulling-mill': *rhyd, y, pandy*
Rhydypandy 1813, 1841, Rhyd y pandy 1852
The road running north from Llangyfelach towards Cynghordy must have once forded Afon Llan here but it had been replaced by a bridge before 1877. There was also a ford immediately east of the ht. in Nant y Milwr.

Rhydypennau ST 186811
Cardiff (Llanisien)
'ford over which packs are carried' or 'ford used by livestock': *rhyd, y,* and *pwn* pl. *pynnau* or *pennau*

Rhud y pynne Farm, Rood y Punny 1767, Reed a penne 1773, Rhydypenna 1831, Rhyd-penna 1833, (fm.) Rhydypennau 1880
The n. of a former fm. preserved in the n. of a school and road. All forms are late and certainty is impossible but two forms favour the first suggestion. Gwynedd Pierce (ADG², 87) prefers the second explanation with *pennau*, literally 'heads', with the sense 'heads of cattle, etc, livestock', i.e. a 'ford over which livestock were driven'. Rhydypennau (SN 6285), in Cardiganshire, has historic forms such as *Redepenne* 1284 (PNCrd 1104).

Rhymni¹ (Rhymney) SO 1107, 1206
Caerphilly
(place) *Rumny* 1826, *Rymni* 1828, *Rumney Works* 1829, *Rhymney Bridge* 1832, *Rhymney, Rumney* 1851, *Rhymney* 1871
Named from the Rhymney Iron Works which appeared in 1800 taking its n. from its proximity to the r. Rhymni² (q.v.). Rhymney was chosen as the n. of the ecclesiastical p. formed 1843.

Rhymni² (Rhymney)
rn.
Caerphilly, Cardiff
'river which bores like an auger', *rhwmp*¹
(r.) *Remni* 1102, *Rempney* 1200, (r.) *Rymni* early 13th cent, (water) *Rompney* 1314, 1590, *avon Rymhi* c.1400, *Rymney* 1541, *Rumney flu:* 1578
Some early forms lack –p- which presumably explains why R.J. Thomas (EANC 164-5) links the rn. with OW †*Gwrymi, Gorymi* GLA (= r. Waycock or a tributary) and compares it with Blaenrhymni near Pontardawe), Rummy, in Radnorshire, recorded in *Pull remmi* 1200, *Pulleremmy* 1215, and *Upper ~, Lower Rummey* 1833, etc, but he was unable to explain *Rhym-* (and *-rym-*) satisfactorily. There is nothing to favour *rhym*, a ghost word reputedly meaning 'what stretches round, that (which extends' (GPNG 28); this notion may lie behind Matthews's suggestion that it 'implies a boundary stream in a flat country' (CR V, 409). Glynrhymni (in Llanfabon) is recorded in (forest of) *Glynrempny* (near Caerphilly)

1429, *Glinrumney Hamlet* 1783, *Glyn-Rumney (Glyn-Rhymni)* 1840 (***glyn***).

Rhyndwyglydach　　　　　　SN 6801, 6901
Swansea (Llangyfelach)
'(administrative area) between the two (rivers) Clydach': (***parsel***), ***rhwng***, ***dwy*** rns. **Clydach**
(Ynysdderw between) *doygludagh* 1495, *Parcell Rhundwy Glydach* 1650, *Parcel rwng dwy Gledach* 1670, *parcell Rhwngdwyglydach* 1695, *parcel of Ryndwy clydach* 1733, *Rhyndwyclydach* 1852
The rs. are Clydach Isaf and Clydach Uchaf (***isaf, uchaf***). ***parsel*** is found in other parts of Wales with the particular sense 'sub-division' often of large ps. (as in this case) and larger administrative units. Variants of ***rhwng*** include *rin* in Glamorgan (GPC).

Risca see **Rhisga**

Riverside　　　　　　　　　　ST 175762
Cardiff (Llandaf)
'(area at) side of river (Taf): E ***river***, E ***side***
Riverside 1884
A modern n. coined for housing constructed from c.1880 between Wellington Street, Ninian Park Road (*Eldon Street* 1901, 1920), Tudor Street and the r. Taf and applied to a local government ward. A direct translation Glanyrafon (***glan, yr, afon***) is in informal use and Glan'rafon is used in EnWales 120. Neither have any historical basis.

Roath, Y Rhath　　　　　　　ST 193776
Cardiff
?'fort, ring-fort': ?Ir ***ráth***
Rad, Rath c.1166, *Raht* c.1178, *Radf, Rat* 1185, *Raad, Raath* early 13th cent, *Roth'* 1296, *Rooth* 1375, *Rath* 1401, *Roath* 1547, *Rothe* 1550, *Roath Bridge, Court ffarm* 1788, *y Raff* c.1566, *Rofe* 1766, (meadow in) *Rothismore* 1516, (lp.) *Roth Dogvile* c.1560, (~) *Roth Dogfeld* 1604, *Rothe Kensum* c.1598, *Rothe Teuxberye* 1570
A castle is recorded in Roath in 1185 which may be the mound described by the antiquarian Rice Merrick in the late 16th cent as *an old Pyle, compassed with a Mote, which is called 'the Court', but now in ruyne*. This presumably refers to a predecessor of Roath Court (ST 198776). The obvious question is why an Ir pn. el. should be employed in south Wales when there were already suitable W terms such as ***caer*** denoting a fort. One possible answer is that there may have been Ir settlement in this area, perhaps in conjunction with Norse settlers. We know of Scand or presumed Scand pns. in the vicinity such as Womanby Street (Cardiff), Lamby and Flatholm, and one pn. Dunraven may be a hybrid of Ir and Scand els. in Celtic word order. Similar hybrids are known in north-west England, the Isle of Man, Ireland and parts of Scotland and are taken as evidence of settlement by gaelicised Norsemen. The alternative explanation is that the pn. is taken from Roath Brook otherwise Nant y Rhath, containing an el. found in *rhathu* 'to scratch, to file', i.e. 'river which scrapes its banks'. This is thought to be the el. found in Amroth and in several minor rns. in Pembrokeshire (PNPemb 465). The difficulty with applying this explanation here is that early forms of Nant y Rhath alias Roath Brook have not been found. Roath/Y Rhath has also been speculatively connected with *Ratostabius fluvii ostia* in Ptolemy's Geography AD 140-150, partly on the apparent similarity of *Rato-* to *Rhath* and partly on linguistic arguments which are now considered untenable (PNGlam 172-4). The former manor of Roath Dogfield (in Llanisien) probably contains a pers.n. Dogwel, Dogfael (< OW *Docmail*) found in the n. of William *Docgevel* c.1155. Roath Keynsham was a manor which included land in Roath, Llanedern, Cardiff, Llandaf and Whitchurch takings its n. from the abbey of Keynsham, Somerset, which held it before the Dissolution. Roath Tewkesbury included Roath ch., Cardiff castle, and the White or Grey Friars in Cardiff, granted to Tewkesbury abbey, Gloucester.

Roath Park, Parc y Rhath　　ST 185792
Cardiff (Llandaf, Llanisien, Roath)
Roath Park (ST 7879) refers to public gardens laid out along the course of Roath Brook below the artificial Roath Park Lake 1887-94 and to

adjoining housing constructed mainly after 1918.

Robertstown, Tresalem SO 000034
Rhondda Cynon Taf (Aberdare)
'settlement named from Roberts': surname *Roberts*, E ***town***; 'settlement near Salem (chp.)': ***tref***,
chapel n.
Robert's Town 1852, *Robert's Town, Mr Robert's Lodge* 1861, *Tresalem* 1865
Probably named from Dr James Lewis Roberts (1810-64), a member of a prominent local landowning family who owned Gadlys Uchaf on which the ht. was built. Salem Independent chp. was built in 1841 (CVPN 84-5; MCPP 81-5). Robertstown was also a former n. for part of Ynysybŵl around Robert Street, giving its n. to a hotel and Robertstown School opened in 1886 between Crawshay Street and Thompson Street. These took their names from Robert Thompson Crawshay (PNIG 29; HLlanwyno[1], 21-22).

Rock ST 179986
Caerphilly (Bedwellte Monmouthshire)
'(settlement near) Rock': E ***rock***
Rock Chapel 1811, *Rockhouse* 1813, *Rock Inn* 1833, *Rock* 1858, (*capel*) *y Rock* 1882
Apparently named directly from the Calvinistic Methodist chp. There are similar chp. ns. elsewhere such as the former Independent chp. in Cwmafan recorded as *Rock* 1856 and *y Rock* 1872 adjoining the hill Craig y Tewgoed, and Rock Particular Baptist chp. (SO 094659) at Llanbadarn Fawr, Radnorshire, referred to as *y Roc* 1778 and *y Rock* 1838 in W sources. Chapel names of this sort might have been inspired by the local topography, a religious association with the Dome of the Rock, or St Peter ('the Rock'). Rock may also have described a broader area including the steep hillside extending northwards from Blackwood overlooking Afon Sirhywi since the OS map drawing 1813 has a ho. *Ty Craig* which must refer to *Rock House* (ST 174975) recorded in 1880 near St Margaret's ch. in Charlestown (Blackwood). OS maps for 1879 also show *Rock Cottage* (ST 174982) in Cwmgelli and *Rock Foundry* (ST 174979) less than a mile from Rock.

Rumney, Tredelerch ST 215794
Cardiff
'(place by r.) Rhymni': rn. **Rhymni**[2]; 'settlement of Telerch', ***tref***, pers.n. *Telerch*
(*de*) *Remneio* c.1160, *Rumia, Remni* c.1194, *Rempney* c.1291, *Remeny* 1295, *Rumeney* 1401, (bridge) *Remeebrygge* 1479, *Pont Remny, Rumnesbridge* c.1523, *Rumpney Mill* 1608, *Rumney in Englisch, in Walsch Tredelerch* c.1538, *tref delerch* c.1566, *Tredelyrch* 1590-1, *Tirdelarch* 1694, *Tredelarch* 1717, *Tredelerch* 1883
Rumney is an anglicised form of the r. *Rhymni*[2]. *Telerch* is composed of the honorific prefix *ty-* and pers.n. *Elerch*, earlier *Eleirch* (PNGlam 195-6; EANC 164-5). Misinterpretation of the n. gave rise to a tale, dating at latest from 1801 and repeated by Mathews (CR V, 425), Bradney (HMON V, 87) and others, that Tredelerch contains a variant form of *eleirch* or *elyrch*, pl. of *alarch* 'a swan', and that Elerch was also an alternative n. of the r. Rhymni. Rumney has also been identified with (ch. of *St Peter,*) *Treberge* 1292 but the ch. here is dedicated to Augustine, not Peter. Rumney was transferred from Monmouthshire to Cardiff County Borough in 1937.

Ruperra Castle see **Rhiwperra**

Ruthin see **Rhuthin**

St Andrews Major to Swffryd

St Donats castle and church, from a nineteenth century print.

Sain, Saint see under **St**

St Andrews Major, Saint Andras ST 138714
Vale of Glamorgan
'greater church of St Andrew': E *saint*, pers.n. Andrew, Lat *major*; W *saint*, pers.n. Andras
(*ecclesiæ*) *Sancti Andreæ* 1242, (~) *Sancti Andree* 1254, *St. Andrew by Cardiff* 1400, *St. Andrews, Dynaspowes* 1439, (p.ch. of) *S'ti Andree* 1535, *Sant Andras* 1554, *Saynt Andros* 1559, *Saint andras* c.1566, *St. Andrews Major* 17th cent, *Llanandras* c.1795
The ch. is dedicated to St Andrew. *Llanandras* is almost certainly an invention of the antiquarian Iolo Morganwg modelled on the genuine W n. Llanandras (*llan*) for Presteigne, Radnorshire. W *saint* seen in sps. for 1554 and c.1566 is derived from the E sing.noun *saint* and is not the pl. of *sant* 'saint'. The qualifier Major seems to occur only from the 17th cent but distinguishes it from St Andrews Minor (SS 928734) recorded as *St. Andros neare Wicke otherwise Clemenstoune* 1586, *St. Andrew Minor* 1661, *St. Andrews minor* 1670.

St Athan, Sain Tathan ST 016680
Vale of Glamorgan
'(ch. of) St Tathan': E *saint*, W *sain*, pers.n. Tathan
(ch. of) *Sancte Thathane* 1254, *St. Thathan* 1349, *Seint Atha* 1307, *Sancta Tathana* 13th cent, *Seint Athan* 1349, *Senathan* 1425, *Seynt Tathan* 1549, *St. Athan* c.1598, *St. Athans* 1670
St Tathan, otherwise known as Meuthi or Meuthin, is also dedicated at Llanfeuthin (q.v.), and is believed to have been an Ir saint who

lived in the 5th cent. His largely legendary 'Life' survives in a manuscript dated c.1200. The E form has lost the initial *T-* through confusion between *-t* and *T-* and misassociation with saints Athanasius of Alexandria and Athanasius the Anchorite. Forms with *Athan* dominate E sources from the late 17th cent but *Tathan* remained current among W-speakers.

St Brides Major, Saint-y-brid SS 895749
Vale of Glamorgan
'greater (ch. of) St Brigid': E *saint*, pers.n. *Bride*, Lat *major*; *saint*, *y*, cymricised pers.n. *Brid*
(ch. of) Ste. Brigide virginis 1138, (~) Stæ Brigidæ 1141, Sancta Brigida superiori 1247, Sancte Brigide majoris 13th cent, St Brides the More 1552, saint y brid c.1566, St. Brydes the greater 1576, Sct: Brides maior 1578, Great S. Brides 1645, St. Brides Majo^r: Parish 1670, Sant-y-Brid 1867
Dedicated to St Bride or Brigid of Ireland (d. c.523), the most-dedicated saint in Ireland after Patrick. The approved W form *Saint-y-brid* (rather than *Sanffraid* or *Ffraid*) appears to be a relatively late borrowing from the E pn., substituting *saint* (from E *saint*) and *Brid* [briːd] for *Bride*. 19th cent sources and current usage, however, favour the form *Sant-y-brid*. The –y- in both cases may be a natural intrusive sound between *-t* and *B-* or may be the def.art. *y* which was sometimes employed by W-speakers in some parts of Glamorgan as a connective particle before unfamiliar non-W pers.ns. Lat *major* distinguishes it from St Brides Minor but the p. was also variously known as St Brides the More (1551/2, 1560) (E *more* 'greater'), St Brides the Greater and Great St Brides.

St Brides Minor, Llansanffraid-ar-Ogwr
SS 897835
Bridgend
'lesser (ch. of) St Brigid: E *saint*, pers.n. *Bride*; 'church of St Brigid on (r.) Ogwr', *llan, san(t)*, pers.n. *Ffraid, ar*, rn. **Ogwr**
(ch. of) Sanctæ Brigidæ c.1168, Sancte Brigide Parve 1254, Sancte Brigide Minoris 13th cent, Brideston̄ c.1348, Lansanfride c.1538, Llansanfrede 1559, ll. san ffred or ogwr c.1566, Sct: Brides sup' ogmore, S. Brides upon Ogur 1578, St. Bridges minor, otherwise Saint Brides super Ogmore 1740, Llansanfryd 1754, St. Brides Minor 1799, Llansan-ffred ar Ocwr 19th cent
Cf. St Brides Major. *san(t)* 'saint' is employed as a prefix often used before the ns. of non-W saints. This need not reflect Norman influence, as Fenn (in VGS4: 117-8) has suggested, because there are at least seventeen dedications to Sanffraid / St Bride in Wales, most in areas where Norman influence was weak. The association between *san(t)* and the distinct el. AN *saint* would, however, have been a natural one in parts of Wales such as the Vale of Glamorgan where Norman and E influence was strong.

St Bride's-super-Ely, Llansanffraid-ar-Elái
ST 097776
Vale of Glamorgan
'(ch. of) St Brigid on (r.) Ely', E *saint*, pers.n. *Bride*, Lat *super*, rn. **Ely**; *llan, san(t)*, pers.n. *Ffraid, ar*, rn. **Elái**
lann sanfreit, Lann Sanbregit c.1170, Lann sant breit inmainaur crucmārc, ecclesiam sancte Brigide c.1145, (ch. of) Sancte Brigide 1254, ll. san ffred c.1566, Sct: bryde 1578, St: Brides are y Laie c.1612, St. Brides-super-Ely 1661, St. Brides on Eley 1781, St. Brides supr. Ely or Llansaintfread 1833, Llansantffraid-ar-lai 1872
Britton 1433, Britton sup(er) Elly 1535, and similar forms down to 1567, have been identified (PNDPH 253-4) with The Drope (q.v.) in St Georges p. which possesses forms such as *Britton-Thorpe* c.1659 and *Brytton Throps.* c.1670. The two groups of names actually refer to different places though both stand for 'bridge settlement' (E *bridge*, ME *-ton*). Britton is unlikely to contain *Bride* because historic forms lack possessive *'s*. *Britton super Elly*, etc would refer to a bridge over the r. Ely and *Britton-Thorpe* in St Georges to one over the stream Nant y Drope. The spelling for c.1145 indicates that St Brides lay in the *maenor* of Crugmarchan, a n. which contains *crug* 'hillock, cairn' (probably recalled in *Pen-crug* 1885 at ST 083784) and *marchan* found also in the fm. Parc-coed-machen (ST 090789). This is *Coidmerchan p(ar)ke* 1578, (park) *Coed Merchann*

c.1580, *Coed Marchan parke* c.1619 and *Parc-coed Machen* 1833 referring to a former park (*parc*) on the south side of the fm. Marchan probably contains **march** 'horse, stallion' with suffix – **an**, in this case perhaps a pers.n. rather than a rn. because there are no large streams in the immediate area apart from Nant Rhych flowing through St-y-Nyll (ST 095091).

St Donats, **Sain Dunwyd** SS 934681
Vale of Glamorgan
'(ch. of) St Donat': E *saint*, pers.n.; *sain(t)*, pers.n. *Dunwyd*
(chp. of) *sancti Donati* c.1178, *(de) Sancto Donato* before 1201, *Seint Donats* 1307, *(de) Sancto Donato Anglicano* 1341, *Seint Donet'* 1390, *Seyntdonattes* 1441, *saint dunwyd* c.1566, *St. Donaddes* 1603, *St. Donat's* 1599, *Sant Dvnawt* 1609, *S^t dynwyd* early 17th cent, *St Dunawd* 1818
The combination of St/Sain with a saint's n. is evidence of E naming patterns, cf. St Andrews Major and St Brides Major, and is typical of the Vale where E settlement was extensive in the Middle Ages. The sps. with *Donat(s)* and *Donatus* etc are likely to be products of association with the Ir saint Donatus of Fiesole (d. 876). *Anglicano* 1341 has Lat *anglicanus* (dative case) 'English' which distinguishes it from Welsh St Donats/Llanddunwyd though there is no evidence that St Donats was ever known as 'English St Donats'. Later W sources have *Dunawt, -d*. The forms Llanywerydd, Glanydon, and Llanweryryd used by Dafydd Morganwg are spurious derived from Iolo Morganwg (1747-1826).

St Fagans, **Sain Ffagan** ST 120772
Cardiff
'(ch. of) St Ffagan': E *saint*, pers.n.; *sain(t)*, pers.n. *Ffagan*
(de) sancto Fagano c.1178, *(~) Sco' Fagan'* c.1291, *Sanctus Faganus* 1307, *Seint Fagan* 1402, *Seyntvagan* 1412, *Sancti Fagani in Wallia* 1429, *Seyntfagan* 1440, *Sain ffagan* c.1566, *Sct Fagans* 1578, *San faganes* 1690, *St. Fagans* 1833
For the use of *sain(t)*, cf. Saint-y-brid (St Brides Major), Sain Siorys (St Georges-super-Ely), etc. Ffagan ['fagan] is said by antiquarians to have been one of four missionaries sent to Britain by Pope Eleutherius c.180 AD at the request of King Lleurwg, a great-grandson of Caractacus (VGS1, 38; CR V, 474, and see Llanfedw and Rhydlafar) but there is no firm historical evidence for this and the pers.n. is in any case Ir. There also appears to be no basis for the form *Llansanffagan* (CR V, 414). *St. Faggans* is the usual spelling of local man William Thomas (1762-95) (in DWT).

St Georges, **Sain Siorys** ST 104766
Vale of Glamorgan
'(ch. of) St George': E *saint*, pers.n. *George*; *sain(t)*, pers.n. *Siorys*
(ch. of) *Sancti Georgii* 1254, *(de) Sco' Georg'* c.1291, *St. Georges* 1292, 1833, *S. George* c.1538, *St. George Maleffaunt* 1540, *Seynt Georgis* 1542, *sain siorys* c.1566, *Saint Syorys, ~ Siorys* 1584, *Sain Sior* early 17th cent, (castle of) *Sant Jorys* 1609
Probably an AN foundation (PNDPH 249-51). The saint's n. is cymricised *Siôr, Siôrs* and more commonly *Siorys* (with intrusive vowel). Iolo Morganwg c.1800 uses the form *St. Iorys* which may perhaps be justified by local pron. but he also has the spurious forms *Caer Luned, Llan Iorys, Llanufelwyn* and *Llanfelwyn* which were accepted by a number of antiquarians including Dafydd Morganwg (HMorg 469). The 1540 spelling has the family n. *Malefa(u)nt(e)*, also appended to St Nicholas (q.v.). The Malefant family held St Nicholas in the 15th cent. Some late sources use the forms St George's and St Georges super Ely; neither are historical.

St Hilary, **Saint Hilari** ST 016732
Vale of Glamorgan
'(ch. of) St Hilary', E *saint*, pers.n. *Hilary*; *sain(t)*, pers.n. *Hilari*
(ch. of) *sancti Hilarii* c.1170, *(de) Sancto Hilario* c.1188, *(de) Sco' Hillar'* c.1291, *Sent Teleri* 1537, *Sain tilari* c.1560, *Sct: Hilerye* 1578, *St. Hillary* 1670, *St. Tillary* 1763
Probably St Hilary of Poitiers (d. c.367) or St Hilary of Arles (d. 449) and evidently an AN adoption. A few sps. such as *Sain tilari* show provection of *-t* in *St* to *Hilary* (the opposite of

Sain Tathan > St Athan) and also shift of stress from *Hil-* to *-ar-* [hɪl'ari:] in pron. by W-speakers. For the W form with *Saint*, cf. Sain Siorys (St Georges) and Sain Ffagan (St Fagans). There is no evidence to support the suggestion that St Hilary was ever known to W-speakers as *Llan-Sant-Elari* (as in HMorg 470).

St Lythans, Llwyneliddon ST 109729
Vale of Glamorgan
'(ch. of) St Eliddon': E *saint*, pers.n; 'grove of Eliddon', *llwyn*, pers.n. *Eliddon ecclesiam Elidon* c.1145, *luin Elidon* c.1170, *(de) Sancto Lythano* c.1291, *St. Lethian* 1400, *Sti' Lithani* 1535, *Lluen Lithan, Lanlithan* c.1538, *Ll. lidan* c.1549, *Llwyn Lyddon* 1550, *ll. liðan* c.1566, *Sct: Lethans* 1578, *St. Lythans* 1619, *Llwyn Ddyddan* 1729, *Llanddiddan* 1739
The E is evidently drawn directly from a former ch. dedication to St Eliddon, a W pers.n. made up of the prefix *El-* 'great, many', *-iudd-* 'lord, prince', and suffix *-on* as in Cynon, Mabon, Iddon, etc (PNDPH 260-2). Loss of the unaccented vowel E- by the mid 13th cent produced sps. such as *Lythan, Lethan, Lyddan* etc. and *llwyn* was then confused in some late sources with *llan*; cf. Llantriddyd. *Llanddiddan* 1739 may have been influenced by *diddan* adj. 'amusing, pleasant'.

St Martin's ST 153865
Caerphilly
'(area near ch. of) St Martin': E *saint*, pers.n. *Martin*
Named from the p.ch. of Caerphilly erected 1878-9 near the ancient chp. of St Martin recorded in 1586. The area developed along St Martin's Road from the 1890s, expanding during the 1930s.

St Mary Church, Llan-fair ST 001715
Vale of Glamorgan
'church of St Mary': E *saint*, pers.n. *Mary*; *llan*, pers.n. *Mair*
(Wm. de) *Seyntemariechurche* 1314, *Seint Marychurch* 1317, *Seyntmarichirche* 1349, *Seynt Merychurche* 1440, *Marychurche* 1541, (ch. of) *Beatæ Mariæ* 1699

The W form is poorly recorded but may be *Lanvaire* 1721 and occurs in a late 19th cent triban as *Llan-fair* (Trib 22). See also Beaupre.

St Mary Hill, Eglwys Fair y Mynydd
SS 961785
Vale of Glamorgan
'(ch. of) St Mary on a hill', E *saint*, pers.n. *Mary*, OE *hyll*, ME *hill*; 'church of (St) Mary on the mountain', *eglwys*, pers.n. *Mair*, *y*, *mynydd*
(ch. of) *Beate Marie super Montem* 1254, (~) *Sce' Marie sup' Monte'* c.1291, (~) *beate Marie supra Montem* c.1348, *Sancta Maria super montem* or *St. Maryes church upon the hill* c.1598, *St. Maryhill* 1535, *Sct: marias hill* 1578, *ll. fair or mynyð* c.1566, *Eglwys Fair y Mynydd* 1612, *Eglwys Vaer or St. Marys Church* 1729
A number of early forms have Lat *super montem* 'on the mountain'. The ch. (SS 957794) is located on a hill north of St Mary Down about a mile from the modern village which is properly Gelli-garn (q.v.). Only one historic form favours Llanfair with *llan*. The proximity of St Mary's to Gelli-garn and refs. such as *St. Mary Hill iuxta Kelligarne* 1640 have led to the supposition that it is the ch. recorded as *Kilthekarn* 1254 and *Sce' Marie juxta Kyltikarn* c.1291 but see Gelli-garn.

St Mellons, Llaneirwg ST 237810
Cardiff
'(ch. of) St Melan', E *saint*, pers.n. *Melan*; 'church of ?Lleirwg', *llan*, pers.n. ?*Lleirwg*
(ch. *de*) *sancto Melano* c.1195, (~) *Sancti Melani* 1254, *Sanctum Melanum* 1314, *Seynt Melen* 1476, *Seynt Melense* 1531, *LL. leirwc* c.1550, *ll. lirwg* c.1566, *Saint Melans* 1594, (*o*) *Lan Leirwg* early 17th cent, *St. Mellans (alias, Llaneurwg)* 1751, *St. Mellons* 1774, *Llaneurwg* 1801, *Llaneirwg* 1838
Also identified with *St. Melan de Porttaske* 1401 but *Porttaske* is unexplained. St Melan or Melaine was a Breton or Frankish bishop of Rennes 6th cent, dedicated as Melyan at St Mellion (*de Sancto Melano* 1198-1280, *Sanctus Melanus* 1259) and Mullion (*Sanctus Melanius* c.1225), in Cornwall, and is widely dedicated in Brittany. Bradney (HMON V, 91) preferred St Melanius, bishop of Rouen, 'to whom the

Norman church was dedicated', but he is evidently referring to a distinct Breton saint better known as Maclou or Malo. The W n. has **llan**, prompting the assumption that the second el. is a pers.n., identified by Matthews as St Lucius, 'the kingly "light-bearer"' (CR V, 268n, and 1414-5). This presumably gave rise to the form *Lleurwg* on the supposition that it contains *lleu* 'bright, shining' as in *Lleu* Llaw Gyffes in the medieval tales of the Mabinogi, although earlier forms of the pn. favour *Lleirwg*, a n. which has so far defied satisfactory explanation. The loss of -*ll*- (probably by dissimilation) seems to be first recorded in 1751 and local pron. was *Llanirwg* according to G.J. Williams (IoloMor 311). There seems to be no reliable evidence that Lleirwg/Lleurwg was a saint, a supposition which seems to begin with the antiquarian Iolo Morganwg c.1800. The area around the p.ch. (ST 228814) is now known as Old St Mellons or Pentref Llaneurwg to distinguish it from the housing constructed east of Newport Road in the 1980s.

St Nicholas, Sain Nicolas   ST 088742
Vale of Glamorgan
'(ch. of) St Nicholas', E **saint**, pers.n. *Nicholas*; **sain(t)**, pers.n. *Nicolas*
(ch. *de*) *Sancta Slichi*, (*de*) *Sto. Nicholao* c.1168, (*apud*) *Sanctum Nicholaum* 1248, (ch. of) *Sancti Nicholai* 1254, *Seynt Colas* 1508, *Saint Niclas* 1556, *sain nikolas* c.1566, *Saint Nikólas*, *Sain i Kólas* c.1613, *St. Nicholas Malefaunte* 1540
A 19th cent poetic triplet ('triban') rhymes *Nicolas* with *priodas* (Trib 318) stressed regularly on the middle vowel and this is confirmed by local testimony. There is a fuller list of sps. and closer analysis by Gwynedd Pierce (PNDPH 274-7). The ch. is dedicated to Nicholas (like Barry), probably St Nicholas (bishop of Myra, 4th cent), the saint of sailors, children, merchants etc, rather than Pope Nicholas (d. 867). The body of St Nicholas was moved from Constantinople to Bari (in Apulia, Italy) in 1087 and the similarity of Bari and Barry and the Norman connections with Apulia may have prompted the dedication to Nicholas. For *Malefaunt* 1540, see St Georges.

A reputed alternative W n. *Llanelnydd* may be a miscopying derived from Iolo Morganwg's *Eglwys Llaneinydd* who also has the otherwise unattested *Llan Nicolas* c.1810.

St Thomas   SS 666932
Swansea
'(chp. of) St Thomas': E **saint**, pers.n. *Thomas* (chp. of) *St. Thomas, Kylveye* 1320, (chp. of) *Sancti Thome Martyris in Kylvei* 1340, *St. Thomas Chappel in the late Burrough of Bettus* 1686, (ht.) *Saint Thomas* 1783
A chp. (in Kilvey, q.v.) which stood near the seashore and Salthouse Point, destroyed by sand dunes, its ruins recorded in 1697 and 1762 and re-discovered in the 1820s during construction of docks at the terminus of the Tennant Canal (Gower 61, 44-50). Described as the 'borough' of Betws (**betws**[1]) in a survey of Gower 1686 but this is almost certainly a misinterpretation of E *burrow*, i.e. 'sand burrow, sand dune'.

Saint-y-brid see **St Brides Major**

Saint-y-nyll   ST 095782
Vale of Glamorgan (St Bride's-super-Ely)
?'(ch. of) St Tylull': **sain(t)**, *Tylull*
Lann dilull 1128 and *Lann týlull* 1129 (c.1170), *S. Nele* c.1538, *St.-y-nyll* c.1560, *Sainct Nyll* 1600, *Santanel Supr. Elay* 1729, *St. Nill* 1737, *Saintnill* 1799, *Saintynyll* 1867
The first two sps. are taken from the Book of Llandaf which in ModW might appear as *Llandylull*, 'church of Tylull' (**llan**). It is possible that Saint-y-nyll developed by way of unrecorded intermediary anglicised forms *Saint Tylull, *Saintylull, and *Saintynull with dissimilation and finally *Saint-y-nyll* through shift of stress to the first syllable and association with the def.art. *y* seen in the modern map form. The large gap in historical evidence between the 12th and 16th centuries is bound to raise questions with this interpretation, however, and further evidence is needed. There is no explicit mention of a ch. here until 1880 when the OS 1:2,500 map shows *Site of Chapel* here and *Human Remains found A.D. 1866* nearby.

Saltmead   ST 174756
Cardiff (Llandaf)
'salt meadow': E *salt, mead*
Saltmead moors 1709, *ye Saltsmead* 1728, *Saltmead, Salt mead newyd* 1788, *Saltmead* 1891
Formerly part of Cardiff West Moors, much of it once affected by tidal flooding. Developed from c.1888. The n. now applies to the north part of Grangetown extending westwards from the r. Taf and Clare Road to the Penarth and Barry railway. Evidently, there was both an unrecorded 'Old Saltmead' and a 'New Saltmead' or Saltmead Newydd (*newydd*).

Sanctuary   SS 488875
Swansea (Penrice)
'sanctuary': E *sanctuary*
(lands) *Sanctuary* 1632, 1698, *the Sanctuarie* 1641, (ho.) *Centry* 1813
Known locally as 'Sentry'. Possibly located on the two acres of land granted by William de Narberth for a sanctuary of the Knights Hospitallers (WGOW IV, 98-101). There are similar pns. elsewhere such as Saintwalls (Llanrhidian) which is recorded as *Seintwar* 1641, *St Wall* 1721, (fm.) *Llodrog alias St Wall* 1764, *Saintwalls* 1879. Gwynedd Pierce (PNGlam 64-5) shows that this is derived from ME *seintuarie* 'sanctuary, holy place' borrowed as W *seintwar* and *seintwal*. Cyntwell (q.v.) is identical in meaning.

Sandfields   SS 742904
Neath Port Talbot (Aberafan)
E *sand*, E *field*
Sandfields 1894, *the Sandfields* 1901, *y Sandfields* 1909
An area of hos. developed from c.1894. The n. was extended to include the housing estate built after 1947 behind Aberafan beach on the levelled sand dunes of Aberavon Burrows (*Aberafon Marsh* 1830, *Aberavon Burrows* 1877).

Sandylane   SS 551888
Swansea (Pennard)
'(house on) lane covered with sand': E *sandy, lane*
Sandylane 1841

The n. referred to a ho. (ST 551889) and ajoining lane leading across what was part of Pennard Burrows and has been transferred to modern housing.

Sarn   SS 901835
Bridgend (St Brides Minor)
'causeway': *sarn*
(ho.) *Sarn fawr* 1813, *Sarn-fawr* 1833, *Sarnfawr, Sarnfach* 1841, *Sarn-fâch* 1877
Sarn-fawr (approx. SS 902836) and Sarn-fach (a little to the south) are distinguished as 'great' and 'little' (*mawr, bach¹*). Both hos. were close to Bryncoch Road leading north to Heol Cwrdy and the r. Ogmore (now bridged at SS 902839) but the causeway could actually refer to the road Sarn Hill leading to St Bride's ch. It gives its n. to housing developed between the World Wars and to Sarn Park Services on the M4.

Sarn Helen   SN 8003, 8205
'causeway of Elen', *sarn*, pers.n. *Elen*
Neath Port Talbot
(causeway) *Cawsy Elen lueddog* c.1700, *Sarn Helen Roman Road* 1833, 'the *Via Helena*, commonly called the *Sarn Helen*' 1840
A Roman road running along the ridge of Hirfynydd from a bridge near Aberdulais (RFWM 326: R622a). Its extension in Breconshire is recorded as *The Sarn Lleon or via Helena* 1809, an antiquarian n. The first ref. is 'causeway of Elen Luyddog' with *cawsai* and the n. of Elen 'the renowned' (*lluyddog*). Elen (from Lat *Helena*) was identified in 'The Dream of Macsen Wledig' (in the medieval tales of the Mabinogion) with Helen, wife of the Emperor Magnus Maximus and mother of Constantine. Elen or Helen is said to have caused high roads to be built 'from one stronghold to another in the Island of Britain'. The evidence for all instances of Sarn Elen/Helen is late and flimsy. The first instance of the n. is thought to be *surne Ellen* 1627 describing a piece of land in Newtown, Montgomeryshire. All other refs. appear to be c.1700 and later suggesting that Sarn Elen/ Helen was propagated as a n. by antiquarians familiar with the tales in the Mabinogion and was applied to Roman roads which had never

borne the n. There is very little evidence to favour the suggestion that the n. is a popular reinterpretation of *sarn halen*, 'salt road' (*halen*), a major road along which salt was carried.

Scurlage SS 464876
Swansea (Knelston)
'(place of family called) Scurlage': AN surname *Scurlage*
Scorlaggeskastel 1306, *Scurlagiscastel, Scurlage Castel* 1361, *Scor- , Scurlacescastell'* 1435, *Skorlages Castell* 1539, *Skurlach or Horton* c.1598, *Scurlage Castle* 1632, *Skurlag* 1650
Named from the family of Richard Scurlage who granted the manor to John Dou in 1361 (NCPN 119). Historic forms properly apply to Scurlage Castle (SS 461881) on the north side of the ht. which developed near Crosshouses from the 1960s. Paterson (AC 1922, 42) identified Scurlage as an ON pers.n. but it may actually derive from OE *Scīrloc* ('someone with 'bright hair') identified in a lost *Scurlagston* (Pwllcrochan), Pembrokeshire, recorded 1326-1608. Scurlage was also an earlier n. for the castle at Trecastell (q.v.), Llanhari, and the manor and fm. Coedcynllan (ST 018810). The n. occurs in Gower and Bridgend area from the mid 12th cent.

Sebastopol (SO 133045) see **Troedrhiw'r-fuwch**

Senghennydd ST 116907
Caerphilly (Eglwysilan)
?'territory associated with *Sangan': pers.n. ?*Sangan*, suffix *–ydd¹*
(land of) *Seinhenit* c.1179, *Seighenith* c.1194, *Seing- , Seynhenyz* 1268, *Seynghenyth* 1271, *Seyngheneth* c.1295, (*patria*) *Seinghenith* 1307, *Senghenyth* 1314, (land) *Seint Genyth* 1326, *Seynthenneth* 1476, *Saing henyð* c.1566
The n. Senghenydd (with one *n*) now applies to the village which developed around the Universal Colliery in the 1890s and is taken from the ancient administrative division. The suffix *–ydd¹* is found also in Eifionydd, Caernarfonshire, Meirionnydd, and Gwrinydd (q.v.) but the pers.n. is hypothetical. It could contain the el. *sang-* found also in *sangu* or *sengi* 'to tread' (ETG 15-16). **Sangan* and *–ydd¹* would produce Senghennydd with stress on -enn- and shift of vowels a-a to e-e; cf. *Mafan* and *–ydd¹* > Mefenydd, the n. of a commote in Cardiganshire (ADG², 90; PNGlam 27-30). The -h- has intruded before the vowel in the stressed syllable. The ancient cantref extended from Whitchurch to Merthyr Tudful and contained two commotes Uwch Caeach 'above (r.) Caeach' (**uwch**) and Is Caeach 'below (r.) Caeach' (**is**). These are recorded as *Senghenyth subtus Caagh* 1281, *Sengh[enith] super Caugh'* 1375, *Kymwt vch Caech, ~ is Caech* mid 14th cent, *Senghenydd sub Kaeach* 1490, *Com. Sengheneth huch, Singhenith ... devidid into Iskaihach, and Huhekaihach* c.1538, *Sain henyd, vwch kayach, is kayach* mid 16th cent (Lat *sub, subtus* 'below', *super, supra* 'above'). For the rn. Caeach see Llancaeach. The pn. has been explained as W **sain(t)** and a pers.n. *Cenydd* which gave rise to the false n. Trecenydd adopted for a housing estate (ST 1487) in Caerphilly in the 1950s (q.v.). Some fanciful tales are recounted by Dafydd Morganwg concerning a Cennydd ab Gildas y Coed Aur who reputedly established a college (*Cor Cennydd*). Some of these can be traced back to David Powel's *Historie of Cambria* 1584 and the false chronicle of Caradoc of Llancarfan. The north gate of Cardiff is called *Porte Singhenith* by John Leland c.1538 because it was the gate (**porth²**) through which the road passed towards Caerphilly and Senghennydd.

Seven Sisters, Blaendulais SN 819089
Neath Port Talbot (Cadoxton-juxta-Neath)
'(village named from) Seven Sisters Colliery': E **seven, sisters**; 'headwaters of (r.) Dulais', **blaen**, rn. *Dulais*
Seven Sisters, ~ Pit (Coal) 1878, (colliery) *Seven Sisters* 1884, *y Seven Sisters* 1908, (grange) *Blayth Tulleys* 1296, *Blaen Deylys* 1541, *Blaen dilas* 1631, *Blaen Dilaies* 1713
The colliery was opened in 1872 by Evan Evans of Neath and his son-in-law David Bevan (Evans & Bevan, Cadoxton), taking its n. from the 'seven sisters' of David Bevan's son Evan Evans Bevan. The village developed during the

1870s-1880s and its n. was in formal use by 1882 (MCPP 86-89; HSeven 49, 52). Similar names are found elsewhere, notably Seven Sisters in north London, named from seven elm trees (a n. in use from 1732) and Two Sisters Colliery or Pit recorded at Swansea in 1871 and 1908. The village lies in the upper part of the Dulais valley hence its formal W n. Blaendulais but it is locally known as *Y Sefn*. Both Christopher Evans (HSeven 3-5) in 1964 and Erastus Jones (HSoar 4) in 1951 state that older inhabitants gave its former n. as Cwmdulais (*cwm*) which appears in pre-1874 p. records of Ystradgynlais and Bryngwrach ch. Cwmdulais was also an alternative n. for Bryndulais fm. recorded as *Bryndylais* 1785 and *Bryn-dulais* 1878 (*bryn*) on the west side of the village.

Sger see **Sker**

Sgeti see **Sketty**

Sgiwen see **Skewen**

Shelf SS 936801
Bridgend (Coychurch)
'shelf, terrace': E *shelf*
(lands) *Tir y Shelf fawr* 1704, *Shelf* 1784, 1813, *Shelph* 1802
Referring to its location above Nant Brynglas. The first ref. has the def.art. *y* and *mawr*, *fawr*, 'the greater', implying a lost *Y Shelf Fach* with *bach¹* len. *fach* 'the lesser'. The same el. is found in fields-ns. such as *the Shilfe* 1711, *Y Shelf* 1741, *Erw Margarett or Shelf* 1708 and *Kaia'r Shelf* 1766 in Newton Nottage (*erw*, pers.n. *Margaret, cae* pl. *caeau, y*).

Shwt SS 890868
Bridgend (Betws)
?'water-course, shoot': *siwt*
Shwt 1877, 1919
siwt is recorded locally for E 'gutter(ing)' but the sense here is probably 'water-course' and is comparable with E dialect *shut* or *shoot* found in Pembrokeshire with the meaning 'water-trough' (PNPemb 714); cf. also the use of *cwter*.

The n. applies to a small group of buildings including Glannant Row which adjoins what appears to be an industrial leat running parallel to part of a former tramroad connecting Llantwit Colliery to a railway running down the Llynfi valley to Bridgend. The water from the leat was probably used to remove top-soil, rocks and vegetation to expose mineral seams in a process known as 'scouring'.

Sigingstone, Tresigin ST 972716
Vale of Glamorgan (Llantwit Major/ Llanmihangel)
'settlement of (man called) Sigin': pers.n. *Sigin*, OE *tūn*; *tref*, pers.n. *Sigin*
(Hugh Sigin of) *Siginestone* c.1260, *Sygynston* 1495, *Sygenstonn* 1531, *Siginstone* 1536, *Siginston* 1601, (well) *Sigiston well, Siginswell* c.1598, *Tresigan* 1764, *Treshigin or Sigginstone Farm* 1791, *Tresigin* c.1800
This may also be the location of (lands) *Sygyns londs* 1488 (*land*). Clark (Cartae II, 655) describes Hugh Sigin c.1260 as 'a Llantwit juror', and says that the family *Siggin* probably entered Glamorgan in the 12th cent or early 13th cent. The pn. should be compared with (land) *Teere Siggen* (at St. Brides Major) 1600 and (~) *Tir Sygyn Ycha* (at Llampha) 1569. *Treshigin* 1791 suggests that it was pronounced with the aspirate *sh* [ʃ] (for *s*) found elsewhere in south Wales.

Sili see **Sully**

Silstwn see **Gileston**

Singleton SS 627921
Swansea
?'(house named from family called) Singleton': surname *Singleton*
(ho.) *Singletons* 1650, (tmt.) *Singleton* 1714, 1754
There seems to be no early evidence for the pn. Probably taken from the family of Robert *de Sengeltone* recorded at the lost Bryn-y-misgl (near Pant-gwyn SS 623927) in 1319 and Thomas *Sengleton'* 1383, ~ *Sengleton* 1399. The n. became more prominent when it was

transferred in the 1820s by John Henry Vivian family to his new ho. Singleton Abbey (now part of Swansea University campus) which he built around an older ho. known as Marino (recorded 1799). Singleton occurs as a pn. in Lancashire ('settlement where shingles are manufactured': OE *scingol*) and Sussex (possibly 'the brushwood farm or estate': OE **sengel*, **sængel*); see CDEPN, ODEPN. The relationship between Singleton and Singlewood recorded as (land) *Single-Wood* 1738 and *Singlewood* 1764 at Oystermouth is unclear but can hardly be coincidental. Singlewood could be elliptical for 'wood belonging to (place called) Singleton'.

Sirhywi (Sirhowy)   SN 1409, 1602, ST 1794
rn. Caerphilly (Monmouthshire)
(r.) *Serewi* c.1190 (1290), *Syrowy*, *Sirowy* 1467, *Sherowy* 1476, *Sirywi* 1479, *Sirrowie* 1718
The meaning is uncertain. The first el. is unidentified though the suffix is probably the common **-wy**[j] as in Conwy, Llugwy, etc. The valley is *Diffrin Serowy* 1536-9 and *Glyn Serwy* 1314 (**dyffryn**, **glyn**). The OS describes it as Sirhowy Valley/Cwm Sirhiwi with **cwm** 'small valley' but this is an inaccurate and unhistoric translation; cf. the use of Cwm Taf for Glyn Taf and Cwm Rhondda for Glyn Rhondda.

Sker, **Y Sger**   SS 795798
Bridgend
'(the) rock': ON **sker**
Blachescerre c.1170, *Blakeskarra*, *Blakeschare* 1208, *le Blackscerr* c.1670, (gr.) *Skerra* c.1175, *Skarra*, *or Sker* c.1291, *Sker* 1535, (gr.) *Skeere in Newton* 1542, *the Sker* 1782, *Rocau'r Scer* 19th cent, (cape) *Sker Point* 1799, *Scarveur House* 1729, *y Scer Fawr* 1874, `r Sger* 1919
Named from Sker Point (SS 787798) and the Sker Rocks which are described as 'a reef of rocks visible on the shore at low water' (BirchN 46); cf. The Sker (at Bishopston, but not current) recorded as *Sker* 1764 and in *Skergrove* 1675. Early refs. have OE **blæc** 'black' possibly distinguishing these rocks from Tusker Rock. Y Scer or Y Scer Fawr (**mawr**, *fawr*) were evidently the local forms. The latter referred to a crag of limestone quarried away in the 17th-18th cents.

Sketty, **Sgeti**   SS 625929
Swansea
'water-meadow of (man called) Ceti': **ynys**, pers.n. *Ceti*
Enesketti 1319, *le Skette* 1400, *Sketty* 1583, *Scetty* 1718, *Sketty Llwyd alias Brinkenol* 1764, (hos.) *Sketty Hall* 1799, (~) *Sketty Green*, *~ Hall* 1832, *Yscetty* 1867, *yr Ysgetty* 1872
The loss of Yn- may be attributed to association with **yn** 'in' comparable with colloquial 'Sforgan' for Ynysforgan, 'Spenllwch' for Ynyspenllwch and 'Stawe' for Ynystawe. The pers.n. is also found in Kilgetty, Pembrokeshire (with **cil**) and in Maen Ceti an alternative n. for Arthur's Stone (SS 491905) on the hill Cefn Bryn (ADG², 10; APNW 190) recorded by the antiquarian Malkin 1807 as *King Arthur's Stone, … in Welsh the Stone of Sketty* (Malkin II, 490) and by Dafydd Morganwg 1874 (HMorg 35) as *Maen Cetti* or *Coeten Arthur* (**maen**).

Skewen, **(Y) Sgiwen**   SS 72594
Neath Port Talbot (Cadoxton-juxta-Neath)
?'river-meadow of ?Cuen', **?ynys**, ?*Cuen*
(rivulet) *Skuen* c.1688, 'r *Skuen* c.1700, *Vaink Scuan* 1784, *Bank y Scuen* 1785, *Askewan* 1813, *Mainc-ysgawen* 1830, *Skewen* 1851, *Sgiwen* 1870, *Sciwen* 1894, *i'r Sciwen* 1908
Cuen is a pers.n. according to Richards (VNeath 330) but may be taken directly from a small stream rising on south side of Mynydd y Drumau running to the ht. and r. Neath. On the analogy of Sketty (q.v.) and Skenfrith, Monmouthshire, it is possible that *Skewen/Sgiwen* is a re-interpretation of an earlier, undocumented *Ynys Cuen* with loss of Yn- through association with **yn** 'in'. Unlike Skenfrith, and perhaps Sketty, the unstressed –*y*- seems to survive in *y Scuen* and the colloquial form *Y Sciwan* in use among W-speakers. Early sps. appear to rule out the pers.n. *Ciwen*, variant *Ciwan*, suggested by R.J. Thomas (EANC 123) though this may have influenced later forms of the pn. Some forms also associate the pn. with *ysgawen* 'elder-tree'. The *mainc*, *fainc* 'bench'

recorded in 1784 and 1830 refers to the low ridge on which the older part of the village lies.

Slade SS 487860
Swansea (Oxwich)
'low, flat valley': E *slade* (OE *slæd*)
Slade, wester Slade alias Lym Slade 1591, *Slade* 1632, 1799, *Slade alias Limeslade* 1671
slade is generally translated as 'a valley' but in Gower it is often applied to a 'low flat valley' (NCPN 125) and was in common colloquial use. Other instances are recorded in Bishopston, Llanrhidian and Penrice, and at least six ps. in the Vale, and further afield in Monmouthshire and Pembrokeshire. Slade on modern OS maps was the 'eastern Slade' (*Easternslade* 1879) in contrast to Western Slade (SS 481860) (*Wester slade* 1632) otherwise Lime Slade which is notable for limestone; cf. Limeslade.

South Cornelly see **Cornelly**

Southerndown SS 882738
Vale of Glamorgan (St Brides Major)
'south, southernmost hill or down': OE *sūðer, dūn*
Southdoune 1361, *Southerdoune* 1501, *Southerndown* 1605, *Northdowne, Sotherdowne* 1631, *Southerdown* 1727, *Setterdown* 1765, *Southern-down* 1833
Charles (NCPN 148) compares Norton in the same p. recorded as *Nortun* 1767, *Norton farm* 1785, *Norton, Sutton* 1833 (*norð, sūð, tūn*).

Southgate SS 550880
Swansea (Pennard)
'south hut', later 'south gate': E *south*, ME *cot* later E *gate*
Southcott 1634, 1709, *Southgate* 1729, (ho.) *South Gate* 1799, *Southgate* 1813
Charles (NCPN 127) locates *Southcourte* 1399 here but the identification is not certain. If reliable, then the second el. is ME *court*, 'court, grange, house'. 'South' may contrast it with Norton. *gate* may have been substituted for *cot* under the influence of the ho.n. Greenlane Gate (SS 557884) on Pennard Road or Widegate (SS 566881) 1km to the east.

Spelter SS 853936
Bridgend
'(place at) spelter works': E *spelter*
Spelter, ~ works 1841, *Spelter* 1868
Named from spelter works built by James H. Allen in 1830 near Y Coegnant (Lloffyn 16-18; HMorg 364). The works were connected to a tramroad – the Dyffryn Llynfi and Porthcawl Railway – and were held by The Llynvi Coal & Iron Co. Ltd. from 1845. Spelter was an alloy of zinc and copper used for soldering or zinc and lead for cheap cast articles such as candlesticks and ornaments.

Splott (Splottlands), **(Y) Sblot** ST 201766
Cardiff (Roath)
'a spot, a plot of land': OE *splott*
the Splott, Splot 1392, *Splot* 1401, *Splot a maner place* c.1538, *the Splote by Cardiff* 1586, *the Splott* 1658, *Splott in Roath* 1702, *Upper ~ , Lower Splot* 1833, *Splotteland terrace* 1868
Cf. Splot (Colwinston), Splott (Penmark) recorded as (meadow) *ye Splot* 13th cent and *Splot* 1587, Splott (St Donats), (meadow) *the Lower splott* (Nicholaston), *Splott* (Penrice) c.1640, *the green splott* (Pennard) 1650, and Heol y Splott (Pyle SS 8380) (*heol*). *splot* is still used in south-west England dialect for 'a plot or little piece of ground' (NCPN 161) and this was evidently the case in those parts of Glamorgan where the E language has been spoken since the Middle Ages. It also provides further evidence for the close relationship between the E language spoken on either side of the Bristol Channel.

Springfield, Maesyffynnon ST 183956
Caerphilly (Mynyddislwyn)
?'field near a spring': E *spring, field*; 'the well field', *maes, y, ffynnon*
Springfield Cottages is applied in 1901 to cottages (ST 181954) on the south side of Pontllan-fraith but later housing development included *Springfield Terrace* 1953 (ST 194961) half-a-mile eastwards and this is the focus of modern Springfield. This lies close to Ton-y-pistyll (q.v.) which raises the possibility that Springfield is a late translation of Tonypistyll,

'unploughed land at the spring', *ton*², *y*, *pistyll*. Maes-y-ffynnon appears to be a late adoption by the local authority.

Stalling Down SS 0174
Vale of Glamorgan (Llanblethian)
?'stallion's down', ?ME ***stalun***, ***down***
Stallingdour 1585, *Stallinge downe* 1645, *y staling downe* 1651, *Staling Thorn* c.1670, *Stallingdown* 1710, 1824, *Stalliondown* 1852
A ref. to horse races on *the Stalling down* in 1764 and a 'Horse Course' in 1792 seem to confirm the suggested meaning. The first el. could perhaps be E *stalling* describing a stall where animals might be kept. In Glamorgan it occurs in a bequest of a dwelling ho. with garden, croft and *stalling court* at Wick in 1750. Any such building, however, has yet to be found on Stalling Down. The W n. is said to be Bryn Owen (GazWPN; BroM 29) 'Owen's hill' (***bryn***, pers.n. *Owen*) on the basis of a reputed battle of Owain Glyndŵr in 1401 shown on OS maps between 1878-1964. The story seems to originate with Iolo Morganwg.

Stanleytown ST 011940
Rhondda Cynon Taf (Llanwynno)
'settlement named from Stanley' or 'settlement near Stanley Hotel': surname *Stanley*, E ***town***
Stanleytown 1896
Built around the Stanley Hotel probably named from the explorer H.M. Stanley (1841-1904). The hotel is recorded from 1898.

Stembridge SS 468918
Swansea (Cheriton and Llangennith)
'bridge made of stones': OE ***stǣniht***, ***brycg***
Steentebrugge 1306, *Stenbridge* 1575, *Bury alias Stenbrige* 16th cent, *Burrey alias Stembridge* 1704, *Stembridge* 1583, 1650, *Stone Bridge* 1813
Over Burry River (SS 468917). See Charles in NCPN 122, and cf. Stembridge (SS 946741), near Llandow, recorded as *Steynesbrugge* 1364 and *Stembridge* 1231, and Stem Bridge, Pembrokeshire (PNPemb 681). The shift from *-n-* to *-m-* is caused by anticipating the following *-b-*.

Stormy SS 840815
Bridgend (Tythegston)
'(place belonging to family called) Sturmi': surname *Sturmi*
(*terra*) *Sturmi* c.1150, (*villa*) *Sturmi* c.1170, *Sturmiestun'*, *Sturmi* 1235, *Sturmy* c.1291, *Courte Bechan...apud Istormy* 1518, *Courtbaghan alias Parva Stormy ... juxta grangiam de Stormy alias Stormy Magna* 1543, *Storme Major, ~ Minor* 1547, *Stormy le more and Stormy le les* 1623, (ho.) *Stormey* 1799, *Stormy, -fawr* 1833
Note Roger *Sturmi* 12th cent and Geoffrey *Esturmi* 1150 x 1166. The property was acquired by Margam abbey between 1154 and 1183 and appears to have consisted of two granges. Gray (BCKenfig 259) identified the ruins of the ch. nearly 800 yards east of Stormy Grange alias Stormy-fawr (SS 849821) (***mawr***). The 1518 and 1543 sps. show that the W n. of Parva Stormy/Little Stormy (now plain Stormy) is Cwrt Bychan, with ***cwrt***¹ in the specific sense of 'farm, grange' and ***bychan***. The hill Stormy Down (SS 848807) is *Mynydd Stormye Common* 1605, *Stormy Down* 1799, and *Stormey Common* 1814 (***mynydd***, ***down***, ***common***).

Sully, **Sili** ST 152683
Vale of Glamorgan
?'(place belonging to family called) Sully': surname or transferred n. *Sully*
(*Walter de*) *Suli* c.1185, *Sully* 1205, *Sulye* 1254, *Silly by Kaerdyf* 1376, *jnsulam vocatam Port Silly id est litille Silly sequitur jnsulam Barry* 1478, *p. sili* c.1566, *Scilley, Scylley* c.1538, *Sellie* 1549, *Sylley a creke for small boats* 1562, *Sylye, ~ Insul* 1578, *Syli, dyffryn Syli* 1584, *Afon Sily, Syli* c.1780, *Sili* 1799
The n. of a p., island (ST 167669) and stream. The manor was held from the late 12th cent by the family de Sully but it is uncertain if they derived their n. from the place or whether the place gave rise to their n. (PNDPH 290-3). Paterson (AC 1920, 46) favoured the meaning 'something cleft or furrowed' with ON *øy* (***ey***) 'island', and *súla*, dialect *sul*, referring to the shape of Sully Head which has raised east and west ends and low ground between them. ON pns. are certainly found along the coast of Wales

but Pierce notes the occurrence of individuals such as *Reymundus de Suly* in Devon who was a contemporary (1205-c.1250) and perhaps identical to a namesake at Sully, Glamorgan. It is also worth noting that all historical refs. before 1254 apply to members of the family rather than the place. As a surname, Sully may have been taken from one of several places called Sully and Silly in France. Modern pron. by E-speakers rhyming the pn. with E 'to sully' ['sʌli:] is difficult to square with forms such as *Silly* 1376, 1478, etc and the W form *Sili*. The answer may lie with forms such as *Syli* in which –*y*- could represent a long vowel similar to W (and Fr) –*û*- [ɨː]. Sps. such as *Sili* would be attempts at representing this vowel with a long -*i*- [iː] or may have been influenced by analogy with the *Scilly* Isles. *Port Silly* 1478, *havenet* c.1538 and *creke* 1562 refer to the area where Sully Brook and Cadoxton River reach the Bristol Channel on the east side of Barry Island. One source describes this as *Abersili* c.1805-10 but this is otherwise uncorroborated. .

Swanbridge ST 164676
Vale of Glamorgan (Lavernock)
?'swan bridge': E *swan*, ?E *bridge*
Swanbury c.1700, *Swanbridge* 1762, 1777
Late sps. favour **bridge** but there is no specific ref. to a bridge here and it could be a re-interpretation. Gwynedd Pierce suggests the spelling with -*bury* may be significant, perhaps from OE *byrig* dat. of **burh**, 'fortified place, fort' (EPNE I, 58-62) or OE *beorg* 'hill, hillock, mound', referring to Hopkin's Mount (PNDPH 47, 48). Swanbridge is described as *Sully Passage* in 1799 since it was the departure point for Sully Island.

Swansea, Abertawe SS 656930
Swansea
?'Sveinn's island': Scand pers.n. *Sveinn*, ?ON *ey*; 'mouth of (r.) Tawe', **aber**, rn. **Tawe**
Sweyneshea c.1187, *Suinesea*, -*hæ* 1190, *Sweinesei* 1210, *Sweineshe*, *Sweynseya* 1234, *Sweyneseye* 1277, *Swanesey*, -*e* 1322, *Sweynesse* 1168 (early 14th cent), *Swaynesey* 1465, *Swannesey in Gower* 1505, *Swansey* 1578, *Abertawe* c.1191, *aber tawe* c.1566, *Abertawi*, *Abertaui* c.1286, *Aber Tawy* c.1400
The second el. could also be Scand *sær* 'sea, ocean' but the occurrence of *ey* in the names of islands such as Bardsey, Ramsey and Anglesey (NCPN 130-1) is more convincing. The actual island has not been certainly identified and the suggestion that it may be identified with *Le Ylond* 1425, *Iselond'* 1432 and *Island* 1641 must be rejected because this evidently referred to a water-meadow further up the r. Tawe. The second suggestion is that it applied to the former tidal sandbank at the mouth of the r. removed in the 1840s and by later dock works but this would have been far too small and perilous to accommodate a settlement. See further Gwynedd Pierce (PNGlam 181-185) and Gerald Gabb (Gower XXXIX). The third possibility is that the island refers to the site of medieval Swansea. Few traces of the city's origins survive but a reconstruction of its lay-out based on historic maps, written and archaeological evidence, shows that the original medieval borough occupied a tongue of land defined on the east by the former course of the r. Tawe and by a ditch and small stream on the west (MedSwans). Some of the more fanciful theories on the meaning of Swansea are collected by the Revd. Thomas Morgan (OPN 154-5) and W.Ll. Morgan (ASEG 221-50). One of the most enduring is that Swan- refers to the bird, hence the nickname of Swansea City FC as 'The Swans' and their white sports clothes.

Swansea Valley, **Cwm Tawe**
Neath Port Talbot and Swansea
'valley near Swansea': pn. *Swansea*, E **valley**; 'valley of (r.) Tawe', **cwm**, rn. **Tawe**
the Vale of Swansea, or rather of Towey 1819, *the Swansea Valley* 1845, *Swansea Valley* 1921
The upper part of the valley was Glyn Tawe (**glyn**) giving its n. to Glyntawe chp. (alias Capel Callwen), in Breconshire, and occasionally used as an alternative n. for Ystradgynlais (PNBre 85). In earlier sources Cwmtawe applied to several tmts. in Llan-giwg recorded as *Cwm Tawe* 1600 and *Cwm Tawy* 1764 and in Ystradgynlais recorded as *Cwmtawey* 1712.

The E n. simply refers to its proximity to Swansea and confirmed by association with the Swansea Canal completed in 1798. The n. was reinforced by the construction of the Swansea Vale Railway up the valley in the 1850s, reaching Ystalyfera in 1861.

Swffryd SO 216988
Caerphilly (Llanhiledd, Monmouthshire)
Uncertain
Sofrydd 1616, 1857, *Soverith farm* 1707, *Swffrid* 1813, *the Soverydd Farm* 1832, *Swffrid Farm, Swffridfach* 1833, *Soverith fach*, ~ *Vawr*, ~ *Isha* 1841, *Soferydd-fach*, ~ -*fawr*, *Lower Soferydd* 1871, *Swffryd* 1880, *Soverydd* 1895

Most historic sources favour *Sofrydd* with a variant *Soferydd*, later displaced by *Swffrid* and *Swffryd* which seem to be confined as written forms to OS maps. These may have been influenced by **swfr** 'murmur; din, noise' which is probably a late back-formation from *syfrdanu* 'to stun, to bewilder; to rave, to babble' (GPC). Earlier evidence is clearly needed but it is possible that the pn. is composed of an authenticated pers.n. *Serw* coupled with the common territorial suffix –**ydd**[1] (as in Gwrinydd and Senghennydd) in the sense 'land of (man called) Serw'. An original **Serwydd* with variant **Serfydd* (displaying alternation of -*w*- and –*f*- as, for example, in *cawod/cafod* 'shower') could have produced **Sefrydd* (by inversion of -*rf*- and –*fr*-) and **Syfrydd* (comparable with the historical forms *Seaverny Hill* 1622, *Craig Syvyrni* c.1700 for Craig Syfyrddin, Monmouthshire) and finally *Sofrydd* (through confusing the similar sounds -*yf*- [əv] and –*of*- [ɔv]) recorded from 1616. Historic forms for the period from 1707 down to 1871 imply a variant *Soferydd* although it is not clear if the middle vowel –*e*- was stressed, i.e. [sɔ'vɛrɪð]. If it was then it is presumably intrusive. The pn. is taken from three hos. distinguished as 'small', 'large' and 'middle' (**bach**[1], **mawr**, **canol**) and applied to the hill (*the Soverydd Mountain* 1853) on which they are located. This has a wooded slope Craig Swffryd (**craig**) on its western side and the form *Graig-y-Seferydd* is applied to its south-eastern slopes in 1833. The suggestion (PNWG 69) that the pn. contains *swf* 'spot or place' with *ffridd* 'mountain pasture or sheepwalk' may be safely rejected. The first el. is not recorded in GPC and the second is typically found in north and mid-Wales.

Taf to Tythegston

Tylorstown. East Road, looking north towards Pendyrys Colliery, c.1925.

Taf (Taff)
rn. Cardiff, Merthyr Tudful, Rhondda Cynon Taf
'flowing (r.)': Brit *tam-*
Taf 1102, *Tamii fluminis* c.1140, *Taf maur, Tafbechan* c.1170, *Taam, Taaph* c.1200, *Tave vechan* 1444, *Taffe vawr* 1461, *Taue uaure flu., Taue uachan flu:* 1578, *Blayne ~ , Great Taf* 1584, (place) *Taue Vaure* late 16th cent, *River of Taffe* c.1598, *Taffe* 1612
Taf belongs to a group of rns., including Thames, Tamar, Tawe (q.v.), Tay, etc. which were once thought to contain IE *tam-* in the supposed sense of 'dark'. The gen. form *Tam-i* developed into *Tyf* by *-i* affection (PNGlam 125-7) and survives in Cardiff (q.v.). The headwaters Taf Fawr and Taf Fechan, recorded as *Taf maur, Tafbechan* c.1145, *Tavevechan* 1651 (**mawr, bechan**), rise on the Brecon Beacons/Bannau Brycheiniog and meet at Cefncoedycymer. There is another Taf in Carmarthenshire and Pembrokeshire recorded as *Tam, taf* c.1145, *Taf* c.1170, *Taph* c.1191.

Taf a Cynon ST 0895
Merthyr Tudful
'(area between) Taf and Cynon': rn. **Taf**, conj. *a*, rn. *Cynon* asp.mut. *Chynon*
(forest between) *Taf and Cavan* (= *Canan*) 1307, *Tavern Kennon* 1670, (ht.) *Taff & Cynon* 1752, *Tâf and Cynon* 1811

a 'and' regularly causes asp.mut. (ch) [χ] but is ignored in historic forms.

Taff Merthyr Garden Village　　ST 106980
Merthyr Tudful
'village near Taff Merthyr (Colliery)': colliery n., E *garden*, E *village*
Established in the 1930s partly on land of Gilfach-maen Isaf fm. after the opening of Taff Merthyr Colliery in 1926. The housing was known locally as Stormtown because of its exposed location on hill-slopes. The modern n. does not appear on OS maps till the 1980s.

Taff's Well, Ffynnon Taf　　ST 122833
Rhondda Cynon Taf (Eglwysilan)
'well near (r.) Taf': rn. *Taf* anglicised *Taff*, E *well*; *ffynnon*, rn. **Taf**
Hot-well, ~ House 1729, (ho.) *Funnon Tave* 1778, *Taf's Well farm* 1795, *Ffynhon Daf, called by some Ffynhon dwym, or the Tepid well* 1814, *Taffs Well* 1825, *Fynnon Tâf, or "the well of Tâf"* 1840, *Ffynon Taf* 1873
Some historical forms favour the form Ffynnon Daf with len. *t* > *d* because **ffynnon** is a nf. Named from a well believed to cure rheumatism. The 'hot well' Ffynnon-dwym is also recorded as *Ffynhon twm* 1795 (**ffynnon**, *twym* 'warm, hot'). The village consisted of only a few hos. in 1851 but expanded to cover both Portobello recorded as *Portybello* 1769, *Portobello* 1811 and the area known as Walnut Tree Bridge (ST 312832) recorded as *Walnutre, Walnut* 1841 and *Walnut Tree Bridge* 1851. Portobello commemorates Porto Belo, in Panama, captured by the English admiral Edward Vernon in 1739. In 1875 it referred to an inn near Sycamore Terrace (now Sycamore Street). The n. subsequently changed to Taff's Well Inn and Portobello was transferred as a n. before 1900 to a former inn in the middle of the village nearly opposite Castle Street. The n. was often given to public hos. such as Portobello (at Ogmore) now known as Portobello House and sometimes to domestic hos. which gave rise to Portobello (a suburb of Edinburgh) and Portobello Road (London). Walnut Tree Bridge is reputedly named from walnut trees said to have been chopped down for railway requirements (PNIG 37). The n. applied to a bridge over the Glamorganshire Canal (*Walnut Bridge* 1833), adjoining hos. in 1841, a bridge over the Taff Vale Railway (*Walnut Tree Bridge* 1875) and the junction of this railway with the New Rhymney Railway.

Taff Vale, Cwm Taf　　ST 0890, 0989, 1184
Cardiff/Rhondda Cynon Taf
A modern n. for what is properly Glyn Taf (see Glyn-taf). In Glamorgan a long, relatively narrow valley is **glyn**; **cwm** typically refers to a small, short valley. Cf. the use of Cwm Rhondda for Glyn Rhondda.

Tai-bach　　SS 775881
Neath Port Talbot (Margam)
'little houses': *tŷ* pl. **tai**, **bach**[1]
(ho., etc) *Taybach* 1773, 1794, *Taibach, Croeswen* 1813, *Tai-bach* 1832
Apparently named from four small thatched hos. that once stood at the bottom of the former Water Street (StTaibach 21, 26-7) and the lower end of St Alban's Terrace. Note also *Tai bach* 1795 in the ht. Heolwermwd, Merthyr Tudful.

Tai'r-gwaith　　SN 720120
Neath Port Talbot (Llan-giwg)
'houses near the works': **tai**, *y* affixed as `r, **gwaith**
Tairgwaith 1903, *Tair Gwaith* 1918
A small ht. which developed in the late 19th cent near Gwaun-cae-gurwen Colliery. Cf. Tai'rheol.

Tai'rheol　　ST 105949
Caerphilly (Llanfabon)
'houses on the road': **tai**, *y* affixed as `r, **heol**
(ho.) *Ty heol* 1813, *Tay yr Heol* 1841, (ht.) *Tai-yr-heol* 1881, *Tairheol* 1888
On Llanfabon Road. The n. distinguished it from a row of four hos. known as *Tai-machine* 1875 (ST 108951) removed during the 1960s

by housing development and re-alignment of Mafon Road. The n. means 'houses at the machine', ***tai***, *y*, and *masîn* nmf. 'machine' but its precise meaning is uncertain since 'machine' might be applied to a variety of industrial apparatus. Tai'r-machine lay near a former branch railway running from Llanbradach and other collieries to the Taff Vale Railway.

Tai'rysgol   SS 693973
Swansea (Llansamlet)
'the school houses': ***tai***, *y* affixed as `*r*, **ysgol**¹*
Tai yr Ysgol 1851, *Tai-yr-ysgol* 1881, *Tai'r Ysgol* 1908
The former school was near Bethel Independent chp. (built 1818) on Bethel Road and was later known as Peniel Green Infants School.

Talbot Green, Tonysguboriau   ST 039828
Rhondda Cynon Taf (Llantrisant)
'open land near Talbot Arms': public ho., E ***green***; 'lay-land near the barns', ***ton***², ***ysgubor*** pl. ***ysgubor(i)au***
Tonisca Borra 1754, *Ton Ysguborau* 1833, *Talbot Town*, ~ *Road* 1875, *Talbot Row* 1885, *Talbot Green* 1956
Talbot Green, earlier Talbot Road, derives in part from a tavern reputedly built 1859, recorded as Talbot Arms 1868 and Talbot Inn in 1872, itself named from the Talbot family of Hensol Castle. The first Talbot at Hensol was Charles Talbot, Lord Chancellor, 1733-9. Morien (HTonyrefail 72) mistakenly refers to it as (i) *Dwyn Ysguborau* as if it contains ***twyn*** 'hillock'. Tonysguboriau is retained in the n. of the primary school opened in 1909.

Tal-y-bont see **Llandeilo Tal-y-bont**

Tal-y-fan (Tir y Stiward) Tal-y-fan cas. ST 021771
Vale of Glamorgan
'end of the hill': ***tal***, *y*, ***ban***¹; 'land of (family called) Siward', ***tir***, surname *Siward*
(castle of) *Thalevon, -van* 1248, (~) *Talvan, Talevan* 1281, *Talavan* 1535, *Tallavan alias Kyre*

Seawarde late 16th cent, *Comm. Meanaur Taluan, Com. Meana[u]r Talyuan* c.1538, (commote) *Maenor Dalyvan* 1559, *Snardislande* 1460, *Tier Stuart, Terstuart, Terstuard* lordship c.1538, (lp.) *Tyr Syward, viz. Sewarde's Land* c.1670
The hill is presumably that on which the castle stands. Cf. Talyfan at Llandeilo Tal-y-bont recorded as *Tal y van* 1650 and *Tâl y van* 1670 centred on the fm. of the same n. (SN 588052) which is *Tal-y-fan-fawr* 1830 (***mawr***) and a nearby (fm.) Talyfan Fach (SN 592050) recorded as *Tallyvan Vach* 1760 and *Tal-y-fan-fach* 1830 (***bach***¹). Seward has been identified (Paterson in AC 1922, 41) with the family of Richard Siward, lord of Tal-y-fan, accused by Richard de Clare, lord of Glamorgan, in 1245 of aiding and abetting rebellion by certain Welshmen. The pers.n. has been displaced by E *steward* in some later sources. Paterson also identifies Seward in Maes-y-ward (ST 038753 in Welsh St. Donats) which is *Maeseard* 1788 but sps. such as *Maes Heyward* 1597 and *Maesheyarte* 1603 tend to favour a surname Heyward, Hayward (see ADG², 64).

Tal-y-garn see **Capel Tal-y-garn**

Tawe
rn. Neath Port Talbot, Swansea
?'flowing one, river': Br ****tam-, -wy***¹
taui 1129 (c.1172), *Tauuỳ* c.1145, *Tawy* 1203, *Thawi, Tawi* 1208, *Tawye* 1433, *Sweynseywater vocata the water of Towee* 1479, *Tawe* c.1538, *Tawy alias Tawe* 1738, *the River Tawy* 1764
Historic sps. suggest that *Tawe* is a later development of the n., perhaps reflecting W local dialect with *–we* for *–wy*. A full discussion of Tawe and similar rns. in Britain and on the Continent is given by Rivet and Smith (PNRB 465). Nicolaisen (BZN VIII, 256-62) traces the n. to a common IE root **ta-, *tə-* 'fliessen' ('to flow'). Melville Richards (NTC 178) prefers a derivation from Brit **Tamou̯i̯ā*, meaning possibly 'water, dark river', accepting the theory – widely discredited – made by other scholars that **tam-* in rns. means 'dark' (ERN 405; OPemb III, 309, n.2).

Thaw, Ddawan see **Aberthaw, Aberddawan**

Thistleboon SS 618876
Swansea (Oystermouth)
?'land cleared of thistles' or ?'land held on condition of clearing weeds': E *thistleboon* (*villa*) *Thistelbon'* 1396, *Fistleboone* 1630, *Ffistleboon* 1650, *Thistleboon* 1742, (ho.) *Thistle Boon* 1799, *Thistle-boon* 1832
A compound of OE *thistel* 'thistle' and perhaps *boon* 'a blessing, a gift' as in 'boon-work' which was a manorial duty to do seasonal work. Thistleboon is also recorded in the north of England as a feudal due for weeding fields and it is possible that the property – variously described as *villa*, place and ho. – may have been held on partial condition of clearing weeds. Confusion of *th* and *f*, *ff* is found in both W and E. Thistleboon House was demolished c.1972.

Thomastown ST 008868
Rhondda Cynon Taf (Llantrisant)
'settlement named from Thomas': surname *Thomas*, E *town*
Thomastown 1909
Built on part of the Ynys-y-plwm estate inherited by William Meyler Thomas (1850-1917) of Ynys-y-plwm House in 1901 (MCPP 95-96). Thomastown appears to have developed after sinking of Coedely coal-mine by The Welsh Navigation Steam Coal Co. 1901-6. The village now extends to the east side of Afon Elái/Ely to include the area around Tylcha-wen recorded as *Talchewen* 1745, *Tulcha wen* 1811 and *Tylca-wen* 1833 possibly meaning 'white sheds (*or* huts)' with *tylc(i)au* pl. of *twlc*[1] nm. 'pig-sty, hut' and *gwen*, although len. is irregular.

Thomas Town SO 052061
Merthyr Tudful
'settlement named from Thomas': surname *Thomas*, E *town*
Thomas Town 1852, *Thomas town* 1868
Built in 1850s on part of the Court estate and named after Dr William Thomas (1794-1858), owner 1827-58 (MCPP 92-94; PNIG 27). He is also recalled in Thomas Street.

Thornhill, Y Ddraenen ST 173828
Cardiff (Llanisien)
'hill covered with thorn-bushes': E *thorn*, E *hill*; 'the thorn-bush', *y*, *draenen*
(ho.) *Dan y Ddrainen* 1729, *the Newhouse*, or *Ty Newydd dan y ddrainen* 1764, *the Newhouse* 1767, (ho.) *Thorn Hill* 1799, (hill) *Thornhill*, (area) *Thornhill* 1885
The n. now refers to a housing estate developed from c.1990 but applied in 1833 to the small ht. which developed around the Traveller's Rest public ho. and the medieval castle Castell Morgraig (ST 160843). Both Thornhill and Craig y Ddraenen referred earlier to the hill extending from Coed y Briwnant (ST 156841) – known as *Craig y draenen* in 1833 (*craig*) – and Cefn Carnau (*Thorn Hill* 1799) to Craig Llanisien (ST 167846) (*Thorn Hill* 1811, *Craig Lanishen* 1833). Tŷ Newydd Dan y Ddraenen, 'new house below the thorn-bush' (*tŷ*, *newydd*, *dan*), recorded in 1764 is now New House Hotel (ST 160840). Draenen Pen-y-graig was the earlier n. of Hill Farm (ST 167842), meaning 'thorn-bush at Pen y graig'. This is *drainen pen y graig* 1720, abbreviated to *Pengraig* in 1813, *Graig* 1833, *Y Graig* 1841 and *Hill Farm* 1852. Pen-y-graig is 'top of the cliff' (*pen*[1], *y*, *craig*).

Three Crosses, Y Crwys SS 573942
Swansea (Llanrhidian)
'three crosses': E *three*, E *cross* pl. *crosses*; 'the crosses', *y*, *crwys*
Y Crooyse 1594, *the Three Crosses* 1642, *the Cruse* 1756, *the three crosses* 1764, *'r Croes* or *Three Crosses* 1830, *y Crwys* 1867
Referring to lost standing-crosses or boundary crosses. *crwys* earlier meant 'a cross' but is also recorded from the 14th cent as a pl. The n. is unlikely to mean 'three crossroads' as it is taken from a fm. where four roads met. As a result of road re-alignment in the 1930s, five roads now meet here.

Tiger Bay ST 1874
Cardiff
'Tiger Bay' 1885, *Tiger Bay* 1917
A n. typically used for disreputable areas such as Bluegate Fields, a 19th cent slum in the east end of London. One or other of London's Tiger Bays appears in the title of a detective novel published by the reputed Order for the Prevention of Vice in 1863; a personal description of crime and poverty in London written in 1865 by Thomas Archer; and in a novel *Girl from Tiger Bay* by Roland Vane (the pseudonym of E.L. McKeag) in 1950. It is clear that Tiger Bay was simply employed as a generic for an area frequented by sailors, and notable for drinking, opium dens, gambling and prostitution. This interpretation is reinforced by similar pns. elsewhere such as the once notorious Tigers Bay, around Mackey Street, in Belfast. Tiger Bay seems to have been propagated as a n. by local newspapers to describe Butetown or parts of Butetown, usually in connection with some criminal offence. In Cardiff, the n. was reinforced by the novels *Once to Tiger Bay* by W. Townend (1929), *Tiger Bay* by David Martin (1946) and *Once in Tiger Bay* by James Morgan Walsh (1947), but it is best known from the movie 'Tiger Bay' 1959, based on the short story *Rodolphe et le Revolver* by Noel Calef (1907-68). A film with an identical n., made in 1934 at Ealing studios, relates to a 'Tiger Bay' set in China. The area has long lost its unpleasant notoriety but the n. was revived – much to the chagrin of local people – to describe Shirley Bassey as 'The Girl from Tiger Bay', though she grew up in Splott. Tiger Bay is said to have been named from a music hall song of the 1860s composed by Harry Moreton (PNIG 9, 13; IHCS 19-20). The song has not been identified among music hall records but Moreton (died 1907) was an amateur concert arranger and comic singer and may well have had such a song in his repertoire.

Tinkinswood ST 094733
Vale of Glamorgan (St Nicholas)
?'wood belonging to (man called) Tinkin': surname or pers.n. *Tinkin*, E **wood**
(old druid cell near) *Tinkin's Wood ... called Carreg Maen Llwyd, called by some Castle Careg* 1765, *Tinkinswd.* 1787, *Tinkins Wood* 1793, *Tickins Wood* 1833
Probably *Tomkins Wood* recorded in 1674. *Tinkin* is recorded as a variant of *Tom(p)kin* (PNDPH 286-7) and *Timkin*. The 'druid cell' refers to a prehistoric chambered cairn. The alternative forms in 1765 are best understood as Carreg y Maenllwyd 'stone at Y Maenllwyd' (*carreg*) qualified by Y Maenllwyd meaning 'the grey boulder' (*maen*, *llwyd*), and the second for 'castle at the stone' (E *castle*, *carreg*) but they are otherwise unattested.

Tircanol SS 673985
Swansea (Llangyfelach)
'middle land': *tir*, *canol*
Tir y velin 1650, *Tyr y Velin alias Tuy Kenol* 1764, *Tircanol* 1813, 1841, (area) *Tir-canol* 1876-9
The earlier n. is 'the mill land' (*tir*, *y*, *melin*, *felin*). Tircanol was a former fm. and the n. was extended to include an industrial site consisting of a coal-pit, lime-kilns and the Morriston tin-plate works.

Tir-coed SN 619000
Swansea (Llangyfelach)
'woodland': *tir*, *coed*
A modern n. for a small ho. estate constructed from the late 1990s at Craig Tyle-du in Penllergaer Forest near Coed-tremig, so spelt 1884 and *Coeddremig* 1813, *Coidtremig* 1841, composed of *coed* and apparently *tremyg* 'contempt, scorn, insult', perhaps in the sense of 'poor, worthless wood'.

Tirdeunaw SS 652971
Swansea (Llangyfelach)
'land paying 18d.': *tir*, (*y*), *deunaw*
Tir y doynaw, *Tyre Doynawe* 1650, *Tir y Deunaw* 1699, *Tyrdoinaw* 1720, *Tir Deunaw* 1794
In 1650 it consisted of two tmts. each paying 9d. rent and local people in 1945 understood the meaning as 'one-and-sixpenny land'. The suggestion by Thomas Morgan (OPN 127) that the n. was replaced by Caersalem Newydd ('New Jerusalem'), a Baptist chp. (SS

65259730) at the north end of the village, is not borne out by the available evidence.

Tir Iarll
'earl's land': *tir*, *iarll*
Bridgend, Neath Port Talbot
Tyrarch 1295, *Tyriartlh alias Tyryartlh* 1296, *Tyryarilth* 1402, *Tieryarll'* 1538, *Teryarlth, Comm. Tir yarll* c.1538, *tir yr Jarll* mid 16th cent, *Tyr yr Iarlh* 1559, *Tyre y Yarll* c.1598, *Erleslande* 1460
Sps. with *-yarlth* etc are best explained as attempts by E and AF scribes at representing –iarll [jarɬ]. Occasional sps. such as *Tiriarth* 1326 suggest association with *garth*, *-(i)arth*, *-arth*. The 'earl' may be Robert the Consul, an illegitimate son of Henry I, who married Mabel, daughter of Robert Fitzhamon, conqueror of Glamorgan. Robert is known to have granted land here to Margam abbey in 1147. The lp. of Tir Iarll covered only Llangynwyd and Betws in the 13th cent (and later) but the commote of Tir Iarll (in the cantref of Gwrinydd) covered a larger area extending to Margam, Pyle, and Kenfig (HLlangynwyd 5). *Tyr yr Yarll* is also recorded in Lisvane in 1712.

Tir-nest SS 675953
Swansea (Llansamlet)
'land of (person called) Nest': *tir*, pers.n. *Nest*
Tir Neast 1762, *Ty'r Nest* 1772, *Tirnest* 1878, *Tir-Nest* 1879
Shown as a small group of hos. between Hanover Square and Pentre'rgaseg 1879. The same n. occurs in Tir Nest Fras (Swansea), a former fm. near Kilvey Hill, at Dan-y-graig, recorded as (land) *Tir Nest Vrase* c.1583, *Tir Neast Vrase* 1686, ~ *otherwise Danygraig Genol* 1764, with qualifier *bras* adj. 'fat, large; rich, prosperous', and in Tir-nest (SN 402167, Llandyfaelog), Carmarthenshire.

Tirpenry SS 673982
Swansea (Llangyfelach)
'land of (man called) Penry': *tir*, pers.n. and surname *Penry, Penri*
Tyr Penry Williams 1764, *Tirpenry* 1841, *Tyrpenry*, *Tyrpendry, Tyrpendre* 1852

Generally a surname derived from the patronymic *ap Henri* 'son of Henri', *mab* etc 'son', but the first historic form favours a given n. with surname Williams.

Tir-phil SO 141032
Caerphilly (Gelli-gaer)
'land of ?', *tir*, ?
Tir Phil 1841, *Tyr Phil otherwise Graig Rhymney* 1855, *Tre Fill* 1858, *Tirphil, Tir-Fill* 1861
A seemingly identical field-name in Llanbadog, Monmouthshire, is recorded as *Tir Phill* c.1613, *Tyr hill* 1613-14 and *Tirevill* 1707. The first el. in both cases is *tir* but the second el. is uncertain. It has been suggested that it may be *ffyll* 'wild, overgrown', a word of doubtful origin (recorded from 1707), possibly found in Nantyffyllon, Montgomeryshire. A more plausible candidate is *ffull²*, *ffill* but its meaning 'bud, blade' is difficult to justify in this context (DPNW 460-1). The difficulty with both suggestions is that there is no clear evidence of forms with *–ll* though there are instances in Glamorgan where *–l* [l] is substituted for *–ll* [ɬ]; cf. Pontsticill. Morgan suggested '*Phil*, an abbreviation of Philip, the n. of the then owner of the land on which the place is situated' (OPN 153) but such an abbreviation is not evidenced elsewhere in W sources. The same objection applies to a field-name *Tyre Phillipp Gwilliam* 1563 which appears to have been located near the bridge in Bargoed. There is no connection with Phillipstown (SO 145035) immediately east of the village. This is named from Nehemiah Phillips, colliery manager, county councillor, and Baptist preacher (MCPP 68).

Tir-y-berth ST 151966
Caerphilly (Llanfabon)
'land of the thicket': *tir*, *y*, **perth**
Tyr y berth 1676, *Tyr-y-berth farm alias Edward Lewis David's mess(uage)* 1698, (ho.) *tir y berth* 1783, *Ty'r berth* 1813, *Tir y Berth* 1833, *Tir-y-berth* 1886
The precise sense may be 'land near a bush or copse'. The n. is taken from the ho. (ST 148967) located near a former ho. recorded as

Teere y bongam 1680 and *Tir-y-bongam* 1877-8, 'crooked tree trunk' (*y*, *bôn¹*, *cam²*).

Tirybrenin SS 5798, 5997
Swansea (Llandeilo Tal-y-bont)
'the king's land': *tir*, *y*, *brenin*
Tyre y brenin, otherwise Tire y Abade 1577, *Tyr-y-Brenin* 1731, *Parcell Tiry Brenin* 1670, (*the parcel of*) *Tyr y Brennin* 1764, (ht.) *Tyrbrenin* 1852
The n. applies to the southerly part of Llandeilo Tal-y-bont and its former tenure by King Henry VIII who acquired it from the abbey of Neath at the dissolution of the monasteries, hence its alternative n. Tiryabad, 'land of the abbot' (*abad*). The 'king' is also recalled in Kingsbridge (SS 592978) otherwise Pontybrenin (*pont*), recorded as *Pont Brenin* 1729, *Pont y Brennin* 1764 and *Kings Bridge* 1799.

Tonbreigam SS 994795
Vale of Glamorgan (Llansanwyr)
'lay-land near Breigam': *ton²*, pn. *Breigam*
Ton 1833, *Ton Brigan, ~ Brigam* 1841, *Ton-brigam* 1875
Breigam (SS 994798) is recorded as *Brigam* 1520, *Brygan* c.1541, *Brygam* 1544, *Brigan* 1571, (*o*) *vraigan* 17th cent, with an adjoining (meadow) *Brigam Moor or Morva Brigam* 1753 (*morfa*) possibly the rough pasture south-east of Ton-breigam and Argoed-ganol. Breigam may also be *uillam breican* c.1145, known to have lain in Gwrinydd (q.v.) (Lat *villa*).

Ton-du SS 893843
Bridgend (Betws/Llangynwyd)
'black or dark lay-land': *ton²*, *du*
Tondu 1525, *Y Toune Dy* 1631, *Tondy* 1699, *Tondu* 1799
'Dark' perhaps from its soil. Named from Ton-du House. Note also John Richard *Tonndduy* recorded at nearby Newcastle and Cefncribwr in 1651.

Tongwynlais ST 1328221
Cardiff (Whitchurch)
'lay-land near (r.) Gwynlais': *ton²*, rn. *Gwynlais*
Tonn Gwenglais 1591, *Tu Gwenlas* 1729, *Tongwnlas* 1758, *Old Furnace farm or Tongwynlais* c.1781, *Tongwynlais* 1809, *Tongwaunlas* 1833
The rn. is *gungleis* c.1145 and occurs in (bridge) *Pont Gwenlas* 1729. Sps. generally favour 'white stream' (*gwyn* alternating with *gwen, glais*). The stream, now shown as Nant y Fforest on OS maps, described as *Fforest Brook* 1875 (in refs. to woodland Fforest Fawr and Fforest Ganol), rises near *Blaen-gwynlais* 1875 (ST 14358413) (*blaen*).

Ton-mawr SS 801963
Neath Port Talbot (Baglan)
'big lay-land': *ton²*, *mawr*
tonn mawre 1574, *Ton Mawr* 1823, *Tonmawr Colliery* 1847, *Ton-mawr* 1884
Perhaps in contrast to Ton-y-grugos (SS 798971) so spelt 1832 meaning 'lay-land at place of abundant heather' (*y*, *grugos*). An identical fm.n. (SS 824862) in Margam occurs as (tmt.) *Ton-mawr* 1727, *Tonmawr* 1766. The village developed next to Ton-mawr fm. (SS 806962) in the late 19th cent near several small coal-mines.

Tonna, Tonnau SS 775990
Neath Port Talbot (Llantwit-juxta-Neath)
'lay-lands': *ton²* pl. *tonnau*
Tonna 1702, (part of) *Tonna alias Ynis Neath* 1737, *Tonne* 1779, *Tonna* 1799, *Tonnau* 1832
Tonna represents the dialect form; cf. *Bedda* for Beddau (q.v.). The alternative n. 1737 is for Ynys Nedd 'river-meadow by the (r.) Nedd/Neath' (*ynys*). Tonnau-uchaf is at SS 778993 (*uchaf*).

Tonpentre (Ton Pentre) SS 971953
Rhondda Cynon Taf (Ystradyfodwg)
'lay-land at the village': *ton²*, *pentref*
Ton ir Ystrade 1541, *Ton yr Ystrad* 1580, (fm.) *Ton* 1833, *Ton, or Ton Pentre, or Ton Ystrad* 1891
The village refers to Ystradyfodwg, hence the earlier description of Ton-yr-ystrad, and distinguishes it from Tonypandy. The abbreviated form of Ystradyfodwg now applies

to the village of Ystrad a mile further down the valley.

Ton-teg   ST 093861
Rhondda Cynon Taf (Llantwit Fardre)
'fine lay-land': *ton², teg*
Tonteg 1861, *Ton-teg* 1885, *y Tonteg* 1904
Cf. Ton-teg (in Cadoxton-juxta-Neath) recorded as *Tonn Tege* 1541 and *Ton teg* 1633. Developed after 1885 between *Mount Pleasant* (ST 093865) and *Three Horseshoes P.H.* 1875 (ST 094868). The n. once applied to a wider area, possibly extending southwards to the former fm.n. Maes-teg (ST 094863) (*maes, teg*) and Salem chp. (ST 089863).

Tonypandy   SS 992928
Rhondda Cynon Taf (Ystradyfodwg)
'lay-land of the fulling-mill': *ton², y, pandy*
Tonypandy 1841, 1868, *Ton-y-pandy, Pandy Bridge* 1881
The mill evidently lay next to Nant Clydach near the bridge (SS 992926) and is probably *Pandy yr Ystrad Tavodog* 1764 from its location in the p. of Ystradyfodwg. *Pandy* applied in 1799 and 1841 to a single ho. The 'lay-land' probably adjoined Rhondda Fawr and the n. was transferred to the n. of the industrial settlement which developed along the Pen-y-graig road from the 1860s.

Tonypistyll   ST 197962
Caerphilly (Mynyddislwyn Monmouthshire)
'lay-land of the well': *ton², y, pistyll*
(ho.) *Ton Pistil* 1813, *Ton Pistyl* 1833, *Ton y Pistill* 1841, *Ton-pistyll* 1879
Two springs are shown on the OS 1:2,500 plan near Pen-y-coedcae (ST 199959) about a third of a mile south-east of Tonypistyll. See also Springfield.

Tonyrefail   ST 009882
Rhondda Cynon Taf (Llantrisant)
'lay-land of the smithy': *ton², yr, gefail*
Tonyrevel 1732, *Ton yr Evail* 1786, *Tonyrefail* 1811, *Ton yr Evil* 1831, *Ton-yr-efail* 1833
The smithy is shown on the OS 1:2,500 map 1875-80 near the crossroads (ST 010882).

The village developed with the arrival of the Llantrisant Junction Railway in 1860 and the opening of Collenna, Glyn and Cilely collieries in the 1870s. Familiarly known as Y Ton.

Townhill   SS 639937
Swansea
'(area on) hill near the town (of Swansea)': E *town, hill*
the Town Hill 1742, 1764, *Town hill* 1852
An area of former common lands occupying a hill above the centre of Swansea enclosed under an Act 1762. *Townhill* and *Hill Farm* 1879 were at the west end of Townhill Road. The Townhill housing estate was first proposed in 1905; work began in 1912 but largely constructed during the 1930s. The former ho.n. *Pen-y-graig* 1879 (approx. SS 644939) suggests that the hill may once have borne the W n. Y Graig 'the cliff' (*y, craig*). Seyler, however, suggests it was Cefncoed (AC 1925: 168).

Traeth Treco see **Trecco Bay**

Trallwn¹   SS 693967
Swansea (Llansamlet)
'(the) boggy place, dirty pool; a soft place on a road': (*y*), *trallwng*
Trallwn 1788, *Trallwyn* 1830, *Trallwm* 1841
The el. is fairly common, both in minor pns. and major pns.; the best known in the second category include Trallong, in Breconshire, and Y Trallwng, the W n. of Welshpool, Montgomeryshire. Colloquial variants include *trallwn* and *trallwm*. The n. probably refers to the area (SS 691968) where Trallwn Road, recorded as *Trallwyn Road* 1878 and *Heol y Trallwm* 1908 (*heol*), crosses a small tributary of the r. Tawe towards Pentredŵr. Other examples of *trallwng* in Glamorgan include Trallwn (SS 980804, in Llanilid) which is *Trallwyn* 1770, *Trallwm* 1833, and Trallwng (Margam) recorded as *Trallwm in Trissent Hamlet* 1760.

Trallwn²   ST 076905
Rhondda Cynon Taf (Eglwysilan)
'(the) boggy place, dirty pool; a soft place on a road': (*y*), *trallwng*

Trallwm 1795, *Trallwn* 1841
A low-lying area, occasionally flooded, which developed from the mid 19th cent as part of Pontypridd on the east side of the r. Taf.

Tramway SN 962053
Rhondda Cynon Taf (Aberdare)
'(place by the) tramway': E *tramway*
Tramway 1877
Named from the Aberdare & Hirwaun (mineral) Tramway linking the railway station and ironworks in Hirwaun with Aberdare.

Tranch, **Transh** SS 855810
Bridgend (Tythegston)
?'way cut through a wood': E *trench* or W *transh*, *trensh*
Trench 1633, 1813, *Tranch* 1841
Similar pns. occur elsewhere in south Wales and in England derived from OFr, ME *trenche*, 'a woodland road with clearings on either side to make the route safe for travellers' (ODEPN) later 'a path or track cut through a wood or forest'. That may well be the meaning here since Tranch is located on a small road running from Haregrove (where there is woodland) over Stormy Down to the A38. This word was borrowed in W as a common noun with the sense 'trench; dyke, bulwark' but in pns. in Glamorgan it generally matches the meanings of E *trench* with the additional sense of 'a way cut through a wood by a stream'. Transh-yr-hebog (ST 178848), for example, at Lisvane, is applied to a valley recorded as *Trench yr Hebog* in 1833 where a stream Nant yr Hebog (*nant*, *yr*, *hebog* 'hawk') passes through woodland known as *Coed Trench-yr-hebog* 1873-7 (*coed*). Three miles away at Llanfedw, the wood Coed y Tranch (ST 229855) is *the Trench* 1732, *Trench Wood* 1833 and *Coed-y-trench* 1875, and is crossed by a small stream Nant y Côr Fawr. The same el. is found in Tyn-y-tranch (ST 008792) in Ystradowen recorded as *le Trenche* 1556, *Tir Tranch* 1580, *the Trench* 1740 and *Tynytranch* 1852 (*tyn*); a wood Coed y Trenches (ST 120794) near Rhydlafar; a forest *Trench Newith* 1574 (*newydd*) mentioned in connection with Garthmaelwg, in Llanharan; and Tranch/Y Transh (SO 273008) near Pontypool, Monmouthshire, recorded as *the trench* 1740, *the Transh* 1765 and *Tranch* 1833.

Trealaw SS 002920
Rhondda Cynon Taf (Ystradyfodwg)
'settlement commemorating Alaw': *tref*, bardic n. *Alaw*
Trealaw Inn 1868, (4 dwellinghouses at) *Trealaw* 1868
Trealaw was developed from c.1865 on land belonging to Gwilym Williams (1839-1906) and named in honour of his father David Williams (1811-63) who bore the bardic n. Alaw Goch ('red lily', *alaw*, **coch**, *goch*), originally of Ystradowen, who opened collieries at Ynyscynon 1842-3, Aberaman, and later Deep Duffryn (Mountain Ash) and elsewhere (MCPP 97-99).

Tre-Aubrey ST 038724
Vale of Glamorgan (Llantrithyd)
'low settlement (or farm)': *tref*, *dre(f)*, **obry**
Dreobry 1728, *Dreobree* 1784, *Tre Obry* c.1800, *Ty-obry* 1833, *Dreobery* 1852, *Tre-Aubrey* 1878
In contrast to Tŷ Fry (= Llantrithyd House) and Tŷ Draw (ST 033727) (*fry* 'above, aloft'; *draw* 'yonder, beyond'). The pn. has clearly been associated with the Aubrey family of Llantrithyd. The surname occurs elsewhere in Glamorgan and Breconshire and has a variant Obray in Pembrokeshire (WS 105).

Trebanog[1] ST 016903
Rhondda Cynon Taf (Llantrisant)
'settlement (or farm) characterised by ?cotton-grass': *tref*, **panog*
Trebannoge 1541, *Trebannock* 1631, *Tire y Drebannog* 1675, *Trebannog* 1732
*panog may be an unrecorded adj. form of *pân* 'cotton-grass' though *panog* or *pannog* also applies to various types of the herb mullein such as *pannog brithgoch* 'purple mullein' and *pannog melyn* 'great mullein' (ECB; EANC 37). Trebanog developed in the mid/late 19th cent along Trebanog Road (SS 016903) extending towards *Trebanog (P.H.)* 1874.

Trebanog[2] SN 945073
Rhondda Cynon Taf (Penderyn Breconshire)
'settlement (or farm) characterised by ?cotton-grass': *tref*, ?**panog*
Tre bannog 1674, *Trebannog, ~ Ishaf, ~ Uchaf* 1776, *Tyr Trebannog, Trebannog Uchaf, Trebannog Isha* 1819, (hos.) *Great ~ , Little Trebanog* 1831, *Trebanog-uchaf, ~ -ganol, ~ -fawr* 1832
Apparently identical in meaning to Trebanog but the n. has also been connected with a rn. *gauanhauc* c.1145, thought to be Gafannog a mile south of Penderyn village. Deric John (CVPN 88-89) favours 'the farm on the high or elevated land' with *bannog*, 'high, elevated; exalted, famous, conspicuous' etc, but this does not explain the lack of len. (b to f) after *tref*.

Trebanos SN 712029
Neath Port Talbot (Llangyfelach)
'settlement (or farm) with an abundance of cotton-grass': *tref, panos*
(mess.) *Ydre bannos yssa* 1688, *Drebanno* 1691, *Alt y Trebannoes alias Clyn y March, Craig Trebannoes* 1764, *Tre-bran-nos* 1832, *Trebannos* [TG] *Gate* 1848, *Trebanos* 1879
panos appears to be a collective form of *pân*[2] 'cotton grass' with the suffix *-os* seen in other pns. such as Bedwas, Rhigos, etc. Cf. also (mess.) *Trebannos* (in Llantwit-juxta-Neath) 1688. Some OS maps from c.1962 use the alternative form Trebannws but there is little evidence for this.

Trebefered see **Boverton**

Tre-boeth SS 652965
Swansea (Llangyfelach)
'burnt (or warm) settlement': *tref, poeth* le. *boeth*
y Dreeboeth 1556, *Treboth, Treboeth* 1650, *y dre boeth* 1686, *Tre-boeth* 1832, *y Drefboeth* 1872
poeth generally means 'hot' but the occurrence of pns. such as Coedpoeth (*coed*), Denbighshire, suggests that it acquired the extended sense of 'burnt, scorched' (DPNW lxiii). Tre-boeth (ST 025884) at Llantrisant is *Tre boeth* 1580 and *Dreboth* 1811 and Tre-boeth (formerly at ST 167860) near Caerphilly is (wood of) *Treboyth*, (forest of) *trepoyth* 1429, *Treboeth* 1467 and *Treboth* 1833. Other instances of Tre-boeth occur in Pembrokeshire and Radnorshire. Cf. Pentre-poeth (q.v.).

Trecastell ST 017814
Rhondda Cynon Taf (Llanhari)
'settlement at the castle': *tref*, (*y*), *castell*
Treer cast: 1578, *Trecastell* 1591, *Tre Castle* c.1659, *Trer Castle* c.1670, *Trecastle* 1682, (manor) *Castelton* 1488
Earlier known as Scurlage castle from the AN family of Scurlage who settled here in the mid 13th cent (MSM 458-9) and recorded as *Scurla castle* 1320, *Scarlag y castell* 1429, *Scurla Castell alias Coyett Kynllan* 1552-3, *Scurlagh castle* c.1659. The n. was gradually displaced by Coedcynllan recorded as *Coyde Kenllan* 1488, *Coyetkynllane* c.1541, *Coed Cynlla* 1789, and (ho.) *Coed-cynllwyn* 1833 with *coed* 'trees, wood' and *Cynllan* – perhaps a lost n. of the stream Nant Felin-fach. A second castle seems to be recalled in Castell-y-mwnws (ST 022806) recorded thus in 1833 and 1876-8 less than 1 mile south-east of Trecastell. This is probably 'the ruinous castle' with *castell*, *y*, *mwnws*, *mynws* coll.n. in the sense 'dust, worthless remains, refuse, rubble'.

Trecco Bay, Traeth Treco SS 831765
Bridgend (Newton Nottage)
E *bay* and *traeth*[1] 'beach'
Traeth Treco 1877, *Traeth Trecco* 1899, 1964, *Treco Bay* 1910, *Trecco Bay* 1916, 1966
Trec(c)o allegedly refers to a ship 'Trecco' wrecked here at an unspecified date (PNIG 41) but this is not recorded in *A Chronology of Bristol Channel Shipwrecks, 1687-1983*. The pn. properly refers to the beach between Rhŷch Point and Newton Point but is better known as the n. of a holiday caravan park on Newton Burrows created after World War II.

Trecenydd ST 145874
Caerphilly (Eglwysilan)
'settlement of Cenydd': *tref*, pers.n. *Cenydd*
Trecenydd 1937
Cenydd, variant Cennydd, is a reputed saint (HMorg 24) but the pn. is ultimately drawn

from a misinterpretation of Senghennydd (q.v.). Development began with suburban housing at *St. Cenydd's Terrace* 1922 on the eastern side of what is now called St Cenydd Road. The latter was also a shortlived n. for the eastern end of Nantgarw Road near Bethel chp. and Bryncenydd.

Trecynon SN 994035
Rhondda Cynon Taf (Aberdare)
'settlement by (r.) Cynon': ***tref***, rn. *Cynon*
Trecynon c.1855, 1860, (district) *Mill-street (or Trecynon)* 1863, *Tre-cynon* 1868
A late n. lacking regular len. of *-cynon* as *-gynon* after ***tref*** (ETG 105). Deric John (CVPN 89-90) says the n. was submitted at an eisteddfod in the 1850s to find a suitable n. for the industrial settlement which developed on Tir Iorin and Gadlys Uchaf. Its earlier n. was Heolyfelin (*Heol-y-felin* 1833), 'the mill road' (***heol***, ***y***, ***melin***, *felin*) so called from Llwydcoed mill on the r. Cynon. The n. is preserved in Mill Street, recorded 1841.

Tredegar Newydd see **New Tredegar**

Tredegarville ST 190770
Cardiff (Roath)
'settlement on Tredegar estate': pn. *Tredegar*, E ***ville***
Tredegarville 1861, *Tredegar Villa*, *Tredegarville House* 1868
An area of housing developed on part of the Tredegar estate between Newport Road, the railway to Caerphilly and City Road. The n. survives in that of Tredegarville Baptist ch. formed in 1861 and opened 1862. For Tredegar, see DPNW 461.

Tredelerch see **Rumney**

Tredodridge, Tredotris ST 052773
Vale of Glamorgan (Pendeulwyn)
'ford of ?Dodridge': ***rhyd***, ?surname *Dodridge*
Redodrys 1573, *Rydd Addris* 1649, *Tredodrish* 1742, *Rhydodris* 1737, *Tretroedrist* 1766, *Rhydodrish Land* 1795, *Tredotris* 1811, *Tre-dotrus* 1833, *Tre-Dodridge* 1879

The first el. has been confused with ***tref*** as Gwynedd Pierce shows (PNGlam 195-6). The second el. may be a locational surname, possibly derived from the pn. Dodridge, in Devon. The form Tredotris has unvoicing –d-/-t- > -tt-, -t- (a characteristic of Glamorgan dialect) and substitution by W-speakers of –is in written forms and –ish [ɪʃ] in spoken forms for –idge. The ford was evidently over a small stream Nant Dodridge recorded as *Nant Tre-Dodridge* 1879 in the village.

Tredogan ST 070678
Vale of Glamorgan (Pen-marc)
'settlement of (man called) ?Trychan': ***tref***, ?pers.n. ?*Trychan*
Dredruckan 1578, *Dredrokan* 1601, *Tredruckan* 1596, *Tredogan* 1721, *Treduchan* 1755, *Treducan* 1784, *Tre-Dwgan* 1879
The pers.n. is also found as *Tirchan, Trican, Trychan* 12th cent, possibly composed of ***twrch*** 'boar' and suffix ***-an***. The same els. may also explain the rn. Trychan, Breconshire (EANC 90). E-speakers have probably substituted –c- [k] for W –ch- [χ]. The alternative suggestion by Gwynedd Pierce (PNDPH 190-1) is that the pn. could contain the pers.n. *Cadwgan* or a derivative form such as *Dwgan*. The pers.n. is known to be one of the sources of the surname Duggan, Dougan. This seems less likely because forms such as *Dredruckan, Tredruckan* are generally earlier and would have to be explained as containing an intrusive *r* with metathesis, i.e. **Tre'rdwgan* > *Tredrwgan*; unvoicing of –g- as –c- is a characteristic of local W dialect.

Tredomen ST 138944
Caerphilly (Llanfabon)
'settlement at the mound': ***tref***, (***y***), ***tomen***, *domen*
Tre yr Doman 1666, *Tredomen* 1733, 1776, *tredomanvach, Tredoman Vaur* 1783
A housing estate developed from the 1930s. The n. also applies to earlier housing constructed around a ho. Brynmynach. Named from the ho. Tredomen (SO 134946); there is a small wooded hillock on its south-eastern side. Local dialect appears to have been 'Tredoman'. There is an identical pn. Tredomen (SO 122316) near

Llanfilo, Breconshire, recorded as *Tredomen* 1595, *Tre-domen* 1832 (PNBre 145).

Trefansel see **Manselton**

Trefechan SO 036089
Merthyr Tudful (Faenor)
'little settlement': ***tref***, ***bechan***
Trefechan 1964
A new n. for a housing estate developed largely on land of Vaynor House after World War II. Cf. the much older Trefechan (SO 096932), in Llanfabon, recorded as *tre Vochan* 1783, *y Trevochan* 1784, *Trefychan* 1885 which contains a variant ***bychan*** for the regular fem. adj. ***bechan***. This variation is also found in some historic forms of Pontneddfechan (q.v.).

Tref Elliot see **Elliots Town**

Trefflemin see **Flemingston**

Trefforest ST 083891
Rhondda Cynon Taf (Llantwit Fardre)
'forest settlement': ***tref***, ***fforest***
Trefforest 1833, 1856, *Tre fforest* 1842, *Treforest* 1851
There are numerous refs. to forests and woodland in this part of the Taf valley such as *Forrest above Taaf* c.1700, *Forrest Issa* 1729 and Fforest, a ht. of Hendredenni. Trefforest was reputedly named from Craig y Fforest, 'the rock of the forest'; this is (slope) *Graig y Fforest* 1833 (approx. ST 087878) (***craig***) but the n. is more likely drawn directly from the ho. Fforest Isaf, 'lower forest' (***isaf***) later known as Forest House. Trefforest was the location of tinplate works 1794-1946 and Lower Forest Ironworks from 1831 (HMorg 368-9; EHOSW 111) later known as the Forest Iron and Steel Works and closed before World War I. The village owes its later expansion to the establishment of the School of Mines (predecessor of Glamorgan Polytechnic and Glamorgan University) and to the industrial estate.

Trefgolych see **Worleton**

Treforgan SN 791060
Neath Port Talbot (Cadoxton-juxta-Neath)
'settlement of Morgan': ***tref***, pers.n. or surname *Morgan*
Treforgan 1899
The identity of Morgan is unknown. Recorded on an OS plan in 1878 but the first hos. appeared in the 1890s, the ht. expanding after the opening of the nearby Llwynon Colliery in 1901.

Treforgan see **Morganstown**

Treforys see **Morriston**

Treganna see **Canton**

Tregantllo see **Candleston**

Tregatwg see **Cadoxton**

Tregibbon, Tregibwn SN 992051
Rhondda Cynon Taf (Aberdare)
'settlement of (man called)': ***tref***, surname *Gibbon*, *Gibwn*
Tregibon 1814, *Tregibbon* 1825, *Tre Gibbon* 1844, *Tregibwn* 1858, *Tre-Gibbon* 1877
Built to accommodate workers at Aberdare Iron Works at Llwydcoed c.1801 by Thomas Jenkin alias Gibbon (probably the same man as Thomas ap Shencin ap Gibbon) of Fforchaman (CVPN 91). This is *Tre Gibwn* in the poem 'Can Hanes Ffair Aberdar' by Thomas Tayler (HTonyrefail 107) late 19th cent. Gibbon/Gibwn may be a familiar form of Gilbert (SW 140-1).

Treglement see **Clemenston**

Tre-gof see **Treguff**

Tregolwyn see **Colwinston**

Treguff, Tre-gof ST 030710
Vale of Glamorgan (Llancarfan)
'settlement with a smith': ***tref***, ?***gof*** or 'settlement of (man called) Cof': ***tref***, ?pers.n. *Cof*, *Gof*
Treigof c.1090, *Treygof* c.1135, *Tregof* 1146, 1263, *Tregoffe* 1521, *Tregoff* 1522, *Dreergosse* 1578, *Tre'r Gowf* c.1659, *Tre'r Gove* c.1678, *Treguff* 1706

Discussed by Gwynedd Pierce (PNDPH 100-2). The first interpretation seems to be confirmed by *Smithton* in 1787-8 but this is otherwise unrecorded and is almost certainly an affectation. If *gof* is correct then Tre-gof would also be irregular since *gof* would normally lenite to *of* after *tref* which is a nf. No len. is required if the pn. is properly Tre'r-gof with the def.art. *y* affixed as *'r* but this does not appear in historic sps. until 1578 and is uncommon even after that date. The second el. may rather be a pers.n. *Cof* recorded in Brittany and Cornwall. There is very little evidence for it in Wales but it does occur as the n. of Cof, a son of Ceidio, in a late 13th cent pedigree, and Cof, a son of Caw of Twrcelyn, in late manuscripts. Tre-gof (lost, SN 690985), at Llansamlet, by contrast, is more likely to derive from Tre'r-gof (*y, gof*) since it is recorded as *Trergove* c.1583, 1686, later *Tregove* 1764 and *Tregof* 1844. E influence might account for W vowel -o- [ō] > [ə] and [ʌ] and unvoicing of W -f [v] as -ff [f] as seen in the modern map form.

Tregŵyr see **Gowerton**

Trehafod ST 045909
Rhondda Cynon Taf (Llanwynno)
'settlement at Hafod': *tref*, pn. *Hafod*
Trehafod 1851
Built on land of Hafod Uchaf otherwise Hafod Fawr fm. (ST 040916) (*mawr*) close to Hafod Colliery. The ho. and Hafod Isaf (ST 045913) are recorded as *Hafod-uchaf, ~ -isaf* 1833 containing **hafod** 'summer dwelling' qualified as 'upper' and 'lower' (*uchaf, isaf*). According to H.C. Jones (PNIG 32) the mineral rights of Hafod Uchaf were first leased in 1809 but Hafod Colliery was not sunk until 1850; the village developed about the same time.

Treharris ST 099970
Merthyr Tudful
'settlement of Harris': *tref*, surname *Harris*
Treharris 1875
Named from Frederick William Harris (1833-1917), an English Quaker, prominent in coal exploitation here (MCPP 100-1). Developed in 1870s after sinking of the Deep Navigation Pits alias Harris's Navigation Colliery 1873 by Harris Navigation Steam Coal Co. and later known as Deep Navigation (closed 1991). Built for sinkers and known initially as the 'huts'. This was not formerly Twyn-y-garreg as H.C. Jones suggests (PNIG 27) which refers to a former ho: (ST 094972) close to Twynygarreg Road at the western edge of the village. This is *Twyn carreg* 1813 and *Twyn* 1833, 'hillock of the rock' (*twyn, y, carreg*).

Treherbert SS 940983
Rhondda Cynon Taf (Ystradyfodwg)
'settlement named from Herbert': *tref*, surname *Herbert*
Tref Herbert, Treherbert 1855, *Tre-Herbert* 1877
Chosen by the marquesses of Bute to honour their predecessors the Herbert earls of Pembroke (MCPP 102-3). The first shaft of the Bute Treherbert Colliery was opened in Cwmsaerbren 1851 by the trustees of the Marquess of Bute II (d. 1848) with a second shaft 1853-5. The town developed rapidly after the opening of the pit, acquiring Independent and Libanus Baptist chps. 1858 and a National School 1861.

Trehill, **Tre-hyl** ST 084742
Vale of Glamorgan (St Nicholas)
'settlement on a hill' or 'settlement called Hill': *tref*, E **hill**
(lp.) *Tree hyll* 1535, *Trehill* 1653, 1755, *Tre hyll* 1697, *Tre-hil* 1874
The first el. has probably been influenced by E *tree*. There are doubts with both explanations but other 'hill' ns. are found in the same p. such as Vianshill (surname *Vian*). Gwynedd Pierce notes (PNDPH 287) the occurrence of other pns. in the area composed of paired W and E els. though these are generally synonymous, eg. Brynhill (Wenvoe) (*bryn*) and Penhill (Llandaf) (*pen¹*).

Trehopcyn see **Hopkinstown**

Tre-Ifor SN 993053
Rhondda Cynon Taf (Aberdare)
'settlement of Ifor': *tref*, pers.n. *Ifor*
Tre-Ifor 1951

A small housing estate constructed from the late 1930s named from Ifor Bryant, surveyor of Aberdare Urban District Council, who was in charge of the project. The location was previously known as Coroner's Field, later as Buxton's Field, and was used by the village football team.

Trelái see **Ely**

Trelales see **Laleston**

Treleision see **Leason**

Trelewis   ST 104974
Merthyr Tudful (Gelli-gaer)
'settlement of Lewis': *tref*, surname *Lewis*
Lewistown 1879, *Tre Lewis*, *Trelewis* 1881
Named from William Lewis of Tir-shag (ST 111972) and Bontnewydd (1828-1903), churchwarden and guardian of Gelli-gaer (MCPP 105-7), who provided land and money for a new ch. in 1886-7. The older part of the village developed near Bontnewydd Colliery from the late 1870s. Lewistown alternates with Trelewis down to c.1905 and was dropped soon afterwards. See also **Lewistown**.

Trelyn see **Fleur-de-lis**

Tremains   SS 912795
Bridgend (Coety)
'settlement near stones': *tref*, *maen* pl. *main*
Dremains 1775, *Tremains* 1789, *Tremains Farm* 1798, (fms.) *Lower ~* , *Upper Tremains* 1813, *Lower ~* , *Upper ~* , *Old Tremaen* 1833, *Tremains House* 1875
Cf. Tre-main, Cardiganshire, recorded as *Tremeyn* 1241, *Tremaen* 1428, *trer main* c.1566, *Trermain* 1602. The E pl. –s may have arisen because Tremains referred to several hos.

Tremorfa   ST 208771
Cardiff (Roath)
'settlement on the sea-shore': *tref*, *morfa*
Tremorfa 1942
morfa earlier meant 'land (*or* marsh) by the sea-shore' later 'wet, marshy land' and sometimes applied to inland locations (PNDPH 344-5). The n. of a housing estate largely built 1939-1942 on Pengam fm. and completed after 1945 on the north side of East Moors next to the Severn estuary.

Treorci (Treorchy)   SS 960967
Rhondda Cynon Taf (Ystradyfodwg)
'settlement by the (r.) Gorci': *tref*, rn. *Gorci*
Treorki 1867, 1894, *Tre-orky,* (ho.) *Aber-gorky* 1884, *Treorchy* 1870, *Treorci* 1872
A n. coined in the 1860s for a new industrial settlement. The rn., marked as Nant Orci on modern OS maps, is also found in Fforch-orci (SS 955985) recorded as *Tyre Forghe Arkye Ighan* 1541 (*bychan*, lens. *fychan*, *ychan*), *fforch Orki* 1666, *fforch Gorky* 1727, (hos.) *Fforch-orchwy* 1833, in the 'fork' (*fforch*) of Nant Ynysfeio and Nant Gorci, and in Abergorci recorded as *Abergorky* 1673, *Abergorchwy* 1833, *Abergorgi* 1841, meaning 'confluence of Gorci (with Rhondda Fawr)' (*aber*). It is possible that Gorci is derived from **Gorgi* composed of *gor-* 'over, exceeding' etc, and *ci* 'dog, hound', perhaps for a r. fancied as running and darting like a dog. Gorci may have a match in the (lost) n. of a mess. *Tall Ardd otherwise Abergorgi* 1782 at Betws, Carmarthenshire. The OS map form Treorchy probably arose through supposition by map makers and others that the rn. was related etymologically to the Scottish rn. Orchy, in Argyll. The form *Gorchwy* used by Dafydd Morganwg (HMorg 13) and others is based on the now discredited belief that *–wy* means 'water'.

Tre-os (Treoes)   SS 944783
Vale of Glamorgan (Llan-gan)
'goose settlement': *tref* displacing OE *gōs*, OE *tūn*
Gaston 1525, *Goston* 1536, *Treoys* 1650, *Treos* 1668, *Velin Treos o(therwise) Treos Mill* 1683, *Goston, ~ Mill* 1712, *Treoes* 1749, *Treose* 1799, *Treôs or Goston* 1833, *Treos* 1849
OE *gōs* is also found in pns. in watery locations such as Gosford, -forth, Gosbrook etc, a description also suiting Tre-os in the Ewenni valley. Cymricised by substituting *tref* for *tūn* but *Gos-* was not replaced by *gwydd* 'goose',

presumably because the meaning of *Gos-* was not understood. It was, however, lenited in the regular fashion after *tref*, a nf. The first written evidence for this is *Tress* c.1598. Late sps. with *-oys, -oes* are over-corrections based on the supposition that *–o-* in forms such as *Treos* stands for *-oe-*. In many parts of south Wales the stressed dipthong oe [ɔi] is often reduced to a long vowel [o:] so that words such as *coed* and *coes* are generally heard as [ko:d] and [ko:s].

Treowen ST 210976
Caerphilly (Mynyddislwyn, Monmouthshire)
The n. apparently recalls Lord Treowen (Ivor John Caradoc Herbert, 1851-1933), owner of Llanarth Court and Treowen (Wonastow). Lord Treowen was the eldest son of John Arthur Edward Herbert and Augusta Hall, heir of Benjamin Hall, 1st Baron Llanover. Augusta's mineral agent William Thomas was father of William Thomas ('Islwyn'), the poet. Members of Lord Treowen's family are recalled in Albertina, Fflorens and Elidyr Roads. Treowen (Wonastow), Monmouthshire, is 'Owen's settlement': *tref*, pers.n. *Owen* (PNGwent 207). Housing development began in the 1930s on the west side of the GWR Vale of Neath Line.

Tre'rannell see **Angelton**

Trerhingyll (Trerhyngyll) ST 005768
Vale of Glamorgan (Llanblethian)
'ringild's farm (or settlement)': *tref, rhingyll*
Trerynghill 1650, *Ringyllston* 1662, *Treringill* 1670, *Trerhingill* 1696, *Tre y Ringyll* 1833, *Trerhingyll* 1846
The form for 1662 seems to be unparalleled and is likely to be a formal usage with no popular currency. A bridge here, probably over the small stream south of the ht., is recorded as *ringyll Seys Bridge* 1625 and *Pont y ringill Seys* 1674 'bridge of the English ringild' (*pont, Sais*) possibly in ref. to local use of E tenurial custom.

Tresalem see **Robertstown**

Tresimwn see **Bonvilston**

Trethomas ST 181887
Caerphilly (Bedwas Monmouthshire)
'settlement of Thomas': *tref*, surname *Thomas*
Trethomas 1913, 1951, *Thomastown* 1914, *Thomastown, Trethomas Station* 1920
Trethomas was developed around Tyn-y-pwll Inn on a green-field site between Glyn-gwyn and the r. Rhymni from c.1911 after sinking of the Bedwas Navigation Colliery by William James Thomas (1867-1945) (later Baron Ynyshir), owner of the Standard Collieries, Ynys-hir (MCPP 108-9). Trethomas is the usual form in W newspapers but on OS maps was initially confined as a n. to the railway station. The form *Tretomas* is the form used in gazetteers (GazWPN, LlEnwau) and *Tretomos* in a local history (NCR 182-4) as W forms but neither has been formally adopted.

Trewalter see **Walterston**

Trewiliam see **Williamstown**

Trewyddfa Fach SS 663973
Swansea (Llangyfelach)
'little Trewyddfa': pn. *Trewyddfa*, **bach**¹
Trewyddfa-fâch 1879, *Trewŷddfa-fâch* 1899
Named from a ho. (SS 663974) contrasting with Trewyddfa-fawr (*mawr, fawr*). Both places are located in the former manor recorded as *Trewithewa* 1319, *Trewydva* 1402, *Trywythva* 1583, *Trevidva* 1508, and *Treoyddeva* 1556 meaning 'settlement in a prominent place' (*tref, gwyddfa*). The second el. is identical to Yr Wyddfa (W n. for Snowdon) (DPNW 443). The n. is also recalled in Graig Trewyddfa (q.v.).

Trinant ST 206999
Caerphilly (Mynyddislwyn Monmouthshire)
'three streams': *tri* (variant *try-*), **nant**
Trenant Colliery 1833; *Trynant* 1841, (area) *Trenant, Tri-nant Level (Coal)* 1879, (village) *Tri-nant* 1886
The masc. form with Tri- (rather than Tair-) would favour the sense 'three valleys' because *nant* in this particular sense is generally a nm. There are exceptions elsewhere, however, such as Trinant (a tributary of Afon Hydfer) which

appears on OS maps from 1884. This has three headwaters rising on Y Fan Foel (SN 821223) in the Black Mountains, Breconshire. The stream at Trinant, Monmouthshire, is earlier called *Nantyglanach* 1813 from its proximity to *Glanach* 1813, *Glanerch Farm* 1833, *Llannerch farm* 1841 (now Llannerch-uchaf) (presumably **llannerch**), and *Tri Nant* 1879-80. *Trenant* 1833 misassociates the n. with **tref**, 'settlement, town'.

Trisaint see **Capel Trisaint**

Troedrhiw'r-fuwch　　　　　SO 130045
Caerphilly (Gelligaer)
'(land at) foot of the cow's slope': (**tir**), **troed, rhiw, y, buwch**
Tire Troed Rhyw yr vuwch 1657, *Troed Rhuw y Fuch* 1830, *Troed-y-rhiw-fuwch* 1833
The n. is applied on late 19th cent OS maps to an area at the foot of the slopes of Cefn y Brithdir. The village developed from the 1860s around Capel Bethania, the Board school and *Troedrhiw'r-fuwch Arms* 1900 extending southwards towards Tir-phil. Some older OS maps show the village as part of the nearby ht. Sebastopol (SO 133045). This takes its n. directly from the Sebastopol Arms commemorating the siege of Sebastopol 1854-5 in the Crimean War. Sebastopol owed its growth to the opening of Powell's Dyffryn Colliery sunk in 1853, later known as Powell Duffryn Colliery and as New Tredegar Colliery. Identical to Sebastopol (ST 2998) at Pontypool, Monmouthshire, and cf. Balaclava (SN 706004), in Llansamlet.

Troedrhiw-trwyn　　　　　ST 058908
Rhondda Cynon Taf (Llanwynno)
'(place at) foot of the slope shaped like a nose': **troed, y, rhiw, trwyn**
(ho.) *Troed Rhiew Yr Trwyn* 1793, *Troed-y-trwyn* 1833, *Troad Rhiw trwyn* 1841, *Troed-rhiw-trwyn* 1874-5
Troed-y-rhiw, variant Troedrhiw, is very common in Glamorgan as a loose compound with the general sense of 'place at the foot of a slope'.

Troed-y-rhiw　　　　　SO 071023
Merthyr Tudful
'(land at) foot of the slope': (**tir**), **troed, y, rhiw**
Tire Troed rywe gunrowyd 1598, *Thre troid Gymrugge* 1615, *Troedyrhiw* 1714, (ho.) *Troed rhiew gwmwrwg, Melintroed y rhiw* 1813, *Troed y rhiw gwmrwg* 1833, (ho.) *Troed-rhiw-gymrwg* 1881
Named from a ho. (SO 07310184) described in 1867 as simply *Troedyrhiw Farm* (HMerth 130), a residence of Sir John Guest, the industrialist. A number of sps. have a qualifier apparently representing *Gymrwg* as a len. of *Cymrwg*. The same el. is found in *Penrhiw-gymro* 1881, *Penrhiw-gymrwg* 1900 (approx. SO 080008) – no longer found on OS maps – which appears to suggest that the intervening hill-slope may once have been *Rhiw Gymrwg*. The qualifier has not been satisfactorily explained.

Trowbridge　　　　　ST 231803
Cardiff (Rumney and St Mellons)
'? bridge': ?, **bridge**
Great Towbridge c.1778, (hos.) *To bridge-fawr, ~ -fach* 1833, *Towbridge bach, Trowbridge* 1841, *Towbridge bach, ~ Mawr* 1869, *Trowbridge-mawr, -bâch* 1887
Trowbridge is the n. of two hos., distinguished as 'great' and 'small' (**mawr, bach¹**) and the n. was adopted for the housing estate developed after 1951 when the area was added to Cardiff County Borough. Earlier forms have To(w)- as if the n. contains E *tow* 'to tow, to haul'. That suggests a bridge over one of the numerous 'reens' or drainage ditches which could be moved aside but further evidence is needed. Later forms suggest association with Trowbridge, Wiltshire, meaning 'tree-trunk bridge' (OE **trēow, brycg**).

Tusker Rock　　　　　SS 840741
Vale of Glamorgan (St Brides Major)
'projecting reef': ON **skot**, ON **sker**
(*the groundes called*) *Skuttskeir* c.1598, *Skuscar I.* 1754, (vessel lost on) *the Wiskar* 1764, *Skuskar I.* 1777, *Tusker Rock* 1833

Cf. Sker. Later forms have been influenced by a fancied resemblance to E *tusk* or *tusker* (DPNW 479).

Tutt SS 626871
Swansea (Oystermouth)
?'look-out (point): ?ME *toot* (headland) *Tutt* 1880-1
The suggested meaning suits its location perfectly but sps. are too late for certainty. Local E also had *tutt* meaning 'a litle heepe of earth' in 1697 which could have influenced the development of *toot*. The n. applies to a rocky headland and a coastguard station between Limeslade Bay and Bracelet Bay.

Twmbarlwm ST 243927
hill Caerphilly (Henllys and Rhisga Monmouthshire)
'hillock (or mound) of bare hill': *twyn*, *bar*², *llwm*
Tuinbarlum c.1538, *Tumberlow hill* 1578, *Tombarlom* 1628, *Pentwynbarlw* 1695, *Twynbarlwm* 1778, *Twyn Barlwm ... vulgarly Tom Balam* 1809, *Twyn barllwm* 1813
William Coxe (Coxe 75n.) in his historical tour in 1801 describes it as 'in Welsh y Twyn a'i var yn Llwm, or the hill with the summit barren or naked' but *twyn* may actually refer to the mound of its prominent motte-and–bailey castle. The -*n* of *Twyn-* has become -*m* through anticipating the following –*b*- as in *Llambed* and *Dimbech* the colloquial forms of Llanbedr Pont Steffan and Dinbych (Denbigh).

Twmpath-mawr SS 850921
Bridgend (Llangynwyd)
'big mound': *twmpath*, *mawr*
Twmp-mawr 1877, *Twmpath-mawr* 1899
The area has been so heavily changed by industrial workings and urban development that it is difficult to identify any mound.

Twrch rn. se **Cwmtwrch Uchaf**

Twyn-yr-odyn¹ SO 053058
Merthyr Tudful
'hillock of the kiln': *twyn*, *yr*, *odyn*

Twynyrodin 1813, *Twyn yr odyn* 1820, *Twyn-yr-odyn* 1845, *Twynyrodyn* 1874
Cf. Twyn-yr-odyn² and Twynyrodyn (Lavernock) recorded as *Twyn-yr-odyn* 1879, and Twynyrodyn in Llangyfelach recorded as *Twyn Odin* 1841 and *Twynyrodyn* 1852.

Twyn-yr-odyn² ST 116137
Vale of Glamorgan (Wenvoe)
'hillock of the kiln': *twyn*, *yr*, *odyn*
Twyn-yr-odyn 1833, *Twynyrodyn* 1839, *Twyn-r-roddyn* 1842
Located near limestone quarries. Limekilns are shown on the OS 1:2,500 plan 1879.

Ty-coch SS 624933
Swansea
'red house': *tŷ*, *coch*
(tmt.) *Coch* c.1718, (ho.) *Tycoch* 1813, *Ty-coch* 1832, *Tŷ-coch* 1879
Named from a fm. (ST 625933). A suburban area which initially developed along Ty-coch Road and Carnglas Road from c.1905. A very common n. with identical examples in Llanedern, Aberafan, and Morriston.

Tydfil's Well, Ffynnon Tudful SO 044069
Merthyr Tudful
'well of (St) Tudful', pers.n. *Tudful*, E *well*, *ffynnon*
ffynon Diffil, ffynondufil 1820, *Tydvil's ~* , *Tydfil's Well, Ffynon Tydfil* 1852, (place) *Tydfil's Well* 1857, *St. Tydfil's Well* 1868, (place) *Tydfil Well* 1873
Recalling a well dedicated to Tudful (see Merthyr Tudful) with an adjoining chp. (SO 040070) on Church Street. Earlier sps. tend to favour the form Ffynnon Dudful with len. One imaginative guide to the town in 1848 describes this as the spot where the saint was murdered by a party of 'Pagan Saxons and Irish Picts'; there is no evidence for this.

Ty-draw SS 680949
Swansea (Llansamlet)
'distant, far house': *tŷ*, *draw*
(ho.) *Tir Llen' ap Ieuan Tew* c.1583, *Tir Lewelin ap Evan Tew* 1650, *Tyr Draw alias Tyr Richard John Llewelyn Tew* 1780, *Tydraw* 1813, *y Tydraw* 1908

The n. has displaced Tir Llywelyn ab Ieuan Tew also recorded as *Tyr Llewelyn Bevan Tew* 1764 referring to a ho. on 'land of Llywelyn son of Ieuan the fat' (*tew* 'fat, thick'). If the 1780 form is reliable, it bore an alternative n. meaning 'land of Richard son of Ieuan son of Llywelyn the fat'. Ty-draw is a very common ho.n. with examples in Aberdare (CVPN 93), Colwinston, Llanedern, Llanfabon, Llanhari, Llantrisant, Llantrithyd, Margam, Roath and other ps. The small group of hos. of Ty-draw appeared during the 19th cent near shallow drift mines and brickworks.

Tyllgoed see **Fairwater**

Tylorstown　　　　　　　　　　ST 010955
Rhondda Cynon Taf (Ystradyfodwg)
'settlement named from Tylor': surname *Tylor*, E *town*
Tylorstown 1882, *Tylor's Tn. Sta.* c.1898, *Tylerstown* 1900
Alfred Tylor (1824-84), a London quaker, married a daughter of Frederick William Harris (see Treharris) 1850. Tylor bought the mineral rights of Pendyrys (q.v.) fm. 1872 and sank the colliery near the top of what later became Tylorstown village which developed during the 1880s and 1890s (MCPP 110-113). The n. has also been attributed to his brother Louis Tylor (1837-1905). The colliery is described as *Pendyrys Colliery* (ST 012958) 1876-84. Glanffrwd says Tylorstown replaced Pont-y-gwaith, but this is a distinct village just below Tylorstown (HLlanwyno[1], 185).

Ty-nant　　　　　　　　　　　ST 063851
Rhondda Cynon Taf (Llantrisant)
'house or homestead near the stream': *tŷ* or *tyn*, (*y*), *nant*
(ho.) *Ty'r-nant* 1833, *Tynant* 1841, *Ty'n-y-nant, ~ Colliery* 1875, *Tyn-y-nant* 1964-5, *Tynant* 1970
Most historic forms favour the second interpretation with loss of the def.art. *y* a characteristic of other pns. in Glamorgan (see Blaen-cwm). The housing estate developed from c.1910 near the former Ida and Ty'n-y-nant collieries and takes its n. from a fm.

(ST 061843), in Llantwit Fardre p., next to a stream Nant Myddlyn recorded in *Blayne Myth Lyne* 1570 and as *Myddlyn* 1833 of uncertain meaning.

Tynewydd[1]　　　　　　　　　SN 827098
Neath Port Talbot (Cadoxton-juxta-Neath)
'new house': *tŷ*, *newydd*
Tuynewidd 1769, (ho.) *Ty-newydd* 1832, 1878
The n. was transferred to an industrial village which developed from c.1910 between Seven Sisters and Dulais Colliery.

Tynewydd[2]　　　　　　　　　SS 931989
Rhondda Cynon Taf (Ystradyfodwg)
'new house': *tŷ*, *newydd*
(tmt.) *Tŷ newydd* 1740, (fm.) *Ty Newydd* 1778, (ho.) *Tynewydd* 1813, *Ty-newydd* 1833
Named from a fm. probably identifiable with *Tŷ newydd* 1740. The village is shown as *Bryn-Wyndham* on OS maps 1877, 1884, a n. later confined to a street. *Tynewydd* reappears in 1900. Tynewydd Colliery was opened in 1852 by the Troedyrhiw Coal Co. and closed in 1901.

Tŷ-newydd[3] (Peterston-super-Montem) see **Newland**

Tyntetown　　　　　　　　　　ST 067967
Rhondda Cynon Taf (Llanwynno)
'settlement named from Tynte', surname *Tynte*, E *town*
Tyntetown 1895, *Tynte Hotel* (P.H.), *Tyntetown* 1900
Built on land part of Ynys-boeth Uchaf (approx. ST 071966) held by Halswell Milborne Kemeys-Tynte (1852-99), son of Charles Kemeys-Tynte (1822-91) (CVPN 95-96). Developed in the 1890s (MCPP 114-5). Tyntetown, pronounced as 'Tin Town' 1914, and informally as 'the Tynte', was alternatively known as Matthewstown (thus 1896) named from Rees Matthews (d. 1915), cashier of Penrikyber Colliery.

Tyn-y-bryn (Ty'n-y-bryn)　　　ST 005877
Rhondda Cynon Taf (Llantrisant)
'homestead at the hill': *tyn*, *y*, *bryn*

Tin y Brin 1768, *Ty yn y bryn* 1841, (fm.) *Ty'n-y-bryn* 1875
A housing estate developed after World War II and named from the former ho. (approx. SS 006879).

Tyn-y-caeau SS 758976
Neath Port Talbot (Neath)
'homestead at the enclosures' or 'house in the enclosures': *tyn* or *tŷ* and *yn*, *cae* pl. *caeau*
Ty'n-y-caeau 1830, *Tyn y caia* 1852
Identical pns. are found in Monknash, St Brides Major, Margam and elsewhere.

Tynycoedcae see **Waterloo**

Tyn-y-cwm SN 630029
Swansea (Llangyfelach)
'house in the valley': *tŷ* or *tyn*, *yn*, *y*, *cwm*
Ty yn y Cwm 1686, *Tuy yn y Cwm* 1764, *Tynycwm* 1813, *Ty'n-y-cwm* 1832, *Tyn y cwm* 1841
From a ho. in the valley Cwm Ysgiach. The modern ht. developed from c.1910 near a ho. Crwca-bach recorded as *Crwca-bâch* 1876 'lesser Crwca' (***bach***[1]) in contrast to Crwca (SN 624023) which is *Crwca* 1830 and *Crwcca* 1841 which is evidently *crwca* adj. 'crooked, bent, curved' probably describing a hillock or a bend in the stream Nant Sgiach. The latter may be a borrowing from Ir *sceach* 'hawthorn'.

Tyn-y-garn SS 894824
Bridgend (Newcastle)
'homestead at the cairn': *tyn*, *y*, *carn*, *garn*
Tyn y Garn 1852, *Tyn y garn* 1868, *Ty'n-y-garn* 1877
No cairn is shown on OS maps but one may be recalled in nearby Rock Cottage (SS 892825) on Penyfái Common/Gwaun Penyfái. Tyn-y-garn was little more than a row of hos. until the construction of a housing estate in the 1960s and 1970s.

Ty-rhiw ST 127836
Rhondda Cynon Taf (Eglwysilan)
'house on a slope': *tŷ*, *rhiw*
Ty-rhiw 1833, 1875
A small housing estate developed from the 1950s immediately below a ho. Tŷ-rhiw (ST 129837) on the north slopes of the wooded hill Fforest Fawr.

Tŷ-sign ST 257904
Caerphilly (Rhisga Monmouthshire)
'house near a sign': *tŷ*, E *sign*
the signe 1654, *yr signe* 1685, *Tir y Signe* 1708, (ho.) *Ty-Sign* 1832, *Ty-sign* 1883
Named from a former ho. (ST 256902) recorded for a short period around 1901 as *Channel View* as it looks towards the Bristol Channel. Historic forms 1708-1776 suggest that *tŷ* has displaced *tir* 'land' and the def.art. *y* with the implication that the 'sign' was an identifiable feature such as a sign-post. The area, however, is now covered by post-war housing and there is nothing very suggestive on early OS maps. The alternative, less likely, explanation is that the 'sign' was the sign of the zodiac marked perhaps on a specific building or ho. (PNWG 73-74). That seems to favour an inn-name but none is recorded here. Ty-sign lay close to Pontymason Lane running from Rogerstone to the northern end of Rhisga. Sign was also the n. of a former ho. (SS 870899), in Laleston, located significantly at crossroads where remains of a cross are marked on OS maps 1899-1965.

Tythegston, Llandudwg SS 857788
Bridgend
'settlement of Tudwg': pers.n., OE *stōw*; 'church of (St) Tudwg': *llan*, pers.n. **Tudwg**
sanctum Tudocum c.1165, (chp. of) *sancti Deducti* c.1178, *Tethegstowe* 1258, *Tedegstowe* 1265, *Tithexton* 1597, *Tythegstowe* c.1600, *Tythegston* 1799, *Landethoge* 1442, *Llandudwg* late 15th cent, *llann dudwc* c.1550, *ll. dydwc* c.1566, *Llandydock* 1578, (o) *Landydwg* 16th cent
This may also be *Landewdduc* early 13th cent and *Landewddich* 1254 which have been identified with Llangewydd and perhaps the chp. of *Sti. Duoti* c.1178 belonging to the ch. of St Leonard of Newcastle. The W n. is poorly represented in early sps. but is likely to be the original. E-speakers first substituted **stōw** with a similar meaning to ***llan*** (cf. Michaelston-le-Pit) which was itself gradually replaced by ME *-ton* (OE

tūn) from the late 16th cent. The antiquarian John Leland c.1538 regarded *Tidug* as a rn. since he says Newton Nottage was 'on the est ripe of Tidug' and that there was a haven for ships' here. This belief is apparently based on a defective part of the original text which says *Tidug* was 'a litle brok [which risith] out of a welle at Llanti-...a ii. miles [by nor]th from Newton'. Tythegston has a small stream, often dry, which runs south from the village only to be lost in the sands of Merthyr Mawr Warren about two miles east of Newton.

Uchelola to Upper Killay

The bridge over the Glamorgan Canal at Upper Boat.

Uchelola see **Highlight**

Uplands　　　　　　　　　　　SS 638929
Swansea
'higher lands': E *up*, *land* pl. *lands*
(ho.) *Upland* 1833, *Upland cottage* 1852, *Uplands* 1868, *Uplands Hotel* 1869
A housing estate developed from c.1880 named from a ho. (SS 640931) near Cwmdonkin Drive and Uplands Crescent on hill slopes above Brynmill.

Upper Boat, **Glan-bad**　　　　ST 105870
Rhondda Cynon Taf (Eglwysilan)
'upper ferry': E *upper*, E *boat*; 'boat side': *glan*, (*y*), *bad*²
the *Upper Boat* 1766, *Upper Boatside* 1769, the *Higher Boat* 1788, *Baduchaf* 1872, *Glanbad* 1879, *Glànybâd* 1887
Other sources suggest an alternative W n. Bad Uchaf (***uchaf***). A ferry over the r. Taf to *Boatside* 1769 here was replaced by a footbridge before 1875 and a road bridge before 1901.

There appears to be no specific mention of a 'Lower Boat' but there were ferries lower down the r. at Nant-garw, Melin Gruffudd and Gabalfa. The village developed along Cardiff Road northwards from Porth-y-glo towards Melin-gorrwg Foundry in the 19th cent.

Upper Forge, Forge-uchaf　　　SN 688019
Swansea (Llangyfelach)
E *upper*, E *forge*; *uchaf*
Forge-uchaf 1832, *Upper Forge* 1841
'upper, uppermost' in contrast to the *Old Forge* (in ruins 1879) on the opposite side and lower down Nant Clydach in the village of Clydach.

Upper Forge was worked until 1864. This may have been otherwise known as Forge Fach, 'little forge' (***bach***[1.] *fach*), which leaves its n. in that of a small street.

Upper Killay, Cilâ Uchaf　　　SS 589925
Swansea (Bishopston)
'upper (part of) Killay': E ***upper***, pn. *Killay*
Upper Killay 1878
Killay in 1799 and 1830 refers to what is now Middle Killay (SS 587922). The other two hos. are distinguished as 'big' (***mawr***, *fawr*) and 'little' (***bach***[1], *fach*). Most of the housing development took place after World War II.

Vale of Glamorgan to Virginia Park

Vale of Glamorgan. Cowbridge, from *Wales Illustrated* by Henry Gastineau (1830).

Vale of Glamorgan, Bro Morgannwg (Y Fro) 'lowland of Glamorgan': E *vale*, *Glamorgan*; 'lowland of Morgannwg': **bro**, *Morgannwg* Bro ... 'the lowe Country,' or, 'the Country in the Vale' c.1670, *the Vale or Champain* c.1800, *Bro Morgannwg* 1820 'lowland'), in contrast to Blaenau Morgannwg (q.v.). To the antiquarian Rice Merrick c.1580 the *Bro* was south of the portway leading west from Cardiff to Cowbridge and Bridgend, i.e. the area first conquered by the Anglo-Normans and largely subject to E law and customs. The W n. also occurs in a 19th cent triban as *y Fro* (Trib 41). Neither Vale nor Bro possessed any widespread currency before the 19th cent and refs. seem to be largely confined to the writings of antiquarians.

Vale of Neath see **Glyn-nedd**

Van see **Fan, Y**

Vardre see **Faerdre**

Varteg Hill see **Farteg Hill**

Vaynor see **Faenor, Y**

Velindre see **Felindre**

Victoria Park ST 154769
Cardiff
'municipal park commemorating Queen Victoria': monarch *Victoria*, E ***park***
Victoria Park 1901
Created in the 1890s taking up the greater part of Ely Common and opened in 1897 (PNIG 14; IHCS 33-37). The n. was extended to include housing constructed around the park during the first half of the 20th cent.

Virginia Park ST 159877
Caerphilly (Eglwysilan)
'housing estate near Virginia House': ho.n. *Virginia House*, E ***park***
Virginia Park 1920
A housing estate developed around a recreation and sports area (in use since 1887) on former pasture land between Pontygwindy Road and Bedwas Road north of Cae'rbragdy from the mid 1960s. Virginia House (ST 15398814), recorded in 1875, was on Pontygwindy Road.

Wallston to Wyndham Park

Whitchurch, Cardiff. Merthyr Road, looking north c.1900.

Wallston   ST 120732
Vale of Glamorgan (Wenvoe)
?'settlement with walls': OE **wall**, **tūn**
Walstone 1598, *Wallston* 1662, *~ house* 1677, *Walston* c.1620, *Walston vach* 1705, (fms.) *Old ~, New Walston* 1798
Gwynedd Pierce also notes (PNDPH 301, 321-2) that similar pns. Wallstone and Walson, in Monmouthshire and Walton East, and perhaps Walton West, in Pembrokeshire, are thought to contain pers.ns. Note in particular Walterston (q.v.). He suggests that if 'walls' is correct it may refer to ruins and notes the lost *Castelton*

Winvo 1540 in this p. A fn. *Walston* is recorded in Llan-maes or Llantwit Major in 1666.

Walterston, Trewalter   ST 068711
Vale of Glamorgan (Llancarfan)
'Walter's farm or settlement': pers.n. **Walter**, **tūn**; **tref** pers.n. **Gwalter**
Waltervilla c.1102, *Walterston* 1541, *Waterston* 1567, *Walterstowne* 1578, *Walston* 1675, *Walterstown* 1696, *Walterston or Trefwalter* 1866
See PNDPH 103-4, and NCPN 155. Probably *Trewalter* 1762, *Tre Walter* 1774 and *Tre(f)walter* c.1810. Iolo Morganwg mistakenly identified

Walter as Walter Map, 12th cent author of *De Nugis Curialum* ('Courtier's Trifles'). *Walston* is a contracted form, cf. *Bolston* for Bonvilston and *Flymston* for Flemingston. There are identical pns. elsewhere in Glamorgan, viz. Walterston (SS 5189), a chp. of Llanrhidian, recorded as (fee of) *villa Walteri in Guer* c.1200, (~) *Villa Walteri in terra de Goher* c.1250, *Walterston* 1583, *Walterstown* 1754, *Waterstown* 1715, and also the lost Walterston, in Laleston, recorded as *Walteristone* c.1283, *Waldereston, Waltereston* 13th cent.

Waterloo, Tynycoedcae ST 195881
Caerphilly (Rhydri, Bedwas)
'(place commemorating) Waterloo', n. of battle *Waterloo*; 'homestead at the hedged enclosure', *tyn*, *y*, *coedcae*
(ho.) *Ty'n-y-coedcae* 1875, (ho. and ht.) *Ty'n-y-coedcae* 1900, 1981, *Waterloo* 1991
The nucleus was Waterloo Row built in 1891 near the former Waterloo Tin Works (closed c.1940) and a small blast furnace ruinous in 1875 and 1900. These hos. and others nearby were known as Tynycoedcae (named from a ho. at ST 193882) down to the 1980s when Waterloo makes its appearance. Waterloo no doubt refers to the battle of Waterloo 1815.

Waterton SS 931788
Bridgend (Coychurch)
'farm near water': OE *wæter*, *tūn*
Watirton 1376, *Watertowne* 1581, *Waterton* 1618, *Walterton, al(ias) Waterston* 1631, (mill) *Watterton* 1665, *Water Town* 1831, (land) *Walter-Towne-Park* 1670
From a former fm. near the r. Ewenni (NCPN 133). A small number of forms suggest association with the pers.n. Walter, variants Wauter, Water. Waterton Park and Waterton Lane appear in the Philip's Street Atlas (2007) in W as *Parc Tredwr* and *Lôn Tre-dwr* (*parc*, *lôn*) but there seems to be no evidence that Waterton was ever known to W-speakers as Tredŵr, 'settlement near water' (*tref*, *dŵr*).

Watford Plas Watford ST 148860
Caerphilly (Eglwysilan)
'homestead by a road *or* ford': *bod¹*, *ffordd*
Tyrebotforde 1541, *Tyr y Voteford* 1570, *Votfordd* 1713, *Tir y Bedfordd* 1717, *Wadford* 1738, *Boddfordd, Bodford, Vodford* 1739, *Watford, Waterford* 1740, *Votffordd* 1778, *Y Fotffordd* 1872
Comparable with Bodffordd, Anglesey, pronounced 'Botffordd' (DNPW 39-40). Some sps. have an E appearance, hence B.G. Charles (NCPN 164) favoured 'a ford which can be crossed by wading' (OE *wæd*, *ford*) and drew a parallel with Watford, Hertfordshire and Northamptonshire. The first is now thought to mean 'hunting ford, a ford used when hunting' with OE *wāth* (CDEPN 656). To find an E pn. here at such an early date, however, seems very unlikely. The evidence favours *bod¹* and *ffordd* either in its early sense of 'ford' or later a 'track, path, road' (ADG², 104; PNGlam 213-5). Watford applies to the location where a road crosses a small stream Nant Ddu so that either meaning would be appropriate. The early sps. *Wotfordesweye* 1313 and *Botfordwey* 1314 clearly refer to the road (OE *wæg*). Sps. such as *Voteford*, *Vodford* probably stand for (Y) Fotffordd (as in 1872) with len. B- > F- [v] which suggests that here at least *bod¹* is a nf. The n. is recorded in that of an Independent chp. and two hos. Plas Watford, formerly Watford Fawr, and Watford Fach (*plas*, *mawr*, *bach¹*). Watford Park is a housing estate (ST 147860).

Wattstown, Aberllechau ST 019938
Rhondda Cynon Taf (Llanwynno)
'settlement named from Watts': surname *Watts*: E *town*; 'mouth of (r.) Llechau': *aber*, rn. *Llechau*
(ho.) *Cwtch or Aber-llechau* 1833, *Aberlecha* 1841, *Aberllechau* 1886, *Wattstown* 1887
Edmund Hannay Watts (1822-1894) was senior partner in Watts, Watts & Company coal exporters, colliery owners, agents and ship-brokers (MCPP 116-8). Located next to the National Colliery at Aberllechau, on the east side of Nant Llechau. A coal mine was sunk here before 1880 (www.welshcoalmines.co.uk) when it was locally known as 'Cwtch' standing for *cwts*, *cwtsh* [kʊtʃ] 'couch, resting-place, little corner, recess' etc, used in a topographical sense. This el. is recorded in

the n. of the bridge over Rhondda Fach as *Pont Rhyd-y-cŵch* 1877, 'bridge at the Cwtsh ford' (*pont*, *rhyd*, *y*). Cwtch/Cwtsh evidently continued in use among Welsh-speakers. The colliery was apparently taken over by the United National Steam Coal Co. and managed through agents Watts, Williams & Co., Cardiff whence the modern n.; cf. Wattsville.

Wattsville   ST 208914
Caerphilly (Mynyddislwyn Monmouthshire)
'settlement of Watts': surname *Watts*, E ***ville***
Wattsville 1884
Built c.1884 between a ho. Dyffryn-isaf, (ho.) *Tŷ-Prince*, the wood *Coed y Prince* 1885 and Afon Sirhywi, to house workers at the United National Collieries, Risca, and named like Wattstown (ST 0193) from Edmund Hannay Watts (1830-1902) (MCPP 119).

Waun, Y see **Heath**

Waunarlwydd   SS 602955
Swansea (Loughor and Swansea)
'the lord's moor': (***y***), ***gwaun***, ***arlwydd***
Gweine Arlloid 'the Lorde's meade' 1585, (field) *Wain Arglwydd* 1764, (tmt. of land) *Gwain Arlwidd* 1795, (?moor) *Waun arlwyd* 1832, *Gwayn Arlwydd Farm* 1837
arlwydd is an old variant of *arglwydd* more often used of a secular lord than the spiritual one. The def.art. *y* appears in (meadow) *Morva'r Arlwydd* (in Trewyddfa) 1650, a moor (***morfa***) lying partly in Loughor, partly in Trewyddfa ht., Swansea. H.C. Jones (PNIG 54) says that Portmead, in Swansea, was divided during the reign of Henry VIII and that Waunarlwydd, 'the lord's moor', was the part retained by the lord of Gower; this is unproven. Cf. the fn. *Wain yrarlwydd* recorded at Gabalfa (Llandaf) 1782.

Waun-gron   SS 653965
Swansea (Llangyfelach)
'round moor': ***gwaun***, ***cron***
(meadow) *Wain gron* 1580, *Waynegron* 1650, *Wain Gron* 1764, *Waun-gron* 1881
An area of housing developed in the 19th cent on a low rise between Heol y Cnap and Llangyfelach Road. The n. is now also applied on OS maps to the area south of Heol Fach.

Wauntreoda see **Gwaun Treoda**

Welsh St Donats, Llanddunwyd ST 028762
Vale of Glamorgan
'(ch. dedicated to) St Dunwyd in Welsh lp.': E ***Welsh***, E ***saint***; 'church dedicated to (St) Dunwyd': ***llan***, pers.n. *Dunwyd*
Welsh Seynt Donats 1482, *Welshe Seint Donettes* 1559, *Walshe Saint Donettes* 1613, *ll. dynwyd* c.1566, *llan ddunwyd* 1590-1, *Llanddynoyd* 1632, *Llanddunwd* 1763, *Llanddynwyd* 1867
Welsh refers to its location within the demesne lp. of Tal-y-fan in contrast to St Donats in lp. of Ogmore in the shire-fee of Glamorgan. Dunwyd was latinised as Donatus, the n. of several continental saints. The absence of early sps. probably reflects its relatively inferior status as a chp. of Llanbleddian but Welsh St Donats was implicitly in existence as a pn. long before 1482 since St Donats (q.v.) is recorded as *Sancto Donato Anglicano* 1341.

Wenallt   ST 149853
hill Cardiff (Whitchurch)
'(the) white wooded-slope': (***y***), ***gwen***, ***allt***.
Y Wenallt 1718, *Wynallt* 1811, (hill) *Craig Wenallt*, (ho.) *Wenallt* 1833, *Wen-allt* 1873
The hill is notable for its whitethorn blossom though now largely afforested as Coed y Wenallt (***coed***). Generally known as 'the Wenallt' ['wɛnəlt, 'wɛnalt] to local E-speakers. Craig (y) Wenallt properly refers to its steep slopes (***craig***). The ho. (Y) Wenallt (ST 152841) – probably *the wenalt* 1664 and *Wennalt* 1783 – is on its north side close to Wenallt Road.

Wenvoe, Gwenfô   ST 122728
Vale of Glamorgan
Uncertain
Wnfa c.1168, (*Roberto de*) *Wnuo* c.1200, *Wunfo* 1254, *Wenvo* c.1262, *Wenfo* 13th cent, *Wonfa* 1307, *Wynnefeo* 1383, *Gwenvoo* 1563, *Gwenfo* c.1566, *Gwaynfo* 1591, *Wenvoe* 1799
Wenvoe is a particularly frustrating pn. because it is so well evidenced (PNDPH 298-301). Local

W pron. was *Gwaun-fo* [guain'vo:] apparently containing **gwaun** 'high and wet level ground, moor, heath' but the rarity of historical forms supporting this el. raises the suspicion that **gwaun** has been substituted for an obscure el. represented as *Wn-*, *Won-*, *Wun-* and *Wen-* in older sources. The variation in the first vowel *e*, *o*, *y*, *i* of many sps. of Wenvoe suggests that clerks and copyists had great difficulty in knowing how to represent what was probably a middle vowel [ə] after w-, gw-, gu-, a feature also found in early forms of Undy, Monmouthshire. The collective evidence for Wenvoe seems to favour **gwyn** 'white, fair' but that still leaves the second el. unexplained. It has been suggested (OPN 154; PNIG 20) that this might be **-fa** 'plain, place' etc, but this does not suit the numerous forms with *-fo, -vo(e)*. These accord better with the final el. found in Cynfoi which is thought to be a pers.n. (see Abercwmboi) as Pierce says. That raises the possibility that the pn. is actually a pers.n., perhaps *Gwynfoi, but further comparative evidence is needed.

Weobley SS 478926
Swansea (Bishopston and Llanrhidian)
'clearing of (man called) Webba': OE pers.n. *Webba*, **lēah**
Webbelegha 1306, *Webley* 1318, *Wybley* 1532, *Wible* 1548, *Wibley* 1583, *Weobley* c.1600, *Webly Cast:* 1729, *Guible* c.1538, *Gwebbley, Gwebley* c.1598, *Gwibli* 1606, *Gweblai* c.1800
Local pron. 'Wibbley' ['wɪbli:] and later forms with *Wyb-*, *Wib-* appear to show association with a pers.n. *Wibba* or *wibba* 'beetle, worm'. Charles (NCPN 123) drew a comparison with Weobley, Herefordshire, and suggested that Weobley, Glamorgan, is identical or named after it although, as he admitted, there is no historical evidence to suggest a connection between them. Weobley, Herefordshire, may have influenced late written forms of Weobley but as a pn. it is now thought to contain the pers.n. *Wiobba (ODEPN). W-speakers have prefixed *G-* to bring Weobley into line with unlenited words with gw-; cf. the treatment of borrowings such as *gwalstod* (< OE *wealh-stōd*),

'interpreter', *gwarden* 'warden'. Sps. generally favour *Gweble* or *Gwebli* but this has not acquired official status. The form *Weble* is given in GazWPN and WATU

Wern-bwll SS 555947
Swansea (Llanrhidian)
'alder-trees pit': **gwern**, **pwll**
Wernbwll 1973
Apparently a new n. for a small group of hos. built in the late 1960s. There was an identical ho.n. (SN 718113) near Tai'r-gwaith recorded as *y Wern bwll* 1610, *Tir y wern bwll* 1681, and *Wernbwll* 1841 in a small, once wooded, dingle, and Wern-bwll near Glais recorded as *Y Werne Bwll* c.1583, *Gwern bwll* 1650.

Wern-ddu ST 170863
Caerphilly (Fan, Bedwas)
'(the) dark alder-tree marsh': (*y*), **gwern**, **du**
(lands) *y Wernddu* 1765, *Wernddu* 1786, (woodland) *Gwern-ddu* 1875, *Wern-ddu* 1885
The n. referred on 19th cent maps to a short row of hos. and is taken from adjoining woodland. A common n. with other instances in Cadoxton-juxta-Neath, Llanharan and Swansea.

Wernffrwd SS 515942
Swansea (Llanrhidian)
'white stream': **gwen**, **ffrwd**
(place) *Wenfroode* 1599, *Gwenffrwd* 1614, *Wenffrood* 1624, *Gwenfrwd* 1852, *Gwernfrwd* 1855, *Wern-ffrŵd* 1878
The first el. is misassociated in late sources with **gwern** 'alder-trees, alder-tree marsh'. The adjoining stream enters the Llwchwr estuary at SS 512950.

Wernolau SS 565957
Swansea (Llanrhidian)
'(the) bright alder-tree marsh': (*y*), **gwern**, with later addition of **golau**
'r *Wern* 1830, *Wern* 1841, *Wern-olau* 1879
golau variant **goleu** also appears in nearby Cefn-goleu fm. (SS 575953) recorded as *Cefn-golau Farm* 1879, *Cefn-goleu Farm* 1938, and Cefn-goleu Parc is *Cefn gole* 1830, *Cefn-golau*

1879, *Cefn-goleu Park* 1938. *Cefngole* 1841 probably refers to both of these hos. Craig Cefn-golau is a small, wooded ridge between them, *craig*.

West Aberthaw (ST 024668) see **Aberthaw**

West Cross SS 610891
Swansea (Oystermouth)
'west crossroad': E *west*, E *cross*
Wess Cross 1716, *West Cross* 1764, *West-cross* 1832
Named from a fm. next to the junction of Westcross Lane and Westcross Avenue; 'west' perhaps in contrast to the old junction of Westcross Lane with Mumbles Road. The area developed as a seaside suburb of Swansea during the 19th cent and includes a post-1960 housing estate.

West End ST 213952
Caerphilly (Mynyddislwyn Monmouthshire)
West End 1879
Located west of r. Ebwy and Aber-carn. The area was developed in the 1870s between the hos. Troed-y-rhiw and Tyle-coch and the railway next to a brass and iron foundry.

West-end Town see **Llantwit Major**

West Town see **East Town** or **Prior's Town**

Westra ST 144710
Vale of Glamorgan (St Andrews Major)
'west row (of houses)': OE *west*, OE *ræw*
Westrewe 1455, *Le Rewe* 1489, *Westrew* 1562, *Westre* 1638, *the Westra* 1762, *Great Westra* 1765, *Little Westra* 1777, *Westra Fawr Farm, Westra House* 1816, *Westra, ~ Vach, ~ fawr* 1852
Gwynedd Pierce (PNDPH 238) compares Southra (about half-a-mile away). There were formerly two fms. distinguished as *great*, *mawr* and *little*, *bach¹*, lens. *fawr, fach*. Southra is *Southrewe* 1455, *Sowthrewe, la Southrewe* 1489, *The Southra Tenement* 1748, *Southra* 1764 (OE *sūð* 'south'). There is record also of a *Northrewe* in the same lp. of Dinas Powys in 1455 (*norð*).

West Village see **Cowbridge**

Whitchurch, Eglwys Newydd ST 154800
Cardiff
'white church': OE *hwit, cirice*; 'the new church': *yr, eglwys, newydd*
Album Monasterium 1296, (*de*) *Albo Monasterio* 1307, *Album Monasterium alias Whitchirch* 1401, *Whytechurch* 1375, *Whitchurch* 1578, *Blaunk Moustier* 1315, *Blankmoster* 1322, *Newchurch* 1472, *Egluis Newith* c.1538, *yr eglwys newyð* c.1566, *or eglwys newydd* 1601, *Eglwys Newydd* c.1800
Many W forms have the def.art. *y* which is normally dropped in official usage but remains in general conversation. Gwynedd Pierce (ADG², 35) shows that Whitchurch and Eglwys Newydd are independent pns., not mistranslations of each other. They may at one time have referred to distinct buildings, i.e. an earlier 'white church' replaced by a 'new church', though not necessarily in different locations. The E n. probably refers to the practice of whitewashing churches (NCPN 163-4). The additional historic names have Lat and Fr *album, blanc, monasterium, mo(u)ster* etc, and may be purely administrative forms with no widespread currency. Sps. with *monasterium* have sometimes been taken as indicating an early monastic establishment (BirchN 174-5; NCDL 13) but *monasterium* sometimes means nothing more than 'church'. *Egluis Newith* in the itinerary of John Leland c.1538 refers to the old ch. on the north side of the village, demolished in 1904, and now a garden, near a *pile or maner place*. This must refer to the former castle mound, next to Clos Treoda, and ruinous c.1580. Traces of a castle were noted here in the 19th cent and in the garden of Treoda House in 1945 but when the ho. and castle were removed in 1966, archaeologists found little apart from a Bronze Age barrow. Treoda is also recalled in Gwaun Treoda (q.v.) otherwise Whitchurch Common. The central shopping area of Whitchurch is described as *Pentref* 1833 meaning '(the) village' (*pentref*) and is still known as 'the Village'.

Whiteford Point SS 448966
Swansea (Llanmadog)
'promontory near white ford': OE *hwit, ford, point*
Whitford poynt 1578, 1648, *Whitford Pt.* 1754, ~ *Point* 1799, *Whiteford Point* 1832
Charles (NCPN 121) noted a local tradition that 'many years ago persons used to cross the r. here from Penbrey on stepping stones' (WGOW II, 46). There is no evidence of stepping stones on 19th cent maps. Any ford would more likely have crossed the r. Burry on the east side of Whiteford Burrows but no obvious feature can be identified among the mud banks and river channels.

Whiterock SS 907787
Bridgend (Oldcastle)
'(place where there is) white rock': E *white, rock*
Whiterock Cottages 1878, *Whiterock* 1892
A housing estate, developed along Ewenni Road and Heronston Lane from the 1930s, and named from the former Whiterock Cottages (SS 90747882) in an area which has exposed carboniferous limestone. Cf. Whiterock (Swansea, Llansamlet) recorded in *White Rock Coal Bank* 1739, *White Rock works* 1772, *Whiterock* 1827.

Wick, (Y) Wîg SS 923721
Vale of Glamorgan
'farm, dairy farm, specialized farm or settlement': OE *wīc*; (*y*), cymricised *Wig*
Wicham c.1144, (ch. of) *sancti Jacobi apud Wicham*, *Wic* c.1165, *La Wyke* 1303, *Weeke Capella* c.1598, *the Wigge* 1623, *Wick parish* 1670, *y wig* c.1566, *Greate Wick* 1611
Wicham probably represents the OE dative pl. *wīcam* 'at the dairy farms', etc, but later forms have the sg. Occasionally recorded with the def.arts. *the, le, la* matched by W *y*. Sps. do not favour *gwig*¹ 'the wood', as suggested by Dafydd Morganwg (HMorg 477) and others but it has influenced the development of the W form. *Great* presumably distinguishes it from Wig-fach (q.v.).

Wig-fach SS 850779
Bridgend (Merthyr Mawr)
'(the) little wood': (*y*), *gwig*¹, *bach*¹
Y Weeg Vach 1755, *Wick fach* 1833, *Wick Vach* 1852, *Wic-fâch* 1876
Also recorded in (place) *Cwm y Wig vach* 1689 and *Cwm y wick vach* 1725 (*cwm*). There does not, however, seem to be a 'Wig-fawr' in this p. so that the comparison may be with Wick (q.v.).

Wild Mill, (Y) Felin-wyllt SS 902813
Bridgend (Coety)
'the wild mill': (*y*), *melin, gwyllt*
Willdmille 1565, *Wild Mill* 1775, *Velyn Wyllte* 1569, (place) *Y Vellin Willt*, (mill) *Y vellin Wyllt* 1586, *Vellyn-wyllt* 1676, *Melin-wyllt* 1833
Probably a 'mill driven fiercely (by a mill-stream)' but note also Parc Gwyllt which is (mess.) *Park Gwyllt* 1767, *Parc-y-wyllt* 1833 and *Parc-gwyllt* 1884-5 (SS 91768262) about one mile eastwards, its n. surviving in that of a hospital. This is 'wild park, wild enclosure' with *parc* – often applied to fairly small enclosed pieces of land as well as much larger areas such as deer-parks. It is also conceivable that Wild Mill and Y Felin-wyllt are eliptical for 'mill near Parc Gwyllt'. The last and *Parc-gwyllt-fâch* (SS 912826) 1885 (incorporated into the hospital grounds) adjoined the rough pastures on the south slopes of Cefn Hirgoed.

Williamstown, Trewiliam ST 003907
Rhondda Cynon Taf (Llantrisant)
'settlement named from Williams': surname *Williams*, E *town*; *tref*
Williamstown 1877, *William's town, Trewiliam* 1895, *Tre-william* 1892, *Trewilliam* 1903
Built from 1870s on land inherited by the Williams family from Walter Coffin (1784-1867), a pioneer of the south Wales coal-trade (MCPP 120-6). Two members of the Williams family are recalled in Arthur Street and Caroline Street. H.C. Jones (PNIG 33) connects it with (fm.) *Hendre Gwilim* 1833 (SS 998910) (*hendref*, pers.n. *Gwilym* = William) but this is an error. Richards (WATU) gives Dinas Isaf as an older n. for the area of

Williamstown but this was the n. of a fm. (ST 009901) at Edmondstown.

Williamstown (Merthyr Tudful) see **Georgetown**.

Winsh-fawr (Winchfawr)   SO 023062
Merthyr Tudful
'big winch': ***winsh***, ***mawr***
Winchfawr pit 1860, (place) *Winchfawr* 1882, *Winch Fawr* 1964
Located at a shaft adjoining a tramway running from coal and ironstone pits around Ochr-y-mynydd to link with a second tramway leading down to Cyfarthfa and was owned by the Cyfarthfa Company in 1860. Permission was granted in 1858 to build hos. here by the Board of Health. The n. was later transferred to a scattering of nearby hos. shown as Ochr-y-mynydd on OS maps down to 1952. This is 'side of the mountain' (***ochr***, ***y***, ***mynydd***) in ref. to Mynydd Aberdâr.

Winsh-wen   SS 682963
Swansea (Llansamlet)
'(the) white winch *or* pit': (***y***), ***winsh***, ***gwen***
Winch-wen 1830, *White Pit* 1841, *Winch Wen* 1896, *Winsh-wen* 1899, 1942, *y Winchwen* 1908
winsh is a borrowing from E *winch* and both els. are known to have sometimes referred to a well rather than simply its wheel; cf. Winchpit (ST 094736 in St Nicholas) recorded as *Winch-Pit* 1820, *Winchpit* 1885 (PNDPH 287). The use of ***winsh*** for a well (rather than ***ffynnon***, for example), however, is unlikely here and tends to favour an industrial winch and, by extension of meaning, 'pit possessing a winch' and 'pit', a supposition borne out by the n. White Pit (SS 682964) which drops off OS maps in 1884; cf. Winsh-fawr.

Woodfieldside   ST 180968
Caerphilly (Mynyddislwyn Monmouthshire)
'(area at) side of Woodfield': ho.n. *Woodfield*, E ***side***
The east side of Blackwood, around Woodfield House recorded in 1832, extending northwards to *Woodfield Park* 1901. Woodfield is recorded at least as early as 1819. Some of the once extensive woods still survive. Note *St. David's Wood* (ST 177972) and *Coed Cariad* 1879-80 (ST 184971). As a n.. Woodfieldside seems to be a post-war adoption, occurring on OS maps from c.1960. The village lacks a W n. though Maes-y-coed (***maes***, ***y***, ***coed***) has apparently been coined as a translation of Woodfield House (ST 178975) around which the housing developed from the 1920s.

Worms Head, **Pen y Pryf** (Pen y Pyrod)
SS 388877
Swansea (Rhosili)
'snake's head, headland shaped like a serpent':
OE ***wyrm***, E ***head***; ***pen***[1], ***y***, ***pryf***
Insula Wormyshede 1478, *Wormeshead* 1400, *Wormes hedd* 1562, *the Wormes head* 1586, *the Worm's head* 1672, *Penprys* 1670, *woomeshed in welsh penypryf*, *wormeshead* 1697
The n. describes the narrow, curving headland detached from the mainland at high water, hence Lat *insula* 1478, and *island* 1689. Two W names are recorded. The first Ynysweryn, now obsolete, appears in the 15th cent 'Life of St. Cenydd' (in John Capgrave's *Nova Legenda Angliæ* 1516) as *Henisweryn*. The scribe interprets the n. in Latin as *insula turbe* ('island of the crowd or mob'), apparently confusing *gwerin* 'folk, people' for ***gweryn***[2] recorded in 1800 as meaning 'a worm or bot, that breeds in the backs of cattle' (GPC). It probably once had the additional sense of 'serpent, snake' (ADG[2], 106). Ynysweryn was displaced among W-speakers by Pen y Pryf – no longer in widespread use – which is similar in meaning to both Ynysweryn and Worms Head. ***pryf*** now means 'insect, fly, maggot' but earlier had the sense of 'reptile, serpent, snake' (PNGlam 219-21). Gazetteers and current usage prefer the W form *Pen Pyrod* but this derives from the unreliable form *Pen y Pyrod* (in HMorg 454). Penrhyngŵyr on current OS maps seems to be unauthenticated (*penrhyn* nm. 'promontory' and Gŵyr, Gower).

Wyllie ST 177940
Caerphilly (Mynyddislwyn Monmouthshire)
'(settlement of) Wyllie': surname *Wyllie*
Pronounced ['waili]. Built on a green-field site below Tyle-gwyn c.1928-29 to house miners of Wyllie Colliery sunk 1924-26 by the Tredegar Iron and Steel Co., and closed in 1968. Named from Lt. Col. Alexander Keith Wyllie (1853-1928) (MCPP 127; www.welshcoalmines.co.uk), a director of the Tredegar Iron and Coal Company and Oakdale Colliery.

Wyndham SS 932914
Bridgend (Llangeinwyr)
'(settlement of) Wyndham': surname *Wyndham*
Developed from 1860s on part of the earl of Dunraven's estate after sinking of the Wyndham pit by John Brogden and Sons seeking coal for their ironworks at Ton-du (MCPP 128-9). The nucleus was a group of about twenty hos. in Wyndham Street near the Wyndham Arms 1875-81 at Nantdyrys. The village subsequently developed southwards with the construction of Dunraven Terrace and Fronwen Terrace on what is now Dunraven Place. Wyndham was adopted on OS maps after 1900. The n. could commemorate Windham Henry Quin (1782-1850), second earl of Dunraven, who married Caroline (daughter of Thomas Wyndham, c.1768-1814) of Dunraven Castle, in 1810, their eldest son Edwin Richard Wyndham-Quin (1812-71), third earl, or simply the family n. The second earl added his wife's surname to Quin in 1815. The earls' other title Viscount Adare is recalled in Adare Street.

Wyndham Park ST 085760
Vale of Glamorgan (Peterston-super-Ely)
'housing estate of Wyndham Ivor Radcliffe': pers.n. *Wyndham*, E *park*
Wyndham Park 1966
Originating as a commuter village known as *Glyn Cory Garden Village* 1909-1965 (*glyn*). The original plans were drawn by Thomas Mawson (1861-1933) who designed the gardens at Dyffryn House, St Nicholas. Construction of the village apparently began in 1907 under the supervision of Thomas Adams, an early pioneer of the modern planning movement, on land owned by John Cory (d. 1910), a partner in Cory Brothers and Co, shipping and coal magnates. In 1961 the estate was acquired by Wyndham Ivor Radcliffe of Evan Thomas, Radcliffe and Company, a Cardiff shipping company, and re-named Wyndham Park (www.wyndhampark.org).

Ynysawdre to Ystumllwynarth

Ynys-y-bŵl. The old village c.1900.

Ynysawdre SS 899845
Bridgend (St Brides Minor)
?'river-meadow belonging to the harvest farm':
ynys, ?***cynhaeaf-dre***
(place) *Ynys Nawdre* 1631, *Ynys Naudre* 1692, *Ynisawdre* 1767, *Ynys mawdre Ycha*, ~ *Issa* 1779, *Ynishawdre* 1799, *Ynys-nawdre* 1833
Gwynedd Pierce (ADG[1], 118; PNGlam 222-4) demonstrates that the –n- found in historic forms such as *Ynys Nawdre* may favour **cynhaeaf-dre** variant *cynhawdre* and that the greater part of the unstressed syllable -gyn- has been lost, i.e. *Ynysgynhaeafdre > Ynysgynhawdre, Ynysgynawdre > Ynysnawdre > Ynysawdre. The variation *hafdre/hawdre* 'summer farm' (***haf***, ***tref***) is found locally in Hawdre (SS 773948, 782951), at Baglan, recorded as *Hawdre Cenoll*, ~ *Yssa*, ~ *Ycha* 1698, *Have dre* 1602, *Middle* ~, *Lower Hafdre* 1791 (***canol***, ***isaf***, ***uchaf***). In pns. **cynaeaf-dre** is probably found in Gwenhafdre (SN 674671) at Lledrod Uchaf, Cardiganshire, with forms that include *Kanavdrey* 1660, *Gynhawdref* 1690, *Canhawdre* c.1757 (PNCrd 832) is best known in and perhaps Cynheidre (Llanelli), Carmarthenshire, recorded as *Kynhaydre* 1583, *Y gynheydrey* 1596 and *Kynhaydrey* 1610 (DPNW 116). In order to explain the historic

–n-, historians such as H.C. Jones (PNIG 92) supposed that *–nawdre* contained *nawdd* 'refuge, protection' and that the pn. meant 'meadow of the protected homestead' but the combination of *-dd* and *d-* would generally produce *–th-* [θ] as in Rhuthin (q.v.).

Ynys-boeth ST 070963
Rhondda Cynon Taf (Llanwynno)
'burnt river-meadow': *ynys, poeth*
Ynys boeth issa 1633, *Ynysboeth Yssa, ~ Ycha* 1636, (2 fms.) *Ynysboeth* 1813, *Ynysboeth-uchaf, ~ -isaf* 1833, *ynis both issa, ~ ycha, Ynis Both Isha, ~ Ucha* 1841
Deric John (CVPN 98-99) suggests 'a sunny river meadow usually with a thin layer of soil ... that bakes and retains the sun's heat' or a ref. to an industrial activity such as charcoal burning; cf. Tre-boeth (q.v.). There were two fms. Ynys-boeth Isaf (ST 071963) and ~ Uchaf (ST 069967) (*isaf, uchaf*). Local pron. is W 'bôth', E 'both' [bo:θ]

Ynys-ddu ST 180924
Caerphilly (Mynyddislwyn, Monmouthshire)
'black (or dark) river-meadow': *ynys, du*
Ynys ddy 1630, *Ynysddy* 1649, *Ynysddu* 1715, *Ynys du* 1813, *Ynys-ddu* 1859
Named from a ho., the former home of the poet Islwyn (William Thomas) (1832-78). The location of a small 'model' settlement founded in the 1820s by John Hodder Moggridge (see Blackwood), a magistrate and industrialist. Identical pns. include Ynys-ddu (ST 033819) at Llanharan recorded as (tmt.) *Ynys Ddye* 1595, *Ynys ddy* 1747, (ho.) *Ynys ddu* 1811.

Ynys-fach SO 044059
Merthyr Tudful
'little river-meadow': *ynys, bach*[1]
(close) *yr ynys-vach* 1691, (lands) *Ynysfach* 1760, *Ynys fach* 1783, *Ynys fach furnaces* 1818, *Ynysfach* 1852
The location of furnaces near r. Taf built by the Crawshay family of industrialists, 1801 (StoryMT 367).

Ynysforgan SS 678996
Swansea (Llangyfelach)
'river-meadow of (man called) Morgan': *ynys*, pers.n. *Morgan*
Ynis vorgan 1650, *Ynnis forgan* 1699, *Ynis Vorgan* 1730, *Ynisvorgan* 1764, *Ynys-forgan* 1832
Morgan is unidentified. Named from a ho., one of the homes of Hopcyn ap Tomas, a major patron of W learning, who arranged for the compilation and copying of the Red Book of Hergest c.1400 (DWB). It is now the site of a caravan park. The village developed from the 1890s near several coal-pits close to the r. Tawe. The same pers.n. is also recalled in a nearby ho.n. Penrhiwforgan (approx. SS 674994)

Ynys-hir SN 024928
Rhondda Cynon Taf (Ystradyfodwg)
'long river-meadow': *ynys, hir*
(lands) *Tyir y rynys hyir, y rynys hyir* 1633, *Ynusshire* 1789, *Ynis Hyr* 1799, *Ynyshir* 1813, (village) *Ynys-hir, ~ Colliery* 1885
Named from Ynyshir Colliery recorded 1865, ultimately taken from a fm. on the west bank of the r. Rhondda. The village developed from the 1870s.

Ynysmaerdy[1] SS 739951
Neath Port Talbot (Briton Ferry)
'river-meadow of the steward's house': *ynys, (y), maerdy*
(ancient house) *Ynismaerdy* c.1700, *Ynysymardy* 1707, *Ynys-y-maerdy* 1830, *Ynys-maerdy* 1878
Cf. Maerdy. An area of housing developed from the 1960s and named from a ho. reputedly built by Lleision ap Rhys mid 16th cent after he secured Neath abbey and its estates.

Ynysmaerdy[2] ST 033845
Rhondda Cynon Taf (Llanharan)
'river-meadow of the steward's house': *ynys, (y), maerdy*
Ynys J Mayarde 1541, *Ynis Ymardu* 1783, *Ynisy mardu* 1795, *Ynys Maerdy* 1833

As Ynysymaerdy[1]. Named from a fm. (ST 033839) near the r. Ely, the area was developed from the 1930s near Llantrisant Colliery.

Ynysmeudwy SN 736054
Swansea (Llan-giwg)
'the hermit's river-meadow': ***ynys***, (***y***), ***meudwy***
Ynys Mydo 1529, *Enes e Meydoo* 1558, *Ynys y meydow* 1605, (tmts.) *Ynis meydow ycha, ~ isha* 1650, *Ynis y medw Ycha, Ynismedw Yssha, Ynis medw Genol* 1764, *Ynis Meidw* 1828, *Ynys-mydw-ganol, ~ -uchaf* 1830
Locally pronounced 'Smitw' ['smɪtu:]. The village occupies the site of Ynysymeudwy Uchaf (***uchaf***). Ynysymeudwy Ganol (***canol***, ***ganol***) is at SN 734059 and Ynysmeudwy-isaf (***isaf***) was apparently near Craig Llan-giwg. The third el. also occurs in Llwynmeudwy-uchaf (SN 725057) and Llwynmeudwy-isaf (SN 728053) recorded as (tmt.) *Llyn y meydow* 1650, *Llwyn y Medw* 1764, *Llwyn-mydw-uchaf, ~ -isaf* 1830, hos. called 'the hermit's grove' (***llwyn***, ***uchaf***, ***isaf***). There seems to be no evidence of a hermitage here and it is possible that Meudwy is simply a lost n. for the stream which flows down the valley Cwm Siôn to the r. Tawe, perhaps one which is hidden away and secluded. ***meudwy*** in its literal sense occurs in Ffynnon-fedw (SS 627031), in Mawr ht., Llangyfelach. This is recorded as *Funnon Mydow* 1764, *Ffynnon-fidw* 1830 and *Finonfidow* 1841, 'the hermit's well' (***ffynnon***, ***y***, ***meudwy*** confused with ***bedw*** 'birch-trees').

Ynysowen see **Merthyr Vale: Ynysowen**

Ynystawe SN 681002
Swansea (Llangyfelach)
'river-meadow by (r.) Tawe': ***ynys***, rn. ***Tawe***
Ynis dawey 1697 (late 18th cent), *Ynis dawy* late 18th cent, *Ynis Tawe* 1799, *Ynys-tawe* 1830
Named from the ancient ho. associated with Hopcyn ap Tomas (see Ynysforgan). A largely mid 19th cent development along Clydach Road.

Ynys-wen SS 948975
Rhondda Cynon Taf (Ystradyfodwg)
'fair river-meadow': ***ynys***, ***gwen***
Enys Wen Naunte 1541, *ynys wen* 1580, (mess.) *Yniswen* 1759, *Ynys-wen* 1833
Named from a former fm. on the west side of Rhondda Fawr. The village developed near the former Ynys-wen Colliery. The form for 1541 has ***nant*** 'stream', apparently a scribal error.

Ynys y Barri see **Barry**

Ynys-y-bŵl ST 060941
Rhondda Cynon Taf (Llanwynno)
'bowl-shaped valley' or 'river-meadow used for the game of bowls': ***ynys***, ***y***, ***bŵl***
Ynys-y-Bool 1739, (dw. ho., smith's forge) *Evail ynis y Bool* 1756, *Ynis y Bwl* 1799, *Ynysybwl* 1813, *Ynysybwl* 1833, (ho.) *Ynys-y-bwll* 1874
See CVPN 97-98. There is also mention of *Bowling green* 1798, confirmed by Glanffrwd in 1888 (HLlanwyno[1], 16, 51-59). This could be a re-interpretation but the sport is recorded elsewhere in names such as Alabowl ('bowling alley') at Waun-fawr, Caernarfonshire, and Alafowlia, in Denbigh, and possibly Ael y Bowl, in Anglesey, all with *ala* 'narrow path, alley' (HE 13-14; HM 18-20). The industrial village developed from about 1868 when the former British School opened, expanding to the area below a ho. Ynysybŵl (ST 055951). *Evail* is 'a smithy', ***gefail***, *efail*. The established form has –bŵl with a long vowel [u:] but locally it is pronounced with –bwl with a mid to short vowel [ʊ].

Ynysymwn (Ynysymond) Ynys-y-mond Uchaf SN 714024
Neath Port Talbot (Cadoxton-juxta-Neath)
?'river-meadow of ?Ymwen': ***ynys***, ?pers.n. **Ymwen*
Enysumwen 1334, *Parcell ynys Sym[m]ond* 1670, *Ymysymon* c.1700, *Ynissymon* 1764, *Ynissimond* 1791, (hos.) *Ynys-y-mwyn-uchaf, ~ -ganol, ~ -isaf* 1830, *Ynysmond* 1885, *Ynysymwn* 1906

Prys Morgan (Morgannwg 53, 174) suggests that *Ymwen* is also found in the n. of a pool above the former Ynyspenllwch weir (SN 704014) just downstream in the r. Tawe recorded as *Llyn Immon* 1764. Some forms of Ynysymwn appear to show association with Sim(m)on(d), a surname recorded locally in Llan-giwg and Swansea 1670. The 1832 sps. misassociate the pn. with the def. art. *y* and *mwyn* 'ore, wealth' etc. There is no connection with the Mond family of industrialists and Mond Nickel Co. established in 1900. Ynysymwn was a division (***parsel***) and township of Cadoxton-juxta-Neath.

Ysgubornewydd SO 057054
Merthyr Tudful
'new barn': ***ysgubor, newydd***
Ysgubor Newydd 1833, *Skybornewydd* 1843, (ho.) *Ysgubor-newydd* 1885
The n. applied in 1919 to a small group of hos. on the south side of Primrose Hill next to a mineral railway but was transferred to a housing estate built after World War II.

Ystalyfera SN 766088
Neath Port Talbot (Llan-giwg)
'meadow at the end of the short share-land': ***ynys, tal*** 'end', ***y, *berran***
Ynys Delverran 1548, *Ynys Tal y Veran* 1582, *Tir Ynystalverran* 1604, *Tyr Stale Verra Ycha, Staleyfere* 1729, *Stallferra Issaf, ~ Uchaf, Stallfera Genol* 1795, *Stalyfera Issa, ~ Ycha, Staly Fera* 1797, *Ystal-y-fera* 1831, *~ Station* 1865
berran is a hypothetical word composed of ***ber*** adj.f. 'short' and *rhan* 'part, share'. 'Share-land' would be land shared by two or more tenants. The alternative is *beran*[1] a dim. of *bêr*[1] nmf. 'spear, lance' and 'spit, skewer' which might be used figuratively for a point or promontory of land, i.e. 'meadow at the end of the promontory'. It is, however, difficult relating that to the local topography. Early forms with *-n* rule out *bera* 'rick, stack' (suggested in PNIG 49). Later loss of the final *–n* can be paralleled elsewhere in Glamorgan, particularly in the Vale.

Ystrad SS 987950
Rhondda Cynon Taf
'valley-bottom (of St Tyfodwg)': ***ystrad***, pers.n. *Tyfodwg*
Istradvadok 1375, *Estrad* 1535, *Ystrate* c.1538, *Estrydiuodok* 1578, *Istradtevodocke* 1578, *Ystradetyvydoge* 1553, *Rustrad* 1639, *Ystradevoducke* 1711, *Ystrad-y-fodwg* 1833, *yr Ystrad* 1839, *Ystrad* or *Ystrad-Rhondda* 1868
Ystrad Tyfodwg > Ystradyfodwg through assimilation of unvoiced –t–. Tyfodwg is also dedicated at Llandyfodwg and Llantrisant. The short form Ystrad is evidenced as early as 1535 as the n. of the p. and seemingly for a stretch of the valley of Rhondda Fawr below Pentre centred on the old ch. dedicated to St John (SS 972954) in what is now known as Ton-pentre (q.v.). The full n. of the p. was confined on OS maps in 1877 and 1884 to the area east of the r. Rhondda Fawr extending along what is now Ystrad Road towards Bodringallt (SS 982952). *Ystrad-Rhondda* was in use as the n. of the railway station at Ton-pentre on OS maps 1900-1947. Ystrad Rhondda (without the hyphen) was chosen as the n. of the new railway station (SS 986948) constructed in the 1980s. The abbreviated form Ystrad does not actually appear on OS maps until 1961 (displacing Bodringallt) but was the n. of the gas-works next to the railway at least as early as 1877 and may have been in informal use as a description for the area extending from Bethel Calvinistic Methodist chp. on William Street to St Stephen's ch. on Gelligaled Road.

Ystrad-fawr SS 898800
Bridgend (Newcastle)
'big valley-bottom': ***ystrad, mawr***
(ho.) *Ystrad fawr* 1813, *Ystrad-fawr* 1833, *Ystrad Fawr* 1899
This may also be freehold land called *Ystrad Vawre* located in this area in the 17th cent. Transferred to a housing estate mainly developed since the mid 1960s and named from a ho. (approx. SS 898800) located next to a small stream Nant Cefn-glas.

Ystradmynach ST 145943
Caerphilly (Llanfabon)
'valley-bottom of the ?monk': *ystrad, mynach¹, manach*
Ystrad manach 1635, *Ystradmanach* 1729, *the Estrad* 1783, *Ystrad Manach* 1799, *Ystrad-y-mynach* 1833
There is no reliable evidence for a monastery here and Mynach could simply be a lost rn., perhaps describing a 'quiet (like a monk) stream'; cf. Castellymynach. There is a r. Mynach at Devil's Bridge, Cardiganshire, but the association there seems to be with the monastery of Strata Florida. *mynach¹* is also found in Brynmynach (ST 140944) taken from a ho. recorded in 1868 but earlier forms have not been found. H.C. Jones (PNIG 24) recounts a local fanciful tale associating the pn. with Gilbert de Clare, lord of Glamorgan, whose wife Alicia reputedly had an affair with a W lord Gruffudd ap Hywel and confessed this to a monk who told Clare. Clare killed the monk and hanged Gruffudd.

Ystradowen ST 012776
Vale of Glamorgan
?'valley-bottom of Owain': *ystrad,* pers.n. *Owain* variant *Owen*
(chp. of) *sancti Euiani de Cherleton'* c.1178, *Stradeuwen* 1263, *Stradowayn* 13th cent, *Straddouwen* c.1291, *Ystradowen* 1507, *Istrodowen'* 1543, *Ystrad Owen, ystrad owain* c.1566
This appears to receive support from the ch. dedication to St Owain which is presumably what *sancti Euiani* represents (if it is correctly identified with Ystradowen because *Cherleton'* seems to be unmatched in other sources). The pn. occurs elsewhere, eg. Ystrad Owen (SO 811003, Llantwit-juxta-Neath) (mess.) recorded as *Ystrad Owen* 1671, 1784.

Ystradyfodwg see **Ystrad**

Ystumllwynarth see **Oystermouth**

LIST OF SUBSCRIBERS

The author and publisher are very grateful to those listed below for their support for this publication.

Individuals

Bevan, Gareth A.
Bird, Margaret
Boyns, Arthur
Briggs, John W.
Broderick, Prof. Dr. George
Childs, Jeff
Clarke, Alex
Coates, Richard
Comeau, Rhiannon
Coplestone-Crow, Bruce
Curry, Delyth
Davies, David Leslie
Davies, John Barry
Davies, Jack
Davies, Jeff
Dolben, William
Duggan, Dr. M.A.K.
Edwards, Keith
Edwards, Kelvin
Emlyn-Jones, Stephen
Evans, Alcwyn Deiniol
Finch, Peter
Flowers, Ness
Foster Evans, Dr. Dylan
Frayling, Dafydd
Freeman, John
Fychan, Angharad
Gabb, Gerald
Gronow, Colin
Gwyndaf, Eleri & Robin
Gwynn, Elinor
Harris, Edward
Hawke, Andrew
Hawkins, Dai
Headon, Mike
Hill, Charles
Hines, John
Hughes, Glyn
Johnston, Prof. Dafydd
James, Brian
James, Heather
Jones, Berwyn Prys
Jones, Denzil
Jones, Handel
Jones, J. Brynmor
Jones, Mary
Jones, Megan
Jones, Pat
Jones, Peter Meurig
Jones, Rhidian
Kidwell, Mathew
Kitson, P.R.
Lewis-Jones, Jeffrey
Lewis-Jones, Keith L.
Linnard, Dr. William
Martin, Dr. Joanna
McMullen, Pedr
Morgan, Anne
Morgan, Prof. Prys
Morgan, Timothy
Morton, Dr. Miranda
Newley, Jinx
Owen, Prof. Hywel Wyn
Owen, John
Owen, Morfydd
Padel, Dr. Oliver

List of Subscribers

Powell, Richard
Raybould, W.H.
Richards, Claire
Richard, Ioan
Richards, Gareth
Roberts, Stephen K.
Sheppard, Margaret
Smith, Peter

Taylor, Prof. Richard
Thomas, Jac
Thorne, David
Thynne, Andrew
Webb, Clifford R.
Williams, Dewi Bowen
Williams, Ifor
Wood, Philip N.

Institutions

National Museum of Wales
Centre for Advanced Welsh and Celtic Studies
Welsh Place-Name Society
Glamorgan Archives

Gower Society
Society for Name Studies in Britain and Ireland
Swansea University Library
West Glamorgan Archive Service

welsh academic press

POLITICAL CHAMELEON
In Search of George Thomas

Martin Shipton

"I picked up this book expecting it to be a hatchet job, but it is a very fair book and a very well researched book. The problem with George Thomas is that one can write a book that is very fair and very well researched yet he still comes out of it very badly."
Vaughan Roderick, BBC Radio Wales

Drawing on previously unpublished material from Thomas' vast personal and political archive in the National Library of Wales, and interviews with many who knew him during his career, award-winning journalist Martin Shipton reveals the real George Thomas, the complex character behind the carefully crafted facade of the devout Christian, and discovers a number of surprising and shocking personae - including the sexual predator - of this ultimate *Political Chameleon*.

978-1-86057-137-4   304pp   £16.99   PB

'YOU ARE LEGEND'
The Welsh Volunteers In the Spanish Civil War

Graham Davies

'Excellent. A paean to the working men and women of Wales who went to Spain to fight in defence of the fledgling Spanish Republic.'
Keith Jones, son of volunteer Tom Jones from Rhosllanerchrugog

'Well researched, and using previously unpublished sources, 'You Are Legend' is recommended reading. It is important that the contribution of the large number of Welsh volunteers continues to be recognised.'
Mary Greening, daughter of volunteer Edwin Greening of Aberdare

'A highly readable and comprehensively researched account of the Welsh Brigaders.'
Alan Warren, Spanish Civil War historian

Almost 200 Welshmen and women volunteered to join the International Brigade and travelled to Spain to fight fascism alongside the Republican government during the 1936-1939 Spanish Civil War. While over 150 returned home, at least 35 died during the brutal conflict. *'You Are Legend'* is their remarkable story.

978-1-86057-130-5   224pp   £19.99   PB

welsh academic press

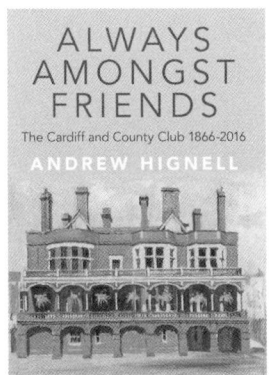

ALWAYS AMONGST FRIENDS
The Cardiff & County Club 1866-2016

Dr. Andrew Hignell

Since its establishment in 1866 by prominent businessmen and the gentry of south Wales, the Cardiff and County Club has played a central role in the commercial, political and sporting life of Cardiff, as it developed from a burgeoning Victorian coal metropolis into the dynamic Welsh capital city of today.

Extensively researched and lavishly illustrated, *Always Amongst Friends* not only traces the fascinating 150-year history of the Club through a scholarly study of the social and economic history of Cardiff, but also celebrates the Cardiff and County Club's colourful characters, their mischievous humour and exudes the warmth and camaraderie so treasured by its members.

978-1-86057-129-9   304pp   £20.00   PB

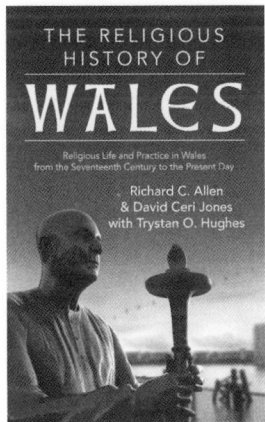

THE RELIGIOUS HISTORY OF WALES
Religious Life and Practice in Wales from the Seventeenth Century to the Present Day

Richard C. Allen & David Ceri Jones, with Trystan O. Hughes

An essential reference guide, this volume draws together an impressive collection of academics and religious practitioners to map out, for the first time, the religious multiplicity and diversity of Wales, manifested in the following religions, beliefs and denominations:

The Church in Wales - Independents (Congregationalists) - Baptists
The Religious Society of Friends (Quakers) - Roman Catholicism
Calvinistic Methodism - Wesleyan Methodism - The Moravian Church
Unitarianism - Salvation Army - Pentecostalism - United Reform
Church Seventh-Day Adventism - The Church of the Latter-Day
Saints (Mormons) - Jehovah's Witnesses - Evangelicalism - Judaism -
Islam Sikhism - Bahá'Í

978-1-86057-079-7   293pp   £25.00   PB

welsh academic press

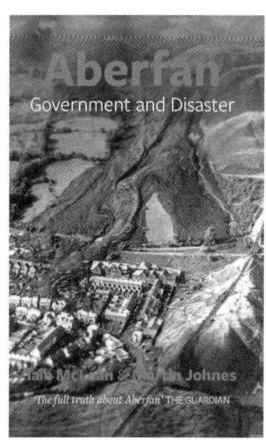

ABERFAN
Government and Disaster
(Second Edition)

Iain McLean & Martin Johnes

'The full truth about Aberfan'
The Guardian

'The research is outstanding...the investigation is substantial, balanced and authoritative...this is certainly the definitive book on the subject...Meticulous.'
John R. Davis, Journal of Contemporary British History

'Excellent...thorough and sympathetic.'
Headway 2000 (Aberfan Community Newspaper)

Aberfan - Government & Disaster is widely recognised as the definitive study of the disaster and, following meticulous research of previously unavailable public records - kept confidential by the UK Government's 30-year rule - the authors explain how and why the disaster happened and why nobody was held responsible.

978-1-86057-133-6   192pp   £19.99   PB

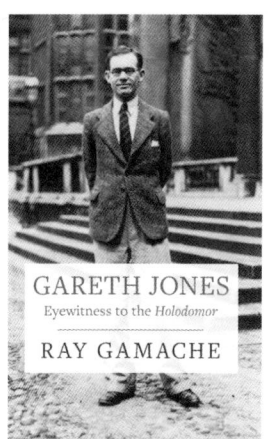

GARETH JONES
Eyewitness to the Holodomor

Ray Gamache

'Excellent ... serves as a warning to journalists not to be taken in by official sources and political ideology but to report what they actually learn through their own efforts.'
Prof. Maurine H. Beasley, Univ. of Maryland

'...meticulously researched book [that] returns Gareth Jones to his rightful status, as one of the most outstanding journalists of his generation'
Nigel Linsan Colley, www.garethjones.org

'Extraordinary ... Jones' articles ... caused a sensation ... Because [his] notebooks record immediate impressions and describe events as they were happening, they have an unusual freshness ... Jones' reputation has revived thanks to the Ukrainian government's broader efforts to tell the history of the famine.'
Anne Applebaum, The New York Review

Gareth Jones (1905-1934), the young Welsh investigative journalist, is revered in Ukraine as a national hero and is now rightly recognised as the first reporter to reveal the horror of the Holodomor, the Soviet Government-induced famine of the early 1930s, which killed millions of Ukrainians.

978-1-86057-122-0   256pp   £19.99   PB

welsh academic press

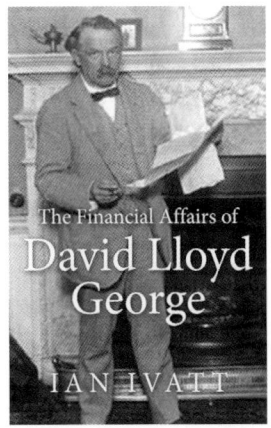

The Financial Affairs of
DAVID LLOYD GEORGE

Ian Ivatt

'*In this important and pioneering study, Ian Ivatt has focussed his attention on a key theme rather neglected by historians and biographers of Lloyd George – his relationship with money and financial resources ... [these] compelling, engrossing themes, central to an understanding of Lloyd George's life, are dissected with a masterly touch by Mr. Ivatt. He has spared no effort to master the ever burgeoning published literature on David Lloyd George, has waded through the various scattered archival sources and scoured the newspaper columns too. He has also conducted personal interviews and undertaken research on the ground. All his enthralling discoveries have been deftly welded into a cohesive, absorbing account*'
J. Graham Jones, from the Foreword

The Financial Affairs of David Lloyd George is the first serious and systematic study to examine, assess and analyse Lloyd George's attitude to money and finance and compellingly illustrates how he accumulated great wealth by fair and more questionable methods.

978-1-86057-125-1   128pp   £19.99   PB

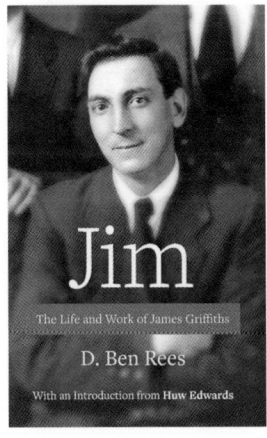

JIM
The Life and Work of Jim Griffiths

D. Ben Rees

'*The remarkable story of James Griffiths takes us all the way from the origins of British Labour to the origins of devolved Wales. Ben Rees has crafted a highly-readable and authoritative account of the life and times of one of Wales' greatest statesmen*'
Huw Edwards

In this, the first full-length biography of James Griffiths in English, Dr D. Ben Rees provides a comprehensive yet very accessible and personal study of one of the towering figures of twentieth-century Welsh and British politics. As Minister for National Insurance in the Atlee post-war government, introduced the Family Allowance in 1946 and became Secretary of State for the Colonies in 1950.

A product of the Welsh radical political tradition, James Griffiths became a miner at 13 and was a conscientious objector during WW1. He rose to become President of the South Wales Miner's Federation, the MP for Llanelli for 34 years, Chairman and then Deputy Leader of the Labour Party and the first Secretary of State for Wales in 1964.

978-1-86057-120-6   400pp

welsh academic press

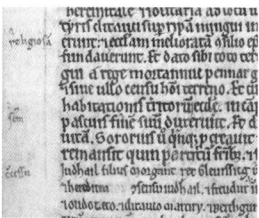

Vitae Sanctorum Britanniae et Genealogiae
The Lives and Genealogies of the Welsh Saints

Edited and translated by A.W. Wade-Evans
New edition edited by Scott Lloyd
Studies in Medieval Wales

VITAE SANCTORUM BRITANNIAE ET GENEALOGIAE
The Lives and Genealogies of the Welsh Saints

Edited and Translated by A.W. Wade-Evans
New edition edited by Scott Lloyd

This work, first published in 1944, provides the most reliable texts of the Lives of Welsh Saints based upon the Cotton MS in the British Library from 1200. Out of print for over 50 years, this work is still the standard edition of these Lives and is still widely used by scholars today. As well as being the major text for our information concerning the Welsh saints it also contains some of the earliest Arthurian material and is the first to make Arthur a king.

This new edition contains six additional genealogical tracts

De Situ Brecheniauc	(Concerning Brycheiniog)
Cognacio Brychan	(Family of Brychan)
Ach Kynauc Sant	(Pedigree of St. Cynog)
Generatio St. Egweni	(Descent of St. Eigion)
Progenies Keredic	(Progeny of Ceredig)
Bonedd y Saint	(Lineage of the Saints)

978-1-86057-089-6   418pp   £60.00   PB

SNP
The History of the Scottish National Party
(Second Edition)

Peter Lynch

'lucid, comprehensive and balanced - an invaluable guide to the SNP'
David Torrance

'There is scholarship on every page. It will become the definitive reference work on the nationalist strand of Scottish politics and Scottish history...the early days in particular are extremely well done, with close attention to original sources... impressive and has never been so well set out before.'
Scottish Affairs

The first full-length history of the Scottish National Party which traces the fortunes of the SNP from its establishment in 1934 to winning power in the Scottish Parliament.

978-1-86057-057-5   319pp   £19.99   PB

welsh academic press

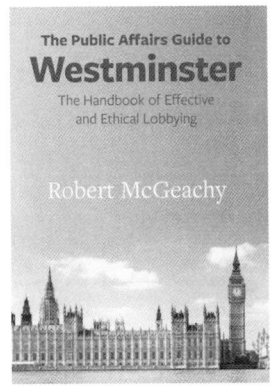

The Public Affairs Guide to
Westminster
The Handbook of Effective and Ethical Lobbying

The Public Affairs Guide to Westminster is the essential handbook for organisations seeking to influence legislation and shape policy development in the UK Parliament and at UK Government level, and is packed with invaluable advice on devising cost effective public affairs strategies and campaigns that achieve success on a limited budget.

Robert McGeachy's step-by-step guide - for private, public and third sector organisations - expertly strips away the mysteries and misconceptions of engaging with the UK Government, Opposition parties, as well as with individual MPs, Peers and the civil service.

The Public Affairs Guide to Westminster will empower campaigners to maximise their influence and to ensure their voice is heard at Westminster.

978-1-86057-134-3   224pp   £19.99   PB

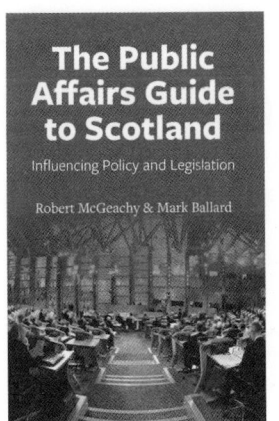

The Public Affairs Guide to
Scotland

'*[an excellent] guide for the newcomer and a 'memory stick' for the expert. It contains all a person needs to know to engage with the Parliament, the Government, local authorities and civic society in an effective and efficient way. This book shows how one can participate in that fast moving and interesting field and will become a tool for all who wish to get involved and achieve success in their endeavours.*'
Michael P Clancy

'*Effective and informed activity by MSPs, the Parliament, the Scottish Government and third sector bodies in taking forward legislation and promoting causes, whilst protecting the most vulnerable is the best way to ensure a truly participatory, power sharing democracy and that is why this guide will be so useful ... Mark Ballard and Robert McGeachy, through the pages of this important book, are therefore doing democracy a service.*'
Michael Russell, MSP for Argyll & Bute
Professor in Scottish Culture & Governance, The University of Glasgow

978-1-86057-126-8   224pp   £19.99   PB

St David's Press

'this rugby spellbound people'
THE BIRTH OF RUGBY IN CARDIFF AND WALES

Gwyn Prescott

"...scrupulously researched [and] well written...Gwyn Prescott has given [rugby in Wales] a history to be proud of."
Huw Richards, scrum.com

"Prescott paints a meticulous picture of Welsh rugby's growth in Victorian Britain"
Rugby World

"...a fascinating piece of research and a major contribution to the history of rugby."
Tony Collins

The Birth of Rugby in Cardiff and Wales is the essential guide to the importance of rugby in Cardiff and to the significance of Cardiff to the development of Welsh rugby in the nineteenth century.

978-1-902719-43-6   304pp   £16.99   PB

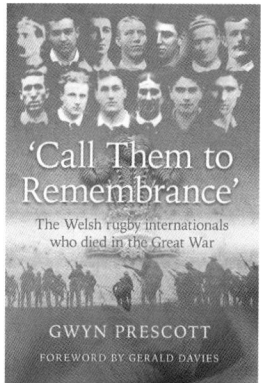

'CALL THEM TO REMEMBRANCE'
The Welsh Rugby Internationals Who Died in the Great War

Gwyn Prescott

This book is [an] acknowledgment of the sacrifice made by 13 Welshmen...Theirs was a sacrifice which needs to be told...[and] Gwyn Prescott, with meticulous and sympathetic attention to detail, tells the story. This narrative is an essential record',
Gerald Davies

'These humbling stories describe thirteen individual journeys which began on muddy yet familiar Welsh playing fields but ended in the unimaginable brutality of the battles of the First World War.'
www.gwladrugby.com

'Call them to remembrance', which includes 120 illustrations and maps, tells the stories of thirteen Welsh heroes who shared the common bond of having worn the famous red jersey of the Welsh international rugby team.

978-1-902719-37-5   170pp   £14.99   PB

St David's Press

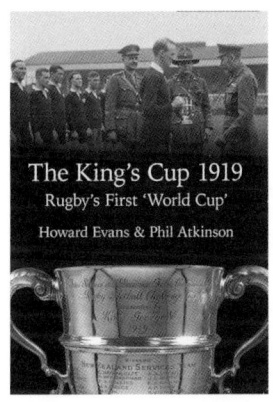

THE KING'S CUP 1919
Rugby's First World Cup

Howard Evans & Phil Atkinson

'An intriguing retelling of a significant but largely forgotten chapter of rugby union history, superbly illustrated.'
Huw Richards

'Howard is an authority on rugby's history and meticulous in his research'
Andy Howell, *Western Mail*

After the Armistice in November 1918 – with the forces of the world's rugby-playing nations and many of their stars still stationed in Britain – and with the public desperate to see competitive rugby played again, an inter-military tournament was organised. King George V was so enthused by the proposed competition that he agreed to have the tournament named after him, and so The King's Cup was born.

The King's Cup 1919 is the first book to tell the full story of rugby's first 'World Cup' and is essential reading for all rugby enthusiasts and military historians.

978-1-902719-44-3   192pp   £14.99   PB

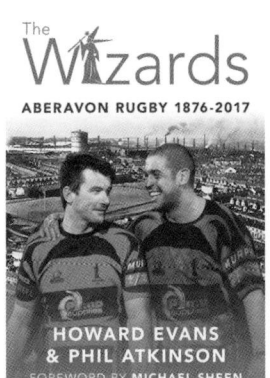

THE WIZARDS
Aberavon Rugby 1876-2017

Howard Evans & Phil Atkinson

'I would rather have played rugby for Wales than Hamlet at the Old Vic. To that town, Aberavon and its rugby team, I pledge my continuing allegiance, until death.'
Richard Burton

One of the traditional powerhouses of Welsh first class rugby, Aberavon RFC has a long, proud and illustrious history, with 50 of its players being capped for Wales, the club winning many league titles and domestic cups, and - with Neath RFC - facing the might of South Africa, Australia and New Zealand. Aberavon RFC is a great rugby club and this is its story.

978-1-902719-66-5   256pp   £19.99   PB

St David's Press

THE BOXERS OF WALES
CARDIFF

'Some of the greatest boxers in Britain have come out of Cardiff and this book is a must read for fight fans, whether you're Welsh or not.'
Colin Hart, *The Sun*

'This book is not just about the famous fighters, it's about the forgotten heroes.'
Steve Bunce, Boxing Broadcaster & Journalist

'A compelling and fascinating study.'
Claude Abrams, Editor, *Boxing News*

978-1-902719-26-9   160pp   £14.99   PB

THE BOXERS OF WALES
MERTHYR
ABERDARE & PONTYPRIDD

'a masterpiece... a must-read for any boxing fan...Compelling stuff.'
Steve Lillis, *News of the World*

'The valleys of south Wales have produced many fighters known worldwide ... but this book reminds us that there were others who lit up the ring in their day.'
Gareth A. Davies, *Daily Telegraph*

978-1-902719-29-0   160pp   £14.99   PB

THE BOXERS OF WALES
RHONDDA

'When Boxing News marked its centenary in 2009 by choosing the best British boxer of the previous 100 years, we opted for the one and only Jimmy Wilde. But the Rhondda produced many other outstanding fighters, as this book reminds us.'
Tris Dixon, Editor, *Boxing News*

'When it comes to in-depth research, they don't come much better than Gareth Jones ... The likes of the great Tommy Farr and Jimmy Wilde get the Jones treatment, along with a host of tales surrounding so many boxers from this mining area that produced such a rich seam of boxing greats.'
Kevin Francis, Boxing Correspondent, *Daily Star*

978-1-902719-33-7   160pp   £14.99   PB

THE BOXERS OF WALES
SWANSEA & LLANELLI

'My co-commentator, Enzo Maccarinelli, keeps telling me what a great fight town Swansea is. And here's the evidence. It's not just about the big names, like Colin Jones, Ronnie James and the Curvises - here you can learn of the only Welsh-speaker ever to win a Scottish title and the Llanelli girl who took on Germany's boxing queen. A great read!'
John Rawling, Commentator, *BoxNation*

'This book is a must for all serious boxing fans.'
Graham Houston, Editor, *Boxing Monthly*

978-1-902719-450   176pp   £14.99   PB

THE BOXERS OF WALES
NEWPORT
THE GWENT VALLEYS AND MONMOUTHSHIRE

'Nobody knows Welsh boxing with quite the depth, understanding and empathy of Gareth Jones.'
Kevin Mitchell, *The Observer*

'Gareth Jones is THE authority on Welsh boxing, and always a joy to read. His exhaustive research uncovers wonderful stories that should not be missed.'
Matt Christie, Editor, Boxing News

978-1-902719-634   192pp   £14.99   PB